INTERNATIONAL LAW AND INTERNATIONAL RELATIONS

MARK WESTON JANIS

WILLIAM F. STARR PROFESSOR OF LAW
UNIVERSITY OF CONNECTICUT SCHOOL OF LAW
VISITING FELLOW AND FORMERLY READER IN LAW
UNIVERSITY OF OXFORD

JOHN E. NOYES

ROGER J. TRAYNOR PROFESSOR OF LAW EMERITUS
CALIFORNIA WESTERN SCHOOL OF LAW
PAST PRESIDENT
AMERICAN BRANCH OF THE INTERNATIONAL LAW ASSOCIATION

WEST
ACADEMIC
PUBLISHING

© 2018 LEG, Inc. d/b/a West Academic
    444 Cedar Street, Suite 700
    St. Paul, MN 55101
    1-877-888-1330

West, West Academic Publishing, and West Academic are trademarks of West Publishing Corporation, used under license.

Printed in the United States of America

ISBN: 978-1-63460-293-8

Table of Sources and Acknowledgments

Some of the cases and materials excerpted in *International Law and International Relations* are reprinted with omissions. Any omitted text is indicated by three ellipses or by brackets. However, the omission of footnotes or citations has not been indicated.

The sources for the images and figures in this book are listed in the Table of Figures. All web site sources, in the Table of Figures and throughout the book, were last visited May 25, 2017.

The authors acknowledge and thank Joan Wood for her typing, Tyler Conklin for her work on the Index, and Heddy Rudd for her help with permissions.

Most of the excerpts in the book are from U.S. government publications, require no permission notice from the publisher, or are in the public domain; those sources are not listed below, but full citations are provided in the text. The authors and publisher have made reasonable efforts to contact all copyright holders, and gratefully acknowledge the copyright holders listed below for their permission to reproduce material. The following acknowledgments are listed in the order the related excerpts appear in the text.

Janis, Mark Weston, International Law (6th ed. 2012). © Mark Janis.

Scripture quotations marked (GNT) are from the Good News Translation in Today's English Version- Second Edition Copyright © 1992 by American Bible Society. Used by Permission.

CONSOLIDATED TREATY SERIES 1648–1919 EDITED AND ANNOTATED BY Clive Parry (1069): Peace of Westphalia (1648); 580 words (p.198) "By Permission of Oxford University Press, USA."

Bederman, David J., *Revivalist Canons and Treaty Interpretation*. First published in *UCLA Law Review* at 41 UCLA L. Rev. 953 (1994).

The Texaco/Libya Arbitration republished with permission of American Society of International Law, from The Texaco/Libya Arbitration Award of 19 Jan. 1977, 17 *International Legal Materials* 1 (1978); permission conveyed through Copyright Clearance Center, Inc.

AM & S Europe Limited v. Commission of the European Communities, European Court of Justice, [1982] E.C.R. 1575. The excerpted material is from an unauthenticated report found at http://curia.europa.eu and is reproduced free of charge. The definitive versions are published in *Reports of Cases before the Court of Justice* or the *Official Journal of the European Union*.

From *Prosecutor v. Furundžija,* Case IT–95–17/1, by Trial Chamber, International Criminal Tribunal for the former Yugoslavia, © 1998 United Nations. Reprinted with the permission of the United Nations.

E. Lauterpacht and C. J. Greenwood (eds.), "*In re* Duchy of Sealand," in *International Law Reports*, Volume 80, 1989, © Sir Elihu Lauterpacht, published by Cambridge University Press, reproduced with permission.

From Aguilar-Amory and Royal Bank of Canada claims. Great Britain *versus* Costa Rica. Washington, October 18, 1923, by 1 *Reports of International Arbitral Awards*, © 2006 United Nations. Reprinted with the permission of the United Nations.

Edis, Richard. (June 1, 1992). A job well done: The founding of the United Nations revisited. *Cambridge Review of International Affairs* copyright © Centre of International Studies reprinted by permission of (Taylor & Francis Ltd, Http://www.tandfonline) on behalf of Centre of International Studies.

From Draft articles on the responsibility of international organizations, with commentaries, by International Law Commission (Report on its Sixty-third Session), © 2011 United Nations. Reprinted with the permission of the United Nations.

Rona, Gabor. (February 2004). The ICRC's Status: In a Class of its Own. *International Committee of the Red Cross (ICRC)*. Retrieved from https://www.icrc.org/eng/resources/documents/misc/5w9fjy.htm. © International Committee of the Red Cross. Reprinted by permission.

Janis, Mark Weston, America and the Law of Nations 1776–1939 (2010). © M.W. Janis.

From Case concerning the differences between New Zealand and France arising from the *Rainbow Warrior* Affair; Ruling of 6 July 1986 by the Secretary-General of the United Nations, by 19 *Reports of International Arbitral Awards*, © 2006 United Nations. Reprinted with the permission of the United Nations.

E. Lauterpacht and C. J. Greenwood (eds.), "Rainbow Warrior (New Zealand v. France) [France-New Zealand Arbitration Tribunal] (1990)," in *International Law Reports*, Volume 82, 1994, © Sir Elihu Lauterpacht, published by Cambridge University Press, reproduced with permission.

Christopher, Warren and Richard M. Mosk. *The Iranian Hostage Crisis and the Iran-U.S. Claims Tribunal: Implications for International Dispute Resolution and Diplomacy*, 7

Pepperdine Dispute Res. L.J. 165, 165–166 (2007). Reprinted with permission by the Pepperdine Law Journal.

Henkin, Louis, "Will the U.S. Supreme Court Fail International Law?," *Newsletter of the American Society of International Law*, Aug.-Sept. 1992, at 1. Reprinted by permission of the American Society of International Law.

The Caroline Dispute, 29 *British and Foreign State Papers* 1129; 30 *British and Foreign State Papers* 195. Reprinted pursuant to United Kingdom Open Government Licence Version 3.0, http://www.nationalarchives.gov.uk/doc/open-government-licence/version/3/.

Louis Henkin, "The Use of Force: Law and U.S. Policy, Right v. Might," in *International Law and the Use of Force* 37 (1989). Reprinted by permission of the Council of Foreign Relations Press.

W. Michael Reisman, "Criteria for the Lawful Use of Force in International Law," 10 *Yale Journal of International Law* 279 (1985). Reprinted by permission of the Yale Journal of International Law.

Republished with permission of American Society of International Law, from Thomas M. Franck & Faiza Patel, "UN Police Action in Lieu of War: The Old Order Changeth," 85 *American Journal of International Law* 63 (1991); permission conveyed through Copyright Clearance Center, Inc.

Republished with permission of American Society of International Law, from Eugene V. Rostow, "Until What? Enforcement Action or Collective Self-Defense?," 85 *American Journal of International Law* 506 (1991); permission conveyed through Copyright Clearance Center, Inc.

Republished with permission of American Society of International Law, from Thomas M. Franck, "Criminals, Combatants, or What? An Examination of the Role of Law in Responding to the Threat of Terror," 98 *American Journal of International Law* 686, 687 (2004); permission conveyed through Copyright Clearance Center, Inc.

The Chilcot Report, *The Report of the Iraq Inquiry*, Section 5 (July 2016). Reprinted pursuant to United Kingdom Open Government Licence Version 3.0, http://www.nationalarchives.gov.uk/doc/open-government-licence/version/3/.

Letter from Deputy Legal Adviser Elizabeth Wilmhurst to Michael Wood, March 18, 2003, available at http://www.iraqinquiry.org.uk/media/242786/2003-03-18-minute-wilmshurst-to-wood-untitled.pdf. Reprinted pursuant to United Kingdom Open Government Licence Version 3.0, http://www.nationalarchives.gov.uk/doc/open-government-licence/version/3/.

Republished with permission of American Society of International Law, from Sean D. Murphy, "Self-Defense and the Israeli Wall Advisory Opinion: An *Ipse Dixit* from the Court?," 99 *American Journal of International Law* 62, 66 (2005); permission conveyed through Copyright Clearance Center, Inc.

From Report of the High-level Independent Panel on Peace Operations on Uniting Our Strengths for Peace, U.N. Doc. A/70/95–S/2015/446, by High-level Independent Panel on Peace Operations on Uniting Our Strengths for Peace, © 2015 United Nations. Reprinted with the permission of the United Nations.

Newton, Mike (2006). The military lawyer: Nuisance or necessity, human dignity protection in armed conflict: Strengthening measures for the respect and implementation of international humanitarian law and other rules protecting human dignity in armed conflict. 107 *International Institute of Humanitarian Law*, Guido Ravasi & Gian Luca Beruto eds. Reprinted by permission of author Mike Newton.

William H. Taft IV, "A View from the Top: American Perspectives on International Law After the Cold War," 31 *Yale Journal of International Law* 503, 509–10 (2006). Reprinted by permission of the Yale Journal of International Law.

From *Prosecutor v. Tadić*, Decision on the Defence Motion for Interlocutory Appeal on Jurisdiction, Case No. IT–94–1, by Appeals Chamber, International Criminal Tribunal for the former Yugoslavia, © 1995 United Nations. Reprinted with the permission of the United Nations.

Mark W. Janis, "Individuals as Subjects of International Law," 17 *Cornell Int'l L.J.* 61 (1984). Reprinted with permission of the Cornell Repository.

Leila Nadya Sadat, "Shattering the Nuremberg Consensus: U.S. Rendition Policy and International Criminal Law," *Yale J. Int'l Aff.* Winter 2008, at 65, 66–67. Reprinted with permission of the Yale Journal of International Affairs.

Republished with permission of the Johns Hopkins University Press, from Thomas Buergenthal, "The Normative and Institutional Evolution of International Human Rights," 19:4 *Human Rights Quarterly* 703 (1997); permission conveyed through Copyright Clearance Center, Inc.

From *Damian Thomas v. Jamaica*, U.N. Human Rights Committee Communication No. 800/1998, U.N. Doc. CCPR/65/D/800/1998, by Human Rights Committee, © 1998 United Nations. Reprinted with the permission of the United Nations.

Leila Nadya Sadat & S. Richard Carden, "The New International Criminal Court: An Uneasy Revolution," 88 *Georgetown L.J.* 381 (2000). Reprinted with permission of the publisher, Georgetown Law Journal, © 2000.

Safer Ships, Cleaner Seas, *Report of Lord Donaldson's Inquiry into the Prevention of Pollution from Merchant Shipping*, Cm. 2560 (1994). Reprinted pursuant to United Kingdom Open Government Licence Version 3.0, http://www.nationalarchives.gov.uk/doc/open-government-licence/version/3/.

Lord Rochdale, Committee of Inquiry into Shipping, *Report 51*, Cmnd. 4337 (1970). Reprinted pursuant to United Kingdom Open Government Licence Version 3.0, http://www.nationalarchives.gov.uk/doc/open-government-licence/version/3/.

M/V "SAIGA" (No. 2) (Saint Vincent and the Grenadines v. *Guinea), Judgment, ITLOS Reports 1999,* Kluwer Law International, p. 10, at pp. 48, 55, paras. 106–107, 130–131. Reprinted with permission of the International Tribunal for the Law of the Sea.

Bernard Oxman, "The Regime of Warships Under the United Nations Convention," 24 *Va. J. Int'l L.* 809, 861–62 (1984). Reprinted with permission of the Virginia Journal of International Law.

Responsibilities and obligations of States with respect to activities in the Area, Advisory Opinion, 1 February 2011, ITLOS Reports 2011, Martinus Nijhoff Publishers, p. 10, at pp. 53–54, 59, paras. 158–159, 161–162, 179–180. Reprinted with permission of the International Tribunal for the Law of the Sea.

Table of Contents

Table of Figures

https://en.wikipedia.org/wiki/United_Nations_Security_Council#/media/File:UN-Sicherheitsrat_-_UN_Security_Council_-_New_York_City_-_2014_01_06.jpg. Neptuul. Licensed under the Creative Commons Attribution-Share Alike 3.0 Unported license: CC BY-SA 3.0. File: UN-Sicherheitsrat - UN Security Council - New York City - 2014 01 06.jpg. Created: 6 January 2014.

https://en.wikipedia.org/wiki/Gulf_War_air_campaign#/media/File:USAF_F-16A_F-15C_F-15E_Desert_Storm_edit2.jpg. Source: U.S. Air Force. File: USAF F-16A F-15C F-15E Desert Storm edit2.jpg. Uploaded: 5 December 2007. Public domain.

https://en.wikipedia.org/wiki/Organisation_for_the_Prohibition_of_Chemical_Weapons#/media/File:HQ_of_OPCW_in_The_Hague.jpg. Licensed under the Creative Commons Attribution-Share Alike 3.0 Unported license: CC BY-SA 3.0. File: HQ of OPCW in The Hague.jpg. Created: 31 December 2006.

Reproduced from Mike Newton, "The Military Lawyer: Nuisance or Necessity?," in *Human Dignity Protection in Armed Conflict: Strengthening Measures for the Respect and Implementation of International Humanitarian Law and Other Rules Protecting Human Dignity in Armed Conflict* 107 (International Institute of Humanitarian Law, Guido Ravasi & Gian Luca Beruto eds. 2006).

https://en.wikipedia.org/wiki/Francis_Lieber#/media/File:Francis_Lieber_-_Brady-Handy.jpg. Mathew Brady, "Prof. Frances [sic] Lieber," between 1855 and 1866. Library of Congress Prints and Photographs Division. Brady-Handy Photograph Collection. http://hdl.loc.gov/loc.pnp/cwpbh.01402. CALL NUMBER: LC-BH82- 4591 C <P&P>[P&P]. File: Francis Lieber - Brady-Handy.jpg. Public domain.

Table of Cases

INTERNATIONAL LAW AND INTERNATIONAL RELATIONS

Introduction

International law has never been more relevant. International law and organizations play significant roles in regulating the international economy, international conflicts, arms control, human rights, the oceans, the international environment, and a myriad of other topics. Diplomats and politicians look to treaties and other international legal norms when they condemn war crimes and evaluate national treatment of refugees and immigrants. International courts and tribunals have ruled in thousands of international disputes.

International Law and International Relations has several missions. First, we explain what international law is. It is not only a body of rules. Our world depends on structures grounded in international law. States, international courts, and other international organizations are not merely factual entities; they are endowed with legal characteristics, legal rights, and legal duties.

Second, we explore the efficacy of international law. How and why does it shape international relations? For diplomats and for lawyers in foreign offices, international law provides a common language. Those who lack legal training soon discover that legal rules, institutions, and processes both help and hinder them.

Third, we introduce the actors who have rights and duties under international law. International law and international relations concern not only interactions among states, but among international organizations and individuals as well. Even the treatment of citizens by their own government or their political and military leaders raises questions of international law and may affect international relations. When individuals or corporations from different countries contest the reach of national laws, they expose conflicts between those laws. International law helps to resolve and accommodate such conflicts and to regulate national actors on the international stage.

Fourth, we highlight the significance of various forums that interpret and apply international law. Different countries treat international law in different ways in their domestic legal systems. International courts and tribunals also differ in their procedures and in the international law they apply.

Throughout the book, we provide historical context explaining modern disputes and applications of international law. Lawyers assess the role of "tradition" or "precedent," while international relations specialists talk about the importance of "path dependency." Regardless of terminology, we recognize that current concepts build on the past. International courts, for example, were not made from whole cloth; their creators drew on earlier theories and reacted to earlier methods of dispute settlement. Moreover, understanding legal disputes means remembering the historical and political contexts within which the disputes arose.

The importance of context leads us to include excerpts from cases and legal debates as important instructional tools. The "case method," a familiar vehicle for instruction in law and business schools, focuses on actual incidents. This focus illustrates how problems in international law and relations arise in particular historical, cultural, and political settings. Our text provides background and raises questions that prompt discussion about the general significance of international law in specific international contexts.

Chapter 1 of this book introduces major themes using two topical cases, one in an international court, the other in a domestic tribunal. In Chapter 2 we examine the sources of international law: treaties, customary international law, general principles of law, natural law, *jus cogens*, and equity. Chapter 3 turns to the theory and practice of international law in diplomacy and international politics. Chapter 4 discusses international courts and arbitration. Chapter 5 looks at the enforcement of international law by domestic courts. The later chapters in the book deal with some of the many substantive issues addressed by international law: Chapter 6 the use of force; Chapter 7 human rights law; and Chapter 8 the law of the sea. These later chapters also reinforce and expand on earlier discussion of international law's sources, processes, and influence on international relations.

CHAPTER 1

The Nature of International Law

International Law and International Relations provides a working knowledge of how international law functions in modern international politics. This chapter introduces international law, looking first a little at its long history, and then at two sample judicial decisions, *McCann* and *Filartiga*, that show how international law is, in the real world, made, adjudicated, and enforced.

When students think of "law," they usually think of domestic law with which international law is sometimes compared unfavorably. Domestic law (which international lawyers sometimes refer to as "municipal law") is ordinarily composed of rules legitimately made by legislatures in statutes or sometimes by judges in their case law; these rules are interpreted and applied by courts, and enforced by executives.

At first glance, international law seems to lack all of these elements. There is no unified international legislature, no generally authoritative international judiciary, and no effective international executive. Yet, whatever its theoretical ambiguities, international law has been practiced by states for centuries. Moreover, international law remains one of the principal tools by which nations order their relationships. Why, with all its faults, is international law so important? Let us briefly explore the foundations of modern international law.

A. THE HISTORY OF INTERNATIONAL LAW

MARK WESTON JANIS, INTERNATIONAL LAW
1–4 (6th ed. 2012)

The roots of international law run deep in history. In early religious and secular writings, there are many evidences of what we now know as international law; there are, for example, the detailed peace treaties and alliances concluded between the Jews and the Romans, Syrians, and Spartans. The Romans knew of a *jus gentium*, a law of nations, which Gaius, in the second century, saw as a law "common to all men," a universal law that could be applied by Roman courts to foreigners when the specific law of their own nation was unknown and when Roman law was inapposite. In the seventeenth century, the Dutch jurist Hugo Grotius argued that the law of nations also established legal rules that bound the sovereign states of Europe, then just emerging from medieval society, in their relations with one another. Grotius' classic of 1625, *The Law of War and Peace*, is widely acknowledged, more than any other work, as founding the modern discipline of the law of nations, a subject that, in 1789, the English philosopher Jeremy Bentham renamed and refashioned as "international law." Nowadays, the terms *the law of nations* and *international law* are often used interchangeably.

At least since the end of the Thirty Years War in 1648, world politics has principally involved the relations of more or less independent sovereign states. An important part of international law has consequently had to do with the establishment of a set of mutually agreed-upon rules respecting the nature of these states and their fundamental rights and obligations *inter se*. If there is a single international legal principle underlying the modern state system, it probably is the one neatly framed by Montesquieu in 1748 and offered to Napoleon in 1806 by Talleyrand: "that nations ought to do to one another in peace, the most good, and in war, the least evil possible."

International law is sometimes conceived to be divided into public and private parts, the first concerning the legal relations of states, the second involving the law governing the foreign transactions of individuals and corporations. However, the public-private division of international law can be misleading. Many of the laws and processes traditionally within the ambit of public international law actually concern private, not public, parties, while much of the domain of private international law covers the transactions of public entities. Nonetheless, the terms *public* and *private* international law are highly popular and, in a rough kind of way, do compartmentalize legal rules addressing two problem areas: Public international law mostly concerns the political interactions of states; private international law relates to legal aspects of the international economy and conflicts and cooperation among national legal systems.

Few deny that the rules of international law actually influence state behavior. Even international law's most famous jurisprudential critic, John Austin, acknowledged in 1832 that international legal rules were effective. At the same time, however, he argued that, because there was no international sovereign to enforce it, international law could not be the same sort of positive law as that enacted by sovereign states for internal application:

[T]he law obtaining between nations is not positive law: for every positive law is set by a given sovereign to a person or persons in a state of subjection to its author. As I have already intimated, the law obtaining between nations is law (improperly so called) set by general opinion. The duties which it imposes are enforced by moral sanctions: by fear on the part of nations, or by fear on the part of sovereigns, of provoking general hostility, and incurring its probable evils, in case they shall violate maxims generally received and respected.

Just a few years later, in 1836, the United States diplomat Henry Wheaton, in the first great English-language treatise on international law, was already grappling with Austin's characterization of the rules governing international politics as being a form of mere "morality." Wheaton accepted Austin's view that international law's principal sanction was "the hazard of provoking the hostility of other communities," but contended that "[e]xperience shows that these motives, even in the worst times, do really afford a considerable security for the observance of justice between States, if they do not furnish the perfect sanction annexed by the lawgiver to the observance of the municipal code of any particular State." Unlike Austin, Wheaton found international law sufficiently law-like to justify calling it "law," a definitional outcome reached by generations of subsequent international lawyers.

Whether the international rules regulating interstate behavior are to be properly termed "legal" or "moral" is in truth a question that can only be answered after one has made more or less arbitrary definitions of what really constitutes "law" and "morality," a sometimes sterile exercise.[12] Suffice it to say at this early stage of our own discussion that there are a great many rules regulating international politics commonly referred to as "international law" and that these rules are usually, for one reason or another, observed in international practice. Moreover, there is no doubt that the norms of international law are frequently applied as rules of decision by law courts, domestic as well as international.

International Law? Note how the discipline of what we now call "international law" has changed its name over its two-thousand-year-old history. However named, the discipline has always fulfilled the same function: providing legal rules and process beyond those of a single state or nation. Newer terms are now sometimes employed: transnational law and global law, for example. Add to this the term in different languages. In French, for

---

[12] "The only intelligent way to deal with a verbal question like that concerning the definition of the word 'law' is to give up thinking and arguing about it." Williams, "International Law and the Controversy Concerning the Word 'Law,' " 22 *British Yearbook of International Law* 146, 163 (1945).

example, one finds *droit des gens* and *droit international.* This is a veritable Tower of Babel from which many confusions can result. Of course, the "babble" characterizes not only international law but all international relationships.

Efficacy. Why does international law work at all? The puzzler in the two cases below is that the decision of the international court, the European Court of Human Rights, is apparently much more efficacious than the judgment of the U.S. Second Circuit Court of Appeals. This seems to contradict expectations; one would think that domestic courts are more powerful than international courts. Keep an eye out for why the applicants in *McCann* and the plaintiffs in *Filartiga* bring their cases. Are they looking to international law for different sorts of results?

B. AN INTERNATIONAL LAW SAMPLER

The two cases that follow explore some of the different ways in which international law is actually made, applied, and enforced. The *McCann Case* illustrates an international legal rule made by a treaty, adjudicated by an international court, and enforced by a regional international legal system. The *Filartiga Case* shows a customary or perhaps fundamental international legal norm adjudicated by a municipal—*i.e.*, a domestic—court and enforced (or not) by the ordinary mechanisms of that domestic legal system.

Following short excerpts from each case, the text introduces issues about the rules, processes, actors, and domains of international law, topics that occupy us throughout the book. Some questions are also posed that may serve as good discussion points.

Facts, Law, and the Judicial Role. The excerpts from *McCann* are in two parts, first the facts, then the law. This is an ordinary way in which courts explain why they decide a case as they do. The facts are the incidents that have prompted one side, here the "applicants," family members of three deceased members of the Irish Republican Army, to sue the other side, here the "Government," the British government whose agents, special forces Army soldiers, killed the three IRA members in Gibraltar, a British dependency at the tip of the Hispanic Peninsula. The role of any court is to determine the facts, and then to interpret and apply the relevant law, here an article of the European Human Rights Convention, and finally to reach a decision.

McCann v. United Kingdom

European Court of Human Rights, Judgment of 27 September 1995,
Series A, No. 324, Application No. 18984/91 (1995) © Council of Europe/European Court of Human
Rights—Conseil de l'Europe/Cour européenne des droits de l'homme

The Facts

The case . . . originated in an application (no. 18984/91) against the United Kingdom of Great Britain and Northern Ireland lodged . . . by Ms. Margaret McCann, Mr. Daniel Farrell and Mr. John Savage, who are all Irish and United Kingdom citizens. They are representatives of the estates of Mr. Daniel McCann, Ms. Mairead Farrell and Mr. Sean Savage. . . .

Before 4 March 1988, and probably from at least the beginning of the year, the United Kingdom, Spanish and Gibraltar authorities were aware that the Provisional IRA (Irish Republican Army—"IRA") were planning a terrorist attack on Gibraltar. It appeared from the intelligence received and from observations made by the Gibraltar police that the target was to be the assembly area south of Ince's Hall where the Royal Anglican Regiment usually assembled to carry out the changing of the guard every Tuesday at 11.00 hours.

[On March 5, 1988, a] briefing by the representative of the Security Services included inter alia the following assessments:

(a) the IRA intended to attack the changing of the guard ceremony in the assembly area outside Ince's Hall on the morning of Tuesday 8 March 1988;

(b) [a group] of three would be sent to carry out the attack, consisting of Daniel McCann, Sean Savage and a third member, later positively identified as Mairead Farrell. McCann had been previously convicted and sentenced to two years' imprisonment for possession of explosives. Farrell had previously been convicted and sentenced to fourteen years' imprisonment for causing explosions. She was known during her time in prison to have been the acknowledged leader of the IRA wing of prisoners. Savage was described as an expert bomb-maker. Photographs were shown of the three suspects;

(c) the three individuals were believed to be dangerous terrorists who would almost certainly be armed and who, if confronted by security forces, would be likely to use their weapons;

(d) the attack would be by way of a car bomb. It was believed that the bomb would be brought across the border in a vehicle and that it would remain hidden inside the vehicle;

(e)   the possibility that a "blocking" car—i.e. a car not containing a bomb but parked in the assembly area in order to reserve a space for the car containing the bomb—would be used had been considered, but was thought unlikely. . . .

Various methods of detonation of the bomb were mentioned at the briefing[.] Use of a remote-control device was considered to be far more likely since it was safer from the point of view of the terrorist who could get away from the bomb before it exploded and was more controllable than a timer which once activated was virtually impossible to stop. . . .

At about 14.50 hours [on March 6], it was reported to the operations room that the suspects McCann and Farrell had met with a second man identified as the suspect Savage and the three were looking at a white Renault car in the car-park of the assembly area.

Witness H stated that the three suspects spent some considerable time staring across to where a car had been parked, as if, in his assessment, they were studying it to make sure it was absolutely right for the effect of the bomb. [Detective Constable] Viagas also witnessed the three suspects meeting in the area of the car-park, stating that all three turned and stared towards where the car was parked. He gave the time as about 14.55 hours. He stated that the Security Services made identification of all three at this moment.

At this moment, the possibility of effecting an arrest was considered. There were different recollections. [Deputy Commissioner] Colombo stated that he was asked whether he would hand over control to the military for the arrest but that he asked whether the suspects had been positively identified; he was told that there was 80% identification. Almost immediately the three suspects moved away from the car through the Southport Gate. He recalled that the movement of the three suspects towards the south gave rise to some discussion as to whether this indicated that the three suspects were on reconnaissance and might return for the car. It was for this reason that the decision was taken not to arrest at this point. . . .

The evidence at the inquest given by the soldiers and Police Officer R and DC Ullger was that the soldiers had practised arrest procedures on several occasions with the police before 6 March 1988. According to these rehearsals, the soldiers were to approach the suspects to within a close distance, cover the suspects with their pistols and shout "Stop. Police. Hands up." or words to that effect. They would then make the suspects lie on the ground with their arms away from their bodies until the police moved in to carry out a formal arrest. Further,

DC Ullger stated that special efforts had been made to identify a suitable place in Gibraltar for the terrorists to be held in custody following their arrest.

On reaching the junction of Smith Dorrien Avenue with Winston Churchill Avenue, the three suspects crossed the road and stopped on the other side talking. Officer R, observing, saw them appear to exchange newspapers. At this point, Soldiers C and D were approaching the junction from Smith Dorrien Avenue. Soldiers A and B emerging from Landport tunnel also saw the three suspects at the junction from their position where the pathway to the tunnel joined Corral Road.

As the soldiers converged on the junction, however, Savage split away from suspects McCann and Farrell turning south towards the Landport tunnel. McCann and Farrell continued north up the right-hand pavement of Winston Churchill Avenue.

Savage passed Soldiers A and B, brushing against the shoulder of B. Soldier B was about to turn to effect the arrest but A told him that they should continue towards suspects McCann and Farrell, knowing that C and D were in the area and that they would arrest Savage. Soldiers C and D, aware that A and B were following suspects McCann and Farrell, crossed over from Smith Dorrien Avenue and followed Savage. . . .

Soldiers A and B continued north up Winston Churchill Avenue after McCann and Farrell, walking at a brisk pace to close the distance. McCann was walking on the right of Farrell on the inside of the pavement. He was wearing white trousers and a white shirt, without any jacket. Farrell was dressed in a skirt and jacket and was carrying a large handbag.

When Soldier A was approximately ten metres (though maybe closer) behind McCann on the inside of the pavement, McCann looked back over his left shoulder. McCann appeared to look directly at A and the smile left his face, as if he had a realisation of who A was and that he was a threat.

Soldier A drew his pistol, intending to shout a warning to stop at the same time, though he was uncertain if words actually came out. McCann's hand moved suddenly and aggressively across the front of his body. A thought that he was going for the button to detonate the bomb and opened fire. He shot one round into McCann's back from a distance of three metres (though maybe it might have been closer). Out of the corner of his eye, A saw a movement by Farrell. Farrell had been walking on the left of McCann on the side of the pavement next to the road. A saw her make a half turn to the right towards McCann, grabbing for her handbag which was under her left arm. A thought that she was also going for a button and shot one round into her back. He did not disagree when it was put to him that the forensic evidence suggested that he may have shot from a distance of three feet. Then A turned back to McCann and shot him once more in the body and twice in the head. A was not aware of B opening fire as this was happening. He fired a total of five shots.

Soldier B was approaching directly behind Farrell on the road side of the pavement. He was watching her. When they were three to four metres away and closing, he saw in his peripheral vision that McCann turned his head to look over his shoulder. He heard what he presumed was a shout from A which he thought was the start of the arrest process. At almost the same instant, there was a firing to his right. Simultaneously, Farrell made a sharp movement to her right, drawing the bag which she had under her left arm across her body. He could not see her hands or the bag and feared that she was going for the button. He opened fire on Farrell. He deemed that McCann was in a threatening position and was unable to see his hands and switched fire to McCann. Then he turned back to Farrell and continued firing until he was certain that she was no longer a threat, namely, her hands away from her body. He fired a total of seven shots.

Both soldiers denied that Farrell or McCann made any attempt to surrender with their hands up in the air or that they fired at the two suspects when they were lying on the ground. At the inquest, Soldier A stated expressly that his intention had been to kill McCann "to stop him becoming a threat and detonating that bomb." . . .

Inside Farrell's handbag was found a key ring with two keys and a tag bearing a registration number MA9317AF. This information was passed at about 17.00 hours to the Spanish police who commenced a search for the car on the suspicion that it might contain explosives. During the night of 6 to 7 March, the Spanish police found a red Ford Fiesta with that registration number in La Linea. Inside the car were found keys for another car, registration number MA2732AJ, with a rental agreement indicating that the car had been rented at 10.00 hours on 6 March by Katharine Smith, the name on the passport carried in Farrell's handbag.

At about 18.00 hours on 8 March, a Ford Fiesta car with registration number MA2732AJ was discovered in a basement car-park in Marbella. It was opened by the Malaga bomb-disposal squad and found to contain an explosive device in the boot concealed in the spare-wheel compartment. The device consisted of five packages of Semtex explosive (altogether 64 kg) to which were attached four detonators and around which were packed 200 rounds of ammunition. There were two timers marked 10 hrs 45 mins and 11 hrs 15 mins respectively. The device was not primed or connected.

In the report compiled by the Spanish police on the device dated Madrid 27 March 1988, it was concluded that there was a double activating system to ensure explosion even if one of the timers failed; the explosive was hidden in the spare-wheel space to avoid detection on passing the Spanish/Gibraltarian customs; the quantity of explosive and use of cartridges as shrapnel indicated the terrorists were aiming for greatest effect; and that it was believed that the device was set to explode at the time of the military parade on 8 March 1988. . . .

An inquest by the Gibraltar Coroner into the killings was opened on 6 September 1988. The families of the deceased (which included the applicants) were represented, as were the SAS [Special Air Service] soldiers and the United Kingdom Government. The inquest was presided over by the Coroner, who sat with a jury chosen from the local population. . . .

The jury returned verdicts of lawful killing by a majority of nine to two.

The applicants were dissatisfied with these verdicts and commenced actions in the High Court of Justice in Northern Ireland against the Ministry of Defence for the loss and damage suffered by the estate of each deceased as a result of their death. The statements of claim were served on 1 March 1990.

[The applicant's claims concerning the events in Gibraltar were disallowed, on the grounds that governing U.K. law excluded proceedings against the British government unless those proceedings arose "in respect of Her Majesty's Government in the United Kingdom." The United Kingdom includes Northern Ireland but not Gibraltar.]

On 28 April 1988 Thames Television broadcast its documentary entitled "Death on the Rock," during which a reconstruction was made of the alleged surveillance of the terrorists' car by the Spanish police and witnesses to the shootings described what they had seen, including allegations that McCann and Farrell had been shot while on the ground. A statement by an anonymous witness was read out to the effect that Savage had been shot by a man who had his foot on his chest. The Independent Broadcasting Authority had rejected a request made by the Foreign and Commonwealth Secretary to postpone the programme until after the holding of the inquest into the deaths. . . .

The applicants lodged their application with the [European Human Rights] Commission on 14 August 1991. They complained that the killings of Daniel McCann, Mairead Farrell and Sean Savage by members of the SAS (Special Air Service) constituted a violation of Article 2 of the [European Human Rights] Convention.

Exhaustion of Domestic Remedies. It is an ordinary rule of international law that one cannot get relief from an international tribunal, like the European Court of Human Rights, until one has "exhausted domestic remedies." Exhaustion respects state sovereignty. Until one has tried all realistic avenues for domestic relief of an alleged violation of international law, one is barred from going to international legal process. Otherwise, the international court will usually dismiss an applicant's case. Can you see how the applicants in *McCann* did all they could to get relief from the British legal system?

European Court of Human Rights. The European Court of Human Rights in Strasbourg, France, can be described as an "international court" in at least two ways. Constitutionally, the Court is established by a treaty: the 1950 European Convention for the Protection of Human Rights and Fundamental Freedoms. Substantively, the rules the Court applies are international law: human rights norms made and protected by the same European Human Rights Convention. As of 2017, some 47 European countries were parties to the European Human Rights Convention and subject to Strasbourg's jurisdiction. More about treaties is found in Chapter 2, and we consider international adjudication in Chapter 4. The structure and substance of European human rights law are more fully explained in Chapter 7.

The Nature of Treaties. As you read the law part of *McCann*, note that the applicable substantive rule is drawn from the 1950 European Human Rights Convention: Article 2 protecting the right to life. The ordinary explanation of the legally binding effect of an international agreement is that a sovereign state may exercise its sovereignty not only by making domestic law but also by making international law. Hence, Article 2 obliges the United Kingdom in international law because of the U.K.'s own consent.

The European Convention on Human Rights thus resembles an international contract among states, but it may also be said to be like an international statute, providing a generally applicable set of rules for all its member states. This helps explain why states are considered to be not only the legislators of international law but also subjects of international law. Of course, since states are sovereign, multilateral treaties, unlike municipal statutes, do not bind non-parties. We consider the nature of the sovereign state in Chapter 3.

―――――――

Figure 1.A
European Court of Human Rights, Strasbourg, France

McCann v. United Kingdom
The Law

In 3 September 1993 the Commission declared the applicants' complaint admissible.

In its report of 4 March 1994 (Article 31), it expressed the opinion that there had been no violation of Article 2 (eleven votes to six). . . .

The Government submitted that the deprivations of life to which the applications related were justified under Article 2 para. 2(a) as resulting from the use of force which was no more than absolutely necessary in defence of the people of Gibraltar from unlawful violence and the Court was invited to find that the facts disclosed no breach of Article 2 of the Convention in respect of any of the three deceased.

The applicants submitted that the Government have not shown beyond reasonable doubt that the planning and execution of the operation was in accordance with Article 2 para. 2 of the Convention. Accordingly, the killings were not absolutely necessary within the meaning of this provision.

The applicants alleged that the killing of Mr. McCann, Ms. Farrell and Mr. Savage by members of the security forces constituted a violation of Article 2 of the Convention which reads:

1.   Everyone's right to life shall be protected by law. No one shall be deprived of his life intentionally save in the execution of a sentence of a court following his conviction of a crime for which this penalty is provided by law.

2.   Deprivation of life shall not be regarded as inflicted in contravention of this Article when it results from the use of force which is no more than absolutely necessary:

    (a)   in defence of any person from unlawful violence;

    (b)   in order to effect a lawful arrest or to prevent the escape of a person lawfully detained;

    (c)   in action lawfully taken for the purpose of quelling a riot or insurrection.

The Court's approach to the interpretation of Article 2 must be guided by the fact that the object and purpose of the Convention as an instrument for the protection of individual human beings requires that its provisions be interpreted and applied so as to make its safeguards practical and effective.

It must also be borne in mind that, as a provision which not only safeguards the right to life but sets out the circumstances when the deprivation of life may be justified, Article 2 ranks as one of the most fundamental provisions in the Convention—indeed one which, in peacetime, admits of no derogation under Article 15. Together with Article 3 of the Convention, it also enshrines one of the basic values of the democratic societies making up the Council of Europe. As such, its provisions must be strictly construed. . . .

While accepting that the Convention institutions are not in any formal sense bound by the decisions of the inquest jury, the Government submitted that the verdicts were of central importance to any subsequent examination of the deaths of the deceased. Accordingly, the Court should give substantial weight to the verdicts of the jury in the absence of any indication that those verdicts were perverse or ones which no reasonable tribunal of fact could have reached. In this connection, the jury was uniquely well-placed to assess the circumstances surrounding the shootings. The members of the jury heard and saw each of the seventy-nine witnesses giving evidence, including extensive cross-examination. With that benefit they were able to assess the credibility and probative value of the witnesses' testimony. The Government pointed out that the jury also heard the submissions of the various parties, including those of the lawyers representing the deceased. . . .

As regards the appreciation of these facts from the standpoint of Article 2, the Court observes that the jury had the benefit of listening to the witnesses first hand, observing their demeanor and assessing the probative value of their testimony.

Nevertheless, it must be borne in mind that the jury's finding was limited to a decision of lawful killing and, as is normally the case, did not provide reasons for the conclusion that it reached. In addition, the focus of concern of the inquest proceedings and the standard applied by the jury was whether the killings by the soldiers were reasonably justified in the circumstances as opposed to whether they were "absolutely necessary" under Article 2 para. 2 in the sense developed above.

Against this background, the Court must make its own assessment whether the facts as established by the Commission disclose a violation of Article 2 of the Convention. . . .

The applicants alleged that there had been a premeditated plan to kill the deceased. While conceding that there was no evidence of a direct order from the highest authorities in the Ministry of Defence, they claimed that there was strong circumstantial evidence in support of their allegation. They suggested that a plot to kill could be achieved by other means such as hints and innuendoes, coupled with the choice of a military unit like the SAS which, as indicated by the evidence given by their members at the inquest, was trained to neutralize a target by shooting to kill. Supplying false information of the sort that was actually given to the soldiers in this case would render a fatal shooting likely. The use of the SAS was, in itself, evidence that the killing was intended. . . .

The Commission concluded that there was no evidence to support the applicant's claim of a premeditated plot to kill the suspects.

The Court observes that it would need to have convincing evidence before it could conclude that there was a premeditated plan, in the sense developed by the applicants.

In the light of its own examination of the material before it, the Court does not find it established that there was an execution plot at the highest level of command in the Ministry of Defence or in the Government, or that Soldiers A, B, C and D had been so encouraged or instructed by the superior officers who had briefed them prior to the operation, or indeed that they had decided on their own initiative to kill the suspects irrespective of the existence of any justification for the use of lethal force and in disobedience to the arrest instructions they had received. Nor is there evidence that there was an implicit encouragement by the authorities or hints and innuendoes to execute the three suspects. . . .

The Court therefore rejects as unsubstantiated the applicants' allegations that the killing of the three suspects was premeditated or the product of a tacit agreement amongst those involved in the operation.

The applicants [also] submitted that it would be wrong for the Court, as the Commission had done, to limit its assessment to the question of the possible justification of the soldiers who actually killed the suspects. It must examine the liability of the Government for all aspects of the operation. Indeed, the soldiers may well have been acquitted at a criminal trial if they could have shown that they honestly believed the ungrounded and false information they were given.

. . . In sum, [the applicants] submitted that the killings came about as a result of incompetence and negligence in the planning and conduct of the anti-terrorist operation to arrest the suspects as well as a failure to maintain a proper balance between the need to meet the threat posed and the right to life of the suspect. . . .

The Commission considered that, given the soldiers' perception of the risk to the lives of the people of Gibraltar, the shooting of the three suspects could be regarded as absolutely necessary for the legitimate aim of the defence of others from unlawful violence. It also concluded that, having regard to the possibility that the suspects had brought in a car bomb which, if detonated, would have occasioned the loss of many lives and the possibility that the suspects could have been able to detonate it when confronted by the soldiers, the planning and execution of the operation by the authorities did not disclose any deliberate design or lack of proper care which might have rendered the use of lethal force disproportionate to the aim of saving lives.

[The Court concludes that "the actions of the soldiers do not, in themselves, give rise to a violation of" Article 2, and then turns to the question "whether the anti-terrorist operation as a whole was controlled and organised in a manner which respected the requirements of Article 2."]

It may be questioned why the three suspects were not arrested at the border immediately on their arrival in Gibraltar and why, as emerged from the evidence given by Inspector Ullger, the decision was taken not to prevent them from entering Gibraltar if they were believed to be on a bombing mission. Having had advance warning of the terrorists' intentions it would certainly have been possible for the authorities to have mounted an arrest operation. Although surprised at the early arrival of the three suspects, they had a surveillance team at the border and an arrest group nearby. In addition, the Security Services and the Spanish authorities had photographs of the three suspects, knew their names as well as their aliases and would have known what passports to look for.

On this issue, the Government submitted that at that moment there might not have been sufficient evidence to warrant the detention and trial of the suspects. Moreover, to release them, having alerted them to the authorities' state of awareness but leaving them or others free to try again, would obviously increase the risks. Nor could the authorities be sure that those three were the only terrorists they had to deal with or of the manner in which it was proposed to carry out the bombing.

The Court confines itself to observing in this respect that the danger to the population of Gibraltar—which is at the heart of the Government's submissions in this case—in not preventing their entry must be considered to outweigh the possible consequences of having insufficient evidence to warrant their detention and trial. In its view, either the authorities knew that there was no bomb in the car—which the Court has already discounted—or there was a serious miscalculation by those responsible for controlling the operation. As a result, the scene was set in which the fatal shooting, given the intelligence assessments which had been made, was a foreseeable possibility if not a likelihood. The decision not to stop the three terrorists from entering Gibraltar is thus a relevant factor to take into account under this head. . . .

Although detailed investigation at the inquest into the training received by the soldiers was prevented by the public interest certificates which had been issued, it is not clear whether they had been trained or instructed to assess whether the use of firearms to wound their targets may have been warranted by the specific circumstances that confronted them at the moment of arrest.

Their reflex action in this vital respect lacks the degree of caution in the use of firearms to be expected from law enforcement personnel in a democratic society, even when dealing with dangerous terrorist suspects, and stands in marked contrast to the standard of care reflected in the instructions in the use of firearms by the police which had been drawn to their attention and which emphasised the legal responsibilities of the individual officer in the light of conditions prevailing at the moment of engagement.

This failure by the authorities also suggests a lack of appropriate care in the control and organisation of the arrest operation.

. . . In sum, having regard to the decision not to prevent the suspects from travelling into Gibraltar, to the failure of the authorities to make sufficient allowances for the possibility that their intelligence assessments might, in some respects at least, be erroneous and to the automatic recourse to lethal force when the soldiers opened fire, the Court is not persuaded that the killing of the three terrorists constituted the use of force which was no more than absolutely necessary in defence of persons from unlawful violence within the meaning of Article 2 para. 2(a) of the Convention.

Accordingly, the Court finds that there has been a breach of Article 2 of the Convention. . . .

FOR THESE REASONS, THE COURT

1. Holds by ten votes to nine that there has been a violation of Article 2 of the Convention;

2. Holds unanimously that the United Kingdom is to pay to the applicants, within three months, £38,700 for costs and expenses incurred in the Strasbourg proceedings, less 37,731 French francs to be converted into pounds sterling at the rate of exchange applicable on the date of delivery of the present judgment;

3. Dismisses unanimously the applicants' claim for damages;

4. Dismisses unanimously the applicants' claim for costs and expenses incurred in the Gibraltar inquest;

5. Dismisses unanimously the remainder of the claims for just satisfaction.

JOINT DISSENTING OPINION OF JUDGES RYSSDAL, BERNHARDT, THOR VILHJALSSON, GÖLCÜKLÜ, PALM PEKKANEN, SIR JOHN FREELAND, BAKA AND JAMBREK

We are unable to subscribe to the opinion of a majority of our colleagues that there has been a violation of Article 2 of the Convention in this case.

As to the section dealing with the application of Article 2 to the facts of the case, we fully concur in rejecting as unsubstantiated the applicants' allegations that the killing of the three suspects was premeditated or the product of a tacit agreement among those involved in the operation.

We also agree with the conclusion . . . that the actions of the four soldiers who carried out the shootings do not, in themselves, give rise to a violation of Article 2. It is rightly accepted that those soldiers honestly believed, in the light of the information which they had been given, that it was necessary to act as they did in order to prevent the suspects from detonating a bomb and causing serious loss of life: the actions which they took were thus perceived by them as absolutely necessary in order to safeguard innocent lives.

We disagree, however, with the evaluation made by the majority of the way in which the control and organisation of the operation were carried out by the authorities. It is that evaluation which, crucially, leads to the finding of violation.

We recall at the outset that the events in this case were examined at the domestic level by an inquest held in Gibraltar over a period of nineteen days between 6 and 30 September 1988. The jury, after hearing the evidence of seventy-nine witnesses (including the soldiers, police officers and surveillance personnel involved in the operation and also pathologists, forensic scientists and experts on the detonation of explosive devices), and after being addressed by the Coroner in respect of the applicable domestic law, reached by a majority of nine to two a verdict of lawful killing. The circumstances were subsequently investigated in depth and evaluated by the Commission, which found in its report, by a majority of eleven to six, that there had been no violation of the Convention.

The finding of the inquest, as a domestic tribunal operating under the relevant domestic law, is not of itself determinative of the Convention issues before the Court. But, having regard to the crucial importance in this case of a proper appreciation of the facts and to the advantage undeniably enjoyed by the jury in having observed the demeanour of the witnesses when giving their evidence under examination and cross-examination, its significance should certainly not be underestimated. Similarly, the Commission's establishment and evaluation of the facts is not conclusive for the Court; but it would be mistaken for the Court, at yet one further remove from the evidence as given by the witnesses, to fail to give due weight to the report of the Commission, the body which is primarily charged under the Convention with the finding of facts and which has, of course, great experience in the discharge of that task.

[The dissenting judges disagree with the legal evaluations of the Court about the alleged failures of the United Kingdom and conclude:]

The accusation of a breach by a state of its obligation under Article 2 of the Convention to protect the right to life is of the utmost seriousness. For the reasons given above, the evaluation in . . . the judgment seems to us to fall well short of substantiating the finding that there has been a breach of the Article in this case. We ourselves follow the reasoning and conclusion of the Commission in its comprehensive, painstaking and notably realistic report. Like the Commission, we are satisfied that no failings have been shown in the organisation and control of the operation by the authorities which could justify a conclusion that force was used against the suspects disproportionately to the purpose of defending innocent persons from unlawful violence. We consider that the use of lethal force in this case, however regrettable the need to resort to such force may be, did not exceed what was, in the circumstances as known at the time, "absolutely necessary" for that purpose and did not amount to a breach by the United Kingdom of its obligations under the Convention.

McCann *and the Court of Public Opinion.* When the British government, then the Conservative government of John Major, complied with the *McCann* judgment and paid the sums ordered by the European Court of Human Rights, it was condemned in the British media. The *Daily Mail*, for example, gave the payment its main headline: "£40,000 PRESENT FOR IRA FAMILIES." The front-page story began as follows: "The Government handed a Christmas gift of nearly £40,000 to relatives of three IRA terrorists." The article said that members of the House of Commons "branded the decision 'appalling' and 'unthinkable'" and that the "[f]amilies of IRA victims were also horrified." *Daily Mail* (London), Dec. 27, 1995, at 1. The *Times* took a more nuanced position, noting that "[o]nly certain aspects of the [Gibraltar] operation have been condemned in this judgment," but still remarking that the "cost of denying the IRA the status of an army is to swallow hard when a continental court wags its finger." *The Times* (London), Sept. 28, 1995, at 21.

The Efficacy of International Law. The British government was originally reluctant to pay the *McCann* judgment. The Prime Minister "had hinted that the Gibraltar case and other setbacks suffered by the United Kingdom before the European Court might cause it to withdraw from the convention." John Cary Sims, "Compliance Without Remands: The Experience under the European Convention on Human Rights," 36 *Arizona State Law Journal* 639, 650 (2004). Why in the end did the U.K. government satisfy the Strasbourg Court's judgment? What "sanction" could have been applied against the U.K. if the government had failed to comply with the ruling? Why should a sovereign state like the United Kingdom voluntarily comply with an international court judgment like *McCann*? What would the United Kingdom lose if it were to be expelled from other European institutions for failure to comply with decisions of the European Court of Human Rights? Could the United Kingdom expect other states to comply with the Convention if it repudiated the Court's judgment? Would repudiation spoil the U.K.'s reputation and make it more difficult for the government to conclude treaties in the future?

The many European countries that are parties to the European Convention on Human Rights have their own domestic legal rules and processes protecting human rights. Why should they also enter into an international legal system establishing European rules about human rights and setting up European institutions to enforce those rules?

Domestic Courts and International Law. Perhaps surprisingly, the great proportion of international law judgments are made, not by international courts like the European Court of Human Rights, but by domestic courts. There are, of course, thousands of domestic courts, and many of them have the authority to interpret and apply the rules of international law. Below in *Filartiga* we watch one such court, the U.S. Court of Appeals for the Second Circuit, interpret a rule of customary international law based on state practice. The rule it expounds was deemed so important that the Second Circuit hinted that what may be at issue is a fundamental legal norm, more powerful than either a customary or a treaty rule.

FILARTIGA V. PENA-IRALA

630 F.2d 876 (2d Cir. 1980)

IRVING R. KAUFMAN, CIRCUIT JUDGE:

Upon ratification of the Constitution, the thirteen former colonies were fused into a single nation, one which, in its relations with foreign states, is bound both to observe and construe the accepted norms of international law, formerly known as the law of nations. Under the Articles of Confederation, the several states had interpreted and applied this body of doctrine as a part of their common law, but with the founding of the "more perfect Union" of 1789, the law of nations became preeminently a federal concern.

Implementing the constitutional mandate for national control over foreign relations, the First Congress established original district court jurisdiction over "all causes where an alien sues for a tort only [committed] in violation of the law of nations." Judiciary Act of 1789, ch. 20, § 9(b), 1 Stat. 73, 77 (1789), *codified at* 28 U.S.C. § 1350. Construing this rarely-invoked provision, we hold that deliberate torture perpetrated under color of official authority violates universally accepted norms of the international law of human rights, regardless of the nationality of the parties. Thus, whenever an alleged torturer is found and served with process by an alien within our borders, § 1350 provides federal jurisdiction. Accordingly, we reverse the judgment of the district court dismissing the complaint for want of federal jurisdiction.

The appellants, plaintiffs below, are citizens of the Republic of Paraguay. Dr. Joel Filartiga, a physician, describes himself as a longstanding opponent of the government of President Alfredo Stroessner, which has held power in Paraguay since 1954. His daughter, Dolly Filartiga, arrived in the United States in 1978 under a visitor's visa, and has since applied for permanent political asylum. The Filartigas brought this action in the Eastern District of New York against Americo Norberto Pena-Irala (Pena), also a citizen of Paraguay, for wrongfully causing the death of Dr. Filartiga's seventeen-year old son, Joelito. Because the district court dismissed the action for want of subject matter jurisdiction, we must accept as true the allegations contained in the Filartigas' complaint and affidavits for purposes of this appeal.

The appellants contend that on March 29, 1976, Joelito Filartiga was kidnapped and tortured to death by Pena, who was then Inspector General of Police in Asuncion, Paraguay. Later that day, the police brought Dolly Filartiga to Pena's home where she was confronted with the body of her brother, which evidenced marks of severe torture. As she fled, horrified, from the house, Pena followed after her shouting, "Here you have what you have been looking for so long and what you deserve. Now shut up." The Filartigas claim that Joelito was tortured and killed in retaliation for his father's political activities and beliefs.

Shortly thereafter, Dr. Filartiga commenced a criminal action in the Paraguayan courts against Pena and the police for the murder of his son. As a result, Dr. Filartiga's attorney was arrested and brought to police headquarters where, shackled to a wall, Pena threatened him with death. This attorney, it is alleged, has since been disbarred without just cause.

During the course of the Paraguayan criminal proceeding, which is apparently still pending after four years, another man, Hugo Duarte, confessed to the murder. Duarte, who was a member of the Pena household, claimed that he had discovered his wife and Joelito *in flagrante delicto*, and that the crime was one of passion. The Filartigas have submitted a photograph of Joelito's corpse showing injuries they believe refute this claim. Dolly Filartiga, moreover, has stated that she will offer evidence of three independent autopsies demonstrating that her brother's death "was the result of professional methods of torture." Despite his confession, Duarte, we are told, has never been convicted or sentenced in connection with the crime.

In July of 1978, Pena sold his house in Paraguay and entered the United States under a visitor's visa. He was accompanied by Juana Bautista Fernandez Villalba, who had lived with him in Paraguay. The couple remained in the United States beyond the term of their visas, and were living in Brooklyn, New York, when Dolly Filartiga, who was then living in Washington, D.C., learned of their presence. Acting on information provided by Dolly the Immigration and Naturalization Service arrested Pena and his companion, both of whom were subsequently ordered deported on April 5, 1979 following a hearing. They had then resided in the United States for more than nine months.

Almost immediately, Dolly caused Pena to be served with a summons and civil complaint at the Brooklyn Navy Yard, where he was being held pending deportation. The complaint alleged that Pena had wrongfully caused Joelito's death by torture and sought compensatory and punitive damages of $10,000,000. The Filartigas also sought to enjoin Pena's deportation to ensure his availability for testimony at trial. The cause of action is stated as arising under "wrongful death statutes; the U.N. Charter, the Universal Declaration on Human Rights; the U.N. Declaration Against Torture; the American Declaration of the Rights and Duties of Man; and other pertinent declarations, documents and practices constituting the customary international law of human rights and the law of nations," as well as 28 U.S.C. § 1350, Article II, sec. 2 and the Supremacy Clause of the U.S. Constitution.

. . . The Filartigas submitted the affidavits of a number of distinguished international legal scholars, who stated unanimously that the law of nations prohibits absolutely the use of torture as alleged in the complaint.[4] Pena, in support of his motion to dismiss on the ground of *forum non conveniens*, submitted the affidavit of his Paraguayan counsel, Jose Emilio Gorostiaga, who averred that Paraguayan law provides a full and adequate civil remedy for the wrong alleged. Dr. Filartiga has not commenced such an action, however, believing that further resort to the courts of his own country would be futile. . . .

The district court continued the stay of deportation for forty-eight hours while appellants applied for further stays. These applications were denied by a panel of this Court on May 22, 1979, and by the Supreme Court two days later. Shortly thereafter, Pena and his companion returned to Paraguay.

Appellants rest their principal argument in support of federal jurisdiction upon the Alien Tort Statute, 28 U.S.C. § 1350, which provides: "The district courts shall have original jurisdiction of any civil action by an alien for a tort only,

---

[4] Richard Falk, the Albert G. Milbank Professor of International Law and Practice at Princeton University, and a former Vice President of the American Society of International Law, avers that, in his judgment, "it is now beyond reasonable doubt that torture of a person held in detention that results in severe harm or death is a violation of the law of nations." Thomas Franck, professor of international law at New York University and Director of the New York University Center for International Studies, offers his opinion that torture has now been rejected by virtually all nations, although it was once commonly used to extract confessions. Richard Lillich, the Howard W. Smith Professor of Law at the University of Virginia School of Law, concludes, after a lengthy review of the authorities, that officially perpetrated torture is "a violation of international law (formerly called the law of nations)." Finally, Myres McDougal, a former Sterling Professor of Law at the Yale Law School, and a past President of the American Society of International Law, states that torture is an offense against the law of nations, and that "it has long been recognized that such offenses vitally affect relations between states."

committed in violation of the law of nations or a treaty of the United States." Since appellants do not contend that their action arises directly under a treaty of the United States, a threshold question on the jurisdictional issue is whether the conduct alleged violates the law of nations. In light of the universal condemnation of torture in numerous international agreements, and the renunciation of torture as an instrument of official policy by virtually all of the nations of the world (in principle if not in practice), we find that an act of torture committed by a state official against one held in detention violates established norms of the international law of human rights, and hence the law of nations.

The Supreme Court has enumerated the appropriate sources of international law. The law of nations "may be ascertained by consulting the works of jurists, writing professedly on public law; or by the general usage and practice of nations; or by judicial decisions recognizing and enforcing that law." *United States v. Smith*, 18 U.S. (5 Wheat.) 153, 160–61 (1820); *Lopes v. Reederei Richard Schroder*, 225 F.Supp. 292, 295 (E.D.Pa.1963). In *Smith*, a statute proscribing "the crime of piracy [on the high seas] as defined by the law of nations," 3 Stat. 510(a) (1819), was held sufficiently determinate in meaning to afford the basis for a death sentence. The *Smith* Court discovered among the works of Lord Bacon, Grotius, Bochard and other commentators a genuine consensus that rendered the crime "sufficiently and constitutionally defined." *Smith, supra*, 18 U.S. (5 Wheat.) at 162.

The Paquete Habana, 175 U.S. 677 (1900), reaffirmed that

> where there is no treaty, and no controlling executive or legislative act or judicial decision, resort must be had to the customs and usages of civilized nations; and, as evidence of these, to the works of jurists and commentators, who by years of labor, research and experience, have made themselves peculiarly well acquainted with the subjects of which they treat. Such works are resorted to by judicial tribunals, not for the speculations of their authors concerning what the law ought to be, but for trustworthy evidence of what the law really is.

Id. at 700. Modern international sources confirm the propriety of this approach. . . .

The United Nations Charter (a treaty of the United States, *see* 59 Stat. 1033 (1945)) makes it clear that in this modern age a state's treatment of its own citizens is a matter of international concern. It provides:

> With a view to the creation of conditions of stability and well-being which are necessary for peaceful and friendly relations among nations . . . the United Nations shall promote . . . universal respect for, and

observance of, human rights and fundamental freedoms for all without distinctions as to race, sex, language or religion.

Id. Art. 55. And further:

All members pledge themselves to take joint and separate action in cooperation with the Organization for the achievement of the purposes set forth in Article 55.

Id. Art. 56.

While this broad mandate has been held not to be wholly self-executing, *Hitai v. Immigration and Naturalization Service*, 343 F.2d 466, 468 (2d Cir. 1965), this observation alone does not end our inquiry. For although there is no universal agreement as to the precise extent of the "human rights and fundamental freedoms" guaranteed to all by the Charter, there is at present no dissent from the view that the guaranties include, at a bare minimum, the right to be free from torture. This prohibition has become part of customary international law, as evidenced and defined by the Universal Declaration of Human Rights, General Assembly Resolution 217(III)(A) (Dec. 10, 1948) which states, in the plainest of terms, "no one shall be subjected to torture."[10] The General Assembly has declared that the Charter precepts embodied in this Universal Declaration "constitute basic principles of international law." G.A.Res. 2625 (XXV) (Oct. 24, 1970).

Particularly relevant is the Declaration on the Protection of All Persons from Being Subjected to Torture, General Assembly Resolution 3452, 30 U.N. GAOR Supp. (No. 34) 91, U.N.Doc. A/1034 (1975)[.] The Declaration expressly prohibits any state from permitting the dastardly and totally inhuman act of torture. Torture, in turn, is defined as "any act by which severe pain and suffering, whether physical or mental, is intentionally inflicted by or at the instigation of a public official on a person for such purposes as . . . intimidating him or other persons." The Declaration goes on to provide that "[w]here it is proved that an act of torture or other cruel, inhuman or degrading treatment or punishment has been committed by or at the instigation of a public official, the victim shall be afforded redress and compensation, in accordance with national law." This Declaration, like the Declaration of Human Rights before it, was adopted without dissent by the General Assembly. Nayar, "Human Rights: The United Nations and United States Foreign Policy," 19 *Harv. Int'l L.J.* 813, 816 n.18 (1978).

---

[10] Eighteen nations have incorporated the Universal Declaration into their own constitutions. 48 *Revue Internationale de Droit Penal* Nos. 3 & 4, at 211 (1977).

These U.N. declarations are significant because they specify with great precision the obligations of member nations under the Charter. Since their adoption, "[m]embers can no longer contend that they do not know what human rights they promised in the Charter to promote." Sohn, "A Short History of United Nations Documents on Human Rights," in *"The United Nations and Human Rights," 18th Report of the Commission* (Commission to Study the Organization of Peace ed. 1968). Moreover, a U.N. Declaration is, according to one authoritative definition, "a formal and solemn instrument, suitable for rare occasions when principles of great and lasting importance are being enunciated." 34 U.N. ESCOR, Supp. (No. 8) 15, U.N. Doc. E/cn.4/1/610 (1962) (memorandum of Office of Legal Affairs, U.N. Secretariat). Accordingly, it has been observed that the Universal Declaration of Human Rights "no longer fits into the dichotomy of 'binding treaty' against 'nonbinding pronouncement,' but is rather an authoritative statement of the international community." E. Schwelb, *Human Rights and the International Community* 70 (1964). Thus, a Declaration creates an expectation of adherence, and "insofar as the expectation is gradually justified by State practice, a declaration may by custom become recognized as laying down rules binding upon the States." 34 U.N. ESCOR, *supra*. Indeed, several commentators have concluded that the Universal Declaration has become, *in toto*, a part of binding, customary international law. Nayar, *supra*, at 816–17; Waldock, "Human Rights in Contemporary International Law and the Significance of the European Convention," *Int'l & Comp. L.Q.*, Supp. Publ. No. 11 at 15 (1965).

Turning to the act of torture, we have little difficulty discerning its universal renunciation in the modern usage and practice of nations. *Smith, supra*, 18 U.S. (5 Wheat.) at 160–61. The international consensus surrounding torture has found expression in numerous international treaties and accords. *E.g., American Convention on Human Rights*, Art. 5, OAS Treaty Series No. 36 at 1, OAS Off. Rec. OEA/Ser 4 v/II 23, doc. 21, rev. 2 (English ed., 1975) ("No one shall be subjected to torture or to cruel, inhuman or degrading punishment or treatment"); International Covenant on Civil and Political Rights, U.N. General Assembly Res. 2200 (XXI)A, U.N. Doc. A/6316 (Dec. 16, 1966) (identical language); European Convention for the Protection of Human Rights and Fundamental Freedoms, Art. 3, Council of Europe, European Treaty Series No. 5 (1968), 213 U.N.T.S. 211 (*semble*). The substance of these international agreements is reflected in modern municipal—*i.e.* national—law as well. Although torture was once a routine concomitant of criminal interrogations in many nations, during the modern and hopefully more enlightened era it has been universally renounced. According to one survey, torture is prohibited, expressly or implicitly, by the constitutions of over fifty-five nations, including both the United States and Paraguay. Our State Department reports a general recognition of this principle:

> There now exists an international consensus that recognizes basic human rights and obligations owed by all governments to their citizens. . . . There is no doubt that these rights are often violated; but virtually all governments acknowledge their validity.

Department of State, *Country Reports on Human Rights for 1979*, published as Joint Comm. Print, House Comm. on Foreign Affairs, and Senate Comm. on Foreign Relations, 96th Cong. 2d Sess. (Feb. 4, 1980), Introduction at 1. We have been directed to no assertion by any contemporary state of a right to torture its own or another nation's citizens. Indeed, United States diplomatic contacts confirm the universal abhorrence with which torture is viewed:

> In exchanges between United States embassies and all foreign states with which the United States maintains relations, it has been the Department of State's general experience that no government has asserted a right to torture its own nationals. Where reports of torture elicit some credence, a state usually responds by denial or, less frequently, by asserting that the conduct was unauthorized or constituted rough treatment short of torture.[15]

Memorandum of the United States as *Amicus Curiae* at 16 n.34.

Having examined the sources from which customary international law is derived—the usage of nations, judicial opinions and the works of jurists[16]—we conclude that official torture is now prohibited by the law of nations. The prohibition is clear and unambiguous, and admits of no distinction between treatment of aliens and citizens. Accordingly, we must conclude that the dictum in *Dreyfus v. Von Finck*, [534 F.2d 24, 31 (2d Cir.), *cert. denied*, 429 U.S. 835 (1976)], to the effect that "violations of international law do not occur when the aggrieved parties are nationals of the acting state," is clearly out of tune with the current usage and practice of international law. The treaties and accords cited above, as

---

[15] The fact that the prohibition of torture is often honored in the breach does not diminish its binding effect as a norm of international law. As one commentator has put it, "The best evidence for the existence of international law is that every actual State recognizes that it does exist and that it is itself under an obligation to observe it. States often violate international law, just as individuals often violate municipal law; but no more than individuals do States defend their violations by claiming that they are above the law." J. Brierly, *The Outlook for International Law* 4–5 (Oxford 1944).

[16] *See also Ireland v. United Kingdom*, Judgment of Jan. 18, 1978 (European Court of Human Rights), *summarized in* [1978] Yearbook, European Convention on Human Rights 602 (Council of Europe) (holding that Britain's subjection of prisoners to sleep deprivation, hooding, exposure to hissing noise, reduced diet and standing against a wall for hours was "inhuman and degrading," but not "torture" within meaning of European Convention on Human Rights).

well as the express foreign policy of our own government, all make it clear that international law confers fundamental rights upon all people vis-á-vis their own governments. While the ultimate scope of those rights will be a subject for continuing refinement and elaboration, we hold that the right to be free from torture is now among them. . . .

In the twentieth century the international community has come to recognize the common danger posed by the flagrant disregard of basic human rights and particularly the right to be free of torture. Spurred first by the Great War, and then the Second, civilized nations have banded together to prescribe acceptable norms of international behavior. From the ashes of the Second World War arose the United Nations Organization, amid hopes that an era of peace and cooperation had at last begun. Though many of these aspirations have remained elusive goals, that circumstance cannot diminish the true progress that has been made. In the modern age, humanitarian and practical considerations have combined to lead the nations of the world to recognize that respect for fundamental human rights is in their individual and collective interest. Among the rights universally proclaimed by all nations, as we have noted, is the right to be free of physical torture. Indeed, for purposes of civil liability, the torturer has become—like the pirate and slave trader before him—*hostis humani generis*, an enemy of all mankind. Our holding today, giving effect to a jurisdictional provision enacted by our First Congress, is a small but important step in the fulfillment of the ageless dream to free all people from brutal violence.

Individuals as Subjects of International Law. Filartiga involved international human rights claims of Paraguayan citizens against an official of the government of Paraguay. *McCann* concerned individuals' international human rights claims against the U.K. government. Why in principle and practice should either the Paraguayan or U.K. government be subject to international law rules or process with respect to complaints by their own or foreign nationals?

J.L. Brierly in his classic British introduction to international law defined the discipline "as the body of rules and principles of action which are binding upon civilized states in their relations with one another." J.L. Brierly, *The Law of Nations* 1 (4th ed. 1949). How well does Brierly's definition describe the law the rules of which were actually applied in *Filartiga* and *McCann*? How might this definition be reformulated in the light of these two cases where individual rights in international law were in issue? More about individual rights under international law is in Chapter 7.

States as Subjects of International Legal Process. In *McCann*, the United Kingdom was subject to the jurisdiction of the European Court of Human Rights because it had ratified an international convention formally and explicitly accepting the jurisdiction of the Court. The U.K. government had agreed that the dispute could go to the Court for judgment. In *Filartiga* why should Paraguayan government officials be subject to the jurisdiction of United States federal courts in New York? If it appeared unlikely that the government of Paraguay would permit the Filartigas to sue in Paraguayan courts, would it be likely that the Paraguayan courts would respect or enforce a U.S. judgment in favor of the Filartigas?

Perspectives on Litigating International Human Rights Law. Each of the participants in *Filartiga* had a particular perspective on the case. Why did the Filartigas sue in a U.S. court? In some cases it was possible for litigants like the Filartigas to win significant monetary damages to redress violations of international law. Professor Murphy pointed out that at one time in Alien Tort Claims Act litigation "the chances for a successful civil suit were substantially greater than those for a successful criminal prosecution." John F. Murphy, "Civil Liability for the Commission of International Crimes as an Alternative to Criminal Prosecution," 12 *Harvard Human Rights Journal* 1, 47 (1999). So too for claims against "perpetrators of international terrorism." John F. Murphy, "Civil Lawsuits as a Legal Response to International Terrorism," in *Civil Litigation Against Terrorism* 37, 44 (John Norton Moore ed. 2004). Probably, the Filartigas' battle was more about political goals and public recognition of their cause than actually to win monetary damages. Roberts B. Owen, the Legal Adviser to the U.S. Department of State at the time of the case, viewed Dr. Filartiga as "one of the leading political opponents of the present [Paraguayan] regime." Roberts B. Owen, "Address at the Annual Dinner of the American Branch of the International Law Association, the Princeton Club, New York City, November 14, 1980," *Proceedings and Committee Reports of the American Branch of the International Law Association 1981–1982*, at 14.

Owen also described how lawyers for the U.S. government were divided about what side to take in *Filartiga*, some feeling that there was "a consensus that customary international law now imposes upon every government an obligation to refrain from torture" and others concerned that "our courts and our government would gradually become self-appointed policemen for the world." Finally, "after much soul-searching and debate," the U.S. government chose to file its *amicus* brief for the plaintiff's position, Owen agreeing "that it is a good thing for the U.S. courts to be available to provide remedies for persons aggrieved by violations of internationally protected rights." *Id.* at 16. When the U.S. government fails to take foreign opinion into account, the United States can lose some of its ability to influence world politics. See Joseph S. Nye, Jr., "The Decline of America's Soft Power: Why Washington Should Worry," 83 *Foreign Affairs*, May/June 2004, at 16.

Over and above his judgment, Judge Kaufman had strong views about the case. He authored an article on *Filartiga* in which he wrote that "the decision breaks new ground in the body of law governing torture." Irving R. Kaufman, "A Legal Remedy for International Torture?," *New York Times Magazine*, Nov. 9, 1980, at 44. Several years later he chose *Filartiga* to conclude an article about his judicial career. Irving R. Kaufman, "The Anatomy of Decisionmaking," 53 *Fordham Law Review* 1, 20–22 (1984). *Filartiga* has been recognized as a "landmark legal precedent." Beth Stephens, "*Filartiga v. Peña-Irala*: From Family Tragedy to Human Rights Accountability," 37 *Rutgers Law Journal* 623 (2006). The case "triggered a sea change in international human rights litigation." Harold Hongju Koh, "*Filartiga v. Peña-Irala*: Judicial Internationalization into Domestic Law of the Customary International Law Norm Against Torture," in *International Law Stories* 45, 46 (John E. Noyes, Laura A. Dickinson & Mark W. Janis eds. 2007).

The lawyers who brought the *Filartiga* case hoped for just this result. They explained that they turned to the Alien Tort Claims Act, "a little-used 200-year old statute," in their search for a way to give lawyers "the opportunity to establish that officials who violate the rights of their own citizens could be brought to justice in U.S. courts." After *Filartiga*, their goal "was to bring more cases, obtain more circuit court opinions in our favor and make the *Filartiga* principle unassailable." They plainly acknowledged that they were "political lawyers, [wanting] to use the *Filartiga* precedent to fight those who were violating human rights." Michael Ratner & Beth Stephens, "The Center for Constitutional Rights: Using Law and the *Filartiga* Principle in the Fight for Human Rights," in American Civil Liberties Union, *International Civil Liberties Report*, Dec. 1993, at 29. For an excellent account of the efforts made by the attorneys in *Filartiga*, see William J. Aceves, *The Anatomy of Torture: A Documentary History of* Filartiga v. Pena-Irala (2007). In general, for the relation between municipal courts and international law, see Chapter 5.

The Fate of Filartiga. On its facts, would *Filartiga* be decided the same way today? The first significant holding of the Supreme Court on the Alien Tort Claims Act, *Sosa v. Alvarez-Machain*, 542 U.S. 692 (2004), seemed to preserve a *Filartiga*-like cause of action. However, a second Supreme Court ATCA judgment, *Kiobel v. Royal Dutch Petroleum Co.*, 569 U.S. 12 (2013), raised doubts about whether the territorial linkages of a case like *Filartiga* would nowadays satisfy the Court's presumption against the extraterritorial application of a U.S. statute. We consider both *Sosa* and *Kiobel* and their implications in Chapter 5.

The Nature of Customary International Law. Whatever the eventual outcome of the Supreme Court's test about the extraterritorial reach of the Alien Tort Claims Act, *Filartiga* remains an excellent introduction to the nature of customary international law. In theory, at least, customary international law is developed as a result of the actual practice of states. If the Paraguayan government and other governments do actually torture their own citizens, how can there be a rule of customary international law proscribing such practice? Is the court in *Filartiga* truly applying customary international law, or is it perhaps finding and applying rules drawn from some sort of fundamental international law, an international human rights law analogous to municipal constitutional guarantees of human rights?

Note the diverse evidences of international law employed by the *Filartiga* court in deciding that international law prohibits torture. Did the court give any one kind of evidence primacy over the others? Did some evidences seem more or less persuasive? Did the judgment demonstrate that Paraguay has consented to the rule prohibiting torture or only that the community of nations generally supports such a rule? Chapter 2 further explores customary international law and the various non-consensual sources of international law, such as *jus cogens*.

The Efficacy of International Law. Although one might assume that national courts, like the U.S. federal courts, are usually more efficacious than international courts, here the expectation was reversed in practice. Though the decision of the international court in *McCann* was respected, the decisions of the national courts in *Filartiga* were not. On remand, the district court imposed a judgment for $10,385,364 against Pena-Irala in order "to reflect adherence to the world community's proscription of torture and to attempt to deter its practice," 577 F.Supp. 860, 867 (E.D.N.Y.1984), but these damages were never paid.

Nonetheless, *Filartiga* had considerable effect as a judicial precedent, spawning many subsequent cases in U.S. courts. The jurisdiction of the Alien Tort Claims Act grew to reach not only individual actors, but also governments and private corporations. Plaintiffs included non-governmental organizations as well as individuals. Moreover, courts in other countries, including Spain, the Netherlands, and the United Kingdom, followed in *Filartiga*'s wake. Association of the Bar of the City of New York, Panel, "The Making of *Filartiga v. Peña*: The

Alien Tort Claims Act After Twenty-Five Years," 9 *New York City Law Review* 249, 267–73 (2006).

CHAPTER 2

The Sources of International Law

International lawyers ordinarily conceive of international law in terms of its "sources," a term introduced in Part A. Each source is then explored in subsequent parts: treaties (B), custom (C), general principles (D), *jus cogens* (E), and equity (F). Besides introducing the sources of international law, this chapter asks how international law is made or "legislated" and why countries and individuals make use of international law in practice.

A. AN OVERVIEW OF SOURCES

In this part we examine the concept of sources of law and look at Article 38 of the Statute of the International Court of Justice, which is often consulted on the issue of sources of international law.

Evidentiary Sources. Sometimes when lawyers refer to "sources" of law they are simply thinking about where to find the evidences of rules of international law. In *McCann* in Chapter 1, the rule was evidenced in a treaty—Article 2 of the European Convention on Human Rights. In *Filartiga*, the evidences for the international law rule proscribing torture were quite varied: customary practice, international judgments and resolutions, fundamental and constitutional norms, and the writings of jurists.

Formal Sources. Different from the question of where to find the law is the question of what may or may not constitute a legitimate rule of international law. For any legal system to function effectively in practice, its participants must agree on the types of rules that amount to "law." Those types of rules are sometimes called "formal" sources.

The question of formal sources arises with respect to national legal systems as well as the international one. In civil law countries, such as France and Germany, participants rely primarily on statutes as a source of law. Common law jurisdictions, such as the United States and the United Kingdom, look both to statutes and to judicial case law. Islamic countries consider religious teachings as a source of legal rules. Some states rely at least in part on customary law, and many countries reflect mixtures of different legal traditions.

When countries differ in their views of legal authority, that often creates no dilemmas. That is, French legal players may agree on one set of rules, and U.S. players on a different set, but if each set of players applies its own rules among themselves on their own turf, there are no conceptual disputes about what counts as law. (There are of course plenty of disputes about how that law should be interpreted and applied!) But it may be harder to agree on the sources of legal authority when questions of international law arise. If there is theoretical disagreement about what international law is, it can be awkward for international lawyers, judges, and jurists, who are all supposed to be playing by the same rules.

Article 38 of the Statute of the International Court of Justice. When international lawyers from most anywhere think about the formal sources of international law, an ordinary starting point is Article 38 of the Statute of the International Court of Justice (an international tribunal that we will look at closely in Chapter 4). Strictly speaking, Article 38 is an instruction only to the judges of the International Court; it does not by its terms apply to other international courts or lawyers. Moreover, Article 38 nowhere mentions "sources." It is, however, often taken to be a listing of the formal sources of international law.

STATUTE OF THE INTERNATIONAL COURT OF JUSTICE, ARTICLE 38

June 26, 1945, 59 Stat. 1031, T.S. No. 993

1.   The Court, whose function is to decide in accordance with international law such disputes as are submitted to it, shall apply:

(a)   international conventions, whether general or particular, establishing rules expressly recognized by the contesting States;

(b)   international custom, as evidence of a general practice accepted as law;

(c)   the general principles of law recognized by civilized nations;

(d)   subject to the provisions of Article 59, judicial decisions and the teachings of the most highly qualified publicists of the various nations, as subsidiary means for the determination of rules of law.

2. This provision shall not prejudice the power of the Court to decide a case *ex aequo et bono*, if the parties agree thereto.

Article 38(1)(a) of the ICJ Statute: Treaties. An "international convention" is another name for a treaty. The lawyers and judges in the *McCann Case* in Chapter 1 relied on a treaty: the European Convention on Human Rights. We examine treaties in Part B of this chapter.

Article 38(1)(b) and (c): International Custom and General Principles of Law. Some international lawyers would consider *Filartiga*'s rule proscribing torture (Chapter 1) to be based on international custom, reflecting a general practice of countries (Article 38(1)(b)). We explore customary international law in Part C. As we suggested in Chapter 1, however, it may be that the rule in *Filartiga* depends on "fundamental norms" not necessarily linked to general practice or custom. Article 38(1)(c)'s "general principles of law," to which we turn in Part D, also does not necessarily encompass the notion of fundamental norms. In short, there may be types of international law beyond the confines of Article 38.

Sources Not Listed in Article 38. Natural law and *jus cogens* are two concepts often linked to the notion of fundamental norms. Neither is listed in Article 38. In practice, however, international lawyers and judges on both the ICJ and other tribunals do use sources of international law other than those listed in Article 38. Additional sources not mentioned in Article 38 include equitable principles and the resolutions of international organizations such as the United Nations. We consider various additional sources of international law alongside customary international law and the general principles of law in this chapter.

Article 38(1)(d): Judicial Decisions. Article 38(1)(d) of the ICJ Statute refers to Article 59, which reads: "The decision of the Court has no binding force except between the parties and in respect of that particular case." This language seems to be meant to limit any inference that the reference to "judicial decisions" allows judicial precedent itself to be a source of international law. Although judicial precedent is quite an ordinary source of law in common law legal systems like those in the United States and England, many civil law legal systems formally restrict the judicial role to merely applying non-judicial law. Article 59 has, however, not prevented the International Court from relying heavily on its own past decisions as a guide in finding customary international law.

Article 38(2): Ex Aequo et Bono. Article 38(2) of the ICJ Statute allows the Court to decide *ex aequo et bono*, by what is equal and good, if the parties agree.

But there has never been such agreement! Neither the International Court of Justice nor its predecessor, the Permanent Court of International Justice, has ever played an *ex aequo et bono* role in the century of their existence. Article 38(2) has, however, caused problems for the Court's use of equity, a topic explored in Part F below.

The Hierarchy of the Sources of International Law. Are some sources more important than others? Are treaties the primary source of international law? Partly because "international conventions" are listed first in Article 38(1), the judges of the ICJ and other international lawyers have often given treaties pride of place among the sources of international law. There are other reasons too for thinking of treaties as primary among the rules of international law. Treaties are ordinarily in written form, and they thus clearly show the legal rule. Moreover, treaties are subject to the explicit acceptance of states. Treaties therefore can often be clearer in their terms and more certain in their acceptance than other sorts of international law sources. Furthermore, especially since the 19th century, treaties have been widely used by states. Many areas that used to be the province of customary international law, *e.g.*, the law of the sea (see Chapter 8), have now been put into conventions. However, treaties do not cover all topics in international law, and rarely do they include all states as parties. Sometimes other forms of international law, especially natural law or *jus cogens*, may even trump treaties; and treaties always need to be interpreted in practice by judges or commentators who will use other sources of international law in their interpretations.

B. TREATIES

The conclusion of treaties between nations is a natural feature of human society. For as long as there have been written records, there have been international compacts. The five sample agreements and one case discussed and excerpted below span more than two thousand years. Among other things, they demonstrate the permanence of treaties as part of the human experience. They prove the point that international law "exists" regardless of any philosophical debate about whether there is or is not international law. States have been making treaties for as long as we have had recorded history and well before anyone was employed either as an academic or a practicing international lawyer!

Treaties concern matters vital to international relations, as well as a host of mundane issues for which international standards are useful. Our examples show treaties as vehicles for: (1) forming military and political alliances; (2) peace-making; (3) creating new states; (4) exchanging territory; (5) controlling international violence; and (6) regulating business and specifying remedies for injuries to individuals. Today, as before, treaties constitute the most frequent sort of international law made in practice. There are thousands of new treaties each year.

The Treaty Between the Jews and the Romans (Circa 160 B.C.). Our first example, a treaty of alliance and mutual defense, we have from the Bible, affirmed in historical sources. The account begins with the treaty's historical background, which helps explain why the Jews sought a treaty.

THE TREATY BETWEEN THE JEWS AND THE ROMANS (CIRCA 160 B.C.)

1 Maccabees 8:9–15, 17–28 (*Good News Bible with Deuterocanonicals/Apocrypha*)

The Background

Judas had heard about the Romans and their reputation as a military power. He knew that they welcomed all those who joined them as allies and that those who came to them could be sure of the friendship of Rome. People had told him about the wars the Romans had fought and their heroic acts among the Gauls, whom they had conquered and forced to pay taxes. He had been told what they had done in Spain when they captured the silver mines and the gold mines there. By careful planning and persistence, they had conquered the whole country, even though it was far from Rome. They had overcome the kings from distant lands who had fought against them; they had defeated them so badly that the survivors had to pay annual taxes. They had fought and conquered Philip and Perseus, kings of Macedonia, and all who had joined them against Rome. They had even defeated Antiochus the Great, king of Syria, who had attacked them with 120 elephants, cavalry, chariots, and a powerful army. They took him alive and forced him and his successors to pay heavy taxes, to give hostages, and to surrender India, Media, Lydia, and some of their best lands. They took these and gave them to King Eumenes.

When the Greeks made plans to attack and destroy them, the Romans learned of the plans and sent a general to fight against them. The Romans killed many of the Greeks, took their wives and children captive, plundered their possessions, occupied their land, tore down their fortresses, and made them slaves, as they are today. They also destroyed or made slaves of other kingdoms, the islands, and everyone who had ever fought against them. But they maintained their friendship with their allies and those who relied on them for protection. They conquered kings near and far, and everyone who heard of their reputation was afraid of them. They helped some men to become kings, while they deposed others; they had become a world power. [Rome's governmental authority rested in its] senate, and each day 320 senators came together to deliberate about the affairs of the people and their well-being. . . .

Judas chose Eupolemus, the son of John and grandson of Accos, and Jason son of Eleazar and sent them to Rome to make a treaty of friendship and alliance with the Romans. He did this to eliminate Syrian oppression, since the Jews clearly saw that they were being reduced to slavery. After a long and difficult journey, Eupolemus and Jason reached Rome and entered the Senate. They addressed the assembly in these terms: "Judas Maccabeus, his brothers, and the Jewish people have sent us here to make a mutual defense treaty with you, so that we may be officially recorded as your friends and allies."

Figure 2.A
The Roman Senate

A Written Record. The Romans accepted the Jewish proposal, and we see below how the treaty was preserved. It is significant that the treaty was in writing, rather than solely a verbal agreement or proclamation. The writing helps make sure the terms were clear. The Jews and Romans probably thought that engraving the treaty in bronze would help ensure its continuing efficacy after those who negotiated the agreement had passed from the scene.

The Treaty Between the Jews and the Romans
The Terms of the Treaty

The Romans accepted the proposal, and what follows is a copy of the letter which was engraved on bronze tablets and sent to Jerusalem to remain there as a record of the treaty:

> May things go well forever for the Romans and for the Jewish nation on land and sea! May they never have enemies, and may they never go to war! But if war is declared first against Rome or any of her allies anywhere, the Jewish nation will come to her aid with whole-hearted support, as the situation may require. And to those at war with her, the Jews shall not give or supply food, arms, money, or ships, as was agreed in Rome. The Jews must carry out their obligations without receiving anything in return.

> In the same way, if war is declared first against the Jewish nation, the Romans will come to their aid with hearty support, as the situation may require. And to their enemies there shall not be given or supplied food, arms, money, or ships, as was agreed in Rome. The Romans must carry out their obligations without deception.

> These are the terms of the treaty that the Romans have made with the Jewish people.

The Historical Permanence of Treaties. We should be cautious about assuming that the Jews and the Romans would have thought of their treaty as creating "legal" obligations in the same way that we think about such obligations today. This difference in historical perspectives, sometimes called the "intertemporal problem" of international law, complicates modern efforts to understand arrangements among peoples from other times and places. Yet despite its antiquity, the Treaty Between the Jews and the Romans has quite a modern ring to it. Think, for example, of the 1949 North Atlantic Treaty, which created the North Atlantic Treaty Organization to provide for the collective self-defense of its members, particularly against threats from the then Soviet Union.

The Efficacy of Treaties. Why did the Jews seek a treaty? The excerpts above provide one explanation, the security of the Jewish state. A modern scholar has suggested another: the Jews also likely "sought acceptance and respectability, and wanted to use their recognition by the most powerful country of the time to establish friendships with states closer to home, who would take their cue from the Roman attitude." Dov Gera, *Judaea and Mediterranean Politics 219 to 161 B.C.E.* 314 (1998). Why did the Romans consent to the treaty? Here the legislative history provides no explicit answer. It may be that even an empire as powerful and widespread as Rome's wanted some stability at its outer reaches. Or perhaps the Romans saw the treaty as a first step toward absorption of the Jewish state, exactly what, in a short time, did occur.

Was the Treaty Between the Jews and the Romans meant to be enforced? If so, how? Can a law be effective if there are no courts and police to enforce it? One can envision the threat of punishment by Rome should the Jewish nation fail to live up to its obligations as an inducement to compliance. But what explains Rome's compliance? If the Romans had not had a good record of respecting their treaty commitments, would the Jews have been as eager to enter this alliance? Reciprocal good faith always seems to have been one of the key components in ensuring the obligatory force of treaties.

The notion that treaties are to be obeyed in good faith—captured in the Latin phrase *pacta sunt servanda*—underpins modern treaty law and how states typically react to treaties. Even when states break a treaty, they usually say they are legally justified in doing so. Why? Largely for the same reasons that one sees in human affairs generally, *e.g.*, in business transactions. If some government or state is seen to go back on its word, no one is quite as likely to trust them the next time. Saying to the world, "I (we) have lied," makes it difficult to strike a deal in the future. Keeping to an agreement that has turned sour is often seen as the price of being able to make a deal the next time.

Religion and International Law. The highly influential Dutch jurist Hugo de Groot (or Grotius) relied heavily on the Bible for evidences of the law of nations in his seminal treatise of 1625, *De Jure Belli Ac Pacis, The Law of War and Peace.* Grotius cited a great number of treaties made between the Jews and their neighbors as proof for his proposition that treaties with those not believing in God were permitted. His other principal evidences were drawn from the great Greek and Roman classical authors.

The Peace of Westphalia (1648). Grotius was writing just before our second sample treaty, the Peace of Westphalia. The Peace of Westphalia is a landmark in the history of international law and relations because of its significance for the concept of the modern nation state.

_____

Figure 2.B
Hugo Grotius

To set the scene: The Roman empire, so powerful at the time of the Treaty between the Jews and Romans, fell due to internal disintegration and external invasions between the third and the fifth centuries. A new and quite different, mostly Germanic, "Holy Roman Empire" emerged in the Middle Ages and remained in the heart of Europe, conceptually unified in the Catholic faith, at least until the 17th century. As a political entity, the Holy Roman Empire, though an important source of authority, was a loose political arrangement. Hundreds of local sovereigns—principalities, free cities, bishoprics, and other territories—also exercised authority within the Empire. See Figure 2.C. During the medieval era, individuals did not owe allegiance only to one territorial ruler.

Instead, that era was "characterized by criss-crossing political, legal, religious, and moral allegiances. The ties of feudalism, of King and baron, of the Holy Roman Empire, of the Catholic Church, indeed of all the settled order of medieval Europe, bound men and women this way and that." Mark Weston Janis, *International Law* 171 (7th ed. 2016).

The Thirty Years War (1618–1648), with its brutality and famines, shattered the medieval political order. The 1648 Peace of Westphalia, which brought to a close the Thirty Years War, was based on two treaties, the Treaty of Osnabrück between Sweden and the Holy Roman Empire and the Treaty of Münster between France and the Empire. The treaties served several different, albeit related, functions. These treaties were, first, peace agreements, concluding hostilities and declaring between the parties "[t]hat there be a Christian, universal and perpetual Peace, and a true and sincere Friendship and Amity." Second, the Peace of Westphalia established an amnesty: former enemies were not to be punished, injured, or hindered in their endeavors. Damages suffered during the War on both sides were not compensable, but were to "be bury'd in perpetual Oblivion." Treaty of Osnabrück, Oct. 24, 1648, arts. I–II, 1 Consolidated Treaty Series 198.

Third, the Peace of Westphalia respected some freedom of religion. One of the central issues of the Thirty Years War was the right of princes and peoples to choose to be Catholic or Protestant. Along with general provisions respecting amity and amnesty, the Peace of Westphalia contained clauses about religious liberty. Even though many associate individual rights under international law with the post-World War II era—we take up modern human rights in Chapter 7—here we see an early provision on "liberty of conscience."

THE PEACE OF WESTPHALIA (1648)

Treaty of Osnabrück, Oct. 24, 1648, 1 Consolidated Treaty Series 198

Liberty of Conscience

It has moreover been found good, that those of the Confession of *Augsburg* [Protestants], who are Subjects of the Catholicks, and the Catholick Subjects of the States of the Confession of *Augsburg*, who had not the public or private Exercise of their religion in any time of the year 1624 and who after the Publication of the Peace shall possess and embrace a Religion different from that of the Lord of the Territory, shall in consequence of the said Peace be patiently suffer'd and tolerated, without any Hindrance or Impediment to attend their Devotions in their Houses and in private, with all Liberty of Conscience, and without any Inquisition or Trouble, and even to assist in their Neighbourhood, as often as they have a mind, at the publick Exercise of their Religion, or send their children to foreign Schools of their Religion, or have them instructed in their Families by private Masters; provided the said Vassals and Subjects do their Duty in all other things, and hold themselves in due Obedience and Subjection, without giving occasion to any Disturbance or Commotion. In like manner Subjects, whether they be Catholicks, or of the Confession of *Augsburg,* shall not be despis'd any where upon account of their Religion, nor excluded from the Community of Merchants, Artizans or Companies, nor depriv'd of Successions, Legacies, Hospitals, Lazar-Houses, or Alms-Houses, and other Privileges or Rights, and far less of Church-yards, and the Honour of Burial; nor shall any more be exacted of them for the Expence of their Funerals, than the Dues usually paid for Burying-Places in Parish-Churches: so that in these and all other the like things they shall be treated in the same manner as Brethren and Sisters, with equal Justice and Protection.

Sovereignty and International Law. For many historians and lawyers, the Peace of Westphalia marks the beginning of the era of "modern international relations" and hence of "modern international law." Yet, the Peace itself was drafted by Europeans already well familiar with international compacts. They probably had little idea that others would view their newly crafted Peace as an innovation. What makes the Peace of Westphalia so compelling as a starting point? Besides ending the Thirty Years War and setting out principles of religious tolerance, the Peace of Westphalia in Article VIII "re-established" rights of the "electors, princes, and states of the Roman Empire." These rights, described as protecting the German states from any "molestation," presage the state sovereignty that was to become the fundamental building block for modern international politics. Here is an excerpt from the Treaty of Osnabrück highlighting some of the rights that the component parts of the Holy Roman Empire were to enjoy:

———

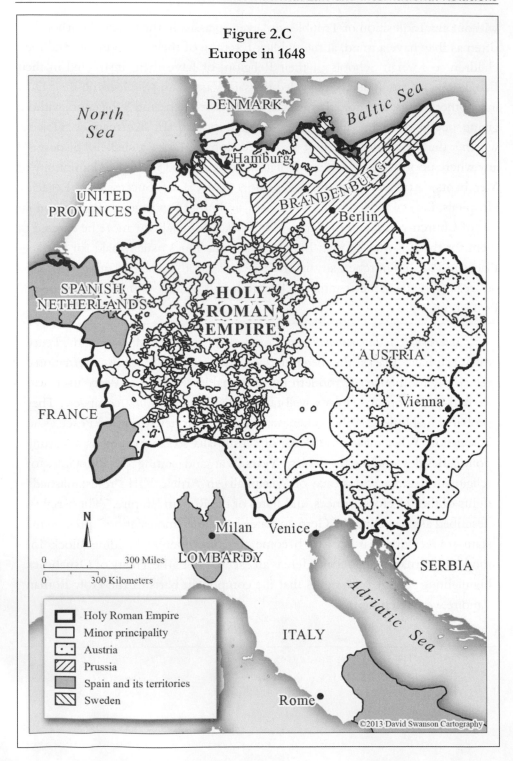

Figure 2.C
Europe in 1648

The Peace of Westphalia (1648)
Principles of Sovereignty

And in order to prevent for the future all Differences in the Political State, all and every the Electors, Princes, and States of the *Roman* Empire shall be so establish'd and confirm'd in their ancient Rights, Prerogatives, Liberties, Privileges, free Exercise of their Territorial Right, as well in Spirituals and Temporals, Seigneuries, Regalian Rights, and in the possession of all these things, by virtue of the present Transaction, that they may not be molested at any time in any manner, under any pretext whatsoever.

That [Electors, Princes, and States of the Holy Roman Empire] enjoy without contradiction the Right of Suffrage in all Deliberations touching the Affairs of the Empire, especially in the manner of interpreting Laws, resolving upon a War, imposing Taxes, ordering Levies and quartering of Soldiers, building for the publick Use new Fortresses in the Lands of the States, and reinforcing old Garisons, making of Peace and Alliances, and treating of other such-like Affairs; so that none of those or the like things shall be done or receiv'd afterwards, without the Advice and Consent of a free Assembly of all the States of the Empire: That, above all, each of the Estates of the Empire shall freely and for ever enjoy the Right of making Alliances among themselves, or with Foreigners, for the Preservation and Security of every one of them: provided nevertheless that these Alliances be neither against the Emperor nor the Empire, nor the publick Peace, nor against this Transaction especially; and that they be made without prejudice in every respect to the Oath whereby every one of them is bound to the Emperor and the Empire.

The Fate of the Holy Roman Empire. The Peace of Westphalia did not formally dissolve the Holy Roman Empire, with which the various "Electors, Princes, and States" remained affiliated; the Empire officially ended only in 1806, after a military defeat at the hands of Napoleon and the French. But the 1648 Peace of Westphalia did signal a move away from a hierarchical political order in which one Empire, linked to the Roman Catholic Church, played a prominent role, and a corresponding move toward a multi-polar world. It is for this reason that the Peace of Westphalia is most often invoked as the start of modern international relations.

International Law and the Sovereign State. Note how ironic it is that states chose to agree in a treaty to limit their freedom of action in order to assure their sovereignty. The success of international law as a political and intellectual discipline over the past five centuries has had much to do with international law's utility in regulating and cementing a world political system based on more or less sovereign states. For more on international law and the sovereign state, see Chapter 3.

The Flexibility of Treaties. Looking at the Treaty between the Jews and the Romans and the Peace of Westphalia, we see how flexible treaties are. Not only may they deal with a wide range of subject matters—mutual self-defense, peace and amity, religious freedom, and preservation of sovereign rights—but they fulfill a variety of functions important to international relations. For example, the treaties seek to promote predictable behavior between the parties, and the Peace of Westphalia's provisions on religious tolerance also set common rules within states. As we proceed with our survey of sample treaties, consider what additional types of functions they serve.

Who Makes Treaties? In the centuries after the Peace of Westphalia, Europe and eventually most of the world came to be organized politically in sovereign nation states. These states often entered into treaties. Indeed, as the Permanent Court of International Justice concluded in 1923, "the right of entering into international engagements is an attribute of State sovereignty." The S.S. "Wimbledon," 1923 P.C.I.J., Ser. A, No. 1, at 15, 25. But that does not mean that treaties today are the exclusive province of states. For example, in Part F of this chapter, the *Cayuga Indians Case* refers to treaties between New York, a component of the United States, and indigenous peoples. Moreover, international organizations sometimes possess treaty-making authority. The European Union is a party to hundreds of treaties, and the United Nations may join treaties as well. Thus, both before and after the Peace of Westphalia, we see non-state entities making treaties.

The Treaty of Paris (1783). Our third sample treaty is the Treaty of Paris, concluded between the United States of America and Great Britain at the end of the Revolutionary War. Three of the founders of the United States—John Adams, Benjamin Franklin, and John Jay—represented the United States in Paris, where they negotiated the Treaty with David Hartley, representing Great Britain. In the Treaty of Paris, the new United States achieved a remarkable diplomatic triumph, giving "the lie to the epigram that 'America never lost a war, or won a peace conference.'" Major American cities—New York and Charleston—were still in British hands. With both the British army and navy superior to U.S. forces, "it is surprising what wide boundaries and favorable terms the United States obtained." Samuel Eliot Morison, Henry Steele Commager & William E. Leuchtenberg, 1 *The Growth of the American Republic* 204 (7th ed. 1980).

The terms of the Peace of Paris were varied. Like the Peace of Westphalia, the Treaty of Paris contained a provision (Article VII) declaring peace and providing for amnesty in the form of a release of prisoners held by both sides. Other provisions set rules governing future activities, such as rights for Americans to take fish in Canadian waters (Article III) and a right of free navigation of the Mississippi River for U.S. and British citizens (Article VIII).

Recognition of the United States. May treaties sometimes serve constitutional functions? Recall from Chapter 1 that the European Convention on Human Rights created an international court, the European Court on Human Rights. The 1783 Treaty of Paris is sometimes thought to have created the United States.

THE TREATY OF PARIS (1783)
United States and Great Britain, 12 Bevans 8

Sovereignty of the United States

Article I. His Britannick Majesty acknowledges the said United States, viz. New Hampshire, Massachusets Bay, Rhode Island and Providence Plantations, Connecticut, New York, New Jersey, Pennsylvania, Delaware, Maryland, Virginia, North Carolina, South Carolina, and Georgia, to be Free, Sovereign and Independent States; that he treats with them as such; and for himself, his heirs and successors, relinquishes all claims to the government, propriety, and territorial rights of the same, and every part thereof.

The United States as a Sovereign State. Did Article I of the Treaty of Paris merely declare Britain's formal recognition of the sovereignty of the United States, already objectively established in 1776 by the United States itself in the Declaration of Independence? U.S. Supreme Court Justice Chase wrote in 1796 that he "considered it as the established doctrine of the United States, that their independence originated from, and commenced with, the declaration of congress, on the 4th of July, 1776; . . . and that all laws made by the legislatures of the several states, after the declaration of independence, were the laws of sovereign and independent governments." Ware v. Hylton, 3 U.S. (3 Dall.) 199, 224 (1796).

Is Justice Chase's view persuasive? Or did the Treaty of Paris itself constitute the sovereignty of the United States as of January 14, 1784, when the Treaty came into force? When preparing to negotiate the Treaty of Paris with the Americans, the British government debated these alternatives, which reflect the theoretical distinction in international law between the "declaratory" and "constitutive" theories of recognition. Some in the British Cabinet thought the Foreign Office should orchestrate the negotiations, on the grounds that the United States was already independent, while others argued that responsibility should rest instead with the Colonial and Home Offices. Britain initially instructed its negotiator to pursue a peace treaty with the representatives of the "Colonies or plantations," but John Jay and Benjamin Franklin refused to proceed until those instructions were changed. See Andrew Cunningham McLaughlin, *The Confederation and the Constitution 1783–1789*, at 6, 12–14 (1905). Regardless of the theoretical debate over whether British recognition merely declared already-existing U.S. sovereignty or constituted that sovereignty, British recognition undoubtedly strengthened the standing of the new United States with other countries—an important effect of the Treaty of Paris. We see more about recognition of states in Chapter 3.

Effect of Treaties on Third Parties. Did the Treaty of Paris affect third parties only politically? Did it also create legal obligations for them? Article II, which delimited the boundaries of the United States in 1783 (see Figure 2.D), was legally binding on the United States and the United Kingdom. But Article II also may have led to international legal obligations, if not treaty obligations, for other countries. After all, other countries by and large recognized the boundaries of the new United States even if they themselves did not enter boundary treaties with the U.S. If those other countries ignored the U.S. boundaries, they would violate international law. One way that treaties may help create legal obligations for nonparties is through customary international law, which we discuss in Part C.

The Treaty of Paris and the U.S. Constitution. International law interacts with municipal law in many ways. When the Treaty of Paris was concluded in 1783, the United States was governed by the Articles of Confederation, which left more authority to the U.S. states than would the 1789 U.S. Constitution. How did the weaker Articles of Confederation affect the negotiation of Articles IV, V, and VI of the Treaty of Paris, excerpted here?

The Treaty of Paris (1783)
The Rights of Individuals

IV. It is agreed, that creditors on either side shall meet with no lawful impediment to the recovery of the full value, in sterling money, of all *bona fide* debts heretofore contracted.

V. It is agreed, that the Congress shall earnestly recommend it to the legislatures of the respective states, to provide for the restitution of all estates, rights, and properties, which have been confiscated, belonging to real British subjects[.] And that Congress shall also earnestly recommend to the several states, that the estates, rights, and properties, of [those whose properties were confiscated] shall be restored to them, they refunding to any persons who may be now in possession the *bona fide* price (where any has been given) which such persons may have paid on purchasing any of the said lands, rights, or properties, since the confiscation.

And it is agreed, that all persons who have any interest in confiscated lands, either by debts, marriage settlements or otherwise, shall meet with no lawful impediment in the prosecution of their just rights.

VI. That there shall be no future confiscations made, nor any prosecutions commenced against any person or persons, for or by reason of the part which he or they may have taken in the present war; and that no person shall, on that account, suffer any future loss or damage either in his person, liberty, or property; and that those who may be in confinement on such charges at the time of the ratification of the treaty in America, shall be immediately set at liberty, and the prosecutions so commenced be discontinued.

Executing the Treaty of Paris. Following the Treaty of Paris, U.S. state courts proved unable or unwilling to protect the rights of British subjects detailed in Articles IV, V, and VI. As a result, Britain remained in occupation of much of what was then the Northwest Territory (later the states of Illinois, Indiana, Michigan, Ohio, and Wisconsin). This in turn was one impetus to the calling of the Constitutional Convention in 1787, to the establishment of U.S. federal courts in 1789 under the new U.S. Constitution, and to the mention of U.S. treaties as part of "the supreme Law of the Land" in the Constitution's Supremacy Clause, Article VI(2). See Chapter 5.

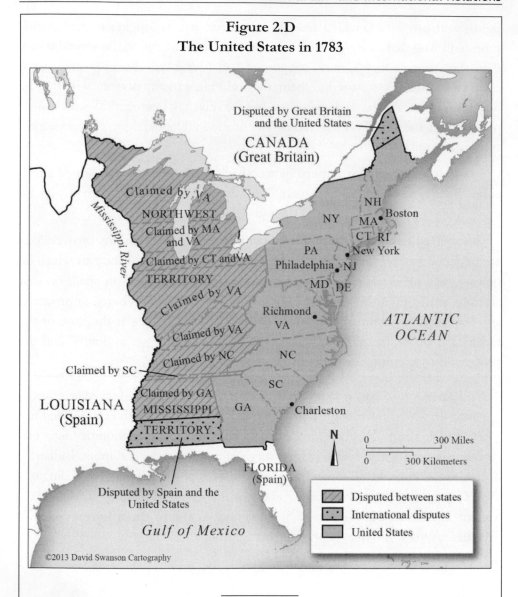

Figure 2.D
The United States in 1783

The Cession of Alaska and the Kellogg-Briand Pact. Our next two sample treaties present quite a contrast in subject matter and function. The 1867 Cession of Alaska was the vehicle by which the United States acquired Alaska from Russia. Here are its core provisions:

THE CESSION OF ALASKA (1867)

11 Bevans 1216, 15 Stat. 539, Treaty Series 301

ARTICLE I.

His Majesty the Emperor of all the Russias agrees to cede to the United States, by this convention, immediately upon the exchange of the ratifications thereof, all the territory and dominion now possessed by his said Majesty on the continent of America and in the adjacent islands, the same being contained within the geographical limits herein set forth, to wit: The eastern limit is the line of demarcation between the Russian and the British possessions in North America, as established by the convention between Russia and Great Britain, of February 28–16, 1825, and described in Articles III and IV of said convention[.] [Article I of the Cession of Alaska also describes in detail the western limit, starting at a point in the Behring Strait and proceeding "due north, without limitation, into the . . . Frozen ocean"; and from the same point proceeding southwest on a course that encompasses the Aleutian Islands.]

ARTICLE VI.

In consideration of the cession aforesaid, the United States agree to pay at the Treasury in Washington, within ten months after the exchange of the ratifications of this convention, to the diplomatic representative or other agent of his Majesty the Emperor of all the Russias, duly authorized to receive the same, seven million two hundred thousand dollars in gold.

A Treaty as Quid Pro Quo Exchange. The Cession for Alaska was not quite so simple as an exchange of land for gold. There also had to be provisions concerning public buildings and archives, churches, removal of troops, and the citizenship of individuals who chose to remain in Alaska after the transfer. Still, the goal of the treaty was straightforward: to strike a bargain between two parties.

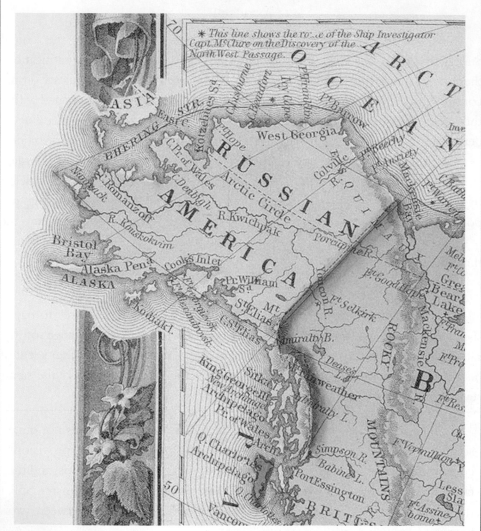

Figure 2.E
Russian America in 1860

The Kellogg-Briand Pact and the Peaceful Settlement of Disputes. The 1928 Kellogg-Briand Pact ambitiously set out new general standards of international law by renouncing war "as an instrument of national policy." It did not purport to outlaw recourse to force in self-defense. Concluded following the devastation of World War I, the Pact entered into force in July 1929 with 46 parties, among them China, France, Germany, Great Britain, Japan, the Soviet Union, Spain, and the United States; several more countries later adhered to the treaty. The excerpt below contains the treaty's preamble and short operative provisions.

THE KELLOGG-BRIAND PACT (1928)

Renunciation of War as an Instrument of National Policy,
2 Bevans 732, 46 Stat. 2343, Treaty Series 796, 94 L.N.T.S. 57

Deeply sensible of their solemn duty to promote the welfare of mankind;

Persuaded that the time has come when a frank renunciation of war as an instrument of national policy should be made to the end that the peaceful and friendly relations now existing between their peoples may be perpetuated;

Convinced that all changes in their relations with one another should be sought only by pacific means and be the result of a peaceful and orderly process, and that any signatory Power which shall hereafter seek to promote its national interests by resort to war should be denied the benefits furnished by this Treaty;

Hopeful that, encouraged by their example, all the other nations of the world will join in this humane endeavor and by adhering to the present Treaty as soon as it comes into force bring their peoples within the scope of its beneficent provisions, thus uniting the civilized nations of the world in a common renunciation of war as an instrument of their national policy; . . .

ARTICLE I

The High Contracting Parties solemnly declare in the names of their respective peoples that they condemn recourse to war for the solution of international controversies, and renounce it as an instrument of national policy in their relations with one another.

ARTICLE II

The High Contracting Parties agree that the settlement or solution of all disputes or conflicts of whatever nature or of whatever origin they may be, which may arise among them, shall never be sought except by pacific means.

The Efficacy of International Law. The Cession of Alaska and the Kellogg-Briand Pact make a nice contrast when discussing the efficacy of international law. It is easy to see how the 1867 Cession of Alaska "worked"—Russia ceded the Alaska Territory to the United States and the United States paid the Tsar $7,200,000 in gold. After the conclusion of the treaty, Russian officials left Alaska, U.S. officials arrived, and money changed hands. It is much more difficult to see how the 1928 Kellogg-Briand Pact "worked." What good were "solemn" renunciations of war, especially in light of the developments in world politics in the 1930s and 1940s: the participation of Germany and the Soviet Union in the Spanish Civil War, the invasion of Ethiopia by Italy, the invasion of Manchuria and China by Japan, the invasion of Czechoslovakia by Germany, the invasion of Poland by Germany and the Soviet Union, the invasion of the Baltic States and Finland by the Soviet Union, the invasion of France, the Netherlands, Belgium, Denmark, Norway, and the Soviet Union by Germany, the German attack on the United Kingdom, the Japanese invasion of Malaya, Indonesia, and the Philippines, and the Japanese attack on the United States? If the Cession of Alaska shows treaties at their most efficacious, the Kellogg-Briand Pact seems to show them at their least efficacious.

Figure 2.F
Calvin Coolidge, Herbert Hoover, and Frank B. Kellogg, standing, with representatives of the governments who have ratified the Kellogg-Briand Pact, in the East Room of the White House

"Hard" and "Soft" International Law. Are both the Cession of Alaska and the Kellogg-Briand Pact the same sort of international law? Some international lawyers distinguish between "hard" and "soft" international law, a distinction with at least two meanings. First, the distinction may refer to the difference between rules of law meant to be followed and norms meant merely to set out preferred outcomes. It seems clear that the Cession of Alaska was meant to be followed. The Kellogg-Briand Pact was more aspirational. Over eighty years ago, Manley Hudson, a Harvard Law School professor and U.S. judge on the World Court, argued that the Kellogg-Briand Pact should be viewed as a "fundamental law" and "approached in a state of mind wholly different from that in which we approach the ordinary international treaty." Hudson argued that "[w]e are holding ahead of us great ideals. We may not succeed in realizing

all of them, but I feel, as a member of this generation, that it will have been a great thing for us who are engaged in such an enterprise." International Law Association, *Report of the Thirty-Eighth Conference (Budapest)* 12, 66 (1934).

Second, the distinction between hard and soft law may refer to the difference between formal sources of law (such as treaties) and instruments that are not formally legal sources (such as mutual declarations of government leaders issued at the end of diplomatic conferences). Such declarations may contain non-binding statements of principle. In Part C of this chapter we examine soft law of this second type and ask whether it can have any legal significance.

Despite its aspirational character, the Kellogg-Briand Pact had some real-world consequences. At the Nuremberg trial after World War II, Nazi war criminals were tried and executed for violating its principles. Was this an appropriate use of the Pact? See Chapter 7.

Bilateral and Multilateral Treaties. It is conceptually possible for issues addressed in a multilateral treaty such as the Kellogg-Briand Pact to be addressed in a series of bilateral agreements. The Kellogg-Briand Pact was initiated when the French Foreign Minister, Aristide Briand, encouraged by some influential U.S. citizens, proposed that the United States and France conclude a bilateral treaty banning war as an instrument of national policy. The United States responded by suggesting a multilateral treaty, and member countries of the League of Nations, which the United States had not joined, accepted the "multilateralization" of negotiations. The Kellogg-Briand Pact resulted. Why was the Pact drawn up as a multilateral treaty? The conclusion of a series of bilateral agreements might well have been too cumbersome. Was the subject matter of the Kellogg-Briand Pact also particularly appropriate for multilateral treatment?

Use of multilateral treaties has increased significantly in the 20th and 21st centuries. Some create international organizations, such as the European Union (see the *AM&S Case* in Part D) and the United Nations (see Chapter 3). Other modern treaties standardize international rules for businesses, *e.g.*, the 1929 Warsaw Convention for the Unification of Certain Rules Relating to International Transportation by Air (see the *Eastern Airlines Case* below), or regulate international environmental matters, *e.g.*, the widely accepted 1967 Montreal Protocol on Substances that Deplete the Ozone Layer. Still other multilateral treaties, such as the 1948 Convention on the Prevention and Punishment of the Crime of Genocide, help develop human rights law.

Terminology. Kellogg-Briand is labeled a "pact." Treaties in fact have various designations: "[T]reaty, convention, agreement, protocol, covenant, charter, statute, act, declaration, *concordat*, exchange of notes, agreed minute, memorandum of agreement, memorandum of understanding, and *modus vivendi*. Whatever their designation, all agreements have the same legal status, except as their provisions or the circumstances of their conclusion indicate otherwise." *Restatement (Third) of the Foreign Relations Law of the United States* § 301, Comment a (1987).

The Flexibility of Treaties. Despite the assertion that all treaties "have the same legal status," treaties are a versatile instrument of international relations and have different sorts of municipal law analogies. Think back to the treaties we have seen thus far. Some—the Treaty Between the Jews and the Romans and the Cession of Alaska—are akin to contracts. Others—the Peace of Westphalia and the Kellogg-Briand Pact—may be analogized to statutes. The analogy between "statutory" treaties and municipal statutes is far from perfect: a treaty may operate like a statute in that each sets out rules to govern future conduct, but there is no global legislature, and a treaty usually does not bind non-parties, whereas a municipal statute can bind citizens who do not agree with it. Still other treaties may play constitutional roles, helping to create new states (the Peace of Westphalia and perhaps the Treaty of Paris) or new international institutions (the European Convention on Human Rights, which created the European Court of Human Rights that decided the *McCann Case* in Chapter 1). Finally, some treaties—Westphalia and Kellogg-Briand—seem to be largely aspirational, articulating goals for the future. Although these four categories—contract, statute, constitution, aspiration—are only really descriptive devices rather than legal categories, they do help signal the flexibility of treaties in international affairs.

Steps in Making Treaties. Formal treaty negotiations have several stages or steps. These various steps have legal significance that may influence the conduct of political leaders. For example, signing a treaty often does not mean that a country has agreed to be bound by the treaty; becoming a party may depend instead on "ratification." However, according to Article 18 of the 1969 Vienna Convention on the Law of Treaties (discussed below), a non-party signatory "is obliged to refrain from acts which would defeat the object and purpose of a treaty . . . until it shall have made its intention clear not to become a party to the treaty." On December 31, 2000, President Clinton signed the Rome Statute establishing the International Criminal Court, which we consider in Chapter 7. After President George W. Bush took office, however, his administration wrote the Secretary-General of the United Nations to inform him "that the United States does not intend to become a party" to the Rome Statute and that "[a]ccordingly, the United States has no legal obligations arising from its signature." *Quoted in* Sean D. Murphy, "Contemporary Practice of the United States Relating to International Law," 96 *American Journal of International Law* 706, 724 (2002).

Some steps in approving a treaty relate to domestic legal requirements rather than to international law prerequisites for treaty making. For example, in the United States, the Constitution specifies that the Senate must give its two-thirds advice and consent before the President may ratify a treaty. We explore how international law fits with the U.S. legal system in Chapter 5.

Entry into Force. Even after a treaty has been approved according to domestic law and accepted internationally, it does not take full legal effect until it has "entered into force." A multilateral treaty may contain provisions making the treaty's entry into force subject to a variety of conditions. For example, Article III of the Kellogg-Briand Pact provides that it enters into force when all the negotiating states have accepted it and deposited their instruments of ratification with the "depositary" (in this case, the U.S. government). The 1982 Convention on the Law of the Sea entered into force in November 1994 in accordance with its Article 308, which provides for the Convention's entry into force "12 months after the date of deposit of the sixtieth instrument of ratification or accession." Twenty-five states with merchant fleets comprising not less than 50 per cent of the world's gross tonnage had to accept the 1974 International Convention for the Safety of Life at Sea before it could enter into force. What factors influence decisions concerning the number or characteristics of accepting states necessary for a treaty's entry into force? Why do treaty negotiators sometimes seek a delay between the final necessary acceptance of a treaty and the date on which it formally enters into force? If a treaty is silent about its entry into force, the general rule is that the treaty enters into force when all the negotiating states have consented to be bound by it.

Lawyering. How do government officials and political leaders obtain advice about international law? In the United States, international lawyers working for the State Department's Office of the Legal Adviser (known as "L") participate in treaty negotiations, process international claims, respond to questions from foreign governments and private lawyers, and advise U.S. officials on a wide range of international legal questions. In earlier times, such distinguished lawyers as Thomas Jefferson, James Madison, and James Monroe personally handled the legal work of the State Department when they served as Secretaries of State. In 1891, some 23 years after the Cession of Alaska, the Office of the Solicitor of the Department of State was created; Congress established the Office of the Legal Adviser in 1931. For an excellent inside account of the work of L and the efficacy of the Legal Adviser's advice, see Michael P. Scharf & Paul R. Williams, *Shaping Foreign Policy in Times of Crisis: The Role of International Law and the State Department Legal Adviser* (2010). In the United States, the Department of Defense and other government agencies also employ lawyers to advise about international legal matters. Other countries have government legal advisors as well. For essays about the work and responsibilities of legal advisors to various governments and to international organizations, see *The Role of Legal Advisers in International Law* (Andraž Zidar & Jean-Pierre Gauci eds. 2017). What role should government lawyers play when they advise political leaders about the legality of a proposed international action? Should the lawyers simply provide "objective" legal advice? Should they try to fashion a legal rationale to justify political leaders' actions?

As we saw in *Filartiga* and *McCann* in Chapter 1, and will see throughout the book, lawyers also advise and represent individuals and companies on matters of international law. The following case, in which an individual sought redress from a company for personal injuries, provides an illustration involving the Warsaw Convention.

The Warsaw Convention. Some treaties regulate business liabilities, providing uniform international standards governing injuries to the persons or property of individuals. The 1929 Warsaw Convention for the Unification of Certain Rules Relating to International Transportation by Air is one example. One goal of the Convention was to establish uniform rules governing claims that arose from international air transportation, especially with respect to claims for personal injuries arising out of accidents, for damaged or lost baggage, and for damages caused by flight delays. Another aim was to balance the interests of passengers seeking recovery with airlines' interests in limiting their liability, resulting in caps on damages. For background on the Warsaw Convention, see Andreas Lowenfeld & Allan I. Mendelsohn, "The United States and the Warsaw Convention," 80 *Harvard Law Review* 497 (1967).

The 1999 Montreal Convention for the Unification of Certain Rules for International Carriage by Air has now largely replaced the Warsaw Convention. The Montreal Convention, *inter alia*, removes limits on air carrier liability for accident victims unless the airline proves that it is not at fault or that a third party was alone responsible for damages. The Montreal Convention entered into force in November 2003; as of May 2017, there were 125 parties, including the United States.

The Warsaw Convention gave rise to litigation in municipal courts, with some disputes, including the *Eastern Airlines Case* below, reaching the U.S. Supreme Court. The case emphasizes two important points introduced in Chapter 1: first, individuals may be directly affected by treaties; and second, some disputes over treaties end up in court, just like some disputes arising under municipal law. As we have seen, treaties may "work" without courts or tribunals, but cases may provide avenues for redress for individuals or states. Cases may also develop aspects of the law governing treaties.

This first excerpt provides background about the *Eastern Airlines* dispute.

EASTERN AIRLINES, INC. V. FLOYD

499 U.S. 530 (1991)

The Facts

JUSTICE MARSHALL delivered the opinion of the Court.

Article 17 of the Warsaw Convention sets forth conditions under which an international air carrier can be held liable for injuries to passengers. This case presents the question whether Article 17 allows recovery for mental or psychic injuries unaccompanied by physical injury or physical manifestation of injury.

On May 5, 1983, an Eastern Airlines flight departed from Miami, bound for the Bahamas. Shortly after takeoff, one of the plane's three jet engines lost oil pressure. The flight crew shut down the failing engine and turned the plane around to return to Miami. Soon thereafter, the second and third engines failed due to loss of oil pressure. The plane began losing altitude rapidly, and the passengers were informed that the plane would be ditched in the Atlantic Ocean. Fortunately, after a period of descending flight without power, the crew managed to restart an engine and land the plane safely at Miami International Airport.

Respondents, a group of passengers on the flight, brought separate complaints against petitioner, Eastern Airlines, Inc. (Eastern), each claiming damages solely for mental distress arising out of the incident. . . . Eastern conceded that the engine failure and subsequent preparations for ditching the plane amounted to an "accident" under Article 17 of the Convention but argued that Article 17 also makes physical injury a condition of liability. . . . The District Court concluded that mental anguish alone is not compensable under Article 17.

The Court of Appeals for the Eleventh Circuit reversed, holding that the phrase "lésion corporelle" in the authentic French text of Article 17 encompasses purely emotional distress. . . . We granted certiorari [and] now hold that Article 17 does not allow recovery for purely mental injuries.

The Law of Treaties. International lawyers and judges often confront a range of issues related to treaties, including how a treaty is made, amended, modified, and terminated. Rules related to these topics are part of an area of general international law known as the law of treaties, more or less the equivalent of the domestic law of contracts.

One important law-of-treaties concern is treaty interpretation, the central issue in *Eastern Airlines*. What rules govern interpretation? The Supreme Court began by taking a close look at the text of the Warsaw Convention. Note that the meaning of treaty terms is not always self-evident.

Eastern Airlines, Inc. v. Floyd
Treaty Interpretation and the Treaty Text

"When interpreting a treaty, we 'begin "with the text of the treaty and the context in which the written words are used." ' " *Volkswagenwerk Aktiengesellschaft v. Schlunk*, 486 U.S. 694, 699 (1988), quoting *Société Nationale Industrielle Aérospatiale v. United States District Court*, 482 U.S. 522, 534 (1987), quoting *Air France v. Saks*, 470 U.S. 392, 397 (1985). . . . Moreover, " 'treaties are construed more liberally than private agreements, and to ascertain their meaning we may look beyond the written words to the history of the treaty, the negotiations, and the practical construction adopted by the parties.' " *Saks, supra*, at 396, quoting *Choctaw Nation of Indians v. United States*, 318 U.S. 423, 431–432 (1943). We proceed to apply these methods in turn.

Because the only authentic text of the Warsaw Convention is in French, the French text must guide our analysis. See *Saks, supra*, at 397–399. The text reads as follows:

> Le transporteur est responsable du dommage survenu *en cas de mort, de blessure ou de toute autre lésion corporelle* subie par un voyageur lorsque l'accident qui a causé le dommage s'est produit à bord de l'aéronef ou au cours de toutes opérations d'embarquement et de débarquement.

The American translation of this text, employed by the Senate when it ratified the Convention in 1934, reads:

> The carrier shall be liable for damage sustained *in the event of the death or wounding of a passenger or any other bodily injury* suffered by a passenger, if

the accident which caused the damage so sustained took place on board the aircraft or in the course of any of the operations of embarking or disembarking.

Thus, under Article 17, an air carrier is liable for passenger injury only when three conditions are satisfied: (1) there has been an accident, in which (2) the passenger suffered "mort," "blessure," "ou . . . toute autre lésion corporelle," and (3) the accident took place on board the aircraft or in the course of operations of embarking or disembarking. As petitioner concedes, the incident here took place on board the aircraft and was an "accident" for purposes of Article 17. Moreover, respondents concede that they suffered neither "mort" nor "blessure" from the mishap. Therefore, the narrow issue presented here is whether, under the proper interpretation of "lésion corporelle," condition (2) is satisfied when a passenger has suffered only a mental or psychic injury.

We must consider the "French legal meaning" of "lésion corporelle" for guidance as to the shared expectations of the parties to the Convention because the Convention was drafted in French by continental jurists. [In order to ascertain the meaning of this phrase, the Court looks extensively at bilingual dictionaries; the "principal sources of French law" relied on by "lawyers trained in French civil law," namely "(1) legislation, (2) judicial decisions, and (3) scholarly writing"; and the structure of Article 17. The Court concludes:]

In sum, neither the Warsaw Convention itself nor any of the applicable French legal sources demonstrates that "lésion corporelle" should be translated other than as "bodily injury"—a narrow meaning excluding purely mental injuries. However, because a broader interpretation of "lésion corporelle" reaching purely mental injuries is plausible, and the term is both ambiguous and difficult, we turn to additional aids to construction.

> Travaux Préparatoires. The Supreme Court next looked at the negotiating history, or *travaux préparatoires*, of the Warsaw Convention. The *travaux* may help illuminate what was the parties' intent in making a treaty. The Court examined in detail the records of the Warsaw Convention's Paris negotiating conference and the work of a committee of experts, and then continued:

Eastern Airlines, Inc. v. Floyd
The *Travaux Préparatoires*

Our review of the documentary record for the Warsaw Conference confirms—and courts and commentators appear universally to agree—that there is no evidence that the drafters or signatories of the Warsaw Convention specifically considered liability for psychic injury or the meaning of "lésion corporelle." Two explanations commonly are offered for why the subject of mental injuries never arose during the Convention proceedings: (1) many jurisdictions did not recognize recovery for mental injury at that time, or (2) the drafters simply could not contemplate a psychic injury unaccompanied by a physical injury. Indeed, the unavailability of compensation for purely psychic injury in many common and civil law countries at the time of the Warsaw Conference persuades us that the signatories had no specific intent to include such a remedy in the Convention. [The Court surveys the status of recovery for mental distress in France, the United Kingdom, U.S. jurisdictions, the Netherlands, Germany, Switzerland, and the Soviet Union.] Because such a remedy was unknown in many, if not most, jurisdictions in 1929, the drafters most likely would have felt compelled to make an unequivocal reference to purely mental injury if they had specifically intended to allow such recovery.

In this sense, we find it significant that, when the parties to a different international transport treaty wanted to make it clear that rail passengers could recover for purely psychic harms, the drafters made a specific modification to this effect. The liability provision of the Berne Convention on International Rail, drafted in 1952, originally conditioned liability on "la mort, les blessures et toute autre atteinte, à l'intégrité corporelle." International Convention Concerning the Carriage of Passengers and Luggage By Rail, Berne, Oct. 25, 1952, 242 U.N.T.S. 355, Article 28, p. 390. The drafters subsequently modified this provision to read "l'intégrité physique *ou mentale*." See Additional Convention to the International Convention Concerning the Carriage of Passengers and Luggage by Rail (CIV) of Feb. 25, 1961, Relating to the Liability of the Railway for Death of and Personal Injury to Passengers, done Feb. 26, 1966, Art. 2 (emphasis added).

The narrower reading of "lésion corporelle" also is consistent with the primary purpose of the contracting parties to the Convention: limiting the liability of air carriers in order to foster the growth of the fledgling commercial aviation industry. Indeed, it was for this reason that the Warsaw delegates imposed a maximum recovery of $8,300 for an accident—a low amount even by 1929 standards. Whatever may be the current view among Convention signatories, in 1929 the parties were more concerned with protecting air carriers and fostering a new industry than providing full recovery to injured passengers, and we read "lésion corporelle" in a way that respects that legislative choice.

Treaty Interpretation and the Conduct of Treaty Parties. Finally, the Supreme Court looked to evidence of the post-1929 conduct of the parties to the Warsaw Convention, concluding that "on balance" that evidence "supports the narrow

> translation of 'lésion corporelle.' " In arriving at this conclusion, the Court examined the views of scholars, the proposals of a 1951 committee of 20 parties to the Warsaw Convention, and the effect of three later protocols to the Convention. Another source of evidence about post-Convention agreement concerning the meaning of a treaty term is how courts in various countries have interpreted it.

Eastern Airlines, Inc. v. Floyd
Treaty Interpretation and the Post-Ratification Conduct of Parties

We must also consult the opinions of our sister signatories in searching for the meaning of a "lésion corporelle." The only apparent judicial decision from a sister signatory addressing recovery for purely mental injuries under Article 17 is that of the Supreme Court of Israel. That court held that Article 17 does allow recovery for purely psychic injuries. See *Cie Air France v. Teichner*, 39 Revue Française de Droit Aérien, at 243, 23 Eur. Tr. L., at 102.

Teichner arose from the hijacking in 1976 of an Air France flight to Entebbe, Uganda. Passengers sought compensation for psychic injuries caused by the ordeal of the hijacking and detention at the Entebbe Airport. While acknowledging that the negotiating history of the Warsaw Convention was silent as to the availability of such compensation, the court determined that "desirable jurisprudential policy" ("la politique jurisprudentielle souhaitable") favored an expansive reading of Article 17 to reach purely psychic injuries. In reaching this conclusion, the court emphasized the post-1929 development of the aviation industry and the evolution of Anglo-American and Israeli law to allow recovery for psychic injury in certain circumstances. In addition, the court followed the view of Miller that this expansive construction was desirable to avoid an apparent conflict between the French and English versions of the Guatemala City Protocol.

Although we recognize the deference owed to the Israeli court's interpretation of Article 17, we are not persuaded by that court's reasoning. Even if we were to agree that allowing recovery for purely psychic injury is desirable as a policy goal, we cannot give effect to such policy without convincing evidence that the signatories' intent with respect to Article 17 would allow such recovery. As discussed, neither the language, negotiating history, nor postenactment interpretations of Article 17 clearly evidences such intent. Nor does the Guatemala City Protocol support the Israeli court's conclusion because nothing in the Protocol purports to amend Article 17 to reach mental injuries. Moreover, although the Protocol reflects a liberalization of attitudes toward passenger recovery in that it provides for strict liability, see Article IV, the fact that the

Guatemala City Protocol is still not in effect after almost 20 years since it was drafted should caution *against* attaching significance to it.

Moreover, we believe our construction of Article 17 better accords with the Warsaw Convention's stated purpose of achieving uniformity of rules governing claims arising from international air transportation. [T]he Montreal Agreement subjects international carriers to strict liability for Article 17 injuries sustained on flights connected with the United States. Recovery for mental distress traditionally has been subject to a high degree of proof, both in this country and others. We have no doubt that subjecting international air carriers to *strict* liability for purely mental distress would be controversial for most signatory countries. Our construction avoids this potential source of divergence.

We conclude that an air carrier cannot be held liable under Article 17 when an accident has not caused a passenger to suffer death, physical injury, or physical manifestation of injury. . . .

The judgment of the Court of Appeals is reversed.

Treaty Text and Treaty Interpretation. How much attention should be paid to the text of a treaty? In 1844, British judge Stephen Lushington, construing a treaty of commerce between Britain and Turkey, said that in such treaties "we cannot expect to find the same nicety of strict definition as in modern documents, such as deeds, or Acts of Parliament[;] it has never been the habit of those engaged in diplomacy to use legal accuracy, but rather to adopt more liberal terms." An interpreter therefore "ought to look at all the historical circumstances attending" the treaties, "in order to ascertain what was the true intention of the contracting parties, and to give the widest scope to the language of the treaties in order to embrace within it all the objects intended to be included." Maltass v. Maltass, 1 Rob. Ecc. 67, 76 (Prerogative Ct. 1844).

The U.S. Supreme Court has not always followed the approach to treaty interpretation set out in *Eastern Airlines*, where the Court turned first to the treaty text. During the first half of the 20th century, for example, the Court "expressly adopted a purposive approach to treaty interpretation designed, fundamentally, to advance amicable relations between the United States and its treaty partners." In addition, the Court at that time "firmly endorsed, and repeatedly applied, a presumption in favor of a liberal recognition of individual rights secured by treaties." Michael P. Van Alstine, "Treaties in the Supreme Court, 1901–1945," in *International Law in the U.S. Supreme Court: Continuity and Change* 191, 193–94 (David L. Sloss, Michael D. Ramsey & William S. Dodge eds. 2011).

Why might some states prefer strict adherence to the text of a treaty? Why might recourse to the *travaux préparatoires* be controversial? To the extent the *travaux* are not generally available, reliance on them could "give an edge" to developed states with large foreign office legal departments and research capabilities.

Should the same treaty interpretation approach be used for all types of treaties? Should a human rights treaty, such as the European Convention on Human Rights, which we considered in the *McCann Case* in Chapter 1 and which we revisit in Chapter 7, be liberally interpreted to further its objectives?

Treaty Interpretation and the Decisions of Foreign Courts. In interpreting a treaty, what use should a municipal court make of foreign judicial interpretations? In his dissenting opinion in *Olympic Airways v. Husain*, interpreting the meaning of the word "accident" in Article 17 of the Warsaw Convention, Justice Scalia cited the Supreme Court's unanimous opinion in *Eastern Airlines* favorably for having "carefully considered foreign case law." Justice Scalia noted the value of looking to other states' interpretations of the same treaty provision:

> We can, and should, look to decisions of other signatories when we interpret treaty provisions. Foreign constructions are evidence of the original shared understanding of the contracting parties. Moreover, it is reasonable to impute to the parties an intent that their respective courts strive to interpret the treaty consistently. (The Warsaw Convention's preamble specifically acknowledges "the advantage of regulating *in a uniform manner* the conditions of . . . the liability of the carrier." (emphasis added).) Finally, even if we disagree, we surely owe the conclusions reached by appellate courts of other signatories the courtesy of respectful consideration.

Olympic Airways v. Husain, 540 U.S. 644, 660-61 (Scalia, J., dissenting).

Uniformity of Treaty Interpretation. Is it possible to reduce the risk of different municipal court interpretations of the same treaty provision? Should a municipal court more or less automatically defer to an interpretation of a treaty provision made by a foreign court? Should a foreign court's decision interpreting a treaty be accorded weight if the foreign court's approach to treaty interpretation differs from the approach of the domestic court? Compare the approaches to treaty interpretation used by the U.S. Supreme Court in *Eastern Airlines* and by the Israeli Supreme Court in *Teichner*, discussed in *Eastern Airlines*.

Would agreement on a standard method of treaty interpretation significantly reduce uncertainty? If not, what would a standard method of treaty interpretation accomplish? Although some answers about the meaning of treaty text are quite straightforward—it seems clear, for example, that Article 17 of the Warsaw Convention applies to physical wounds—other questions will be debatable. Modern interpreters inevitably apply their own values to current circumstances when they determine what a treaty means. Although most interpreters place considerable importance on the intent of treaty drafters, the process of interpretation necessarily involves judgment. Perhaps using a uniform approach to treaty interpretation can be valuable—even if different interpreters may construe a treaty differently—because it leads interpreters to ask the same questions and consider similar factors. For more discussion, see Alex Glashauser, "Difference and Deference in Treaty Interpretation," 50 *Villanova Law Review* 25 (2005); John E. Noyes, "Memorializing UNCLOS III, Interpreting the Law of the Sea Convention, and the *Virginia Commentary*," in *Peaceful Order in the World's Oceans* 218 (Myron Nordquist & Michael Lodge eds. 2014).

Could treaty negotiators themselves promote more uniform interpretations by municipal courts? How? When the drafters of the Warsaw Convention provided that only the French text was authentic, they arguably eliminated some ambiguity that could arise from having multiple official language versions.

Comparing Statutory Interpretation and Treaty Interpretation. Do differences in how treaties and domestic statutes are made suggest that they should be interpreted using different methodologies? Professor Bederman has explored how to cure ambiguities in U.S. statutes and in treaties. If a statute is constitutional, "Congress always has the last word in construction. Congress can and does fix its drafting mistakes after being prompted by the courts." However, with respect to treaties, "there is no convenient way to cure defects in construction." If a U.S. court were to adopt "an interpretation at variance with our treaty partners," the interpretation would be binding in U.S. law but could well leave the United States "in default of its international obligations. To reconcile the internal and international meanings of a treaty, the United States government would be forced to renegotiate the agreement. Because any process of negotiation is consensual, there is no guarantee that a reconciliation could occur." David J. Bederman, "Revivalist Canons and Treaty Interpretation," 41 *UCLA Law Review* 953, 1023–24 (1994). What are the implications of the different ways in which statutes and treaties may be changed—the first by congressional action and the second by international negotiation? One could argue that the difficulty in changing treaties means that municipal courts should have considerable freedom to construc treaties in ways that are fair in light of contemporary circumstances. Alternatively, perhaps municipal courts should stick closely to the treaty text and the intent of the drafters, because the "legislator" cannot readily reenter the picture to cure any "defects" in interpretation.

The Vienna Convention on the Law of Treaties. To find rules about treaty interpretation and other law-of-treaties issues, lawyers often consult the 1969 Vienna Convention on the Law of Treaties. This Convention was drafted by the International Law Commission, a body of legal experts created by the U.N. General Assembly pursuant to Article 13 of the U.N. Charter to encourage "the progressive development of international law and its codification." The Vienna Convention is binding as treaty law for those states that have accepted it—114 (not including the United States) as of May 2017.

What rules govern the law of treaties for non-parties to the Vienna Convention? What rules applied for parties to the Convention before it entered into force? Many Vienna Convention rules are regarded as customary international law, which we examine in Part C; customary international law governed the law of treaties prior to the Vienna Convention. Although the United States is not a party to the Vienna Convention, U.S. courts and the U.S. State Department have invoked it with respect to various law-of-treaties issues. In *Chubb & Son, Inc. v. Asiana Airlines*, a federal court viewed the Vienna Convention "as an authoritative guide to the customary international law of treaties" and noted that "[t]he United States Department of State considers the Vienna Convention in dealing with day-to-day treaty problems and recognizes the Vienna Convention as in large part the authoritative guide to current treaty law and practice." 214 F.3d 301, 308–09 (2d Cir. 2000), *cert. denied*, 533 U.S. 928 (2001).

Treaties and the Law of State Responsibility. For some topics that arise in international treaty disputes, including remedies for breaches, the law of state responsibility, another branch of general international law, also contains important rules. We explore state responsibility later in the book, especially in Chapters 4 and 7.

Reservations to Treaties and International Relations. Some law-of-treaties issues reflect debates about the nature of treaties and international relations. For example, in the 1951 *Reservations to the Genocide Convention Case*, 1951 I.C.J. 15, the International Court of Justice issued an advisory opinion concerning whether a party to a multilateral treaty could validly make reservations to it. Reservations are unilateral statements purporting to exclude or modify the legal effect of particular treaty articles for the reserving country. The ICJ permitted reservations if the treaty did not prohibit them and if they did not violate the treaty's "object and purpose"; the Vienna Convention on the Law of Treaties later echoed the ICJ's approach. This approach might encourage widespread acceptance of a multilateral treaty. However, permitting reservations means that a multilateral treaty could well reflect a complex web of different "contractual" relationships: As between two states parties that make no reservations, the treaty would apply in full; if a state party accepts reservations made by another party, the treaty articles subject to reservations do not apply between those states; and if a state party rejects reservations and declares that it does not consider itself bound by the treaty *vis-à-vis* the reserving state, those states have no treaty relationship at all. A treaty with multiple parties, multiple reservations, and multiple reactions to those reservations may be complex indeed!

Four dissenting judges in the *Genocide Case* "believe[d] that the integrity of the terms of the [1948 Genocide] Convention is of greater importance than mere universality in its acceptance." *Id.* at 31, 46. The dissenters would have required states parties, as members of the international community, to accept the whole of the Convention in order to be bound by it. In short, they viewed the Convention as akin to uniform "legislation," rather than as a web of bilateral agreements. In a multilateral treaty with a significant moral mission like the Genocide Convention, should community sentiment play a larger role than in a more transactional bilateral agreement, say the Cession of Alaska?

C. CUSTOMARY INTERNATIONAL LAW

At first glance, one might think that treaties provide all that international law needs by way of rules. Nowadays, there are tens of thousands of international agreements, most all of which offer the distinct advantages of explicitly expressing international norms and the consent of sovereign states. However, other sorts of international law remain just as important as before. This is so for at least two reasons. First, treaty provisions need to be interpreted and, if treaty interpretation is not to be pure discretion, some guidance from other forms of law is called for. Second, treaties almost never bind all states, and there need to be some rules of more general application.

Next to treaties, international lawyers work most often with customary international law, to which we now turn. Our first two examples involve maritime incidents, historically an important cause of foreign relations disputes; our third example concerns the nationalization of foreign investments. As you read this part, evaluate the role of decision makers in determining rules of custom and how their decisions impact international relations. Consider too whether custom is best viewed as a consensual source of international law—an implicit sort of international agreement—or instead is better viewed as not based on the consent of states.

The Spanish-American War. Our first example of customary international law, the *Paquete Habana Case*, emerged from the 1898 Spanish-American War. Professor Dodge described the setting:

> Cuba was then a colony of Spain. For three years Spanish authorities had struggled to put down a Cuban insurgency, most notoriously with a policy of "reconcentration" that forced people from the countryside into fortified areas where thousands died from unsanitary conditions. Reports of atrocities in the American "yellow press," reaching a public already hostile to European involvement in the Western hemisphere and sympathetic to U.S. expansion, produced strong anti-Spanish feelings. Then, on February 15, 1898, an enormous explosion ripped through the battleship *Maine*, sending her to the bottom of Havana harbor, with a loss of 266 lives. From then on, "Cuban issues consumed the body politic, displacing all other concerns."

> After negotiations failed to convince Spain to grant Cuba independence, President McKinley sent a message to Congress on April 11 asking for authority to intervene. Congress responded on April 20, 1898, with a joint resolution declaring "[t]hat the people of the Island of Cuba are, and of right ought to be, free and independent"; demanding "that the Government of Spain at once relinquish its authority and government in the Island of Cuba and withdraw its land and naval forces from Cuba and Cuban waters"; and directing the President "to use the entire land and naval forces of the United States, and to call into the actual service of the United States the militia of the several States, to such an extent as may be necessary to carry these resolutions into effect."

William S. Dodge, "The Paquete Habana: Customary International Law as Part of Our Law," in *International Law Stories* 175, 176–77 (John E. Noyes, Laura A. Dickinson & Mark W. Janis eds. 2007).

Figure 2.G
Wreckage of the USS *Maine*, Havana Harbor, 1898

The U.S. Seizure of Spanish Coastal Fishing Vessels and the Paquete Habana *Dispute.* The *Paquete Habana Case* arose out of the seizure of two Spanish fishing vessels by the U.S. Navy during the war between the United States and Spain over Cuba.

THE PAQUETE HABANA

175 U.S. 677 (1900)

The Facts

MR. JUSTICE GRAY delivered the opinion of the court.

These are two appeals from decrees of the District Court of the United States for the Southern District of Florida, condemning two fishing vessels and their cargoes as prize of war.

Each vessel was a fishing smack, running in and out of Havana, and regularly engaged in fishing on the coast of Cuba; sailed under the Spanish flag; was owned by a Spanish subject of Cuban birth, living in the city of Havana; was commanded by a subject of Spain, also residing in Havana; and her master and crew had no interest in the vessel, but were entitled to shares, amounting in all to two thirds, of her catch, the other third belonging to her owner. Her cargo consisted of fresh fish, caught by her crew from the sea, put on board as they were caught, and kept and sold alive. Until stopped by the blockading squadron, she had no knowledge of the existence of the war, or of any blockade. She had no arms or ammunition on board, and made no attempt to run the blockade after she knew of its existence, nor any resistance at the time of the capture. . . .

Both the fishing vessels were brought by their captors into Key West [in Florida]. A libel for the condemnation of each vessel and her cargo as prize of war was there filed on April 27, 1898; a claim was interposed by her master, on behalf of himself and the other members of the crew, and of her owner; evidence was taken, showing the facts above stated; and on May 30, 1898, a final decree of condemnation and sale was entered, "the court not being satisfied that as a matter of law, without ordinance, treaty or proclamation, fishing vessels of this class are exempt from seizure."

Each vessel was thereupon sold by auction; the Paquete Habana for the sum of $490; and the Lola for the sum of $800. . . .

The Paquete Habana, as the record shows, was a fishing sloop of 25 tons burden[.] Her crew consisted of but three men, including the master[.] On her last voyage, she sailed from Havana along the coast of Cuba about 200 miles and fished for 25 days off the cape at the west end of the island within the territorial waters of Spain and was going back to Havana with her cargo of live fish, when she was captured by one of the blockading squadron on April 25, 1898. She had no arms or ammunition on board; she had no knowledge of the blockade or even of the war until she was stopped by a blockading vessel; she made no attempt to run the blockade and no resistance at the time of the capture; nor was there any evidence whatever of likelihood that she or her crew would aid the enemy.

In the case of the Lola, [slight] differences in the facts . . . afford no ground for distinguishing the two cases.

. . . Although [the Lola] extended her fishing trip across the Yucatan Channel and fished on the coast of Yucatan, we cannot doubt that each was engaged in the coast fishery[.]

Suing the United States. The *Paquete Habana Case* was not a case between the U.S. government and the Spanish government. Instead, private parties—the Spanish owners of two seized Spanish vessels, each commanded by a Spanish citizen and crewed by men subject to service in Spain's armed forces—brought the lawsuit against the United States in a U.S. court.

What non-legal arguments might the attorney for the owners of the *Lola* and the *Paquete Habana* have raised with the U.S. government to release the vessels before they were auctioned? Counsel for the Cuban citizens may well first have tried simply to persuade the U.S. Navy and then the Executive Branch not to condemn the vessels. How might foreign relations have informed their arguments? The condemnation of the fishing boats was unlikely to build support for the United States as it liberated Cuba from centuries of Spanish rule. At best, the U.S. government's condemnation of the *Paquete Habana* and the *Lola* was a short-sighted move in U.S. foreign policy.

In the event, informal arguments did not avoid condemnation of the vessels. Litigation ensued.

The Rule in the Case. The issue facing the U.S. Supreme Court was whether the two fishing vessels were legally subject to capture by the U.S. Navy during the U.S. war with Spain. The end result in the *Paquette Habana Case* was that the U.S. Supreme Court held against its own government for the U.S. wartime actions, basing its ruling on international law. Look at the rule the Court articulated:

The Paquete Habana
The Rule in the Case

By an ancient usage among civilized nations, beginning centuries ago, and gradually ripening into a rule of international law, coast fishing vessels, pursuing their vocation of catching and bringing in fresh fish, have been recognized as exempt, with their cargoes and crews, from capture as prize of war. . . .

The doctrine . . . exempts coast fishermen with their vessels and cargoes from capture as prize of war[.]

[C]oast fishing vessels, with their implements and supplies, cargoes and crews, unarmed, and honestly pursuing their peaceful calling of catching and bringing in fresh fish, are exempt from capture as prize of war. . . .

Upon the facts proved in either case, it is the duty of this court, sitting as the highest prize court of the United States, and administering the law of nations, to declare and adjudge that the capture was unlawful, and without probable cause; and it is therefore, in each case,

Ordered, that the decree of the District Court be reversed, and the proceeds of the sale of the vessel, together with the proceeds of any sale of her cargo, be restored to the claimant, with damages and costs.

Customary International Law as Unwritten Law. It is striking that Justice Gray's formulation of the governing rule is not identical throughout his decision! This result is perhaps not so surprising when we recognize that the customary rule— unlike a treaty rule—is unwritten (until a judge or some other decision maker writes it down). If a rule of customary international law is unwritten, where does the rule come from, and how does it fit with other rules of law?

Customary International Law as a Gap Filler. International courts and other international actors often turn to customary international law when there is no governing treaty rule. Municipal courts, such as the U.S. Supreme Court, also use customary international law as a gap filler, though, unlike international courts, they may look to both international and municipal law in their search for a rule. Indeed, the lawyers representing the owners of the Cuban fishing vessels most likely would have first thought to reverse the U.S. government's act on grounds of domestic law, seeking a U.S. statute or regulation that denied the Navy authority to seize the boats. And, if not successful at domestic law, the lawyers might have looked for a treaty with Cuba or Spain that protected private parties like the Cuban fishermen. Customary international law probably came to the rescue, as it so often does, to fill gaps when no easier, more definite rule proved to be available. Justice Gray recognized this "gap filling" role in one of the most famous passages about international law in U.S. case law:

The Paquete Habana
International Law and U.S. Law

International law is part of our law, and must be ascertained and administered by the courts of justice of appropriate jurisdiction, as often as questions of right depending upon it are duly presented for their determination. For this purpose, where there is no treaty, and no controlling executive or legislative act or judicial decision, resort must be had to the customs and usages of civilized nations[.]

Statutory Reference. Sometimes a "controlling legislative act" incorporates customary international law by reference. That is, a U.S. court may turn to customary international law when a U.S. statute specifically refers to "international law" or the "law of nations," as in *Filartiga* in Chapter 1. There was no such statutory incorporation of customary international law in *Paquete Habana*.   *gesetzlich*

What is Customary International Law and How is it Found? Justice Gray described the rule proscribing seizure of coastal fishing vessels as derived from "an ancient usage among civilized nations, beginning centuries ago, and gradually ripening into a rule of international law." Customary international law thus includes two components: first, the practice of states, and, second, a "ripening" or transformation into law. Consider first the practice component and some of the evidence of practice in *Paquete Habana*.

The Paquete Habana
The Practice of States

[N]o complete collection of the instances illustrating [the rule prohibiting the seizure of coastal fishing vessels] is to be found, so far as we are aware, in a single published work, although many are referred to and discussed by the writers on international law, notably [Ortolan, Calvo, De Boeck, and Hall]. It is therefore worth the while to trace the history of the rule, from the earliest accessible sources, through the increasing recognition of it, with occasional setbacks, to what we may now justly consider as its final establishment in our own country and generally throughout the civilized world.

The earliest acts of any government on the subject, mentioned in the books, either emanated from, or were approved by, a King of England.

In 1403 and 1406, Henry IV issued orders to his admirals and other officers, entitled "Concerning Safety for Fisherman—*De Securitate pro Piscatoribus*." By an order of October 26, 1403, reciting that it was made pursuant to a treaty between himself and the King of France; and for the greater safety of the fishermen of either country, and so that they could be, and carry on their industry, the more safely on the sea, and deal with each other in peace; and that the French King had consented that English fishermen should be treated likewise; it was ordained that French fishermen might, during the then pending season for the herring fishery, safely fish for herrings and all other fish, from the harbor of Gravelines and the island of Thanet to the mouth of the Seine and the harbor of Hautoune. [The Court reviews a similar order of 1406.]

The treaty made October 2, 1521, between the Emperor Charles V and Francis I of France, through their ambassadors, recited that a great and fierce war had arisen between them, because of which there had been, both by land and by sea, frequent depredations and incursions on either side, to the grave detriment and intolerable injury of the innocent subjects of each; and that a suitable time for the herring fishery was at hand, and, by reason of the sea being beset by the enemy, the fishermen did not dare to go out, whereby the subject of their industry, bestowed by heaven to allay the hunger of the poor, would wholly fail for the year, unless it were otherwise provided[.] And it was therefore agreed that the subjects of each sovereign, fishing in the sea, or exercising the calling of fishermen, could and might, until the end of the next January, without incurring any attack, depredation, molestation, trouble or hindrance soever, safely and freely, everywhere in the sea, take herrings and every other kind of fish, the existing war by land and sea notwithstanding; and further that, during the time aforesaid, no subject of either sovereign should commit, or attempt or presume to commit, any depredation, force, violence, molestation or vexation, to or upon such fishermen, or their vessels, supplies, equipments, nets and fish, or other goods soever truly appertaining to fishing. . . .

The herring fishery was permitted, in time of war, by French and Dutch edicts in 1536. Bynkershoek Quæstiones Juris Publicæ, lib. 1, c. 3; 1 Emerigon des Assurances, c. 4, sect. 9; c. 12, sect. 19, § 8.

France, from remote times, set the example of alleviating the evils of war in favor of all coast fishermen. [The Court discusses French ordinances from 1543 and 1584, and a compilation of laws and customs of the sea published by Cleirac in 1661.]

The same custom would seem to have prevailed in France until towards the end of the seventeenth century. For example, in 1675, Louis XIV and the States General of Holland, by mutual agreement, granted to Dutch and French fishermen the liberty, undisturbed by their vessels of war, of fishing along the coasts of France, Holland and England. D'Hauterive et De Cussy, Traités de Commerce, pt. 1, vol. 2, p. 278. But by the ordinances of 1681 and 1692 the practice was discontinued, because, Valin says, of the faithless conduct of the enemies of France, who, abusing the good faith with which she had always observed the treaties, habitually carried off her fishermen, while their own fished in safety. 2 Valin sur l'Ordonnance de la Marine, (1776) 689, 690; 2 Ortolan, 52; De Boeck, § 192.

The doctrine which exempts coast fishermen with their vessels and cargoes from capture as prize of war has been familiar to the United States from the time of the War of Independence. [The Court reviews a 1779 letter from the U.S. ally Louis XVI of France, confirmed in a 1780 royal order, and notes "the capture and ransom, by a French cruiser, of *The John and Sarah*, an English vessel, coming from Holland, laden with fresh fish, were pronounced to be illegal." The Court also concludes, after reviewing English judicial orders and the statements of jurists, that "England, as well as France, during the American Revolutionary War, abstained from interfering with the coast fisheries." Similarly, fishermen and "others whose occupations are for the common subsistence and benefit of mankind" are exempt from "hostile molestation or seizure" under U.S.-Prussia treaties of 1785, 1799, and 1828. And according to a commentator:] "In many treaties and decrees, fishermen catching fish as an article of food are added to the class of persons whose occupation is not to be disturbed in war." Wheaton's International Law, (8th ed.) § 345, note 168. . . .

In the war with Mexico in 1846, the United States recognized the exemption of coast fishing boats from capture. [The Court reviews U.S. naval records.]

> *The Practice of States.* We cannot, of course, see states "practicing," but we can follow their paper trail. What features about the usage or practice component of customary international law emerge from this survey? The practice here is indeed "ancient," although it is not always essential that practice be ancient or longstanding in order to provide the basis for a rule of customary international law. The practice must be "international," in the *Paquete Habana Case* relating to the acts of a government toward foreigners' fishing vessels. The practice seems generally consistent, though it is not 100 percent uniform. What counts as "practice"? Justice Gray referred to treaties, executive branch or royal decrees, judicial pronouncements, and legislative ordinances.
>
> *The Role of Publicists.* It is unlikely that either the attorneys for the vessel owners or the Supreme Court justices had copies of King Henry's 1406 orders on their bookshelves. Where could they find information about state practice? Probably in the scholarly literature. Recall that Article 38(1)(d) of the Statute of the International Court of Justice, quoted in Part A's discussion of sources, refers to "judicial decisions and the teachings of the most highly qualified publicists of the various nations, as subsidiary means for the determination of rules of law." Justice Gray echoed the importance of referring to the writings of publicists and jurists to ascertain the "customs and usages of civilized nations":

The Paquete Habana
The Role of Jurists and Commentators

[A]s evidence of these [customs and usages, we look] to the works of jurists and commentators, who by years of labor, research and experience, have made themselves peculiarly well acquainted with the subjects of which they treat. Such works are resorted to by judicial tribunals, not for the speculations of their authors concerning what the law ought to be, but for trustworthy evidence of what the law really is.

Wheaton places, among the principal sources of international law, "Text-writers of authority, showing what is the approved usage of nations, or the general opinion respecting their mutual conduct, with the definitions and modifications introduced by general consent." As to these he forcibly observes: "Without wishing to exaggerate the importance of these writers, or to substitute, in any case, their authority for the principles of reason, it may be affirmed that they are generally impartial in their judgment. They are witnesses of the sentiments and usages of civilized nations, and the weight of their testimony increases every time that their authority is invoked by statesmen, and every year that passes without the rules laid down in their works being impugned by the avowal of contrary principles." Wheaton's International Law, (8th ed.) § 15.

Chancellor Kent says: "In the absence of higher and more authoritative sanctions, the ordinances of foreign States, the opinions of eminent statesmen, and the writings of distinguished jurists, are regarded as of great consideration on questions not settled by conventional law. In cases where the principal jurists agree, the presumption will be very great in favor of the solidity of their maxims; and no civilized nation, that does not arrogantly set all ordinary law and justice at defiance, will venture to disregard the uniform sense of the established writers on international law." 1 Kent Com. 18.

[The Court cites numerous French, English, Argentinian, German, Dutch, Austrian, Spanish, Portuguese, and Italian jurists.]

This review of the precedents and authorities on the subject appears to us abundantly to demonstrate that at the present day, by the general consent of the civilized nations of the world, and independently of any express treaty or other public act, it is an established rule of international law, founded on considerations of humanity to a poor and industrious order of men, and of the mutual convenience of belligerent States, that coast fishing vessels, with their implements and supplies, cargoes and crews, unarmed, and honestly pursuing their peaceful calling of catching and bringing in fresh fish, are exempt from capture as prize of war.

The exemption, of course, does not apply to coast fishermen or their vessels, if employed for a warlike purpose, or in such a way as to give aid or information to the enemy; nor when military or naval operations create a necessity to which all private interests must give way. . . .

The position taken by the United States during the recent war with Spain was quite in accord with the rule of international law, now generally recognized by civilized nations, in regard to coast fishing vessels.

. . . On April 22, [1898] the President issued a proclamation, declaring that the United States had instituted and would maintain [a] blockade [of the north coast of Cuba] "in pursuance of the laws of the United States, and the law of nations applicable to such cases." 30 Stat. 1769. And by the act of Congress of April 25, 1898, it was declared that the war between the United States and Spain existed on that day, and had existed since and including April 21.

On April 26, 1898, the President issued another proclamation, which, [while] making no mention of fishing vessels[,] clearly manifests the general policy of the Government to conduct the war in accordance with the principles of international law sanctioned by the recent practice of nations.

Opinio Juris. Although consistent state practice, often seen in evidence collected by publicists and jurists, is one component of customary international law, there is also a second component. The practice needs to "ripen" into law or somehow become legally binding.

We know when a treaty becomes legally binding on the parties. We can date its ratification or acceptance and its entry into force. With custom, there is no such date certain. Justice Gray of course did not need to know exactly when the consistent practice or "usages" of states had "ripened" into a legal rule prohibiting the seizure of foreign coastal fishing vessels during wartime. He just needed to know that the rule existed when the *Paquete Habana* and the *Lola* had been seized.

But how do the consistent usages of states ripen into rules of customary international law? Why should such a transformative proposition be valid? With treaties, international lawyers agree that a state's consent has legally binding effect. With custom, why should states or courts give such "ripened usages" the force of law and apply them as rules of decision in cases before them?

Some "positivists," who believe that international law derives from the law-making acts of states, think that custom's "ripening" component depends on state acceptance. Ordinarily in positivist theory, it is said that customary international law is based on consistent state practice plus *opinio juris*, the belief that states act in a certain way because required to do so by law or necessity. Some equate *opinio juris* with "acceptance as law." Is there any proof of *opinio juris* in *Paquete Habana*? *Opinio juris* is vital if custom is to be deemed the implicit agreement of states. When a suggested rule is prohibitory (do not seize coastal fishing vessels), how can we be assured that states by non-action satisfy the requirement of *opinio juris*? States may in practice refuse to seize coastal fishing vessels, but they rarely say their refusal is required by international law. Non-action may be due to some other motivation, such as considerations of humanity or a lack of available resources.

A study by the International Committee of the Red Cross argued that "[w]hen there is sufficiently dense practice, an *opinio juris* is generally contained within that practice and, as a result, it is not usually necessary to demonstrate separately the existence of an *opinio juris*." Jean-Marie Henckaerts, "Study on Customary International Humanitarian Law: A Contribution to the Understanding and Respect for the Rule of Law in Armed Conflict," 87 *International Review of the Red Cross* 175, 182 (2005). Does that assertion in effect suggest that *opinio juris* is a fiction, something to be presumed? When *opinio juris* is a legal fiction, what is the real nature of customary international law? Does state practice without clear *opinio juris* constitute a consensual source of international law? Customary international law and the non-consensual sources all rely especially heavily on judges and publicists. Perhaps this makes judges and publicists sometimes the real "legislators" of international law. The ordinary difficulty in "proving" *opinio juris* contributes to a sense that determining custom is something of an art form, with much discretion left in the hands of judges and other decision makers.

Regional and Particular Custom. If there can be regional and bilateral treaties, may there also be regional and bilateral rules of customary international law? The International Court of Justice accepted an argument based on a non-universal customary rule in the *Anglo-Norwegian Fisheries Case*, respecting Norway's assertion of a wider than ordinary exclusive fishing zone: "The notoriety of the facts, the general toleration of the international community, Great Britain's position in the North Sea, her own interest in the question, and her prolonged abstention would in any case warrant Norway's enforcement of her system against the United Kingdom." 1951 I.C.J. 116, 139.

Customary International Law and the U.S. Legal System. We have been particularly concerned with what *Paquete Habana* has to teach about the manner of determining rules of customary international law. The case also is often cited with respect to two other propositions. The first is the way in which customary international law is incorporated into the municipal law of the United States. As noted above, the Supreme Court held that "international law is part of our law," an important statement about such incorporation. The Supreme Court reaffirmed that proposition in 2004, with a citation to *Paquete Habana*. Sosa v. Alvarez-Machain, 542 U.S. 692, 729–30 (2004).

The second proposition concerns the proper relationship between the U.S. courts and the Executive Branch in legal matters touching on international relations. The *Paquete Habana* Court noted that it was "the general policy of the Government to conduct the war in accordance with the principles of international law," citing two presidential proclamations to that effect. That assertion leaves some important questions of U.S. constitutional law unanswered. Did the Supreme Court have the constitutional authority to use customary international law to trump the Navy's decision to seize vessels, which after all carried experienced sailors whom Spain might have pressed into military service? Had both the President and the Court agreed that the actions of the Executive ought in any case be subject to customary international law? May the President legally, at U.S. law, act in contravention of customary international law? We consider the incorporation of customary international law in the U.S. legal system, and the balance of powers in foreign relations among the President, the Congress, and U.S. courts, in Chapter 5.

The Lotus Case. We continue our exploration of customary international law with the *Lotus Case*. *Lotus* involved a collision between a French vessel and a Turkish ship on the high seas off the coast of Turkey. France and Turkey referred the dispute to the Permanent Court of International Justice, which first determined the facts:

THE LOTUS CASE
France v. Turkey, 1927 P.C.I.J., Ser. A, No. 10

The Facts

On August 2nd, 1926, just before midnight, a collision occurred between the French mail steamer *Lotus*, proceeding to Constantinople, and the Turkish collier *Boz-Kourt*, between five and six nautical miles to the north of Cape Sigri (Mitylene). The *Boz-Kourt*, which was cut in two, sank and eight Turkish nationals who were on board perished. After having done everything possible to succour the shipwrecked persons, of whom ten were able to be saved, the *Lotus* continued on its course to Constantinople, [Turkey,] where it arrived on August 3rd.

At the time of the collision, the officer of the watch on board the *Lotus* was Monsieur Demons, a French citizen, lieutenant in the merchant service and first officer of the ship, whilst the movements of the *Boz-Kourt* were directed by its captain, Hassan Bey, who was one of those saved from the wreck. . . .

On August 5th, Lieutenant Demons was requested by the Turkish authorities to go ashore to give evidence. The examination, the length of which incidentally resulted in delaying the departure of the *Lotus*, led to the placing under arrest of Lieutenant Demons—without previous notice being given to the French Consul-General—and Hassan Bey, amongst others. This arrest, which has been characterized by the Turkish Agent as arrest pending trial (*arrestation préventive*), was effected in order to ensure that the criminal prosecution instituted against the two officers, on a charge of manslaughter, by the Public Prosecutor of Stamboul . . . should follow its normal course.

The case was first heard by the Criminal Court of Stamboul on August 28th. On that occasion, Lieutenant Demons submitted that the Turkish Courts had no jurisdiction; the Court, however, overruled his objection. . . .

On September 15th, the Criminal Court delivered its judgment, the terms of which have not been communicated to the Court by the Parties. It is, however, common ground, that it sentenced Lieutenant Demons to 80 days' imprisonment and a fine of 22 pounds, Hassan Bey being sentenced to a slightly more severe penalty. . . .

The action of the Turkish judicial authorities with regard to Lieutenant Demons at once gave rise to many diplomatic representations and other steps on the part of the French Government or its representatives in Turkey, either protesting against the arrest of Lieutenant Demons or demanding his release, or with a view to obtaining the transfer of the case from the Turkish Courts to the French Courts.

As a result of these representations, the Government of the Turkish Republic declared on September 2nd, 1926, that "it would have no objection to the reference of the conflict of jurisdiction to the Court at The Hague."

The French Government having, on the 6th of the same month, given "its full consent to the proposed solution," the two Governments appointed their plenipotentiaries with a view to the drawing up of the special agreement to be submitted to the Court; this special agreement was signed at Geneva on October 12th, 1926, as stated above, and the ratifications were deposited on December 27th, 1926.

> *The International Court of Justice and its Jurisdiction.* The *Lotus Case* is a judgment of the Permanent Court of International Justice, created as a part of the League of Nations after World War I and the predecessor of the International Court of Justice. The ICJ, technically a new court inaugurated at the end of World War II as a part of the United Nations, is almost identical in

structure and operation to the Permanent Court. Only states may be parties in contentious cases at the International Court. More about the ICJ appears in Chapter 4.

As suggested by the excerpt above, the authority of the PCIJ to hear a contentious case depended on the mutual consent of the states involved; the same remains true for the ICJ. In the *Lotus Case*, that mutual consent took the form of a French-Turkish "special agreement," a treaty that also specified the issue that the parties wanted the Court to decide. The terms of any special agreement under which the International Court takes jurisdiction are carefully negotiated. Contrast municipal litigation practice, in which one party (the "plaintiff") unilaterally brings a lawsuit and frames (in a "complaint") the issues that the defendant and the court must consider.

According to the special agreement in the *Lotus Case*, the International Court was to decide whether Turkey violated Article 15 of the 1923 Convention of Lausanne by instituting criminal proceedings under Turkish law against Lieutenant Demons, the French officer of the watch on the *Lotus* when the vessels collided. Article 15 required "all questions of jurisdiction" between Turkey and the other treaty parties to "be decided in accordance with the principles of international law"—language the Court read as referring to customary international law. The legal issue thus boiled down to whether Turkey could apply its municipal criminal law to the French officer Demons consistently with customary international law principles of jurisdiction. Before seeing how the Court construed customary international law, a word about the jurisdiction of states is in order.

Jurisdiction. In international law, "jurisdiction" refers not only to the authority of courts to hear cases, but to the authority of states to determine or affect legal relationships. In *Lotus* the issue concerned Turkey's legislative jurisdiction, *i.e.*, its authority to apply its criminal law to Lieutenant Demons. A 1926 Turkish statute provided that authority as a matter of Turkish law. The statute called for the punishment of a "foreigner" committing "an offence abroad to the prejudice of Turkey or of a Turkish subject, for which offence Turkish law prescribes a penalty involving loss of freedom for a minimum period of not less than one year." But the issue before the Court was not whether Turkey correctly applied its own law. Instead, the issue was whether the institution of Turkish criminal proceedings comported with customary international law.

One traditional international law basis for applying a country's laws is territoriality, where both proscribed conduct and its consequences occur within that country's territory. Here Lieutenant Demons's acts took place on a French vessel, and the accident occurred on the "high seas," outside Turkey's "territorial sea" (concepts we explore in Chapter 8). (Turkish authorities arrested Demons in Turkey, but that post-accident exercise of "enforcement jurisdiction" did not make Turkey's exercise of "legislative jurisdiction" with respect Demons's acts on the high seas territorial.) Another traditional basis for exercising legislative jurisdiction is nationality, where the offender is a national of the prosecuting country. But Demons was French, not Turkish. You can begin to see why Turkey's prosecution might be controversial at international law. How might it be justified? One possible argument was that the effects of Demons's conduct were felt in Turkish territory, even though he acted outside Turkey. But such "effects" or "objective territorial" jurisdiction was not well established in 1926, and in any event application of that theory would depend on the fiction of treating the Turkish vessel *Boz-Kourt* as a floating bit of Turkish territory. Another possible argument was that international law permitted jurisdiction to be based on the nationality of the victim, rather than the offender. Why might it be difficult if one country's citizen has to follow a second country's laws, with respect to his actions outside that second country? The *Lotus* Court ultimately ruled in Turkey's favor, but the issue was close: the judges were equally divided, and the President of the Court cast the deciding vote.

The finding that Turkey could, consistently with international law, apply its criminal law to Lieutenant Demons did not mean that France lacked concurrent jurisdiction to prosecute Demons under French law. What international law basis of legislative jurisdiction could France assert? The legality of one country's application of its laws, and how to resolve conflicts of jurisdiction in cases, like *Lotus*, of concurrent municipal jurisdiction, are often sources of international tensions and disputes.

The Significance of the Lotus Case. *Lotus* "attracted more attention among international lawyers than any other decision of the 1920s, at the time and ever since." Ole Spiermann, *International Legal Argument in the Permanent Court of International Justice: The Rise of the International Judiciary* 247 (2005). The case's notoriety has related not to the jurisdictional issue involved, but to a far broader lesson that the PCIJ sought to teach. The judgment became one of the most usually cited positivist opinions about the essential nature of international law.

The Lotus Case
Positivism

The Court, having to consider whether there are any rules of international law which may have been violated by the prosecution in pursuance of Turkish law of Lieutenant Demons, is confronted in the first place by a question of principle which . . . has proved to be a fundamental one. The French Government contends that the Turkish Courts, in order to have jurisdiction, should be able to point to some title to jurisdiction recognized by international law in favour of Turkey. On the other hand, the Turkish Government takes the view that Article 15 [of the Treaty of Lausanne] allows Turkey jurisdiction whenever such jurisdiction does not come into conflict with a principle of international law.

The latter view [is] dictated by the very nature and existing conditions of international law.

International law governs relations between independent States. The rules of law binding upon States therefore emanate from their own free will as expressed in conventions or by usages generally accepted as expressing principles of law and established in order to regulate the relations between these co-existing independent communities or with a view to the achievement of common aims. Restrictions upon the independence of States cannot therefore be presumed.

Now the first and foremost restriction imposed by international law upon a State is that—failing the existence of a permissive rule to the contrary—it may not exercise its power in any form in the territory of another State. In this sense jurisdiction is certainly territorial; it cannot be exercised by a State outside its territory except by virtue of a permissive rule derived from international custom or from a convention.

It does not, however, follow that international law prohibits a State from exercising jurisdiction in its own territory, in respect of any case which relates to acts which have taken place abroad, and in which it cannot rely on some permissive rule of international law. . . . Far from laying down a general prohibition to the effect that States may not extend the application of their laws and the jurisdiction of their courts to persons, property and acts outside their territory, [international law] leaves them in this respect a wide measure of discretion which is only limited in certain cases by prohibitive rules; as regards other cases, every State remains free to adopt the principles which it regards as best and most suitable. . . .

In these circumstances, all that can be required of a State is that it should not overstep the limits which international law places upon its jurisdiction; within these limits, its title to exercise jurisdiction rests in its sovereignty.

It follows from the foregoing that the contention of the French Government to the effect that Turkey must in each case be able to cite a rule of international law authorizing her to exercise jurisdiction, is opposed to the generally accepted international law to which Article 15 of the Convention of Lausanne refers.

Positivism and International Law. The PCIJ's positivist attitude is embodied in the claim that "rules of law binding upon States . . . emanate from their own free will as expressed in conventions or by usages generally accepted as expressing principles of law." The ruling half of an evenly divided Court in *Lotus* maintained that all international legal rules are based on state consent: "Restrictions upon the independence of States cannot therefore be presumed." No room was given to general principles, fundamental norms, natural law, or equity as sources of international law; state sovereignty was seen as the fundamental principle of international law from which all other international legal principles and rules are derived. Looking at other cases above, *e.g.*, *Filartiga* and *Paquete Habana*, and below, *e.g.*, *Texaco/Libya*, *AM & S*, *Smith*, and *North Sea Continental Shelf*, is the strict positivism of the *Lotus* judgment too restrictive? If a treaty rule and a rule of customary international law are absent or unclear, need one necessarily default to the notion that states have freedom to act as they wish?

Opinio Juris *and the Proof of Customary International Law.* With France having to demonstrate that Turkey could not exercise jurisdiction, France's task became much more difficult, and, indeed, France ultimately lost the case. (One can easily imagine that if Turkey had had to prove that its exercise of jurisdiction *complied* with international law, the equally divided Court would have tipped the other way.) The French government advanced three arguments. First, "[i]nternational law does not allow a State to take proceedings with regard to offenses committed by foreigners abroad, simply by reason of the nationality of the victim; and such is the situation in the present case because the offence must be regarded as having been committed on board the French vessel." This argument failed because France could establish no rule of international law forbidding "Turkey to take into consideration the fact that the offence produced its effects on the Turkish vessel and consequently in a place assimilated to Turkish territory"; Turkish criminal law could be applied, "even in regard to offenses committed there by foreigners."

France also did not prevail in its second argument, which was that "[i]nternational law recognizes the exclusive jurisdiction of the State whose flag is flown as regards everything which occurs on board a ship on the high seas." The following excerpt concerns France's third argument, that the principle of exclusive flag state jurisdiction "is especially applicable in a collision case." Note how the difficulty of proving *opinio juris* may complicate efforts to establish a rule of customary international law.

The Lotus Case
The Result in the Case

It only remains to examine the third argument advanced by the French Government and to ascertain whether a rule specially applying to collision cases has grown up, according to which criminal proceedings regarding such cases come exclusively within the jurisdiction of the State whose flag is flown.

In this connection, the Agent for the French Government has drawn the Court's attention to the fact that questions of jurisdiction in collision cases, which frequently arise before civil courts, are but rarely encountered in the practice of criminal courts. He deduces from this that, in practice, prosecutions only occur before the courts of the State whose flag is flown and that circumstance is proof of a tacit consent on the part of States and, consequently, shows what positive international law is in collision cases.

In the Court's opinion, this conclusion is not warranted. Even if the rarity of the judicial decisions to be found among the reported cases were sufficient to prove in point of fact the circumstance alleged by the Agent for the French Government, it would merely show that States had often, in practice, abstained from instituting criminal proceedings, and not that they recognized themselves as being obliged to do so; for only if such abstention were based on their being conscious of having a duty to abstain would it be possible to speak of an international custom. The alleged fact does not allow one to infer that States have been conscious of having such a duty; on the other hand, as will presently be seen, there are other circumstances calculated to show that the contrary is true.

So far as the Court is aware there are no decisions of international tribunals in this matter; but some decisions of municipal courts have been cited. [T]he decisions quoted sometimes support one view and sometimes the other. Whilst the French Government have been able to cite the *Ortigia-Oncle-Joseph* case before the Court of Aix and the *Franconia-Strathclyde* case before the British Court for Crown Cases Reserved, as being in favour of the exclusive jurisdiction of the state whose flag is flown, on the other hand the *Ortigia-Oncle-Joseph* case before the

Italian Courts and the *Ekbatana-West-Hinder* case before the Belgian Courts have been cited in support of the opposing contention.

[A]s municipal jurisprudence is thus divided, it is hardly possible to see in it an indication of the existence of the restrictive rule of international law which alone could serve as a basis for the contention of the French Government. . . .

Consequently, Turkey, by instituting, in virtue of the discretion which international law leaves to every sovereign State, the criminal proceedings in question, has not, in the absence of such principles, acted in a manner contrary to the principles of international law within the meaning of the special agreement.

Tacit Consent and the Formation of Rules of Customary International Law. In order to establish that Turkey was bound by some rule of international law prohibiting its prosecution of Lieutenant Demons, would France have had to establish that Turkey itself, in its international relations, affirmatively consented to that prohibitory rule? The *Lotus* Court did not insist on that extreme voluntarist position. Under the positivist conception of universal custom set out in *Lotus*, it would have sufficed to establish expressions of consent to a rule by some or many states, coupled with the silence of other states. Has a silent state necessarily "tacitly consented" to the rule? Does a consensual account of customary international law accurately reflect how it develops?

Reversal of the Rule in Lotus. France's concern in pursuing the *Lotus Case* was only partly its interest in Lieutenant Demons; a broader principle important to a maritime power such as France was at issue. As a matter of maritime law, many observers disagreed with the *Lotus* decision, feeling that it could expose shipboard officers to double prosecution and lead to unnecessary delays in maritime traffic. In the 1958 Geneva Convention on the High Seas, Article 11(1) provides that in cases involving collisions on the high seas, only the flag state or the national state of the accused may prosecute the officer in a case of a collision on the high seas. The same anti-*Lotus* rule resurfaced in Article 97(1) of the 1982 Convention on the Law of the Sea. These articles illustrate how a treaty may sometimes reverse a rule of customary international law. Should custom ever be able to reverse a treaty rule?

The Significance of the Forum. Compare *Paquete Habana* and *Lotus*, both decided during the early 20th century. Why did the *Lotus* Court take a stricter state-centric positivist view? Why was the *Paquete Habana* Court more willing to infer a rule of customary international law from state practice, indeed not even explicitly mentioning the traditional requirement of *opinio juris*? And why did that Court not limit the application of international law to states? In *Paquete*

Habana the Court found that rules of international law may be invoked by, and may apply to, individuals.

The fact that a different forum decided each case suggests answers. The U.S. Supreme Court, deciding *Paquete Habana*, was acting in the U.S. common law tradition, which emphasizes the importance of "reasonableness." That tradition, along with the customary U.S. respect for the rights of individuals, could help explain the Supreme Court's positions.

Compare the forum in *Lotus*. The Permanent Court of International Justice was established by states to hear disputes between them. It is perhaps not surprising that this Court, especially in the early 20th century, was deferential to states' freedom of action. In addition, many PCIJ judges were trained in the civil law tradition, which regards state-made codes rather than judicial opinions as the starting point for analyzing legal problems. Perhaps civil law-trained judges are more disposed to look primarily to the state as a source of legal authority.

The Texaco/Libya Case. Our third example illustrating the use of customary international law comes from yet a different forum, an arbitral tribunal. As is also true with contentious cases in the International Court, arbitration depends on the mutual consent of the parties, here the country of Libya and two Western oil companies, California Asiatic Oil Company and Texaco Overseas Petroleum Company. The parties had entered "deeds of concession" between 1955 and 1966, allowing the oil companies to explore for and extract oil in Libya. Libya promised to ensure that the companies enjoyed all the rights conferred by the concessions and that the contractual rights created by the concessions "shall not be altered except by mutual consent of the parties." Libyan nationalization of the companies' oil wells in 1973 and 1974 led to a legal dispute. The deeds of concession authorized arbitration of such disputes, and the arbitrator eventually ruled that Libya had breached the deeds of concession and violated customary international law.

"Mixed" *International Arbitrations*. One advantage of international arbitration is that it can be tailor-made to fit specific cases. The deeds of concession at issue in the *Texaco-Libya Case* provided that an aggrieved party could request the President of the International Court of Justice to appoint a sole arbitrator if the other party refused to make an appointment to a three-judge panel. Appointment by the President of the International Court of Professor René-Jean Dupuy as the sole arbitrator did not, of course, make this

an ICJ proceeding. Here, because both private and public parties were involved, the procedure was a "mixed" form of international arbitration.

Why would the parties drafting the deeds of concession have chosen international arbitration to settle their disputes? Compare the alternatives of litigation in Libyan courts and litigation in U.S. courts. A neutral forum is one virtue of international arbitration.

Historical Context. Why did Libya nationalize the property of foreign oil companies? What had changed between the signing of the oil concession contracts, primarily in the 1950's, and Libya's 1973 and 1974 nationalization decrees, and how might those changes have affected Libya's attitude towards the contracts? Note the following: First, the oil companies had discovered and were producing oil. The success of the petroleum exploitation project allowed Libya to assert leverage over the companies, which had considerable sunk costs in the country. Second, scores of former European colonies had gained their independence. Many poorer, newly independent states pursued a political agenda known as the New International Economic Order, explored below, which stressed state control over natural resources. Third, the government of Libya had changed. Itself a former Italian colony, Libya became independent in 1951 under the rule of King Idris, a pro-Western monarch. In 1969, Colonel Muammar Qaddafi seized power in a coup; his dictatorship stressed themes of Arab nationalism, opposition to neo-colonialism, and socialism. Qaddafi remained in power until 2011, when a rebel militia killed him.

Individuals and International Law. How did customary international law come to apply in the case? The short answer, explored in the excerpt below, is that the parties were allowed to specify the governing law—a typical arrangement in international business contracts—and they in part chose international law to displace Libyan law. But could international law even apply to individuals? Was the arbitrator limited by the state-centric conception of international law set out in the *Lotus Case*? Here is Arbitrator Dupuy's conclusion:

The Texaco/Libya Arbitration

Award of 19 January 1977, 17 *International Legal Materials* 1 (1978)

Individuals and International Law

> B.   *How did the parties to these Deeds of Concession deal with the question of the applicable law? . . .*

What was the law applicable to these contracts? It is this particular question that the parties intended to resolve in adopting Clause 28 of the Deeds of Concession in a form which must be recalled here:

> This concession shall be governed by and interpreted in accordance with the principles of the law of Libya common to the principles of international law and in the absence of such common principles then by and in accordance with the general principles of law, including such of those principles as may have been applied by international tribunals.

Thus, a complex system to determine the law applicable or the "choice of law" has been provided by the contracting parties involving a two-tier system:

—the principles of Libyan law were applicable to the extent that such principles were common to principles of international law;

—alternatively, in the absence of such conformity, reference was made to general principles of law. . . .

1.   First question: Did the parties have the right to choose the law or the system of law which was to govern their contract?

[W]hile the old case law [of the Permanent Court of International Justice] viewed the contract as something which could not come under international law because it could not be regarded as a treaty between States, under the new concept treaties are not the only type of agreements governed by such law. [A]lthough they are not to be confused with treaties, contracts between States and private persons can, under certain conditions, come within the ambit of a particular and new branch of international law: the international law of contracts.

A Rejection of State-Centric Positivism. In his decision, the Arbitrator, Professor Dupuy, reviewed and rejected the positivist doctrine of the 19th and early 20th centuries that held that international law could only bind states. Neither the classical law of nations of the 17th and 18th centuries nor the modern international law of the later 20th and early 21st centuries holds such a restrictive view. Both permit individuals, including private corporations, as well as states to be subjects of international law. The Arbitrator found that under modern international law, contracts may be "delocalized" from municipal law and "internationalized." More on individuals as subjects of international law is to be found in Chapter 7.

United Nations General Assembly Resolutions and the New International Economic Order. Our primary concern is with what the *Texaco/Libya* opinion has to teach about the legal effect of United Nations General Assembly resolutions. In considering whether Libya had breached the deeds of concession, Arbitrator Dupuy considered, *inter alia*, whether Libya's nationalization could be justified on the basis of "the present status of international law, and in particular from certain resolutions concerning natural resources and wealth as adopted, in the last few years, by the United Nations." He surveyed several potentially relevant General Assembly resolutions, the most recent of which from 1973 and 1974 proclaimed the "New International Economic Order" (NIEO). In the following excerpt from Dupuy's opinion, see if you can identify NIEO features.

The Texaco/Libya Arbitration
U.N. General Assembly Resolutions

This Tribunal has stated that it intends to rule on the basis of positive law, but now it is necessary to determine precisely the content of positive law and to ascertain the place which resolutions by the General Assembly of the United Nations could occupy therein.

[According to a 1974 Libyan Government Memorandum:]

Nationalization is an act related to the sovereignty of the State. This fact has been recognized by the consecutive Resolutions of the United Nations on the sovereignty of States over their natural resources, the last being Resolution No. 3171 of the United Nations General Assembly adopted on December 13, 1973, as well as paragraph (4/E) of Resolution No. 3201 (S–VI) adopted on 1 May, 1974. The said Resolutions confirm that every State maintains complete right to exercise full sovereignty over its natural resources and recognize Nationalization as being a legitimate and internationally recognized method to ensure the sovereignty of the State upon such resources. Nationalization, being related to the sovereignty of the State, is not subject to foreign jurisdiction. Provisions of the International Law do not permit a dispute with a State to be referred to any Jurisdiction other than its national Jurisdiction. In affirmance of this principle, Resolutions of the General Assembly provide that any dispute related to

Nationalization or its consequences should be settled in accordance with provisions of domestic law of the State.

. . . This Tribunal wishes first to recall the relevant passages for this case of Resolution 1803 (XVII) entitled "Permanent Sovereignty over Natural Resources," as adopted by the General Assembly on 14 December 1962:

> In cases where authorization is granted, the capital imported and the earnings on that capital shall be governed by the terms thereof, by the national legislation in force, and by international law. . . .

> Nationalization, expropriation or requisitioning shall be based on grounds or reasons of public utility, security or the national interest which are recognized as overriding purely individual or private interests, both domestic and foreign. In such cases the owner <u>shall</u> be paid appropriate compensation, in accordance with the rules in force in the State taking such measures in the exercise of its sovereignty and in accordance with international law. . . .

The Memorandum of the Libyan Government which has just been quoted relies, however, on more recent Resolutions of the General Assembly (3171 and 3201 (S–VI), in particular) which, according to this Government would as a practical matter rule out any recourse to international law and would confer an exclusive and unlimited competence upon the legislation and courts of the host country.

Although not quoted in the Libyan Memorandum, since subsequent to the date of 26 July 1974, Resolution 3281 (XXIX), proclaimed under the title "Charter of Economic Rights and Duties of the States" and adopted by the General Assembly on 12 December 1974, should also be mentioned with the two Resolutions in support of the contention made by the Libyan Government. Two portions of such Resolutions are of particular interest in the present case:

—Resolution 3201 (S–VI) adopted by the General Assembly on 1 May 1974 under the title "Declaration on the Establishment of a New International Economic Order," Article 4, paragraph (e):

> Full permanent sovereignty of every State over its natural resources and all economic activities. In order to safeguard these resources, each State is entitled to exercise effective control over them and their exploitation with means suitable to its own situation, including the right to nationalization or transfer of ownership to its nationals, this right being an expression of the full permanent sovereignty of the State. No State

may be subjected to economic, political or any other type of coercion to prevent the free and full exercise of this inalienable right.

—Article 2 of Resolution 3281 (XXIX):

    1.   Every State has and shall freely exercise full permanent sovereignty, including possession, use and disposal, over all its wealth, natural resources and economic activities.

    2.   Each State has the right . . .

    c)   To nationalize, expropriate or transfer ownership of foreign property, in which case appropriate compensation should be paid by the State adopting such measures, taking into account its relevant laws and regulations and all circumstances that the State considers pertinent. In any case where the question of compensation gives rise to a controversy, it shall be settled under the domestic law of the nationalizing State and by its tribunals, unless it is freely and mutually agreed by all States concerned that other peaceful means be sought on the basis of the sovereign equality of States and in accordance with the principal [sic] of free choice of means.

[handwritten margin note: should instead of shall]

Substantial differences thus exist between Resolution 1803 (XVII) and the subsequent Resolutions as regards the role of international law in the exercise of permanent sovereignty over natural resources.

Conflicting General Assembly Resolutions. The excerpt above concerns Libya's contention that international law permitted the Libyan Government to nationalize foreign investments without reference to any substantive standards of foreign or international law. The 1973 and 1974 NIEO resolutions conflicted with U.N. General Assembly Resolution 1803 (XVII) of 1962, which recited that in the case of nationalization "the owner shall be paid appropriate compensation, in accordance with the rules in force in the State taking such measures in the exercise of its sovereignty, and in accordance with international law." The NIEO resolutions seemed to leave such compensation questions simply to the law of the nationalizing state. As the Arbitrator wrote, there were "substantial differences" between the rules in the 1962 and NIEO resolutions.

[handwritten margin note: later resolutions remove all international law connection, is all in national hand ↳ their votes not as wide spread a spread of states that are uncomfortable with vote]

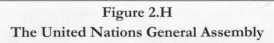

Figure 2.H
The United Nations General Assembly

U.N. General Assembly Resolutions and Customary International Law. Which, if any, of the General Assembly resolutions discussed above reflected international law? Why should any such resolutions have any legal value? Here is Arbitrator Dupuy's analysis:

The Texaco/Libya Arbitration
Determining the Legal Relevance of General Assembly Resolutions

[T]his Tribunal is obligated to consider the legal validity of the above-mentioned Resolutions and the possible existence of a custom resulting therefrom.

The general question of the legal validity of the Resolutions of the United Nations has been widely discussed by the writers. This Tribunal will recall first that, under Article 10 of the U.N. Charter, the General Assembly only issues "recommendations," which have long appeared to be texts having no binding force and carrying no obligations for the Member States.

[I]t is impossible to deny that the United Nations' activities have had a significant influence on the content of contemporary international law. In appraising the legal validity of the above-mentioned Resolutions, this Tribunal will take account of the criteria usually taken into consideration, *i.e.*, the examination of voting conditions and the analysis of the provisions concerned.

Vorschriften

With respect to the first point, Resolution 1803 (XVII) of 14 December 1962 was passed by the General Assembly by 87 votes to 2, with 12 abstentions. It is particularly important to note that the majority voted for this text, including many States of the Third World, but also several Western developed countries with market economies, including the most important one, the United States. The principles stated in this Resolution were therefore assented to by a great many States representing not only all geographical areas but also all economic systems.

[T]he affirmative vote of several developed countries with a market economy was made possible in particular by the inclusion in the Resolution of two references to international law, and one passage relating to the importance of international cooperation for economic development. According to the representative of Tunisia:

> the result of the debate on this question was that the balance of the original draft resolution was improved—a balance between, on the one hand, the unequivocal affirmation of the inalienable right of States to exercise sovereignty over their natural resources and, on the other hand, the reconciliation or adaptation of this sovereignty to international law, equity and the principles of international cooperation.

The reference to international law, in particular in the field of nationalization, was therefore an essential factor in the support given by several Western countries to Resolution 1803 (XVII).

On the contrary, it appears to this Tribunal that the conditions under which Resolutions 3171 (XVIII), 3201 (S–VI) and 3281 (XXIX) (Charter of the Economic Rights and Duties of States) were notably different:

—Resolution 3171 (XVIII) was adopted by a recorded vote of 108 votes to 1, with 16 abstentions, but this Tribunal notes that a separate vote was requested with respect to the paragraph in the operative part mentioned in the Libyan Government's Memorandum whereby the General Assembly stated that the application of the principle according to which nationalizations effected by States as the expression of their sovereignty implied that it is within the right of each State to determine the amount of possible compensation and the means of their payment, and that any dispute which might arise should be settled in conformity with the national law of each State instituting measures of this kind. As a consequence of a roll-call, this paragraph was adopted by 86 votes to 11 (Federal Republic of Germany, Belgium, Spain, United States, France, Israel, Italy, Japan, The Netherlands, Portugal, United Kingdom), with 28 abstentions (South Africa, Australia, Austria, Barbados, Canada, Ivory Coast, Denmark, Finland, Ghana,

Greece, Haiti, India, Indonesia, Ireland, Luxembourg, Malawi, Malaysia, Nepal, Nicaragua, Norway, New Zealand, Philippines, Rwanda, Singapore, Sri Lanka, Sweden, Thailand, Turkey).

This specific paragraph concerning nationalizations, disregarding the role of international law, not only was not consented to by the most important Western countries, but caused a number of the developing countries to abstain.

—Resolution 3201 (S–VI) was adopted without a vote by the General Assembly, but the statements made by 38 delegates showed clearly and explicitly what was the position of each main group of countries. [T]he most important Western countries were opposed to abandoning the compromise solution contained in Resolution 1803 (XVII).

—The conditions under which Resolution 3281 (XXIX), proclaiming the Charter of Economic Rights and Duties of States, was adopted also show unambiguously that there was no general consensus of the States with respect to the most important provisions and in particular those concerning nationalization. Having been the subject matter of a roll-call vote, the Charter was adopted by 118 votes to 6, with 10 abstentions. The analysis of votes on specific sections of the Charter is most significant insofar as the present case is concerned. From this point of view, paragraph 2(c) of Article 2 of the Charter, which limits consideration of the characteristics of compensation to the State and does not refer to international law, was voted by 104 to 16, with 6 abstentions, all of the industrialized countries with market economies having abstained or having voted against it.

[T]he legal value of the resolutions which are relevant to the present case can be determined on the basis of circumstances under which they were adopted and by analysis of the principles which they state:

—With respect to the first point, the absence of any binding force of the resolutions of the General Assembly of the United Nations implies that such resolutions must be accepted by the members of the United Nations in order to be legally binding. In this respect, the Tribunal notes that only Resolution 1803 (XVII) of 14 December 1962 was supported by a majority of Member States representing all of the various groups. By contrast, the other Resolutions mentioned above, and in particular those referred to in the Libyan Memorandum, were supported by a majority of States but not by any of the developed countries with market economies which carry on the largest part of international trade.

With respect to the second point, to wit the appraisal of the legal value on the basis of the principles stated, it appears essential to this Tribunal to distinguish

[margin note:] "red flag" → is can't rely on fact that old (widely accepted) rule was replaced as not consistent uniformed practice

between those provisions stating the existence of a right on which the generality of the States has expressed agreement and those provisions introducing new principles which were rejected by certain representative groups of States and having nothing more than a *de lege ferenda* value only in the eyes of the States which have adopted them; as far as the others are concerned, the rejection of these same principles implies that they consider them as being *contra legem*. With respect to the former, which proclaim rules recognized by the community of nations, they do not create a custom but confirm one by formulating it and specifying its scope, thereby making it possible to determine whether or not one is confronted with a legal rule. . . .

On the basis of the circumstances of adoption mentioned above and by expressing an *opinio juris communis*, Resolution 1803 (XVII) seems to this Tribunal to reflect the state of customary law existing in this field. Indeed, on the occasion of the vote on a resolution finding the existence of a customary rule, the States concerned clearly express their views. The consensus by a majority of States belonging to the various representative groups indicates without the slightest doubt universal recognition of the rules therein incorporated, *i.e.*, with respect to nationalization and compensation of the use of the rules in force in the nationalizing State, but all this in conformity with international law. . . .

Such an attitude is further reinforced by an examination of the general practice of relations between States with respect to investments. [A] great many investment agreements entered into between industrial States or their nationals, on the one hand, and developing countries, on the other, state, in an objective way, the standards of compensation and further provide, in case of dispute regarding the level of such compensation, the possibility of resorting to an international tribunal. In this respect, it is particularly significant in the eyes of this Tribunal that no fewer than 65 States, as of 31 October 1974, had ratified the Convention on the Settlement of Investment Disputes between States and Nationals of other States, dated March 18, 1965.

The Relationship Between General Assembly Resolutions and Customary International Law. The Arbitrator in the *Texaco-Libya Case* explored whether General Assembly resolutions could pass into customary international law. What theory justifies treating some General Assembly resolutions as customary international law? As a matter of law-finding, what are their advantages and disadvantages *vis-à-vis* other possible forms of customary international law? Certainly they are easy to find, since in writing; and, if viewed as "instant custom," they could allow for quick responses to new developments. But do General Assembly resolutions reflect either state practice or *opinio juris*? Some observers conclude that "words alone," absent concrete practice, are a misleading guide to customary international law. Since Article 10 of the U.N. Charter deems General Assembly resolutions "recommendations," some also argue that it violates the spirit as well as the letter of the Charter to give resolutions, by any logic, the force of law.

Evaluating General Assembly Resolutions. In looking at General Assembly voting, was Arbitrator Dupuy right in disregarding majority voting and relying instead on consensus? Was the Arbitrator right in putting great weight on the fact that the 1962 Resolution was "assented to by a great many states representing not only all geographical areas but also all economic systems"? He concluded that "[o]n the basis of the circumstances of [its] adoption . . . and by expressing an *opinio juris communis*, Resolution 1803 (XVII) seems to this Tribunal to reflect the state of customary law existing in this field." Even if only such a consensus could elevate a resolution from a recommendation to a custom, did not the voting for the NIEO resolutions at least demonstrate that most states no longer supported the 1962 rule? Was it possible that the General Assembly actions in 1973–1974 destroyed the old customary rule but failed to establish a new rule? Arbitrator Dupuy's analysis, and his ultimate conclusion that Libya had breached the deeds of concession and violated international law, avoided leaving a *Lotus*-like gap in international law. Dupuy denied that Libya had the sovereign discretion to use only its own 1970s law, which allowed nationalization of foreign oil company assets without compensation. Was the Arbitrator simply giving effect to the expectations of the parties, interpreting the original deeds of concession between them, rather than applying a strictly positivist, consensual international law?

The General Assembly as a Legislature? As a formal matter, as noted above, the U.N. Charter provides that General Assembly resolutions are merely recommendations. What, if anything, would be wrong with amending the Charter to grant the U.N. General Assembly the authority to enact binding international legislation, dispensing with the need to debate whether General Assembly resolutions may have legal authority as a matter of customary international law? At present, each member state of the United Nations has one vote in the General Assembly. If Assembly resolutions were to be treated as legislation, should the votes of some states be given proportionately greater weight? This could be based on population, economic or political power, or contributions to the U.N. budget.

General Assembly Resolutions vs. Security Council Decisions. Contrast the legal status of General Assembly resolutions and Security Council decisions. The

U.N. Security Council is composed of 15 states, five of which (China, France, Russia, the United Kingdom, and the United States) are permanent members. U.N. Security Council decisions, adopted by nine members of the Council without the opposition of any of the permanent members, do have formal legal effect. The U.N. Charter, a treaty accepted by 193 countries, provides in Article 25 that "[t]he Members of the United Nations agree to accept and carry out the decisions of the Security Council in accordance with the present Charter." Article 103 further provides that "[i]n the event of a conflict between the obligations of the Members of the United Nations under the present Charter and their obligations under any other international agreement, their obligations under the present Charter shall prevail." We study the United Nations and the legal and political roles of the Security Council in Chapters 3 and 6.

The Efficacy of the Texaco-Libya Arbitral Award. On September 25, 1977, Libya agreed to pay Texaco and Standard Oil of California $76 million in crude oil to compensate them for the nationalization of their subsidiaries. The agreement effectively terminated the international arbitral proceedings. "Libya to Compensate Two U.S. Companies," *New York Times*, Sept. 26, 1977, at 55. What induced Libya finally to compensate the American oil companies? What difference might the arbitral award have made? There are several possible explanations for Libya's compliance with the arbitral award. Perhaps Libya was looking to reassure potential new foreign investors, or perhaps Libya feared diplomatic pressure after the arbitral award.

Libya might also have been afraid of recognition and enforcement actions brought on the basis of the arbitral judgment in third countries and seeking to attach Libyan accounts or assets in those countries. The 1958 New York Convention on the Recognition and Enforcement of Foreign Arbitral Awards (in force for 157 parties as of May 2017) in fact does provide for the recognition and enforcement of many foreign arbitral awards by national courts, and is widely used in commercial cases. Why has it been difficult for countries to negotiate and accept a treaty providing for the recognition and enforcement of foreign judicial judgments? The 2005 Hague Choice of Court Convention, which entered into force only in 2015, provides for the recognition and enforcement of certain foreign judicial decisions, but as of May 2017 the only parties are the European Union, Mexico, and Singapore.

Treaties and Foreign Investment Disputes. Today treaties play a significant role in investment disputes. Over 2,500 bilateral investment treaties (BITs) set standards of nondiscrimination, non-arbitrary treatment, and fair and equitable treatment to protect foreign companies investing in host countries. Many BITs authorize mixed arbitrations under the auspices of the International Centre for Investment Disputes (ICSID), connected with the World Bank headquartered in Washington, DC. As of May 2017, over 400 ICSID arbitrations brought by investors against host countries have been concluded. According to Article 54 of the 1965 ICSID Convention—a treaty Arbitrator Dupuy noted in his opinion, and to which 153 states were parties as of May 2017—"[e]ach Contracting State shall recognize an award rendered pursuant to this Convention as binding and enforce the pecuniary obligations imposed by that award within its territories as if it were a final judgment of a court in that State."

Claims, Counterclaims, and Customary International Law. Countries sometimes disagree about what rules of customary international law govern a dispute. Even when a rule of customary international law is clear—few if any international lawyers will contest, for example, that a country's territorial sea may extend no farther than 12 nautical miles from its coastal baselines—there may be debate about how the law applies in particular circumstances. Countries do not usually litigate their differences over customary international law. No third-party decision maker may have jurisdiction to rule on competing contentions. How are competing claims about the content or application of customary international law asserted when there is no third-party decision maker? One traditional method is a formal diplomatic protest followed by a diplomatic response. Even though such competing claims may not be definitively resolved, countries still use legal language. This claim/counterclaim process may affect international relations by framing the legal dimension of disputes. Does the claim/counterclaim process also help clarify the content of international law, even absent a third-party decision maker? How?

NOTE: SOFT LAW

International lawyers often talk about "soft law," which may be of different types. We have already seen one example of soft law in Part B: the Kellogg-Briand Pact. Its norms, though aspirational and indeterminate ("soft"), are embodied in a legal instrument, a treaty ("law"). Our concern in this Note is with various non-treaty instruments that also are termed soft law.

One example of a non-treaty soft law instrument is the 1992 Rio Declaration on Environment and Development. The Rio Declaration was one product of the U.N. Conference on Environment and Development (the Earth Summit), a major event in the history of international environmental law. The Declaration contains "principles"; Principle 2, for example, provides that countries have "the responsibility to ensure that activities within their jurisdiction or control do not cause damage to the environment of other States or of areas beyond the limits of national jurisdiction." But the makers of the Declaration did not regard it as legally binding. Non-treaty soft law may take a variety of other forms, including memoranda of understanding and codes of conduct, *e.g.*, the Food and Agriculture Organization's 1995 Code of Conduct for Responsible Fisheries.

Why might international actors prefer soft law to a treaty? Sometimes soft law such as the Rio Declaration may usefully conclude a diplomatic conference, facilitating agreement on a non-binding instrument when conclusion of a treaty text would be impossible. From a municipal law perspective, a government's executive branch may prefer soft law instruments because they do not require legislative approval, as treaties often do.

Soft law may help pave the way for later treaties. Soft law instruments such as the Rio Declaration set aspirational goals that are later developed in more concrete treaty form. A soft law instrument may serve as the starting point— an agreed-upon mindset—for the negotiation of treaties. Some Rio principles have found their way into subsequent treaties, sometimes in clauses that exactly track the Rio Declaration language and sometimes in clauses that include more determinate or contextual obligations. Furthermore, soft law also may usefully supplement existing treaties, providing glosses or understandings concerning treaty provisions.

However, treaties serve some functions that soft law usually cannot. Conclusion of a treaty gives rise to a formally binding obligation, and the legally binding effect of treaties may signal particularly significant political as well as legal commitment. When a country wants to help ensure that municipal or international legal dispute settlement mechanisms take account of an international instrument, the country will prefer a treaty over soft law. And treaties carry with them a well-developed "law of treaties," introduced in Part B above, which does not apply to non-treaty soft law.

Some treaties explicitly authorize states or a treaty-compliance body to make non-binding recommendations. General Assembly resolutions, considered in the *Texaco-Libya Case*, are one example, for the U.N. Charter authorizes the Assembly to issue recommendations in the form of resolutions. Article IX of the 1959 Antarctic Treaty, considered in Chapter 3, provides a mechanism for recommendations regarding a range of issues, including facilitation of scientific research, rights of inspection, preservation of living resources, and the use of Antarctica for peaceful purposes. Those recommendations set out sometimes-detailed guidelines that supplement treaty law, shape behavior, and help form expectations.

May norms contained in non-binding resolutions (such as General Assembly resolutions) or non-treaty declarations (such as the Rio Declaration) ever count as binding international law? For many international lawyers, such as the Arbitrator in the *Texaco-Libya Case*, they count as law only if they rise to the level of customary international law. What is the relationship between soft law and customary international law? Soft law instruments such as General Assembly resolutions or the Rio Declaration may spur action—by civil society as well as governments—that can help develop customary international law. Whether a soft law instrument itself constitutes state practice or *opinio juris* is, however, a contentious point, as we saw in our discussion of the *Texaco-Libya Case*.

If the Rio Declaration or General Assembly resolutions do not articulate rules of customary international law, should their norms nonetheless be regarded as "law"? May a court charged with applying international law rely on soft law when it does not constitute a traditional source of international law? Many judges and other decision makers take the traditional position that they may determine which international norms are legally binding only by referring to accepted categories such as treaties and customary international law. Such judges agree that in any society, non-legal norms may affect behavior, sometimes giving rise to strong community expectations, but those judges would limit the materials on which they could draw in making their legal determinations. However, as in the *Texaco-Libya Case*, international courts and tribunals occasionally invoke soft law instruments in their decisions, and states sometimes refer to such instruments in their legal arguments—reasons why international lawyers should be aware of soft law, even in formal legal settings.

D. GENERAL PRINCIPLES OF LAW

Sometimes neither treaties nor custom provides a rule to decide a case involving international law. Then the judge or other seeker may look outside the theoretically consensual sources to non-consensual sources. The first such source we examine is general principles of law, listed in Article 38(1)(c) of the Statute of the International Court of Justice (see Part A). We illustrate what general principles are and how they work by looking at a case from the European Court of Justice (ECJ), *AM & S Europe Limited v. Commission of the European Communities*.

The AM & S Case *and EC Competition Law.* The European Community (now the European Union) has a comprehensive system of competition (antitrust) law and procedure. The EC Commission, a body created by a treaty designed to promote economic integration among European countries, has the power to investigate and to prosecute possible monopolistic and anti-competitive economic activities. In *AM & S*, the Commission was investigating a British company for violating EC competition law. The company, AM & S, became subject to EC law when the United Kingdom joined the European Common Market a few years prior to the investigation. In the case, AM & S was urging the ECJ to find an international legal rule protecting lawyer-client confidentiality. The company wanted to shield from the EC Commission sensitive correspondence with the company's lawyers that might help show AM & S's non-compliance with EC competition law.

The case excerpt below begins with the opinion of Sir Gordon Slynn, one of the EC's Advocates General, who provided background analysis of the issue being litigated. In ECJ cases the opinions of the Advocates General—a position unknown in the U.S. legal system—ordinarily are published both because they amplify ECJ opinions and because they have some persuasive value of their own. Note that the Advocate General first looked to see whether a rule protecting lawyer-client confidentiality could be found in the European Community's governing treaty or in regulations adopted pursuant to that treaty.

THE AM & S CASE

AM & S Europe Limited v. Commission of the European Communities,
European Court of Justice, [1982] E.C.R. 1575

The Search for a Rule of Law

Opinion of Advocate General Sir Gordon Slynn
Delivered on 26 January 1982

In February 1979, officials of the [European Community's] Commission required the applicants to make available documents which they wished to see in connection with an investigation being conducted pursuant to Article 14(1) of Council Regulation 17 of 6 February 1962. This was said to be an investigation of competitive conditions concerning the production and distribution of zinc metal and its alloys and zinc concentrates in order to verify that there is no infringement of Articles 85 and 86 of the EEC Treaty [relating to the EC competition law]. The applicants produced copies of most of the documents. Some, however, were not produced; so far as relevant, on the basis that they were covered by legal confidentiality, which entitled the applicants to withhold them. . . .

The parties were invited to state . . . their views on the law as to, and legal opinions relating to, the existence and extent of the protection granted in investigative proceedings instituted by public authorities for the purpose of detecting offenses of an economic nature, especially in the field of competition, to correspondence passing between

(a)   two lawyers,

(b)   an independent lawyer and his client,

(c)   an undertaking and a lawyer in a permanent contractual relationship, or who is an employee of the undertaking,

(d)   a legal adviser to, and an employee of, an undertaking or an employee of an associated undertaking,

(e)   employees of an undertaking, or different but associated undertakings, where the correspondence mentions legal advice given by an independent lawyer or legal adviser serving one of the undertakings or other undertakings in the same group. . . .

The Commission's investigative powers for the purpose of carrying out the duties assigned to it by Article 89 of the EEC Treaty, and provisions adopted under Article 87 of the Treaty, are so far as relevant conferred by Article 14 of Regulation 17. It may "undertake all necessary investigations into undertakings and associations of undertakings" and, to that end, its authorised officials are empowered to examine books and business records, to take copies of them, and to ask for oral explanations. There is no reference to any exemption or protection which may be claimed on the basis of legal confidence. Is that silence conclusive that no such protection is capable of applying in any form and in any situation? In my view it is not. The essential enquiry is, first, whether there is a principle of Community law existing independently of the regulation, and, secondly, whether the regulation does on a proper construction restrict the application of that principle. The question is not whether a principle of Community law derogates from Article 14, but whether Article 14 excludes the application of a principle of Community law.

Gaps in the Law. EC competition law is, of course, a form of international law. It is constituted fundamentally by treaty rules like Articles 85–89 of the Treaty of Rome and partly by rules like Council Regulation 17 generated by delegated powers given to the institutions making up the EC, a regional international organization. The legal question in this case was what to do when there was a gap (a *lacuna*) in international law. Here neither the Rome Treaty nor the rules made by the EC institutions determined whether there was a right to lawyer-client confidentiality in EC law, and if there was such a right how it was defined. If there had been a customary European international practice establishing lawyer-client privilege as a rule, that could have been used, but apparently no such custom existed at the time of the case. Should international courts like the ECJ be more or less reluctant than municipal courts to fill gaps when formal sources are silent? Some municipal legal systems (often in the common law tradition) profess to be more willing than others (often in the civil law tradition) to let courts fill gaps in law.

To fill the gap in EC law, Advocate General Slynn and then the European Court turned to "general principles of law." Where did they find such principles? Consider the following excerpt.

Figure 2.1
Court of Justice of the European Union, Luxembourg

The AM & S Case
The Search for a General Principle of Law

[The Advocate General's opinion continues:] That general principles which have not been expressly stated in the Treaty or in subordinate legislation may exist as part of Community law, the observance of which the Court is required to ensure, needs no emphasis. . . . It does not seem to me that the principle is limited to "fundamental rights[.]" It has a broader base. Such indeed appears to be accepted by both parties to this application. The Commission argue that there has to be a consensus among the laws of all the Member States, and that the Court cannot establish a principle which goes beyond that accepted by any one of the Member States. It cited no specific authority for that proposition, nor indicated what is the necessary level or degree of consensus required to establish the existence of a general principle. The [Consultative Committee of the Bars and Law Societies of the European Community], whose views broadly on the point were adopted by the applicants, submits that the aim of Community law is to find the best solution in qualitative terms, having regard to the spirit, orientation and general tendency of the national laws. . . .

That national law may be looked at on a comparative basis as an aid to consideration of what is Community law is shown in many cases[.] Such a course is followed not to import national laws as such into Community law, but to use it as a means of discovering an *unwritten* principle of Community law. . . .

In looking at national laws it does not seem to me that it can be a pre-condition of the existence of a rule of Community law that the principle should be expressed identically, or should be applied in identical form, in all of the Member States. Unanimity, as to a subject which is relevant to a Community law problem, may well be a strong indication of the existence of a rule of Community law. Total unanimity of expression and application is not, however, necessary. It is at best unlikely, not least as the Community grows in size. . . .

The Court has been provided with extracts from legislation, case decisions and the opinions of academic authors and a welter of case references. [The Advocate General summarizes the law respecting confidential communications between lawyers and their clients in Belgium, and then in turn the law in Denmark, France, Germany, Greece, Ireland, Italy, Luxembourg, and the Netherlands.]

[I]t is plain, as indeed seems inevitable, that the position in all the Member States is not identical. It is to my mind equally plain that there exists in all the Member States a recognition that the public interest and the proper administration of justice demand as a general rule that a client should be able to speak freely, frankly and fully to his lawyer. . . . Whether it is described as the right of the client or the duty of the lawyer, this principle has nothing to do with the protection or privilege of the lawyer. It springs essentially from the basic need of a man in a civilized society to be able to turn to his lawyer for advice and help, and if proceedings begin, for representation; it springs no less from the advantages to a society which evolves complex law reaching into all the business affairs of persons, real and legal, that they should be able to know what they can do under the law, what is forbidden, where they must tread circumspectly, where they run risks.

Decision [by the European Court of Justice]

The application is based on the submission that in all the Member States written communications between lawyer and client are protected by virtue of a principle common to all those States, although the scope of that protection and the means of securing it vary from one country to another.

. . . Community law . . . must take into account the principles and concepts common to the laws of those States concerning the observance of confidentiality, in particular, as regards certain communications between lawyer and client. That confidentiality serves the requirement, the importance of which is recognized in all of the Member States, that any person must be able, without constraint, to consult a lawyer whose profession entails the giving of independent legal advice to all those in need of it. . . .

Whilst in some of the Member States the protection against disclosure afforded to written communications between lawyer and client is based principally on a recognition of the very nature of the legal profession, inasmuch as it contributes towards the maintenance of the rule of law, in other Member States the same protection is justified by the more specific requirement (which, moreover, is also recognized in the first-mentioned States) that the rights of the defence must be respected.

Apart from these differences, however, there are to be found in the national laws of the Member States common criteria inasmuch as those laws protect, in similar circumstances, the confidentiality of written communications between lawyer and client provided that, on the one hand, such communications are made for the purposes and in the interests of the client's rights of defence and, on the other hand, they emanate from independent lawyers, that is to say, lawyers who are not bound to the client by relationship of employment.

[A]lthough . . . the Commission [has the power under written EC law] to require . . . production of the business documents the disclosure of which it considers necessary, including written communications between lawyer and client, for proceedings in respect of any infringements of Articles 85 and 86 of the Treaty, that power is, however, subject to a restriction imposed by the need to protect confidentiality, on the conditions defined above, and provided that the communications in question are exchanged between an independent lawyer, that is to say one who is not bound to his client by a relationship of employment, and his client.

The EC and General Principles of Law. In *AM & S,* the European Court of Justice (today officially known as the Court of Justice of the European Union) turned to general principles of law to fill a gap. Are general principles of law a type of positive international law, made or consented to by states? Certainly, the various countries comprising the European Community had individually enacted or otherwise made laws concerning lawyer confidentiality. But did the fact that municipal legal systems used certain similar rules make it plain that states had consented to establishing a rule in international law? What are other consensual arguments justifying the use of general principles to find or develop rules of international law? Does the fact that the United Kingdom and other members of the European Community joined the treaty establishing the Community and the ECJ establish their consent to this and other general principles?

Alternatively, it may be more accurate to describe general principles of law as a non-consensual source of international law. The Advocate General sought to avoid a gap in consensual international (EC) law when he looked at national laws "not to import national laws as such into Community law," but to "discover[ ] an *unwritten* principle of Community law." Was this "discovery" really just a justification for a form of judicial discretion and law-making? What values did the Advocate General see as underpinning the general principle articulated in *AM & S*? Note his reference to the "basic need of a man in a civilized society to be able to turn to his lawyer for advice and help." The theory underlying general principles of law is that some legal principles are so general or fundamental that they are to be found in all or nearly all legal systems. In *AM & S* the presumption was that if rules protecting lawyer-client communication could be found in every municipal legal system within the European Community, then such rules were to be presumed to be included within the body of EC law.

The ECJ has found quite a number of other general principles of law to close gaps and create a new and coherent legal order for Europe. Other ECJ-recognized general principles include the principle of equal treatment, the principle of proportionality, the principle of legal certainty, and the principle of the protection of fundamental rights. Takis Tridimas, *The General Principles of EC Law* 4 (2007).

The Comparative Law Search and the Problem of In-house and Foreign Lawyers. The search for common legal rules in *AM & S* was conducted on the assumption that only the minimum content of rules found in all relevant European municipal legal systems would be presumed to exist in EC law. This "lowest common denominator" approach excluded lawyer-client communications not related to "rights of defence."

The lowest common denominator approach also excluded communications with certain kinds of lawyers. Some European countries do not allow in-house counsel employed by a business (as opposed to "independent" lawyers who work at law firms) to be members of the bar, fully subject to rules of legal professional ethics. The Advocate General, in a portion of his opinion not excerpted above, analyzed the position of in-house counsel in various countries and concluded that "in some Member States full-time employment is incompatible with the full professional status of a lawyer (apparently in Belgium, France, Italy, and Luxembourg)," whereas "in others the employed lawyer remains subject to professional discipline and ethics." In addition, some European countries also do not allow foreign lawyers to be members of the bar. These distinctions among independent, in-house, and foreign lawyers point to one of the challenges in the practice of international law: conceptions of who may be a lawyer may differ from country to country! The principles declared in *AM & S* may well affect to whom companies turn for legal advice; outside counsel working at law firms may see their business increase as a result of the ECJ's decision.

After accepting the concept of general principles of law, conducting a comparative law search, and identifying the general principle at issue, it remained only for the ECJ to apply that general principle to the particular AM & S communications. Here is the Court's conclusion concerning the confidentiality of the documents at issue:

The AM & S Case
Applying the General Principle Governing Lawyer Confidentiality

It appears that the communications in question were drawn up during the period preceding, and immediately following, the accession of the United Kingdom to the Community, and that they are principally concerned with how far it might be possible to avoid conflict between the applicant and the Community authorities on the applicant's position, in particular with regard to the Community provisions on competition. [T]he communications [fall] within the context of the rights of the defence and the lawyer's specific duties in that connection. They must therefore be protected from disclosure.

In view of that relationship and in the light of the foregoing considerations the written communications at issue must accordingly be considered, in so far as they emanate from an independent lawyer entitled to practise his profession in a Member State, as confidential and on that ground beyond the Commission's power of investigation under Article 14 of Regulation No. 17.

Judicial Discretion and International Law. Is the formulation of a general principle really a result of employing a scientific comparative method? Is an element of judicial rule-making involved? A court must determine whether it is appropriate to translate a common municipal practice into an international norm. Why was it appropriate to do so in *AM & S*? In part this was so because the European system deals with the same types of problems, involving consultations between attorneys and individuals or corporations, as do municipal legal systems. But the Advocate General and the ECJ may also have been motivated by the belief that the attorney-client privilege is just or sensible. The Advocate General invoked "the public interest," "the proper administration of justice," and "the basic need of a man in a civilized society" to support his argument for an attorney-client privilege. If there is a measure of judicial rule-making here, perhaps the comparative method suggests at least some constraint on the range of rules that judges may make; after all, the method requires identifying common rules in municipal legal systems.

Is there more judicial discretion employed in a general principles case like *AM&S* than in a customary international case like *Paquete Habana*? Can you identify some exercise of judicial discretion even in the allegedly strictly positivist judgment in *Lotus*? Do even cases involving treaties involve the exercise of judicial discretion? Recall the discussion of treaty interpretation in the *Eastern Airlines Case* in Part B.

Universal General Principles and the Comparative Law Search. AM & S was a case before the European Court of Justice, a regional international court, and accordingly the ECJ needed only compare the domestic practices of the nine states then members of the European Community. To how many municipal legal systems should the International Court of Justice, or another international tribunal not applying regional law, be obliged to turn in order to discern a general principle? The Appeals Chamber of the International Criminal Tribunal for the former Yugoslavia (ICTY) faced this question in a 1997 case, *Prosecutor v. Erdemović*, asking whether duress was a complete defense for a soldier charged with a war crime or a crime against humanity involving the killing of innocent individuals. The Tribunal's Statute is silent on the issue. In their Joint Separate Opinion, Judges McDonald and Vohrah also found no customary international law rule on point. They then turned to a general principles search. Noting the "practical impossibility" of conducting a "comprehensive survey of all legal systems of the world," they surveyed only "those jurisdictions whose jurisprudence is, as a practical matter, accessible to us in an effort to discern a general trend, policy or principle underlying the concrete rules of that jurisdiction which comports with the object and purpose of the establishment of the International Tribunal." They grouped countries by type of legal system and asked whether duress was a complete defense in civil law systems (Belgium, Chile, Finland, France, Germany, Italy, Mexico, the Netherlands, Nicaragua, Norway, Panama, Poland, Spain, Sweden, Venezuela, and the former Yugoslavia); in common law systems (Australia, Canada, England, India, Malaysia, Nigeria, South Africa, the United Kingdom, and the United States); and in the law of "other states" (China, Ethiopia, Japan, Morocco, and Somalia). Judges McDonald and Vohrah concluded that the "positions of the principal legal systems of the world" differ, and that "no consistent rule" applies. Did this mean there was a gap in international law? Prompted by their view that "the law . . . must serve broader normative purposes in light of its social, political and economic role," and that the issue before the Tribunal concerned "the most heinous crimes known to humankind," they joined a 3–2 majority, holding that "duress cannot afford a complete defence to a soldier charged with crimes against humanity or war crimes in international law involving the taking of innocent lives." Case No. IT–96–22–A (1997), ¶¶ 57, 72, 75, 88.

When the judges found "no consistent rule" governing the defense of duress, should they then have left a gap in the law? When they instead drew on "broader normative purposes" and pointed to the heinousness of crimes against humanity and war crimes, were they really turning to natural law to support the rule that duress is not a complete defense to such crimes? We consider natural law and the related concept of *jus cogens* in Part E.

"*Civilized Nations.*" General principles of law are included among the sources of international law that the International Court of Justice is permitted to apply. Article 38(1)(c) of the ICJ Statute authorizes the Court to use "the general principles of law recognized by civilized nations." When the clause was originally drafted for the Permanent Court of International Justice in 1920, the term "civilized nations" was meant to exclude some non-European nations; nowadays that limitation has been rejected by commentators and judges alike.

Domestic Courts and International Law. Note that decisions of municipal courts play two distinct roles as sources of international law. First, as we saw in Part C, domestic judgments are sometimes employed to demonstrate state practice; they are evidences to be weighed in determining customary international law. Second, as we see in this part, the holdings of municipal judges may be crucial to the comparative law search to fill gaps using general principles of law. Moreover, as we explore in Chapter 5, municipal judgments play an important third role in international law: enforcing international legal norms of any sort at the domestic level. Domestic judges, when they determine and apply international law, may play significant and sensitive roles in international relations.

E. NATURAL LAW AND *JUS COGENS*

We have now explored the three principal formal sources of international law set forth in Article 38(1) of the Statute of the International Court of Justice; these are the rules that the Court "shall apply" as it decides "in accordance with international law such disputes as submitted to it": "(a) international conventions, whether general or particular, establishing rules expressly recognized by the contesting states" (Treaties, Part B); "(b) international custom, as evidence of a general practice accepted as law" (Customary International Law, Part C); and "(c) the general principles of law recognized by civilized nations" (General Principles of Law, Part D). Although the first two sources—treaty and custom—may be said by positivists to be more or less consensual among states, the third source— general principles of law—involves, as we have seen, some judicial or doctrinal initiative beyond a search for inter-state agreement on rules. Indeed, the same may well be true even for most rules of customary international law.

Historically, the oldest and one of the most important sources of the law of nations was natural law, but nowadays the function of this avowedly non-consensual source has been largely replaced by the notion of *jus cogens* or compelling norm. Are these sources suspect because neither is mentioned in Article 38 of the ICJ Statute? Strictly speaking, Article 38 only binds the fifteen judges on the ICJ. For all the rest of us, it is not formally a restriction on where we may look to find international legal rules, although it is often consulted because few alternative authoritative listings are so generally shared among so many countries. The fact that many 19th- and early 20th-century international lawyers rejected natural law explains why it was not listed in Article 38, formulated in

1919–1920. However, we think natural law remains important, not simply historically but in understanding modern international law.

An 1820 U.S. Supreme Court piracy judgment, *United States v. Smith*, illustrates a classic use of natural law. We then turn to a 2000 decision by the International Tribunal for the former Yugoslavia and a 2002 report from the Inter-American Commission on Human Rights to explore *jus cogens* and the related concept of obligations *erga omnes*. A good question to keep in mind throughout this part is what role should non-consensual norms or natural law play in modern international law?

> United States v. Smith. In *United States v. Smith*, a criminal case prosecuting the defendant for piracy, the U.S. Supreme Court consulted "the law of nations." A U.S. statute called for application of that law in piracy trials. We start with a statement of the facts of the case.

UNITED STATES V. SMITH
18 U.S. (5 Wheat.) 153 (1820)

The Facts

This was an indictment for piracy against the prisoner Thomas Smith, before the Circuit Court of Virginia, on the act of Congress, of the 3d of March, 1819, c.76.

The jury found a special verdict as follows: "We, of the jury, find, that the prisoner, Thomas Smith, in the month of March, 1819, and others, were part of the crew of a private armed vessel, called the Creollo, (commissioned by the government of Buenos Ayres, a colony then at war with Spain,) and lying in the port of Margaritta; that in the month of March, 1819, the said prisoner and others of the crew mutinied, confined their officer, left the vessel, and in the said port of Margaritta, seized by violence a vessel called the Irresistible, a private armed vessel, lying in that port, commissioned by the government of Artigas, who was also at war with Spain; that the said prisoner and others, having so possessed themselves of the said vessel, the Irresistible, appointed their officers, proceeded to sea on a cruize, without any documents or commission whatever; and while on that cruize, in the month of April, 1819, on the high seas, committed the offence charged in the indictment, by the plunder and robbery of the Spanish vessel therein mentioned. If the plunder and robbery aforesaid be piracy under the act of the Congress of the United States, entitled, 'An act to protect the commerce of the United States, and punish the crime of piracy,' then we find the said prisoner guilty; if the plunder and robbery, above stated, be not piracy under the said act of Congress, then we find him, not guilty."

United States v. Smith *and the Law of Piracy*. The lower court divided on whether Smith's conduct amounted to "piracy as defined by the law of nations," and the Supreme Court took up the issue. As you read Justice Story's legal analysis, pay particular attention to where he turns for evidence of the international law concept of piracy.

United States v. Smith
The Law

MR. JUSTICE STORY delivered the opinion of the court. The act of Congress upon which this indictment is founded provides, "that if any person or persons whatsoever, shall, upon the high seas, commit the crime of piracy, as defined by the law of nations, and such offender or offenders shall be brought into, or found in the United States, every such offender or offenders shall, upon conviction thereof, &c. be punished with death."

. . . The constitution declares, that Congress shall have power "to define and punish piracies and felonies committed on the high seas, and offences against the law of nations."

[S]upposing Congress were bound in all the cases included in the clause under consideration to define the offence, still there is nothing which restricts it to a mere logical enumeration in detail of all the facts constituting the offence. Congress may as well define by using a term of a known and determinate meaning, as by an express enumeration of all the particulars included in that term. That is certain which is by necessary reference made certain. . . . To define piracies, in the sense of the constitution, is merely to enumerate the crimes which shall constitute piracy; and this may be done either by a reference to crimes having a technical name, and determinate extent, or by enumerating the acts in detail, upon which the punishment is inflicted.

It is next to be considered, whether the crime of piracy is defined by the law of nations with reasonable certainty. What the law of nations on this subject is, may be ascertained by consulting the works of jurists, writing professedly on public law; or by the general usage and practice of nations; or by judicial decisions recognising and enforcing that law. There is scarcely a writer on the law of nations, who does not allude to piracy as a crime of a settled and determinate nature; and whatever may be the diversity of definitions, in other respects, all writers concur, in holding, that robbery, or forcible depredations upon the sea, *animo furandi*, is piracy. The same doctrine is held by all the great writers on maritime law, in terms that admit of no reasonable doubt. The common law, too, recognises and punishes piracy as an offence, not against its own municipal code, but as an offence against the law of nations, (which is part of the common law,) as an offence against the universal law of society, a pirate being deemed an enemy of the human race. . . . Sir Charles Hedges, . . . in the [English] case of Rex v. Dawson, (5 *State Trials*,) declared in emphatic terms, that "piracy is only a sea term for robbery, piracy being a robbery committed within the jurisdiction of the admiralty." Sir Leoline Jenkins, too, on a like occasion, declared that "a robbery, when committed upon the sea, is what we call a 'piracy' "; and he cited the civil law writers, in proof. And it is manifest from the language of Sir William Blackstone,[a] in his comments on piracy, that he considered the common law definition as distinguishable in no essential respect from that of the law of nations. So that, whether we advert to writers on the common law, or the maritime law, or the law of nations, we shall find that they universally treat of piracy as an offence against the law of nations, and that its true definition by that law is robbery upon the sea. And the general practice of all nations in punishing all persons, whether natives or foreigners, who have committed this offence against any persons whatsoever, with whom they are in amity, is a conclusive proof that the offence is supposed to depend, not upon the particular provisions of any municipal code, but upon the law of nations, both for its definition and punishment. We have, therefore, no hesitation in declaring, that piracy, by the law of nations, is robbery upon the sea, and that it is sufficiently and constitutionally defined by the fifth section of the act of 1819. . . .

It is to be certified to the Circuit Court, that upon the facts stated, the case is piracy, as defined by the law of nations, so as to be punishable under the act of Congress of the 3d of March, 1819.

> *An Enemy of All Mankind.* Remember the next-to-last line of the *Filartiga* judgment in Chapter 1: "Indeed, for purposes of civil liability, the torturer has become—like the pirate and the slave trader before him—*hostis humani generis*, an enemy of all mankind." The sense that certain behavior is universally to be

---

[a]   To show that piracy is defined by the law of nations, the following citations are deemed sufficient: [Story fills almost eighteen pages with citations at length from, *inter alia*, Grotius, Bynkershoek, Azuni, Bacon, Martens, Rutherforth, Woodeson, Bulamaqui, Calvinus, Bouchard, Bonnemant, Valin, Straccha, Casaregis, Brown, Beames, Molloy, Marshall, Viner, Cowell, Comyn, Coke, Jenkins, Targa, Hawkins, Blackstone, Hedges, Holt, Ward, and Erskine. He concludes:] The foregoing collection of doctrines, extracted from writers on the civil law, the law of nations, the maritime law, and the common law, in the most ample manner confirms the opinion of the Court in the case in the text; and it is with great diffidence submitted to the learned reader to aid his future researches in a path, which, fortunately for us, it has not been hitherto necessary to explore with minute accuracy.

why it is important to find universal norms in IL rather than leaving problems

condemned is a feature of natural law reasoning. How is a judge to ascertain such law? *Smith* was one of the two principal cases relied on by the *Filartiga* court to demonstrate that rules of the law of nations "may be ascertained by consulting the works of the jurists, writing professedly on public law; or by the general usage and practice of nations; or by judicial decisions recognizing and enforcing that law." The other was *Paquete Habana*. The similarities between *Filartiga* and *Smith* are great, even greater than between *Filartiga* and *Paquete Habana*. In *Paquete Habana* the guilty party was a state. Both *Smith* and *Filartiga* held that an individual could be found guilty of violating the law of nations. Pirate, slave trader, torturer—all were viewed as acting so contrary to fundamental norms that their actions were seen to be universally proscribed and their persons subject to punishment by all courts.

*Custom? General Principle? Natural Law? Fundamental Principle (*Jus Cogens*)?* Another similarity between *Filartiga* and *Smith* is their mutual confusion about what the source of the rule is. In contrast, *Paquete Habana* and *AM & S* are clearer: *Paquete Habana* weighed evidences of state practice to find custom, and *AM & S* examined comparative municipal law rules to find a general principle. Can you spot traces of custom, general principles, and natural law or fundamental principle in *Filartiga* and *Smith*?

Smith and *Filartiga* were both cited in *Beanal v. Freeport-McMoran, Inc.*, a 1999 U.S. case in which the court rejected an Indonesian citizen's claims that environmental degradation amounted to cultural genocide because it destroyed a tribe's cultural and social framework. The legal evidence presented described only an "amorphous right . . . devoid of discernable means to define or identify conduct that constitutes a violation of international law." The *Beanal* court, like the courts in *Smith* and *Filartiga*, did not make it clear whether it was looking for a rule of customary international law, general principles of law, natural law, or *jus cogens*, but its language, like that of *Smith* and *Filartiga*, looked for some sort of universality: "it would be imprudent for a United States tribunal to declare an amorphous cause of action under international law that has failed to garner universal acceptance." 197 F.3d 161, 168 (5th Cir. 1999).

It seems that *Smith*, *Filartiga*, and *Beanal* all looked to find some non-treaty international law rule general or universal enough to bind apparently non-consenting states. How well does this kind of search fit into the positivist insistence in *Lotus* that all rules of international law must be based on state consent? Why is it important to find universal norms in international law, rather than leaving problems—even atrocities—to be resolved by recourse to national laws or to rules specified by treaty?

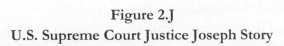

Figure 2.J
U.S. Supreme Court Justice Joseph Story

Defining International Criminal Law. Some positivists rejected the notion that international law provided a substantive definition of the crime of piracy. In 1932, a Harvard research project proposed a treaty premised on the view "that piracy is not a crime by the law of nations." Instead, piracy "is the basis of an extraordinary jurisdiction in every state to seize and to prosecute and punish persons, and to seize and dispose of property, for factual offenses which are committed outside the . . . ordinary jurisdiction of the prosecuting state and which do not involve attacks on its peculiar interests." Harvard Research Project, 26 *American Journal of International Law Supplement* 739, 760 (1932).

However, modern international criminal law has followed the logic behind *Smith*, recognizing that customary and other non-consensual international legal rules can in some instances serve as the foundation for criminal prosecutions. In the words of Judge Meron, it is "realistic to expect a would-be offender to be aware of well-established principles of the law of nations. After all, customary humanitarian law for the most part prohibits acts that everyone would assume to be criminal anyway: rape, murder, torture, deportations, pillage, attacking civilians, and so forth." Judge Meron, describing the approach of the International Tribunal for the former Yugoslavia (ICTY), argued that "customary law can provide a safe basis for a conviction, but only if genuine care is taken to determine that the legal principle was firmly established at the time of the offense so that the offender could have identified the rule he was expected to obey." Theodor Meron, "Revival of Customary Humanitarian Law," 99 *American Journal of International Law* 816, 821 (2005). We look at the ICTY when we consider the *Furundžija Case* later in this part.

Piracy in U.S. Law. The statute used to convict Thomas Smith remains in the U.S. Code at 18 U.S.C. § 1651. Would section 1651, which today carries a mandatory life sentence rather than the death penalty, now support a U.S. criminal conviction? The issue is not hypothetical. An upsurge in pirate attacks in recent years, especially off Somalia in northeast Africa, has led to the capture of some pirates with trials in different national courts. In 2012 the U.S. federal Fourth Circuit Court of Appeals affirmed the convictions under section 1651 of several Somalis for "the crime of piracy as defined in the law of nations." United States v. Dire, 680 F.3d 446 (4th Cir. 2012), *cert. denied*, 133 S. Ct. 982 (2013). See Chapter 8.

Jus Cogens *and Obligations* Erga Omnes. Many international lawyers accept the modern concept of *jus cogens*, which may trump inconsistent rules of international law. Following are a note on the history of *jus cogens* and two cases that explore and apply *jus cogens* and the related concept of obligations *erga omnes*. Consider in what respects these concepts are similar to the natural law seen in *Smith*.

Jus Cogens *Norms.* In the late 19th and early 20th centuries, prominent theories conceptualized international law solely in state-centric positivist terms and regarded international law as created by the consent of states and applicable only to states. In the 1930s and 1940s, the horrors of Nazi-occupied Europe catapulted natural law in the guise of fundamental norms to the forefront of legal thought. As one leading textbook put it not long after World War II:

> In so far as the revival of the authority of natural law, in its modern connotation, has tended to undermine the rigid positivism of the nineteenth century, that development received an accession of strength[.] The rise of the German and the other totalitarian dictatorships, trampling upon the rights of man and universally accepted notions of law, once more tended to bring into prominence the importance and the vitality of legal standards which, though they may not be enforceable before municipal courts, are of an enduring validity transcending the positive law of any one sovereign State.

L. Oppenheim, *International Law: A Treatise: Volume I—Peace* 108 (H. Lauterpacht ed., 8th ed. 1955). To what extent do beliefs in legal positivism and in the notion that states alone are legitimate sources of legal rules depend on an unrealistic expectation that governments will always act responsibly?

Alfred von Verdross, an Austrian professor of international law, challenged views that read moral and natural law out of municipal and international law. His 1937 article, "Forbidden Treaties in International Law," rejected absolute positivism, arguing that there were necessary non-consensual rules of international law. 31 *American Journal of International Law* 571 (1937). (The quotes in the following two paragraphs are from pages 574–75; all emphasis is in the original.)

This article was one important step in the development of modern conceptions of peremptory norms of international law. Verdross identified, as a category of compulsory norms, what he called *jus cogens* rules prohibiting immoral treaties (treaties *contra bonos mores*). As examples of invalid treaties *contra bonos mores*, Verdross noted treaties binding a state "to reduce its police or its organization of courts in such a way that it is no longer able to protect at all or in an adequate manner, the life, the liberty, the honor or the property of men on its territory," "to reduce its army in such a way as to render it defenseless against external attacks," or "to close its hospitals or schools, to extradite or sterileze its women, to kill its children, to close its factories, to leave its fields unploughed, or in other ways to expose its population to distress." In general, Verdross asserted, "everywhere such treaties are regarded as being *contra bonos mores* which *restrict the liberty of one contracting party in an excessive or unworthy manner or which endanger its most important rights.*"

Verdross regarded *contra bonos mores* norms as stemming from general principles of law recognized by civilized nations. He granted that the ethics of democratic, fascist, and socialist regimes were different, but he argued that there was at least an "ethical minimum" to them all. Given the record of World War II, should a *jus cogens* norm need meet even such an "ethical minimum"? Does it make sense to treat such norms as general principles *à la* 38(1)(c) of the ICJ Statute? A logical alternative is simply to accept them as a form of natural or fundamental law.

Jus Cogens, *Obligations* Erga Omnes, *and the Rights of Individuals.* Following World War II and the Nuremberg trials, which we consider in Chapter 7, compulsory or *jus cogens* norms have been invoked to protect the rights of individuals. Our two illustrations of the modern concept of *jus cogens* and the related concept of *erga omnes* are the *Furundžija Case*, decided by the International Tribunal for the former Yugoslavia (ICTY), and the *Domingues Case*, decided by the Inter-American Commission on Human Rights. We look first at *Furundžija* and the ICTY.

The International Tribunal for the former Yugoslavia. The ICTY, which decided the *Furundžija Case*, sits in The Hague in the Netherlands. See http://www.icty. org. Established by the United Nations Security Council to prosecute individuals under international criminal law for crimes committed in the former Yugoslavia since 1991, the ICTY is one of several forums in which individuals may be prosecuted for violating international law. For more on international criminal law, see the discussion of the Nuremberg Tribunal and the International Criminal Court in Chapter 7. We examine the U.N. Security Council in Chapter 6.

The Furundžija Case. Anto Furundžija, the commander of a unit of the Croatian Defence Council, was tried in the ICTY for the torture and rape of a Bosnian Muslim woman during the conflict in Bosnia-Herzegovina in the early 1990s. In convicting Furundžija, a Trial Chamber of the ICTY found that torture was a violation of customary international law. The Chamber cited, *inter alia*, the *Filartiga Case* featured in Chapter 1 for its assertion that "the torturer has become . . . an enemy of all mankind." The Chamber went on to explore obligations *erga omnes* and *jus cogens* norms. First, obligations *erga omnes*:

PROSECUTOR V. FURUNDŽIJA

Case No. IT–95–17/1–T (Trial Chamber, International Criminal Tribunal for the former Yugoslavia, 1998)

Obligations *Erga Omnes*

[T]he prohibition of torture imposes upon States obligations *erga omnes*, that is, obligations owed towards all the other members of the international community, each of which then has a correlative right. In addition, the violation of such an obligation simultaneously constitutes a breach of the correlative right of all members of the international community and gives rise to a claim for compliance accruing to each and every member, which then has the right to insist on fulfilment of the obligations or in any case to call for the breach to be discontinued.

Defining Obligations Erga Omnes. The nature of obligations *erga omnes* has been widely debated. In 1970, in the *Barcelona Traction Case*, the International Court of Justice recognized the concept of obligations *erga omnes*—"the obligations of a State towards the international community as a whole." Case Concerning the Barcelona Traction, Light and Power Co., Limited (Belgium v. Spain), 1970 I.C.J. 3, ¶ 33. The Court cited, as examples, the international legal proscriptions against interstate aggression, genocide, slavery, and racial discrimination. In 1976 the International Law Commission endorsed both the concept and the *Barcelona Traction* examples of obligations *erga omnes*, and added obligations based on the prohibition of colonial domination by force and obligations essential to preserve the human environment, such as those prohibiting massive pollution of the seas or the atmosphere. U.N. Doc. A/31/10 (1976), art. 19(3), *reprinted in* 2 *Yearbook of the International Law Commission* 73, U.N. Doc. A/CN.4/Ser.A/1976/Add.1 (1976). One definition is that obligations *erga omnes* "articulate basic interests and needs as well as fundamental values of the international community as a whole." Jost Delbrück, " 'Laws in the Public Interest'—Some Observations on the Foundations and Identification of *Erga Omnes* Norms in International Law," in *Liber Amicorum Günther Jaenicke—Zum 85. Geburstag* 17, 18 (Volkmar Götz *et al.* eds. 1998).

Furundžija *and* Jus Cogens. The ICTY in *Furundžija* turned next to *jus cogens*, a fundamental peremptory or "trumping" norm of international law. As you read the excerpt, consider how *jus cogens* relates to the concept of *erga omnes* and to historic notions of natural law as seen in *United States v. Smith*.

Prosecutor v. Furundžija
Jus Cogens Norms

While the *erga omnes* nature just mentioned appertains to the area of international enforcement . . . the other major feature of the principle proscribing torture relates to the hierarchy of rules in the international normative order. Because of the importance of the values it protects, this principle has evolved into a peremptory norm or *jus cogens*, that is, a norm that enjoys a higher rank in the international hierarchy than treaty law and even "ordinary" customary rules. The most conspicuous consequence of this higher rank is that the principle at issue cannot be derogated from by States through international treaties or local or special customs or even general customary rules not endowed with the same normative force.

Clearly, the *jus cogens* nature of the prohibition against torture articulates the notion that the prohibition has now become one of the most fundamental standards of the international community. Furthermore, this prohibition is designed to produce a deterrent effect, in that it signals to all members of the international community and the individuals over whom they wield authority that the prohibition of torture is an absolute value from which nobody must deviate.

The fact that torture is prohibited by a peremptory norm of international law has other effects at the inter-state and individual levels. At the inter-state level, it serves to internationally de-legitimize any legislative, administrative or judicial act authorizing torture. It would be senseless to argue, on the one hand, that on account of the *jus cogens* value of the prohibition against torture, treaties or customary rules providing for torture would be null and void *ab initio*, and then be unmindful of a State say, taking national measures authorizing or condoning torture or absolving its perpetrators through an amnesty law. If such a situation were to arise, the national measures, violating the general principle and any relevant treaty provision, would produce the legal effects discussed above and in addition would not be accorded international legal recognition. Proceedings could be initiated by potential victims if they had *locus standi* before a competent international or national judicial body with a view to asking it to hold the national measure to be internationally unlawful; or the victim could bring a civil suit for damage in a foreign court, which would therefore be asked *inter alia* to disregard the legal value of the national authorizing act. What is even more important is that perpetrators of torture acting upon or benefiting from those national measures may nevertheless be held criminally responsible for torture, whether in a foreign State, or in their own State under a subsequent regime. In short, in spite of possible national authorization by legislative or judicial bodies to violate the principle banning torture, individuals remain bound to comply with that principle. As the International Military Tribunal at Nuremberg put it: "individuals have international duties which transcend the national obligations of obedience imposed by the individual State."

Furthermore, at the individual level, that is, that of criminal liability, it would seem that one of the consequences of the *jus cogens* character bestowed by the international community upon the prohibition of torture is that every State is entitled to investigate, prosecute and punish or extradite individuals accused of torture, who are present in a territory under its jurisdiction. Indeed, it would be inconsistent on the one hand to prohibit torture to such an extent as to restrict the normally unfettered treaty-making power of sovereign States, and on the other hand bar States from prosecuting and punishing those torturers who have engaged in this odious practice abroad. This legal basis for States' universal jurisdiction over torture bears out and strengthens the legal foundation for such jurisdiction found by other courts in the inherently universal character of the crime. It has been held that international crimes being universally condemned wherever they occur, every State has the right to prosecute and punish the authors of such crimes. As stated in general terms by the Supreme Court of Israel in *Eichmann*, and echoed by a USA court in *Demjanjuk*, "it is the universal character of [international crimes] which vests in every State the authority to try and punish those who participated in their commission."

The Fate of Furundžija. The ICTY sentenced Anto Furundžija to ten years in prison, giving him credit for his time in prison since his 1997 arrest. Furundžija appealed, but an ICTY Appeals Chamber affirmed his conviction in 2000. Furundžija was transferred to Finland to serve out his sentence—international criminal courts must rely on countries to help carry out sentences—but in 2004 was released early from prison.

Defining Jus Cogens. How do we know what is and is not a peremptory norm of international law (*i.e., jus cogens*)? The International Court of Justice has declared that the prohibition of genocide is "assuredly" a *jus cogens* norm. Case Concerning Armed Activities on the Territory of the Congo (Democratic Republic of Congo v. Rwanda), 2006 I.C.J. 6, ¶ 64. In the 1986 *Military and Paramilitary Activities In and Against Nicaragua Case*, the Court cited authorities indicating that Article 2(4) of the U.N. Charter condemning the use of force had moved from treaty rule to a norm of *jus cogens*. 1986 I.C.J. 14, ¶ 190. We explore Article 2(4) in Chapter 6.

The availability of a forum to interpret and apply the concept of *jus cogens* may be of critical importance. One study concluded that "without a procedure for ascertaining its content and applying it to concrete cases, *jus cogens* will continue to be more of a mission statement than a practicable legal instrument." Andreas L. Paulus, "*Jus Cogens* in a Time of Hegemony and Fragmentation," 74 *Nordic Journal of International Law* 297, 330 (2005). What would be an appropriate procedure for deciding what should or should not be a *jus cogens* rule? As you read the *Domingues Case*, next, note the forum at issue—the Inter-American Commission on Human Rights—and also consider whether the asserted *jus cogens* violation is a firm rule of international law.

The Inter-American Commission on Human Rights. The Inter-American Commission on Human Rights, which decided the *Domingues Case* below, may hear individual petitions concerning the 1948 American Declaration of the Rights and Duties of Man pursuant to the Charter of the Organization of American States, a treaty to which the United States is a party. The Commission is authorized only to deliver a non-legally-binding Report. (The Commission also may hear cases pursuant to the 1969 American Convention on Human Rights, which the United States has not accepted.) There is also an Inter-American Court of Human Rights, which has a more limited jurisdiction than the European Court of Human Rights; for example, the Inter-American Court cannot hear individual petitions unless referred by a state or the Commission. We met the European Court in the *McCann Case* in Chapter 1 and explore it further in Chapter 7.

The Domingues Case. Michael Domingues was convicted in Nevada state court of two murders committed when he was 16 years old. He was sentenced to death, a sentence affirmed by the Supreme Court of Nevada, despite Dominigues's claim that the death penalty for juveniles 16 years old violated the International Covenant on Civil and Political Rights (ICCPR) and customary international law. After the United States Supreme Court refused to review the case, Domingues petitioned the Inter-American Commission on Human Rights. Following are excerpts from the Argument of the United States in 2001 and from the Report of the Inter-American Commission in 2002.

The United States first argued that Nevada's imposition of the death penalty on juvenile offenders violated neither any treaty obligation of the United States nor any rule of customary international law. The United States then turned to its legal status as a persistent objector and to *jus cogens*. This first excerpt from the case introduces the international law concept of persistent objection.

THE MICHAEL DOMINGUES CASE: ARGUMENT OF THE UNITED STATES

Office of the Legal Adviser, United States Department of State, *Digest of United States Practice in International Law 2001*, at 303 (Sally J. Cummins & David P. Stewart eds. 2002)

Persistent Objection

Even if the execution of sixteen and seventeen-year-old offenders were prohibited by customary international law—which it is not—the United States has consistently and persistently objected to the application of such a principle to the United States. It is generally accepted that a state may contract out of a custom in the process of formation by persistent objection. *See* Restatement (Third) Foreign Relations Law of the United States 102 cmt. d ("In principle a dissenting state which indicates its dissent from a practice while the law is still in the process of development is not bound by that rule of law even after it matures.") On this basis, therefore, the United States would not be bound by such principle if it existed.

As a matter of domestic law, the laws of many states within the United States provide for the prosecution of juveniles as adults for the most serious crimes, either automatically or after a transfer review process. Half of the states in the United States permit juveniles to be prosecuted as adults in certain capital cases: five states have chosen age seventeen as the minimum age and, in eighteen states, sixteen is the minimum age. Persons under sixteen years of age at the time of the crime may not be subject to capital punishment in the United States, as the U.S. Supreme Court held that such executions would violate the U.S. Constitution.

[T]he United States has persistently asserted its right to execute juvenile offenders in multiple international fora, such as the United Nations General Assembly, the United Nations Commission on Human Rights, responses to the U.N. Special Rapporteurs, the Council of Europe, the Organization for Security and Cooperation in Europe, the Organization of American States, and the Inter-American Commission on Human Rights.

The Persistent Objector. Is a state bound by a rule of customary international law if it has persistently objected to the rule? The U.S. argument to this effect in the *Domingues Case* finds support in the 1951 *Anglo-Norwegian Fisheries Case*. In that case the International Court of Justice concluded that even if an asserted rule capping the length of baselines across the mouths of bays at ten miles had been a general rule of international law—it was not—the rule would "be inapplicable as against Norway inasmuch as she has always opposed any attempt to apply it to the Norwegian coast." 1951 I.C.J. 116, 131.

A state may file diplomatic protests or assert its position in international fora to try to prevent a rule of customary international law from ripening, as well as to ensure that it will not be bound by the rule even if it does become recognized as custom. A state may also take actions "on the ground" for these reasons. For example, the United States has sent warships into, and flown planes over, waters in the South China Sea claimed by China, in order to preserve navigational freedoms under international law.

What are the advantages and disadvantages of the persistent objector rule? It certainly fits with the notion that countries may not be bound by a rule of customary international law without their consent, albeit they must affirmatively assert their lack of consent. What practical difficulties is a state likely to face if it continues to assert its status as a persistent objector?

Should persistent objection be able to overcome *jus cogens*? Consider that question as you read the remainder of the U.S. argument in the *Domingues Case* and then the report of the Inter-American Commission. Note that the United States accepted the reality of the concept of *jus cogens*, even though disputing that execution of juveniles was a *jus cogens* violation.

The Michael Domingues Case: Argument of the United States
Jus Cogens

A *jus cogens* norm holds the highest hierarchical position among all other international norms and principles. As a consequence, *jus cogens* norms are deemed to be non-derogable. Shaw, Malcolm N., *International Law* (4th) 1997, at 544. For a norm to be *jus cogens*, the international community of States as a whole must accept and recognize not only the norm but also its peremptory character. Vienna Convention on the Law of Treaties, art 53; *see also* Restatement of Foreign Relations Law of the United States (Third) § 102(3). . . .

There is no *jus cogens* norm that establishes eighteen years as the minimum age at which an offender can receive a sentence of death. In order to so hold, the Commission would have to decide that this alleged prohibition has similar force to prohibitions such as those against piracy and genocide. There is simply no support for this proposition.

THE MICHAEL DOMINGUES CASE: REPORT OF THE INTER-AMERICAN COMMISSION ON HUMAN RIGHTS

IACHR, Report No. 62/02, Case 12.285, Merits (publication), Michael Domingues, October 22, 2002

Jus Cogens

[T]he Commission is satisfied . . . that [a rule prohibiting the execution of offenders under the age of 18 years at the time of their crime is not only a rule of customary international law, but] has been recognized as being of a sufficiently indelible nature to now constitute a norm of *jus cogens*[.] [N]early every nation state has rejected the imposition of capital punishment to individuals under the age of 18. They have done so through ratification of the ICCPR, U.N. Convention on the Rights of the Child, and the American Convention on Human Rights, treaties in which this proscription is recognized as non-derogable, as well as through corresponding amendments to their domestic laws. The acceptance of this norm crosses political and ideological boundaries and efforts to detract from this standard have been vigorously condemned by members of the international community as impermissible under contemporary human rights standards. Indeed, it may be said that the United States itself, rather than persistently objecting to the standard, has in several significant respects recognized the propriety of this norm by, for example, prescribing the age of 18 as the federal standard for the application of capital punishment and by ratifying the Fourth Geneva Convention without reservation to this standard. On this basis, the Commission considers that the United States is bound by a norm of *jus cogens* not to impose capital punishment on individuals who committed their crimes when they had not yet reached 18 years of age. As a *jus cogens* norm, this proscription binds the community of States, including the United States. The norm cannot be validly derogated from, whether by treaty or by the objection of a state, persistent or otherwise.

Interpreting the terms of the American Declaration in light of this norm of *jus cogens*, the Commission therefore concludes in the present case that the United States has failed to respect the life, liberty and security of the person of Michael Domingues by sentencing him to death for crimes that he committed when he was 16 years of age, contrary to Article I of the American Declaration.

The Fate of Domingues. Michael Domingues remained on death row in Nevada until 2005, when the U.S. Supreme Court ruled in *Roper v. Simmons*, 543 U.S. 551 (2005), that the juvenile death penalty violated the U.S. Constitution. International and foreign law played a part in the analysis of the *Roper* majority. In Chapter 5 we explore the roles of international law in the U.S. legal system.

Comparing Jus Cogens *Norms and Obligations* Erga Omnes. Are the obligations in *Furundžija* and *Domingues jus cogens* norms, obligations *erga omnes*, or both? Do the references of the United States and the Inter-American Commission in *Domingues* to the "acceptance" of *jus cogens* norms mean that *jus cogens* is a type of positive international law, or are *jus cogens* and *erga omnes* really forms of natural law? To the extent that both concepts focus on universal application and fundamental values, the concepts link to the natural law tradition.

An independent study group led by Professor Koskenniemi, considering the general topic of the fragmentation of international law, concluded that although all *jus cogens* norms were also *erga omnes* obligations, "the reverse is not necessarily true." For example, some rules concerning navigation on the oceans that are not "established by peremptory norms of general international law" have *erga omnes* status. Michael J. Matheson, "The Fifty-Eighth Session of the International Law Commission," 101 *American Journal of International Law* 407, 425 (2007). An obligation to keep maritime straits open to all vessels under a regime of transit passage through straits (see Chapter 8) is arguably an obligation owed to all. That obligation, however, likely could be modified or eliminated by bilateral agreement between a particular coastal state and a state that transports dangerous materials, whereas a *jus cogens* norm could not be modified bilaterally. Are human rights norms like those in *Furundžija* and *Domingues* more likely to be both *jus cogens* norms and obligations *erga omnes* than are other kinds of international rules?

Even when the substance of obligations *erga omnes* and *jus cogens* norms is identical, the focus of the concepts is different. As noted in the *Furundžija Case*, the concept of *erga omnes* relates to whom obligations are owed and who correspondingly may raise a claim for compliance; *jus cogens* describes the peremptory effect and higher rank of certain rules of international law.

Persistent Objection and Jus Cogens. Did the Inter-American Commission's conclusion in *Domingues* that the norm against juvenile execution was *jus cogens* put the question outside the realm of an argument about the status of the persistent objector *vis-à-vis* customary international law? Professor Shelton submitted that "although the idea of *jus cogens* originated solely as a limitation on the treaty-making power of states, today an assertion that a norm is *jus cogens* seems more often intended to over-ride the will of persistent objectors to the emergence of the norm as customary international law." Dinah Shelton, "Normative Hierarchy in International Law," 100 *American Journal of International Law* 291, 304 (2006).

More broadly, the debate about *jus cogens* and other non-consensual sources of international law is, in a way, about the respect (or not) to be paid to state freedom of action. How much authority should the international community in general and international or domestic judges in particular have to evaluate the international legality of an act of a sovereign state when the state chooses to declare itself not bound by international law? Should stronger sovereign states have more freedom to disregard international legal rules than weaker states? Should all states be allowed equally to opt out of an international legal rule when it no longer suits them? These questions are central to the on-going controversy in the United States and elsewhere about the meaning and efficacy of international law.

F. EQUITY

Although equity is not explicitly mentioned as a source of law in Article 38(1) of the Statute of the International Court of Justice, international lawyers and tribunals—including the ICJ itself—sometimes apply equity. With respect to the materials in this part, consider what authority there is for the use of equity, its content, and the relationship between equity and other sources of international law.

The Cayuga Indians Case. Our first illustration of the use of equity comes from a 1926 arbitration between the United States and Great Britain, with the British then governing Canada. The focus is on the entitlement of the indigenous Cayuga people in New York and Canada to payments owed them by treaty. We start with the facts.

THE CAYUGA INDIANS CASE

American and British Claims Arbitration under Agreement of August 8, 1910
(Fred K. Nielson, Reporter, U.S. Government Publishing Office, 1926)

The Facts

This is a claim of Great Britain, on behalf of the Cayuga Indians in Canada, against the United States by virtue of certain treaties between the State of New York and the Cayuga Nation in 1789, 1790, and 1795, and the Treaty of 1814 between the United States and Great Britain, known as the Treaty of Ghent.

At the time of the American Revolution, the Cayugas, a tribe of the Six Nations or Iroquois, occupied that part of Central New York lying about Cayuga Lake. During the Revolution, the Cayugas took the side of Great Britain, and as a result their territory was invaded and laid waste by Continental troops. Thereupon the greater part of the tribe removed to Buffalo Creek, and after 1784 a considerable portion removed thence to the Grand River in Canada. By 1790 the majority of the tribe were probably in Canada. In 1789 the State of New York entered into a treaty with the Cayugas who remained at Cayuga Lake, recognized as the Cayuga Nation, whereby the latter ceded the lands formerly occupied by the Tribe to New York and the latter covenanted to pay an annuity of $500 to the nation. In this treaty a reservation at Cayuga Lake was provided for. As there was much dissatisfaction with this treaty on the part of the Indians, who asserted that they were not properly represented, it was confirmed by a subsequent treaty in 1790 and finally by one in 1795, executed by the principal chiefs and warriors both from Buffalo Creek and from the Grand River. By the terms of the latter treaty, in which, as we hold, the covenants of the prior treaties were merged, the State covenanted, among other things, with the "Cayuga Nation" to pay to the said "Cayuga Nation" 1800 dollars a year forever thereafter, at Canandaigua, in Ontario County, the money to be paid to "the Agent of Indian Affairs under the United States for the time being, residing within this State" and, if there was no such agent, then to a person to be appointed by the Governor. Such agent or person appointed by the Governor was to pay the money to the "Cayuga Nation," taking the receipt of the nation and also a receipt on the counterpart of the treaty, left in the possession of the Indians, according to a prescribed form. By this treaty the reservation provided for in the Treaty of 1789 was sold to the State.

[From 1795 through 1810] the only persons who can be identified among those to whom the money was paid, and the only persons who can be shown to have held prominent positions in the tribe, were then living in Canada. . . . Since [1811] no part of the moneys paid under the treaty has come in any way to the Cayugas in Canada, but the whole has been paid to Cayugas in the United States, and since 1829 in accordance with treaties in which the Canadian Cayugas had no part or in accordance with legislation of New York. The claim is: (1) That the Cayugas in Canada, who assert that they have kept up their tribal organization and undoubtedly have included in their number the principal personages of the tribe according to its original organization, are the "Cayuga Nation," covenantees in the Treaty of 1795, and that as such they, or Great Britain on their behalf, should receive the whole amount of the annuity from 1810 to the present. In this connection it is argued that the covenant could only be discharged by payment to those in possession of the counterpart of the treaty and indorsement of a receipt thereon, as in the treaty prescribed. (2) In the alternative, that the Canadian Cayugas, as a part of the posterity of the original nation, and numerically the greater part, have a proportion of the annuity for the future and a proportion of the payments since 1810, to be ascertained by reference to the relative numbers in the United States and in Canada for the time being.

As the occasion of the change that took place in and after 1811 was the division of the tribe at the time of the War of 1812, those in the United States and those in Canada taking the part of the United States and of Great Britain, respectively, Great Britain invokes Article IX of the Treaty of Ghent, by which the United States agreed to restore to the Indians with whom that Government had been at war "all the possessions, rights, and privileges which they may have enjoyed or been entitled to" in 1811 before the war. . . .

It can not be doubted that until the Cayugas permanently divided, all the sachems and warriors, wherever they lived, whether at Cayuga Lake, Buffalo Creek, or the Grand River in Canada, were regarded as entitled to and did share in the money paid on the annuity. Indeed it is reasonably certain that the larger number and the more important of those who signed the Treaty of 1795 were then, or were soon thereafter, permanently established in Canada. It is clear that the greater number and more important of those who signed the annuity receipts from the date of the treaty until 1810 were Canadian Cayugas. [D]own to the division the money was regarded as payable to and was paid to and divided among the Cayugas as a people.

Equity and the Definition of the "Cayuga Nation." To resolve the question of the Cayugas' entitlement, the arbitral tribunal turned to equity. As you read the tribunal's analysis below, consider what prompted this recourse to equity. One explanation may well have related to the difficulty of defining the "Cayuga Nation." As one looks at the agreements of 1789, 1790, and 1795 between the state of New York and the Cayuga Nation, at the 1814 Treaty of Ghent between the United States and Great Britain, and at arguments about the implementation of treaty rights by various governmental entities, one can identify different legal systems that plausibly could supply a definition of the "Cayuga Nation." Possibilities include New York law, U.S. federal law, Ontario law, British law, Cayuga law (both of tribes in the U.S. and Canada), and international law. The Cayugas' entitlement could well vary depending on which law is used. The arbitral tribunal's use of equity avoids the need to give a definitive answer to the "choice-of-law problem" of picking which governing law would define the "Cayuga Nation."

The Cayuga Indians Case

Equity Gerechtigkeit

The claim of the Canadian Cayugas, who are in fact the greater part of that people, is founded in the elementary principle of justice that requires us to look at the substance and not stick in the bark of the legal form.

But there are special circumstances making the equitable claim of the Canadian Cayugas especially strong.

In the first place, the Cayuga Nation had no international status. As has been said, it existed as a legal unit only by New York law. It was a *de facto* unit, but *de jure* was only what Great Britain chose to recognize as to the Cayugas who moved to Canada and what New York recognized as to the Cayugas in New York or in their relations with New York. As to the annuities, therefore, the Cayugas were a unit of New York law, so far as New York law chose to make them one. When the tribe divided, this anomalous and hard situation gave rise to obvious claims according to universally recognized principles of justice.

In the second place, we must bear in mind the dependent legal position of the individual Cayugas. Legally they could do nothing except under the guardianship of some sovereign. They could not determine what should be the nation, nor even whether there should be a nation legally. New York continued to deal with the New York Cayugas as a "nation." Great Britain dealt with the Canadian Cayugas as individuals. The very language of the treaty was in this sense imposed on them. What to them was a covenant with the people of the tribe and its posterity had to be put into legal terms of a covenant with a legal unit that might and did come to be but a fraction of the whole. American Courts have agreed from the beginning in pronouncing the position of the Indians an anomalous one. When a situation legally so anomalous is presented, recourse must be had to generally recognized principles of justice and fair dealing in order to determine the rights of the individuals involved. The same considerations of equity that have repeatedly been invoked by the courts where strict regard to the legal personality of a corporation would lead to inequitable results or to results contrary to legal policy, may be invoked here. In such cases courts have not hesitated to look behind the legal person and consider the human individuals who were the real beneficiaries. Those considerations are even more cogent where we are dealing with Indians in a state of pupilage toward the sovereign with whom they were treating.

There is the more warrant for so doing under the terms of the treaty by virtue of which we are sitting. It provides that decision shall be made in accordance with principles of international law and of equity. Merignhac considers that an arbitral tribunal is justified in reaching a decision on universally recognized principles of justice where the terms of submission are silent as to the grounds of decision and even where the grounds of decision are expressed to be the "principles of international law." He considers, however, that the appropriate formula is that "international law is to be applied with equity." *Traité théorique et pratique de l'arbitrage international*, § 303. It is significant that the present treaty uses the phrase "principles of international law and equity." When used in a general arbitration treaty, this can only mean to provide for the possibility of anomalous cases such as the present.

An examination of the provisions of arbitration treaties shows a recognition that something more than the strict law must be used in the grounds of decision of arbitral tribunals in certain cases; that there are cases in which—like the courts of the land—these tribunals must find the grounds of decision, must find the right and the law, in general considerations of justice, equity, and right dealing guided by legal analogies and by the spirit and received principles of international law.

. . . Our conclusion on this branch of the cause is that, according to general and universally recognized principles of justice and the analogy of the way in which English and American courts, on proper occasions, look behind what in such cases they call "the corporate fiction" in the interests of justice or of the policy of the law, on the division of the Cayuga Nation the Cayuga Indians permanently settled in Canada became entitled to their proportionate share of the annuity and that such share ought to have been paid to them from 1810 to the present time.

Individual and Group Rights in International Law. The arbitral panel looked behind the "legal person" of the Cayuga Nation so it could protect "human individuals who were the real beneficiaries" of the treaties. The Cayuga Nation was a "nation" but not a "state," and thus in the 1920s unable to vindicate its own international legal rights via arbitration. Only later did "mixed arbitrations" between states and non-state entities, such as the *Texaco-Libya Case* in Part C, become common; the *Cayuga Indians* arbitration was conducted between the United States and Great Britain. In 2010, a committee of the International Law Association characterized the *Cayuga Indians* decision as a "down" because it "denied indigenous peoples the status of a 'legal unit of international law.'" ILA Committee on the Rights of Indigenous Peoples, "Interim Report," in International Law Association, *Report of the Seventy-Fourth Conference (The Hague)* 834, 835 (2010). Questions about the relationship of individuals to international law and their international legal rights and obligations *vis-à-vis* their own and other states are raised in Chapter 7. The group rights of "peoples," highlighted in Chapter 3, are also an increasing area of concern in international law. Today, a forum for considering the rights and concerns of indigenous peoples exists at the United Nations, and cases involving group rights may be litigated in the Inter-American human rights system, introduced in the *Domingues Case.*

The Authority to Use Equity. The treaty providing for the resolution of the *Cayuga Indians* dispute explicitly called for the application of "the principles of international law and of equity." This treaty provision does not really help us know exactly what equity is, but the provision does settle concerns about where the tribunal gets the authority to apply equity. Some international lawyers find recourse to equity without clear authorization to be controversial.

The Varieties of Equity. Given the explicit authorization to use equity, the arbitral tribunal was not concerned that its use of equity necessarily be within the rules of international law, *i.e.,* that it be equity *intra legem*. Use of equity *intra legem* to reach a fair result is often less controversial than applying equity to fill gaps in the law, *i.e.,* equity *praeter legem,* or using equity that is contrary to the law, *i.e.,* equity *contra legem.* Although the *Cayuga Indians* tribunal had a general warrant to use "equity," did it really venture beyond equity *intra legem* to fill gaps in international law or to reverse international law? The arbitrators might well have felt uncomfortable entirely ignoring or rewriting the treaty by, for example, increasing the total dollars owed the Cayuga Nation under the treaty above the $1,800 specified.

The arbitral tribunal was persuaded that "as a matter of justice" the Canadian Cayugas had a good claim against the United States: "The claim of the Canadian Cayugas, who are in fact the greater part of that people, is founded in the elementary principle of justice that requires us to look at the substance and not stick in the bark of the legal form." Should international law be more or less able than municipal law "to look at the substance" of disputes and "not stick in the bark of the legal form"? On the one hand, formal agreements among sovereign states may deserve special respect. On the other hand, without municipal-type legislative organs, international law may become especially rigid.

The Meuse Case. Our next example of a use of equity is the *Meuse Case,* decided by the Permanent Court of International Justice in 1937. The Netherlands challenged the legality, under an 1863 treaty, of Belgium's drawing water from the River Meuse by the Neerhaeren Lock, and sought an order that Belgium discontinue this conduct. Belgium replied that the Netherlands had lost the right to invoke the treaty against Belgium, because the Netherlands had taken water from the River Meuse by operating a lock at Bosscheveld—an operation also not permitted under the treaty. We excerpt part of the opinion of Judge Manley Hudson, who was the U.S. judge on the PCIJ from 1931 to 1945.

THE MEUSE CASE

Judge Hudson's Opinion, 1937 P.C.I.J., Ser. A/B, No. 70, at 73

Equity and Law

What are widely known as principles of equity have long been considered to constitute a part of international law, and as such they have often been applied by international tribunals. Mérignhac, *Traité théorique et pratique de l'Arbitrage international* (1895), p. 295; Ralston, *Law and Procedure of International Tribunals* (new ed., 1926), pp. 53–57. A sharp division between law and equity, such as prevails in the administration of justice in some States, should find no place in international jurisprudence; even in some national legal systems, there has been a strong tendency towards the fusion of law and equity. Some international tribunals are expressly directed by the *compromis* which control them to apply "law and equity." See the Cayuga Indians Case, Nielsen's Report of the United States-British Claims Arbitration (1926), p. 307. Of such a provision, a special tribunal of the Permanent Court of Arbitration said in 1922 that "the majority of international lawyers seem to agree that these words are to be understood to mean general principles of justice as distinguished from any particular systems of jurisprudence." Proceedings of the United States-Norwegian Tribunal (1922), p. 141. Numerous arbitration treaties have been concluded in recent years which apply to differences "which are justiciable in their nature by reason of being susceptible of decision by the application of the principles of law or equity." Whether the reference in an arbitration treaty is to the application of "law and equity" or to justiciability dependent on the possibility of applying "law or equity," it would seem to envisage equity as a part of law.

Justifying a Recourse to Equity. Unlike the arbitrators in the *Cayuga Indians Case*, Judge Hudson had no explicit charge from the states involved to apply equity as well as law to the dispute. How then did Hudson justify his use of equity? He noted the "strong tendency toward the fusion of law and equity." If principles of equity are part of international law, an "international law and equity" authorization *à la Cayuga Indians* would arguably have been simply redundant. The European Court of Human Rights also turned to equity without an explicit agreement in a recent determination of damages: "[Our] guiding principle is equity which above all involves flexibility and an objective consideration of what is just, fair and reasonable in all the circumstances of the case." Al-Jedda v. United Kingdom, European Court of Human Rights, Judgment of 7 July 2011, ¶ 14.

Judge Hudson also noted that a principle of equity could be a "general principle of law," which the Court is authorized to apply under Article 38(1)(c) of its Statute:

The Meuse Case
Equity and General Principles

The Court has not been expressly authorized by its Statute to apply equity as distinguished from law. Nor, indeed, does the Statute expressly direct its application of international law, though as has been said on several occasions the Court is "a tribunal of international law." Series A, No. 7, p. 19; Series A, Nos. 20/21, p. 124. Article 38 of the Statute expressly directs the application of "general principles of law recognized by civilized nations," and in more than one nation principles of equity have an established place in the legal system. The Court's recognition of equity as a part of international law is in no way restricted by the special power conferred upon it "to decide a case *ex aequo et bono*, if the parties agree thereto." It must be concluded, therefore, that under Article 38 of the Statute, if not independently of that Article, the Court has some freedom to consider principles of equity as part of the international law which it must apply.

It would seem to be an important principle of equity that where two parties have assumed an identical or a reciprocal obligation, one party which is engaged in a continuing non-performance of that obligation should not be permitted to take advantage of a similar non-performance of that obligation by the other party. The principle finds expression in the so-called maxims of equity which exercised great influence in the creative period of the development of the Anglo-American law. Some of these maxims are, "Equality is equity"; "He who seeks equity must do equity." It is in line with such maxims that "a court of equity refuses relief to a plaintiff whose conduct in regard to the subject-matter of the litigation has been improper." 13 Halsbury's *Laws of England* (2nd ed., 1934), p. 87. A very similar principle was received into Roman Law. The obligations of a vendor and a vendee being concurrent, "neither could compel the other to perform unless he had done, or tendered, his own part." Buckland, *Text Book of Roman Law* (2nd ed., 1932), p. 493. The *exceptio non adimpleti contractus* required a claimant to prove that he had performed or offered to perform his obligation. Girard, *Droit romain* (8th ed., 1929), p. 567; Saleilles, in 6 *Annales de Droit commercial*, (1892), p. 287, and 7 *id.*

(1893), pp. 24, 97 and 175. This conception was the basis of Articles 320 and 322 of the German Civil Code, and even where a code is silent on the point Planiol states the general principle that "dans tout rapport synallagmatique, chacune des deux parties ne peut exiger la prestation qui lui est due que si elle-offre elle-même d'exécuter son obligation." Planiol, *Droit civil*, Vol. 2 (6th ed., 1912), p. 320. . . .

One result of applying the principle will be that even if the Court should be of the opinion that the Belgian action with regard to the functioning of the Neerhaeren Lock is contrary to the Treaty of 1863, it should nevertheless refuse in this case to order Belgium to discontinue that action. In equity, the Netherlands is not in a position to have such relief decreed to her. Belgium cannot be ordered to discontinue the operation of the Neerhaeren Lock when the Netherlands is left free to continue the operation of the Bosscheveld Lock.

Searching for General Principles. How thorough a review of municipal law did Judge Hudson make in search of his general principle? How did his review compare to Advocate General Slynn's search of municipal law in the *AM & S Case*? Was Hudson's search meant to be universal? Hudson limited his comparative search to "Anglo-American law," Roman law, and French and German law. Hudson's result would have been more persuasive, even in 1937, had he surveyed a wider variety of legal systems in the world.

The Effect of Applying Equity. What was the effect of Judge Hudson's application of equity to the facts of the *Meuse Case*? What were the parties supposed to do if they accepted Hudson's decision? By not finding that Belgium had breached the 1863 treaty, and instead refusing to allow the case to proceed on the equitable grounds that the Netherlands had "unclean hands," Judge Hudson left the two states in an equal negotiating position.

Ex Aequo et Bono. By Article 38(2) of its Statute, the International Court of Justice may decide a case *ex aequo et bono,* by what is "equal and good," but only if the states party to the dispute specifically authorize it to do so. The Court has never been so authorized. What in practice would be the difference between applying equitable principles pursuant to Article 38(1)(c) and deciding *ex aequo et bono* pursuant to Article 38(2)? Both avenues appear to call for application of considerable judicial discretion. However, an *ex aequo* authorization could, in theory, allow the Court entirely to disregard any existing treaties or other law, applying equity *contra legem* if doing so seemed fair and just.

The North Sea Continental Shelf Cases. Our last case in this chapter both illustrates the use of equity in international law and provides a review of other sources of international law. The Federal Republic of Germany, Denmark, and the Netherlands had unsuccessfully tried to negotiate continental shelf boundaries in the North Sea. The continental shelf, which we explore in Chapter 8, comprises a portion of the seabed and subsoil of the ocean beyond a narrow coastal territorial sea. The countries brought their dispute to the International Court of Justice, specifying the issue on which they sought a ruling. See Alex G. Oude Elferink, *The Delimitation of the Continental Shelf Between Denmark, Germany, and the Netherlands* (2013). We start with the factual background.

THE NORTH SEA CONTINENTAL SHELF CASES

Federal Republic of Germany v. Denmark; Federal Republic of Germany v. Netherlands, 1969 I.C.J. 3

The Facts

Articles 1 to 3 of the Special Agreement between the Governments of Denmark and the Federal Republic of Germany [and another between the Governments of the Netherlands and the Federal Republic, both dated February 2, 1967, provide] as follows:

ARTICLE 1

(1) The International Court of Justice is requested to decide the following question:

> What principles and rules of international law are applicable to the delimitation as between the Parties of the areas of the continental shelf in the North Sea which appertain to each of them beyond the partial boundary determined by [1964 and 1965 treaties]?

(2) The Governments of [the Netherlands and] the Kingdom of Denmark and of the Federal Republic of Germany shall delimit the continental shelf in the North Sea as between their countries by agreement in pursuance of the decision requested from the International Court of Justice.

[T]he North Sea, which lies between continental Europe and Great Britain in the east-west direction, is roughly oval in shape and stretches from the straits of Dover northwards to a parallel drawn between a point immediately north of the Shetland Islands and the mouth of the Sogne Fiord in Norway, about 75 kilometres above Bergen, beyond which is the North Atlantic Ocean. In the extreme northwest, it is bounded by a line connecting the Orkney and Shetland island groups; while on its north-eastern side, the line separating it from the entrances to the Baltic Sea lies between Hanstholm at the north-west point of Denmark, and Lindesnes at the southern tip of Norway. . . . Thus, the North Sea has to some extent the general look of an enclosed sea without actually being one. Round its shores are situated, on its eastern side and starting from the north, Norway, Denmark, the Federal Republic of Germany, the Netherlands, Belgium and France; while the whole western side is taken up by Great Britain, together with the island groups of the Orkneys and Shetlands. From this it will be seen that the continental shelf of the Federal Republic is situated between those of Denmark and the Netherlands.

The waters of the North Sea are shallow, and the whole seabed consists of continental shelf at a depth of less than 200 metres, except for the formation known as the Norwegian Trough, a belt of water 200–650 metres deep, fringing the southern and south-western coasts of Norway to a width averaging about 80–100 kilometres. Much . . . of this continental shelf has already been the subject of delimitation by . . . agreements concluded between the United Kingdom [and] Norway, Denmark and the Netherlands. These three delimitations were carried out by the drawing of what are known as "median lines" which . . . may be described as boundaries drawn between the continental shelf areas of "opposite" States, dividing the intervening spaces equally between them. . . .

In addition to the partial boundary lines Federal Republic/Denmark and Federal Republic/Netherlands, which . . . were respectively established by the agreements of 9 June 1965 and 1 December 1964, and which are shown as lines A–B and C–D on Map 3 [Figure 2.K,] another line has been drawn in this area, namely that represented by the line E–F on that map. This line, which divides areas respectively claimed (to the north of it) by Denmark, and (to the south of it) by the Netherlands, is the outcome of an agreement between those two countries dated 31 March 1966, reflecting the view taken by them as to what are the correct boundary lines between their respective continental shelf areas and that of the Federal Republic, beyond the partial boundaries A–B and C–D already drawn. These further and unagreed boundaries to seaward, are shown on [Figure 2.K] by means of . . . lines B–E and D–E. They are the lines, the correctness of which in law the Court is in effect, though indirectly, called upon to determine. Also shown on [Figure 2.K] are the two . . . lines B–F and D–F, representing approximately the boundaries which the Federal Republic would have wished to obtain in the course of the negotiations that took place between the Federal Republic and the other two Parties prior to the submission of the matter to the Court. . . .

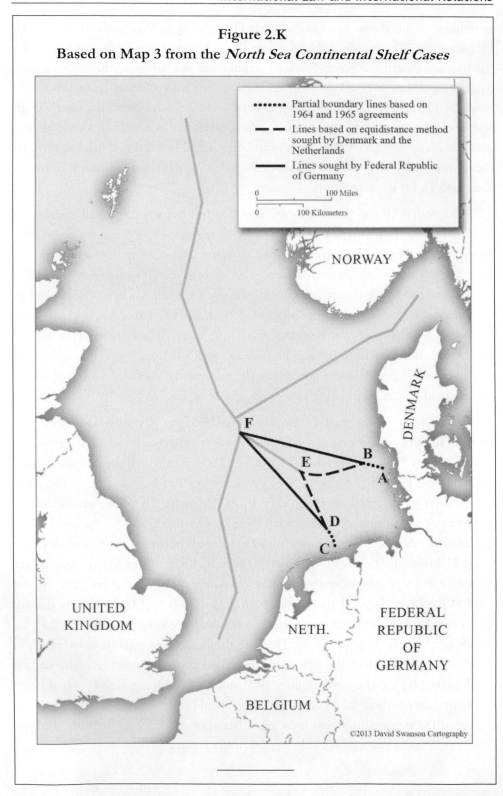

Figure 2.K
Based on Map 3 from the *North Sea Continental Shelf Cases*

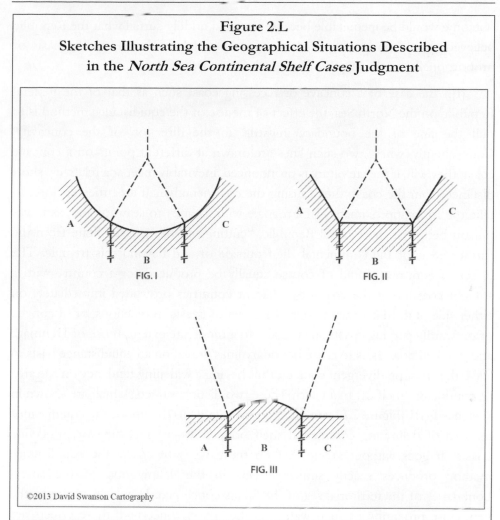

Figure 2.L
Sketches Illustrating the Geographical Situations Described
in the *North Sea Continental Shelf Cases* Judgment

FIG. I

FIG. II

FIG. III

©2013 David Swanson Cartography

Under the agreements of December 1964 and June 1965, already mentioned, the partial boundaries represented by the map lines A–B and C–D had . . . been drawn mainly by application of the principle of equidistance[.] [A]n "equidistance line" . . . leaves to each of the parties concerned all those portions of the continental shelf that are nearer to a point on its own coast than they are to any point on the coast of the other party. An equidistance line may consist either of a "median" line between "opposite" States, or of a "lateral" line between "adjacent" States. . . .

The further negotiations between the Parties for the prolongation of the partial boundaries broke down mainly because Denmark and the Netherlands respectively wished this prolongation also to be effected on the basis of the equidistance principle,—and this would have resulted in . . . lines B–E and D–E, shown on [Figure 2.K]; whereas the Federal Republic considered that such an outcome would be inequitable because it would unduly curtail what the Republic believed should be its proper share of continental shelf area, on the basis of proportionality to the length of its North Sea coastline. . . .

[I]n the case of a concave or recessing coast such as that of the Federal Republic on the North Sea, the effect of the use of the equidistance method is to pull the line of the boundary inwards, in the direction of the concavity. Consequently, where two such lines are drawn at different points on a concave coast, they will, if the curvature is pronounced, inevitably meet at a relatively short distance from the coast, thus causing the continental shelf area they enclose, to take the form approximately of a triangle with its apex to seaward and, as it was put on behalf of the Federal Republic, "cutting off" the coastal State from the further areas of the continental shelf outside of and beyond this triangle. The effect of concavity could of course equally be produced for a country with a straight coastline if the coasts of adjacent countries protruded immediately on either side of it. In contrast to this, the effect of coastal projections, or of convex or outwardly curving coasts such as are, to a moderate extent, those of Denmark and the Netherlands, is to cause boundary lines drawn on an equidistance basis to leave the coast on divergent courses, thus having a widening tendency on the area of continental shelf off that coast. These two distinct effects, which are shown in sketches I–III [Figure 2.L], are directly attributable to the use of the equidistance method of delimiting continental shelf boundaries off recessing or projecting coasts. It goes without saying that on these types of coasts the equidistance method produces exactly similar effects in the delimitation of the lateral boundaries of the territorial sea of the States concerned. However, owing to the very close proximity of such waters to the coasts concerned, these effects are much less marked and may be very slight[.]

After [negotiations] failed to result in any agreement about the delimitation of the boundary extending beyond the partial one already agreed, [the parties] decided to submit the matter to the Court.

The Need to Delimit the Continental Shelf. Note the geographical elements of the problem as sketched in Figure 2.K. Because of the indentation of the German shore, delimitation by the equidistance method would bend the line along the route D–E–B. Germany preferred D–F–B. Why did the states involved so vigorously contest the delimitation lines? Why had it not been important to delimit the shelf prior to the 1960's? By the 1960s, major oil deposits had been discovered under the North Sea, and technology capable of drilling for oil on the continental shelf had been developed. It was important to know which state could license exploration and exploitation for the valuable resource.

Figure 2.M
Tyra Field, Danish Sector of North Sea, Discovered 1968

The North Sea Cases*: A Treaty Obligation?* The *North Sea* judgment provides an excellent resume of the sources of international law, beginning with treaties, moving to other sources, and ending with equity. Did treaty law mandate the use of an equidistance rule in setting continental shelf boundaries? Denmark and the Netherlands contended that the 1958 Geneva Convention on the Continental Shelf bound all the parties, and that the Court must interpret Article 6 of that Convention. Article 6(2) reads:

> Where the same continental shelf is adjacent to the territories of two adjacent States, the boundary of the continental shelf shall be determined by agreement between them. In the absence of agreement, and unless another boundary line is justified by special circumstances, the boundary shall be determined by application of the principle of equidistance from the nearest points of the baselines from which the breadth of the territorial sea of each State is measured.

Denmark and the Netherlands were parties to the Continental Shelf Convention, but the Federal Republic was not. That pretty much ended any possibility that the treaty was binding on Germany as a matter of treaty law.

The North Sea Cases: *A General Principle of Law?* Denmark and the Netherlands nevertheless contended that the Article 6 regime had "become binding on the Federal Republic" because Germany "by conduct, by public statements and proclamations, and in other ways . . . has unilaterally assumed the obligations of the Convention; or has manifested its acceptance of the conventional régime." The ICJ acknowledged that, in theory, a principle of "estoppel" could be used to establish that Germany was "now precluded from denying the applicability of the conventional régime, by reason of past conduct, declarations, etc., which not only clearly and consistently evinced acceptance of that régime, but also had caused Denmark or the Netherlands, in reliance on such conduct, detrimentally to change position or suffer some prejudice." Estoppel, which is used in municipal legal systems, has been recognized internationally as a general principle of law, grounded in the notion of good faith. The estoppel argument was, however, unavailing, since "there is no evidence whatever in the present case" of clear and consistent German conduct accepting Article 6 obligations, or of detrimental reliance by Denmark or the Netherlands on any such German conduct.

The North Sea Cases: *A Customary International Law Rule?* The Court also asked whether an equidistance-special circumstances rule bound Germany as a matter of general or customary international law. The Court considered whether there was a positive law basis for an equidistance-special circumstances rule, based on the work of "international legal bodies, on state practice and on the influence attributed to the Geneva Convention itself,—the claim being that these various factors have cumulatively evidenced or been creative of the *opinio juris sive necessitatas*, requisite for the formation of new rules of customary international law."

Customary international law might relate to Article 6 of the Continental Shelf Convention in at least three ways. First, it might declare an existing rule of customary international law; Denmark and the Netherlands did not make this contention. Second, the process of preparing drafts of the Convention and negotiating its provisions might "crystallize" an emerging customary rule. The Court rejected this claim, noting that the International Law Commission, whose draft provided the basis for the Convention, regarded the equidistance-special circumstances rule as "new law," not emerging customary international law. In addition, Article 6 permitted reservations (see the discussion of reservations at the end of Part B), which seemed inconsistent with crystallization of a general rule of custom. Third, the equidistance-special circumstances rule of Article 6 might have developed after the conclusion of the Geneva Convention. The Court rejected that assertion too. Article 6 was not a "norm-creating provision" that had "passed into the general *corpus* of international law." The Court noted that countries had based some 15 maritime delimitations, including four in the North Sea, on the equidistance method but dismissed the relevance of those delimitations to the subsequent development of a rule of custom.

The North Sea Continental Shelf Cases
A Restrictive View of Custom

To begin with, over half the [delimiting countries] were or shortly became parties to the Geneva Convention, and were therefore presumably . . . acting actually or potentially in the application of the Convention. From their action no inference could legitimately be drawn as to the existence of a rule of customary international law in favour of the equidistance principle. As regards those States, on the other hand, which were not, and have not become parties to the Convention, the basis of their action can only be problematical and must remain entirely speculative. Clearly, they were not applying the Convention. But from that no inference could justifiably be drawn that they believed themselves to be applying a mandatory rule of customary international law. There is not a shred of evidence that they did and . . . there is no lack of other reasons for using the equidistance method, so that acting, or agreeing to act in a certain way, does not of itself demonstrate anything of a juridical nature. . . .

The legal situation therefore is that the Parties are under no obligation to apply either the 1958 Convention, which is not opposable to the Federal Republic, or the equidistance method as a mandatory rule of customary law, which it is not.

Evaluating the Three-step Process. How convincing was the Court's analysis of the ways in which customary international law might relate to Article 6(2) of the 1958 Continental Shelf Convention? The three-step process went: the Convention might (1) "embody" or codify the custom, (2) "crystallize" the custom, or (3) contribute to the subsequent development of the custom. Was the Court's rejection of possibility (3) as persuasive as its rejection of (1) and (2)? Looking at *North Sea*, Professor Schachter pointed out that a new treaty might not only itself contribute to the development of custom but might also generate complying practice that contributed to custom. Oscar Schachter,

"Entangled Treaty and Custom," in *International Law at a Time of Perplexity* 717, 723–29 (Yoram Dinstein ed. 1989).

The North Sea Cases: *Equity?* Having found no basis for an equidistance-special circumstances rule in the sources listed in Article 38(1) of its Statute, the ICJ turned to equity. As you read the excerpt below, ask how the Court justified its application of equity, and whether the Court's reasoning was persuasive.

The North Sea Continental Shelf Cases
The Recourse to Equity

But as between States faced with an issue concerning the lateral delimitation of adjacent continental shelves, there are still rules and principles of law to be applied; and in the present case it is not the fact either that rules are lacking, or that the situation is one for the unfettered appreciation of the Parties. Equally, it is not the case that if the equidistance principle is not a rule of law, there has to be as an alternative some other single equivalent rule.

[T]he essential reason why the equidistance method is not to be regarded as a rule of law is that, if it were to be compulsorily applied in all situations, this would not be consonant with certain basic legal notions which . . . have from the beginning reflected the *opinio juris* in the matter of delimitation; those principles being that delimitation must be the object of agreement between the States concerned, and that such agreement must be arrived at in accordance with equitable principles. On a foundation of very general precepts of justice and good faith, actual rules of law are here involved which govern the delimitation of adjacent continental shelves—that is to say, rules binding upon States for all delimitations;—in short, it is not a question of applying equity simply as a matter of abstract justice, but of applying a rule of law which itself requires the application of equitable principles, in accordance with the ideas which have always underlain the development of the legal régime of the continental shelf in this field, namely:

(*a*) the parties are under an obligation to enter into negotiations with a view to arriving at an agreement, and not merely to go through a formal process of negotiation as a sort of prior condition for the automatic application of a certain method of delimitation in the absence of agreement; they are under an obligation so to conduct themselves that the negotiations are meaningful, which will not be the case when either of them insists upon its own position without contemplating any modification of it;

(*b*) the parties are under an obligation to act in such a way that, in the particular case, and taking all the circumstances into account, equitable principles are applied,—for this purpose the equidistance method can be used, but other methods exist and may be employed, alone or in combination, according to the areas involved;

(c) ... the continental shelf of any State must be the natural prolongation of its land territory and must not encroach upon what is the natural prolongation of the territory of another State. ...

The Court comes next to the rule of equity. The legal basis of that rule in the particular case of the delimitation of the continental shelf as between adjoining States has already been stated. [However,] the rule rests also on a broader basis. Whatever the legal reasoning of a court of justice, its decisions must by definition be just, and therefore in that sense equitable. Nevertheless, when mention is made of a court dispensing justice or declaring the law, what is meant is that the decision finds its objective justification in considerations lying not outside but within the rules, and in this field it is precisely a rule of law that calls for the application of equitable principles. There is consequently no question in this case of any decision *ex aequo et bono*, such as would only be possible under the conditions prescribed by Article 38, paragraph 2, of the Court's Statute.

The Recourse to Equity in North Sea. Compare the source of equitable principles to the source of such principles in *Meuse. North Sea* showed no borrowing from municipal legal systems. Whence then came the equitable rule? Did it really emerge from customary international law, as the Court seemed to suggest by its reference to *opinio juris* in the excerpt above? Did the Court cite any evidence of state practice?

Note that the ICJ was asked to decide what "principles and rules of international law" were applicable to the delimitation of continental shelf between West Germany and Denmark, and between West Germany and the Netherlands. The parties could have asked the Court to decide the case *ex aequo et bono* pursuant to Article 38(2) of the ICJ Statute, but they did not. To use its Article 38(2) power, the ICJ must have the specific agreement of the parties to the case; in *North Sea* there was no such consent. Would the Court have had any extra power with an *ex aequo et bono* authorization? *North Sea*'s equity seems to be more like Article 38(2)'s *ex aequo et bono* than like Article 38(1)(c)'s general principles of law. But perhaps there is a third sort of equity, based neither on Article 38(2) nor on general principles *à la Meuse*, but instead on some residual, inherent judicial rule-making power.

A Hierarchy of Sources? Did the ICJ's ordering of the sources reflect a necessary hierarchy of the sources of international law, *i.e.*, do treaties necessarily "trump" custom and general principles, which in turn "trump" equity? Where would natural law or *jus cogens* fit into a hierarchy of sources? Although many international lawyers and judges rely heavily on treaties and customary international law today, it does not necessarily follow that they may not apply other sources, or that other sources do not sometimes provide a governing rule or principle.

The Content of Equitable Principles. What principles of equity did the Court use in *North Sea*? The Court concluded by considering that issue.

The North Sea Continental Shelf Cases
Equity in Context

[I]n certain geographical circumstances which are quite frequently met with, the equidistance method, despite its known advantages, leads unquestionably to inequity, in the following sense:

(*a*)   The slightest irregularity in a coastline is automatically magnified by the equidistance line as regards the consequences for the delimitation of the continental shelf. Thus it has been seen in the case of concave or convex coastlines that if the equidistance method is employed, then the greater the irregularity and the further from the coastline the area to be delimited, the more unreasonable are the results produced. So great an exaggeration of the consequences of a natural geographical feature must be remedied or compensated for as far as possible, being of itself creative of inequity.

(*b*)   In the case of the North Sea in particular, where there is no outer boundary to the continental shelf, it happens that the claims of several States converge, meet and intercross in localities where, despite their distance from the coast, the bed of the sea still unquestionably consists of continental shelf. A study of these convergences, as revealed by the maps, shows how inequitable would be the apparent simplification brought about by a delimitation which, ignoring such geographical circumstances, was based solely on the equidistance method. . . .

Equity does not necessarily imply equality. There can never be any question of completely refashioning nature, and equity does not require that a State without access to the sea should be allotted an area of continental shelf, any more than there could be a question of rendering the situation of a State with an extensive coastline similar to that of a State with a restricted coastline. Equality is to be reckoned within the same plane, and it is not such natural inequalities as these that equity could remedy. But in the present case there are three States whose North Sea coastlines are in fact comparable in length and which, therefore, have been given broadly equal treatment by nature except that the configuration of one of the coastlines would, if the equidistance method is used, deny to one of these

States treatment equal or comparable to that given the other two. Here indeed is a case where, in a theoretical situation of equality within the same order, an inequity is created. What is unacceptable in this instance is that a State should enjoy continental shelf rights considerably different from those of its neighbours merely because in the one case the coastline is roughly convex in form and in the other it is markedly concave, although those coastlines are comparable in length. It is therefore not a question of totally refashioning geography whatever the facts of the situation but, given a geographical situation of quasi-equality as between a number of States, of abating the effects of an incidental special feature from which an unjustifiable difference of treatment could result. . . .

The Court, by eleven votes to six, finds that, in each case,

(A) the use of the equidistance method of delimitation not being obligatory as between the Parties; and

(B) there being no other single method of delimitation the use of which is in all circumstances obligatory;

(C) the principles and rules of international law applicable to the delimitation as between the Parties of the areas of the continental shelf in the North Sea which appertain to each of them beyond the partial boundary determined by the agreements of 1 December 1964 and 9 June 1965, respectively, are as follows:

(1) delimitation is to be effected by agreement in accordance with equitable principles, and taking account of all the relevant circumstances, in such a way as to leave as much as possible to each Party all those parts of the continental shelf that constitute a natural prolongation of its land territory into and under the sea, without encroachment on the natural prolongation of the land territory of the other;

(2) if, in the application of the preceding sub-paragraph, the delimitation leaves to the Parties areas that overlap, these are to be divided between them in agreed proportions or, failing agreement, equally, unless they decide on a régime of joint jurisdiction, user, or exploitation for the zones of overlap or any part of them;

(D) in the course of the negotiations, the factors to be taken into account are to include:

(1) the general configuration of the coasts of the Parties, as well as the presence of any special or unusual features;

(2)   so far as known or readily ascertainable, the physical and geological structure, and natural resources, of the continental shelf areas involved;

(3)   the element of a reasonable degree of proportionality, which a delimitation carried out in accordance with equitable principles ought to bring about between the extent of the continental shelf areas appertaining to the coastal State and the length of its coast measured in the general direction of the coastline, account being taken for this purpose of the effects, actual or prospective, of any other continental shelf delimitations between adjacent States in the same region.

Evaluating the ICJ's Equitable Principles in North Sea. If it would be inequitable to give comparable coastlines different allotments of continental shelf, why was it equitable to deprive land-locked countries of all continental shelf belonging to their continent? Why was this a better kind of equity than one based on equidistance or on population, economic need, or use? In a subsequent maritime delimitation case, the ICJ observed: "Equity as a legal concept is a direct emanation of the idea of justice." Tunisia/Libya Continental Shelf Case, 1982 I.C.J. 18, 60. Does this observation simply beg the question how one determines the content of an equitable rule? Does the substance of the equitable principle in *North Sea* ultimately depend solely on judicial discretion? As it was said of English equity, does an equitable result depend only on the length of the Chancellor's foot?

Different Meanings of Equity. Note the use of equity in the Charter of Economic Rights and Duties of States considered by Professor Dupuy in the *Texaco/Libya Arbitration* in Part C. There are at least 12 references to equity in the Charter: "the development of international economic relations on a just and equitable basis," "a new system of international economic relations based on equity, sovereign equality, and interdependence of the interests of developed and developing countries," a "new international economic order, based on equity," "equitable benefits for all peace-loving states," "a just and equitable economic and social order," "more rational and equitable international economic relations," "mutual and equitable benefit" (twice), "remunerative and equitable prices," "equitable development of the world economy," "share equitably," and "stable, equitable and remunerative prices for primary products." What did these references to equity mean? In the Charter of Economic Rights and Duties, references to equity connoted an economic "sharing" or redistribution of wealth to developing countries from former colonial powers. Compare the use of "equity" in promoting the New

International Economic Order with the concept's use in international arbitral and judicial decisions like *Cayuga Indians*, *Meuse*, and *North Sea*.

The Gap Problem and Judicial Law-making. What were the perils if the ICJ simply came up empty handed in its search for an applicable rule? Was the Court willing to rule that international law provided no guidance for Germany, Denmark, and the Netherlands? Would such a finding of a *lacuna* or gap have fulfilled the expectations of the three countries when they entrusted the dispute to the Court? The parties, having decided to bring their dispute to the ICJ, probably expected that the Court would help surmount the roadblocks that blocked diplomatic negotiations. Had the Court, *Lotus*-like, found no guidance for the parties, then not only would the parties be disappointed, but the prestige of the Court could have diminished, with states becoming increasingly reluctant to submit cases to the ICJ.

Was it the expectation of the parties that the ICJ would make new international law? Professor Cassese wrote: "Whenever an international court or tribunal applies equity, it creates law between the parties in dispute." Antonio Cassese, *International Law* 155 (2001). Looking at the judicial reasoning in *Cayuga Indians*, *Meuse*, and *North Sea*, do you agree?

Article 38(1)(d) of the ICJ Statute. Once rendered, the *North Sea* judgment became part of the corpus of evidence of international law. Other courts deciding continental shelf cases could and did rely on *North Sea* as a subsidiary source of international law per Article 38(1)(d). The work of respected scholars also may, like judicial opinions, be used "as subsidiary means for the determination of rules of law" under Article 38(1)(d). Recall Justice Gray's reference in *Paquete Habana* (Part C above) to evidence of "the customs and usages of civilized nations" found by consulting "the works of jurists and commentators, who by years of labor, research and experience, have made themselves peculiarly well acquainted with the subjects of which they treat."

The Parties' Delimitation of the North Sea Continental Shelf. The *North Sea* judgment left it to Germany, Denmark, and the Netherlands to agree on the delimitation of the continental shelf taking into account the Court's statement of applicable equitable principles; the Court itself was not asked to draw maritime boundaries for the parties, as was true in some later cases. As shown in Figure 2.N, the parties eventually negotiated a division of the continental shelf that gave Germany more area than it would have had using just the equidistance method.

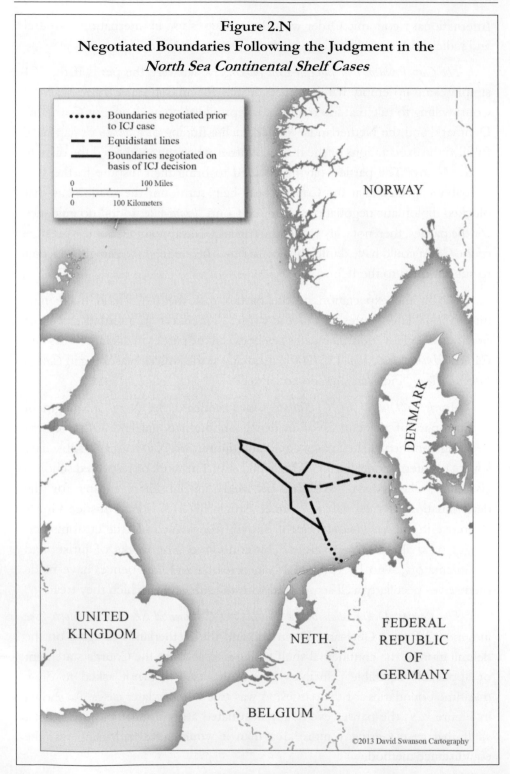

Figure 2.N
Negotiated Boundaries Following the Judgment in the
North Sea Continental Shelf Cases

CHAPTER 3

States and International Institutions

This chapter explores the role international law plays in international relations, especially in the relations between independent sovereign states. Since there is no universal sovereign to make or enforce international law, the responsibility for legislating and applying international law lies, in great measure, with no court, municipal or international, but with the principal subjects of that law, the sovereign states themselves. This is especially so with respect to the more or less constitutional and political rules of international relations, for example, those that set out the fundamental character and the rights and duties of states and international institutions, and those that strive to govern the use of force.

Part A introduces the principles of state sovereignty and explores the relationship of international law to the conduct of international relations. Part B considers how international law defines a "state" and a "government." Finally, Part C looks at the important roles international institutions, non-governmental organizations, and international regimes now play in international law and relations. We turn to international law and the use of force in Chapter 6.

A. SOVEREIGN STATES AND INTERNATIONAL LAW

Sovereignty and international law are at first sight antagonistic. The notion behind sovereignty is the proposition that a state ought to govern itself, free from outside interference. Underpinning international law is the idea that external rules should limit state behavior. In the real world, neither sovereignty nor international law could reign absolutely without vanquishing the other. A lesson of history seems to be that in practice, neither sovereignty nor international law ever completely wins out. Rather, a balance is struck between the two, an accommodation that makes up an essential aspect of the constitution of the international political system at any point in time.

To illuminate this accommodation, we move chronologically through six of the great theories about the interplay between sovereign states and international law. We start with Hobbes and Grotius, who in the 17th century helped set the intellectual framework for our modern international construct. We then turn to Vattel and Wheaton to catch sight of how the international constitutional framework worked and was perceived in the 18th and 19th centuries. Finally, we introduce Oppenheim, who captured an optimistic "scientific" image of international law and relations just before the cataclysm of 1914, and Morgenthau, who, in the light of the debacle of World War II, asked whether international law still played any role at all in the relations among sovereign states. A seventh explanatory theory, constructivism, is introduced in Part C when we explore international regimes. All these theories have carried weight with diplomats and jurists.

1. Hobbes and Grotius

MARK WESTON JANIS, INTERNATIONAL LAW

169–72 (6th ed. 2012)

In 1648, the Peace of Westphalia ushered in a new period of international relations for which new legal and moral principles were needed. These principles Thomas Hobbes' *Leviathan*, a celebration of the sovereign state, supplied. Hobbes [1588–1679] was an Oxford-educated classicist-turned-philosopher and one-time tutor to both the Earl of Devonshire and the young prince who became Charles II. Writing in 1651 in exile in Paris, he was a refugee from Cromwell and the English Civil War.

The medieval era, which the bloody Thirty Years War shattered, had been characterized by crisscrossing political, legal, religious, and moral allegiances. The ties of feudalism, of King and baron, of the Holy Roman Empire, of the Catholic Church, indeed of all the settled order of medieval Europe, bound men and women this way and that. That such ties could pull in contradictory ways is, for example, the lesson in Anouilh's *Becket*, the story of a medieval man tugged one way by his King and another by his Church. The conflicting allegiances of Europe had contributed to the terrible toll of confusion, death, and destruction from 1618 to 1648. In the mid-seventeenth century, many Europeans sought a simpler and, it was hoped, safer set of loyalties.

When in 1618 the Bohemians (today's Czechs) threw the despised agents of a despised Holy Roman Emperor from a window onto a dung heap, the defenestration of Prague signaled not only their scorn for the Emperor, not only the onset of a terrible religious war of Christian Europe, but also an assertion of Bohemian nationalism. The Bohemian claim was that a people of a certain language, society, and tradition had a right to choose their own religion and to govern themselves, free from the competing universalistic claims of Emperor and Pope. Though hotly disputed for three awful decades (some estimate that half of Germany died as a result of war, siege, starvation, pillage, and disease), similar sovereign assertions were embodied in the two peace treaties of Münster and Osnabrück. The Peace of Westphalia legitimated the right of sovereigns to govern their peoples free of outside interference, whether any such external claim to interfere was based on political, legal, or religious principles. The two 1648 peace treaties elaborated in great detail which sovereign ruled what. The Peace was a great property settlement for Europe, a quieting of title across the continent. It stilled many of the competitions for land and loyalty that had devastated much of what otherwise would have been the prizes of war.

What 1648 most significantly inaugurated (and what Thomas Hobbes most significantly conceptualized) was the organizing principle of the state, particularly the sovereign state. Sovereignty as a concept formed the cornerstone of the edifice of international relations that 1648 raised up. Sovereignty was the crucial element in the peace treaties of Westphalia, the international agreements that were intended to end a great war and to promote a coming peace. The treaties of Westphalia enthroned and sanctified sovereigns, gave them powers domestically and independence externally. But what exactly did "sovereignty" mean? How did being a "sovereign" work? Because Hobbes in 1651 provided answers to these questions raised so critically in 1648, *Leviathan* took on the lasting importance it did.

Hobbes crafted and fit a crucial puzzle piece into an emerging picture of the new Europe. Hobbes' lasting contribution was the envisioning, in his own words, of "that great Leviathan, or rather (to speak more reverently) of that Mortall God, to which we owe under the *Immortall God*, our peace and defence." Rather than believing in any number of loyalties, Hobbes believed that all men required "a Common Power, to keep them in awe, and to direct their actions to the Common Benefit." This Common Power, the Leviathan, required a single authoritarian state:

> The only way to erect such a Common Power, as may be able to defend them from the invasion of Forraigners, and the injuries of one another, and thereby to secure them in such sort, as that by their owne industrie, and by the fruites of the Earth, they may nourish themselves and live contentedly; is, to conferre all their power and strength upon

one Man, or upon one Assembly of men, that may reduce all their Wills, by plurality of voices, unto one Will: which is as much as to say, to appoint one Man, or Assembly of men, to beare their Person; and every one to owne, and acknowledge himselfe to be Author of whatsoever he that so beareth their Person, shall Act, or cause to be Acted, in those things which concerne the Common Peace and Safetie; and therein to submit their Wills, everyone to his Will, and their Judgments, to his Judgment.

This "Multitude so united in one Person, is called a Commonwealth in latine Civitas . . . that great Leviathan." The person, be it one man or an assembly, in whom is united the multitude, commonwealth, civitas, or leviathan "is called Soveraigne, and said to have soveraigne power; and everyone besides, his Subject."

Hobbes' celebration of the Leviathan, the sovereign state, provided a crucial bit of the ideological machinery necessary to operate the structure of world politics crafted at Westphalia. Given the long traditions of loyalty to Church as well as to King, to guild as well as to city, to baron as well as to empire, there needed to be some sort of solvent to dissolve these old ties and some sort of glue to fasten a new and simpler allegiance. Hobbes offered both solvent and glue, proffering the notion that the key actor on the world's stage was the sovereign state to which all loyalty was due internally and which was unrestrained externally.

So successful was the political settlement of Westphalia and so useful was Hobbes' concept of Leviathan and the sovereign state that they became deeply imbedded in the public consciousness. It is difficult now even to conceive that a world of sovereign states is an intellectual abstraction, a humanly devised creation, albeit one of tremendous force and utility for more than three centuries.

As Hobbes offered a plausible vision of a sovereign state at the right place at the right time, so Hugo Grotius was timely on the same scene with a workable theory of a law and order for inter-state relations. In 1625, 26 years before *Leviathan*, Grotius' *De Jure Belli ac Pacis* was published in the midst of terrible slaughter. That the excesses of the Thirty Years War motivated Grotius is plain from the book's Prologue:

Figure 3.A
Thomas Hobbes's *Leviathan*

I have had many and weighty reasons for undertaking to write upon this subject. Throughout the Christian world I observed a lack of restraint in relation to war, such as even barbarous races should be ashamed of; I observed that men rush to arms for slight causes, or no cause at all, and that when arms have once been taken up there is no longer any respect for law, divine or human; it is as if, in accordance with a general decree, frenzy had openly been let loose for the committing of all crimes.

Confronted with such utter ruthlessness, many men who are the very furthest from being bad men, have come to the point of forbidding all use of arms to the Christian, whose rule of conduct above everything else comprises the duty of loving all men. To this opinion sometimes John Ferus and my fellow countryman Erasmus seem to incline, men who have the utmost devotion to peace in both Church and State; but their purpose, as I take it, is, when things have gone in one direction, to force them in the opposite direction, as we are accustomed to do, that they may come back to a true middle ground. But the very effort of pressing too hard in the opposite direction is often so far from being helpful that it does harm, because in such arguments the detection of what is extreme is easy, and results in weakening the influence of other statements which are well within the bounds of truth. For both extremes therefore a remedy must be found that men may not believe either that nothing is allowable, or that everything is.

But was there any such remedy? Grotius [1583–1645] had not been by any means the first to write or to speculate about what would become modern international law.[9] The antecedents of the discipline—treaties, diplomacy, arbitration, laws of war—go back thousands of years. Grotius himself owed an intellectual debt to a number of sixteenth-century Spanish theologians—Vitoria, Suárez, and others—who sought to apply the Catholic Church's medieval theories of natural law to the new realities of international politics as they urged that the Spanish Crown deal justly with the natives that Spain had found and conquered in the Americas.

Some have argued that in light of the Spanish tradition, Grotius' truly distinctive contribution was that he "secularized" international law. Indeed, it is true that Grotius, unlike the Spaniards, presumed to write outside a single Christian denomination, seeking to fashion a law of nations that could appeal to and bind Catholics and various denominational Protestants alike. However, it is doubtful, given his times and his character, that Grotius meant to effect a strictly secular refashioning of the medieval Catholic natural law tradition. His approach was very different from a truly secular author like Machiavelli, who felt that princes ought to be fundamentally irreligious and faithfully unscrupulous. Machiavelli believed that Christianity was a less desirable religion for princes than

---

[9]   The actual term "international law" was only invented in 1789 by the English philosopher Jeremy Bentham in a flurry of new legal definitions. Janis, Jeremy Bentham and the Fashioning of "International Law," 78 *American Journal of International Law* 405 (1984).

were the pagan faiths of ancient times because Christianity placed "the supreme happiness in humility, lowliness, and a contempt for worldly objects." . . .

Grotius' ideas were quite different. His basic notion was that there was an authentic law of nations, which was based on the "mutual consent" of sovereigns acting in the context of a "great society of states." Though meant to be religiously neutral, Grotius' vision of the law of nations was not secular, but rather was a liberal Christian pronouncement. Theologically, Grotius [accepted the view that all] could receive God's grace if they believed in God's law. It was this liberal, more or less universalist, doctrine that ultimately led to Grotius' arrest and imprisonment when the Remonstrants were repressed by Prince Maurits and the Calvinist party in the Netherlands. When Grotius wrote *De Jure Belli ac Pacis*, he was in exile in France, as Hobbes would be 26 years later when Leviathan was published.

. . . Grotius believed that sovereigns not only made rules, but also were obliged to live with the rules one made, *pacta sunt servanda*. The covenants or contracts of sovereigns were legally and morally binding and not just Machiavellian temporary arrangements of mutual convenience. As men and women could bind themselves together in religious communities and to the law of God, so could sovereigns bind themselves to the law of nations. That there was anything transitory to or hypocritical in commitments made in the law of nations was a notion alien to Grotius. God and the law of nature obliged promisors to keep their promises and makers of contracts to honor their commitments. . . .

Compared to private contracts, treaties were a "more excellent kind of agreement" and, though made by the sovereign, binding on the whole of the people. Treaties were to be fulfilled and interpreted in good faith. Even between enemies, good faith, either expressed or implied, was the foundation for all promises.

That Grotius in particular and Protestants in general should put faith in law and covenant as means to moderate the cruelties attending the relations of states should come as no surprise. A respect for law runs deep in the Protestant tradition. . . .

Not only were the laws of nations legally and morally binding, but also they were rationally calculated to lead to the long-term advantage of sovereign states. Here, again, Grotius treated the sovereign state as a person and a reasonable person at that:

> [T]he national who in his own country obeys its laws is not foolish, even though, out of regard for that law, he may be obliged to forgo

certain things advantageous for himself, so that nation is not foolish which does not press its own advantage to the point of disregarding the laws common to nations. The reason in either case is the same. For just as the national, who violates the law of his country in order to obtain an immediate advantage, breaks down that by which the advantages of himself and his posterity are for all future time assured, so the state which transgresses the laws of nature and of nations cuts away also the bulwarks which safeguard its own future peace.

Grotius' argument was based on natural law in the sense that he believed that sovereign states, like individuals, naturally relied upon communities for their well-being. The pacts made within these communities needed to be respected for the benefit of all, even the greatest individual or state. "[L]aw is not founded on expedience alone, there is no state so powerful that it may not some time need the help of others outside itself, either for purposes of trade, or even to ward off the forces of many foreign nations united against it." "[N]o association of men can be maintained without law . . . surely also that association which binds together the human race, or binds many nations together, has need of law."

Grotius, a diplomat as well as a jurist, was no starry-eyed idealist. His approach to international law and order was quite different from the utopian proposals of the Abbé de Saint-Pierre who, almost a century later, would suggest a peace-keeping league of the principal European powers. Grotius acknowledged that war, as well as law, was a natural feature of human society. His belief was that war and law were inextricably intertwined:

> Least of all should that be admitted which some people imagine, that in war all laws are in abeyance. On the contrary war ought not to be undertaken except for the enforcement of rights; when once undertaken, it should be carried on only within the bounds of law and good faith. Demosthenes well said that war is directed against those who cannot be held in check by judicial processes. For judgements are efficacious against those who feel that they are too weak to resist; against those who are equally strong, or think they are, wars are undertaken. But in order that wars may be justified, they must be carried on with no less scrupulousness than judicial processes are wont to be.

Grotius' ideas, like those of Hobbes, emerged at a critical moment. To settle the Catholic-Protestant disputes underlying the Thirty Years War, the Treaties of Westphalia of 1648 acknowledged the sovereign authority of Europe's individual princes and nations in matters both religious and political. Not only the authority of the Emperor, but also the temporal jurisdiction of the Church, including its power to regulate and moderate wars, were much restricted in theory and practice. If international conflicts were to be controlled, the Emperor and the Church, through their edicts and regulations, could no longer be counted on as principal instruments of moderation. Rather, sovereign states would have to restrain themselves. Grotius' suggestion that the states could do so with a positive law of nations grounded on moral notions of covenant caught hold in the imagination of those conducting world affairs. Three centuries later, it holds on still.

The Concept of the State. How do we conceive of the state? Has the concept changed over time? Jean Bodin, a French philosopher, writing in 1576, conceptualized European political authority in terms of the unified control of monarchs. Bodin identified "markes of Soveraignetie" that concerned especially a monarch's internal authority. These "markes" included the rights, subject to "the Laws of God and nature," to make laws, name magistrates, hear final appeals, grant pardons, coin money, set weights and measures, impose taxes, wage war, and exact "liege fealtie and homage." See Jean Bodin, *The Six Bookes of a Commonweale* (1606 English trans. of *République,* Kenneth Douglas McRae ed. 1962). Compare Bodin's Sovereign with Hobbes's Leviathan.

Sovereignty and International Law. Look again at the 1648 Peace of Westphalia in Chapter 2. What measures of autonomy and authority did the Peace of Westphalia grant to states? How were states limited? How is state sovereignty consistent with the notion that international law regulates when and how a state may use force against another state? Does the acquiescence of each independent state in rules of international law concerning territorial integrity and protections for diplomats and citizens travelling abroad help establish and preserve the rights of every other state? May international law limit a sovereign state's freedom of action even with respect to its own internal affairs? Does international law restrict how a state may treat is own citizens within its own territory? Are such limits consistent with the concept of sovereignty? See the discussion of international human rights law in Chapter 7.

The Development of the State System in International Relations. Following the Peace of Westphalia, sovereign states with defined boundaries became the predominant form of political organization in Europe. Outside of Europe as well, states evolved from other forms of political relationships. In some regions, territorially bounded states are even more modern phenomena. Decolonization in the 20th century resulted in the creation of many new states. See the discussion of self-determination in Part B below.

Legal Rights and Duties of Sovereign States. What does it mean to say that a state is "sovereign"? How do we reconcile state sovereignty with the notion that states exercise rights and are subject to duties under international law? Is state sovereignty itself a product of international law? Is there one system of international law for all states? To explore these questions, we look at the work of Emer de Vattel (1714–1767), the influential 18th-century Swiss international law theorist, and Henry Wheaton (1785–1848), a 19th-century American lawyer and diplomat, who wrote the first English-language international law treatise. As early as the 1700s and the 1800s the international political system took on much of the form that it displays today. What might Vattel and Wheaton describe that does not ring true in the early 21st century?

2.   Vattel and Wheaton

E. DE VATTEL, THE LAW OF NATIONS
3–7, 11 (1758 ed., Charles G. Fenwick trans. 1916; reprinted 1964)

Nations or States are political bodies, societies of men who have united together and combined their forces, in order to procure their mutual welfare and security.

Such a society has its own affairs and interests; it deliberates and takes resolutions in common, and it thus becomes a moral person having an understanding and a will peculiar to itself, and susceptible at once of obligations and of rights.

[L]iberty and independence belong to man by his very nature, and . . . they can not be taken from him without his consent. Citizens of a State, having yielded them in part to the sovereign, do not enjoy them to their full and absolute extent. But the whole body of the Nation, the State, so long as it has not voluntarily submitted to other men or other Nations, remains absolutely free and independent.

As men are subject to the laws of nature, and as their union in civil society can not exempt them from the obligation of observing those laws, since in that union they remain none the less men, the whole Nation, whose common will is but the outcome of the united wills of the citizens, remains subject to the laws of nature and is bound to respect them in all its undertakings.

[W]hen men have agreed to act in common, and have given up their rights and submitted their will to the whole body as far as concerns their common good, it devolves thenceforth upon that body, the State, and upon its rulers, to fulfill the duties of humanity towards outsiders in all matters in which individuals are no longer at liberty to act, and it peculiarly rests with the State to fulfill these duties towards other States.

. . . Hence the end of the great society established by nature among all nations is likewise that of mutual assistance in order to perfect themselves and their condition.

The first general law, which is to be found in the very end of the society of Nations, is that each Nation should contribute as far as it can to the happiness and advancement of other Nations.

But as its duties towards itself clearly prevail over its duties towards others, a Nation owes to itself, as a prime consideration, whatever it can do for its own happiness and advancement. (I say whatever it *can* do, not meaning *physically* only, but *morally* also, what it can do lawfully, justly, and honestly.) . . .

Since Nations are free and independent of one another as men are by nature, the second general law of their society is that each Nation should be left to the peaceable enjoyment of that liberty which belongs to it by nature. The natural society of nations can not continue unless the rights which belong to each by nature are respected. . . .

Since men are by nature equal, and their individual rights and obligations the same, as coming equally from nature, Nations, which are composed of men and may be regarded as so many free persons living together in a state of nature, are by nature equal and hold from nature the same obligations and the same rights. Strength or weakness, in this case, counts for nothing. A dwarf is as much a man as a giant is; a small Republic is no less a sovereign State than the most powerful Kingdom.

From this equality it necessarily follows that what is lawful or unlawful for one Nation is equally lawful or unlawful for every other Nation. . . .

From the fact that [individuals form] a society in which they have common interests and must act in concert it is necessary that a public authority be set up, which shall regulate and prescribe the duties of each member with respect to the object of the association. This public authority constitutes the *sovereignty*; and he, or they, in whom it is vested is the *sovereign*. . . .

Every Nation which governs itself, under whatever form, and which does not depend on any other Nation, is a *sovereign State*. Its rights are, in the natural order, the same as those of every other State. Such is the character of the moral persons who live together in a society established by nature and subject to the Law of Nations. To give a Nation the right to a definite position in this great society, it need only be truly sovereign and independent; it must govern itself by its own authority and its own laws.

HENRY WHEATON, ELEMENTS OF INTERNATIONAL LAW

51, 43–45 (1st ed. 1836)

The subjects of international law are separate political societies of men living independently of each other, and especially those called Sovereign States.

A sovereign state is generally defined to be any nation or people, whatever may be the form of its internal constitution, which governs itself independently of foreign powers. . . .

If states are moral beings capable of contracting by direct and positive consent, and still more if their consent to consider each other as moral beings may be implied from the general acquiescence of mankind, they are equally capable of binding themselves by that tacit convention which is fairly to be implied from the approved usage and practice of nations, and their general acquiescence in certain positive rules for the regulation of their mutual intercourse. But it has been asserted that such an approved usage and general acquiescence can only spring up among nations of the same class or family, united by the ties of similar origin, manners, and religion. . . .

There is . . . no universal, immutable law of nations, binding upon the whole human race—which all mankind in all ages and countries, ancient and modern, savage and civilized, Christian and pagan, have recognised in theory or in practice, have professed to obey, or have in fact obeyed;—no law of nations similar to that right of reason of which Cicero speaks, "which is congenial to the feelings of nature, diffused among all men, uniform, eternal, commanding us to our duty and prohibiting every violation of it;—one eternal and immortal law, which can neither be repealed nor derogated from, addressing itself to all nations and all ages, deriving its authority from the common Sovereign of the universe, seeking no other lawgiver and interpreter, carrying home its sanctions to every breast by the inevitable punishment he inflicts on its transgressors." If there be any such universal law acknowledged by all nations, it must be that of reciprocity, of amicable or vindictive retaliation, as the case may require the application of either. The ordinary *jus gentium* is only a particular law, applicable to a distinct set or family of nations, varying at different times with the change in religion, manners, government, and other institutions, among every class of nations. Hence the international law of the civilized, Christian nations of Europe and America, is one thing; and that which governs the intercourse of the Mohammedan nations of the East with each other, and with Christians, is another and a very different thing.

The Equality of States. Vattel asserted that each state has the same legal rights as other states. In making this claim, was he drawing on some precept of natural law? The principle of juridical equality of states is enshrined in Article 4 of the Montevideo Convention, reproduced below, and in Article 2(1) of the United Nations Charter. According to Chief Justice Marshall of the U.S. Supreme Court, "No principle of general law is more universally acknowledged, than the perfect equality of nations." The Antelope, 23 U.S. (10 Wheat.) 66, 122 (1825). Does the equality principle simply mean that the weakness of a state provides no legal justification for violating its legal rights? Should this fundamental principle ever be varied? If so, when and why? For example, how well does the principle of equality of states fit with the legal power of the five permanent members at the U.N. Security Council to veto resolutions, an issue discussed in Part C below?

Civilized States? Recall from Chapter 2 that the ICJ Statute, echoing language in the 1920 Statute of the Permanent Court of International Justice, lists as a source of international law "general principles of law recognized by civilized nations." The "civilized" limitation is rarely invoked today. In the 19th and early 20th centuries, however, European international law doctrine generally considered that the "family of nations" was open only to European states and to those entities outside Europe that achieved a certain degree of civilization and of interaction with states that were already part of the "family." In the decades after the American Revolution, the United States was eager to demonstrate that it was part of that European "family of nations," but were Americans willing to include states that did not spring from European roots? How did Wheaton handle this question?

Vattel and Wheaton. Vattel was frequently cited in 18th- and 19th-century U.S. jurisprudence. Wheaton, writing in the early to mid 19th century, was also influential, both in America and abroad, where his work was translated into several languages. Compare the views of Vattel and Wheaton. How did their conceptions of sovereignty and international law differ? How did each of their views differ from those of Bodin, discussed above? From the views of Grotius and Hobbes?

Modern Challenges to State Sovereignty. The sovereign state has been criticized on many fronts. Some, for example, stressing the importance of economics in the modern world, see states as imposing artificial boundaries that impede the efficient operation of markets. Others argue that states may be either too large or too small to respond well to current challenges; management problems may require structures larger than the state, while entities smaller than the state may more effectively produce political legitimacy. In light of such criticisms of the state, what justifies its continuing central role in international law? Do states retain legitimate authority today only insofar as they act as "trustees for the people committed to their care," operating to further a "peaceful and ordered world"? Jeremy Waldron, "The Rule of International Law," 30 *Harvard Journal of Law and Public Policy* 15, 24 (2006).

Should international law adopt a functional view of authority, under which the state competes as just one of several actors in efforts to regulate international activities?

3. Oppenheim

Lassa Oppenheim (1858–1919) wrote just before World War I, the so-called Great War. It was the period of the greatest general optimism about the role of international law, an optimism that Oppenheim reflected. Born and educated in Germany, Oppenheim moved to England in 1895, and taught and wrote mostly at Cambridge. His textbook on international law had a first edition in 1905 and, through subsequent editions (later edited by others), became the principal English-language international law treatise of the early and middle 20th century. Oppenheim is often held out as a prime example of the modern legal positivist school of international law. As you will see, Oppenheim tried to make international law a hard science. Ask how well he succeeded.

MARK WESTON JANIS, AMERICA AND THE LAW OF NATIONS 1776–1939
126–30 (2010)

Oppenheim, having moved to England, penned the international law treatise that, through a number of editions, came to dominate the English-speaking world for most of the twentieth century. Oppenheim became to the twentieth century, what Grotius was to the seventeenth century, Vattel to the eighteenth and Wheaton to the nineteenth: the definitive commentator on international law with whom one had to reckon whether to revere or revile. . . .

It was Oppenheim . . . who most captured turn-of-the-century imagination. In the preface to his first edition published in 1905, Oppenheim . . . put himself on record as accepting the challenge of a positivistic subject: "I have tried to the best of my power to build my system and my doctrines on a thorough jurisprudential, which is equivalent to a positive, basis. My definitions are as sharp as possible." Typically, Oppenheim made a positivist presumption about the distinction between morality and law, a presumption he based on the means of enforcement: "A rule is a rule of morality, if by common consent of the community it applies to conscience and to conscience only; whereas, on the other hand, a rule is a rule of law, if by common consent of the community it shall eventually be enforced by external power." . . . Following Wheaton, Oppenheim submitted that international law, too, was real law. However, rather than relying, as had Wheaton, on the Christian community of nations for efficacy, Oppenheim thought that the enforcement of international law depended upon self-help: "Self-help and the help of the other states which sympathize with the wronged one are the means by which the rules of the Law of Nations can be and actually are enforced." . . .

In a revealing article, "The Science of International Law: Its Task and Method," published in 1908, in the second volume of the *American Journal of International Law*, Oppenheim . . . never defined the "science" of international law. Instead, he seemed to presume that what his article described was indeed the science of the subject. . . . As a science, international law is not "an end in itself," but rather "merely a means to certain ends: [P]rimarily, peace among the nations and the governance of their intercourse by what makes for order and is right and just; secondarily, the peaceable settlement of international disputes; lastly the establishment of legal rules for the conduct of war and for the relations between belligerents and neutrals. . . .

Oppenheim devoted much of the article to an exposition of what he viewed as the seven "tasks to which our science must devote itself." These were the "exposition of the existing rules of law," "historical research," "criticism of the existing law," "preparation of codification," "distinction between the old customary and the new conventional law," "fostering of arbitration," and "popularization of international law."

Oppenheim was ready to "exclude the law of nature and what is called 'natural' international law" to embrace " 'real' international law," i.e. "the method to be applied by the science of international law . . . no other than the positive method."

4. Morgenthau

Like Oppenheim, Hans Morgenthau (1904–1980) was born and educated in Germany. Also like Oppenheim, Morgenthau emigrated to an English-speaking country where he worked for most of his professional life. Trained as an international lawyer in Germany, Morgenthau became disillusioned with the discipline when faced with Nazi international lawlessness and atrocities in his native land. Emigrating to the United States in 1937, he turned to the new discipline of international politics. Morgenthau taught principally at the University of Chicago, and wrote what became a classic text on the new subject: *Politics Among Nations: The Struggle for Power and Peace*. In this work, Morgenthau penned an influential critique of international law. First published in 1948, *Politics Among Nations* appeared in four more editions by Morgenthau himself in 1954, 1960, 1967, and 1973; with new editors, sixth and seventh editions were added in 1985 and 2005. To introduce Morgenthau's perspective on international law, we employ his third edition of 1960, published in the midst of the dangerous Cold War (1945–1989) between the United Sates and the Soviet Union.

Morgenthau's View of International Relations and International Law. Morgenthau's first chapter, "A Realist Theory of International Politics," has been widely understood to be a depiction of the "realist" school of international politics, set out as an alternative to the "utopian" or "idealist" school of the discipline. Morgenthau enunciated six principles of political realism, a theory for all politics, not only international politics. The first principle is that "[p]olitical realism believes that politics, like society in general is governed by objective laws that have their root in human nature." Second, the "main signpost that helps political realism to find its way through the landscape of international politics is the concept of interest defined in terms of power." The remaining four principles explain that interest and power have no fixed meanings. A nation's moral aspirations do not reflect universal values, and it is the duty of statesmen to try to align their policies with their nation's real interests.

How, if at all, does international law fit into Morgenthau's realist perspective? This answer comes in Part Six, "Limitations of National Power: International Law," in the heart of the book. Sharing earlier historical views, including those of Grotius, Wheaton, and Oppenheim, Morgenthau wrote that the "modern system of international law is the result of the great political transformation that marked the transition from the Middle Ages to the modern period of history [i.e.,] the transformation of the feudal system into the territorial state." In the new international political system, monarchs no longer shared legal authority with either feudal lords or the Church, but became "legally speaking, completely independent of each other." In "one word, they were sovereign." To attain "a certain measure of peace and order," there had to be a "core of rules of international law." It was Grotius who set forth the basic model of international law in the 17th century. The 18th, 19th, and 20th centuries "built an imposing edifice, consisting of thousands of treaties, hundreds of decisions of international tribunals, and innumerable decisions of domestic courts."

So, "international law exists," but because it is based on a decentralized system of international politics, it is not particularly effective. It is a primitive law. Domestic law may be created and enforced by the state, but international law is merely "the result of objective social forces." "In the international field, it is the subjects of the law themselves that not only legislate for themselves but are also the supreme authority for interpreting and giving concrete meaning to their own legislative enactments." The consequences of decentralization are extreme. Morgenthau put international law at the lowest rung of law enforcement: "There can be no more primitive and no weaker system of law enforcement than this; for it delivers the enforcement of the law to the vicissitudes of the distribution of power between the violator of the law and the victim of the violation."

Fundamentally, Morgenthau believed that international law does have a role to play in modern international relations, but it is a very limited role. When there is an attempt to centralize either the legislative, judicial, or executive functions of international law, "the decentralized character of international law . . . reasserts itself." The "essence of international law is decentralization." The reality, according to Morgenthau, is that state sovereignty makes decentralization inevitable, leaving international law a very weak kind of law.

The Scientific and Realist Schools. How similar are the scientific school of Oppenheim and the realist school of Morgenthau? Note that both claim to be good at enunciating, not the soft aspirations of dreamers, but the hard realities of the world. Both are critical of utopian views. What in Grotius, Vattel, or Wheaton would be especially utopian? Are Oppenheim and Morgenthau attacking an idealistic strawman of international law who does not actually personify the theorists of the 17th, 18th, and 19th centuries? Was Morgenthau a frustrated idealist? Might he, as a young scholar, have expected too much of international law? Note that Grotius, like Morgenthau, had to personally deal with mass slaughter in Europe, the Thirty Years War. Contrast the path each took in reaction to extreme international savagery.

Kennan's Critique of American Legalism-Moralism. Perhaps it should come as no surprise that another famous critique of international law was delivered in a series of lectures in 1951 at Morgenthau's University of Chicago. The distinguished U.S. diplomat and historian George Kennan (1904–2005) attacked what he called "the legalist-moralistic approach to international problems" as "the most serious fault of American foreign policy." George Kennan, *American Diplomacy 1900–1950*, at 82 (1951). Kennan argued that legal rules cannot realistically "suppress the chaotic and dangerous aspirations of governments in the international field." Morality, Kennan felt, makes matters worse because carrying "over into the affairs of state . . . concepts of right and wrong" makes one "indignant," making war more dreadful. *Id.* at 86–87. Was Kennan even more dismissive of international law than Morgenthau, who at least acknowledged that both law and morality play a useful, if limited, role in world politics?

The Judicial Core of International Law. Although international law may fail Kennan's realist critique, realists (though probably not Morgenthau) often forget that international law has a definite judicial hard core. In both domestic and international litigation, international law is taken seriously. In fields as diverse as the international economy and human rights, practicing lawyers and judges in national and international courts and tribunals turn to international legal rules to decide real cases. Look, for example, at the next part.

International Regimes and Other Subjects of International Law. As you read the materials in the rest of this book, consider whether Morgenthau's views accurately describe the modern world. Do states remain the central actors in the international legal system? Is international law a "decentralized system"? Does Morgenthau's theory accommodate the "international personality" of international organizations and of individuals, the roles of international courts and tribunals, and the impact of numerous treaty-based international regimes?

B. DEFINING STATES AND GOVERNMENTS

Remarkably enough, it is sometimes not so clear just what is a "state" or a "government." Does a state's existence depend on recognition by other states, or is it a matter of objective fact? What are the legal consequences when states break apart or merge? Changes in the governments of states are even more common than changes in states. When should a new government be recognized as having international legal rights and duties? Here is the Montevideo Convention, providing a classic definition of the "state."

THE MONTEVIDEO CONVENTION

Convention on Rights and Duties of States, Dec. 26, 1933, 49 Stat. 3097, 165 L.N.T.S. 19

Article 1

The state as a person of international law should possess the following qualifications: *a)* a permanent population; *b)* a defined territory; *c)* government; and *d)* capacity to enter into relations with the other states.

Article 2

The federal state shall constitute a sole person in the eyes of international law.

Article 3

The political existence of the state is independent of recognition by the other states. Even before recognition the state has the right to defend its integrity and independence, to provide for its conservation and prosperity, and consequently to organize itself as it sees fit, to legislate upon its interests, administer its services, and to define the jurisdiction and competence of its courts.

The exercise of these rights has no other limitation than the exercise of the rights of other states according to international law.

Article 4

States are juridically equal, enjoy the same rights, and have equal capacity in their exercise. The rights of each one do not depend upon the power which it possesses to assure its exercise, but upon the simple fact of its existence as a person under international law.

Article 5

The fundamental rights of states are not susceptible of being affected in any manner whatsoever.

Article 6

The recognition of a state merely signifies that the state which recognizes it accepts the personality of the other with all the rights and duties determined by international law. Recognition is unconditional and irrevocable.

Article 7

The recognition of a state may be express or tacit. The latter results from any act which implies the intention of recognizing the new state.

Article 8

No state has the right to intervene in the internal or external affairs of another.

> *The Montevideo Convention.* The years after World War I saw a growth in multilateral codification promoting broad principles of interstate relations. Recall the Kellogg-Briand Pact in Chapter 2. The Montevideo Convention was adopted in 1933 at the 7th International Conference of American States. The Convention reflected Latin American concerns with the intervention of major powers in their internal and external affairs. In a similar vein, the 1930 "Estrada Doctrine," proclaimed by Mexico's Secretary of Foreign Relations, provided that Mexico would end the "insulting practice" of recognizing new governments:
>
> > [I]n addition to the fact that it offends the sovereignty of other nations, [this practice] implies that judgment of some sort may be passed upon the internal affairs of those nations by other governments, inasmuch as the latter assume, in effect, an attitude of criticism, when they decide, favorably or unfavorably, as to the legal qualifications of foreign régimes.
>
> 2 Marjorie Whiteman, *Digest of International Law* 85 (1963). The United States and 15 Latin American states accepted the Montevideo Convention.
>
> *The Constitutive and Declaratory Theories of Recognition.* The Montevideo Convention rejects the view that recognition by already-existing states was necessary in order to "constitute" a new state. Such a constitutive theory was the preference of Oppenheim, writing in the early 20th century: "a new State before its recognition cannot claim any right which a member of the Family of Nations has towards other members. . . . Through recognition only and exclusively a State becomes an International Person and a subject of International Law." 1 Lassa Oppenheim, *International Law* § 71 (1905). What difficulties does the constitutive theory of recognition create? Would the view that recognition is "constitutive" of statehood mean, for example, that international law rules forbidding transborder use of force do not apply to invasions of unrecognized "states"? How many, or what categories of, existing states need to recognize an entity before it legally becomes a state?
>
> An alternative to the constitutive view is the "declaratory" theory of statehood, the position reflected in Articles 3 and 6 of the Montevideo Convention. But who then determines whether an entity is a state? Do existing states owe a legal duty to recognize an entity that has attained the objective

characteristics of a state? There are also constitutive and declaratory theories about the recognition of governments. See the *Tinoco Arbitration* below.

States and Admission to the United Nations. Is admission to the United Nations an indication of statehood? Might U.N. admission be an example of "collective recognition"? "States" cannot unilaterally accede to the U.N. Charter. According to Article 4 of the U.N. Charter, "peace-loving states" that accept the Charter's obligations and "are able and willing to carry out" those obligations may be admitted by action of the U.N. Security Council and General Assembly. Virtually every state belongs to the United Nations, which as of May 2017 had 193 members. Does U.N. membership assure statehood status? Were the Byelorussian S.S.R. and the Ukrainian S.S.R.—Union Republics in the Soviet Union that were among the 51 original members of the United Nations—really states in the international sense? Does nonmembership in the United Nations necessarily mean that an entity is not a state? Somewhat surprisingly, Switzerland did not join the United Nations until 2002. Is Sealand in the next case really or legally a "state," even though not a member of the United Nations?

IN RE DUCHY OF SEALAND

Case No. 9 K 2565/77 (Federal Republic of Germany,
Administrative Court of Cologne, 1978), 80 *International Law Reports* 683

The Facts

On 14 November 1975 the plaintiff, a German citizen by birth, received a document issued on 26 August 1975 which granted him citizenship of the so-called "Duchy of Sealand." The "Duchy" is a former British anti-aircraft platform situated approximately eight nautical miles off the southern coast of Great Britain. After the end of the Second World War the British abandoned this platform. It constitutes a small island which is situated outside the British three-mile zone. In 1967 a British Major, R.B., occupied the former anti-aircraft platform and proclaimed the "Duchy of Sealand." This "Duchy" is connected to the sea-bed by strong concrete pillars and has a surface area of approximately 1300 square metres. At present 106 persons possess the so-called "citizenship of Sealand." In 1975 R.B. issued a constitution for the former anti-aircraft platform, designating himself as "Roy of Sealand." The plaintiff holds the post of "Foreign Secretary" and "Chairman of the Council of State" of the "Duchy."

On 2 August 1976 the plaintiff [applied] to the defendant for the determination of his citizenship. After the defendant had established the date on which the plaintiff had been issued with the so-called "naturalization document" by the "Duchy of Sealand," the plaintiff was notified that he had not lost his German citizenship because the "Duchy of Sealand" did not constitute a State within the meaning of international law. . . .

The plaintiff instituted proceedings challenging the decision on the basis that the "Duchy of Sealand" was an independent State. . . .

The island was permanently inhabited by between thirty and forty persons who were responsible for the defence of the miniature island and the maintenance of the community. Furthermore, he contended, his island was on the verge of being recognized as a State by Ceylon, Paraguay and Cyprus. The plaintiff seeks a declaration that he has lost his German citizenship as a result of his acquisition of the citizenship of the so-called "Duchy of Sealand" from 14 November 1975.

New "States" at Sea. Sealand is only one of several would-be states situated outside the territorial sea, a narrow band of the oceans over which a coastal state exercises sovereignty. Other statehood candidates have included the Grand Capri Republic and Atlantis, Isle of Gold, off the Florida coast; the Republic of Minerva, planned for coral reefs in the Pacific Ocean; and the short-lived Republic of Rose Island in the Adriatic Sea.

In re Duchy of Sealand
The Law

The plaintiff's action for a declaration . . . is unfounded. . . .

According to [German law] a German who is neither domiciled nor permanently resident within the country loses his citizenship if he acquires a foreign citizenship, if the acquisition of the new citizenship is at his own request. . . . Although, since 28 October 1975, [the plaintiff] has been neither domiciled nor permanently resident in the Federal Republic of Germany, nevertheless he has not lost his German citizenship since he has not acquired any foreign citizenship.

Since the so-called "Duchy of Sealand" does not constitute a State within the meaning of international law, the plaintiff did not acquire foreign nationality when he was issued with a document by the "Duchy of Sealand" on 14 November 1975.

International law lays down three essential attributes for Statehood. The State must have a territory, that territory must be inhabited by a people and that people must be subject to the authority of a Government.

The "Duchy of Sealand" fails to satisfy even the first condition as it does not possess a State territory within the meaning of international law.

The former anti-aircraft platform is not situated on any fixed point of the surface of the earth. Rather, the miniature island has been constructed on concrete pillars.

. . . State territory within the meaning of international law must be either "mother earth" or something standing directly thereon. . . .

In addition to the lack of State territory, the so-called "Duchy" also lacks a State people within the meaning of international law. At present the "Duchy" has 106 "citizens." [T]he size of a people is irrelevant to the question of whether or not it constitutes a State. Nevertheless, in the case of the "Duchy of Sealand" it cannot be accepted that there is a "people" within the meaning of international law since the life of a community is lacking.

The State, as an amalgamation of many individuals, complements the family . . . and has the duty to promote community life. This duty does not merely consist of the promotion of a loose association aimed at the furtherance of common hobbies and interests. Rather it must be aimed at the maintenance of an essentially permanent form of communal life in the sense of sharing a common destiny.

The so called "nationals" of the "Duchy of Sealand" do not satisfy these criteria for community life. Apart from the 30 to 40 persons permanently living on the platform, who are responsible for its defence and the maintenance of its installations, the presence of the other so-called "nationals" is limited to occasional visits. The territorial extent of the "Duchy" of merely 1300 square metres does not satisfy the requirements for the permanent residence of all its "nationals." Even if the plans of "Roy of Sealand" to extend the size of the platform to approximately 13,000 square metres were to come to fruition, there would still not be suitable living space for all "nationals." The life of the State is not limited to the provision of casinos and places of entertainment. Rather a State community must play a more decisive role in serving the other vital human needs of people from their birth to their death. These needs include education and professional training, assistance in all the eventualities of life and the provision of subsistence allowances where necessary. The so-called "Duchy of Sealand" fails to satisfy any of these requirements.

[T]he "nationals" of the "Duchy" . . . have not acquired their "nationality" in order to live with one another and handle all aspects of their lives on a collective basis, but on the contrary they continue to pursue their individual interests outside the "Duchy." The common purpose of their association is limited to a small part of their lives, namely their commercial and tax affairs. This degree of common interest cannot be regarded as sufficient for the recognition of a "people" within the meaning of international law.

Figure 3.B
Sealand

When is a "State" a State? Does Sealand meet the criteria of the Montevideo Convention? Must Sealand's inhabitable territory be a part of the surface of the earth rather than connected to that surface by pillars at sea? Must a state have any defined territory at all? Should Sealand's small population preclude it from being a state? The Republic of Nauru, an eight-square-mile South Pacific island with a population of approximately 9,600 (as of 2016), joined the United Nations in 1999. When might Germany be bound at international law to recognize a foreign nationality? See the discussion of "genuine link" in the *Nottebohm Case* in Chapter 7.

The Variety of States. Is it possible to definitely determine the number and identity of countries in the world? What makes statehood problematic in the following situations?

a.   *Dependent "States."* International law historically regarded some states as not fully independent. These dependent states, although often maintaining some independent relations with third states, were largely under the control of one "protecting power" or "suzerain." The precise status of dependent states varied. According to the Permanent Court of International Justice, "[t]he extent of the powers of a protecting state . . . depends, first, upon the treaties between the protecting state and the protected state establishing the protectorate, and, secondly, upon the conditions under which the protectorate has been recognized by third powers[.]" Nationality Decrees in Tunis and Morocco, 1923 P.C.I.J. Ser. B, at 4, 27. Today, some states or entities have elected to rely on more powerful countries to conduct their foreign relations. The Principality of Liechtenstein (62 square miles; population 37,900), which was admitted to the United Nations in 1990, has delegated to Switzerland much responsibility for its defense, customs affairs, and diplomatic relations with other states.

b.   *Subjugated "States."* Approximately 200,000 Navajos live within a large, clearly bounded territory in the southwestern United States. In 1849, the Navajos acknowledged that the tribe "was lawfully placed under the exclusive jurisdiction and protection" of the United States. The Navajo Nation has its own constitution, however, and exercises domestic self-governance within boundaries set by an 1868 treaty. Is the Navajo nation a state? Estonia became independent in 1918, but was overrun and annexed by the Soviet Union in 1940, and only regained its independence in 1991. Was Estonia a state between 1940 and 1991?

c.   *"Failed States."* In 1991, Somalia's central government collapsed, contributing to widespread pillage and fighting among rival clans. In 1992, the United States and other countries sent troops to Somalia. These forces were deployed, pursuant to U.N. Security Council Resolution 794, to provide humanitarian relief to displaced persons, to help restore peace and stability, and to act with "a view to facilitating the process of a political settlement under the auspices of the United Nations." Efforts to negotiate an end to this civil war proved unavailing, and the involvement of the United Nations and other non-Somali entities in efforts to rebuild Somalia has been controversial. Somalia continues to be plagued by violence, and clan militias control various regions of Somalia. Does the situation in Somalia over the last quarter century suggest the extinction of that state, or rather "merely" a crisis of government?

d.   *States in Economic and Strategic Unions.* The best-known example of a functioning, highly integrated economic union of states is the European Union, but numerous other looser unions also exist. For instance, the Commonwealth of Independent States (C.I.S.) was formed in 1991 when the Soviet Union disintegrated. Armenia, Azerbaijan, Belarus, Kazakhstan, Kyrgystan, Moldova, the Russian Federation, Tajikistan, and Uzbekistan are full C.I.S. member states; Georgia, an original member, withdrew from the C.I.S. in 2008 following Russia's invasion of the South Ossetia region of Georgia. The C.I.S.

contemplates unified command of strategic military forces, joint control over nuclear weapons, joint decisions on military training and the use of peacekeeping forces, and an economic union. Is the C.I.S. to any degree "sovereign"?

e.   *Federal States*. Australia, Brazil, Canada, Germany, India, the Russian Federation, Switzerland, and the United States are all examples of federal states. May the components of a federal state themselves be deemed "states" under international law? What is the position of the United States? See Chapter 5.

f.   *Palestine and the Holy See*. Palestine, or the Palestinian Territories, adjoin Israel and comprise the Gaza Strip and the West Bank. See the *Wall Case* in Chapter 4. Is Palestine a state? What is the significance of the October 2011 resolution by the United Nations Educational, Scientific and Cultural Organization, one of the specialized agencies of the United Nations, to admit Palestine as a member state? 51 *International Legal Materials* 610 (2012). In November 2012, the U.N. General Assembly also accorded Palestine the status of a non-member observer state (replacing its former status as an observer "entity"); the vote was 138 to 9, with 41 states abstaining. Palestine has not, however, been admitted as a member state of the United Nations. May Palestine now become a party to treaties?

The Holy See refers to the seat of Saint Peter, occupied by successive Popes of the Roman Catholic Church. The Holy See is located territorially in the Vatican City, an entity of about 100 acres created by a 1929 treaty between Italy and the Holy See. The Holy See is not solely a religious entity. It maintains diplomatic relations with almost all states, has permanent observer status at the United Nations, and is a full member of several other international organizations. Even if Palestine and the Holy See are not states, do they possess "international personality"? See the *Reparation Case* in Part C below.

Succession of States and Governments. When new states emerge after an older state disintegrates, as was true for the Austrian and Ottoman Empires after World War I, and more recently for the Soviet Union and Yugoslavia, or when a new government takes control of a state following a revolution, a range of difficult legal questions arise. What happens to the former regime's treaties, contracts, property, and memberships in international organizations?

The next two cases focus on succession to contracts and property rights. Pay close attention to the significance or not of recognition.

THE TINOCO ARBITRATION

Aguilar-Amory and Royal Bank of Canada claims. Great Britain *versus* Costa Rica. Washington, October 18, 1923, Opinion and Award of William H. Taft, Sole Arbitrator, Washington, D.C., 1 *Reports of International Arbitral Awards* 369 (2006)

The Facts

This is a proceeding under a treaty of arbitration between Great Britain and Costa Rica. . . .

In January, 1917, the Government of Costa Rica, under President Alfredo Gonzalez, was overthrown by Frederico Tinoco, the Secretary of War. Gonzalez fled. Tinoco assumed power, called an election, and established a new constitution in June, 1917. His government continued until August, 1919, when Tinoco retired, and left the country. His government fell in September following. [T]he old constitution was restored and elections held under it. The restored government is a signatory to this treaty of arbitration.

On the 22nd of August, 1922, the Constitutional Congress of the restored Costa Rican Government passed a law known as Law of Nullities No. 41. It invalidated all contracts between the executive power and private persons, made with or without approval of the legislative power . . . covering the period of the Tinoco government. It also nullified the legislative decree No. 12 of the Tinoco government, dated June 28, 1919, authorizing the issue of the 15 million colones currency notes. The colon is a Costa Rican gold coin or standard nominally equal to 46 1/12 cents of an American dollar, but it is uncoined and the exchange value of the paper colon actually in circulation is much less. The Nullities Law also invalidated the legislative decree of the Tinoco government of July 8, 1919, authorizing the circulation of notes of the nomination of 1000 colones, and annulled all transactions with such colones bills between holders and the state, directly or indirectly, by means of negotiation or contract, if thereby the holders received value as if they were ordinary bills of current issue.

The claim of Great Britain is that the Royal Bank of Canada and the Central Costa Rica Petroleum Company are British corporations whose shares are owned by British subjects; that the Banco Internacional of Costa Rica and the Government of Costa Rica are both indebted to the Royal Bank in the sum of 998,000 colones, evidenced by 998 one thousand colones bills held by the Bank; that the Central Costa Rica Petroleum Company owns, by due assignment, a grant by the Tinoco government in 1918 of the right to explore for and exploit oil deposits in Costa Rica, and that both the indebtedness and the concession have been annulled without right by the Law of Nullities and should be excepted from its operation. She asks an award that she is entitled on behalf of her subjects to have the claim of the bank paid, and the concession recognized and given effect by the Costa Rican Government.

The Government of Costa Rica denies its liability for the acts or obligations of the Tinoco government and maintains that the Law of Nullities was a legitimate exercise of its legislative governing power. It further denies the validity of such claims on the merits, unaffected by the Law of Nullities.

The Arbitrator. William Howard Taft, the sole arbitrator in the *Tinoco Case*, was President of the United States (1909–1913) and Chief Justice of the U.S. Supreme Court (1921–1930). As President, he, along with other leading public figures, supported treaties of general arbitration, applicable even to questions of "vital interests" and "national honor." Taft was a charter member of the American Society of International Law and the Honorary President of the American Branch of the International Law Association. See John E. Noyes, "William Howard Taft and the Taft Arbitration Treaties," 106 *Villanova Law Review* 535 (2011).

The Tinoco Arbitration
The Law

Coming now to the general issues applicable to both claims, Great Britain contends, first, that the Tinoco government was the only government of Costa Rica *de facto* and *de jure* for two years and nine months; that during that time there is no other government disputing its sovereignty, that it was in peaceful administration of the whole country, with the acquiescence of its people.

Second, that the succeeding government could not by legislative decree avoid responsibility for acts of that government affecting British subjects, or appropriate or confiscate rights and property by that government except in violation of international law; that the act of Nullities is as to British interests, therefore itself a nullity, and is to be disregarded, with the consequence that the contracts validly made with the Tinoco government must be performed by the present Costa Rican Government, and that the property which has been invaded or the rights nullified must be restored.

To these contentions the Costa Rican Government answers: First, that the Tinoco government was not a *de facto* or *de jure* government according to the rules of international law. This raises an issue of fact.

Second, that the contracts and obligations of the Tinoco government, set up by Great Britain on behalf of its subjects, are void, and do not create a legal obligation, because the government of Tinoco and its acts were in violation of the constitution of Costa Rica of 1871.

Third, that Great Britain is stopped by the fact that it did not recognize the Tinoco government during its incumbency, to claim on behalf of its subjects that Tinoco's was a government which could confer rights binding on its successor. . . .

Dr. John Bassett Moore, now a member of the Permanent Court of International Justice, in his *Digest of International Law,* Volume I, p. 249, announces the general principle which has had such universal acquiescence as to become well settled international law:

> Changes in the government or the international policy of a state do not as a rule affect its position in international law. A monarchy may be transformed into a republic or a republic into a monarchy; absolute principles may be substituted for constitutional, or the reverse; but though the government changes, the nation remains, with rights and obligations unimpaired. . . .

> The principle of the continuity of states has important results. The state is bound by engagements entered into by governments that have ceased to exist; the restored government is generally liable for the acts of the usurper.

First, what are the facts to be gathered from the documents and evidence submitted by the two parties as to the *de facto* character of the Tinoco government?

In January, 1917, Frederico A. Tinoco was Secretary of War under Alfredo Gonzalez, the then President of Costa Rica. On the ground that Gonzalez was seeking reelection as President in violation of a constitutional limitation, Tinoco used the army and navy to seize the government, assume the provisional headship of the Republic and become Commander-in-Chief of the army. Gonzalez took refuge in the American Legation, thence escaping to the United States. Tinoco constituted a provisional government at once and summoned the people to an election for deputies to a constituent assembly on the first of May, 1917. At the same time he directed an election to take place for the Presidency and himself became a candidate. An election was held. Some 61,000 votes were cast for Tinoco and 259 for another candidate. Tinoco then was inaugurated as the President to administer his powers under the former constitution until the creation of a new one. A new constitution was adopted June 8, 1917, supplanting the constitution of 1871. For a full two years Tinoco and the legislative assembly under him peaceably administered the affairs of the Government of Costa Rica, and there was no disorder of a revolutionary character during that interval. No other government of any kind asserted power in the country. The courts sat, Congress legislated, and the government was duly administered. Its power was fully established and peaceably exercised. The people seemed to have accepted Tinoco's government with great good will when it came in, and to have welcomed the change. [T]hroughout the record as made by the case and counter case, there is no substantial evidence that Tinoco was not in actual and peaceable administration without resistance or conflict or contest by anyone until a few months before the time when he retired and resigned. . . .

It is not important, however, what were the causes that enabled Tinoco to carry on his government effectively and peaceably. The question is, must his government be considered a link in the continuity of the Government of Costa Rica? I must hold that from the evidence that the Tinoco government was an actual sovereign government.

But it is urged that many leading Powers refused to recognize the Tinoco government, and that recognition by other nations is the chief and best evidence of the birth, existence and continuity of succession of a government. Undoubtedly recognition by other Powers is an important evidential factor in establishing proof of the existence of a government in the society of nations. What are the facts as to this? The Tinoco government was recognized by [20 nations: Bolivia, Argentina, Chile, Haiti, Guatemala, Switzerland, Germany, Denmark, Spain, Mexico, Holland, the Vatican, Colombia, Austria, Portugal, El Salvador, Romania, Brazil, Peru, and Ecuador.]

What were the circumstances as to the other nations?

The United States, on February 9, 1917, two weeks after Tinoco had assumed power, took this action:

> The Government of the United States has viewed the recent overthrow of the established government in Costa Rica with the gravest concern and considers that illegal acts of this character tend to disturb the peace of Central America and to disrupt the unity of the American continent. In view of its policy in regard to the assumption of power through illegal methods, clearly enunciated by it on several occasions during the past four years, the Government of the United States desires to set forth in an emphatic and distinct manner its present position in regard to the actual situation in Costa Rica which is that it will not give recognition or support to any government which may be established unless it is clearly proven that it is elected by legal and constitutional means.

And again on February 24, 1917:

> In order that citizens of the United States may have definite information as to the position of this Government in regard to any financial aid which they may give to, or any business transaction which they may have with those persons who overthrew the constitutional Government of Costa Rica by an act of armed rebellion, the Government of the United States desires to advise them that it will not consider any claims which may in the future arise from such dealings, worthy of its diplomatic support.

[The U.S. State Department reaffirmed its nonrecognition of the Tinoco regime in April 1918.]

Probably because of the leadership of the United States in respect to a matter of this kind, her then Allies in the war, Great Britain, France and Italy, declined to recognize the Tinoco government. Costa Rica was, therefore, not permitted to sign the Treaty of Peace at Versailles, although the Tinoco government had declared war against Germany.

The merits of the policy of the United States in this non-recognition it is not for the arbitrator to discuss, for the reason that in his consideration of this case, he is necessarily controlled by principles of international law, and however justified as a national policy non-recognition on such a ground may be, it certainly has not been acquiesced in by all the nations of the world, which is a condition precedent to considering it as a postulate of international law.

The non-recognition by other nations of a government claiming to be a national personality, is usually appropriate evidence that it has not attained the independence and control entitling it by international law to be classed as such. But when recognition *vel non* of a government is by such nations determined by inquiry, not into its *de facto* sovereignty and complete governmental control, but into its illegitimacy or irregularity of origin, their non-recognition loses something of evidential weight on the issue with which those applying the rules of international law are alone concerned. What is true of the non-recognition of the United States in its bearing upon the existence of a *de facto* government under Tinoco for thirty months is probably in a measure true of the non-recognition by her Allies in the European War. Such non-recognition for any reason, however, cannot outweigh the evidence disclosed by this record before me as to the *de facto* character of Tinoco's government, according to the standard set by international law.

Second. It is ably and earnestly argued on behalf of Costa Rica that the Tinoco government cannot be considered a *de facto* government, because it was not established and maintained in accord with the constitution of Costa Rica of 1871. To hold that a government which establishes itself and maintains a peaceful administration, with the acquiescence of the people for a substantial period of time, does not become a *de facto* government unless it conforms to a previous constitution would be to hold that within the rules of international law a revolution contrary to the fundamental law of the existing government cannot establish a new government. This cannot be, and is not, true. The change by revolution upsets the rule of the authorities in power under the then existing fundamental law, and sets aside the fundamental law in so far as the change of rule makes it necessary. To speak of a revolution creating a *de facto* government, which conforms to the limitations of the old constitution is to use a contradiction in terms. The same government continues internationally, but not the internal law of its being. . . . The question is, has [the new government] really established itself in such a way that all within its influence recognize its control, and that there is no opposing force assuming to be a government in its place? Is it discharging its functions as a government usually does, respected within its own jurisdiction? . . .

Third. It is further objected by Costa Rica that Great Britain by her failure to recognize the Tinoco government is estopped now to urge claims of her subjects dependent upon the acts and contracts of the Tinoco government. . . . The contention here . . . precludes a government which did not recognize a *de facto* government from appearing in an international tribunal in behalf of its nationals to claim any rights based on the acts of such government. . . .

I do not understand the arguments on which an equitable estoppel in such case can rest. The failure to recognize the *de facto* government did not lead the succeeding government to change its position in any way upon the faith of it. . . . An equitable estoppel to prove the truth must rest on previous conduct of the person to be estopped, which has led the person claiming the estoppel into a position in which the truth will injure him. There is no such case here. . . .

It is urged that the subjects of Great Britain knew of the policy of their home government in refusing to recognize the Tinoco régime and cannot now rely on protection by Great Britain. This is a question solely between the home government and its subjects. That government may take the course which the United States had done and refuse to use any diplomatic offices to promote such claims and thus to leave its nationals to depend upon the sense of justice of the existing Costa Rican Government, as they were warned in advance would be its policy, or it may change its conclusion as to the *de facto* existence of the Tinoco government and offer its subjects the protection of its diplomatic intervention. It is entirely a question between the claimants and their own government. It should be noted that Great Britain issued no such warning to its subjects as did the United States to its citizens in this matter.

. . . The decision [on the merits] must be governed by the answer to the question whether the claims would have been good against the Tinoco government as a government, unaffected by the Law of Nullities, and unaffected by the Costa Rican Constitution of 1871.

[Taft turns to the claim brought on behalf of the Royal Bank of Canada. Costa Rican law provided for a Costa Rican bank to issue credit, to be used for such purposes as rural farm loans, payments to army veterans, and road construction and repair. This bank deposited credit instruments ("bills") in the Royal Bank of Canada on which the Costa Rican government could draw. Taft finds that the Royal Bank honored some requests for funds from Tinoco government officials that the British government, espousing the claim of the Royal Bank, should not now be entitled to recover:]

It thus appears that the present claim of the bank rests on its payment of $200,000 to the Tinocos, $100,000 to Frederico Tinoco, "for expenses of representation of the Chief of State in his approaching trip abroad," and $100,000 to Jose Joaquin Tinoco, as Minister of Costa Rica to Italy for four years' salary and expenses of the Legation of Costa Rica in Italy, to which post the latter had been appointed by his brother. The Royal Bank cannot here claim the benefit of the presumptions which might obtain in favor of a bank receiving a deposit in regular course of business and paying it out in the usual way upon checks bearing no indication on their face of the purpose. The whole transaction here was full of irregularities. There was no authority of law, in the first place for making the Royal Bank the depositary of a revolving credit fund. . . . The case of the Royal Bank depends not on the mere form of the transaction but upon the good faith of the bank in the payment of money for the real use of the Costa Rican Government under the Tinoco régime. It must make out its case of actual furnishing of money to the government for its legitimate use. It has not done so. The bank knew that this money was to be used by the retiring president, F. Tinoco, for his personal support after he had taken refuge in a foreign country. It could not hold his own government for the money paid to him for this purpose.

The case of the money paid to the brother, the Secretary of War, and the appointed Minister to Italy, is much the same. . . .

The claim of the Royal Bank against the Costa Rican Government has, however, been given a better status than as decided above, to the extent of one-half of it, by the act of the existing Government of Costa Rica in December, 1922. [After Jose Joaquin Tinoco was killed during anti-Tinoco protests in August 1919, the current government sued his estate for $100,000 in Costa Rican court. In 1922 the government secured a mortgage for $100,000.] This should enure to the benefit of the Royal Bank. Proceeding in this matter *ex aequo et bono*, therefore, I must hold that the bank is subrogated to the title of Costa Rica in the mortgage[.]

[With respect to the petroleum concession, the arbitrator disallows recovery because the concession violated Costa Rica's 1917 constitution. Because of this violation, even Tinoco's government could have defeated the concession. Thus, when the Law of Nullities deemed the concession to be invalid, it worked no injury to the British companies of which Great Britain could complain.]

The Identity of a State. Does the *Tinoco Case* demonstrate that even a radical change in government will not by itself affect the identity of a state? The state of Costa Rica survived when Tinoco seized power, and continued when he was deposed. Does the continued existence of Costa Rica settle the question whether the contract obligations of the Tinoco regime must be honored?

Government Succession to Obligations. Taft's basic position was that, as a matter of international law, a new government is generally bound by the legal commitments of an old government. Could there be any practical alternative to this rule? It is difficult to see how there could be any legally binding commitments of states if international obligations could be repudiated simply by forming or declaring a new government. Should an exception be made to permit the repudiation of national commitments when there has been a radical change in government? If so, who determines whether the change is radical enough?

Should the contracts of a government that seized control in an extraconstitutional coup, in violation of the wishes of the people who are governed, be considered binding? Did Taft occupy a middle, "rule of law" ground between, on the one hand, finding all obligations of a predecessor government binding, and, on the other, refusing to enforce any foreign contracts of an undemocratic predecessor government? How sensible is Taft's approach today?

De Facto *and* De Jure *Governments.* Taft needed to establish whether the Tinoco regime was the actual government of Costa Rica when it entered into the banking and oil concession arrangements with the British companies. He discussed the categories of *de facto* and *de jure* governments. What is the difference between them? Taft seemed to look most at the factor of popular acquiescence to determine whether the Tinoco regime was the *de facto* government of Costa Rica. What evidences would a judge or lawyer consider in evaluating the popular support for a government? If Taft had found that the Tinoco regime lacked popular support, would he necessarily have concluded it was not the *de facto* government?

There were about 50 governments worldwide in 1917; the Tinoco regime was recognized by 20 of them. Was this number enough to establish Tinoco as the *de jure* government of Costa Rica under the constitutive theory? Would the answer depend on the degree to which non-recognizing foreign governments both opposed the Tinoco regime and still supported the old Gonzalez regime?

The Relative Importance of De Facto *Control and* De Jure *Recognition.* What if the evidences of *de facto* control conflict with the evidences of *de jure* recognition? Which should govern in determining the legitimate government of a state? Could there be different answers to this question depending on the forum and depending on whether the forum looks to an answer in international law or one or another municipal law? Is the distinction between *de facto* and *de jure* governments another way of stating the conflict between declaratory and constitutive theories of recognition?

Estoppel. How persuasive was Taft in his estoppel argument? Should Great Britain have been permitted to insist that the Tinoco regime was the government of Costa Rica when it had failed to recognize the Tinoco regime? The Tinoco regime probably could not have availed itself of the British courts because it was unrecognized. Should there be one answer as to the status of the Tinoco regime *vis-à-vis* Great Britain in British municipal courts and another in an international tribunal?

Succession to Treaties. When a new state or government emerges, it may enter agreements with the treaty partners of its predecessor state or government to confirm the continuing effect of the treaty. Absent such agreements, a change in government—even a revolutionary change—generally does not affect the continuing validity of a state's treaties at international law. See the *Diplomatic and Consular Staff Case* in Chapter 4 below. The situation is more complicated when an entirely new state emerges. There are sometimes devolution agreements between a predecessor and successor state, specifying which of the predecessor state's treaties the successor will accept. Could such an agreement bind third-state treaty parties? If not, what is the practical significance of such devolution agreements? And what happens if the new state does not indicate the treaties to which it is willing to be bound? Should only some new states, *e.g.*, those emerging from colonialism, be entitled to begin life with a "clean slate"? What values and practical reasons support a general presumption that treaties should continue in force for all successor states?

Comparing the Succession of States and the Succession of Governments. Is it always easy to distinguish changes in states from changes in governments? Should different consequences attach to changes in governments and changes in states? In the view of Professor Daniel O'Connell,

> the solution of the problem raised by political change cannot be left to the hazard of characterizing the event as a succession of States or a succession of governments. There is evident at the present time a developing pressure in the direction of assimilating these two categories of events, and as the nineteenth-century theory of the State, with its concomitant metaphysics of political personality, loses its cogency, legal theory will tend more and more to return to its eighteenth-century position.

1 D.P. O'Connell, *State Succession in Municipal Law and International Law* 7 (1967). The 18th-century position to which O'Connell referred called for a succession to commitments without drawing a distinction between states and governments. In the following case is it an alleged succession of states or of governments that is at issue?

AUTOCEPHALOUS GREEK-ORTHODOX CHURCH OF CYPRUS v. GOLDBERG & FELDMAN FINE ARTS, INC.

917 F.2d 278 (7th Cir. 1990), *cert. denied*, 502 U.S. 941 (1991)

The Facts

BAUER, CHIEF JUDGE.

In this appeal, we consider the fate of several tangible victims of Cyprus' turbulent history: specifically, four Byzantine mosaics created over 1400 years ago. The district court awarded possession of these extremely valuable mosaics to plaintiff-appellee, the Autocephalous Greek-Orthodox Church of Cyprus ("Church of Cyprus" or "Church"). Defendants-appellants, Peg Goldberg and Goldberg & Feldman Fine Arts, Inc. (collectively "Goldberg"), claim that in so doing, the court committed various reversible errors. We affirm.

I. BACKGROUND

In the early sixth century, A.D., a large mosaic was affixed to the apse of the Church of the Panagia Kanakaria ("Kanakaria Church") in the village of Lythrankomi, Cyprus. The mosaic, made of small bits of colored glass, depicted Jesus Christ as a young boy in the lap of his mother, the Virgin Mary, who was seated on a throne. Jesus and Mary were attended by two archangels and surrounded by a frieze depicting the twelve apostles. The mosaic was displayed in the Kanakaria Church for centuries, where it became, under the practices of Eastern Orthodox Christianity, sanctified as a holy relic. It survived both the vicissitudes of history, and, thanks to restoration efforts, the ravages of time.

Testimony before Judge Noland established that the Kanakaria mosaic was one of only a handful of such holy Byzantine relics to survive into the twentieth century. Sadly, however, war came to Cyprus in the 1970s, from which the mosaic could not be spared.

The Cypriot people have long been a divided people, approximately three-fourths being of Greek descent and Greek-Orthodox faith, the other quarter of Turkish descent and Muslem [*sic*] faith. No sooner had Cyprus gained independence from British rule in 1960 than this bitter division surfaced. Civil disturbances erupted between Greek and Turkish Cypriots, necessitating the introduction of United Nations peacekeeping forces in 1964. (U.N. forces still remain in Cyprus.) Through the 1960s, the Greek Cypriots, concentrated in the southern part of the island, became increasingly estranged from the Turkish Cypriots, concentrated in the north.

The tensions erupted again in 1974, this time with more violent results. In July, 1974, the civil government of the Republic of Cyprus was replaced by a government controlled by the Greek Cypriot military. In apparent response, on July 20, 1974, Turkey invaded Cyprus from the north. By late August, the Turkish military forces had advanced to occupy approximately the northern third of the island. The point at which the invading forces stopped is called the "Green Line." To this day, the heavily-guarded Green Line bisects Nicosia, the capital of the Republic, and splits the island from east to west.

The Turkish forces quickly established their own "government" north of the Green Line. In 1975, they formed what they called the "Turkish Federated State of Cyprus" ("TFSC"). In 1983, that administration was dissolved, and the "Turkish Republic of Northern Cyprus" ("TRNC") was formed. These "governments" were recognized immediately by Turkey, but all other nations in the world—including the United States—have never recognized them, and continue to recognize the Republic of Cyprus ("Republic"), plaintiff-appellee in this action, as the only legitimate government for all Cypriot people.

The Turkish invasion led to the forced southern exodus of over 100,000 Greek Cypriots who lived in northern Cyprus. Turkish Cypriots living in southern Cyprus (and tens of thousands of settlers from mainland Turkey) likewise flooded into northern Cyprus, resulting in a massive exchange of populations.

Lythrankomi is in the northern portion of Cyprus that came under Turkish rule. Although the village and the Kanakaria Church were untouched by the invading forces in 1974, the villagers of Greek ancestry were soon thereafter "enclaved" by the Turkish military. Despite the hostile environment, the pastor and priests of the Kanakaria Church continued for two years to conduct religious services for the Greek Cypriots who remained in Lythrankomi. Hardy as they must have been, these clerics, and virtually all remaining Greek Cypriots, were forced to flee to southern Cyprus in the summer of 1976. Church of Cyprus officials testified that they intend to re-establish the congregation at the Kanakaria Church as soon as Greek Cypriots are permitted to return safely to Lythrankomi. (Thirty-five thousand Turkish troops remain in northern Cyprus.)

When the priests evacuated the Kanakaria Church in 1976, the mosaic was still intact. In the late 1970s, however, Church of Cyprus officials received increasing reports that Greek Cypriot churches and monuments in northern Cyprus were being attacked and vandalized, their contents stolen or destroyed. . . . In November, 1979, a resident of northern Cyprus brought word to the Republic's Department of Antiquities that this fate had also befallen the Kanakaria Church and its mosaic. Vandals had plundered the church, removing anything of value from its interior. The mosaic, or at least its most recognizable and valuable parts, had been forcibly ripped from the apse of the church. Once a place of worship, the Kanakaria Church had been reduced to a stable for farm animals.

Upon learning of the looting of the Kanakaria Church and the loss of its mosaics (made plural by the vandals' axes), the Republic of Cyprus took immediate steps to recover them. [T]hese efforts took the form of contacting and seeking assistance from many organizations and individuals, including the United Nations Educational, Scientific and Cultural Organization ("UNESCO"); the International Council of Museums; the International Council of Museums and Sites; Europa Nostra (an organization devoted to the conservation of the architectural heritage of Europe); the Council of Europe; international auction houses such as Christie's and Sotheby's; Harvard University's Dumbarton Oaks Institute for Byzantine Studies; and the foremost museums, curators and Byzantine scholars throughout the world. The Republic's United States Embassy also routinely disseminated information about lost cultural properties to journalists, U.S. officials and scores of scholars, architects and collectors in this country, asking for assistance in recovering the mosaics. The overall strategy behind these efforts was to get word to the experts and scholars who would probably be involved in any ultimate sale of the mosaics. These individuals, it was hoped, would be the most likely (only?) actors in the chain of custody of stolen cultural properties who would be interested in helping the Republic and Church of Cyprus recover them.

The Republic's efforts have paid off. In recent years, the Republic has recovered and returned to the Church of Cyprus several stolen relics and antiquities. The Republic has even located frescoes and other works taken from the Kanakaria Church, including the four mosaics at issue here. These four mosaics, each measuring about two feet square, depict the figure of Jesus, the busts of one of the attending archangels, the apostle Matthew and the apostle James.

To understand how these pieces of the Kanakaria mosaic resurfaced, we must trace the actions of appellant Peg Goldberg and the other principals through whose hands they passed in 1988.

Peg Goldberg is an art dealer and gallery operator. Goldberg and Feldman Fine Arts, Inc., is the Indiana corporation that owns her gallery in Carmel, Indiana. In the summer of 1988, Peg Goldberg went to Europe to shop for works for her gallery. Although her main interest is 20th century paintings, etchings and sculptures, Goldberg was enticed while in The Netherlands by Robert Fitzgerald, another Indiana art dealer and "casual friend" of hers, to consider the purchase of "four early Christian mosaics." [The court details Goldberg's efforts to buy the mosaics. The sale was concluded by the exchange of the mosaics for $1,080,000 in $100 bills at the airport in Geneva, Switzerland.]

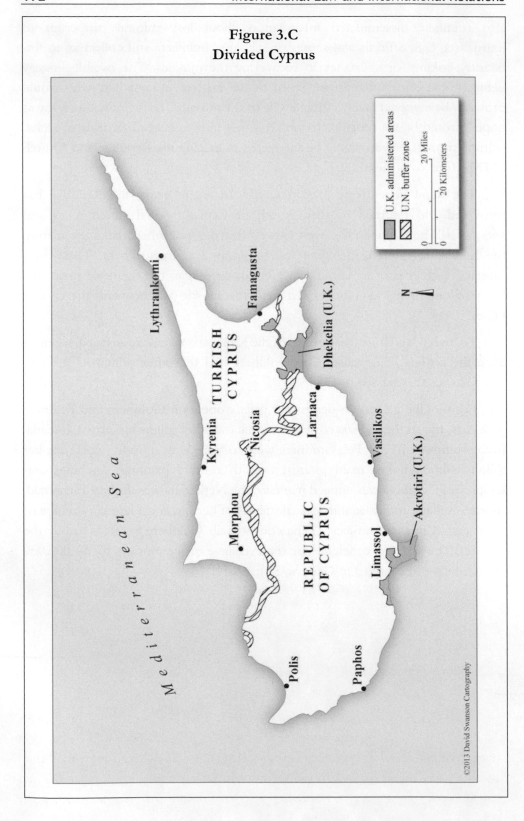

Figure 3.C
Divided Cyprus

©2013 David Swanson Cartography

Peg Goldberg's efforts soon turned to . . . the resale of these valuable mosaics. She worked up sales brochures about them, and contacted several other dealers to help her find a buyer. Two of these dealers' searches led them both to Dr. Marion True of the Getty Museum in California. When told of these mosaics and their likely origin, the aptly-named Dr. True explained to the dealers that she had a working relationship with the Republic of Cyprus and that she was duty-bound to contact Cypriot officials about them. Dr. True called Dr. Vassos Karageorghis, the Director of the Republic's Department of Antiquities and one of the primary Cypriot officials involved in the worldwide search for the mosaics. Dr. Karageorghis verified that the Republic was in fact hunting for the mosaics that had been described to Dr. True, and he set in motion the investigative and legal machinery that ultimately resulted in the Republic learning that they were in Goldberg's possession in Indianapolis.

After their request for the return of the mosaics was refused by Goldberg, the Republic of Cyprus and the Church of Cyprus (collectively "Cyprus") brought this suit in the Southern District of Indiana for the recovery of the mosaics. . . . Judge Noland awarded possession of the mosaics to the Church of Cyprus. [Goldberg appealed the trial court's decision.]

Illicit Trafficking in Cultural Property. Those who steal art and antiquities often destroy archaeological and other significant cultural information. Moreover, the economic losses from illicit trafficking in cultural property, although difficult to measure, are enormous. "[T]he annual illicit flow of cultural property totals well above $1 billion." James A.R. Nafziger, "Protection of Cultural Property," in 1 *International Criminal Law* 977, 1011 (M. Cherif Bassiouni ed., 3d ed. 2008). Countries have sometimes persuaded museums to return some stolen art treasures, and have also sued individuals allegedly conspiring in illegal art transactions.

Autocephalous Greek-Orthodox Church of Cyprus v. Goldberg & Feldman Fine Arts, Inc.
The Law

[The court concludes that no statute of limitations bars the action, and that applicable rules of replevin allow the plaintiff Church to recover the mosaics.]

Finally, Goldberg argues that several decrees of the TFSC (the entity established in northern Cyprus by the Turkish military immediately after the 1974 invasion) divested the Church of title to the mosaics. Goldberg asks us to honor these decrees under the notion that in some instances courts in the United States can give effect to the acts of nonrecognized but "*de facto*" regimes if the acts relate to purely local matters. The TFSC decrees at issue, all propagated in 1975, are principally these: 1) the "Abandoned Movable Property Law," which provided that all movable property within the boundaries of the TFSC abandoned by its owner because of the owner's "departure" from northern Cyprus "as a result of the situation after 20th July 1974" now belongs to the TFSC "in the name of the Turkish Community" and that the TFSC "is responsible for the possession and control of such property"; and 2) the "Antiquities Ordinance," which provided that all religious buildings and antiquities, including specifically "synagogues, basilicas, churches, monasteries and the like," located north of the Green Line, as well as any and all "movable antiquities" contained therein, are now the property of the TFSC. Because these decrees were enacted before the Kanakaria Church was looted and its mosaics stolen, the argument concludes, the Church cannot here claim to hold title to the mosaics.

It is helpful to note at the outset what is *not* being claimed here. First, Goldberg does not (and cannot) suggest that this court should pass on the validity of the Turkish administration in northern Cyprus. We repeat here precepts that are well-established in the law of this country:

> [T]he conduct of foreign relations was committed by the Constitution to the political departments of the government, and the propriety of what may be done in the exercise of this political power [is] not subject to judicial inquiry or decision, . . . [and] who is the sovereign of a territory is not a judicial question, but one the determination of which by the political departments conclusively binds the courts[.]

United States v. Belmont, 301 U.S. 324, 328 (1937). Indeed, Goldberg herself supports the district court's decision to deny the TRNC's motion to intervene in this case, which decision was based on the TRNC's continued status as a nonrecognized entity.

Second, this is not a case in which one party is claiming title under the laws of a state that has been entirely displaced, and the other is claiming title under the laws of the new, displacing regime. All Goldberg can hope to gain from the invocation of these TFSC edicts is a finding that the Church's claim of title is defective; she has no plausible claim of valid title in herself based on these edicts. . . .

What Goldberg is claiming is that the TFSC's confiscatory decrees, adopted only one year after the Turkish invasion, should be given effect by this court because the TFSC and its successor TRNC should now be viewed as the "*de facto*" government north of the Green Line. This we are unwilling to do. We draw on two lines of precedent as support for our decision. First, we note that, contrary to the New York court's decision in *Salimoff* [*v. Standard Oil Co.*, 262 N.Y. 200, 186 N.E. 679 (1933)], several courts of the same era refused to give effect to the nationalization decrees of the as-yet-unrecognized Soviet Republics. These courts relied on a variety of grounds, including especially the fact that the political branches of our government still refused to recognize these entities. . . . Similarly, as regards the Turkish administration in northern Cyprus, the United States government (like the rest of the non-Turkish world) has not recognized its legitimacy, nor does our government "recognize that [the Turkish administration] has functioned as a de facto or quasi government . . . , ruling within its own borders."

Second, we are guided in part by the post-Civil War cases in which courts refused to give effect to property-affecting acts of the Confederate state legislatures. In one such case, *Williams v. Bruffy*, 96 U.S. 176 (1878), the Supreme Court drew a helpful distinction between two kinds of "*de facto*" governments. The first kind "is such as exists after it has expelled the regularly constituted authorities from the seats of power and the public offices, and established its own functionaries in their places, so as to represent in fact the sovereignty of the nation." This kind of *de facto* government, the Court explained, "is treated as in most respects possessing rightful authority, . . . [and] its legislation is in general recognized." The second kind of *de facto* government "is such as exists where a portion of the inhabitants of a country have separated themselves from the parent State and established an independent government. The validity of its acts, both against the parent State and its citizens or subjects, depends entirely upon its ultimate success. . . . If it succeed, and become recognized, its acts from the commencement of its existence are upheld as those of an independent nation." (The Court held that the Confederacy was a government of the second type that ultimately failed.) Goldberg argues that the TFSC and its successor TRNC have achieved the level of "ultimate success" contemplated by this standard, because they have maintained control of the territory north of the Green Line for over fifteen years. We will not thus equate simple longevity of control with "ultimate success." The Turkish forces, despite their best efforts, did not completely supplant the Republic nor its officers. Instead, the TFSC and the TRNC, neither of which has ever been recognized by the non-Turkish world, only acceded to the control of the northern portion of Cyprus. The Republic of Cyprus remains the only recognized Cypriot government, the sovereign nation for the entire island. [W]e conclude that the confiscatory decrees proffered by Goldberg do not divest the Church of its claim of title.

. . . Those who plundered the churches and monuments of war-torn Cyprus, hoarded their relics away, and are now smuggling and selling them for large sums, are . . . blackguards. The Republic of Cyprus, with diligent effort and the help of friends like Dr. True, has been able to locate several of these stolen antiquities; items of vast cultural, religious (and, as this case demonstrates, monetary) value. Among such finds are the pieces of the Kanakaria mosaic at issue in this case. Unfortunately, when these mosaics surfaced they were in the hands not of the most guilty parties, but of Peg Goldberg and her gallery. Correctly applying Indiana law, the district court determined that Goldberg must return the mosaics to their rightful owner: the Church of Cyprus. Goldberg's tireless attacks have not established reversible error in that determination, and thus, for the reasons discussed above, the district court's judgment is AFFIRMED.

[T]hose who wish to purchase art work on the international market, undoubtedly a ticklish business, are not without means by which to protect themselves. Especially when circumstances are as suspicious as those that faced Peg Goldberg, prospective purchasers would do best to do more than make a few last-minute phone calls. . . . In such cases, dealers can (and probably should) take steps such as a formal IFAR [International Foundation for Art Research] search; a documented authenticity check by disinterested experts; a full background search of the seller and his claim of title; insurance protection and a contingency sales contract; and the like. If Goldberg would have pursued such methods, perhaps she would have discovered in time what she has now discovered too late: the Church has a valid, superior and enforceable claim to these Byzantine treasures, which therefore must be returned to it.

Divided Cyprus. How should we characterize the Turkish Republic of Northern Cyprus (TRNC), labeled "Turkish Cyprus" in Figure 3.C? Is it a state? The widespread refusal of existing states to recognize the Turkish Federated State of Cyprus (TFSC) or its successor, the TRNC, has been explained as a reaction to Turkey's unlawful use of force in northern Cyprus. The European Court of Human Rights also has imputed to Turkey various human rights violations in northern Cyprus. Cyprus v. Turkey, 2001–IV Eur. Ct. H.R. 1.

There have been proposals to establish a federal Cypriot government, with the northern and southern regions of the island each exercising extensive internal competences. However, such efforts to end the division of Cyprus have so far proved unsuccessful. Despite recent reunification talks, "the road to a deal remains mined with misgivings and disagreements over territory, power sharing and security guarantees." "Why There Are Fresh Hopes of a United

Cyprus," *The Economist*, Apr. 25, 2016, at 51. The Greek-dominated Republic of Cyprus joined the European Union in 2004.

Giving Effect to the Laws of Unrecognized States and Governments. How does the *Goldberg* court's treatment of recognition compare to that of Arbitrator Taft in the *Tinoco Case*? In *Goldberg*, we see some effects of nonrecognition in a municipal court. The U.S. Seventh Circuit Court of Appeals refused to give effect to a law of an entity that the United States had not recognized as a state. If the TFSC and the TRNC had been recognized by many states, but not by the United States, would the court have given effect to the confiscatory TFSC decrees? Or did the *Goldberg* court refuse to give effect to the TFSC's decrees simply because the court found them objectionable? Should acts taken under *un*objectionable laws of an unrecognized state—perhaps laws specifying rules of intestate (without a will) succession—be denied effect in U.S. courts?

Access of Unrecognized States and Governments to U.S. Courts. The *Goldberg* district court also refused to allow the TRNC to intervene directly in the case, stating that to do so "would create the incongruous result of having the Judicial Branch implicitly recognize that entity as a legitimate government in the face of explicit nonrecognition by the Executive Branch." Autocephalous Greek-Orthodox Church of Cyprus v. Goldberg & Feldman Fine Arts, Inc., No. IP 89–304–C (S.D. Ind. May 31, 1989), *quoted in* 86 *American Journal of International Law* 128, 129 (1992).

U.S. courts have not always refused to allow unrecognized entities to pursue their claims. In *National Petrochemical Co. v. M/T Stolt Sheaf*, 860 F.2d 551 (2d Cir. 1988), *cert. denied*, 489 U.S. 1081 (1989), the Second Circuit reversed the district court's dismissal of a suit brought by a corporation wholly owned by the government of Iran. Although the United States did not recognize Iran at the time, the court accepted the view of the U.S. Justice and State Departments, which argued in an *amicus* brief that this plaintiff should have access to U.S. courts. Should unrecognized governments be permitted to litigate in U.S. courts unless the executive branch expressly objects?

Recognition and the Maintenance of Diplomatic Relations. Recognition by the executive branch is ordinarily a prerequisite for the establishment of diplomatic relations. Nonrecognition traditionally meant that the unrecognized state or government could not sue in U.S. court. Should a recognized government with which the United States does not maintain diplomatic relations be similarly barred? The U.S. Supreme Court addressed the issue in *Banco Nacional de Cuba v. Sabbatino*, 376 U.S. 398, 410 (1964):

Respondents, pointing to the severance of diplomatic relations, commercial embargo, and freezing of Cuban assets in this country, contend that relations between the United States and Cuba manifest such animosity that unfriendliness is clear, and that the courts should be closed to the Cuban Government. We do not agree. This Court would hardly be competent to undertake assessments of varying degrees of friendliness or its absence, and, lacking some definite touchstone for determination, we are constrained to consider any relationship, short of war, with a recognized sovereign power as embracing the privilege of resorting to United States courts. . . . Severance [of diplomatic relations] may take place for any number of political reasons, its duration is unpredictable, and whatever expression of animosity it may imply does not approach that implicit in a declaration of war.

Self-determination. A sometimes-important feature in the definition of a state is self-determination. Article 1(2) of the U.N. Charter provides that one purpose of the United Nations is "to develop friendly relations among nations based on respect for the principle of equal rights and self-determination of peoples," a goal also elaborated in widely accepted treaties and U.N. General Assembly declarations.

Self-determination was a crucial issue at the Paris Peace Conference concluding World War I. U.S. President Woodrow Wilson believed that achieving national self-determination was vital in maintaining a peaceful international society. Wilson's notion of self-determination had both an internal aspect (promotion of democratic institutions, respecting the consent of the governed) and an external aspect (freedom from foreign rule). Wilson particularly championed self-determination in breaking up the Austro-Hungarian and Ottoman empires. The Russian leader, Vladimir Lenin, also forcefully espoused self-determination, at least on the international level. Lenin condemned colonialism, arguing that peoples under colonial rule had the right to gain their independence, a position closely tied to his more fundamental goal of advancing socialism on a global basis. While Wilson too thought that self-determination should be taken into account in settling colonial claims, he sought to balance self-determination with the interests of colonial powers to achieve self-determination in an orderly, nonviolent manner.

The diplomats at the Paris Peace Conference consulted with various European groups seeking self-determination. The Conference agreed to allow residents along some borders to hold plebiscites to help determine new boundaries between states. Belief in self-determination facilitated the establishment of Poland and Czechoslovakia as independent states. However, the economic, strategic, and geopolitical interests of the principal Allied powers often proved more important. When it proved impossible to divide all of Europe up into perfectly homogenous states, the Allies concluded peace treaties obliging new states to protect the rights of ethnic, religious, and linguistic minorities.

The League of Nations, also a product of the Paris Peace Conference, grappled with self-determination in the 1920s and 1930s. For example, a League-designated Committee of Jurists investigated the status of the Åland Islands, asking whether the Ålands, which had previously been controlled by Finland, "should, according to International Law, be entirely left to the domestic jurisdiction of Finland." "Report of the International Committee of Jurists on the Legal Aspects of the Aaland Islands Question," *League of Nations Official Journal*, Special Supp. No. 3, at 3 (1920). Åland inhabitants sought to align with Sweden because of linguistic, cultural, and ethnic ties. According to the Committee of Jurists, the principle of self-determination, though recognized in some treaties, did not rest "upon the same footing as a positive rule of the Law of Nations." Nonetheless, self-determination was an important, though not necessarily dispositive, consideration in this case, because Finland, emerging from under Russian control, itself faced an unsettled political situation. The Åland Island situation suggested to some observers that a right to self-determination during this period applied only in "abnormal" situations. Ultimately, the Ålands remained part of Finland, although the Islanders were accorded significant autonomy.

Again responding to claims of self-determination, the Covenant of the League of Nations created "mandates," authorizing European powers to govern certain territories under certain conditions. Pursuant to Article 22 of the Covenant, colonies that had been governed by states defeated in World War I and that were "inhabited by peoples not yet able to stand by themselves under the strenuous conditions of the modern world" could be administered subject to "the principle that the well-being and development of such peoples form a sacred trust of civilization." Class A mandates, for territories closest to statehood, comprised "[c]ertain communities formerly belonging to the Turkish Empire"—Mesopotamia (later Iraq), Syria, and Palestine—that had "reached a stage of development where their existence as independent nations can be provisionally recognized subject to the rendering of administrative advice and assistance by a Mandatory until such time as they are able to stand alone." Other classes of mandates, located in Africa and the South Pacific, were deemed to require more control by a Mandatory.

Mandates ended with the dissolution of the League of Nations after World War II. In their place, the United Nations and states implemented the principle of self-determination enshrined in the U.N. Charter and treaty law. Look at the *Secession of Quebec Case* below, and ask how adequately international law establishes rules or principles determining whether a "people" have a legal right to their own state.

The Secession of Quebec Case *in Context.* In October 1995, a proposal calling for Quebec's secession from Canada was narrowly defeated in a provincial referendum. Canadian political leaders, upset at the close vote, determined they had been insufficiently attentive to separatist arguments in Quebec. The national government countered aggressively, stressing the social and economic disadvantages of secession and questioning whether a referendum on the future of Canada in which only Quebecers would vote could ever be legitimate. The national government asked the Canadian Supreme Court for an advisory opinion on the legality of Quebec's secession. In doing so, "the federal Government wanted to reassert the relevance of law to the shaping of democratic governance within Canada. Less charitably, the Government may also have hoped that Quebecers"—who showed little sympathy for revolutionary movements—would "be frightened by a judicial declaration that secession by the province would be an 'illegal' act." Stephen J. Troope, "International Decision," 93 *American Journal of International Law* 519, 520 (1999). Quebec's Attorney General refused to participate in the case, and the Court appointed a separatist lawyer as an *amicus curiae.*

In rendering its advisory opinion, the Canadian Supreme Court first determined that Canadian constitutional law did not permit unilateral secession, although a constitutional duty to negotiate would arise if Quebecers voted for secession by "a clear majority on a clear question." The Court then turned to the second question:

> Does international law give the National Assembly, legislature or government of Quebec the right to effect the secession of Quebec from Canada unilaterally? In this regard, is there a right to self-determination under international law that would give the National Assembly, legislature or government of Quebec the right to effect the secession of Quebec from Canada unilaterally?

Note the phrasing of the international law questions the Court addressed in the *Secession of Quebec Case*. How might the Court have dealt with the question, "If Quebec were to secede from Canada, would it be a state in international law?" According to Professor Crawford, the Court's unanimous opinion, which found no legal right of unilateral secession but a constitutional duty to negotiate for independence if Quebecers clearly voted for secession, achieved an "astute balance" that helped "reduce tension." James Crawford, *The Creation of States in International Law* 412 (2d ed. 2006). In light of the Court's determination that Quebec had no right to secede under either Canadian constitutional law or international law, the Court did not address another question that was asked of it: would the Canadian Constitution or international law have priority in case of a conflict?

REFERENCE RE SECESSION OF QUEBEC

Supreme Court of Canada, Aug. 20, 1998,
37 *International Legal Materials* 1340 (1998)

(1)   *Secession at International Law*

[I]nternational law does not specifically grant component parts of sovereign states the legal right to secede unilaterally from their "parent" state. . . . Given the lack of specific authorization for unilateral secession, proponents of the existence of such a right at international law are therefore left to attempt to found their argument (i) on the proposition that unilateral secession is not specifically prohibited and that what is not specifically prohibited is inferentially permitted; or (ii) on the implied duty of states to recognize the legitimacy of secession brought about by the exercise of the well-established international law right of "a people" to self-determination. . . .

(a)   *Absence of a Specific Prohibition*

International law contains neither a right of unilateral secession nor the explicit denial of such a right, although such a denial is, to some extent, implicit in the exceptional circumstances required for secession to be permitted under the right of a people to self-determination, e.g., the right of secession that arises in the exceptional situation of an oppressed or colonial people, discussed below. As will be seen, international law places great importance on the territorial integrity of nation states and, by and large, leaves the creation of a new state to be determined by the domestic law of the existing state of which the seceding entity presently forms a part. Where, as here, unilateral secession would be incompatible with the domestic Constitution, international law is likely to accept that conclusion subject to the right of peoples to self-determination, a topic to which we now turn.

defined as in the following statement from the *Declaration on Friendly Relations, supra,* as

> The establishment of a sovereign and independent State, the free association or integration with an independent State or the emergence into any other political status freely determined by a *people* constitute modes of implementing the right of self-determination by *that people.* (Emphasis added.)

The international law principle of self-determination has evolved within a framework of respect for the territorial integrity of existing states. The various international documents that support the existence of a people's right to self-determination also contain parallel statements supportive of the conclusion that the exercise of such a right must be sufficiently limited to prevent threats to an existing state's territorial integrity or the stability of relations between sovereign states.

The *Declaration on Friendly Relations, supra,* [the U.N. General Assembly's *Declaration on the Occasion of the Fiftieth Anniversary of the United Nations,* G.A. Res. 50/6 (1995), and the *Vienna Declaration and Programme of Action,* A/Conf.157/24 (1993), which was adopted by the U.N. World Conference on Human Rights,] are specific. They state, immediately after affirming a people's right to determine political, economic, social and cultural issues, that such rights are *not* to ["]be construed as authorizing or encouraging any action which would dismember or *impair, totally or in part, the territorial integrity or political unity of sovereign and independent States conducting themselves in compliance with the principle of equal rights and self-determination of peoples* as described above and thus possessed of a government representing the whole people belonging to the territory without distinction. . . . " (Emphasis added.)

Similarly, while the concluding document of the Vienna Meeting in 1989 of the Conference on Security and Co-operation in Europe on the follow-up to the *Helsinki Final Act* again refers to peoples having the right to determine "their internal and *external* political status" (emphasis added), that statement is immediately followed by express recognition that the participating states will at all times act, as stated in the *Helsinki Final Act,* "in conformity with the purposes and principles of the Charter of the United Nations and with the relevant norms of international law, *including those relating to territorial integrity of states*" (emphasis added).

[T]he reference in the *Helsinki Final Act* to a people determining its external political status is interpreted to mean the expression of a people's external political status through the government of the existing state, save in the exceptional circumstances discussed below. As noted by Cassese, *supra*, at p. 287, given the history and textual structure of this document, its reference to external self-determination simply means that "no territorial or other change can be brought about by the central authorities of a State that is contrary to the will of the whole people of that State."

While the *International Covenant on Economic, Social and Cultural Rights, supra,* and the *International Covenant on Civil and Political Rights, supra*, do not specifically refer to the protection of territorial integrity, they both define the ambit of the right to self-determination in terms that are normally attainable within the framework of an existing state. There is no necessary incompatibility between the maintenance of the territorial integrity of existing states, including Canada, and the right of a "people" to achieve a full measure of self-determination. A state whose government represents the whole of the people or peoples resident within its territory, on a basis of equality and without discrimination, and respects the principles of self-determination in its own internal arrangements, is entitled to the protection under international law of its territorial integrity.

(iii) Colonial and Oppressed Peoples

Accordingly, the general state of international law with respect to the right to self-determination is that the right operates within the overriding protection granted to the territorial integrity of "parent" states. However, as noted by Cassese, *supra*, at p. 334, there are certain defined contexts within which the right to the self-determination of peoples does allow that right to be exercised "externally," which, in the context of this Reference, would potentially mean secession: . . .

The right of colonial peoples to exercise their right to self-determination by breaking away from the "imperial" power is now undisputed, but is irrelevant to this Reference.

The other clear case where a right to external self-determination accrues is where a people is subject to alien subjugation, domination or exploitation outside a colonial context. This recognition finds its roots in the *Declaration on Friendly Relations, supra*[.]

A number of commentators have further asserted that the right to self-determination may ground a right to unilateral secession in a third circumstance. Although this third circumstance has been described in several ways, the underlying proposition is that, when a people is blocked from the meaningful exercise of its right to self-determination internally, it is entitled, as a last resort, to exercise it by secession. The *Vienna Declaration, supra*, requirement that governments represent "the whole people belonging to the territory without distinction of any kind" adds credence to the assertion that such a complete blockage may potentially give rise to a right of secession.

. . . Even assuming that the third circumstance is sufficient to create a right to unilateral secession under international law, the current Quebec context cannot be said to approach such a threshold. . . .

The population of Quebec cannot plausibly be said to be denied access to government. Quebecers occupy prominent positions within the government of Canada. Residents of the province freely make political choices and pursue economic, social and cultural development within Quebec, across Canada, and throughout the world. The population of Quebec is equitably represented in legislative, executive and judicial institutions. In short, to reflect the phraseology of the international documents that address the right to self-determination of peoples, Canada is a "sovereign and independent state conducting itself in compliance with the principle of equal rights and self-determination of peoples and thus possessed of a government representing the whole people belonging to the territory without distinction."

[W]e cannot conclude under current circumstances that [the Canadian constitutional arrangements presently in effect] place Quebecers in a disadvantaged position within the scope of the international law rule.

In summary, the international law right to self-determination only generates, at best, a right to external self-determination in situations of former colonies; where a people is oppressed, as for example under foreign military occupation; or where a definable group is denied meaningful access to government to pursue their political, economic, social and cultural development. In all three situations, the people in question are entitled to a right to external self-determination because they have been denied the ability to exert internally their right to self-determination. Such exceptional circumstances are manifestly inapplicable to Quebec under existing conditions. Accordingly, neither the population of the province of Quebec, even if characterized in terms of "people" or "peoples," nor its representative institutions, the National Assembly, the legislature or government of Quebec, possess a right, under international law, to secede unilaterally from Canada.

Self-determination and Decolonization. The United Nations has supported the right of self-determination of "peoples" in the context of decolonization. See, *e.g.*, the 1970 Declaration on Friendly Relations, cited in the *Secession of Quebec*

Case, and the Declaration on the Granting of Independence to Colonial Countries and Peoples, G.A. Res. 1514 (XV) (1960), which was adopted with no dissenting votes. In Resolution 1514, the U.N. General Assembly declared that "subjection of peoples to alien subjugation, domination and exploitation" violates the U.N. Charter, and that "[a]ll peoples have the right to self-determination." It also called for the immediate transfer of "all powers to the peoples" in "territories which have not yet attained independence," in order to enable such peoples "to enjoy complete independence and freedom." The territories of concern were colonies designated as "non-self-governing territories" pursuant to General Assembly Resolution 1541 (XV) (1960). A non-self-governing territory was one both geographically separate and ethnically or culturally distinct from its administering power. According to the ICJ, "the right of peoples to self-determination, as it evolved from the Charter and from United Nations practice, has an *erga omnes* character." Case Concerning East Timor (Portugal v. Australia), 1995 I.C.J. 90, 102. See Chapter 2 for discussion of obligations *erga omnes*.

Consequences of a Right of Self-Determination. When a right of decolonial self-determination applies, what consequences follow? The ICJ has stressed that self-determination "requires a free and genuine expression of the will of the peoples concerned." Advisory Opinion on the Western Sahara, 1975 I.C.J. 12, 32. How should the "will of the peoples" in non-self-governing territories be ascertained? Since 1954, the United Nations has organized and supervised plebiscites or elections in many such territories. The ultimate result most often has been independence: 70 non-self-governing territories became independent between 1945 and 1979, with a few more gaining independence since then.

Not all of these new states gained their independence peacefully. When a white minority government in Southern Rhodesia seized power and proclaimed independence from Britain in 1965, the Security Council immediately called on all states not to assist or recognize the "illegal racist minority régime," S.C. Res. 216 (1965), and then imposed comprehensive economic sanctions against Southern Rhodesia. *E.g.*, S.C. Res. 232 (1966); S.C. Res. 253 (1968).

Most non-self-governing territories that achieved independence did so without any changes in their territorial boundaries, many of which were drawn by European powers in the late 19th century. Should the United Nations have more actively promoted territorial autonomy for sub-state ethnic groups within newly independent states?

The U.N. Trusteeship Council. The U.N. Trusteeship Council, one of the principal organs of the United Nations, also helped promote self-government or independence for territories that were run by "administering authorities" pursuant to the U.N. Charter. Article 76 of the Charter sets out the trusteeship system's goals, which include "to promote the political, economic, social, and educational advancement of the inhabitants of the trust territories, and their progressive development towards self-government or independence," and "to encourage respect for human rights and for fundamental freedoms for all without distinction as to race, sex, language, or religion." U.N. trust territories included some former colonies of Italy and Japan—countries defeated in World War II—as well as territories previously administered under League of Nations mandates. When Palau became independent in 1994, the last U.N. trusteeship was dissolved. The U.N. Trusteeship Council is now dormant.

Self-determination Outside the Colonial Context. In an omitted portion of the *Secession of Quebec Case*, the Court acknowledged "the rights and concerns of aboriginal peoples in the event of a unilateral secession," but found that those rights required no further exploration in the case. Should indigenous peoples have the right to self-determination? If so, what form should it take? Recall the *Cayuga Indians Case* in Chapter 2.

C. INTERNATIONAL INSTITUTIONS

Along with states, other entities and groups participate in the international legal arena. These include both international institutions, the focus of this Part C; courts and tribunals, explored in Chapters 4 and 5; and individuals, to whom we turn in Chapter 7. Here we examine several sorts of international institutions, including international organizations, created by treaties among states; non-governmental organizations, chartered under municipal law; and international regimes, issue-oriented international legal systems, typically created by treaty.

1. International Organizations

Early international organizations were usually designed to develop and administer common standards for specialized and largely technical matters. Among several such organizations created in the 19th century were the 1856 European Danube Commission, the 1865 Universal Telegraphic Union (now the International Telecommunications Union), and the 1874 Universal Postal Union. Most of today's hundreds of international organizations focus on specialized subject areas, providing administrative continuity and expertise.

Global international organizations designed to address broader issues, such as the use of force and world peace, were in practice though not in theory slower to develop. Ideas about peaceful universal unions of people can be found in the writings of ancient Greek and Roman thinkers. Subsequent European political philosophers, including Erasmus, Thomas More, Jean-Jacques Rousseau, Immanuel Kant, and Jeremy Bentham, all devised and espoused utopian proposals involving international organizations. The League of Nations, formed in 1919 after World War I, was the first general association of states concerned with dispute settlement and the promotion of peace. We introduce the League of Nations and the United Nations, the successor to the League, asking what sort of "international personality" international organizations and other non-state entities may have.

MARK WESTON JANIS, INTERNATIONAL LAW
215–17 (6th ed. 2012)

American enthusiasm for international government, at least in theory, ran high in the early years of the twentieth century. The onset of the Great War in 1914 only quickened the pace. Notables at a meeting of the First Annual National Assemblage of the League to Enforce Peace in Washington, D.C., in 1916 included the former President of the United States, William Howard Taft; the president of Harvard, A. Lawrence Lowell; the director of the Chamber of Commerce of the United States, Edward Filene; the president of the American Federation of Labor, Samuel Gompers; the senator from Massachusetts, Henry Cabot Lodge; the president of the Federal Council of Churches of Christ in America, Shailer Matthews; and the former president of Princeton and the then-President of the United States, Woodrow Wilson. It was Wilson who put the longstanding aspirations for international government into concrete form, proposing in the last of his Fourteen Points on January 8, 1918, that "[a] general association of nations must be formed under specific covenants for the purpose of affording mutual guarantees of political independence and territorial integrity to great and small States alike." Wilson and others believed that an international organization devoted to collective security could better guarantee the peace than could traditional balance-of-power politics, which not only had failed to prevent the outbreak of war in 1914, but also, because of its triggering system of alliances, had contributed to the expansion of the conflict.

The Versailles Treaty establishing the League "had been constructed on the assumption that the United States would be not merely a contracting but an actively executant party." Unfortunately, or as put politely by a Frenchman, "by a strange paradox," the U.S. Senate refused to consent to the ratification of the Treaty, and the United States stayed out of its own plan to keep the peace.

For a decade, from 1920 to 1930, the League, based in Geneva, even without the United States and also without the new Soviet Union, made real contributions to international law, world health, the protection of minorities, and the settlement of international disputes (for example, the pacific settlement of the dispute between Greece and Bulgaria in 1925). Unfortunately, the next decade was disastrous for the League. The turning point was probably the Japanese invasion of Manchuria on September 18, 1931, which the League proved powerless to stop. The League finally condemned the Japanese occupation of Manchuria on February 24, 1933, and Japan simply left the League the next month. Dedicated to the prevention of aggression, the League watched helplessly as Italy invaded Ethiopia in 1934 and as Germany marched into the Rhineland, Austria, and Czechoslovakia between 1936 and 1938. Finally, when Germany and Russia attacked Poland in 1939, Britain and France took action, but it was too late. Poland was lost, then France itself, and the nations descended into the twentieth century's second world war.

By the time of the invasion of Poland in 1939, the League was, in large measure, already a forgotten institution. Poland, France, and Great Britain made no attempt to involve the League in the new world war. For a year, the functionaries of the League carried on in Geneva, a situation described by the Deputy Secretary-General of the League as a "situation of abnormal normality." In the summer and autumn of 1940, the League's officials departed Geneva, where they feared a German or Italian invasion, for safer locations. A large part of the Secretariat was based at Princeton University, a fitting, if ironic, twist on the origins of the League with Woodrow Wilson. Almost a year after the foundation of the United Nations in June 1945, diplomats reconvened at Geneva, where on April 8, 1946, Lord Robert Cecil closed his speech to the League Assembly as follows: "The League is dead, Long live the United Nations." Ten days later, the Assembly unanimously voted to dissolve the League and to transfer its powers, functions, buildings, library, and archives to the United Nations.

RICHARD EDIS, A JOB WELL DONE: THE FOUNDING OF THE UNITED NATIONS REVISITED

6 Cambridge Review of International Affairs 29 (1992)

There was no inevitability that there would be a world organisation at the end of the Second World War, or indeed about the form that it should take. [A]n exclusive directorate of the principal victors to call the shots in the post-war world was a distinct possibility, and indeed was contemplated. On the other hand, the League could have been revived; or a regionally-based system might have been tried.

The UN Charter as it emerged in June 1945 reflected many strands, layers and influences[:] the agendas of the leading anti-Axis powers; the views and idiosyncracies of their leaders, especially Franklin Delano Roosevelt and Winston Churchill; the perceptions and pre-conceptions of their advisers and officials; public opinion as expressed by legislatures, the media and NGO's; and, to a greater extent than is often appreciated, the demands of the medium and smaller powers, who were by no means all "western" in outlook. . . .

The three major Allies brought different agendas to the question of a future world organisation. The British approach could be characterised as a blend of national self-interest and pragmatism admixed with a measure of decency and even vision. The primary British aim was to involve the United States fully in a post-war security system. . . .

The American approach was undoubtedly the most idealistic of the Three, even though the military intruded hard-headed considerations at times. Although Roosevelt thought initially in terms of an Anglo-American condominium, later expanded to include the other two leading anti-Axis powers—the famous "Four Policemen" concept—it was the idea of a worldwide "New Deal" that soon gripped American imagination. There was a crusading wish to end the rotten old system of "balance of power" and "spheres of influence." Concepts such as human rights, freedom for colonial peoples (especially in Asia) and free trade (on the grounds that economic nationalism bred conflict) were prominent in American thinking. Roosevelt became increasingly obsessed with the need to win [Soviet leader Joseph] Stalin's engagement in the new venture, even at the expense of British interests and his relations with Churchill. The US was also a strong supporter of a leading role for China, which was regarded with less than enthusiasm by the British and Russians.

A major factor in the American approach was domestic public opinion which after the experience of the Senate's rejection of the Covenant of the League of Nations in 1920 despite President Woodrow Wilson's key role, was judged to be hostile to or at least suspicious of foreign entanglements. . . .

Although little has emerged about the thinking behind the Soviet approach to the new world organisation, it is not hard to surmise that their agenda was more limited and more motivated by *realpolitik* than either the Americans or the British. The nature of the Soviet system and Stalin's style in particular left little scope for idealism. The main Russian aim was to prevent the revival of Germany and to establish Soviet security and influence more widely. . . .

The Dumbarton Oaks meeting took place in Washington in the Georgetown house of the same name during five weeks in August and September 1944. It was attended at senior official level by representatives of the US, UK and USSR[.]

The basic structure of the new organisation had already been thought through and caused little debate. The framework of the League of Nations with its Council, Assembly, Secretariat and International Court was regarded as sound and new nomenclature readily agreed. The Russians saw no need for an economic and social role for the organisation which they envisaged as having a purely security role. The Americans and the British, however, argued that security issues could not be divorced from the overall economic and social background, and also that the new organisation needed a positive and progressive element which would offer the prospect of human development. . . .

By far the most important question which had to be settled was how to maintain . . . "international peace and security." The League of Nations security system set out in the Covenant, which had been designed to prevent a reoccurrence of 1914 by a process of mediation, cooling-off periods, and voluntary sanctions, had patently failed. It was common ground that the new system needed to be given "teeth" but how? The basic concept was that the executive arm of the new organisation needed to be a policeman rather than as under the League a magistrate and a mediator. In Roosevelt's memorable description "a policeman would not be a very effective policeman if, when he saw a felon break into a house, he had to go down to the town hall and call a town meeting to issue a warrant before the felon could be arrested."

To achieve this, the role of the Security Council was clearly differentiated from that of the General Assembly. In contrast to the situation under the Covenant, the Council was to be given the ability to act quickly and effectively by avoiding elaborate preliminary procedures, including largely cutting out a role for legal mechanisms, and by introducing the device of majority voting in place of the League Council's requirement of unanimity. The Council was also to be given real power to enforce its decisions by being able to require armed forces to be put at its disposal. These forces were to consist of national military contingents, including airforce units on immediate standby, rather than a mixed international force which was regarded as unworkable. Coordination and control [were] to be exercised by the Chiefs of Staff of the major military powers through a Military Staff Committee.

[I]t was envisaged that the strongest military powers, that is the leading Allied nations acting in concert, would provide the muscle to enforce the decisions of the Council. It was regarded as only realistic to accept that the major powers would not be willing to bear the burden of combating future threats to international peace and security, as they were carrying the brunt of the struggle against the Axis powers, unless there were adequate safeguards for their perceived essential interests.

All the Big Three at Dumbarton Oaks were agreed that the Great Powers who would be Permanent Members of the Security Council should have the powers of veto over its decisions in certain cases. But in what cases? Britain argued strongly that if the new system was to attract the adherence of the other powers, the veto could only be used in restricted circumstances and not, for example, in situations to which a Permanent Member was a party. The Soviet Union, on the other hand, maintained that Permanent Members' right to veto should apply to any and all activity in the Security Council. The US, initially undecided, came round to the British position. Despite strenuous efforts, the meeting proved unable to resolve the issue, to the despair of Western participants. . . .

The San Francisco conference which was to finalise the drafting of the United Nations Charter opened on April 25th 1945 and was attended by the fifty countries who were signatories of the UN Declaration or "associated powers." . . .

If the Great Powers were under any illusion that the other powers would show their gratitude by muting their demands, this was soon dissipated. . . . The San Francisco conference, which took two months from beginning to end, cannot in any sense be described as a rubber stamp. . . .

The non-great powers accepted, albeit somewhat grudgingly, the basic concept that the leading powers in the victorious Allied coalition should be accorded a special position in the new international security system. However, they subjected the proposed veto power to detailed scrutiny and applied considerable ingenuity to efforts to whittle it down, as well as to accord themselves a greater influence. . . .

While ready to make concessions in other areas, the sponsoring powers were adamant in opposing any significant lessening of the veto power and in the end made it clear that without the veto there would be no United Nations. . . . However, there was one significant change to the proposed security system as a result of the discussion at San Francisco, which was the addition to the enforcement procedure of a range of measures falling short of the use of force, i.e. economic and diplomatic sanctions, military demonstrations and blockade.

Other issues which reflected the particular concerns of the non-great powers related to the powers of the Security Council were the status of existing and future regional arrangements and the protection of national sovereignty. . . . The outcome was some primarily cosmetic changes to the existing regional provisions of the draft but much more significantly the addition of a new article [51] which reserved the right of individual and collective defence. . . .

Foiled in their attempt to diminish the position of the Great Powers in the Security Council, the other states were more successful in extending the status and responsibilities of those parts of the organisation in which all members were on the same footing. The right of the General Assembly to discuss all matters within the scope of the Charter, including those relating to international peace and security unless the Security Council was formally seized of the issue, was established. And the Economic and Social Council's role was enhanced. It was given the status of a principal organ and ambitious hopes were entertained for its activities in the economic and social field. Greater prominence was also attached to human rights and to social issues such as the status of women.

The deferred issue of Trusteeship and colonial territories was settled by a series of compromises. [L]ed by Britain the colonial powers refused to make explicit the notion of full independence for colonial territories, preferring the term "self-government." This option was however recognised for Trusteeship territories and a separate Trusteeship Council on which neither the Great Powers nor the colonial powers had any special privilege was set up as a principal organ.

In the judicial area, the existing Permanent Court of International Justice was effectively maintained under a new name as the International Court of Justice[.] Finally, Russian attempts to neuter the Secretary General's independence were unsuccessful. . . .

In establishing a system of international peace and security it was realistic of the founding fathers to recognise that great powers will not be prepared to participate in an organisation in which they have to shoulder much of the burden without safeguards for their essential interests. Without the veto, who can doubt that the Soviet Union and the United States would not have been tempted to walk out of the UN as great powers had done from the League? At the same time, there was no question of giving such states unbridled power. Even in the Security Council, the non-permanent members could if united constitute a sixth veto and had in any case to form part of a voting majority. And the Permanent Members were given no privileged role in the other parts of the organisation.

The pragmatic approach was matched by a wider vision. The Preamble of the Charter sets out an inspirational world view which speaks to men and women everywhere today as much as it did in 1945.

CHARTER OF THE UNITED NATIONS

June 26, 1945, 59 Stat. 1031, T.S. No. 993, 3 Bevans 1153

WE THE PEOPLES OF THE UNITED NATIONS DETERMINED

> to save succeeding generations from the scourge of war, which twice in our lifetime has brought untold sorrow to mankind, and

> to reaffirm faith in fundamental human rights, in the dignity and worth of the human person, in the equal rights of men and women and of nations large and small, and

> to establish conditions under which justice and respect for the obligations arising from treaties and other sources of international law can be maintained, and

> to promote social progress and better standards of life in larger freedom,

AND FOR THESE ENDS

> to practice tolerance and live together in peace with one another as good neighbors, and

> to unite our strength to maintain international peace and security, and

> to ensure, by the acceptance of principles and the institution of methods, that armed force shall not be used, save in the common interest, and

> to employ international machinery for the promotion of the economic and social advancement of all peoples,

HAVE RESOLVED TO COMBINE OUR EFFORTS TO ACCOMPLISH THESE AIMS.

Accordingly, our respective Governments, through representatives assembled in the city of San Francisco, who have exhibited their full powers found to be in good and due form, have agreed to the present Charter of the United Nations and do hereby establish an international organization to be known as the United Nations.

Article 1

The Purposes of the United Nations are:

1.   To maintain international peace and security, and to that end: to take effective collective measures for the prevention and removal of threats to the peace, and for the suppression of acts of aggression or other breaches of the peace, and to bring about by peaceful means, and in conformity with the principles

of justice and international law, adjustment or settlement of international disputes or situations which might lead to a breach of the peace;

2.   To develop friendly relations among nations based on respect for the principle of equal rights and self-determination of peoples, and to take other appropriate measures to strengthen universal peace;

3.   To achieve international cooperation in solving international problems of an economic, social, cultural, or humanitarian character, and in promoting and encouraging respect for human rights and for fundamental freedoms for all without distinction as to race, sex, language, or religion; and

4.   To be a center for harmonizing the actions of nations in the attainment of these common ends.

Article 25

The Members of the United Nations agree to accept and carry out the decisions of the Security Council in accordance with the present Charter.

Article 103

In the event of a conflict between the obligations of the Members of the United Nations under the present Charter and their obligations under any other international agreement, their obligations under the present Charter shall prevail.

The United Nations. In the second decade of the 21st century, more than seventy years after the establishment of the United Nations, are the U.N. Charter's goals and purposes still essential? Should the Organization's ambitions be modified? Might any of the purposes of the United Nations be achieved nowadays without this form of global cooperation?

The U.N. Security Council, now composed of 15 members, with China, France, Russia, the United Kingdom, and the United States as permanent members, is one of the six "principal organs" created by the U.N. Charter. Does it still make sense to accord legal supremacy to the decisions of the U.N. Security Council in accordance with Articles 25 and 103 of the U.N. Charter? The other five principal U.N. organs are the General Assembly, the Secretariat (headed by the Secretary-General), the International Court of Justice, the Economic and Social Council, and the now-dormant Trusteeship Council. Many other U.N. subsidiary organs and committees were subsequently created. For example, the General Assembly's subsidiary bodies include the United Nations Environment Programme, the United Nations Conference on Trade and Development, and the Office of the United Nations High Commissioner for Refugees. In addition, Articles 57 and 63 of the U.N. Charter provide for relationships between the United Nations and various "specialized agencies," created by separate treaties and addressing a range of subject matters. The International Monetary Fund, the International Maritime Organization, the Food and Agriculture Organization, and the World Health Organization are some of the specialized agencies. Hence, the term "U.N. system" actually refers to more than just one integrated international organization.

The International Law Commission (ILC), a body of legal experts appointed by the General Assembly pursuant to Article 13 of the U.N. Charter, helps to codify international law. For example, the ILC prepared drafts of Vienna Convention on the Law of Treaties (discussed in Chapter 2) and the 2001 Draft Articles on State Responsibility (Chapter 2 and elsewhere). The relationship between the United Nations and the use of force, introduced in this chapter, is explored more thoroughly in Chapter 6. U.N. organs and agencies have also contributed significantly to international environmental law and the international law of the sea. See Chapter 8. For an excellent introduction to U.N. law and its underlying themes and principles, see *Law and Practice of the United Nations* (Simon Chesterton, Thomas M. Franck & David M. Malone eds. 2008).

The U.N. Budget. As of 2016, approximately 40,000 people from most of the 193 U.N. member states worked for the Secretariat. See "Composition of the Secretariat," U.N. Doc. A/71/360, Table 2 (2016). The U.N. budget is proposed by the Secretary-General, reviewed by budgetary committees, and approved by the General Assembly pursuant to Article 17 of the U.N. Charter. Paying for U.N. staff, basic infrastructure, and Organization activities, the U.N. budget was $5.4 billion for the 2016–2017 biennium, or $2.7 billion per year, funded through member states' assessed and voluntary contributions. U.N. peacekeeping operations, which we introduce below and in Chapter 6, are financed through a separate system of member state assessments. The peacekeeping budget for the July 2016–June 2017 fiscal year was $6.8 billion, less than half of one percent of world military expenditures. "Financing Peace-keeping," http://www.un.org/en/peacekeeping/operations/financing.shtml.

Changes to the U.N. Charter. It is possible to amend the U.N. Charter pursuant to Articles 108 or 109, and a few amendments have been adopted. Consistent practice may also effectively change the Charter. For example, an abstention by a permanent member of the Security Council is not now regarded as a veto of a Council decision, despite the literal language of Article 27(3) of the Charter. How else may the Charter change? What changes should be made? For discussions of possible U.N. reforms, see Report of the High-Level Panel on Threats, Challenges and Change, *A More Secure World: Our Shared Responsibility*, U.N. Doc. A/59/586 (2004); Anne-Marie Slaughter, "Security, Solidarity, and Sovereignty: The Grand Themes of UN Reform," 99 *American Journal of International Law* 619 (2005).

International Personality. One theme in the material below is the constitutional evolution of the international political system. Constitutional law is always a complex subject. It becomes even more so in an international context with so many states and legal cultures involved. Some important constitutional questions are: Does an international organization have an "international personality"? Are its powers limited to those expressly delegated by its member states in the organization's charter? To explore these questions, let us turn to the International Court of Justice's *Reparation Case*.

The Reparation Case *in Context.* In April 1947 the United Kingdom, which administered a League of Nations mandate over Palestine (formerly part of the Ottoman Empire), asked the U.N. General Assembly to consider the future of Palestine. The General Assembly recommended that Palestine be divided into independent Arab and Jewish states; Jerusalem was to be administered under international control. Skirmishes in the region led the U.N. Security Council, in April 1948, to call for a ceasefire in Palestine and to establish a Truce Commission. The U.N. General Assembly appointed Count Folke Bernadotte, a Swedish national, to be U.N. Mediator in Palestine. On September 17, 1948, several months after the Provisional Government of Israel proclaimed Israel to be a state, Count Bernadotte and another U.N. observer, Colonel Serot of France, were assassinated in the Israeli-held zone of Jerusalem by men in Israeli army uniforms. The assassins were members of the Stern Gang, an extremist group opposed to outside interference in Israel.

On December 3, 1948, the U.N. General Assembly decided to ask the International Court of Justice for an advisory opinion:

> In the event of an agent of the United Nations in the performance of his duties suffering injury in circumstances involving the responsibility of a State, has the United Nations, as an Organization, the capacity to bring an international claim against the responsible *de jure* or *de facto* government with a view to obtaining the reparation due in respect of the damage caused (*a*) to the United Nations, (*b*) to the victim or to persons entitled through him?

THE REPARATION CASE

Reparation for Injuries Suffered in the Service of the United Nations, 1949 I.C.J. 174

Competence to bring an international claim is, for those possessing it, the capacity to resort to the customary methods recognized by international law for the establishment, the presentation and the settlement of claims. Among these methods may be mentioned protest, request for an enquiry, negotiation, and request for submission to an arbitral tribunal or to the Court in so far as this may be authorized by the Statute. . . .

But, in the international sphere, has the Organization such a nature as involves the capacity to bring an international claim? In order to answer this question, the Court must first enquire whether the Charter has given the Organization such a position that it possesses, in regard to its Members, rights which it is entitled to ask them to respect. In other words, does the Organization possess international personality? . . .

To answer this question, which is not settled by the actual terms of the Charter, we must consider what characteristics it was intended thereby to give to the Organization.

The subjects of law in any legal system are not necessarily identical in their nature or in the extent of their rights, and their nature depends upon the needs of the community. Throughout its history, the development of international law has been influenced by the requirements of international life, and the progressive increase in the collective activities of States has already given rise to instances of action upon the international plane by certain entities which are not States. This development culminated in the establishment in June 1945 of an international organization whose purposes and principles are specified in the Charter of the United Nations. But to achieve these ends the attribution of international personality is indispensable.

The Charter has not been content to make the Organization created by it merely a centre "for harmonizing the actions of nations in the attainment of these common ends" (Article I, para. 4). It has equipped that centre with organs, and has given it special tasks. It has defined the position of the Members in relation to the Organization by requiring them to give it every assistance in any action undertaken by it (Article 2, para. 5), and to accept and carry out the decisions of the Security Council; by authorizing the General Assembly to make recommendations to the Members; by giving the Organization legal capacity and privileges and immunities in the territory of each of its Members; and by providing for the conclusion of agreements between the Organization and its Members.

Practice—in particular the conclusion of conventions to which the Organization is a party—has confirmed this character of the Organization, which occupies a position in certain respects in detachment from its Members, and which is under a duty to remind them, if need be, of certain obligations. It must be added that the Organization is a political body, charged with political tasks of an important character, and covering a wide field namely, the maintenance of international peace and security, the development of friendly relations among nations, and the achievement of international co-operation in the solution of problems of an economic, social, cultural or humanitarian character (Article I); and in dealing with its Members it employs political means. The "Convention on the Privileges and Immunities of the United Nations" of 1946 creates rights and duties between each of the signatories and the Organization. It is difficult to see how such a convention could operate except upon the international plane and as between parties possessing international personality.

In the opinion of the Court, the Organization was intended to exercise and enjoy, and is in fact exercising and enjoying, functions and rights which can only be explained on the basis of the possession of a large measure of international personality and the capacity to operate upon an international plane. It is at present the supreme type of international organization, and it could not carry out the intentions of its founders if it was devoid of international personality. It must be acknowledged that its Members, by entrusting certain functions to it, with the attendant duties and responsibilities, have clothed it with the competence required to enable those functions to be effectively discharged.

Accordingly, the Court has come to the conclusion that the Organization is an international person. That is not the same thing as saying that it is a State, which it certainly is not, or that its legal personality and rights and duties are the same as those of a State. Still less is it the same thing as saying that it is "a super-State," whatever that expression may mean. It does not even imply that all its rights and duties must be upon the international plane, any more than all the rights and duties of a State must be upon that plane. What it does mean is that it is a subject of international law and capable of possessing international rights and duties, and that it has capacity to maintain its rights by bringing international claims.

The Aftermath of the Reparation Case. Following the ICJ's opinion in the *Reparation Case*, the U.N. General Assembly authorized the Secretary-General to bring a claim for reparations against allegedly responsible states for injuries incurred in the service of the United Nations. Arbitration was contemplated if negotiation did not lead to a settlement. G.A. Res. 365 (IV) (1949). Israel paid over $50,000 in reparations for the deaths of Count Bernadotte and Colonel

Serot. For more background on the *Reparation Case*, see David J. Bederman, "The *Reparation for Injuries* Case: The Law of Nations is Transformed into International Law," in *International Law Stories* 307 (John E. Noyes, Laura A. Dickinson & Mark W. Janis eds. 2007).

International Personality. According to Professor Bederman, the opinion in the *Reparation Case* "conclusively ushered in a new era of international law, fully diversified with multiple subjects and objects." David J. Bederman, "The Souls of International Organizations: Legal Personality and the Lighthouse at Cape Spartel," 36 *Virginia Journal of International Law* 275, 367 (1996). Why did the Court find that the United Nations had "international personality"? If, as the ICJ suggested, international personality depends on a subject being "capable of possessing international rights and duties" and having "capacity to maintain its rights by bringing international claims," what is the source of that capability and capacity? Do the United Nations and other international organizations have international legal rights only because they are authorized in treaties? What underpins the "international personality" of other entities, such as states or individuals?

Capacity of the United Nations to Bring International Claims. In the *Reparation Case*, the capacity of the United Nations to bring a claim for the death of Count Bernadotte did not follow automatically once the Court concluded the Organization had international personality. The Court separately found that the United Nations could bring an international claim against a responsible government to obtain reparations on behalf of a U.N. employee or his survivors. Should the ICJ have left it to Sweden, Count Bernadotte's state of nationality, to pursue any claims related to his death? See the *Nottebohm Case* in Chapter 7.

Judge Hackworth dissented from the part of the Court's opinion finding that the United Nations had the capacity to sponsor an international claim on behalf of one of its agents. He said in part:

> There is no impelling reason, if any at all, why the Organization should become the sponsor of claims on behalf of its employees, even though limited to those arising while the employee is in line of duty. These employees are still nationals of their respective countries, and the customary methods of handling such claims are still available in full vigour.

UN acting in behalf of members instead of their respective nations?

1949 I.C.J. at 198. Should the Court have advised that the U.N. Charter be amended to authorize the United Nations to espouse claims on behalf of nationals of member states in service of the Organization?

Other Types of Legal Capacity. What other international legal rights does the United Nations have, in addition to the right to make claims for injuries to the Organization and its agents? Although Articles 1 and 2 of the Vienna Convention on the Law of Treaties do not define "treaties" to include agreements made by international organizations, the United Nations may enter into international agreements. For example, as discussed below, the United States and the United Nations have a Headquarters Agreement. There is a 1986 Vienna Convention on the Law of Treaties between States and International Organizations or between International Organizations, modeled on the Vienna Convention on the Law of Treaties. However, the United Nations does not have all the rights of a state. For example, the Organization is not permitted to be a party in contentious cases before the International Court of Justice.

Not every international organization has the same legal attributes. The Permanent Court of International Justice, in its *Advisory Opinion of February 7, 1923, on Nationality Decrees in Tunis and Morocco*, suggested that the legal authority of apparently similar entities may differ. The Court, while noting some common features of protectorates under international law, also stressed that "they have individual legal characteristics resulting from the special conditions under which they were created, and the stage of their development." 1923 P.C.I.J., Ser. B, No. 4, at 27.

The United Nations and Nonmember States. One issue in the *Reparation Case* was whether the United Nations had legal rights *vis-à-vis* nonmember states. In a portion of the *Reparation Case* not excerpted above, the International Court concluded "that fifty States, representing the vast majority of the members of the international community, had the power, in conformity with international law, to bring into being an entity possessing objective international personality, and not merely personality recognized by them alone, together with capacity to bring international claims." 1949 I.C.J. at 185. Why should the United Nations have the capacity to bring international claims even against a nonmember state? May the Organization take other steps with respect to nonmember states, such as sanctioning them for conduct that threatens international peace and security? See Article 2(6) of the U.N. Charter and Chapter 6.

The United Nations and Municipal Legal Systems. The United Nations relies on its member states to accord the Organization and its employees and agents certain rights, privileges, and immunities. On the international level, these measures are furthered by treaties, such as Articles 104 and 105 of the 1945 U.N. Charter and the 1946 Convention on the Privileges and Immunities of the United Nations. On the municipal level, a state defines the "legal personality" of international organizations for municipal legal purposes. States enact legislation to provide privileges, immunities, and protections to U.N. missions, to U.N. officials, and to diplomats representing their states at U.N. offices. The United States, for example, enacted the International Organizations Immunities Act, 22 U.S.C. §§ 288–288f, in 1945, and the Act for the Prevention and Punishment of Crimes Against Internationally Protected Persons, 18 U.S.C. § 112, in 1976 (implementing a convention that addresses such crimes). The bilateral U.S.-U.N. Agreement Regarding the Headquarters of the United Nations was implemented by a 1947 joint congressional resolution.

Responsibility of International Organizations. If international organizations have rights at international law, do they also have duties? The International Court of Justice, in its advisory opinion in the *Immunity from Legal Process Case*, although affirming the immunity of a U.N. agent, found that "the United Nations may be required to bear responsibility for the damage arising from" acts performed by the Organization "or by its agents acting in their official capacity." Difference Relating to Immunity from Legal Process of a Special Rapporteur of the Commission on Human Rights, 1999 I.C.J. 62, 88–89.

In 2001 the International Law Commission (ILC) completed its Draft Articles on State Responsibility, which we discuss elsewhere, especially in Chapter 7. In 2002 the ILC decided to pursue the parallel topic of responsibility of international organizations. In 2011 the ILC adopted Draft Articles on that topic.

DRAFT ARTICLES ON THE RESPONSIBILITY OF INTERNATIONAL ORGANIZATIONS

Report of the International Law Commission on its Sixty-third Session,
U.N. GAOR, 66th Sess., Supp. No. 10, U.N. Doc. A/66/10, at 52 (2011)

*Article 4: Elements of an internationally wrongful act
of an international organization*

There is an internationally wrongful act of an international organization when conduct consisting of an action or omission:

(a)   is attributable to the international organization under international law; and

(b)   constitutes a breach of an international obligation of that international organization.

Commentary

[T]he attribution of conduct to an international organization is one of the two essential elements for an internationally wrongful act to occur. . . .

A second essential element . . . is that conduct constitutes the breach of an obligation under international law. The obligation may result either from a treaty binding the international organization or from any other source of international law applicable to the organization. As the International Court of Justice noted in its advisory opinion on the *Interpretation of the Agreement of 25 March 1951 between the WHO and Egypt*, international organizations

> are bound by any obligations incumbent upon them under general rules of international law, under their constitutions or under international agreements to which they are parties.

A breach is thus possible with regard to any of these international obligations.

[The Commission's general commentary concerning attribution of conduct to an international organization includes the following text:]

Although it may not frequently occur in practice, dual or even multiple attribution of conduct cannot be excluded. Thus, attribution of a certain conduct to an international organization does not imply that the same conduct cannot be attributed to a State; nor does attribution of conduct to a State rule out attribution of the same conduct to an international organization.

[T]he present draft articles . . . do not point to cases in which conduct cannot be attributed to the organization. For instance, the articles do not say, but only imply, that conduct of military forces of States or international organizations is not attributable to the United Nations when the Security Council authorizes States or international organizations to take necessary measures outside a chain of command linking those forces to the United Nations.

Article 6: Conduct of organs or agents of an international organization

1. The conduct of an organ or agent of an international organization in the performance of functions of that organ or agent shall be considered as an act of that organization under international law whatever position the organ or agent holds in respect of the organization. . . .

Article 7: Conduct of organs of a State or organs or agents of an international organization placed at the disposal of another international organization

The conduct of an organ of a State or an organ or agent of an international organization that is placed at the disposal of another international organization shall be considered under international law an act of the latter organization if the organization exercises effective control over that conduct.

Commentary

When an organ of a State is placed at the disposal of an international organization, the organ may be fully seconded to that organization. In this case the organ's conduct would clearly be attributable only to the receiving organization [and] the general rule set out in Article 6 would apply. Article 7 deals with the different situation in which the seconded organ or agent still acts to a certain extent as organ of the seconding State or as organ or agent of the seconding organization. This occurs for instance in the case of military contingents that a State places at the disposal of the United Nations for a peacekeeping operation, since the State retains disciplinary powers and criminal jurisdiction over the members of the national contingent. In this situation the problem arises whether a specific conduct of the seconded organ or agent is to be attributed to the receiving organization or to the seconding State or organization. . . .

The criterion for attribution of conduct either to the contributing State or organization or to the receiving organization is based according to article 7 on the factual control that is exercised over the specific conduct taken by the organ or agent placed at the receiving organization's disposal. . . .

The United Nations assumes that in principle it has exclusive control of the deployment of national contingents in a peacekeeping force. This premise led the United Nations Legal Counsel to state:

> As a subsidiary organ of the United Nations, an act of a peacekeeping force is, in principle, imputable to the Organization, and if committed in violation of an international obligation entails the international responsibility of the Organization and its liability in compensation.

This statement sums up United Nations practice relating to the United Nations Operation in the Congo (ONUC), the United Nations Peace-keeping Force in Cyprus (UNFICYP) and later peacekeeping forces. In a [2011] comment, the United Nations Secretariat observed that "[f]or a number of reasons, notably political," the practice of the United Nations had been that of "maintaining the principle of United Nations responsibility vis-à-vis third parties" in connection with peacekeeping operations.

Practice relating to peacekeeping forces is particularly significant in the present context because of the control that the contributing State retains over disciplinary and criminal matters. This may have consequences with regard to attribution of conduct. . . .

As has been held by several scholars, when an organ or agent is placed at the disposal of an international organization, the decisive question in relation to attribution of a given conduct appears to be who has effective control over the conduct in question.

International Organizations and Breaches of International Obligations. For what sorts of international obligations may an international organization be responsible? The U.N. Secretary-General in 1999 instructed forces under U.N. command and control to respect international humanitarian law. The United Nations also accepted responsibility, subject to certain temporal and financial limitations, for tortious damage caused by U.N. peacekeepers while performing their official duties. See Committee on Accountability of International Organizations, "Final Report," in International Law Association, *Report of the Seventy-First Conference (Berlin)* 164 (2004). The United Nations has been criticized, however, for failing to assume responsibility for the contributions of Nepalese peacekeepers to a cholera epidemic in Haiti. See Transnational Development Clinic, Yale Law School *et al.*, *Peacekeeping Without Accountability* (Aug. 2013), *available at* http://www.law.yale.edu/system/files/documents/pdf/Clinics/Haiti_TDC_Final_Report.pdf. Are international organizations in breach only when their agents violate the organization's rules or governing treaty? May the United Nations be liable for violating international human rights law or customary international law?

Attributing Responsibility to International Organizations. The European Court of Human Rights relied on the notion of "ultimate control" rather than "effective control" in attributing conduct to the United Nations in the *Behrami* and *Saramati Cases*. Behrami and Behrami v. France; Saramati v. France, Germany and Norway, App. Nos. 71412/01 & 78166/01 (Grand Chamber, 2007). Which approach is preferable? How should we determine who exercises "effective control" in peacekeeping situations? In *Behrami* children were killed and injured when they played with undetonated cluster bombs left over from a 1999 North Atlantic Treaty Organization (NATO) bombing in Kosovo; members of the U.N. Mission in Kosovo (UNMIK), a U.N. peacekeeping force, had not cleaned up the bombs. *Saramati* involved an individual who was detained by a NATO operation authorized by the United Nations to maintain order in Kosovo. Alleging violations of the European Convention on Human Rights, the applicants in *Behrami* brought a claim against France, which led UNMIK in the relevant sector of Kosovo, while Saramati sought recovery from the governments whose nationals had ordered his detention. The European Court's reliance on the "ultimate control" test meant that the peacekeepers' conduct was not attributable to France, Germany, or Norway. What would happen if the injured parties then asserted a claim against the United Nations?

Attributing responsibility to an international organization has meant that injured claimants could not obtain relief in some cases. Consider, for example, *J.H. Rayner Ltd. v. Department of Trade and Industry*, [1990] 2 App. Cas. 418, 81 *International Law Reports* 671 (House of Lords, 1989), and related litigation involving the International Tin Council (ITC). In the 1980s the ITC, an international organization established to buy and sell tin to stabilize the price of that commodity, ran out of funds to pay for tin it had purchased. Creditors sued the ITC and tried to implead its member states. The British House of Lords ruled that, given the ITC's separate international personality, its member states were not responsible for the ITC's debts. Should states be able to shield themselves from liability by operating through an international organization?

Some courts have decided that the United Nations did not exercise effective control over the actions of its peacekeeping forces and instead attributed control to the troop-contributing state. See Marko Milanovic, "Al Skeini and Al-Jedda in Strasbourg," 23 *European Journal of International Law* 121 (2012). In 2013 the Dutch Supreme Court found the Netherlands responsible for actions of Dutch forces (the Dutchbat) assigned to a U.N. peacekeeping mission. Operating in the former Yugoslavia in 1995, the Dutchbat had refused to allow male family members of a Yugoslav translator to take refuge in a Dutch military compound; those family members were murdered by Bosnian Serbs at Srebenica. Netherlands v. Nuhanović, Case 12/03324 (Supreme Court of the Netherlands, 2013). The Court relied on the ILC's Draft Articles on Responsibility of International Organizations to determine that the Netherlands exercised effective control over the Dutchbat, concluding that Article 7 applied where, as in the *Nuhanović Case*, "a State places troops at the disposal of the United Nations in the context of a UN peace mission, and command and control is transferred to the United Nations, but the disciplinary powers and criminal jurisdiction (the 'organic command') remain vested in the seconding State." *Id.* ¶ 3.10.2. Ought the conduct of the Dutchbat forces also

> be attributed to the United Nations? The Dutch court left open the possibility of such dual attribution. See *id.* ¶ 3.11.2 and Article 48(1) of the ILC Draft Articles.

2.   Non-Governmental Organizations

Non-governmental organizations (NGOs) are created under municipal law rather than by treaty. There are thousands of international NGOs working on a wide range of economic, social, human rights, and environmental issues. Although some NGOs have links to governments or receive government grants, most are private, not-for-profit entities, receiving the large part of their support from individual members or private contributions. As we saw in the *Texaco/Libya Arbitration* in Chapter 2, business corporations, which are also creatures of municipal law, may use international law and international legal process to try to obtain redress when their economic interests have been harmed. International NGOs, by contrast, often have as primary goals the development of international legal norms and the implementation and enforcement of those norms on the international and municipal levels.

In this section, we look at some of the roles of private organizations in international law and process. We first consider the International Committee of the Red Cross, which provides assistance to victims of armed conflicts. Later text concerns actual and potential functions of NGOs in developing and enforcing international environmental law. These materials explore questions about the international legal personality of NGOs and their recognition by other entities.

GABOR RONA, THE ICRC'S STATUS: IN A CLASS OF ITS OWN

Feb. 2004, *available at* http://www.icrc.org

NGOs are private organizations such as associations, federations, unions, institutes, and other groups; they are not established by a government or by intergovernmental agreement. NGOs can play a role in international affairs by virtue of their activities, but they do not necessarily possess any official status, nor do they have a mandate for their existence or activities.

Where an organization's membership or activity is limited to a specific country, it's considered a national NGO; if its activities cross borders, it becomes an international NGO. Some of the best-known international NGOs include Médécins Sans Frontières, Amnesty International, Human Rights Watch, Oxfam, and so on.

. . . Unlike NGOs, intergovernmental organizations by definition have a mandate from governments for their existence and activities and enjoy certain working facilities known in diplomatic parlance as "privileges and immunities."

The ICRC has a hybrid nature. As a private association formed under the Swiss Civil Code, its existence is not in itself mandated by governments. And yet its functions and activities—to provide protection and assistance to victims of conflict—are mandated by the international community of States and are founded on international law, specifically the Geneva Conventions, which are among the most widely ratified treaties in the world.

Because of this the ICRC, like any intergovernmental organization, is recognized as having an "international legal personality" or status of its own. It enjoys working facilities (privileges and immunities) comparable to those of the United Nations, its agencies, and other intergovernmental organizations. Examples of these facilities include exemption from taxes and customs duties, inviolability of premises and documents, and immunity from judicial process.

The ICRC can only do its job of providing protection and assistance to conflict victims if its working principles of impartiality, independence and neutrality are respected. It is through recognition of the ICRC's privileges and immunities that States and international organizations acknowledge their respect for those principles. Thus, in line with its international legal mandate, the ICRC's privileges and immunities are widely recognized by governments, by the United Nations and by other organizations. This means that the ICRC is . . . treated as . . . an intergovernmental organization for the work it does under its international mandate.

The legal basis for the ICRC's essential privileges and immunities [is] recognized in various ways, including:

- *Headquarters Agreements between the ICRC and governments, or state legislation.* In the nearly 80 countries in which the ICRC carries out significant operations, its international legal personality, judicial immunity and testimonial privilege (right not to be called as a witness) [are] recognized either by treaty or by legislation.

- *Judicial decisions.* Several domestic and international tribunals have ruled on the ICRC's judicial immunity and testimonial privileges. Recently, the International Criminal Tribunal for the former Yugoslavia (ICTY) distinguished the ICRC from NGOs by citing its international legal mandate and status, including its right to decline to testify. The rules of procedure and evidence of the newly established International Criminal Court also reflect the position of the more than one hundred states that drafted the document, that the ICRC enjoys testimonial immunity.

- *The United Nations and other international organizations.* The ICRC has been granted observer status at the UN General Assembly [pursuant to General Assembly Resolution 45/6 (1990)] and enjoys similar status with other international, intergovernmental organizations.

The ICRC and the International Red Cross and Red Crescent Movement. The founding of the International Committee of the Red Cross was largely due to the efforts of Henry Dunant, who observed the suffering of thousands of wounded troops during an 1859 battle in the War of Italian Unification. The ICRC was formed under Swiss law in 1863, and its governing body is composed of Swiss nationals. See http://www.icrc.org.

The ICRC is one component of what is known as the International Red Cross and Red Crescent Movement. Another part is the International Federation of Red Cross and Red Crescent Societies (formerly the League of Red Cross Societies), founded in 1919 and, like the ICRC, headquartered in Geneva. The Federation supports the activities of national societies, promoting and coordinating relief operations for natural or technological disasters. As of May 2017, there were 190 national Red Cross and Red Crescent societies, of which the American Red Cross—a corporation formed and supported by the U.S. government (see 36 U.S.C. §§ 300101–300113)—is one. The ICRC itself has multiple functions: assessing whether new national societies meet conditions for recognition; providing international relief services to soldiers and civilians in armed conflicts; assisting national societies in such situations; and developing and promoting international humanitarian law. See "The International Committee of the Red Cross (ICRC): Its Mission and Work," 91 *International Review of the Red Cross*, No. 824 (2009). In 1977 the "International Red Cross" was described as "a transnational movement with two heads and many arms. [T]he heads do not control the arms, and the heads are not always looking in the same direction." David P. Forsythe, *Humanitarian Politics: The International Committee of the Red Cross* 5 (1977).

The ICRC and the Geneva Conventions. The ICRC has contributed to the negotiation of international humanitarian law treaties, including the four 1949 Geneva Conventions, which concern the protection and humane treatment of prisoners of war (POWs), of wounded and sick members of the armed forces in the field and at sea, and of civilians in time of war. Treaties also explicitly provide roles for the Committee. For example, according to Article 5 of the 1977 Protocol Additional (No. I) to the Geneva Conventions, the ICRC may serve as a "Protecting Power," monitoring implementation, *e.g.*, by visiting POWs or conflict zones. Similar authority is granted to the ICRC under the four Geneva Conventions. Why might a government prefer to have the ICRC, rather than a neutral government or the United Nations, act as a Protecting Power? Has the ICRC's confidentiality helped or harmed its ability to fulfill humanitarian functions? See Steven R. Ratner, "Behind the Flag of Dunant: Secrecy and the Compliance Mission of the International Committee of the Red Cross," in *Transparency in International Law* 297 (Andrea Bianchi & Anne Peters eds. 2013). More on the Geneva Conventions and international humanitarian law (also known as *jus in bello*) appears in Chapter 6.

The ICRC's International Personality. Gabor Rona, in the excerpt above, noted other aspects of the ICRC's international personality. For example, the ICRC has entered into headquarters agreements with states where the Committee conducts its activities. These agreements give the ICRC much the same sorts of privileges and immunities that international organizations enjoy pursuant to agreement. For instance, the 1993 Agreement Between the International Committee of the Red Cross and the Swiss Federal Council To Determine the Legal Status of the Committee in Switzerland provides that the ICRC's premises and archives are inviolable and that the ICRC is, with certain exceptions, immune from legal process. According to Article 1 of the Agreement, Switzerland "recognizes the international juridical personality and the legal capacity in Switzerland" of the ICRC.

The International Personality of NGOs. As you read the following comments, consider whether NGOs generally possess some degree of international personality. What differences among international organizations, individuals (Chapter 7), and NGOs help explain the status of NGOs at international law? If all have important roles with respect to international law, should we stop attempting to classify entities as either "subjects" with international legal personality or "objects" without it? Should we instead characterize all influential entities as "participants" in a global legal process? See Rosalyn Higgins, *Problems and Process: International Law and How We Use It* 49–50 (1994).

NGOs and International Law Litigation. What role should international law play in authorizing NGOs to participate in environmental or human rights litigation? The *Friends of the Earth Case*, Bund für Umwelt und Naturschutz Deutschland, Landesverband Nordrhein-Westfalen eV v. Bezitksregierung

Armsberg, [2011] EUECJ C–115/09 (European Court of Justice, Fourth Chamber), concerned one such initiative, the Aarhus Convention. The Convention, negotiated within the United Nations Economic Commission for Europe, entered into force on October 30, 2001, and as of May 2017 numbered 47 parties. Core principles of the Aarhus Convention include citizen access to environmental information, public participation in environmental decision-making, and access to judicial or administrative procedures to promote adherence to environmental law and the Convention's principles. See Vera Rodenhoff, "The Aarhus Convention and its Implications for the 'Institutions' of the European Community," 11 *Review of European Community and International Environmental Law* 343 (2002). The *Friends of the Earth Case* held that the European Union regulations implementing the Aarhus Convention gave the NGO Friends of the Earth standing to appear in German judicial proceedings in order to challenge environmental rulings. Pursuant to that holding, the German Parliament amended German law, giving effect to the judgment. See John Blain & Sharon Long, "Standing of Environmental NGOs: New Measures to Fast-track Proceedings," *Lexology*, Mar. 5, 2013, *available at* http://www.lexology.com/library/.

Should NGOs be able to participate directly in cases brought before international tribunals? For a review of practice concerning NGO participation in international environmental litigation, see Tim Stephens, *International Courts and Environmental Protection* 252–64 (2009). Stephens noted "a host of political impediments in commencing environmental litigation in the community interest." Although efforts by non-state actors to gain access to international litigation "have begun to yield results," these results "have been relatively modest in comparison with gains in environmental diplomacy generally, where civil society groups have become active and valued participants." *Id.* at 269–70.

Even without the impetus of a treaty such as the Aarhus Convention, municipal legal rules sometimes allow non-governmental organizations to participate in litigation. For example, Amnesty International was allowed to intervene in a case before the British House of Lords, in support of Spain's effort to extradite Chile's former dictator, General Augusto Pinochet, in order to prosecute him for human rights offenses. The House of Lords' 1998 decision denying Pinochet immunity with respect to alleged instances of torture and hostage-taking was, however, set aside when it was discovered that one of the Law Lords sitting on the case had links to Amnesty International (as chair and a director of a separate organization, Amnesty International Charity Limited). Following hearings before a new panel of judges, the House of Lords ruled that

Pinochet could be extradited to Spain. Although the British government released him on medical grounds, he faced trial in Chile following his return there. See William J. Aceves, "Liberalism and International Legal Scholarship: The Pinochet Case and the Move Toward a Universal System of Transnational Law Litigation," 41 *Harvard Journal of International Law* 129 (2000). Human rights NGOs also participate in cases in municipal courts in which international human rights law is litigated by filing *amicus curiae* briefs, which courts sometimes cite in their judgments. See, *e.g.*, Ma v. Reno, 208 F.3d 815, 829–30 (9th Cir. 2000).

The Contributions of NGOs to International Law. By gathering facts, lobbying, and providing technical expertise, NGOs contribute to the development and implementation of treaties and other international legal norms, to the work of international organizations, and to the international legal activities of national governments. See Steve Charnovitz, "Two Centuries of Participation: NGOs and International Governance," 18 *Michigan Journal of International Law* 183 (1997). Treaties occasionally specify a direct role for NGOs in international organizations. For example, the Constitution of the International Labor Organization, established in 1919, provides for direct NGO participation. Each ILO member state is represented in the ILO's plenary body by two representatives from government, one representative from management, and one from labor. For the United States, the U.S. Council for International Business represents employers, and the AFL-CIO represents workers. Does this tripartite ILO structure help achieve consensus positions? See Recommendation and Report on the International Labor Organization, in *The United Nations at 50: Proposals for Improving Its Effectiveness* 107 (John E. Noyes ed. 1997).

International organizations may also allow non-governmental organizations to participate in their work even absent explicit "constitutional" authorization. The International Atomic Energy Agency (IAEA), a U.N. specialized agency created in 1957, has long accorded consultative status to NGOs with "special competence in the field," allowing those NGOs to observe meetings, submit certain statements, and gain access to some IAEA documents. See IAEA, Rules on Consultative Status of Non-governmental Organizations with the Agency, IAEA Doc. INFCIRC/14 (1959); Sheel Kant Sharma, "The IAEA and the UN Family: Networks of Nuclear Co-operation," 37 *IAEA Bulletin*, No. 3, Sept. 1995, at 10.

Accountability and Recognition of NGOs. It may be easy to form an NGO, a step typically accomplished by satisfying a state's requirements for forming a not-for-profit entity. A small group of individuals may make decisions on behalf of an NGO. Will an NGO be accountable to its membership? Are NGOs more or less accountable than states? Should NGOs be externally accountable to other international actors for their roles in international systems? See the essays by Paul Wapner, Peter J. Spiro, Debora Spar and James Dail, and Benedict Kingsbury in Vol. 3, No. 1 of the *Chicago Journal of International Law* (2002). Are concerns about input from members, the accuracy and impartiality of positions espoused, and transparency in decision making assuaged if there is competition from other groups and individuals? Are such concerns adequately addressed if an NGO is "recognized" by an international legal person with which it deals?

The U.N. Economic and Social Council, acting pursuant to Article 71 of the U.N. Charter, has adopted criteria for establishing consultative relationships with NGOs. ECOSOC Res. 1996/31. These provide that an NGO must focus on matters within ECOSOC's competence, have purposes in conformity with the U.N. Charter, and disclose its sources of revenue to ECOSOC. As of September 2016, over 4,500 NGOs had entered into consultative status with ECOSOC. See the website of the NGO Branch of the U.N. Department of Economic and Social Affairs at http://www.csonet.org.

Global Civil Society. Do NGOs contribute to the development of a global or world civil society, a concept competing with a state-centric view of international law and relations? Professor Christenson defined global civil society as comprising "individuals and groups in voluntary association without regard to their identities as citizens of any particular country, and outside the political and public dominion of the community of nations." Gordon A. Christenson, "World Civil Society and the International Rule of Law," 19 *Human Rights Quarterly* 724, 731 (1997). Do the media, academia, and transnational corporations also contribute to an emerging global civil society? See *Our Global Neighborhood: The Report of the Commission on Global Governance* (1995). It has been suggested that the origins of the concept of global civil society may be found in the American missionary movement of the 19th century. Walter Russell Mead, *Special Providence: American Foreign Policy and How It Changed the World* 145–46 (2001).

NGOs, interacting with each other and with other entities, form networks of advocacy groups. As we will see in Chapter 7, NGOs collaborated to promote the International Criminal Court. Networking has been aided by developments in information technology.

3. Treaty Regimes

International lawyers and international relations theorists sometimes refer to "regimes" when discussing formal and informal international political arrangements. According to one international relations definition, regimes are

> sets of implicit principles, norms, rules and decision-making procedures around which actors' expectations converge in a given area of international relations. Principles are beliefs of fact, causation and rectitude. Norms are standards of behavior defined in terms of rights and obligations. Rules are specific prescriptions or proscriptions for action. Decision-making procedures are prevailing practices for making and implementing collective choice.

Stephen D. Krasner, "Structural Causes and Regime Consequences: Regimes as Intervening Variables," in *International Regimes* 1, 2 (Stephen D. Krasner ed. 1983). Under this definition, non-binding soft law declarations—such as the Rio Principles noted in Chapter 2—may be elements of regimes. More formal international legal regimes are treaty-based, typically employing both general standards and precise rules. International organizations sometimes administer regimes. Some regimes provide roles for technical or limited-role "treaty bodies" that do not have international personality.

Constructivism. Generally, modern regime theory is promoted as an alternative to both the classical "positivistic" views of scholars like Oppenheim and the perspectives of "realists" like Morgenthau. This alternative account of the nature of international law is sometimes called "constructivism." One definition of constructivism is that world politics and international law are "socially constructed—i.e., constructed by the very ideas that actors share with themselves and others about the world they live in, and (given these 'things'), what they can and should do." David Armstrong, Theo Farrell & Hélène Lambert, *International Law and International Relations* 100 (2d ed. 2012).

The Antarctic Regime. As we explore one important example of a regime—Antarctica—consider how and why this regime evolved, the role that it plays, and potential alternatives. The 1959 Antarctic Treaty, excerpted below, is a cornerstone of the regime. What are its other elements? Is it useful to think of the Antarctic regime as being "socially constructed"?

THE ANTARCTIC TREATY

Dec. 1, 1959, 12 U.S.T. 794, 402 U.N.T.S. 71

The Governments of Argentina, Australia, Belgium, Chile, the French Republic, Japan, New Zealand, Norway, the Union of South Africa, the Union of Soviet Socialist Republics, the United Kingdom of Great Britain and Northern Ireland, and the United States of America,

Recognizing that it is in the best interest of all mankind that Antarctica shall continue forever to be used exclusively for peaceful purposes and shall not become the scene or object of international discord;

Acknowledging the substantial contributions to scientific knowledge resulting from international cooperation in scientific investigation in Antarctica;

Convinced that the establishment of a firm foundation for the continuation and development of such cooperation on the basis of freedom of scientific investigation in Antarctica as applied during the International Geophysical Year accords with the interests of science and progress of all mankind;

Convinced also that a treaty ensuring the use of Antarctica for peaceful purposes only and the continuance of international harmony in Antarctica will further the purposes and principles embodied in the Charter of the United Nations;

Have agreed as follows:

Article I

1.   Antarctica shall be used for peaceful purposes only. There shall be prohibited, *inter alia*, any measures of a military nature, such as the establishment of military bases and fortifications, the carrying out of military maneuvers, as well as the testing of any type of weapons.

2.   The present Treaty shall not prevent the use of military personnel or equipment for scientific research or for any other peaceful purpose.

Article II

Freedom of scientific investigation in Antarctica and cooperation toward that end, as applied during the International Geophysical Year, shall continue, subject to the provisions of the present Treaty.

Article III

1.   In order to promote international cooperation in scientific investigation in Antarctica, as provided for in Article II of the present Treaty, the Contracting Parties agree that, to the greatest extent feasible and practicable:

(a) information regarding plans for scientific programs in Antarctica shall be exchanged to permit maximum economy and efficiency of operations;

(b) scientific personnel shall be exchanged in Antarctica between expeditions and stations;

(c) scientific observations and results from Antarctica shall be exchanged and made freely available.

2. In implementing this Article, every encouragement shall be given to the establishment of cooperative working relations with those Specialized Agencies of the United Nations and other international organizations having a scientific or technical interest in Antarctica.

Article IV

1. Nothing contained in the present Treaty shall be interpreted as:

(a) a renunciation by any Contracting Party of previously asserted rights of or claims to territorial sovereignty in Antarctica;

(b) a renunciation or diminution by any Contracting Party of any basis of claim to territorial sovereignty in Antarctica which it may have whether as a result of its activities or those of its nationals in Antarctica, or otherwise;

(c) prejudicing the position of any Contracting Party as regards its recognition or nonrecognition of any other State's right of or claim or basis of claim to territorial sovereignty in Antarctica.

2. No acts or activities taking place while the present Treaty is in force shall constitute a basis for asserting, supporting or denying a claim to territorial sovereignty in Antarctica or create any rights of sovereignty in Antarctica. No new claim, or enlargement of an existing claim, to territorial sovereignty in Antarctica shall be asserted while the present Treaty is in force.

Article V

1. Any nuclear explosions in Antarctica and the disposal there of radioactive waste material shall be prohibited. . . .

Article VI

The provisions of the present Treaty shall apply to the area south of 60° South Latitude, including all ice shelves, but nothing in the present Treaty shall prejudice or in any way affect the rights, or the exercise of the rights, of any State under international law with regard to the high seas within that area.

Article VII

1.   In order to promote the objectives and ensure the observance of the provisions of the present Treaty, each Contracting Party whose representatives are entitled to participate in the meetings referred to in Article IX of the Treaty shall have the right to designate observers to carry out any inspection provided for by the present Article. Observers shall be nationals of the Contracting Parties which designate them. The names of observers shall be communicated to every other Contracting Party having the right to designate observers, and like notice shall be given of the termination of their appointment.

2.   Each observer designated in accordance with the provisions of paragraph 1 of this Article shall have complete freedom of access at any time to any or all areas of Antarctica. . . .

Article IX

1.   Representatives of the Contracting Parties named in the preamble to the present Treaty shall meet at the City of Canberra within two months after the date of entry into force of the Treaty, and thereafter at suitable intervals and places, for the purpose of exchanging information, consulting together on matters of common interest pertaining to Antarctica, and formulating and considering, and recommending to their Governments, measures in furtherance of the principles and objectives of the Treaty, including measures regarding:

(a)   use of Antarctica for peaceful purposes only;

(b)   facilitation of scientific research in Antarctica;

(c)   facilitation of international scientific cooperation in Antarctica;

(d)   facilitation of the exercise of the rights of inspection provided for in Article VII of the Treaty;

(e)   questions relating to the exercise of jurisdiction in Antarctica;

(f)   preservation and conservation of living resources in Antarctica.

2.   Each Contracting Party which has become a party to the present Treaty by accession under Article XIII shall be entitled to appoint representatives to participate in the meetings referred to in paragraph 1 of the present Article, during such time as that Contracting Party demonstrates its interest in Antarctica by conducting substantial scientific research activity there, such as the establishment of a scientific station or the despatch of a scientific expedition.

3.   Reports from the observers referred to in Article VII of the present Treaty shall be transmitted to the representatives of the Contracting Parties participating in the meetings referred to in paragraph 1 of the present Article.

4.   The measures referred to in paragraph 1 of this Article shall become effective when approved by all the Contracting Parties whose representatives were entitled to participate in the meetings held to consider those measures. . . .

Article X

Each of the Contracting Parties undertakes to exert appropriate efforts, consistent with the Charter of the United Nations, to the end that no one engages in any activity in Antarctica contrary to the principles or purposes of the present Treaty.

Acquiring Territory in Antarctica. One generally accepted way for states to acquire new territory is by discovery and occupation of *terra nullius*, a label used to describe uninhabited territory such as Antarctica. Jurists in the early 20th century argued that discovery alone provided only an "inchoate" title, which in order to become effective against other states had to be followed by occupation and concrete acts exercising authority. See, *e.g.,* T.J. Lawrence, *The Principles of International Law* § 74 (1915). However, in the 19th and early 20th centuries, European explorers, engaged in surveying and conducting scientific investigations, laid claim to parts of Antarctica on behalf of their states, without establishing permanent settlements in that harsh environment. For example, in 1929 Great Britain's King George commissioned explorer Douglas Mawson to lead an expedition to Antarctica, "plant the British flag wherever . . . practicable to do so, . . . read the proclamation of annexation[,] attach a copy of the proclamation to the flagstaff, and place a second copy of the proclamation in a tin at the foot of the flagstaff." *Reprinted in* Anna Bemrose, *Mawson's Last Survivor* 25 (2011). In light of the practical difficulties of establishing permanent settlements in Antarctica, should discovery alone have sufficed to establish state sovereignty?

More controversial than discovery plus effective occupation as grounds for asserting sovereignty over portions of Antarctica are the contiguity theory, propounded by several states geographically close to Antarctica, and the sector theory. Under the sector theory, Antarctic territorial boundaries ought to correspond to longitudinal lines that converge on the South Pole. The longitudinal lines either are extensions of the mainland boundaries of a nearby claimant state, or are drawn from the ends of a stretch of Antarctic coast claimed by the state.

By the 1950s, Argentina, Australia, Chile, France, New Zealand, Norway, and the United Kingdom exercised or claimed territorial sovereignty over "pie slice" sectors of Antarctica that meet at the South Pole. The United States and the Soviet Union made no claims to territory in Antarctica but reserved their right to assert claims in the future. These "nonclaimant states" also refused to recognize the territorial claims of other states. As shown in Figure 3.D, one area of Antarctica remains unclaimed. For more about international law and the acquisition of territory, see the *Minquiers and Echrehos Case* and its accompanying text in Chapter 4.

Disputed Claims. After laying claim to portions of Antarctica, governments occasionally debated the nature and validity of their asserted sovereignty. For example, the British ambassador in Washington and the U.S. Secretary of State exchanged diplomatic notes on the issue in 1934 and 1935. Initially, Britain expressed concern about U.S. airplane flights over, and the establishment of a wireless station and postal facilities in, the Ross Dependency, now an area of Antarctica claimed by New Zealand. If the United States were to establish a post office in this area or to sanction the use of U.S. postage stamps there without permission, the British ambassador claimed, "such acts could not be regarded otherwise than as infringing the British sovereignty." The United States responded that discovery—the basis of the British Antarctic claim— could not, "unaccompanied by occupancy and use," lead to sovereignty. The British replied that they had no objection to a U.S. expedition to the Antarctic and its associated commemorative postal activities. The United States in turn noted the British reply and stated that it "reserves all rights which this country or its citizens may have with respect to the matter." 1 Hackworth, *Digest of International Law* 457–59 (1940). Was this diplomatic exchange part of the claim-counterclaim process used in the formation of customary international law we studied in Chapter 2?

Some disputes over territory in Antarctica led to tense incidents. The claims of Argentina, Chile, and the United Kingdom overlap, and in the areas of overlap there were occasional displays of naval power and even the firing of shots by military personnel. For discussion about claims to Antarctica before the Antarctic Treaty, and conflicts and diplomatic maneuvers concerning those claims, see David Day, *Antarctica: A Biography* (2013).

The International Geophysical Year and the Antarctic Treaty. The 1957 International Geophysical Year (IGY), a cooperative effort of 66 states including all the major powers except the People's Republic of China, provided impetus for the Antarctic Treaty. IGY scientists allocated scientific stations in

Antarctica to states and arranged cooperative ventures concerning mapping, collection of weather data, and exchanges of scientific personnel. The entry of the Soviet Union into Antarctic activities beginning in 1955 contributed to an international arrangement for Antarctica that helped preserve the continent as a laboratory for cooperative scientific research and as a region to be used only for peaceful purposes. Following the IGY, representatives of the 12 states active in the Antarctic work of the IGY met regularly in Washington, D.C., for preparatory treaty talks and a formal negotiating conference. The Antarctic Treaty was signed on December 1, 1959, and entered into force June 23, 1961. The Treaty helped stabilize the situation on the continent, providing the foundation of the Antarctic regime. According to the Treaty, what principles underlie this regime?

Freezing Territorial Claims. One core principle is set forth in Article IV, which "freezes" territorial and sovereignty claims. Why have states found this arrangement acceptable? What problems might be anticipated as time goes on?

Effect on Nonparties. Does the Antarctic Treaty create legal obligations for nonparties? Would such obligations be *erga omnes*? See Chapter 2 and the *Reparation Case* above. What would be the reaction if a nonparty to the Antarctic Treaty were to claim sovereignty over the "unclaimed sector" or some other portion of Antarctica?

Classes of Parties to the Antarctic Treaty. The Antarctic Treaty distinguishes between Consultative Parties and other parties. The 12 original parties to the Antarctic Treaty joined as Consultative Parties, entitled to decision-making roles in periodic international meetings. See Article IX of the Treaty. As of May 2017, 53 states were parties to the Antarctic Treaty, but only 29 of them were Consultative Parties. What justifies the Treaty's two-tiered system? Among the Consultative Parties, should some special status be accorded those states that have asserted territorial claims?

Figure 3.D
Map of National Claims in Antarctica

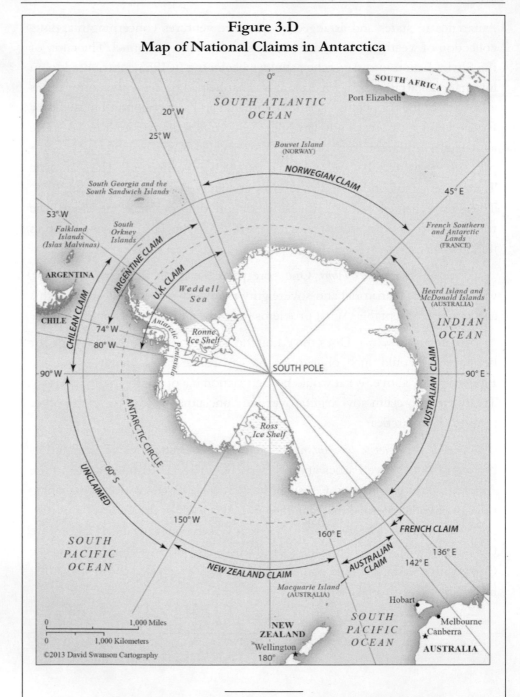

The United Nations and Antarctica. The issue of U.N. involvement with Antarctica was first posed shortly after World War II. India raised the question again in 1956, and Malaysia brought the issue before the U.N. General Assembly in 1982. In 1989 the General Assembly resolved that regimes to protect the Antarctic environment "must be negotiated with the full participation of all members of the international community," urged bans on prospecting and mining in Antarctica, and asked all members of the international community to ensure that activities in Antarctica "are for the benefit of all mankind." G.A. Res. 44/124, ¶¶ 4–5 (1989) (adopted by a vote of 108 states in favor, 0 opposed, and 6 abstaining). This resolution was one of a series expressing regret that the U.N. Secretary-General had not been invited to Antarctic Treaty Consultative Party (ATCP) meetings, and calling on the Consultative Parties "to invite the Secretary-General or his representative to all meetings." *Id.* ¶ 2. In 1996 the General Assembly welcomed "invitations to the Executive Director of the United Nations Environment Programme to attend Antarctic Treaty Consultative Meetings in order to assist such meetings" and "also the practice whereby the Antarctic Treaty Consultative Parties regularly provide the Secretary-General with information on the consultative meetings and on their activities in Antarctica." G.A. Res. 51/56, ¶¶ 3–4 (1996). In 2005 Malaysia abandoned its attempt to involve the United Nations more in Antarctic territorial matters. "As a result . . . the Question of Antarctica was made a sleeping beauty on the UN agenda." Marie Jacobsson, "The Antarctic Treaty System: Legal and Environmental Issues—Future Challenges for the Antarctic Treaty System," in *Antarctica: Legal and Environmental Challenges for the Future* 1, 3 (Gillian Triggs & Anna Riddell eds. 2008). What might spur non-ATCP states again to press for alternative governance arrangements for Antarctica? See Peter J. Beck, "The United Nations and Antarctica, 2005: The End of the 'Question of Antarctica'?," 42 *Polar Records* 217 (2006).

The Common Heritage Principle. During the U.N. debate about Antarctica in the 1990s, Malaysia urged that the "elements of the common heritage concept—peaceful use, non-appropriation, preservation for future generations, . . . international management and benefit-sharing"—should apply to Antarctica. Should the U.N. General Assembly declare Antarctica the "common heritage of mankind"? What would be the legal implications of such a resolution? Would it be effective? Does the *Texaco/Libya Case* in Chapter 2 provide some answers? The common heritage principle is most often associated with the regime for mining the seabed beyond the limits of national jurisdiction, a topic we explore in Chapter 8. For more on this principle, see John E. Noyes, "The Common Heritage of Mankind: Past, Present, and Future," 40 *Denver Journal of International Law and Policy* 447 (2011).

NGOs and Antarctica. What roles do non-governmental organizations usefully play with respect to Antarctica? NGO access to meetings and NGO participation concerning Antarctic issues have increased over the years. One regular and respected NGO observer at ATCP meetings is the Scientific Committee on Antarctic Science. See Richard A. Herr, "The Changing Roles of Non-governmental Organisations in the Antarctic Treaty System," in *Governing the Antarctic: The Effectiveness and Legitimacy of the Antarctic Treaty System* 91 (Olav Schram Stokke & Davor Vidas eds. 1996).

"Governing" Antarctica. How is Antarctica to be managed under the 1959 Antarctic Treaty? The ATCPs meet each year and, pursuant to Article IX of the Antarctic Treaty, adopt non-binding "resolutions," "measures" that become legally binding once all the ATCPs approve them in their municipal legal systems, and "decisions" concerning internal organizational matters. (Prior to 1995, resolutions, measures, and decisions were collectively known as recommendations.) In 2012, for example, the ATCPs adopted four decisions, 11 measures concerning Antarctic historic sites and management plans, and 11 resolutions concerning such matters as cooperation in expeditions, vessel safety, and coordination in search and rescue operations, as well as guidelines for visitors. See 1 *Final Report of the Thirty-fifth Antarctic Treaty Consultative Meeting* (2012), *available at* http://www.ats.aq/documents/ATCM35/fr/ATCM35_fr001 _e.pdf.

The 2011 General Guidelines for Visitors to the Antarctic took the form of an ATCP resolution. The ATCPs' representatives recommended that "their Governments endorse" detailed guidelines concerning respect for Antarctic animals, vegetation, and historic sites, non-interference with scientific research, waste disposal, safety, and landing and transport requirements. The representatives also recommended that "their Governments urge all those intending to visit sites in Antarctica to ensure that they are fully conversant with and adhere to the advice in" the guidelines. Resolution 3 (2011), ATCM XXXIV—CEP XIV, Buenos Aires. Is Resolution 3 an example of "soft law"? See Chapter 2. How effective would you expect such a resolution to be? See Kees Bastmeijer and Ricardo Roura, "Recent Development: Regulating Antarctic Tourism and the Precautionary Principle," 98 *American Journal of International Law* 763 (2004).

What laws govern individuals' activities in Antarctica? Article VIII of the Antarctic Treaty suggests a partial answer, providing that, "in respect of" their Antarctic activities, observers and scientific personnel "shall be subject only to the jurisdiction of the Contracting Party of which they are nationals."

The Antarctic Secretariat. The Antarctic Treaty is silent about any role for international organizations or institutions. After much debate, the ATCPs decided to form an Antarctic Secretariat to assist with preparing Consultative

Meetings, maintaining records, preparing reports, circulating information among the ATCPs, and disseminating information about activities in Antarctica. See ATCP Measure XXVI–1 and Decisions XXVI–1 to 4 (2003); http://www.ats.aq. The Secretariat, described as an "organ without a body," Patrizia Vigni, "The Secretariat of the Antarctic Treaty: Achievements and Weaknesses Three Years After its Establishment," in *Antarctica: Legal and Environmental Challenges for the Future* 17, 18 (Gillian Triggs & Anna Riddell eds. 2007), began operating in 2004 and is headquartered in Buenos Aires, Argentina. Why have the ATCPs narrowly circumscribed the activities of the Secretariat, denying this treaty body international personality? Might a stronger institutional structure promote the legitimacy of the international legal system applicable to Antarctica? See Karen Scott, "Institutional Developments Within the Antarctic Treaty System," 52 *International and Comparative Law Quarterly* 473 (2003).

The Antarctic Treaty System. The legal regime governing Antarctica involves more than the Antarctic Treaty, the Antarctic Secretariat, and the ATCPs' resolutions, measures, and decisions. Other notable treaties include the 1991 Madrid Protocol on Environmental Protection, the 1972 Convention for the Conservation of Antarctic Seals, and the 1980 Convention for the Conservation of Antarctic Marine Living Resources.

Alternatives for Governing Antarctica. What are alternatives to the current regime or to international administration of Antarctica as a common heritage regime? What would be the advantages and disadvantages of, for example, a territorial regime in which claimant states asserted control over their pie-shaped claims? Of a condominium regime, pursuant to which the Antarctic Treaty parties establish a system of joint sovereignty over the continent? Of turning Antarctica into a "world park"? For an overview of alternatives, see S.K.N. Blay, R.W. Piotrowicz & B.M. Tsamenyi, *Antarctica After 1991: The Legal and Policy Options* 13–19 (1989). Assuming that no fundamental change is made to the framework established by the Antarctic Treaty, what steps should be taken to respond to increased international interest in Antarctica and its mineral and living resources?

The Complexity of International Regimes. Some international programs are considerably more complex than the regime governing Antarctica. Consider, for example, the one for combating depletion of the ozone layer, established pursuant to the 1985 Vienna Convention on Substances that Deplete the Ozone Layer and the 1987 Montreal Protocol—each with 197 parties—and later amendments. This regime encompasses a range of governance mechanisms. There are roles for a Multilateral Fund, which has administered billions of dollars of contributions to assist developing states in reducing their production and consumption of ozone-depleting substances; an Implementation Committee that monitors compliance; an Ozone Secretariat that carries out administrative functions; and a Conference of the Parties (COP) that is authorized to make certain adjustments to the ozone regime without ratification by states parties. There are, as well, links to the United Nations Environment Programme, the World Health Organization, the World Bank, and other U.N. specialized agencies. Qualified non-governmental organizations may observe COP meetings and monitor the work of the Implementation Committee. The regime has achieved near-universal participation of states and has succeeded in reducing ozone depletion. See Richard Elliott Benedick, *Ozone Diplomacy* (enlarged ed. 1998); UNEP Ozone Secretariat, *Handbook for the Montreal Protocol on Substances that Deplete the Ozone Layer* (11th ed. 2017), *available at* http://ozone.unep.org. We see an example of a complex regime, concerning deep seabed mining, at the end of Chapter 8.

CHAPTER 4

International Courts and Tribunals

Articles 2(3) and 33 of the United Nations Charter enshrine the legal obligation that international disputes be settled peacefully. The most common method to achieve this end is negotiation. Other dispute settlement mechanisms include mediation, conciliation, fact-finding commissions of inquiry, arbitration, and adjudication. Our focus in this book is primarily on arbitral tribunals and courts, forums that render legally binding decisions and help develop international law.

The process of interpreting, applying, and enforcing international law employs both national courts (see Chapter 5) and various international courts and tribunals. In Part A of this chapter we introduce public international arbitration and, in Part B, the International Court of Justice (ICJ), which is the judicial organ of the United Nations. The ICJ and its immediate predecessor, the Permanent Court of International Justice (PCIJ), have never had a heavy caseload, averaging a little over two adjudicated cases a year. However, PCIJ and ICJ cases have been a very influential source of international law in the 20th and 21st centuries. Finally, in Part C, we look at questions raised by the proliferation of new international courts and tribunals.

While reading the material below, keep in mind the question, when and why do states agree to submit disputes to international arbitration or adjudication? As infrequent as such submissions are, there is no doubt that governments sometimes do desire their disagreements to be settled by international arbiters or judges. What makes an international dispute "court-friendly" or "court-unfriendly"? A plausible answer to this question might help us predict not only which international disputes are likely to go to formal international dispute settlement procedures but also which international decisions, once rendered, will be respected by states in practice.

A. PUBLIC INTERNATIONAL ARBITRATION

Our story begins with public international arbitration. The 1872 *Alabama Claims* arbitration between the United States and the United Kingdom was perhaps the pinnacle of 19th-century aspirations for international law and dispute settlement. Among other things, *Alabama Claims* inspired the creation of the Permanent Court of Arbitration (PCA), established in 1899 in The Hague, the Netherlands. A 1905 PCA case, *Dogger Bank* between the United Kingdom and Russia, comes next, a good example of the kind of cases that permanent arbitral institutions decided in the years before the First World War. Following are two decisions related to a more modern case, the 1985 *Rainbow Warrior* incident between New Zealand and France, examples of the continuing utility of public international arbitration.

The Alabama *Arbitration.* The *Alabama* arbitration of 1872 resolved a high-profile controversy between the United States and Great Britain related to Britain's support for the Confederacy during the U.S. Civil War. It was conducted in a political climate of much public enthusiasm for arbitration as an alternative to war.

MARK WESTON JANIS, THE *ALABAMA* ARBITRATION

America and the Law of Nations 1776–1939, at 131–34 (2010)

Optimism About Public International Arbitration

After the Civil War, some Americans thought that war's days might well be numbered. The great codifier, David Dudley Field remarked at the 1876 Centennial Celebration in Philadelphia:

> The history of international law since July 4, 1776, shows that, notwithstanding the prevalence of almost universal war during the last quarter of the past century and the first fifteen years of the present, there has been a general tendency of the nations to approach each other more closely, to avoid war as much as possible, and to diminish its severity, when it occurs.

In 1910, John W. Foster, Benjamin Harrison's Secretary of State and grandfather of Dwight Eisenhower's Secretary of State, John Foster Dulles, opined that all three of America's nineteenth-century foreign wars—the War of 1812, the 1846 Mexican War, and the 1898 Spanish-American War—could have been avoided if the disputes precipitating them had "been submitted to arbitration and decided without recourse to war." . . .

Field and Foster seemed not to be merely pipe-dreaming. International arbitration had had a remarkable record in the nineteenth century. Beginning with the 536 awards of the Jay Treaty arbitrations between 1799 and 1804, there had been hundreds of international arbitrations, many involving the United States. America was a party to the establishment of international arbitral tribunals along the lines of those introduced in the Jay Treaty with Ecuador, Mexico, Peru, Spain, and Venezuela. The busiest of these, the United States-Mexican Mixed Claims Commission of 1868, heard more than 2,000 claims between 1871 and 1876. As Foster noted in a little book in 1904, "[t]he nineteenth century was more fruitful than any similar era in the submission to the adjudication of special arbitration tribunals of the differences of nations insolvable by diplomatic methods."

Most important of all for the optimism of the time was the judgment of the *Alabama* arbitral tribunal, probably the most influential event of nineteenth-century American international law. Delivered in 1872, . . . the *Alabama* judgment was the work of an *ad hoc* tribunal composed of five judges . . . named by each of the United States, Great Britain, Italy, Switzerland, and Brazil. The panel had been empowered by Great Britain and America in 1871 to decide whether Britain had violated international law when it permitted British companies to build Confederate warships, notably the cruisers *Alabama, Florida,* and *Shenandoah*, which preyed on Union shipping during the American Civil War.

Mutual Consent to Arbitration. As you read next about the *Alabama* tribunal's decision and its aftermath, consider what induced both the United States and Britain to agree to arbitrate their dispute. In any international arbitration, the parties must mutually consent to the procedure. In this case, perhaps part of the reason for accepting international arbitration was the shared legal heritage between Britain and America. Both countries were accustomed to the settlement of many domestic disputes, even political disputes, by judges and the common law.

Mark Weston Janis, The *Alabama* Arbitration
The Decision and Its Aftermath

[T]he *Alabama* tribunal ruled that though Britain had owed the United States a duty of "active due diligence" to prevent private parties from supplying the southern rebels, she had failed to observe her international obligations as a neutral state. In relevant part, the judgment read:

And whereas, with respect to the vessel called the *Alabama*, it clearly results from all the facts relative to the construction of the ship, at first designated by the number '290,' in the port of Liverpool, and its equipment and armament in the vicinity of Terceira, through the agency of the vessels called the *Agrippina* and the *Bahama*, dispatched from Great Britain to that end, that the British Government failed to use due diligence in the performance of its neutral obligations, and especially that it omitted, notwithstanding the warnings and official representations made by the diplomatic agents of the United States during the construction of the said number '290,' to take in due time any effective measures of prevention, and that those orders which it did give at last, for the detention of the vessel, were issued so late that their execution was not practicable;

And whereas, after the escape of that vessel, the measures taken for its pursuit and arrest were so imperfect as to lead to no result, and therefore cannot be considered sufficient to release Great Britain from the responsibility already incurred;

And whereas, in despite of the violations of the neutrality of Great Britain, committed by the '290,' this same vessel, later known as the Confederate cruiser *Alabama*, was on several occasions freely admitted into the ports of the colonies of Great Britain, instead of being proceeded against as it ought to have been in any and every port within British jurisdiction in which it might have been found;

And whereas the Government of Her Britannic Majesty cannot justify itself for a failure in due diligence on the plea of insufficiency of the legal means of action which it possessed;

Four of the arbitrators for the reasons above assigned, and the fifth, for reasons separately assigned by him, are of opinion that Great Britain has in this case failed, by omission, to fulfill the duties prescribed in the first and the third of the rules, established by the sixth article of the treaty of Washington. [These rules specify the due diligence obligations of neutrals.]

The United States claimed about $21 million in direct and $4 million in indirect damages caused by the attacks of the *Alabama* and her sister Confederate raiders; the United Kingdom acknowledged only about $8 million in direct damages. The arbitrators split the difference, ordering the United Kingdom to pay the United States some $15,500,000. The full sum was proffered in British Treasury Bonds on September 9, 1873. The American receipt was framed and hung in 10 Downing Street.

The *Alabama* arbitration was an exceptionally encouraging development for American international law enthusiasts. Some years earlier, in 1865, Lord Russell, the British Foreign Secretary, had refused to arbitrate the *Alabama* claims on the grounds that the British government were "sole guardians of their own honor." War between the two countries was not an outlandish possibility. The United States and Great Britain had already fought twice—the Revolutionary War (1775–1783) and the War of 1812 (1812–1815). It seemed credible that a third Anglo-American conflict might break out, a struggle not only about compensation for the Confederate maritime attacks, but also to settle possession of Canada, a part of the British Empire much coveted by some Americans.

The eventual success of the *Alabama* arbitration became an important popular demonstration that it was possible for powerful states to arbitrate important disputes and thereby avoid war. General Ulysses S. Grant (1822–1885), President of the United States during the *Alabama* arbitration, was so encouraged by the tribunal's deeds that the old warrior predicted "an epoch when a court recognized by all nations will settle international differences instead of keeping large standing armies." David Dudley Field turned to the *Alabama* proceedings to demonstrate the probability of the eventual success of international arbitration. The *Alabama* judgment, now largely forgotten, was at the time profoundly influential. In the words of Samuel Eliot Morison, "never before had disputes involving such touchy subjects of national honor been submitted to the majority vote of an international tribunal."

Avoiding War. *Alabama* was the kind of dispute that 19th-century international law enthusiasts hoped would be settled by arbitration rather than by war. Tom Bingham, Lord Chief Justice of England and Wales between 1996 and 2000, described the *Alabama* arbitration "as the greatest the world had ever seen."

> The *Alabama* arbitration is . . . one of the very few instances in history when the world's leading nation, in the plenitude of its power, has agreed to submit an issue of great national moment to the decision of a body in which it could be, as it was, heavily outvoted. [British Prime Minister William] Gladstone did not see the arbitration as righting a wrong. Rather, "[h]e saw the process as exemplifying the means by which two civilized nations could settle differences, without either having to admit being in the wrong."

Tom Bingham, "The *Alabama* Claims Arbitration," 54 *International and Comparative Law Quarterly* 1, 24 (2005).

Figure 4.A
The CSS *Alabama*

Compensation. In *Alabama*, Britain paid the full award of $15,500,000, a sum that corresponds to approximately $300,000,000 today. Would Britain have been better off to have simply paid damages at the outset? The payment could have been made "*ex gratia*," with no formal admission of responsibility. Perhaps, however, the lapse of time and the decision of an arbitral panel made the payment of damages more palatable.

The Dogger Bank Incident. The Dogger Bank incident threatened to disrupt peaceful relations in Europe in 1905. It was resolved through a third-party procedure that proponents of arbitration applauded. The case introduces us to the Permanent Court of International Arbitration. We start with the factual background.

RICHARD NED LEBOW, ACCIDENTS AND CRISES: THE DOGGER BANK AFFAIR

31 *Naval War College Review*, No. 1, at 66 (Summer 1978)

The Facts

Russian expansion into Manchuria in the latter part of the 19th century brought her into conflict with Japan. Russian penetration of Korea, which directly challenged Japan's economic and political primacy in that country, brought the conflict to a head. St. Petersburg's intransigence made a mockery of negotiations and Japan broke relations with Russia on 8 February 1904.

That very morning Japanese torpedo boats and destroyers launched a daring surprise attack against the Russian Pacific Squadron in its moorings at Port Arthur. The attack was followed up the next day by a long-range naval bombardment of the Russian anchorage. When the smoke had cleared the Japanese Navy was supreme in the Far East. They inflicted a further defeat upon the Russians at Chemulpo in August. On land, the Japanese were equally successful. Their army moved into Manchuria and forced the Russians to retreat down the Liaotung Peninsula. By 14 May they had invested Port Arthur.

The relief of Port Arthur became Moscow's most urgent objective. General Kuropatkin, the Russian Commander-in-Chief, ordered the navy to ready its idle Baltic Fleet for service in the Pacific. Departure of the armada awaited completion of four new battleships, during which time the Baltic Fleet, considered to be the least seaworthy component of the navy, received special training. The deteriorating military situation in the Far East forced Admiral Rozhestvensky to cut his training exercises short and on 14 October 1904 the 42 ships of the hastily assembled Second Pacific Squadron departed the Baltic port of Libau for the 10,000 mile journey to Port Arthur.

As the fleet steamed through the Baltic it was warned to be on the lookout for Japanese torpedo boats disguised as trawlers which were planning an ambush somewhere between The Skaw and English Channel. This far-fetched notion had gained credence in St. Petersburg because of the reports of a Captain Hartling, sent to Copenhagen sometime earlier to organize a Russian counterintelligence network. Hartling's agents, anxious to justify their expense, had reported the existence of suspicious vessels in isolated Danish and Norwegian harbors. Rumors of a Japanese "suicide squadron" had also been picked up by the European press which speculated about the effect of Britain's assumed collusion with her Japanese ally upon Anglo-Russian relations.

According to all reports the prospect of a torpedo attack reduced Admiral Rozhestvensky, a man with no command experience, to a state of extreme anxiety. He doubled all watches, arranged to have searchlights sweep the surrounding sea at night and instructed guncrews to remain by their stations around the clock. The admiral ordered that "No vessel of any sort whatsoever must be allowed to get in amongst the fleet." Approaching merchantmen were warned away, often by a shot across their bows. Tension rose on the evening of 20 October, following receipt of a warning that unidentified torpedo boats had departed from secret bases in Norway. Later that night, *Navarin* reported sighting enemy reconnaissance balloons.

The expected attack failed to materialize and as morning broke the fleet steamed into the North Sea, ominously shrouded by fog. More alarming intelligence came in during the day warning of floating mines and trawlers with torpedo tubes preparing to attack the fleet. At dusk, the cruiser *Kamchatka*, which had become separated from the main body of the fleet, reported that it was under attack by eight torpedo boats and was returning fire. Ninety minutes later action stations were sounded aboard the flagship *Suvorov* in response to two flares sighted from the bridge. Shortly thereafter the order to engage the enemy was flashed down the line as searchlights revealed ships barely a half mile away. Battleships and cruisers opened fire and kept up an intensive barrage for 20 minutes until the admiral could discern only a few battered trawlers bobbing hopelessly in the water. The fleet steamed off concluding that the torpedo boats had fled from the scene.

The "enemy" engaged by Russian gunners was the Gamecock fleet of fishing boats which had left Hull for the Dogger Bank 2 days before and was then 200 miles northeast of the Spurn. They were identifiable as trawlers by their sails and red, white and green lights. These lights were probably the flares sighted on the bridge of *Suvorov*. When the firing began, one of the deckhands, illuminated by the searchlights, held up a plaice while his mate displayed a large haddock in the hope of signaling their peaceful intent. Their efforts were unsuccessful and when the barrage finally ceased one trawler had been sent to the bottom and five damaged. Two seamen were dead and six seriously wounded. Fortunately for the fishermen Russian gunnery had proven extremely inaccurate.

Figure 4.B
Damaged Trawlers, Hull Harbor, 1904

RUSSIAN OUTRAGE ON HULL TRAWLERS. SCENE AT ST ANDREWS DOCK HULL. S.R.&.C Ltd

SHOT HOLES

News of the incident reached London on Monday, 23 October. The next day the M.P. from Hull brought a deputation of fishermen to the Foreign Office where they produced shell splinters to substantiate their story. The Wednesday morning papers carried a more detailed account of the incident and public opinion was so incensed that the Russian Ambassador needed a police escort to leave his Embassy. Trafalgar Square was filled with protesters and the evening papers demanded strong action. The *Standard* raised the question that was on everybody's mind: was the "wretched Baltic fleet with its inefficient commanders, its drafts of raw landsmen, its blundering navigators and incompetent engineers" to be permitted to continue on its journey? The czarist regime was unpopular in England and as more details were released to the press public sentiment was adamant in favor of going after the Russian Fleet. Valentine Chirol, foreign editor of *The Times*, warned the foreign office that "the feeling in this country is such that no government can trifle with it."

The Balfour government, about to face an election, was particularly susceptible to popular pressure. However, the Cabinet did not act solely in response to public opinion. The majority were hostile to Russia and quite prepared to retaliate against her fleet. The Earl of Selbourne, First Lord of the Admiralty, was the most bellicose but Walter Long and Gerald Balfour, neither of whom normally displayed any interest in foreign affairs, also urged military action unless the Russians put into port and removed the officers responsible for the outrage. Admiral Fisher, who had recently been promoted to First Sea Lord, thought it a superb opportunity to destroy the Russian Fleet. It "is ours," he informed Selbourne, "whenever we like to take it." The King himself referred to the incident as "a most dastardly outrage" and urged a military response although he later moderated his position, fearing that war with Russia would only be in Germany's interest.

Lord Lansdowne, the Foreign Secretary, would have had support for any action against Russia he proposed. But he was an advocate of détente with Russia and was intent on resolving the incident peaceably. Lansdowne was nevertheless as outraged as his colleagues and thought Rozhestvensky's failure to stop and search for survivors particularly reprehensible. He was not convinced of the accidental nature of the incident, attributing it instead to the Russian propensity to "shoot first and ask questions later." In his opinion this trigger happy policy made a mockery of maritime law which Britain more than any other nation was dependent upon for her survival. Lansdowne believed that such incidents were likely to recur unless Russia was compelled to adhere to the established rules and customs that governed maritime behavior. Like other members of the Cabinet he also believed that Britain's reputation as a great power was at stake.

. . . Unwilling to let the hostage fleet escape the prime minister and foreign secretary agreed that Russia must be sent an ultimatum demanding that Rozhestvensky call at the Spanish port of Vigo and put ashore the officers responsible for the incident along with witnesses. The Russians were also to give satisfaction that the investigation of the incident would be complete and impartial. . . .

The Royal Navy had already begun preparations for a showdown. Six battleships of the Home Fleet had been ordered to Gibraltar and the reserve fleet of six battleships was being readied for action. Cruisers were sent to shadow the Russian Fleet, Gibraltar was put on a war footing, and the powerful Mediterranean Fleet was hurriedly recalled from the Austrian and Italian ports it was visiting. By the evening of 26 October, 28 battleships, 44 cruisers and their supporting vessels stood poised off Gibraltar ready to intercept the Russian Fleet which in the graphic words of First Sea Lord Fisher had become the "ham of a strategic sandwich."

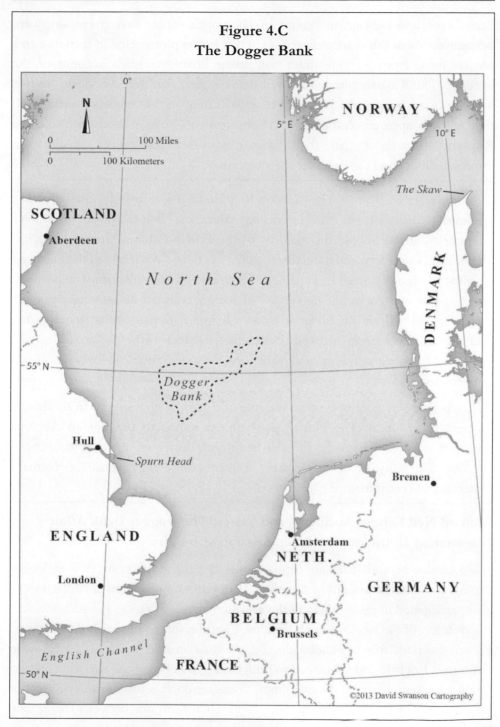

Figure 4.C
The Dogger Bank

On 27 October, [Russian Foreign Minister] Lamsdorff called on Hardinge [the British Minister in St. Petersburg] to warn that "he considered the general purport [of the ultimatum] to be humiliating and unacceptable to a Great Power."

Lansdowne and Balfour, in receipt of Hardinge's report that afternoon, were pessimistic about the chances for peace. Their hopes plummeted in response to a second cable from St. Petersburg containing Rozhestvensky's account of the incident. The Russian admiral claimed that his fleet had been set upon by two torpedo boats but that he had tried to avoid firing on the trawlers even though they were in apparent complicity with the torpedo boats. Lansdowne told the Russian Ambassador that the admiral's version "seemed to bristle with improbabilities" and did not alter the situation.

Incentives to Arbitrate. The decision to arbitrate a sensitive dispute involves political calculation in the interested countries. British public opinion demanded strong action; the majority of the British Cabinet "were hostile to Russia and quite prepared to retaliate against her fleet." What tipped the balance against the use of force? In Britain, an international commission of inquiry—leading to a written, public decision—let the government defuse angry public opinion and still air British grievances. An international third-party dispute settlement mechanism proved preferable to such other alternatives as continued negotiation, economic sanctions, national commissions of inquiry, or recourse to force.

As the story continues, note the role of France, which sought to promote a peaceful solution. The French government hoped to prevent an Anglo-Russian conflict that might threaten a future alliance of all three countries against Germany. What overcame Russian misgivings about a formal international commission?

Richard Ned Lebow, Accidents and Crises: The Dogger Bank Affair
Negotiating an International Commission of Inquiry

Lansdowne and [Russian Ambassador] Benckendorff conferred at length exploring possible ways out of the crisis. Paul Cambon, the French Ambassador, also participated in these talks. As the representative of France, Russia's ally, and the architect of the Anglo-French Entente, Cambon shared the trust of both sides. He acted as translator, as Benckendorff spoke Russian and French but Lansdowne knew only English, and attempted to bridge the gap between the two men created by their uncomplementary personalities. "Benckendorff is too vague, Lansdowne too reserved," he confided to his son, "and when I am not between them, they inhabit different planets."

The main impediment to a solution was the British demand for an inquiry in which British officers would participate. This was seen as humiliating by the Russians. Cambon nevertheless urged acceptance as did the French Foreign

Minister in Paris. On the 27th, the three men agreed that an inquiry conducted by some august international body might be more palatable to the Czar as he had urged the creation of boards of arbitration at the Hague Conference. The suggestion, attributed by Benckendoff to Cambon, was cabled to Lamsdorff who cleverly presented it to the Czar as his own idea in order to secure the autocrat's approval.

No word had been received from St. Petersburg when it came time for Balfour to depart for Southampton on the morning of the 28th. The mood at the Foreign Office was gloomy and remained so until a cable arrived from Hardinge reporting that the Czar approved of an international court of inquiry. A second cable contained the welcome news that Rozhestvensky had received orders to send the ships involved in the attack on the fishing boats to Vigo, that the guilty parties, as determined by the international board of inquiry, would be punished by Russian courts and that measures would be implemented to prevent further incidents. In return Lamsdorff requested that Balfour give credit to Russia in his speech for having expressed its prompt regrets and offering to pay proper compensation.

Upon his arrival at Southampton Balfour was handed a telegram reporting the Russian capitulation. Much relieved, the Prime Minister deleted those parts of his speech which were the equivalent to a declaration of war and told the good news to the cheering crowd. The Royal Navy remained on a war footing until her cruisers had "escorted" Rozhestvensky's fleet half way down the coast of Africa.

The Composition of Arbitral Panels. Note in the account of the *Dogger Bank* proceedings, which follows, that the arbitral commission was composed not of lawyers or judges but of naval officers. What were the advantages and disadvantages of employing admirals instead of jurists as arbitrators? Would Britain or Russia be the more disposed to appoint admirals? Both countries had to agree on the composition of the panel. Britain may have thought admirals would most credibly emphasize the importance of maritime customs and behavior essential to Britain's commercial interests, exposing, in the words of the *Standard*, the Russian fleet's "inefficient commanders, drafts of raw landsmen, blundering navigators and incompetent engineers." Russia may have believed that admirals would be more sympathetic to the Russian officers' wartime reactions in their nocturnal encounter with British fishing vessels. The use of admirals suggests how flexible in form and composition international arbitral tribunals may be—this one technically a "commission of inquiry" tasked with clarifying the factual circumstances of the Dogger Bank incident.

The fact that states choose their arbitrators is an ordinary feature of public international arbitration. Indeed, party choice of the tribunal is probably the most important general distinction between arbitration and adjudication as forms of dispute settlement, whether public (between states) or private (as in most commercial disputes).

Arbitrators may be less bound than judges to apply strict rules of law to their cases, but, sometimes, arbitrators may be just as rule-minded as judges. Did the *Dogger Bank* decision makers see their role as applying strict rules of international law, or did they rely more on some sort of "common sense"? Although the focus of the *Dogger Bank* commission was primarily on finding and analyzing facts, the admirals also determined responsibility. Look back to the *Alabama Claims* arbitration and consider whether that decision reflected a strict application of rules of law.

THE DOGGER BANK CASE

Great Britain v. Russia, Report of February 26, 1905,
The Hague Court Reports 403 (James Brown Scott ed. 1916)

The commissioners [five admirals from Britain, Russia, the United States, France, and Austria], after a minute and prolonged examination of the whole of the facts brought to their knowledge in regard to the incident submitted to them for inquiry by the declaration of St. Petersburg of the 12th (25th) November, 1904, have proceeded to make, in this report, an analysis of these facts in their logical sequence. . . .

Toward 1 o'clock in the morning of 9th (22d) October, 1904, the night was rather dark, a slight, low fog partly clouding the air. The moon only showed intermittently between the clouds. A moderate wind blew from the southeast, raising a long swell, which gave the ships a roll of 5° on each side.

The course followed by the squadron toward the southwest would have taken the last two divisions, as the event proved, close past the usual fishing ground of the fleet of Hull trawlers, which was composed of some thirty of these small steamboats, and was spread over an area of several miles.

It appears from the concordant testimony of the British witnesses that all these boats carried their proper lights, and were trawling in accordance with their usual rules, under the direction of their "admiral," and in obedience to the signals given by the conventional rockets.

Judging from the communications received by wireless telegraphy, the divisions which preceded that of Admiral Rojdestvensky across these waters had signaled nothing unusual.

It became known afterward, in particular, that Admiral Folkersam, having been led to pass round the fishing fleet on the north, threw his electric searchlight on the nearest trawlers at close quarters, and, having seen them to be harmless vessels, quietly continued his voyage.

A short time afterwards the last division of the squadron, led by the *Souvoroff* flying Admiral Rojdestvensky's flag, arrived in its run close to the spot where the trawlers were fishing.

The direction in which this division was sailing led it nearly toward the main body of the fleet of trawlers, round which and to the south of which it would therefore be obliged to sail, when the attention of the officers of the watch on the bridges of the *Souvoroff* was attracted by a green rocket, which put them on their guard. This rocket, sent up by the "admiral" of the fishing fleet, indicated in reality, according to regulation, that the trawlers were to trawl on the starboard tack.

Almost immediately after this first alarm, and as shown by the evidence, the lookout men, who, from the bridges of the *Souvoroff*, were scanning the horizon with their night glasses, discovered "on the crest of the waves on the starboard bow, at an approximate distance of 18 to 20 cables," a vessel which aroused their suspicions because they saw no light, and because she appeared to be bearing down upon them.

When the suspicious-looking vessel was shown up by the searchlight, the lookout men thought they recognized a torpedo boat proceeding at great speed.

It was on account of these appearances that Admiral Rojdestvensky ordered fire to be opened on this unknown vessel.

The majority of the commissioners express the opinion, on this subject, that the responsibility for this action and the results of the fire to which the fishing fleet was exposed are to be attributed to Admiral Rojdestvensky.

Almost immediately after fire was opened to starboard, the *Souvoroff* caught sight of a little boat on her bow barring the way, and was obliged to turn sharply to the left to avoid running it down. This boat, however, on being lit up by the searchlight, was seen to be a trawler.

To prevent the fire of the ships being directed against this harmless vessel, the searchlight was immediately thrown up at an angle of 45°.

The admiral then made the signal to the squadron "not to fire on the trawlers."

But at the same time that the searchlight had lit up this fishing vessel, according to the evidence of witnesses, the lookout men on board the *Souvoroff* perceived to port another vessel, which appeared suspicious from the fact of its presenting the same features as were presented by the object of their fire to starboard.

Fire was immediately opened on this second object, and was, therefore, being kept up on both sides of the ship, the line of ships having resumed their original course by a correcting movement without changing speed.

According to the standing orders of the fleet, the Admiral indicated the objects against which the fire should be directed by throwing his searchlight upon them; but as each vessel swept the horizon in every direction with her own searchlights to avoid being taken by surprise, it was difficult to prevent confusion.

The fire, which lasted from ten to twelve minutes, caused great loss to the trawlers. Two men were killed and six others wounded; the *Crane* sank; the *Snipe*, the *Mino*, the *Moulmein*, the *Gull*, and the *Majestic* were more or less damaged.

On the other hand, the cruiser *Aurora* was hit by several shots.

The majority of the commissioners observe that they have not sufficiently precise details to determine what was the object fired on by the vessels; but the commissioners recognize unanimously that the vessels of the fishing fleet did not commit any hostile act; and, the majority of the commissioners being of opinion that there were no torpedo boats either among the trawlers nor anywhere near, the opening of the fire by Admiral Rojdestvensky was not justifiable.

The Russian commissioner, not considering himself justified in sharing this opinion, expresses the conviction that it was precisely the suspicious-looking vessels approaching the squadron with hostile intent which provoked the fire.

Settlement of the Dogger Bank Case. Resolution of the *Dogger Bank Case* involved the payment of damages. James Brown Scott, the editor of the *Reports* of the Permanent Court of Arbitration, noted that "Russia accepted the decision and paid damages to the extent of about $300,000." *The Hague Court Reports* 403 (James Brown Scott ed. 1916). Why did Russia pay? Was payment easier for Russia to accept after the Commission's decision than before? Complying with a negative result in international dispute settlement may permit a state to abide by its international obligations even while protesting its innocence, both to the world and to its own citizens.

Professor Merrills observed, "The *Dogger Bank* episode furnishes a striking example of the value of the international inquiry commission as an instrument of dispute settlement. Had the issue been investigated by two national inquiries, it is almost certain that . . . they would have exacerbated matters by coming to opposite conclusions." J.G. Merrills, *International Dispute Settlement* 43 (5th ed. 2011).

The Evolution of Interstate Arbitration. Neither *Alabama* nor *Dogger Bank* lived up to expectations as harbingers of a continued substitution of the courtroom for the battlefield. Lord Bingham concluded that *Alabama* "did not, regrettably, herald a century in which judicial arbitration of international differences became the norm." Tom Bingham, "The *Alabama* Claims Arbitration," 54 *International and Comparative Law Quarterly* 1, 24 (2005). Professor Koopmans found that *Dogger Bank* engendered just a few subsequent commissions of inquiry, mostly employed "for technical aspects of maritime disputes." Sven M.G. Koopmans, *Diplomatic Dispute Settlement: The Use of Inter-State Conciliation* 28–29 (2008).

However, there has been considerable evolution in the forms of binding third-party dispute settlement. *Alabama* and the influential tradition of *ad hoc* public international arbitration in the 19th century bridged to the establishment of the Permanent Court of Arbitration in 1899; *Dogger Bank* was decided at the PCA, which we discuss below. There followed the Permanent Court of International Justice in 1921 and, in 1945, the International Court of Justice, which we study in Part B. In a way, the present ICJ is thus the fourth generation of formal international dispute settlement. International lawyers have for over two hundred years sought to employ international arbitral panels and international courts as pacific alternatives to war for the settlement of international conflict.

Despite the emergence of the PCIJ and the ICJ, public international arbitrations still occur. Some are *ad hoc, e.g., Rainbow Warrior*, below. Some rely on the Permanent Court of Arbitration for its facilities and administrative services. Still others use mechanisms established by treaty. For example, since 1995 over 500 interstate trade-related cases have been filed with the Dispute Settlement Body of the World Trade Association. See World Trade Organization, "Dispute Settlement," https://www.wto.org/english/tratop_e/dispu_e/dispu_e.htm#disputes.

The Permanent Court of Arbitration. Founded by the 1899 Hague Peace Conference, the Permanent Court of Arbitration was the world's first permanent and universal court of arbitration. Did the availability of permanent international arbitral machinery at The Hague make it more likely that the parties in *Dogger Bank* would go to arbitration? What might be done to make it even more likely that states use a form of international arbitration in a time of crisis? The *Dogger Bank* tribunal in fact spent considerable time in 1905 deciding its rules of procedure. One of the efforts of the 1907 Hague Convention was to supplement the 1899 Hague provisions on arbitration with articles on procedure and tribunal organization, with a view toward expediting the work of future tribunals.

After the Permanent Court of International Justice was established in 1921, the Permanent Court of Arbitration fell into desuetude. It administered only 34 cases during its first century. Lately, however, the PCA has reinvented itself. In 2015 alone, it provided administrative assistance for some 138 cases, 42 of which were new that year. Eight of the 138 cases were state-to-state arbitrations, while most others involved states or state-controlled entities as one of the parties. Some recent arbitrations have been politically charged. In 2008–2009, for example, the PCA administered a case between Sudan and an armed movement operating in the country (the Sudan People's Liberation Movement). And during 2013-2016, the PCA hosted the South China Sea arbitration between the Philippines and China, which involved sensitive political issues. The PCA has concluded host country agreements with Argentina, Chile, China (respecting Hong Kong), Costa Rica, India, Mauritius, Singapore, South Africa, and Viet Nam to support PCA-run proceedings conducted in those countries. The PCA's Secretary-General also acts as the appointing authority under many arbitral agreements. See Permanent Court of Arbitration, *Annual Report 2015*, *available at* http://www.pca-cpa.org/.

Comparing Public and Private International Arbitration. Private or commercial international arbitration (between private litigants) and mixed international arbitration (between a state and a private litigant) are even more frequent nowadays than is public (interstate) arbitration. There are thousands of such cases a year. We have seen an example of mixed international arbitration in the *Texaco/Libya Case* in Chapter 2.

Public international arbitration differs from international arbitration between private parties in at least three ways. First, in private arbitration, the courts of the state where the arbitration is held typically exercise some oversight to help ensure that the arbitral tribunal carries out its functions with at least minimal procedural fairness. In public international arbitration, however, the process is "denationalized," set up and controlled by the parties themselves or by some international institution. Any concerns about a lack of procedural fairness in public international arbitrations may translate into a lower level of compliance with tribunal decisions or less willingness to resort to a tribunal.

Second, rulings in private arbitration are widely enforceable through municipal courts, as required by the 1965 ICSID Convention and the 1958 New York Convention on the Recognition and Enforcement of Foreign Arbitral Awards (both noted in our discussion of the *Texaco/Libya Case* in Chapter 2). A state's decision to comply (or not) with an adverse ruling of a public arbitral tribunal or an international court normally will depend on other factors.

Third, consider what motivates states to submit to international arbitration. In private party transactions, a major concern, usually of each party, is to provide for a neutral forum, rather than to risk being subjected to a lawsuit in the other party's municipal court. In municipal litigation, some judges might be biased against foreign litigants, and municipal laws and procedures may be unfamiliar or unfavorable to those litigants. However, in non-commercial interstate disputes foreign states are not likely to be subject to jurisdiction in national courts, pursuant to the well-established doctrine of "sovereign immunity." There must be some reasons other than the risk of municipal litigation for a state to submit to public international arbitration.

The Rainbow Warrior *Incident.* Despite the rise of private and mixed international arbitration and the multiplication of international courts (see Part C below), there are still occasional public international arbitrations. One such began when French government agents sank the *Rainbow Warrior* in the harbor in Auckland, New Zealand in July 1985, sparking a tense international dispute between New Zealand and France. The *Rainbow Warrior* belonged to Greenpeace, a non-governmental organization (see Chapter 3) that had been protesting French nuclear testing in the South Pacific. France's nuclear tests had begun well before 1985. Indeed, New Zealand and Australia had challenged the legality of France's nuclear testing before the International Court of Justice in 1973. France refused to appear in the cases, but its public statements that its 1974 series of atmospheric tests would be its last persuaded the Court to dismiss the cases. The Court concluded that the objectives of New Zealand and Australia had "in effect been accomplished, inasmuch as the Court finds that France has undertaken the obligation to hold no further nuclear tests in the South Pacific." Nuclear Tests Case (New Zealand v. France), 1974 I.C.J. 457, 475; Nuclear Tests Case (Australia v. France), 1974 I.C.J. 253, 270. However, France subsequently withdrew its acceptance of the compulsory jurisdiction of the ICJ and resumed nuclear testing, albeit underground.

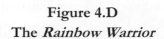

Figure 4.D
The *Rainbow Warrior*

France's Actions. France conducted a nuclear test at Morurua atoll in the South Pacific just two months before the sinking of the *Rainbow Warrior.* Greenpeace was planning to sail the vessel to the French nuclear testing area in protest later in 1985. On September 22, 1985, the French Prime Minister confirmed that agents of the French secret service had acted on official orders and had sunk the vessel. It was later reported that French President François Mitterand apparently personally approved the attack. Henry Samuel, "Sinking of the Rainbow Warrior was personally sanctioned by Mitterand," *The Telegraph* (London), July 11, 2005, at 12. New Zealand arrested the French agents.

French officials expressed regret and indicated that France stood ready to make reparations to New Zealand. According to France's submission to the U.N. Secretary-General, excerpted below, France "recognize[d] that the attack carried out against the *Rainbow Warrior* took place in violation of the territorial sovereignty of New Zealand and that it was therefore committed in violation of international law."

Recourse to International Legal Process. In many highly politicized interstate controversies, one or both sides may not want to participate in a third-party binding proceeding. Why were conditions for arbitration propitious in 1986?

What did France and New Zealand hope to achieve via third-party dispute settlement? France wanted its prisoners released from custody. New Zealand, wronged under international law by the actions of French agents in New Zealand territory, likely wanted a public forum to protest French actions, compensation for the incident, and assurance that France would not disrupt New Zealand's trade with Europe.

On June 19, 1986, following an appeal by Prime Minister Lubbers of the Netherlands, France and New Zealand asked U.N. Secretary-General Javier Pérez de Cuéllar, formerly a professor of international law, to make a binding, "equitable and principled" ruling on matters arising from the sinking of the *Rainbow Warrior*. This first excerpt from his decision highlights events leading up to the case.

THE RAINBOW WARRIOR CASE (1986)

Case concerning the differences between New Zealand and France arising from the
Rainbow Warrior Affair; Ruling of 6 July 1986 by the Secretary-General of the United Nations,
19 *Reports of International Arbitral Awards* 199 (2006)

The Facts

On 10 July 1985 a civilian vessel, the *Rainbow Warrior*, not flying the New Zealand flag, was sunk at its moorings in Auckland Harbor, New Zealand, as a result of extensive damage caused by two high explosive devices. One person, a Netherlands citizen, Mr. Fernando Pereira, was killed as a result of this action; he drowned when the ship sank.

On 12 July, two agents of the French Directorate General of External Security (DGSE) were interviewed by the New Zealand Police and subsequently arrested and prosecuted. On 4 November they pleaded guilty in the District Court in Auckland, New Zealand, to charges of manslaughter and wilful damage to a ship by means of an explosive. They were sentenced to ten years imprisonment each; they are presently serving their sentences in New Zealand prisons.

A communiqué issued on 22 September 1985 by the Prime Minister of France confirmed that the *Rainbow Warrior* had been sunk by agents of the DGSE upon instructions. On the same day, the Minister of External Affairs of France pointed out to the Prime Minister of New Zealand that France was ready to undertake reparations for the consequences of that action. He also declared he was ready, as the Prime Minister of New Zealand had already suggested, to meet with the Deputy Prime Minister of New Zealand on 23 and 25 September in New York. Such a meeting did take place for the purpose of discussing the possible ways to find a solution to the problems arising from the *Rainbow Warrior* affair.

A number of subsequent meetings took place between officials of the two countries in the months that followed, but it did not prove possible to reach a settlement.

In June 1986 I was formally approached by the Governments of France and New Zealand, who referred to me all the problems between them arising from the *Rainbow Warrior* affair for a ruling which both sides agreed to abide by. I then informed both Governments that I was prepared to undertake such a task. . . .

After I had received . . . written statements of the New Zealand and French positions, I then made contact, through diplomatic channels, with each of the two Governments. I did so in order to satisfy myself that I had a full and complete understanding of their respective positions and to be sure that I am able to produce a ruling on all aspects of the affair which in terms of the agreement announced in Paris, Wellington and New York on 19 June, is both equitable and principled.

The Secretary-General's Ruling. France and New Zealand in fact negotiated many of the provisions of the Secretary-General's ruling behind the scenes. Why did they desire his assistance? One unsettled issue was compensation. France argued that compensation should be limited to material damage, *e.g.,* New Zealand's costs for cleaning up Auckland harbor and for the police inquiry, trial, and detention of the two French agents. New Zealand submitted that, in addition, it was "entitled to compensation for the violation of sovereignty and the affront and insult that that involved." The Secretary-General decided the amount of compensation, and included some compensation for non-material damage.

Here is the Secretary-General's ruling on compensation and several other issues:

The Rainbow Warrior Case (1986)
The U.N. Secretary-General's Ruling

The issues that I need to consider are limited in number. I set out below my ruling on them which takes account of all the information available to me. My ruling is as follows:

Apology

New Zealand seeks an apology. France is prepared to give one. My ruling is that the Prime Minister of France should convey to the Prime Minister of New Zealand a formal and unqualified apology for the attack, contrary to international law, on the *Rainbow Warrior* by French service agents which took place on 10 July 1985.

Compensation

New Zealand seeks compensation for the wrong done to it and France is ready to pay some compensation. The two sides, however, are some distance apart on quantum. New Zealand has said that the figure should not be less than US Dollars 9 million, France that it should not be more than US Dollars 4 million. My ruling is that the French Government should pay the sum of US Dollars 7 million to the Government of New Zealand as compensation for all the damage it has suffered.

The Two French Service Agents

It is on this issue that the two Governments plainly had the greatest difficulty in their attempts to negotiate a solution to the whole issue on a bilateral basis before they took the decision to refer the matter to me.

The French Government seeks the immediate return of the two officers. It underlines that their imprisonment in New Zealand is not justified, taking into account in particular the fact that they acted under military orders and that France is ready to give an apology and to pay compensation to New Zealand for the damage suffered.

The New Zealand position is that the sinking of the *Rainbow Warrior* involved not only a breach of international law, but also the commission of a serious crime in New Zealand for which the two officers received a lengthy sentence from a New Zealand court. The New Zealand side states that their release to freedom would undermine the integrity of the New Zealand judicial system. In the course of bilateral negotiations with France, New Zealand was ready to explore possibilities for the prisoners serving their sentences outside New Zealand.

But it has been, and remains, essential to the New Zealand position that there should be no release to freedom, that any transfer should be to custody, and that there should be a means of verifying that.

The French response to that is that there is no basis either in international law or in French law on which the two could serve out any portion of their New Zealand sentence in France, and that they could not be subjected to new criminal proceedings after a transfer into French hands.

On this point, if I am to fulfil my mandate adequately, I must find a solution in respect of the two officers which both respects and reconciles these conflicting positions.

My ruling is as follows:

(*a*)   The Government of New Zealand should transfer Major Alain Mafart and Captain Dominique Prieur to the French military authorities. Immediately thereafter, Major Mafart and Captain Prieur should be transferred to a French military facility on an isolated island outside of Europe for a period of three years.

(*b*)   They should be prohibited from leaving the island for any reason, except with the mutual consent of the two Governments. They should be isolated during their assignment on the island from persons other than military or associated personnel and immediate family and friends. They should be prohibited from any contact with the press or other media whether in person or in writing or in any other manner. These conditions should be strictly complied with and appropriate action should be taken under the rules governing military discipline to enforce them.

(*c*)   The French Government should every three months convey to the New Zealand Government and to the Secretary-General of the United Nations, through diplomatic channels, full reports on the situation of Major Mafart and Captain Prieur in terms of the two preceding paragraphs in order to allow the New Zealand Government to be sure that they are being implemented.

(*d*)   If the New Zealand Government so requests, a visit to the French military facility in question may be made, by mutual agreement by the two Governments, by an agreed third party.

(*e*)   I have sought information on French military facilities outside Europe. On the basis of that information, I believe that the transfer of Major Mafart and Captain Prieur to the French military facility on the isolated island of Hao in French Polynesia would best facilitate the enforcement of the conditions which I have laid down in paragraphs (*a*) to (*d*) above. My ruling is that that should be their destination immediately after their transfer.

Trade Issues

The New Zealand Government has taken the position that trade issues have been imported into the affair as a result of French action, either taken or in prospect. The French Government denies that, but it has indicated that it is willing to give some undertakings relating to trade, as sought by the New Zealand Government. I therefore rule that France should:

(*a*)   Not oppose continuing imports of New Zealand butter into the United Kingdom in 1987 and 1988 at levels proposed by the Commission of the European Communities in so far as these do not exceed those mentioned in document COM(83)574 of 6 October 1983 that is to say, 77,000 tonnes in 1987 and 75,000 tonnes in 1988; and

(*b*) Not take measures that might impair the implementation of the agreement between New Zealand and the European Economic Community on Trade in Mutton, Lamb and Goatmeat which entered into force on 20 October 1980 (as complemented by the exchange of letters of 12 July 1984).

> *Agreement on Interstate Arbitration of Future Disputes.* New Zealand also was eager to create a mechanism to help ensure that France did not violate the Secretary-General's ruling on treatment of the French agents and on trade issues. The Secretary-General decided that the two countries should enter an agreement on arbitration.

The Rainbow Warrior Case (1986)
The Ruling on Arbitral Mechanisms

Arbitration

The New Zealand Government has argued that a mechanism should exist to ensure that any differences that may arise about the implementation of the agreements concluded as a result of my ruling can be referred for binding decision to an arbitral tribunal. The Government of France is not averse to that. My ruling is that an agreement to that effect should be concluded and provide that any dispute concerning the interpretation or application of the other agreements, which it has not been possible to resolve through the diplomatic channel, shall, at the request of either of the two Governments, be submitted to an arbitral tribunal under the following conditions:

(*a*) Each Government shall designate a member of the tribunal within 30 days of the date of the delivery by either Government to the other of a written request for arbitration of the dispute, and the two Governments shall, within 60 days of that date, appoint a third member of the tribunal who shall be its chairman;

(*b*) If, within the times prescribed, either Government fails to designate a member of the tribunal or the third member is not agreed, the Secretary-General of the United Nations shall be requested to make the necessary appointment after consultations with the two Governments by choosing the member or members of the tribunal;

(*c*) A majority of the members of the tribunal shall constitute a quorum and all decisions shall be made by a majority vote;

(*d*) The decisions of the tribunal, including all rulings concerning its constitution, procedure and jurisdiction, shall be binding on the two Governments.

The two Governments should conclude and bring into force as soon as possible binding agreements incorporating all of the above rulings. These agreements should provide that the undertaking relating to an apology, the payment of compensation and the transfer of Major Mafart and Captain Prieur should be implemented at the latest on 25 July 1986.

The Transfer of the French Agents. On July 9, 1986, three days after U.N. Secretary-General Pérez de Cuéllar made his ruling, France and New Zealand entered into three agreements to implement the ruling, including the transfer of Major Mafart and Captain Prieur to the island of Hao.

Compromissory Clauses in Treaties. Many treaties contain so-called "compromissory clauses," which authorize arbitrators to hear disputes concerning the treaty in question. The July 9, 1986 agreement that France and New Zealand entered to implement the Secretary-General's decision concerning arbitration served a compromissory function with respect to the two other bilateral agreements that carried out his substantive ruling. Either state could then unilaterally commence arbitral proceedings alleging a breach of a substantive agreement. Indeed, as we see below, New Zealand instituted an arbitration after France released the prisoners from Hao. Do compromissory clauses serve only to provide the basis for consent to arbitration? Sometimes they may also encourage states to comply with treaties, since breaches could be widely publicized in arbitral proceedings.

Does a compromissory clause preclude measures other than third-party proceedings to counteract the breach of a treaty? That is, could New Zealand legally have taken steps other than instituting arbitration to respond to France's alleged breach of its obligation to confine Mafart and Prieur to Hao? Most authorities conclude that, even after a state has instituted an arbitration, it is entitled to pursue legal countermeasures against the state with which it has a dispute. See the discussion of countermeasures in Chapter 6.

The 1990 Rainbow Warrior *Arbitration.* A 1990 arbitral decision, excerpted below, evaluated the legality of France's evacuation of Major Mafart and Captain Prieur from Hao to France before their three-year detention period had run. Mafart left Hao for France in December 1987 for health reasons, and Prieur left in May 1988 after France sought New Zealand's consent on the ground that she was pregnant. France agreed to an independent examination of Prieur in Hao by New Zealand doctors, but Prieur left the day before the doctors arrived, France claiming that Prieur's father was dying. Neither Mafart nor Prieur ever returned to Hao.

New Zealand unilaterally instituted this second arbitration pursuant to one of its 1986 agreements with France, arguing that Mafart's and Prieur's departures from Hao were illegal. The two countries then in 1989 concluded a Supplementary Agreement designating three arbitrators (one appointed by each state and one appointed jointly by both states) and specifying Tribunal procedures. The Supplementary Agreement also specified that the Tribunal's decisions would be based on the 1986 France-New Zealand agreements and on "applicable rules and principles of international law." As we see in the excerpt below, the arbitrators applied aspects of the law of treaties and the law of state responsibility, both topics introduced at the end of Chapter 2, Part B. We further consider state responsibility in Chapter 7.

THE RAINBOW WARRIOR CASE (1990)

New Zealand v. France, France-New Zealand Arbitration Tribunal, 82 *International Law Reports* 500 (1990)

The Law

[F]or the decision of the present case, both the customary Law of Treaties and the customary Law of State Responsibility are relevant and applicable. The customary Law of Treaties, as codified in the Vienna Convention, proclaimed in Article 26, under the title "*Pacta sunt servanda*" that

> Every treaty in force is binding upon the parties to it and must be performed by them in good faith.

This fundamental provision is applicable to the determination whether there have been violations of that principle and in particular, whether material breaches of treaty obligations have been committed.

Moreover, certain specific provisions of customary law in the Vienna Convention are relevant in this case such as Article 60 which gives a precise definition of the concept of a material breach of a treaty, and Article 70, which deals with the legal consequences of the expiry of a treaty.

On the other hand, the legal consequences of a breach of a treaty, including the determination of the circumstances that may exclude wrongfulness (and render the breach only apparent) and the appropriate remedies for breach, are subjects that belong to the customary Law of State Responsibility.

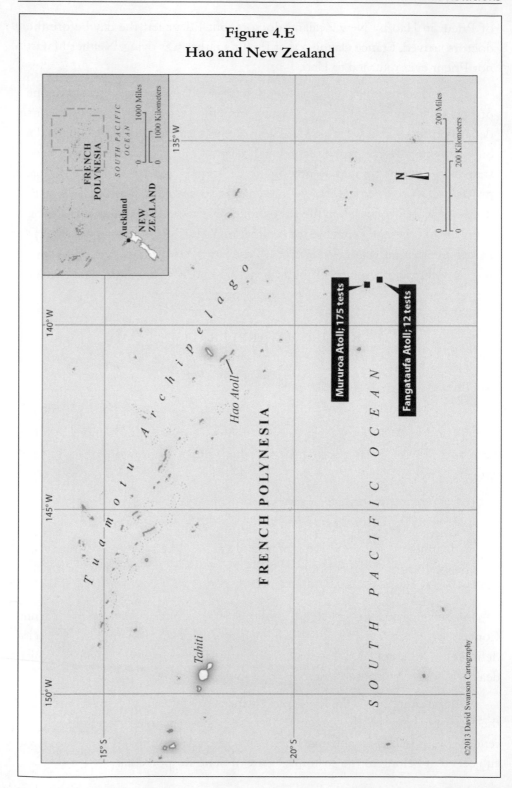

Figure 4.E
Hao and New Zealand

©2013 David Swanson Cartography

The reason is that the general principles of International Law concerning State responsibility are equally applicable in the case of breach of treaty obligation, since in the international law field there is no distinction between contractual and tortious responsibility, so that any violation by a State of any obligation, of whatever origin, gives rise to State responsibility and consequently, to the duty of reparation. . . .

Under the title "Circumstances Precluding Wrongfulness" the International Law Commission proposed in Articles 29 to 35 [of the Commission's Draft Articles on State Responsibility] a set of rules which include three provisions on *force majeure* and fortuitous event (Article 31), distress (Article 32), and state of necessity (Article 33), which may be relevant to the decision on this case. [The Tribunal focuses on distress.]

The question [is] whether the circumstances of distress in a case of extreme urgency involving elementary humanitarian considerations affecting the acting organs of the State may exclude wrongfulness in this case.

[T]he International Law Commission explains that "'distress' means a situation of extreme peril in which the organ of the State which adopts that conduct has, at that particular moment, no means of saving himself or persons entrusted to his care other than to act in a manner not in conformity with the requirements of the obligation in question." . . .

In accordance with the previous legal considerations, three conditions would be required to justify the conduct followed by France in respect to Major Mafart and Captain Prieur:

1) The existence of very exceptional circumstances of extreme urgency involving medical or other considerations of an elementary nature, provided always that a prompt recognition of the existence of those exceptional circumstances is subsequently obtained from the other interested party or is clearly demonstrated.

2) The reestablishment of the original situation of compliance with the assignment in Hao as soon as the reasons of emergency invoked to justify the repatriation had disappeared.

3) The existence of a good faith effort to try to obtain the consent of New Zealand in terms of the 1986 Agreement.

Deciding the Case. How should these principles be applied to the facts? With respect to Major Mafart, the Tribunal found there had been an urgent medical need to evacuate him from Hao and that France had notified New Zealand of the circumstances. These factors led the Tribunal to declare that France "did not breach its obligations to New Zealand by removing Major Mafart from the island of Hao on 13 December 1987." However, France did commit "a material and continuing breach of its obligations to New Zealand by failing to order the return of Major Mafart to the island of Hao as from 12 February 1988," when he had recovered from his illness. The following excerpt concerns the 1990 Tribunal's reasoning with respect to Captain Prieur.

The Rainbow Warrior Case (1990)
The Tribunal's Findings of Breach

The facts . . . show that New Zealand would not oppose Captain Prieur's departure, if that became necessary because of special care which might be required by her pregnancy. They also indicated that France and New Zealand agreed that Captain Prieur would be examined by Dr. Brenner, a New Zealand physician, before returning to Paris.

[D]uring the day of 5 May the French Government suddenly decided to present the New Zealand Government with the *fait accompli* of Captain Prieur's hasty return for a new reason, the health of Mrs. Prieur's father, who was seriously ill, hospitalized for cancer. Indisputably the health of Mrs. Prieur's father, who unfortunately would die on 16 May, and the concern for allowing Mrs. Prieur to visit her dying father constitute humanitarian reasons worthy of consideration by both Governments under the 1986 Agreement. But the events of 5 May (French date) prove that the French Republic did not make efforts in good faith to obtain New Zealand's consent. First of all, it must be remembered that France and New Zealand agreed that Captain Prieur would be examined in Hao on 6 May, which would allow her to return to France immediately. For France, in this case, it was only a question of gaining 24 or 36 hours. Of course, the health of Mrs. Prieur's father, who had been hospitalized for several months, could serve as grounds for such acute and sudden urgency: but, in this case, New Zealand would have had to be informed very precisely and completely, and not be presented with a decision that had already been made.

. . . New Zealand was really not asked for its approval, as compliance with France's obligations required even under extremely urgent circumstances: it was indeed demanded so firmly that it was bound to provoke a strong reaction from New Zealand.

[T]he Tribunal:

–   declares that the French Republic committed a material breach of its obligations to New Zealand by not endeavoring in good faith to obtain on 5 May 1988 New Zealand's consent to Captain Prieur's leaving the island of Hao;

—   declares that as a consequence the French Republic committed a material breach of its obligations by removing Captain Prieur from the island of Hao on 5 and 6 May 1988;

—   declares that the French Republic committed a material and continuing breach of its obligations to New Zealand by failing to order the return of Captain Prieur to the island of Hao.

Remedies. The Tribunal next turned to appropriate remedies. Its analysis provides a good introduction to the international law of remedies, including satisfaction, restitution, and damages. Note that New Zealand did not seek monetary compensation for France's breach of its international law obligations. Why not, especially given the Secretary-General's 1986 determination that a monetary award might be made for non-material harm? More broadly, what did New Zealand hope to gain by instituting the 1990 arbitration? New Zealand likely did not want any appearance of concern with financial gain to detract from what it perceived to be significant issues of national honor and international law, including respect for the legally binding solution set forth in the 1986 agreement to confine the French officials to Hao.

The Rainbow Warrior Case (1990)
Remedies

In the present case the Tribunal must find that the infringement of the special regime designed by the Secretary-General to reconcile the conflicting views of the Parties has provoked indignation and public outrage in New Zealand and caused a new, additional non-material damage. This damage is of a moral, political and legal nature, resulting from the affront to the dignity and prestige not only of New Zealand as such, but of its highest judicial and executive authorities as well.

It follows from the foregoing findings that New Zealand is entitled to appropriate remedies. It claims certain declarations, to the effect that France has breached the First Agreement. But New Zealand seeks as well an order for the return of the agents. . . .

For its part, the French Republic maintains that adequate reparation for moral or legal damage can only take the form of satisfaction, generally considered as the remedy *par excellence* in cases of non-material damage. Invoking the decisions of the International Court of Justice, France maintains that whenever the damage suffered amounts to no more than a breach of the law, a declaration by the judge of this breach constitutes appropriate satisfaction. France points out, moreover, that, rather than *restitutio*, what New Zealand is demanding is the cessation of the denounced behaviour[.]

The recent jurisprudence of the International Court of Justice confirms that an offer for the cessation or discontinuance of wrongful acts or omissions is only justified in case of continuing breaches of international obligations which are still in force at the time the judicial order is issued.

It would be . . . illogical to issue the order requested by New Zealand [because the French conduct], namely to keep the two agents in Paris, is no longer unlawful, since the international obligation expired on 22 July 1989. Today, France is no longer obliged to return the two agents to Hao and submit them to the special regime. . . .

On the other hand, the French contention that satisfaction is the only appropriate remedy for non-material damage is also not justified in the circumstances of the present case.

The granting of a form of reparation other than satisfaction has been recognized and admitted in the relations between the parties by the Ruling of the Secretary-General of 9 July 1986, which has been accepted and implemented by both Parties to this case.

In the Memorandum presented to the Secretary-General, the New Zealand Government requested compensation for non-material damage, stating that it was "entitled to compensation for the violation of sovereignty and the affront and insult that involved."

The French Government opposed this claim, contending that the compensation "could concern only the material damage suffered by New Zealand, the moral damage being compensated by the offer of apologies."

But the Secretary-General did not make any distinction, ruling instead that the French Government "should pay the sum of U.S. dollars 7 million to the Government of New Zealand as *compensation for all the damage it has suffered.*"

[T]he compensation constituted a reparation not just for material damage—such as the cost of the police investigation—but for non-material damage as well, regardless of material injury and independent therefrom. . . .

New Zealand has not however requested the award of monetary compensation—even as a last resort should the Tribunal not make the declarations and orders for the return of the agents.

[T]he Tribunal has decided not to make an order for monetary compensation. . . .

There is a long established practice of States and international Courts and Tribunals of using satisfaction as a remedy or form of reparation (in the wide sense) for the breach of an international obligation. This practice relates particularly to the case of moral or legal damage done directly to the State, especially as opposed to the case of damage to persons involving international responsibilities. . . .

Satisfaction in this sense can take and has taken various forms [including] regrets, punishment of the responsible individuals, safeguards against repetition, the payment of symbolic or nominal damages or of compensation on a broader basis, and a decision of an international tribunal declaring the unlawfulness of the State's conduct.

It is to the last of these forms of satisfaction for an international wrong that the Tribunal now turns. . . . The Tribunal accordingly . . .

— declares that the condemnation of the French Republic for its breaches of its treaty obligations to New Zealand, made public by the decision of the Tribunal, constitutes in the circumstances appropriate satisfaction for the legal and moral damage caused to New Zealand. . . .

Th[e] important relationship [between New Zealand and France], the nature of the decisions made by the Tribunal, and the earlier discussion of monetary compensation lead the Tribunal to make a recommendation. The recommendation, addressed to the two Governments, is intended to assist them in putting an end to the present unhappy affair. . . .

The power of an arbitral tribunal to address recommendations to the parties to a dispute, in addition to the formal finding and obligatory decisions contained in the award, has been recognized in previous arbitral decisions. . . .

For the foregoing reasons the Tribunal:

— in light of the above decisions, recommends that the Governments of the French Republic and of New Zealand set up a fund to promote close and friendly relations between the citizens of the two countries, and that the Government of the French Republic make an initial contribution equivalent to US Dollars 2 million to that fund.

The Variety of Arbitral Functions. The 1986 and 1990 *Rainbow Warrior* decisions illustrate the flexibility in form and function of international third-party dispute settlement. How do the roles and functions of the U.N. Secretary-

General in his 1986 decision differ from those of the Tribunal in the 1990 arbitration? The Secretary-General was charged with fashioning an equitable ruling and showed political sensitivity in building on agreements between France and New Zealand. The 1990 opinion was, by contrast, highly legalistic, involving technical points of the law of state responsibility and remedies. Despite the controversial political matters at the heart of the legal dispute, lawyers had to fashion arguments for the Tribunal, as well as advise government officials about how the Tribunal was likely to be constituted, to approach its task, and to decide the case. Did the 1990 Tribunal also exhibit political sensitivity in its ruling? Note the Tribunal's decision that France was "no longer obliged to return the two agents to Hao" and its recommendation concerning "a fund to promote close and friendly relations."

The Legal Complexity of the Rainbow Warrior *Incident.* Besides the two proceedings excerpted above, many other legal processes were engaged by one aspect or another of the *Rainbow Warrior* incident. First, there was the 1974 International Court of Justice *Nuclear Test Case* between New Zealand and France. Second, New Zealand brought domestic criminal proceedings against the French secret agents. Third, individuals pursued five claims against France, including a 1985–1986 negotiated settlement whereby France paid 2.3 million French francs to the widow, children, and parents of the crew member killed aboard the *Rainbow Warrior*, as well as 1995 challenges to France in the European Court of Human Rights and in the Human Rights Committee organized under a protocol to the International Covenant for Civil and Political Rights. Fourth, there were four claims brought by Greenpeace, a non-governmental organization, against France, including a 1987 arbitration resulting in an order for France to pay Greenpeace $8.1 million, and legal challenges to France made by Greenpeace in 1995 at Euratom and at the French Conseil d'Etat. Fifth, France and New Zealand each made or threatened trade reprisals, involving both the World Trade Organization and the European Union. See Christopher Harding, "Vingt Ans Après: Rainbow Warrior, Legal Ordering and Legal Complexity," 10 *Singapore Year Book of International Law* 99 (2006). Such complexity can be a characteristic of modern international legal process; no one case or forum may be able to resolve all aspects of an international legal dispute. The multiplicity of legal proceedings raises questions about how to reconcile conflicting legal systems, a topic we consider in Part C below.

The Aftermath. France complied almost immediately with the arbitral tribunal's recommendation to contribute $2 million to a fund to promote friendly relations. Michael Rocard, the French Prime Minister, also visited New Zealand in May 1991 and formally apologized for the 1985 bombing.

Nevertheless, tensions continued. France resumed its nuclear testing in the South Pacific, and New Zealand expressed outrage when, in July 1991, France awarded Alain Mafart a medal for distinguished service. A new round of French nuclear testing in 1995 led New Zealand and other Pacific states to protest anew. New Zealand complained to the International Court of Justice that the testing contravened the 1974 *Nuclear Tests Case*. The Court disagreed, however, noting that the earlier case concerned atmospheric testing, whereas the more recent French testing was non-atmospheric. See Request for an Examination of the Situation in Accordance with Paragraph 63 of the Court's Judgment of 20 December 1974 in the Nuclear Tests (New Zealand v. France) Case, 1995 I.C.J. 288. France finally halted its nuclear program in 1996 after conducting over 140 tests at Pacific atolls, and in 1998 France ratified the 1996 Comprehensive Test Ban Treaty.

Greenpeace's political activism continues to upset governments. In September 2013, Russia seized a Greenpeace vessel, the *Arctic Sunrise*, that was protesting at a Russian offshore oil rig in the Arctic Ocean. In November 2013 the International Tribunal for the Law of the Sea (ITLOS) ordered Russia to release the ship and her crew on the posting of a bond. Arctic Sunrise Case (Netherlands v. Russia), ITLOS Case No. 22, *available at* http://www.itlos.org. For background on the ITLOS, see Chapter 8. At the merits stage, an arbitral tribunal ruled that Russia's seizure of the vessel violated the 1982 Convention on the Law of the Sea. Arctic Sunrise Arbitration (Netherlands v. Russia), Award (Annex VII United Nations Convention on the Law of the Sea Arbitral Tribunal, 2015), *available at* https://pcacases.com/web/sendAttach/1438.

B. THE INTERNATIONAL COURT

The failure of diplomacy and the Permanent Court of Arbitration (PCA) to solve the problems prompting the 1914 outbreak of the First World War inspired the 1919 Paris Peace Conference to create the Permanent Court of International Justice (PCIJ) as the judicial arm of the new League of Nations. However, the League and the PCIJ failed to arrest the onset of the Second World War. In 1944–1945 new peacemakers established both the United Nations and, as the judicial organ of that organization, the International Court of Justice (ICJ). In form and function, there are few differences between the PCIJ (1921–1945) and the ICJ (1945 on). Together they are commonly known as the "International Court" or the "World Court." Both have been housed at The Hague in the Netherlands in the Peace Palace, also still the home of the PCA.

1. The Jurisdiction of the International Court

We can better understand the kinds of disputes that come before the International Court of Justice by carefully reading the exact delegations of jurisdiction made to the Court by its constituting treaty. In general, jurisdiction, as a legal term, refers to power or competence. In this context jurisdiction refers to the competence of the Court to decide certain types of cases. There is a contentious jurisdiction based on Article 36 of the Court's Statute, which is an integral part of the United Nations Charter. Only states may be parties in contentious cases, which we explore in Section 2. The Court also has jurisdiction to render advisory opinions to some international organizations pursuant to Article 65 of its Statute and Article 96 of the U.N. Charter itself. See Section 3.

Figure 4.F
The Peace Palace, The Hague, the Netherlands
Seat of the International Court of Justice and
the Permanent Court of Arbitration

STATUTE OF THE INTERNATIONAL COURT OF JUSTICE, ARTICLES 36, 65

June 26, 1945, 59 Stat. 1031, T.S. No. 993

Article 36

1.   The jurisdiction of the Court comprises all cases which the parties refer to it and all matters specially provided for in the Charter of the United Nations or in treaties and conventions in force.

2.   The states parties to the present Statute may at any time declare that they recognize as compulsory *ipso facto* and without special agreement, in relation to any other state accepting the same obligation, the jurisdiction of the Court in all legal disputes concerning:

    a.   the interpretation of a treaty;

    b.   any question of international law;

    c.   the existence of any fact which, if established, would constitute a breach of an international obligation;

    d.   the nature or extent of the reparation to be made for the breach of an international obligation.

3.   The declarations referred to above may be made unconditionally or on condition of reciprocity on the part of several or certain states, or for a certain time. . . .

6.   In the event of a dispute as to whether the Court has jurisdiction, the matter shall be settled by the decision of the Court.

Article 65

1.   The Court may give an advisory opinion on any legal question at the request of whatever body may be authorized by or in accordance with the Charter of the United Nations to make such a request.

2.   Questions upon which the advisory opinion of the Court is asked shall be laid before the Court by means of a written request containing an exact statement of the question upon which an opinion is required, and accompanied by all documents likely to throw light upon the question.

CHARTER OF THE UNITED NATIONS, ARTICLE 96

June 26, 1945, 59 Stat. 1031, T.S. No. 993

1.   The General Assembly or the Security Council may request the International Court of Justice to give an advisory opinion on any legal question.

2.   Other organs of the United Nations and specialized agencies, which may at any time be so authorized by the General Assembly, may also request advisory opinions of the Court on legal questions arising within the scope of their activities.

Compulsory ICJ Jurisdiction in Contentious Cases. What does it mean to say that the International Court may exercise "compulsory" jurisdiction, a term used in Article 36(2) of the Court's Statute? Will the ICJ have jurisdiction any time one member state of the United Nations brings a suit against any other member state? During the 19th and early 20th centuries, members of popular peace societies and many European and U.S. leaders favored not only the codification of international law but the development of a world court with jurisdiction to hear cases brought unilaterally by states. According to a 1920 proposal of the Committee of Jurists, which prepared the Statute of the Permanent Court of International Justice, the Court would have been able to exercise jurisdiction in a contentious case when one state unilaterally applied to it. However, this Committee proposal was not included in the PCIJ Statute. The idea of such true compulsory jurisdiction resurfaced when the U.N. Charter and the Statute of the International Court of Justice were drafted. Many delegations favored subjecting U.N. member states to such compulsory jurisdiction. As finally adopted, however, the ICJ Statute requires the consent of all litigating states if the Court is to have jurisdiction over them in a contentious case. How, then, does the Court obtain "compulsory" jurisdiction?

Other Bases for ICJ Jurisdiction in Contentious Cases. In addition to so-called compulsory jurisdiction, how else may the ICJ obtain jurisdiction in contentious cases? Broadly, states must mutually consent to the Court's jurisdiction. As you read the cases in Section 2, consider how the states involved consented to ICJ jurisdiction and how the basis for jurisdiction relates to the efficacy of the Court's rulings.

The Judges on the International Court. According to Article 2 of the Statute of the International Court of Justice, judges must be "persons of high moral character, who possess the qualifications required in their respective countries for appointment to the highest judicial offices, or are jurisconsults of recognized competence in international law." Many of the Court's 15 judges, who are charged with acting independently, have had significant professional experience as government officials in the countries of their nationality. Judges are elected for nine-year terms by majority vote both of the U.N General Assembly and of the Security Council. As of May 2017, five judges were from the U.N.'s "Western Europe and Other Group" (including one from Australia and one from the United States), two were from Eastern Europe, three from

Asia, three from Africa, and two from Latin America. By tradition, a national of each permanent member of the U.N. Security Council (China, France, Russia, the United Kingdom, and the United States) always serves as a member of the Court.

2. Contentious Cases at the International Court

As with public international arbitration, seen in the *Alabama*, *Dogger Bank*, and *Rainbow Warrior* cases, keep in mind key questions as we explore the International Court. When and why do sovereign states agree to submit disputes to third-party legal settlement? When and why are governments willing to be bound by the decisions of international tribunals? To explore these questions we look first at the *Minquiers and Ecrehos Case* between France and the United Kingdom and next at the *Diplomatic and Consular Staff Case* between the United States and Iran.

ICJ Judges in Contentious Cases. The question "who will judge" factors into a state's decision to allow the International Court to hear a dispute. If the Court's judges do not include a national of a party to a contentious case, that state may appoint an *ad hoc* judge to sit on the case. What explains this rule? After all, a party to litigation in municipal court does not get to appoint a judge to help rule in his or her case. Is the appointment of *ad hoc* judges consistent with the independent judicial character of the Court? States likely would be less willing to accept the Court's jurisdiction without this feature, which ensures that at least one member of the Court is able to explain to other judges the reasons that might justify a country's actions. A judge of the nationality of a state party usually sides with that state. However, the French judge in our first case, *Minquiers and Echrehos*, voted against France.

The Minquiers and Ecrehos Case. The *Minquiers and Ecrehos Case* involved a dispute concerning sovereignty over islets in the English Channel. Territorial and boundary disputes—especially disputes concerning islands and maritime boundaries—are a favorite kind of issue for international adjudication. Note in *Minquiers and Ecrehos* that France's and Britain's consent to ICJ jurisdiction came *after* the dispute had already arisen. Look carefully at their Special Agreement submitting their case to the Court.

THE MINQUIERS AND ECREHOS CASE

France/United Kingdom, 1953 I.C.J. 47

The Special Agreement

By a letter dated December 5th, 1951, the British Ambassador to the Netherlands transmitted to the Registry on behalf of his Government a certified copy of a Special Agreement concluded between the Government of the United Kingdom of Great Britain and Northern Ireland and the Government of the French Republic, signed on December 29th, 1950, the instruments of ratification in respect of which were exchanged at Paris on September 24th, 1951. . . .

By Article I of the Special Agreement, signed on December 29th, 1950, the Court is requested

> to determine whether the sovereignty over the islets and rocks (in so far as they are capable of appropriation) of the Minquiers and Ecrehos groups respectively belongs to the United Kingdom or the French Republic.

Having thus been requested to decide whether these groups belong either to France or to the United Kingdom, the Court has to determine which of the Parties has produced the more convincing proof of title to one or the other of these groups, or to both of them. By the formulation of Article I the Parties have excluded the status of *res nullius* as well as that of *condominium*. . . .

These groups lie between the British Channel Island of Jersey and the coast of France and consist each of two or three habitable islets, many smaller islets and a great number of rocks. The Ecrehos group lies north-east of Jersey, 3.9 sea-miles from that island, measured from the rock nearest thereto and permanently above water, and 6.6 sea-miles from the coast of France, measured in the same way. The Minquiers group lies south of Jersey, 9.8 sea-miles therefrom and 16.2 sea-miles from the French mainland, measured in the same way. This group lies 8 sea-miles from the Chausey Islands which belong to France.

> *The Decision to Adjudicate.* Why was the Minquiers and Ecrehos dispute susceptible to resolution by the International Court? What did the governments of the United Kingdom and France each gain and lose by suspending diplomatic negotiations while the Court heard the case? As you read the excerpts below, consider whether it was likely that each state believed it had the better claim and would win. In many situations, hope of success or fear of failure may affect a state's willingness to submit a case to the ICJ.

Did the *Minquiers and Ecrehos Case* concern an issue of high political importance? In the real world, sovereignty over even small, uninhabited islands may be significant. The sovereign state is entitled to offshore zones in which it may control fishing and exercise other rights. See Chapter 8. However, before the ICJ was notified about the Special Agreement to submit the *Minquiers and Echrehos Case*, France and the United Kingdom concluded a treaty allocating important fishing rights off the islets, "without prejudice to the determination of the question of sovereignty" over the islets themselves. 1951 Agreement Regarding Rights of Fishery in Areas of the Ecrehos and Minquiers. This Agreement may well have facilitated the countries' decision to adjudicate, since the eventual decision on sovereignty would have little economic consequence. Significant fishing rights were allocated; the islets were not otherwise economically important, for agriculture or industry, or as a place for people to live permanently.

In short, sovereignty over the Minquiers and Ecrehos may not have been a major political issue. The United Kingdom and France were not about to go to war over these islets! The two countries, politically unable to negotiate a settlement of this dispute, may have turned to international adjudication because it was nevertheless desirable to reach *some* resolution of the question of sovereignty over the islets.

Shaping the Legal Issue. Note how France and the United Kingdom, in their Special Agreement, formulated the specific question the Court was authorized to answer. By minimizing the possibility that the Court would find the islets either *terra nullius* or subject to a potentially complicated joint condominium regime, the parties seemingly maximized the possibility that the Court would rule that only one or the other state had sovereignty over the islets. Countries submitting contentious cases to the ICJ can shape the issues before the Court.

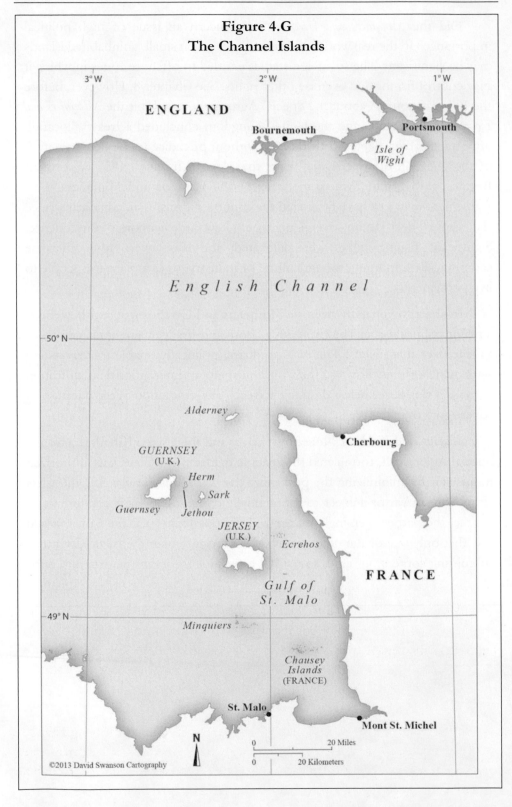

**Figure 4.G
The Channel Islands**

Territorial Sovereignty. Questions about territory have long troubled interstate relations. We met the issue in Chapters 2 (the Peace of Westphalia, the Peace of Paris, and the Cession of Alaska) and 3 (Antarctica), and see it again in Chapter 6 (use of force). International law recognizes several ways in which states may acquire new territory: discovery and occupation of *terra nullius*, a label used to describe uninhabited territory such as newly discovered islands; cession from another state; accretion, *i.e.*, the increase of land, as through new geological formations; and acquiescence or prescription, *i.e.*, a continuous, uncontested display of control. Subjugation—conquest followed by annexation—was historically another method of territorial acquisition, but today may violate the U.N. Charter's proscription against the use of force. As you read the excerpts below, ask which territorial theories France, the United Kingdom, and the International Court employed in *Minquiers and Ecrehos.*

The International Court as Finder of Fact. Municipal courts typically provide some avenue for appealing an adverse legal judgment. In the U.S. federal system, for example, a federal district court hears evidence, determines facts based on that evidence, and then applies the law to those facts. The losing party may appeal to a federal circuit court of appeals and ultimately to the U.S. Supreme Court; these appellate courts review the law and how it is applied in the case but may not, as a general rule, overturn the trial court's findings of facts. While this is the general rule in common law legal systems, it is not so in most countries. Most legal systems are based on the civil law, where matters of fact may be reviewed on appeal.

The International Court of Justice does not hear appeals, either from municipal courts or from any "lower" international court. The International Court is a "one stop" forum that evaluates evidence, finds facts, and applies the law. The following excerpts from the *Minquiers and Ecrehos Case* illustrate the kinds of proof British and French government lawyers needed to collect and argue; the Court's fact-finding function; and the importance of the factual record to the legal inquiry.

The Minquiers and Ecrehos Case
Evidence of Historic Title

Both Parties contend that they have respectively an ancient or original title to the Ecrehos and the Minquiers, and that their title has always been maintained and was never lost. The present case does not therefore present the characteristics of a dispute concerning the acquisition of sovereignty over *terra nullius*.

The United Kingdom Government derives the ancient title invoked by it from the conquest of England in 1066 by William Duke of Normandy. By this conquest England became united within the Duchy of Normandy, including the Channel Islands, and this union lasted until 1204 when King Philip Augustus of France drove the Anglo-Norman forces out of Continental Normandy. But his attempts to occupy also the Islands were not successful, except for brief periods when some of them were taken by French forces. On this ground the United Kingdom Government submits the view that all of the Channel Islands, including the Ecrehos and the Minquiers, remained, as before, united with England and that this situation of fact was placed on a legal basis by subsequent Treaties concluded between the English and French Kings.

The French Government does not dispute that the Islands of Jersey, Guernsey, Alderney, Sark, Herm and Jethou continued to be held by the King of England; but it denies that the Ecrehos and Minquiers groups were held by him after the dismemberment of the Duchy of Normandy in 1204. After that event, these two groups were, it is asserted, held by the King of France together with some other islands close to the continent, and reference is made to the same medieval Treaties as those which are invoked by the United Kingdom Government.

In such circumstances it must be examined whether these Treaties, invoked by both Parties, contain anything which might throw light upon the status of the Ecrehos and the Minquiers. [The Court examines the 1217 Treaty of Lambeth, the 1259 Treaty of Paris, the 1360 Treaty of Calais, and the 1420 Treaty of Tropes, and concludes that they do not elucidate the question.]

There are, however, other documents which provide some indication as to the possession of the islets in dispute.

By a Charter of January 14th, 1200, King John of England granted to one of his Barons, Piers des Préaux, the Islands of Jersey, Guernsey and Alderney "to have and to hold of us by service of three knights' fees." Three years later, by a Charter of 1203, Piers des Préaux granted to the Abbey of Val-Richer "the island of Escrehou in entirety," stating that the King of England "gave me the islands" (*insulas mihi dedit*). This shows that he treated the Ecrehos as an integral part of the fief of the Islands which he had received from the King. [The Court discusses whether a 1258 Order from the English King, 1360 royal Letters Patent, the 1471 Truce of London with France, a 1500 Papal Bull, and two commercial treaties of 1606 and 1655 refer to control over the Minquiers and Ecrehos. The Court also reviews the political history of the Channel Islands and concludes:] What is of decisive importance, in the opinion of the Court, is not indirect presumptions deduced from events in the Middle Ages, but the evidence which relates directly to the possession of the Ecrehos and Minquiers groups.

[The Court turns first to the Ecrehos.]

The grant of the Ecrehos [from Piers des Préaux to the Abbey of Val-Richer in the 1203 Charter] was in frankalmoin. The French Government contends that such a grant had the effect of severing the feudal link between Piers des Préaux and the Abbey, so that the Ecrehos no longer formed a part of the fief of the Channel Islands. The view submitted by that Government is that the Ecrehos remained subject to the Duke of Normandy through the intermediary of the Abbey of Val-Richer, which was situated on the French mainland, and that, when the King of France succeeded to the rights of the Duke after the occupation of Continental Normandy in 1204, the Abbey "passed under his protection, as did the Ecrehos, whose overlord he became."

This contention renders it necessary to consider the Charter of 1203 more closely. It provided the following: . . .

> Know ye all that I, having regard to the mercy of God, have granted and given and by my present charter have confirmed to God and to the church of St. Mary of Val-Richer and to the monks there serving God, for the salvation of the soul of John, illustrious king of England, who gave me the islands, and for the salvation of the souls of myself and of my father and mother and of all my ancestors, the island of Escrehou in entirety, for the building there of a church in honour of God and of the blessed Mary, so that the divine mysteries be daily celebrated there, to have and possess [it] and whatever in the same island they shall be able to increase and build, freely and quietly, fully and honourably, in free pure and perpetual alms. I have further granted to the aforesaid monks whatever by my men of Jersey, and of Guernsey, and of Alderney, having regard to charity, shall be reasonably given to them, saving my right.

It appears clearly from the *Grand Coutumier de Normandie* of the thirteenth century . . . that land held in frankalmoin was a tenure, and that such a grant in frankalmoin to an ecclesiastical institution did not have the effect of severing feudal ties. The text . . . shows that the grantor retained the "patronal domain" (*dominium patronale*). According to this ancient Norman custom, Piers des Préaux did not by his grant drop out of the feudal chain as far as the Ecrehos was concerned. He continued to hold the Ecrehos as a part of his fief of the Channel Islands, with the Abbot of Val-Richer as his vassal and the King of England as his overlord, and the King continued to exercise his justice and levy his rights in the land so put in alms. By granting the Ecrehos in frankalmoin to the Abbey, Piers des Préaux did not, and could not, alienate the island from the fief of the Channel Islands; it remained a part of that fief.

This view is contested by the French Government on the ground that Piers des Préaux had not in the Charter reserved any feudal service and that he therefore had not created any feudal tenure. [E]ven assuming that a condition or reservation was required [—an assumption that the Court disputes—] the grant to the Abbey did contain such a condition or reservation. As is seen from the text of the Charter, the Abbey was to build a church in the Ecrehos "so that the divine mysteries be daily celebrated there," and when the grant was said to be given "for the salvation of the soul of John, illustrious king of England ... and for the salvation of the souls of myself and of my father and mother and all my ancestors," this could, in view of the custom at that time, only mean that a service of prayers was reserved in the Charter. ... The Assize Rolls [from 1309] show that a chapel had in fact been built in the Ecrehos, and that the Prior of that chapel, appearing before the Justices, gave evidence that he and his fellow monk, dwelling in the chapel throughout the whole year, "always celebrate for the lord the King and his progenitors." These records show that the Prior himself as well as the Justices called the grant a *tenura*.

Shortly after his grant of 1203 Piers de Préaux forfeited the fief of the Channel Islands, which thereupon reverted to the English King and were administered by Wardens appointed by that King, except for certain periods in the thirteenth and the beginning of the fourteenth century, when the Islands were again granted in fee. Up to 1309, there is no indication that any change had occurred as to the connection of the Ecrehos with the Channel Islands.

The object of [English legal] proceedings of 1309 ... was to enquire into the property and revenue of the English King. These proceedings, which were numerous, took the form of calling upon persons to justify their possession of property. The Abbot of Val-Richer was summoned before the King's Justices to answer regarding a mill and the *advocatio* of the Priory of the Ecrehos as well as a rent. [This summons must have been premised] on the ground that the Ecrehos ... was within the domain of the English King. And when the Prior of the Ecrehos appeared as the Abbot's attorney in answer to the summons, jurisdiction in respect of the Ecrehos was exercised by the Justices, who decided that "it is permitted to the said Prior to hold the *premissa* as he holds them as long as it shall please the lord the King."

Territorial Sovereignty and the Principle of Effectivity. The ICJ places great emphasis on effective control of territory. In some modern disputes, effective control clashes with prohibitions on the use of force, which we will examine in Chapter 6. For example, Russia's February 2014 annexation of Crimea involved, in the eyes of many international lawyers, a blatantly illegal use of force against the sovereign state of Ukraine in contravention of Article 2(4) of the U.N. Charter. When effective control derives from an illegal use of force, self-defense, sanctions, or other countermeasures may be legally acceptable responses.

In *Minquiers and Ecrehos*, there was no indication of any unlawful use of force; the Court's concern was primarily with evidence of effective control. After the Court reviewed more history, it found that later in the Middle Ages, the Priory "was abandoned and the chapel fell into ruins." From the 16th through the 18th centuries, the Ecrehos were more or less abandoned. As we see in the final case excerpt below, the Court placed considerable emphasis on evidence of exercises of authority over the islets during the 19th century. The Court's consideration of the evidence in *Minquiers and Ecrehos* suggests how it probably will approach future territorial disputes. France, Britain, and other states may well be reassured that the Court focuses on specific evidence of control over territory—at least evidence that is not trumped up by a party to bolster its claim after a dispute over sovereignty has crystallized—rather than pronouncing broad new rules of universal applicability or basing its decision on political biases.

The Minquiers and Ecrehos Case
Evidence of Effective Control

From the beginning of the nineteenth century the connection between the Ecrehos and Jersey became closer again because of the growing importance of the oyster fishery in the waters surrounding the islets, and Jersey authorities took, during the subsequent period, action in many ways in respect of the islets. Of the manifold facts invoked by the United Kingdom Government, the Court attaches, in particular, probative value to the acts which relate to the exercise of jurisdiction and local administration and to legislation.

In 1826 criminal proceedings were instituted before the Royal Court in Jersey against a Jerseyman for having shot at a person on the Ecrehos. Similar judicial proceedings in Jersey in respect of criminal offences committed on the Ecrehos took place in 1881, 1883, 1891, 1913 and 1921. On the evidence produced the Court is satisfied that the Courts of Jersey, in criminal cases such as these, have no jurisdiction in the matter of a criminal offence committed outside the Bailiwick of Jersey, even though the offence be committed by a British subject resident in Jersey, and that Jersey authorities took action in these cases because the Ecrehos were considered to be within the Bailiwick. These facts show therefore that Jersey courts have exercised criminal jurisdiction in respect of the Ecrehos during nearly a hundred years.

Evidence produced shows that the law of Jersey has for centuries required the holding of an inquest on corpses found within the Bailiwick where it was not clear that death was due to natural causes. Such inquests on corpses found at the Ecrehos were held in 1859, 1917 and 1948 and are additional evidence of the exercise of jurisdiction in respect of these islets.

Since about 1820, and probably earlier, persons from Jersey have erected and maintained some habitable houses or huts on the islets of the Ecrehos, where they have stayed during the fishing season. Some of these houses or huts have, for the purpose of parochial rates, been included in the records of the Parish of St. Martin in Jersey, which have been kept since 1889, and they have been assessed for the levying of local taxes. Rating schedules for 1889 and 1950 were produced in evidence.

A register of fishing boats for the port of Jersey shows that the fishing boat belonging to a Jersey fisherman, who lived permanently on an islet of the Ecrehos for more than forty years, was entered in that register in 1872, the port or place of the boat being indicated as "Ecrehos Rocks," and that the licence of that boat was cancelled in 1882. According to a letter of June, 1876, from the Principal Customs Officer of Jersey, an official of that Island visited occasionally the Ecrehos for the purpose of endorsing the licence of that boat.

It is established that contracts of sale relating to real property on the Ecrehos islets have been passed before the competent authorities of Jersey and registered in the public registry of deeds of that island. Examples of such registration of contracts are produced for 1863, 1881, 1884 and some later years.

In 1884, a custom-house was established in the Ecrehos by Jersey customs authorities. The islets have been included by Jersey authorities within the scope of their census enumerations, and in 1901 an official enumerator visited the islets for the purpose of taking the census.

These various facts show that Jersey authorities have in several ways exercised ordinary local administration in respect of the Ecrehos during a long period of time.

By a British Treasury Warrant of 1875, constituting Jersey as a Port of the Channel Islands, the "Ecrehou Rocks" were included within the limits of that port. This legislative Act was a clear manifestation of British sovereignty over the Ecrehos at a time when a dispute as to such sovereignty had not yet arisen. The French Government protested in 1876 on the ground that this Act derogated from the Fishery Convention of 1839. But this protest could not deprive the Act of its character as a manifestation of sovereignty.

Of other facts which throw light upon the dispute, it should be mentioned that Jersey authorities have made periodical official visits to the Ecrehos since 1885, and that they have carried out various works and constructions there, such as a slipway in 1895, a signal post in 1910 and the placing of a mooring buoy in 1939.

The French Government, in addition to the alleged original feudal title considered above, has invoked the fact that the States of Jersey in 1646 prohibited the inhabitants of Jersey from fishing without special permission at the Ecrehos and the Chausey Islands, and that they restricted visits to the Ecrehos in 1692 because of the war between England and France. This shows, it is contended, that the Ecrehos were not considered as British territory. But the Court does not consider that this is the necessary or natural inference to be drawn from these facts.

In the course of the diplomatic exchanges between the two Governments in the beginning of the nineteenth century concerning fisheries off the coast of Cotentin, the French Ambassador in London addressed to the Foreign Office a Note, dated June 12th, 1820, attaching two charts sent from the French Ministry of Marine to the French Ministry of Foreign Affairs purporting to delimit the areas within which the fishermen of each country were entitled to exclusive rights of fishery. In these charts a blue line marking territorial waters was drawn along the coast of the French mainland and round the Chausey Islands, which were indicated as French, and a red line marking territorial waters was drawn round Jersey, Alderney, Sark and the Minquiers, which were indicated as British. No line of territorial waters was drawn round the Ecrehos group, one part of which was included in the red line for Jersey and consequently marked as belonging to Great Britain and the other part apparently treated as *res nullius*. When the French Government in 1876 protested against the British Treasury Warrant of 1875 and challenged British sovereignty over the Ecrehos, it did not itself claim sovereignty, but continued to treat the Ecrehos as *res nullius*. In a letter of March 26th, 1884, from the French Ministry of Foreign Affairs to the French Minister of Marine, it was stated that the British Government had not ceased to claim the Ecrehos as a dependency to the Channel Islands, and it was suggested that French fishermen should be prohibited access to the Ecrehos. It does not appear that any such measure was taken, and subsequently, in a Note to the Foreign Office of December 15th, 1886, the French Government claimed for the first time sovereignty over the Ecrehos "*à la lumière des nouvelles données historiques et géologiques.*"

The Court being now called upon to appraise the relative strength of the opposing claims to sovereignty over the Ecrehos in the light of the facts considered above, finds that the Ecrehos group in the beginning of the thirteenth century was considered and treated as an integral part of the fief of the Channel Islands which were held by the English King, and that the group continued to be under the dominion of that King, who in the beginning of the fourteenth century exercised jurisdiction in respect thereof. The Court further finds that British authorities during the greater part of the nineteenth century and in the twentieth century have exercised State functions in respect of the group. The French Government, on the other hand, has not produced evidence showing that it has any valid title to the group. In such circumstances it must be concluded that the sovereignty over the Ecrehos belongs to the United Kingdom.

[The Court examines the claims to the Minquiers in similar detail.]

The Court, unanimously, finds that the sovereignty over the islets and rocks of the Ecrehos and Minquiers groups, in so far as these islets and rocks are capable of appropriation, belongs to the United Kingdom.

State Practice and Customary International Law. Compare the emphasis on state practice in customary international law with the focus in *Minquiers and Ecrechos* on factual evidence of control. Does customary international law necessarily follow common arrangements at which states have already arrived? Could such an emphasis give too much weight to powerful states in making law? Or too little emphasis to community interests or normative values? As discussed in Chapter 2, non-consensual sources of law, including some interpretations of customary international law, challenge the notion that all non-treaty law must be grounded in state practice.

The Choice of Forum. Why did France and the United Kingdom choose the International Court rather than an *ad hoc* panel of international arbitrators? Perhaps the prestige of a decision by the World Court, a highly visible institution tied to the United Nations, would make the result more palatable to the losing state's citizens. Perhaps France and Britain, both permanent members of the U.N. Security Council, sought to provide an occasion for the Court—the U.N.'s judicial arm—to prove itself useful in its early years. For some states, the fact that the ICJ is funded through contributions from all member states of the United Nations may also be significant; only the parties to an international arbitration typically share the fees of the arbitrators and the other costs of the arbitral proceeding.

The choice of forum usually involves political calculations. When delimiting the continental shelf in the 1970s, France and Britain appointed an arbitral tribunal unrelated to the ICJ. States may sometimes prefer the relative flexibility of arbitration to the prestige, procedures, and fixed panel of judges of the ICJ.

Chambers at the International Court. Another ICJ procedural option is to submit a case to a chamber, typically composed of five judges and constituted at the request of the parties. Parties exercise considerable discretion with respect to the composition of a chamber. In a case brought before a chamber— as in cases before the full Court—a state party may appoint a judge *ad hoc* if a national of that state is not already a member of the Court. Although the other judges in a chamber must be members of the ICJ, the Court in practice defers to the parties' recommendations concerning which judges are to sit.

Since the first ICJ chamber was constituted in 1982, there have been only six chambers cases. Five have involved maritime or territorial boundary delimitations, one between Canada and the United States, one between Burkina Faso and Mali, two between El Salvador and Honduras, and one between Benin and Niger. See, respectively, 1984 I.C.J. 246, 1985 I.C.J. 6, 1992 I.C.J. 351 and 2004 I.C.J. 392, and 2005 I.C.J. 90. The sixth chambers case, the 1989 *ELSI Case*, 1989 I.C.J. 15, was a foreign investment dispute between Italy and the United States.

Why has this flexible chambers procedure not been employed more often? Perhaps one reason for the lack of chamber business at the ICJ is simply that there are many other ways in which parties can now go to formal international dispute settlement if they desire a legally binding third-party decision. Arbitration remains available, an option allowing parties to choose decision makers likely to be sympathetic to their arguments or to have expertise concerning the subject matter of their dispute. Other international judicial tribunals may also be available. We explore the proliferation of international courts and tribunals in Part C of this chapter.

Compliance with ICJ Decisions. Why are states likely to comply with ICJ decisions such as that in *Minquiers and Ecrehos*? It seems likely that both states meant to comply with any eventual judgment when they consented to the *compromis* in their Special Agreement. If either France or the United Kingdom ran a significant risk of losing the case in the ICJ (and, with the advantage of hindsight, one can say that the risk fell significantly on France), the risk may have been worth running because it might be easier politically for the government to give up the islets in a court case than in diplomatic negotiations. Does the ICJ sometimes serve a "scapegoat function"? It is plausible that the two countries turned to the International Court as a face-saving device, believing that the Court would offer an authoritative decision likely effective to resolve the dispute without leading to charges that a government unilaterally "gave away national territory."

The Norman Invasion. On July 10, 1994, the Ecrehos were "invaded" by 150 French citizens from Normandy who sought to reopen the dispute about the ownership of the islets at a time when Jersey was seeking to extend its territorial waters from three to 12 miles. Despite assurances from the government of Jersey that traditional French fishing rights would not be impaired, the Norman party came to the Ecrehos to protest. They were restrained from tearing down the Union Jack, but Jersey authorities permitted them to hold a mass and to plant a Norman flag of two yellow lions rampant on a red ground beside a temporary altar. Marcus Binney & Michael Hornsby, "Jersey Police Outwit Norman Invasion," *The Times* (London), July 11, 1994, at 5.

"Consensual" Submissions to the ICJ. Although in a formal sense all contentious cases in the ICJ are based on mutual consent of the parties, sometimes consent is given after, sometimes before, the dispute arises. In *Minquiers and Ecrehos* consent was given after the dispute arose, and both France and Britain wanted to go to the International Court when the case began. Note how different "consent" is in the *Diplomatic and Consular Staff Case* below. Iran's consent to ICJ jurisdiction was given prior to any dispute with the United States, and, at the time of the case, Iran resisted the ICJ proceedings.

The Diplomatic and Consular Staff Case *in Context.* The *Diplomatic and Consular Staff Case* arose out of the 1979 seizure in Tehran of U.S. diplomatic and consular staff, whom Iran then held as hostages. The movie *Argo*, winner of the 2013 Oscar for best picture, is a Hollywood dramatization of the hostage crisis. Former U.S. Secretary of State Warren Christopher and former Iran-U.S. Claims Tribunal Judge Richard Mosk summarized events leading up to the crisis:

> In 1925 Reza Khan, a semi-literate military officer, ousted the existing dynasty of Iran and had himself enthroned as Reza Shah Pahlavi. Early in World War II, British and Soviet troops, in effect,

occupied Iran and secured the Iranian oil fields for Allied use. The Shah had become too pro German for the Allies. So they had Mohammad Reza Pahlavi, Reza Shah Pahlavi's son, replace him at the age of 22.

In the early 1950s, Mohammed Mossadegh, an elected leftist prime minister, nationalized British and American oil operations in Iran and refused to pay compensation. The Shah did not back Mossadegh, and mobs called for the Shah's removal. He fled Iran.

In 1953, the Iranian military, with C.I.A. support, overthrew Mossadegh, and the Shah was restored to the throne. With a grateful Shah in power, the United States and Iran signed a Treaty of Amity.

In 1963, the Shah began his "White Revolution" of reform. Clerics led by Ayatollah Khomeini challenged the Shah's reform programs. Rioting in Qom was suppressed, and in 1964, Ayatollah Khomeini was exiled to Iraq.

By 1972, the United States decided to allow Iran access to U.S. military weapons. In return, the Shah became a strong ally of the United States in the Gulf region. Meanwhile, American businesses invested heavily, and did substantial business in Iran. The Shah began to increase his powers and used a feared secret police apparatus, SAVAK.

President Carter had criticized the Shah's abuses of human rights but determined that his value as a military ally outweighed his autocratic measures. . . .

After the Government-controlled press published an article [in 1978] ridiculing Khomeini, rioting erupted in Qom. . . .

In January 1979, the Shah left Iran on an "extended vacation[.]" On February 1, the Ayatollah Khomeini triumphantly returned to Iran and was deemed the Imam. The revolution was completed as the Islamic Republic of Iran was declared. . . . The revolution can be traced to the repressive and corrupt regime of the Shah, the perception of Iranians that the Shah was a threat to their culture and religion, and the real and perceived intervention by foreign powers into Iranian internal affairs.

On October 22, 1979, the exiled Shah left Mexico and arrived in New York to undergo treatment for cancer at New York Hospital-

Cornell Medical Center. On November 1, 1979, Khomeini's office in Qom issued a statement encouraging Iranian students to "expand their attacks" against the United States to force the U.S. to return the deposed Shah.

Warren Christopher & Richard M. Mosk, "The Iranian Hostage Crisis and the Iran-U.S. Claims Tribunal: Implications for International Dispute Resolution and Diplomacy," 7 *Pepperdine Dispute Resolution Law Journal* 165, 165–67 (2007).

The ICJ Proceedings. On November 29, 1979, the United States commenced proceedings against Iran in the International Court of Justice. The Court first considered the U.S. application for "provisional measures" to protect the hostages. Iran refused to plead or argue before the International Court. On December 15, 1979, the ICJ delivered an order instructing Iran to release the hostages immediately, 1979 I.C.J. 7, but Iran failed to comply. The case went forward on the merits stage. This first excerpt from the ICJ's merits decision explains some of the immediate factual background:

THE DIPLOMATIC AND CONSULAR STAFF CASE
United States v. Iran, 1980 I.C.J. 3

The Facts

At approximately 10:30 a.m. on 4 November 1979, during the course of a demonstration of approximately 3,000 persons, the United States Embassy compound in Tehran was overrun by a strong armed group of several hundred people. The Iranian security personnel are reported to have simply disappeared from the scene; at all events it is established that they made no apparent effort to deter or prevent the demonstrators from seizing the Embassy's premises. The invading group (who subsequently described themselves as "Muslim Student Followers of the Imam's Policy," and who will hereafter be referred to as "the militants") gained access by force to the compound and to the ground floor of the Chancery building. Over two hours after the beginning of the attack, and after the militants had attempted to set fire to the Chancery building and to cut through the upstairs steel doors with a torch, they gained entry to the upper floor; one hour later they gained control of the main vault. The militants also seized the other buildings, including the various residences, on the Embassy compound. In the course of the attack, all the diplomatic and consular personnel and other persons present in the premises were seized as hostages, and detained in the Embassy compound; subsequently other United States personnel and one United States private citizen seized elsewhere in Tehran were brought to the compound and added to the number of hostages.

During the three hours or more of the assault, repeated calls for help were made from the Embassy to the Iranian Foreign Ministry, and repeated efforts to secure help from the Iranian authorities were also made through direct discussions by the United States Chargé d'affaires, who was at the Foreign Ministry at the time, together with two other members of the mission. From there he made contact with the Prime Minister's Office and the Foreign Ministry officials. A request was also made to the Iranian Chargé d'affaires in Washington for assistance in putting an end to the seizure of the Embassy. Despite these repeated requests, no Iranian security forces were sent in time to provide relief and protection to the Embassy. In fact when Revolutionary Guards ultimately arrived on the scene, despatched by the Government "to prevent clashes," they considered that their task was merely to "protect the safety of both the hostages and the students," according to statements subsequently made by the Iranian Government's spokesman, and by the operations commander of the Guards. No attempt was made by the Iranian Government to clear the Embassy premises, to rescue the persons held hostage, or to persuade the militants to terminate their action against the Embassy.

The premises of the United States Embassy in Tehran have remained in the hands of the militants; and the same appears to be the case with the Consulates at Tabriz and Shiraz. Of the total number of United States citizens seized and held as hostages, 13 were released on 18–20 November 1979, but the remainder have continued to be held up to the present time. The release of the 13 hostages was effected pursuant to a decree by the Ayatollah Khomeini addressed to the militants dated 17 November 1979, in which he called upon the militants to "hand over the blacks and the women, if it is proven they did not spy, to the Ministry of Foreign Affairs so that they may be immediately expelled from Iran."

The persons still held hostage in Iran include, according to the information furnished to the Court by the United States, at least 28 persons having the status, duly recognized by the Government of Iran, of "member of the diplomatic staff" within the meaning of the Vienna Convention on Diplomatic Relations of 1961; at least 20 persons having the status, similarly recognized, of "member of the administrative and technical staff" within the meaning of that Convention; and two other persons of United States nationality not possessing either diplomatic or consular status. Of the persons with the status of member of the diplomatic staff, four are members of the Consular Section of the Mission.

Allegations have been made by the Government of the United States of inhumane treatment of hostages; the militants and Iranian authorities have asserted that the hostages have been well treated, and have allowed special visits to the hostages by religious personalities and by representatives of the International Committee of the Red Cross. The specific allegations of ill-treatment have not however been refuted. Examples of such allegations, which are mentioned in some of the sworn declarations of hostages released in November 1979, are as follows: at the outset of the occupation of the Embassy some were paraded bound and blindfolded before hostile and chanting crowds; at least during the initial period of their captivity, hostages were kept bound, and frequently blindfolded, denied mail or any communication with their government or with each other, subjected to interrogation, threatened with weapons.

Those archives and documents of the United States Embassy which were not destroyed by the staff during the attack on 4 November have been ransacked by the militants. Documents purporting to come from this source have been disseminated by the militants and by the Government-controlled media.

The Decision to Litigate. Why did the United States bring the *Diplomatic and Consular Staff Case* to the International Court? According to Professor Merrills, in bringing the case the United States may have been signaling its willingness to "depoliticise" the hostages dispute, seeking settlement through peaceful judicial means. J.G. Merrills, *International Dispute Settlement* 160 (5th ed. 2011). But was it likely that Iran would comply with an adverse judgment? What could the United States gain if Iran disregarded the judgment? After all, the United States could publicly make strong arguments that Iran had violated international law, even without the Court giving its imprimatur to the U.S. arguments. Did the United States have anything to lose by bringing the case?

According to Roberts B. Owen, State Department Legal Adviser during the Carter administration, "it was generally recognized that . . . it was unlikely that Iran would obey." Should the U.S. government be faulted for bringing this case to the Court, contributing to the sense that the Court is powerless and ineffectual? U.S. government officials "nonetheless believed strongly . . . that quick condemnatory action by the World Court would help us mobilize world opinion against Iran's irresponsible action." *Quoted in* Michael P. Scharf & Paul R. Williams, *Shaping Foreign Policy in Times of Crisis: The Role of International Law and the State Department Legal Adviser* 49 (2010). The United States may have sought "to use the Court's decision as a means for translating a dispute between Iran and the United States specifically into one between Iran and the international community generally." M.W. Janis, "The Role of the International

Court in the Hostages Crisis," 13 *Connecticut Law Review* 263, 280 (1981). It could also be that the United States was mostly trying to impress its own citizens, in an effort to appear to be doing something—anything—to try to end a crisis that was front-page news in the United States for over a year.

The Non-participation of States in ICJ Litigation. Iran did not participate in the ICJ litigation. The Iranian government filed no pleadings and did not appear to make oral arguments. Nevertheless, under the Court's rules, one party's non-appearance cannot by itself preclude the case from moving ahead.

Iran is not the only state to have boycotted an ICJ case. France, Iceland, Turkey, and the United States have also refused to appear before the Court in cases in which the Court found that the parties had consented in advance to jurisdiction. The practice of non-appearing states raises concern about a lack of respect for the Court and could undercut its ability to perform essential judicial functions.

In the *Diplomatic and Consular Staff Case*, Iran, although not a formal participant, made known through letters that it thought the circumstances surrounding the events in the case made it too "political" to proceed. As you read Iran's argument on this point, and the Court's rejection of the argument, consider whether the Court was wise in proceeding with the case, even though it seemed likely that Iran would refuse to appear and to comply with the ICJ's orders.

The Diplomatic and Consular Staff Case
Iran's Position

The position of [the Iranian] Government was . . . defined in [two letters, one dated 9 December 1979 and the second] dated 16 March 1980 and received on 17 March 1980, the text of which . . . reads as follows:

[*Translation from French*] . . .

> The Government of the Islamic Republic of Iran wishes to express its respect for the International Court of Justice, and for its distinguished Members, for what they have achieved in the quest for a just and equitable solution to legal conflicts between States, and respectfully draws the attention of the Court to the deep-rootedness and the essential character of the Islamic Revolution of Iran, a revolution of a whole oppressed nation against its oppressors and their masters, the examination of whose numerous repercussions is essentially and directly a matter within the national sovereignty of Iran.

The Government of the Islamic Republic of Iran considers that the Court cannot and should not take cognizance of the case which the Government of the United States of America has submitted to it, and in the most significant fashion, a case confined to what is called the question of the "hostages of the American Embassy in Tehran."

For this question only represents a marginal and secondary aspect of an overall problem, one such that it cannot be studied separately, and which involves, *inter alia*, more than 25 years of continual interference by the United States in the internal affairs of Iran, the shameless exploitation of our country, and numerous crimes perpetrated against the Iranian people, contrary to and in conflict with all international and humanitarian norms.

The problem involved in the conflict between Iran and the United States is thus not one of the interpretation and the application of the treaties upon which the American Application is based, but results from an overall situation containing much more fundamental and more complex elements. Consequently, the Court cannot examine the American Application divorced from its proper context, namely the whole political dossier of the relations between Iran and the United States over the last 25 years.

[Despite Iran's non-appearance,] the Court, in applying Article 53 of its Statute, must first take up, *proprio motu*, any preliminary question, whether of admissibility or of jurisdiction, that appears from the information before it to arise in the case and the decision of which might constitute a bar to any further examination of the merits of the Applicant's case. The Court will, therefore, first address itself to the considerations put forward by the Iranian Government in its letters of 9 December 1979 and 16 March 1980, on the basis of which it maintains that the Court ought not to take cognizance of the present case.

The Iranian Government in its letter of 9 December 1979 drew attention to what it referred to as the "deep rootedness and the essential character of the Islamic Revolution of Iran, a revolution of a whole oppressed nation against its oppressors and their masters." The examination of the "numerous repercussions" of the revolution, it added, is "a matter essentially and directly within the national sovereignty of Iran." However, as the Court pointed out in its Order of 15 December 1979,

a dispute which concerns diplomatic and consular premises and the detention of internationally protected persons, and involves the interpretation or application of multilateral conventions codifying the international law governing diplomatic and consular relations, is one which by its very nature falls within international jurisdiction.

The Court . . . in its Order of 15 December 1979, made it clear that the seizure of the United States Embassy and Consulates and the detention of internationally protected persons as hostages cannot be considered as something "secondary" or "marginal," having regard to the importance of the legal principles involved. It also referred to a statement of the Secretary-General of the United Nations, and to Security Council resolution 457 (1979), as evidencing the importance attached by the international community as a whole to the observance of those principles in the present case as well as its concern at the dangerous level of tension between Iran and the United States. The Court, at the same time, pointed out that no provision of the Statute or Rules contemplates that the Court should decline to take cognizance of one aspect of a dispute merely because that dispute has other aspects, however important. It further underlined that, if the Iranian Government considered the alleged activities of the United States in Iran legally to have a close connection with the subject-matter of the United States' Application, it was open to that Government to present its own arguments regarding those activities to the Court either by way of defence in a Counter-Memorial or by way of a counter-claim.

The Iranian Government, notwithstanding the terms of the Court's Order, did not file any pleadings and did not appear before the Court. By its own choice, therefore, it has forgone the opportunities offered to it under the Statute and Rules of Court to submit evidence and arguments in support of its contention in regard to the "overall problem." [The Government of Iran] has provided no explanation of the reasons why it considers that the violations of diplomatic and consular law alleged in the United States' Application cannot be examined by the Court separately from what it describes as the "overall problem" involving "more than 25 years of continual interference by the United States in the internal affairs of Iran." Nor has it made any attempt to explain, still less define, what connection, legal or factual, there may be between the "overall problem" of its general grievances against the United States and the particular events that gave rise to the United States' claims in the present case which, in its view, precludes the separate examination of those claims by the Court. [L]egal disputes between sovereign States by their very nature are likely to occur in political contexts, and often form only one element in a wider and long-standing political dispute between the States concerned. Yet never has the view been put forward before that, because a legal dispute submitted to the Court is only one aspect of a political dispute, the Court should decline to resolve for the parties the legal questions at issue between them. Nor can any basis for such a view of the Court's functions or jurisdiction be found in the Charter or the Statute of the Court; if the Court were, contrary to its settled jurisprudence, to adopt such a view, it would impose a far-reaching and unwarranted restriction upon the role of the Court in the peaceful solution of international disputes.

It follows that the considerations and arguments put forward in the Iranian Government's letters of 9 December 1979 and 16 March 1980 do not, in the opinion of the Court, disclose any ground on which it should conclude that it cannot or ought not to take cognizance of the present case.

Mutual Consent and the Jurisdiction of the International Court. The ICJ in the *Diplomatic and Consular Staff Case* also had to satisfy itself that it had "jurisdiction," that is, that the United States and Iran had mutually consented to bring a dispute to the Court. Review the treaty that provided the mutual consent of France and Britain to ICJ jurisdiction in *Minquiers and Ecrehos*, and note when it was concluded. How does the basis for jurisdiction in *Diplomatic and Consular Staff* compare? As we see in the excerpt below, the Court based its jurisdiction on clauses in two multilateral treaties to which Iran and the United States were parties, and on a bilateral U.S.-Iran treaty. Iran had consented to these three treaties when the Shah's government was in power, many years before the Iranian revolution. In 1979, however, the new government of Iran did not want the ICJ to hear the *Diplomatic and Consular Staff Case.*

Yet the principle that treaties—including treaties providing for the jurisdiction of a court or tribunal—survive even radical changes in governments is well established in international law. Why should that be? Recall the principle of *pacta sunt servanda* discussed in Chapter 2, and the importance of "states" (rather than "governments") as fundamental components of the international legal order. See Chapter 3, Part B, and the Peace of Westphalia in Chapter 2.

Note too, in the following case excerpt, how the treaties that provided the basis for the Court's jurisdiction helped define the scope of the issues the Court was authorized to decide.

The Diplomatic and Consular Staff Case
The U.S. Claims and the ICJ's Jurisdiction

[T]he principal claims of the United States relate essentially to alleged violations by Iran of its obligations to the United States under the Vienna

Conventions of 1961 on Diplomatic Relations and of 1963 on Consular Relations. With regard to these claims the United States has invoked as the basis for the Court's jurisdiction Article I of the Optional Protocols concerning the Compulsory Settlement of Disputes which accompany these Conventions. [B]oth Iran and the United States [are] parties to the Vienna Conventions of 1961 and 1963, [and] also to their accompanying Protocols concerning the Compulsory Settlement of Disputes, and in each case without any reservation to the instrument in question. The Vienna Conventions, which codify the law of diplomatic and consular relations, state principles and rules essential for the maintenance of peaceful relations between States and accepted throughout the world by nations of all creeds, cultures and political complexions. . . .

The terms of Article I [of each Optional Protocol provide:]

Disputes arising out of the interpretation or application of the Convention shall lie within the compulsory jurisdiction of the International Court of Justice and may accordingly be brought before the Court by an application made by any party to the dispute being a Party to the present Protocol.

The United States' claims here in question concern alleged violations by Iran of its obligations under several articles of the Vienna Conventions of 1961 and 1963 with respect to the privileges and immunities of the personnel, the inviolability of the premises and archives, and the provision of facilities for the performance of the functions of the United States Embassy and Consulates in Iran. In so far as its claims relate to two private individuals held hostage in the Embassy, the situation of these individuals falls under the provisions of the Vienna Convention of 1961 guaranteeing the inviolability of the premises of embassies, and of Article 5 of the 1963 Convention concerning the consular functions of assisting nationals and protecting and safeguarding their interests. By their very nature all these claims concern the interpretation or application of one or other of the two Vienna Conventions.

[T]he United States also presents claims in respect of alleged violations by Iran . . . of the Treaty of Amity, Economic Relations, and Consular Rights of 1955 between the United States and Iran, which entered into force on 16 June 1957. With regard to these claims the United States has invoked paragraph 2 of Article XXI of the Treaty as the basis for the Court's jurisdiction. The claims of the United States under this Treaty overlap in considerable measure with its claims under the two Vienna Conventions and more especially the Convention of 1963.

. . . The very purpose of a treaty of amity . . . is to promote friendly relations between the two countries concerned, and between their two peoples, more especially by mutual undertakings to ensure the protection and security of their nationals in each other's territory. It is precisely when difficulties arise that the treaty assumes its greatest importance, and the whole object of Article XXI, paragraph 2, of the 1955 Treaty was to establish the means for arriving at a friendly settlement of such difficulties by the Court or by other peaceful means. It would, therefore, be incompatible with the whole purpose of the 1955 Treaty if recourse to the Court under Article XXI, paragraph 2, were now to be found not to be open to the parties precisely at the moment when such recourse was most needed. Furthermore, although the machinery for the effective operation of the 1955 Treaty has, no doubt, now been impaired by reason of diplomatic relations between the two countries having been broken off by the United States, its provisions remain part of the corpus of law applicable between the United States and Iran.

Attribution and the Law of State Responsibility. Were the acts about which the United States complained in the *Diplomatic and Consular Staff Case* those of Iran? After all, "militants," rather than Iranian government agents, stormed the U.S. embassy and seized U.S. personnel and documents. The United States nonetheless claimed that the government of Iran was responsible for breaching international law. In modern international law, the issue of "attribution" of acts to a country is one aspect of the law of state responsibility. We considered other aspects of the modern law of state responsibility, namely excuses and remedies, in the 1990 *Rainbow Warrior Case* earlier in this chapter, and we revisit the topic in Chapter 7.

The Court merged its discussion of attribution with its analysis of the substance of Iran's treaty obligations to protect diplomats, consular officials, diplomatic premises, and diplomatic archives and documents.

The Diplomatic and Consular Staff Case
Attributing Responsibility to Iran

The events which are the subject of the United States' claims fall into two phases which it will be convenient to examine separately.

The first of these phases covers the armed attack on the United States Embassy by militants on 4 November 1979, the overrunning of its premises, the seizure of its inmates as hostages, the appropriation of its property and archives and the conduct of the Iranian authorities in the face of those occurrences. The attack and the subsequent overrunning, bit by bit, of the whole Embassy premises, was an operation which continued over a period of some three hours without any body of police, any military unit or any Iranian official intervening to try to stop or impede it from being carried through to its completion. The result of the attack was considerable damage to the Embassy premises and property, the forcible opening and seizure of its archives, the confiscation of the archives and other documents found in the Embassy and, most grave of all, the seizure by force of its diplomatic and consular personnel as hostages, together with two United States nationals.

No suggestion has been made that the militants, when they executed their attack on the Embassy, had any form of official status as recognized "agents" or organs of the Iranian State. Their conduct in mounting the attack, overrunning the Embassy and seizing its inmates as hostages cannot, therefore, be regarded as imputable to that State on that basis. Their conduct might be considered as itself directly imputable to the Iranian State only if it were established that, in fact, on the occasion in question the militants acted on behalf of the State, having been charged by some competent organ of the Iranian State to carry out a specific operation. The information before the Court does not, however, suffice to establish with the requisite certainty the existence at that time of such a link between the militants and any competent organ of the State.

Previously, it is true, the religious leader of the country, the Ayatollah Khomeini, had made several public declarations inveighing against the United States as responsible for all his country's problems. In so doing, it would appear, the Ayatollah Khomeini was giving utterance to the general resentment felt by supporters of the revolution at the admission of the former Shah to the United States. [In a November 1, 1979] message the Ayatollah Khomeini had declared that it was "up to the dear pupils, students and theological students to expand with all their might their attacks against the United States and Israel, so they may force the United States to return the deposed and criminal shah, and to condemn this great plot" (that is, a plot to stir up dissension between the main streams of Islamic thought). In the view of the Court, however, it would be going too far to interpret such general declarations of the Ayatollah Khomeini to the people or students of Iran as amounting to an authorization from the State to undertake the specific operation of invading and seizing the United States Embassy. To do so would, indeed, conflict with the assertions of the militants themselves who are reported to have claimed credit for having devised and carried out the plan to occupy the Embassy. Again, congratulations after the event, such as those reportedly telephoned to the militants by the Ayatollah Khomeini on the actual evening of the attack, and other subsequent statements of official approval, though highly significant in another context shortly to be considered, do not alter the initially independent and unofficial character of the militants' attack on the Embassy.

The first phase, here under examination, of the events complained of also includes the attacks on the United States Consulates at Tabriz and Shiraz. Like the attack of the Embassy, they appear to have been executed by militants not having an official character, and successful because of lack of sufficient protection.

The conclusion just reached by the Court, that the initiation of the attack on the United States Embassy on 4 November 1979, and of the attacks on the Consulates at Tabriz and Shiraz the following day, cannot be considered as in itself imputable to the Iranian State does not mean that Iran is, in consequence, free of any responsibility in regard to those attacks; for its own conduct was in conflict with its international obligations. By a number of provisions of the Vienna Conventions of 1961 and 1963, Iran was placed under the most categorical obligations, as a receiving State, to take appropriate steps to ensure the protection of the United States Embassy and Consulates, their staffs, their archives, their means of communication and the freedom of movement of the members of their staffs.

Thus, after solemnly proclaiming the inviolability of the premises of a diplomatic mission, Article 22 of the 1961 Convention continues in paragraph 2:

> *The receiving State is under a special duty to take all appropriate steps to protect the premises of the mission against any* intrusion or damage and to prevent any disturbance of the peace of the mission or impairment of its dignity. (Emphasis added.)

So, too, after proclaiming that the person of a diplomatic agent shall be inviolable, and that he shall not be liable to any form of arrest or detention, Article 29 provides:

> The receiving State shall treat him with due respect and *shall take all appropriate steps to prevent any attack on his person, freedom or dignity.* (Emphasis added.)

The obligation of a receiving State to protect the inviolability of the archives and documents of a diplomatic mission is laid down in Article 24, which specifically provides that they are to be "inviolable at any time and wherever they may be." Under Article 25 it is required to "accord full facilities for the performance of the functions of the mission," under Article 26 to "ensure to all members of the mission freedom of movement and travel in its territory," and under Article 27 to "permit and protect free communication on the part of the mission for all official purposes." Analogous provisions are to be found in the 1963 Convention regarding the privileges and immunities of consular missions and their staffs. In the view of the Court, the obligations of the Iranian Government here in question are not merely contractual obligations established by the Vienna Conventions of 1961 and 1963, but also obligations under general international law.

The facts . . . establish . . . that on 4 November 1979 the Iranian Government failed altogether to take any "appropriate steps" to protect the premises, staff and archives of the United States' mission against attack by the militants, and to take any steps either to prevent this attack or to stop it before it reached its completion. They also show that on 5 November 1979 the Iranian Government similarly failed to take appropriate steps for the protection of the United States Consulates at Tabriz and Shiraz. In addition they show, in the opinion of the Court, that the failure of the Iranian Government to take such steps was due to more than mere negligence or lack of appropriate means. . . .

This inaction of the Iranian Government by itself constituted clear and serious violation of Iran's obligations to the United States under the provisions of Article 22, paragraph 2, and Articles 24, 25, 26, 27 and 29 of the 1961 Vienna Convention on Diplomatic Relations, and Articles 5 and 36 of the 1963 Vienna Convention on Consular Relations. Similarly, with respect to the attacks on the Consulates at Tabriz and Shiraz, the inaction of the Iranian authorities entailed clear and serious breaches of its obligations under the provisions of several further articles of the 1963 Convention on Consular Relations. So far as concerns the two private United States nationals seized as hostages by the invading militants, that inaction entailed, albeit incidentally, a breach of its obligations under Article II, paragraph 4, of the 1955 Treaty of Amity, Economic Relations, and Consular Rights which, in addition to the obligations of Iran existing under general international law, requires the parties to ensure "the most constant protection and security" to each other's nationals in their respective territories.

[In the second phase of the events, which "occurred following the completion of the occupation of the United States Embassy by the militants, and the seizure of the Consulates at Tabriz and Shiraz," the Court also found that Iran was responsible for breaching the treaties at issue.]

The occupation having taken place and the diplomatic and consular personnel of the United States' mission having been taken hostage, the action required of the Iranian Government by the Vienna Conventions and by general international law was manifest. Its plain duty was at once to make every effort, and to take every appropriate step, to bring these flagrant infringements of the inviolability of the premises, archives and diplomatic and consular staff of the

United States Embassy to a speedy end, to restore the Consulates at Tabriz and Shiraz to United States control, and in general to re-establish the status quo and to offer reparation for the damage.

No such step was, however, taken by the Iranian authorities. At a press conference on 5 November the Foreign Minister, Mr. Yazdi, [announced] that the action of the students "enjoys the endorsement and support of the government, because America herself is responsible for this incident." . . .

The seal of official government approval was finally set on this situation by a decree issued on 17 November 1979 by the Ayatollah Khomeini. His decree began with the assertion that the American Embassy was "a centre of espionage and conspiracy" and that "those people who hatched plots against our Islamic movement in that place do not enjoy international diplomatic respect." He went on expressly to declare that the premises of the Embassy and the hostages would remain as they were until the United States had handed over the former Shah for trial and returned his property to Iran. [An exception was made only for 13 women and minorities, "if it is proven that they did not spy."]

[Iranian] judicial authorities . . . and the Minister of Foreign Affairs have frequently [threatened to have] some of the hostages submitted to trial before a court or some other body. [I]f the intention to submit the hostages to any form of criminal trial or investigation were to be put into effect, that would constitute a grave breach by Iran of its obligations under Article 31, paragraph 1, of the 1961 Vienna Convention. This paragraph states in the most express terms: "A diplomatic agent shall enjoy immunity from the criminal jurisdiction of the receiving State." Again, if there were an attempt to compel the hostages to bear witness, a suggestion renewed at the time of the visit to Iran of the Secretary-General's Commission, Iran would without question be violating paragraph 2 of that same Article of the 1961 Vienna Convention which provides that: "A diplomatic agent is not obliged to give evidence as a witness."

[T]he Court finds that Iran, by committing successive and continuing breaches of the obligations laid upon it by the Vienna Conventions of 1961 and 1963 on Diplomatic and Consular Relations, the Treaty of Amity, Economic Relations, and Consular Rights of 1955, and the applicable rules of general international law, has incurred responsibility towards the United States. As to the consequences of this finding, it clearly entails an obligation on the part of the Iranian State to make reparation for the injury thereby caused to the United States. Since however Iran's breaches of its obligations are still continuing, the form and amount of such reparation cannot be determined at the present date.

The Judicial Role and Efficacy of the International Court of Justice. When the ICJ is used as a public forum to bring a case against a non-appearing state, does the Court still serve a judicial role? May ICJ decisions be efficacious even when a losing party does not comply with them?

The question of the "efficacy" of international court decisions is a complicated one. A party's noncompliance with a judgment will affect public attitudes about judicial efficacy. However, one should also consider how judgments affect non-parties, the Court itself, any regimes or institutions with which the Court is connected, and the development of international law.

Is it enough to say that, whatever the circumstances, the Court can usefully add the words of a new judgment to the corpus of international law doctrine? As we have noted, the *Diplomatic and Consular Staff Case* concerned the issue of attribution in the law of state responsibility, the succession of the treaty obligations of a state following a radical change in its government, and the interpretation and application of specific treaty provisions. In the following excerpt the ICJ also emphasized the fundamental significance to the international community of rules of general international law protecting diplomats, consular officials, and diplomatic premises. Legal protections for diplomats have been important in international law since antiquity. See the *De Longchamps Case* in Chapter 5.

The Diplomatic and Consular Staff Case
The Importance of Protecting Diplomats and the Court's Judgment

Wrongfully to deprive human beings of their freedom and to subject them to physical constraint in conditions of hardship is in itself manifestly incompatible with the principles of the Charter of the United Nations, as well as with the fundamental principles enunciated in the Universal Declaration of Human Rights. But what has above all to be emphasized is the extent and seriousness of the conflict between the conduct of the Iranian State and its obligations under the whole corpus of the international rules of which diplomatic and consular law is comprised, rules the fundamental character of which the Court must here again strongly affirm. In its Order of 15 December 1979, the Court made a point of stressing that the obligations laid on States by the two Vienna Conventions are of cardinal importance for the maintenance of good relations between States in the interdependent world of today. "There is no more fundamental prerequisite for the conduct of relations between States," the Court there said, "than the inviolability of diplomatic envoys and embassies, so that throughout history nations of all creeds and cultures have observed reciprocal obligations for that purpose." The institution of diplomacy, the Court continued, has proved to be "an instrument essential for effective co-operation in the international community, and for enabling States, irrespective of their differing constitutional and social systems, to achieve mutual understanding and to resolve their differences by peaceful means."

[T]his case is unique and of very particular gravity because here it is not only private individuals or groups of individuals that have disregarded and set at naught the inviolability of a foreign embassy, but the government of the receiving State itself. . . . Such events cannot fail to undermine the edifice of law carefully constructed by mankind over a period of centuries, the maintenance of which is vital for the security and well-being of the complex international community of the present day, to which it is more essential than ever that the rules developed to ensure the ordered progress of relations between its members should be constantly and scrupulously respected.

[The Court's operative judgment comprised six legally binding decisions:]

THE COURT,

By thirteen votes to two,

Decides that the Islamic Republic of Iran, by the conduct which the Court has set out in this Judgment, has violated in several respects, and is still violating, obligations owed by it to the United States of America under international conventions in force between the two countries, as well as under long-established rules of general international law; . . .

By thirteen votes to two,

Decides that the violations of these obligations engage the responsibility of the Islamic Republic of Iran towards the United States of America under international law; . . .

Unanimously,

Decides that the Government of the Islamic Republic of Iran must immediately take all steps to redress the situation resulting from the events of 4 November 1979 and what followed from these events, and to that end:

(*a*)   must immediately terminate the unlawful detention of the United States Chargé d'affaires and other diplomatic and consular staff and other United States nationals now held hostage in Iran, and must immediately release each and every one and entrust them to the protecting Power (Article 45 of the 1961 Vienna Convention on Diplomatic Relations);

(*b*) must ensure that all the said persons have the necessary means of leaving Iranian territory, including means of transport;

(*c*) must immediately place in the hands of the protecting Power the premises, property, archives and documents of the United States Embassy in Tehran and of its Consulates in Iran;

Unanimously,

Decides that no member of the United States diplomatic or consular staff may be kept in Iran to be subjected to any form of judicial proceedings or to participate in them as a witness;

By twelve votes to three,

Decides that the Government of the Islamic Republic of Iran is under an obligation to make reparation to the Government of the United States of America for the injury caused to the latter by the events of 4 November 1979 and what followed from these events; . . .

By fourteen votes to one,

Decides that the form and amount of such reparation, failing agreement between the Parties, shall be settled by the Court, and reserves for this purpose the subsequent procedure in the case.

Resolving the Hostages Crisis. Efforts to resolve the hostages crisis proceeded not only before the ICJ but through diplomatic channels, at the U.N. Security Council, by the freezing of Iranian assets in the United States and abroad, and by a failed U.S. helicopter rescue mission. The ICJ found the rescue effort problematic, because it was undertaken while the Court was preparing its judgment in the case; the effort appeared "calculated to undermine respect for the judicial process in international relations," particularly since the Court, in its order concerning provisional measures, "had indicated that no action was to be taken by either party which might aggravate the tension between the two countries." 1980 I.C.J. 3, ¶ 93. However, the question of the legality of the attempted helicopter rescue was not formally before the Court, and did not affect the Court's findings concerning the legality of Iran's conduct.

Should the United States have done more, or acted differently, to try to pressure Iran to release the hostages? For example, the United States might have responded by seizing the Iranian embassy in Washington, DC and taking Iranian diplomats hostage. Why did it not do so?

Ultimately, in January 1981, a U.S.-Iranian treaty, negotiated through the good offices of Algeria, resulted in the release of the U.S. hostages, the unfreezing of Iranian assets, and the establishment of the Iran-U.S. Claims Tribunal to decide disputes among Iran, the United States, and nationals of those countries. *Dames & Moore*, a U.S. case related to the creation of the Iran-U.S. Claims Tribunal and the unfreezing of Iranian assets, appears in Chapter 5.

Compliance with ICJ Decisions. Although Iran eventually released the hostages, had Iran "complied" with the Court's judgment? How does one measure compliance? Does a losing state comply with a judgment if it significantly delays or takes only some of the steps required by the Court? The ICJ has no formal mechanism for monitoring compliance.

How strong is the correlation between compliance and the basis for ICJ jurisdiction? Will a losing state almost always resist complying with an ICJ decision if the parties have mutually agreed on jurisdiction in advance of the dispute, as in the *Diplomatic and Consular Staff Case*? What could the Court itself do to prompt states to comply with ICJ decisions, even when consent to jurisdiction is given well in advance of a case? For example, if a decision finds a procedural international law violation, *e.g.*, a failure to negotiate, rather than a serious substantive violation as in the *Diplomatic and Consular Staff Case*, the losing party might find it palatable to remedy its procedural default.

What are the prospects for formal institutional enforcement of ICJ judgments? The U.N. Security Council may impose legally binding measures, such as trade sanctions, to pressure a state to comply with an ICJ judgment. U.N. Charter, art. 94(2). However, the Council has never exercised this authority. In 1980, U.S.-Soviet Cold War tensions would likely have led the Soviet Union to veto any proposed Security Council decisions to enforce the ICJ's *Diplomatic and Consular Staff* judgment. We explore Security Council decisions further in Chapter 6. Some ICJ judgments might also in theory be enforced in national courts. See *Medellín* in Chapter 5.

The ICJ's Compulsory Jurisdiction. As we saw in the *Diplomatic and Consular Staff Case*, states may consent to the ICJ's jurisdiction in advance of a dispute by accepting treaties that provide for such jurisdiction. However, there is another way to consent to the Court's jurisdiction in advance of a dispute. The ICJ may also exercise jurisdiction if two states that are parties to a dispute have filed with the Court declarations accepting the Court's so-called "compulsory jurisdiction" under Article 36(2) of the ICJ Statute, reproduced in Section 1 above.

What is the utility of the ICJ's compulsory jurisdiction clause? Only about one-third of all states have filed 36(2) declarations, preferring instead to maintain their control over which forums may be available to hear disputes concerning their international legal obligations. Would it be better if the ICJ relied solely on *ad hoc* submissions on the lines of *Minquiers and Ecrehos*?

Here is an example of an Article 36(2) compulsory clause declaration:

DECLARATION OF MALAWI RECOGNIZING THE COMPULSORY JURISDICTION OF THE ICJ

International Court of Justice, *Yearbook 2006–2007*, No. 61, at 146 (2007)

On behalf of the Government of Malawi, I declare under Article 36, paragraph 2, of the Statute of the International Court of Justice that I recognize as compulsory *ipso facto* and without special agreement, in relation to any other State accepting the same obligation, on condition of reciprocity, the jurisdiction of the International Court of Justice in all legal disputes which may arise in respect of facts or situations subsequent to this declaration concerning:

(a)   the interpretation of a treaty;

(b)   any question of international law;

(c)   the existence of any fact which, if established, would constitute a breach of an international obligation;

(d)   the nature or extent of the reparation to be made for the breach of an international obligation:

Provided that this declaration shall not apply to—

(i)   disputes with regard to matters which are essentially within the domestic jurisdiction of the Republic of Malawi as determined by the Government of Malawi;

(ii)   disputes in regard to which the parties of the dispute have agreed or shall agree to have recourse to some other method of peaceful settlement; or

(iii)   disputes concerning any question relating to or arising out of belligerent or military occupation.

The Government of Malawi also reserves the right at any time, by means of a notification addressed to the Secretary-General of the United Nations, to add to, amend, or withdraw any of the foregoing reservations or any that may hereafter be added. Such notification shall be effective on the date of their receipt by the Secretary-General of the United Nations.

Given under my hand in Zomba this 22nd day of November 1966.

(SIGNED) H. Kamuzu Banda,
President and
Minister for External Affairs.

Attaching Conditions to 36(2) Declarations. As Malawi's declaration illustrates, some states attach conditions—often referred to as reservations—to their 36(2) declarations. Note especially Malawi's self-judging domestic jurisdiction reservation. Should the Court accept such a reservation as valid? One concern is that automatically giving effect to a self-judging domestic jurisdiction reservation would deprive the Court of an inherent judicial role, namely the authority to construe limits on its own competence. Should the Court at least subject a state's invocation of a self-judging domestic reservation to a reasonableness test?

Concerns with reciprocity have led the Court to allow a respondent state to invoke conditions attached to an applicant state's declaration in order to deprive the Court of jurisdiction. The respondent state may achieve this result even if its own 36(2) declaration would otherwise subject it to jurisdiction.

The United States and 36(2) Jurisdiction. On August 14, 1946, President Harry S. Truman signed a declaration accepting the Article 36(2) jurisdiction of the International Court of Justice. The declaration contained three reservations. The first provided that acceptance would not apply to "disputes the solution of which the parties shall entrust to other tribunals by virtue of agreements already in existence or which may be concluded in the future." The second was a self-judging domestic jurisdiction reservation, labeled the Connally Amendment after U.S. Senator Tom Connally, who had proposed it; Malawi's self-judging exception was modeled on this U.S. reservation. Because of the reciprocity concerns discussed above, the Connally Amendment prevented the United States from using Article 36(2) to bring claims to the International Court. For example, when in 1955 Bulgaria attacked a commercial airliner with U.S. passengers on board and the United States sought to bring a case to the ICJ, Bulgaria invoked the U.S. Connally Amendment. The third reservation, known as the Vandenberg Amendment (after another U.S. senator), provided that the U.S. 36(2) declaration would not apply to "disputes arising under a multilateral treaty" unless all other treaty parties "affected by the decision are also parties to the case before the Court." In the ICJ's 1986 *Case Concerning Military and*

Paramilitary Activities In and Against Nicaragua (Nicaragua v. United States), involving Nicaragua's challenge to U.S. military activities and support for rebels in Nicaragua, the Vandenberg Amendment precluded claims alleging violations of the U.N. Charter; Nicaragua could pursue only claims for violations of customary international law and of a bilateral treaty.

On October 7, 1985, following the ICJ's determination that it had jurisdiction in the *Nicaragua Case*, the United States terminated its Article 36(2) declaration, effective six months later, the period of notice specified in the 1946 U.S. declaration. The United States is not the only Western power that has terminated a 36(2) declaration. France took the same step following cases brought to the International Court by Australia and New Zealand in the 1970s that challenged the legality of French nuclear testing in the Pacific. See the discussion about the context of the *Rainbow Warrior Case* in Part A of this chapter. Should the United States reaccept the Article 36(2) compulsory jurisdiction of the ICJ? If so, what reservations, if any, should it attach to its acceptance?

The United States remains bound by numerous treaties containing clauses that authorize a state party to refer to the ICJ a dispute relating to the interpretation or application of the treaty. For a list, see *Medellín v. Texas*, 552 U.S. 491, 569–75 (2008) (Appendix B) (Breyer, J., dissenting).

3. Advisory Opinions at the International Court

As we saw in Section 1, the ICJ has authority pursuant to Article 96 of the U.N. Charter and Article 65 of its Statute to render advisory opinions. These are only given at the request of designated international organizations and, unlike judgments in the ICJ's contentious cases, are not legally binding. In practice, however, many advisory opinions have served functions rather similar to Court judgments. One such example is the *Wall Case* below. Consider especially why states sought to persuade the U.N. General Assembly to request an advisory opinion from the Court, and the role of the Court in a sensitive matter of international relations.

The Infrequency of Advisory Proceedings. During the over 70 years of its existence, 1945 to 2017, the ICJ has delivered only 23 advisory opinions, about one every three years. Why has resort to advisory proceedings been so rare? First, recall from Article 96 of the U.N. Charter (reproduced in Section 1) that not every international organization may seek an advisory opinion. There are over 250 intergovernmental organizations in the world, and thousands more non-governmental organizations. See Chapter 3. However, only the U.N. Security Council, the General Assembly, and other U.N. organs and specialized agencies (when authorized by the General Assembly) may ask the ICJ for an advisory opinion. One of the questions we consider in Part C of this chapter is whether changes should be made to the ICJ's advisory jurisdiction to allow referrals from other courts or from a broader array of international organizations on questions of international law.

Second, bureaucracies, including international bureaucracies, prefer to settle their legal problems outside the gaze of the public. ICJ cases are usually well-publicized. Many advisory opinion requests that reach the ICJ involve situations where some states want publicity for some purpose and can muster enough votes in the U.N. General Assembly or Security Council to support their quest.

In the *Wall Case*, the request for an advisory opinion came from the General Assembly. The request sought the International Court's advice concerning the legality of an Israeli wall or security fence in "Occupied Palestinian Territory" east of a 1949 armistice line between Arab and Israeli forces and west of the Jordan River, in a region known as the West Bank. See Figure 4.H. The Court first considered several objections to its jurisdiction. One, examined in the excerpt below, concerned whether the U.N. General Assembly was competent to request an advisory opinion on a matter related to international peace and security. More on the roles of the U.N. General Assembly and Security Council appears in Chapters 2 (the *Texaco-Libya Case*), 3, and 6.

The Political Context of the Wall Case. The *Wall Case* was decided in a highly politicized context. Palestinians and Israelis held radically different and deeply-felt views. At the 2004 ICJ hearings on the case, Nasser al-Kidwa, a Palestinian observer at the United Nations, argued that the Palestinian people "for too long have been denied the right to self-determination and sovereignty over their land." The Palestinians, "half of whom remain refugees[,] have been subject to a military occupation for almost 37 years. They have been dehumanized and demonized, humiliated and demeaned, dispossessed and dispersed, and brutally punished by their occupier." Since September 2000, "Israeli occupying forces have directly killed, including many by extrajudicial execution, a total of 2,770 Palestinian civilians, including children, women and men." Introductory Statement, Verbatim Record, Feb. 23, 2004, ¶¶ 2, 20, ICJ Doc. CR 2004/1, at 19, *available at* http://www.icj-cij.org/docket/files/131/1503.pdf.

Israeli officials viewed the circumstances far differently, stressing that the "security fence" was a necessary response to "Palestinian terrorism." An "evil campaign" had since 2000 "taken the lives of nearly 1,000 Israelis in over 20,000 attacks" and wounded "thousands more, leaving broken families, widows, and orphans." As long as such terrorism continued, Israel had "a moral and legal obligation" to defend its citizens. "Israel calls on the international community not to lend its hand to the ongoing Palestinian attempts to use international forums to avoid fulfilling their own commitment to fight terrorism." Israeli Statement on ICJ Advisory Opinion on Israel's Security Fence, July 9, 2004, http://www.mfa.gov.il/mfa/pressroom/2004/pages/statement%20on%20icj %20advisory%20opinion%209-july-2004.aspx.

LEGAL CONSEQUENCES OF THE CONSTRUCTION OF A WALL IN THE OCCUPIED PALESTINIAN TERRITORY

2004 I.C.J. 136

The Advisory Opinion Request, the Authority of the U.N. General Assembly, and the Court's Jurisdiction

The question on which the advisory opinion of the Court has been requested is set forth in resolution ES–10/14 adopted by the General Assembly of the United Nations (hereinafter the "General Assembly") on 8 December 2003 at its Tenth Emergency Special Session. . . . The resolution reads as follows: . . .

The General Assembly . . .

Decides, in accordance with Article 96 of the Charter of the United Nations, to request the International Court of Justice, pursuant to Article 65 of the Statute of the Court, to urgently render an advisory opinion on the following question:

What are the legal consequences arising from the construction of the wall being built by Israel, the occupying Power, in the Occupied Palestinian Territory, including in and around East Jerusalem, as described in the report of the Secretary-General, considering the rules and principles of international law, including the Fourth Geneva Convention of 1949, and relevant Security Council and General Assembly resolutions? . . .

When seised of a request for an advisory opinion, the Court must first consider whether it has jurisdiction to give the opinion requested and whether, should the answer be in the affirmative, there is any reason why it should decline to exercise any such jurisdiction. . . .

It is for the Court to satisfy itself that the request for an advisory opinion comes from an organ or agency having competence to make it. In the present instance, the Court notes that the General Assembly, which seeks the advisory opinion, is authorized to do so by Article 96, paragraph 1, of the Charter, which provides: "The General Assembly or the Security Council may request the International Court of Justice to give an advisory opinion on any legal question."

Although the above-mentioned provision states that the General Assembly may seek an advisory opinion "on any legal question," the Court has sometimes in the past given certain indications as to the relationship between the question the subject of a request for an advisory opinion and the activities of the General Assembly.

The Court will so proceed in the present case. The Court would observe that Article 10 of the Charter has conferred upon the General Assembly a competence relating to "any questions or any matters" within the scope of the Charter, and that Article 11, paragraph 2, has specifically provided it with competence on "questions relating to the maintenance of international peace and security brought before it by any Member of the United Nations . . . " and to make recommendations under certain conditions fixed by those Articles. [T]he question of the construction of the wall in the Occupied Palestinian Territory was brought before the General Assembly by a number of Member States in the context of the Tenth Emergency Special Session of the Assembly, convened to deal with what the Assembly, in its resolution ES–10/2 of 25 April 1997, considered to constitute a threat to international peace and security. . . .

On 27 October 2003, the General Assembly adopted resolution ES–10/13, by which it demanded that "Israel stop and reverse the construction of the wall in the Occupied Palestinian Territory, including in and around East Jerusalem, which is in departure of the Armistice Line of 1949 and is in contradiction to relevant provisions of international law."

[O]n 19 November 2003, the Security Council adopted resolution 1515 (2003), by which it "*Endorse[d]* the Quartet Performance-based Roadmap to a Permanent Two-State Solution to the Israeli-Palestinian Conflict." The Quartet consists of representatives of the United States of America, the European Union, the Russian Federation and the United Nations. That resolution "*Call[ed] on* the parties to fulfil their obligations under the Roadmap in cooperation with the Quartet and to achieve the vision of two States living side by side in peace and security." Neither the "Roadmap" nor resolution 1515 (2003) contained any specific provision concerning the construction of the wall, which was not discussed by the Security Council in this context.

. . . Article 12, paragraph 1, of the Charter provides that: "While the Security Council is exercising in respect of any dispute or situation the functions assigned to it in the present Charter, the General Assembly shall not make any recommendation with regard to that dispute or situation unless the Security Council so requests." A request for an advisory opinion is not in itself a "recommendation" by the General Assembly "with regard to [a] dispute or situation." It has however been argued in this case that the adoption by the General Assembly of resolution ES–10/14 was *ultra vires* as not in accordance with Article 12. The Court thus considers that it is appropriate for it to examine the significance of that Article, having regard to the relevant texts and the practice of the United Nations.

Under Article 24 of the Charter the Security Council has "primary responsibility for the maintenance of international peace and security." In that regard it can impose on States "an explicit obligation of compliance if for example it issues an order or command . . . under Chapter VII" and can, to that end, "require enforcement by coercive action" (*Certain Expenses of the United Nations (Article 17, paragraph 2, of the Charter), Advisory Opinion, I.C.J. Reports 1962,* p. 163). However, the Court would emphasize that Article 24 refers to a primary, but not necessarily exclusive, competence. The General Assembly does have the power, *inter alia,* under Article 14 of the Charter, to "recommend measures for the peaceful adjustment" of various situations. . . .

[T]he interpretation of Article 12 has evolved[.] In response to a question posed by Peru during the twenty-third session of the General Assembly, the Legal Counsel of the United Nations confirmed that the Assembly interpreted the words "is exercising the functions" in Article 12 of the Charter as meaning "is exercising the functions at this moment." [T]here has been an increasing tendency over time for the General Assembly and the Security Council to deal in parallel with the same matter concerning the maintenance of international peace and security. . . .

The Court considers that the accepted practice of the General Assembly, as it has evolved, is consistent with Article 12, paragraph 1, of the Charter. The Court is accordingly of the view that the General Assembly, in adopting resolution ES–10/14, seeking an advisory opinion from the Court, did not contravene the provisions of Article 12, paragraph 1, of the Charter. The Court concludes that by submitting that request the General Assembly did not exceed its competence.

Other Jurisdictional Challenges. The Court also rejected other jurisdictional challenges, including assertions that the question posed was "political" and that it was imprecise and overly abstract. The Court concluded that it "has jurisdiction to give the advisory opinion requested by resolution ES–10/14 of the General Assembly." That finding did not, however, end the debate about the propriety of proceeding. Although the Court technically had jurisdiction, it also had the discretion to refuse to exercise that jurisdiction if it found that "specific aspects of the General Assembly's request . . . would render the exercise of the Court's jurisdiction improper and inconsistent with the Court's judicial function." We turn next to some of the arguments about whether it was proper for the Court to proceed.

A Contentious Case? The *Wall Case*, an advisory proceeding, was not, like the *Diplomatic and Consular Staff Case*, a contentious bilateral case that could lead to a binding judgment. Israel has been careful not to consent to the ICJ's jurisdiction; recall that mutual consent of states parties is necessary for the Court to have jurisdiction in contentious cases. Should the ICJ have refused to proceed in the *Wall Case* on the grounds that it was really a contentious bilateral dispute in advisory opinion disguise? As seen in the following excerpt, the International Court was not persuaded by this argument. The Court found that the question on which its advice was sought had a significant multilateral dimension and that the Court would not be fulfilling one of its own important roles under the U.N. Charter if it refused to render an opinion. Might the Court's multilateral emphasis have led it to fail to address bilateral factors important to a more complete understanding of the issues? Should Israel have had the right to name its own *ad hoc* judge, as it would have had in a contentious case?

The Wall Case
The ICJ's Discretion to Decline to Give an Advisory Opinion and the Principle of Consent to Judicial Settlement of Disputes

The Court has recalled many times in the past that Article 65, paragraph 1, of its Statute, which provides that "The Court *may* give an advisory opinion . . ." (emphasis added), should be interpreted to mean that the Court has a discretionary power to decline to give an advisory opinion even if the conditions of jurisdiction are met. The Court however is mindful of the fact that its answer to a request for an advisory opinion "represents its participation in the activities of the Organization, and, in principle, should not be refused." Given its responsibilities as the "principal judicial organ of the United Nations" (Article 92 of the Charter), the Court should in principle not decline to give an advisory opinion. In accordance with its consistent jurisprudence, only "compelling reasons" should lead the Court to refuse its opinion.

The present Court has never, in the exercise of this discretionary power, declined to respond to a request for an advisory opinion. . . .

The first such argument is to the effect that the Court should not exercise its jurisdiction in the present case because the request concerns a contentious matter between Israel and Palestine, in respect of which Israel has not consented to the exercise of that jurisdiction. According to this view, the subject-matter of the question posed by the General Assembly "is an integral part of the wider Israeli-Palestinian dispute concerning questions of terrorism, security, borders, settlements, Jerusalem and other related matters." Israel has emphasized that it has never consented to the settlement of this wider dispute by the Court or by any other means of compulsory adjudication; on the contrary, it contends that the parties repeatedly agreed that these issues are to be settled by negotiation, with the possibility of an agreement that recourse could be had to arbitration. It is accordingly contended that the Court should decline to give the present Opinion[.]

[T]he Court does not consider that the subject-matter of the General Assembly's request can be regarded as only a bilateral matter between Israel and Palestine. Given the powers and responsibilities of the United Nations in questions relating to international peace and security, it is the Court's view that the construction of the wall must be deemed to be directly of concern to the United Nations. The responsibility of the United Nations in this matter also has its origin in the Mandate and the Partition Resolution concerning Palestine [discussed in an excerpt below]. Within the institutional framework of the Organization, this responsibility has been manifested by the adoption of many Security Council and General Assembly resolutions, and by the creation of several subsidiary bodies specifically established to assist in the realization of the inalienable rights of the Palestinian people.

The object of the request before the Court is to obtain from the Court an opinion which the General Assembly deems of assistance to it for the proper exercise of its functions. The opinion is requested on a question which is of particularly acute concern to the United Nations, and one which is located in a much broader frame of reference than a bilateral dispute. In the circumstances, the Court does not consider that to give an opinion would have the effect of circumventing the principle of consent to judicial settlement, and the Court accordingly cannot, in the exercise of its discretion, decline to give an opinion on that ground. . . .

It was also put to the Court by certain participants that the question of the construction of the wall was only one aspect of the Israeli-Palestinian conflict, which could not be properly addressed in the present proceedings. The Court does not however consider this a reason for it to decline to reply to the question asked. The Court is indeed aware that the question of the wall is part of a greater whole, and it would take this circumstance carefully into account in any opinion it might give. At the same time, the question that the General Assembly has chosen to ask of the Court is confined to the legal consequences of the construction of the wall, and the Court would only examine other issues to the extent that they might be necessary to its consideration of the question put to it.

Participants in the Proceedings. Note the Court's reference to "participants" in the proceedings. Although there are no formal parties to an advisory case, states and other entities may still participate, *e.g.*, by submitting comments. Israel informed the ICJ in writing of its reasons for opposing the request for an advisory opinion; Israel did not, however, present arguments concerning the merits of the case. Other countries and entities, including Palestine (recall from Chapter 3.B its debated status at international law), were invited to file statements presenting their views. The Court received timely written statements (in order of their receipt) from Guinea, Saudi Arabia, the League of Arab States, Egypt, Cameroon, Russia, Australia, Palestine, the United Nations, Jordan, Kuwait, Lebanon, Canada, Syria, Switzerland, Israel, Yemen, the United States, Morocco, Indonesia, the Organization of the Islamic Conference, France, Italy, Sudan, South Africa, Germany, Japan, Norway, the United Kingdom, Pakistan, the Czech Republic, Greece, Ireland on its own behalf, Ireland on behalf of the European Union, Cyprus, Brazil, Namibia, Malta, Malaysia, the Netherlands, Cuba, Sweden, Spain, Belgium, Palau, the Federated States of Micronesia, the Marshall Islands, Senegal, and the Democratic People's Republic of Korea. Many countries and Palestine also made oral statements during the Court's hearings.

The Factual Record. As we saw in the *Diplomatic and Consular Staff Case*, when a party fails to appear and does not present evidence in a contentious case, the ICJ may still render a judgment, although under its Statute the Court must satisfy itself "that the claim is well founded in fact and law." In advisory proceedings, the Court shall be "guided by" the Statute's provisions that "apply in contentious cases to the extent to which [the Court] recognizes them to be applicable." ICJ Statute, arts. 53(2), 68. In the *Wall Case* Israel could have presented the Court with facts related to threats to its security and the placement of the wall/security fence, but chose not to do so. Should the ICJ have refused to render an advisory opinion on the grounds that important facts were missing? The Court evaluated that argument:

The Wall Case
The ICJ's Discretion to Decline to Give an Advisory Opinion and the Requirement of Sufficient Evidence

Several participants in the proceedings have raised the further argument that the Court should decline to exercise its jurisdiction because it does not have at its disposal the requisite facts and evidence to enable it to reach its conclusions. . . . According to Israel, if the Court decided to give the requested opinion, it would be forced to speculate about essential facts and make assumptions about arguments of law. More specifically, Israel has argued that the Court could not rule on the legal consequences of the construction of the wall without enquiring, first, into the nature and scope of the security threat to which the wall is intended to respond and the effectiveness of that response, and, second, into the impact of the construction for the Palestinians. This task [would be] complicated in an advisory proceeding, particularly since Israel alone possesses much of the necessary information and has stated that it chooses not to address the merits. . . .

In the present instance, the Court has at its disposal [the report of the Secretary-General issued on November 24, 2003, and prepared pursuant to General Assembly resolution ES–10/13 (hereinafter the "report of the Secretary-General")], as well as a voluminous dossier submitted by him to the Court, comprising not only detailed information on the route of the wall but also on its humanitarian and socio-economic impact on the Palestinian population. The dossier includes several reports based on on-site visits by special rapporteurs and competent organs of the United Nations. The Secretary-General has further submitted to the Court a written statement updating his report, which supplemented the information contained therein. Moreover, numerous other participants have submitted to the Court written statements which contain information relevant to a response to the question put by the General Assembly. The Court notes in particular that Israel's Written Statement, although limited to issues of jurisdiction and judicial propriety, contained observations on other matters, including Israel's concerns in terms of security, and was accompanied by corresponding annexes; many other documents issued by the Israeli Government on those matters are in the public domain.

The Court finds that it has before it sufficient information and evidence to enable it to give the advisory opinion requested by the General Assembly. Moreover, the circumstance that others may evaluate and interpret these facts in a subjective or political manner can be no argument for a court of law to abdicate its judicial task.

[The Court considers that its advice would serve a useful purpose, because the General Assembly had deemed such advice useful and because the "Assembly has not yet determined all the possible consequences of its own resolution." The Court would seek "to determine in a comprehensive manner the legal consequences of the construction of the wall, while the General Assembly—and the Security Council—may then draw conclusions from the Court's findings."]

In the light of the foregoing, the Court concludes not only that it has jurisdiction to give an opinion on the question put to it by the General Assembly, but also that there is no compelling reason for it to use its discretionary power not to give that opinion.

The ICJ's Discretion Not to Render an Advisory Opinion. As we have seen, the *Wall* Court refused to use its discretion to foreclose an advisory opinion. Should the Court have proceeded? Why did it not treat this case as a non-justiciable political question, or a contentious case in disguise (to which Israel had not consented), or a case with an insufficient factual record? Certainly part of the explanation lies in the fact that the ICJ is the judicial arm of the United Nations. The Court sees itself as the proper forum for examining legal issues facing the United Nations when one of the organs authorized to request an advisory opinion makes such a request. The ICJ emphasized the multilateral legal issues of consequence to the United Nations, rather than bilateral, Israeli-Palestinian, aspects of the wall/security fence.

The ICJ's View of the Facts: Israel's Wall/Security Fence in Occupied Territory. The ICJ described Israel's wall or security fence as constructed in "Occupied Palestinian Territory." In the next excerpt the Court explained the territory's status and set out its understanding of the facts concerning the construction of the wall/security fence.

The Wall Case
History and Facts

Palestine was part of the Ottoman Empire. At the end of the First World War, a class "A" Mandate for Palestine was entrusted to Great Britain by the

League of Nations, pursuant to paragraph 4 of Article 22 of the Covenant, which provided that:

> Certain communities, formerly belonging to the Turkish Empire have reached a stage of development where their existence as independent nations can be provisionally recognized subject to the rendering of administrative advice and assistance by a Mandatory until such time as they are able to stand alone.

[I]n its Advisory Opinion on the *International Status of South West Africa,* [the Court found] that "two principles [related to mandates] were considered to be of paramount importance: the principle of non-annexation and the principle that the well-being and development of . . . peoples [not yet able to govern themselves] form[ed] 'a sacred trust of civilization' " ([*I.C.J. Reports 1950*], p. 131).

The territorial boundaries of the Mandate for Palestine were laid down by various instruments, in particular on the eastern border by a British memorandum of 16 September 1922 and an Anglo-Transjordanian Treaty of 20 February 1928.

In 1947 the United Kingdom announced its intention to complete evacuation of the mandated territory by 1 August 1948, subsequently advancing that date to 15 May 1948. In the meantime, the General Assembly had on 29 November 1947 adopted resolution 181(II) on the future government of Palestine, which "*Recommends* to the United Kingdom . . . and to all other Members of the United Nations the adoption and implementation . . . of the Plan of Partition" of the territory, as set forth in the resolution, between two independent States, one Arab, the other Jewish, as well as the creation of a special international régime for the City of Jerusalem. The Arab population of Palestine and the Arab States rejected this plan, contending that it was unbalanced; on 14 May 1948, Israel proclaimed its independence on the strength of the General Assembly resolution; armed conflict then broke out between Israel and a number of Arab States and the Plan of Partition was not implemented.

By resolution 62 (1948) of 16 November 1948, the Security Council decided that "an armistice shall be established in all sectors of Palestine" and called upon the parties directly involved in the conflict to seek agreement to this end. In conformity with this decision, general armistice agreements were concluded in 1949 between Israel and the neighbouring States through mediation by the United Nations. In particular, one such agreement was signed in Rhodes on 3 April 1949 between Israel and Jordan. Articles V and VI of that Agreement fixed the armistice demarcation line between Israeli and Arab forces (often later called the "Green Line" owing to the colour used for it on maps; hereinafter the "Green Line").

In the 1967 armed conflict, Israeli forces occupied all the territories which had constituted Palestine under British Mandate (including those known as the West Bank, lying to the east of the Green Line).

On 22 November 1967, the Security Council unanimously adopted resolution 242 (1967), which emphasized the inadmissibility of acquisition of territory by war and called for the "Withdrawal of Israel armed forces from territories occupied in the recent conflict," and "Termination of all claims or states of belligerency."

From 1967 onwards, Israel took a number of measures in these territories aimed at changing the status of the City of Jerusalem. The Security Council, after recalling on a number of occasions "the principle that acquisition of territory by military conquest is inadmissible," condemned those measures and, by resolution 298 (1971) of 25 September 1971, confirmed in the clearest possible terms that: "all legislative and administrative actions taken by Israel to change the status of the City of Jerusalem, including expropriation of land and properties, transfer of populations and legislation aimed at the incorporation of the occupied section, are totally invalid and cannot change that status."

Later, following the adoption by Israel on 30 July 1980 of the Basic Law making Jerusalem the "complete and united" capital of Israel, the Security Council, by resolution 478 (1980) of 20 August 1980, stated that the enactment of that Law constituted a violation of international law and that "all legislative and administrative measures and actions taken by Israel, the occupying Power, which have altered or purport to alter the character and status of the Holy City of Jerusalem . . . are null and void." It further decided "not to recognize the 'basic law' and such other actions by Israel that, as a result of this law, seek to alter the character and status of Jerusalem."

Subsequently, a peace treaty was signed on 26 October 1994 between Israel and Jordan. That treaty fixed the boundary between the two States "with reference to the boundary definition under the Mandate as is shown in Annex 1*(a)* . . . without prejudice to the status of any territories that came under Israeli military government control in 1967" (Article 3, paragraphs 1 and 2). Annex 1 provided the corresponding maps and added that, with regard to the "territory that came under Israeli military government control in 1967," the line indicated "is the administrative boundary" with Jordan.

Lastly, a number of agreements have been signed since 1993 between Israel and the Palestine Liberation Organization imposing various obligations on each Party. Those agreements *inter alia* required Israel to transfer to Palestinian authorities certain powers and responsibilities exercised in the Occupied Palestinian Territory by its military authorities and civil administration. Such transfers have taken place, but, as a result of subsequent events, they remained partial and limited.

[U]nder customary international law as reflected in Article 42 of the Regulations Respecting the Laws and Customs of War on Land annexed to the Fourth Hague Convention of 18 October 1907, territory is considered occupied when it is actually placed under the authority of the hostile army, and the occupation extends only to the territory where such authority has been established and can be exercised.

The territories situated between the Green Line and the former eastern boundary of Palestine under the Mandate were occupied by Israel in 1967 during the armed conflict between Israel and Jordan. Under customary international law, these were therefore occupied territories in which Israel had the status of occupying Power. Subsequent events in these territories have done nothing to alter this situation. All these territories (including East Jerusalem) remain occupied territories and Israel has continued to have the status of occupying Power.

It is essentially in these territories that Israel has constructed or plans to construct the works described in the report of the Secretary-General. The Court will now describe those works, basing itself on that report. For developments subsequent to the publication of that report, the Court will refer to complementary information contained in the Written Statement of the United Nations, which was intended by the Secretary-General to supplement his report (hereinafter "Written Statement of the Secretary-General").

The report of the Secretary-General states that "The Government of Israel has since 1996 considered plans to halt infiltration into Israel from the central and northern West Bank. . . ." [O]n 14 April 2002, the [Israeli] Cabinet adopted a decision for the construction of works, forming what Israel describes as a "security fence," 80 kilometres in length, in three areas of the West Bank.

According to the Written Statement of the Secretary-General, the first part of these works (Phase A), which ultimately extends for a distance of 150 kilometres, was declared completed on 31 July 2003. It is reported that approximately 56,000 Palestinians would be encompassed in enclaves. During this phase, two sections totalling 19.5 kilometres were built around Jerusalem. . . .

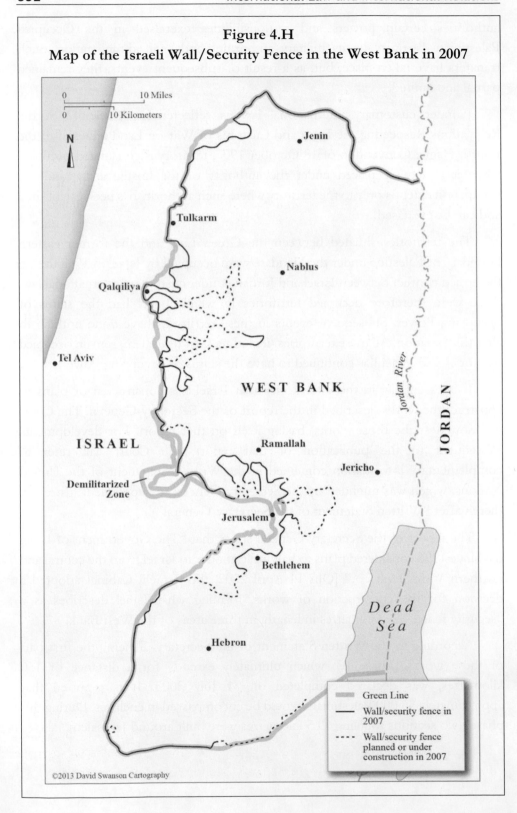

Figure 4.H
Map of the Israeli Wall/Security Fence in the West Bank in 2007

According to the description in the report and the Written Statement of the Secretary-General, the works planned or completed have resulted or will result in a complex consisting essentially of:

(1)   a fence with electronic sensors;

(2)   a ditch (up to 4 metres deep);

(3)   a two-lane asphalt patrol road;

(4)   a trace road (a strip of sand smoothed to detect footprints) running parallel to the fence;

(5)   a stack of six coils of barbed wire marking the perimeter of the complex.

The complex has a width of 50 to 70 metres, increasing to as much as 100 metres in some places. "Depth barriers" may be added to these works.

The approximately 180 kilometres of the complex completed or under construction as of the time when the Secretary-General submitted his report included some 8.5 kilometres of concrete wall. These are generally found where Palestinian population centres are close to or abut Israel (such as near Qalqiliya and Tulkarm or in parts of Jerusalem).

[A]pproximately 975 square kilometres (or 16.6 per cent of the West Bank) would, according to the report of the Secretary-General, lie between the Green Line and the wall. This area is stated to be home to 237,000 Palestinians. If the full wall were completed as planned, another 160,000 Palestinians would live in almost completely encircled communities, described as enclaves in the report. As a result of the planned route, nearly 320,000 Israeli settlers (of whom 178,000 in East Jerusalem) would be living in the area between the Green Line and the wall.

[T]he construction of the wall has been accompanied by the creation of a new administrative régime. Thus in October 2003 the Israeli Defence Forces issued Orders establishing the part of the West Bank lying between the Green Line and the wall as a "Closed Area." Residents of this area may no longer remain in it, nor may non-residents enter it, unless holding a permit or identity card issued by the Israeli authorities. According to the report of the Secretary-General, most residents have received permits for a limited period. Israeli citizens, Israeli permanent residents and those eligible to immigrate to Israel in accordance with the Law of Return may remain in, or move freely to, from and within the Closed Area without a permit. Access to and exit from the Closed Area can only be made through access gates, which are opened infrequently and for short periods.

Figure 4.I
Portion of the Israeli Wall/Security Fence in the West Bank

Evaluating the ICJ's Factual Account. To what might Israel have objected in the ICJ's account of the historical record and the wall/security fence? The U.S. judge on the Court, Thomas Buergenthal, the sole dissenting judge on most of the Court's conclusions, was troubled by what he saw as an insufficient factual record:

The Wall Case
Judge Buergenthal's Declaration

It may well be . . . that on a thorough analysis of all relevant facts, a finding could well be made that some or even all segments of the wall being constructed by Israel on the Occupied Palestinian Territory violate international law. But to reach that conclusion with regard to the wall as a whole without having before it or seeking to ascertain all relevant facts bearing directly on issues of Israel's legitimate right of self-defence, military necessity and security needs, given the repeated deadly terrorist attacks in and upon Israel proper coming from the Occupied Palestinian Territory to which Israel has been and continues to be subjected, cannot be justified as a matter of law. The nature of these cross-Green

Line attacks and their impact on Israel and its population are never really seriously examined by the Court, and the dossier provided the Court by the United Nations on which the Court to a large extent bases its findings barely touches on that subject. I am not suggesting that such an examination would relieve Israel of the charge that the wall it is building violates international law, either in whole or in part, only that without this examination the findings made are not legally well founded.

The Substantive Legal Issues. The *Wall Case* involved several complex questions related to subjects we explore in other chapters: self-determination of peoples (Chapter 3); international human rights law (Chapter 7); international humanitarian law, which applies in armed conflicts and to occupying powers (Chapter 6); and the law governing self-defense and resort to use of force (Chapter 6). The Court looked at rules and principles in the United Nations Charter, other treaties, customary international law, and relevant U.N. General Assembly and Security Council resolutions. The case excerpt below gives the flavor of the Court's reasoning and sets out the Court's reply to the question on which the General Assembly had sought advice.

The ICJ's analysis and conclusions concerning the substantive issues in the *Wall Case* have been much debated. The fact that 14 of 15 judges agreed on a wide range of conclusions represents a significant consensus on the Court. However, other actors have disagreed with the ICJ's analysis, at least in part. The Israeli Supreme Court, in a decision handed down just days before the ICJ's advisory opinion, applied customary international law and ruled that although the wall/security fence was intended to protect Israeli security, portions of it were illegal because they disproportionately affected Palestinian civilians. HCJ/2056/04, Beit Sourik Village Council v. Israel, 43 *International Legal Materials* 1099 (2004). Some observers have also complained that the Court should more thoroughly have explained its reasoning concerning difficult legal issues. For example, ICJ Judge Rosalyn Higgins, in her separate opinion in the *Wall Case*, concluded that the Court's analysis of international humanitarian law was insufficiently detailed. She chided the ICJ for not "follow[ing] the tradition of using advisory opinions as an opportunity to elaborate and develop international law." Separate Opinion of Judge Higgins, ¶ 23.

The Wall Case
The Law and the Court's Advice

Whilst the Court notes the assurance given by Israel that the construction of the wall does not amount to annexation and that the wall is of a temporary nature, it nevertheless cannot remain indifferent to certain fears expressed to it that the route of the wall will prejudge the future frontier between Israel and Palestine, and the fear that Israel may integrate the settlements and their means of access. The Court considers that the construction of the wall and its associated régime create a "fait accompli" on the ground that could well become permanent, in which case, and notwithstanding the formal characterization of the wall by Israel, it would be tantamount to *de facto* annexation.

[T]he route chosen for the wall gives expression *in loco* to the illegal measures taken by Israel with regard to Jerusalem and the settlements, as deplored by the Security Council. There is also a risk of further alterations to the demographic composition of the Occupied Palestinian Territory resulting from the construction of the wall inasmuch as it is contributing . . . to the departure of Palestinian populations from certain areas. That construction, along with measures taken previously, thus severely impedes the exercise by the Palestinian people of its right to self-determination, and is therefore a breach of Israel's obligation to respect that right. . . .

To sum up, the Court is of the opinion that the construction of the wall and its associated régime impede the liberty of movement of the inhabitants of the Occupied Palestinian Territory (with the exception of Israeli citizens and those assimilated thereto) as guaranteed under Article 12, paragraph 1, of the International Covenant on Civil and Political Rights. They also impede the exercise by the persons concerned of the right to work, to health, to education and to an adequate standard of living as proclaimed in the International Covenant on Economic, Social and Cultural Rights and in the United Nations Convention on the Rights of the Child. Lastly, the construction of the wall and its associated régime, by contributing to the demographic changes referred to . . . above, contravene Article 49, paragraph 6, of the Fourth Geneva Convention and [various] Security Council resolutions[.]

[T]he Court, from the material available to it, is not convinced that the specific course Israel has chosen for the wall was necessary to attain its security objectives. The wall, along the route chosen, and its associated régime gravely infringe a number of rights of Palestinians residing in the territory occupied by Israel, and the infringements resulting from that route cannot be justified by military exigencies or by the requirements of national security or public order. The construction of such a wall accordingly constitutes breaches by Israel of various of its obligations under the applicable international humanitarian law and human rights instruments. . . .

The fact remains that Israel has to face numerous indiscriminate and deadly acts of violence against its civilian population. It has the right, and indeed the duty, to respond in order to protect the life of its citizens. The measures taken are bound nonetheless to remain in conformity with applicable international law.

In conclusion, the Court considers that Israel cannot rely on a right of self-defence or on a state of necessity in order to preclude the wrongfulness of the construction of the wall[.] The Court accordingly finds that the construction of the wall, and its associated régime, are contrary to international law.

[B]oth Israel and Palestine are under an obligation scrupulously to observe the rules of international humanitarian law, one of the paramount purposes of which is to protect civilian life. Illegal actions and unilateral decisions have been taken on all sides, whereas, in the Court's view, this tragic situation can be brought to an end only through implementation in good faith of all relevant Security Council resolutions, in particular resolutions 242 (1967) and 338 (1973). The "Roadmap" approved by Security Council resolution 1515 (2003) represents the most recent of efforts to initiate negotiations to this end. The Court . . . draw[s] the attention of the General Assembly, to which the present Opinion is addressed, to the need for these efforts to be encouraged with a view to achieving as soon as possible, on the basis of international law, a negotiated solution to the outstanding problems and the establishment of a Palestinian State, existing side by side with Israel and its other neighbours, with peace and security for all in the region.

[The Court replies] in the following manner to the question put by the General Assembly:

By fourteen votes to one,

The construction of the wall being built by Israel, the occupying Power, in the Occupied Palestinian Territory, including in and around East Jerusalem, and its associated régime, are contrary to international law;

By fourteen votes to one,

Israel is under an obligation to terminate its breaches of international law; it is under an obligation to cease forthwith the works of construction of the wall being built in the Occupied Palestinian Territory, including in and around East Jerusalem, to dismantle forthwith the structure therein situated, and to repeal or render ineffective forthwith all legislative and regulatory acts relating thereto[;]

By fourteen votes to one,

Israel is under an obligation to make reparation for all damage caused by the construction of the wall in the Occupied Palestinian Territory, including in and around East Jerusalem;

By thirteen votes to two,

All States are under an obligation not to recognize the illegal situation resulting from the construction of the wall and not to render aid or assistance in maintaining the situation created by such construction; all States parties to the Fourth Geneva Convention relative to the Protection of Civilian Persons in Time of War of 12 August 1949 have in addition the obligation, while respecting the United Nations Charter and international law, to ensure compliance by Israel with international humanitarian law as embodied in that Convention;

By fourteen votes to one,

The United Nations, and especially the General Assembly and the Security Council, should consider what further action is required to bring to an end the illegal situation resulting from the construction of the wall and the associated régime, taking due account of the present Advisory Opinion.

The Efficacy of the Court's Advice. What is the efficacy of the Court's opinion? Do the functions of the Court in the *Wall Case* differ from those in the *Diplomatic and Consular Staff Case*, a contentious case? In each, the Court served as a public forum in which grievances over the actions of one state were raised. In each, the Court expounded relevant international law. In each, the ICJ's decision or opinion also did not lead to immediate cessation of the behavior deemed to violate international law. In the years since the ICJ's 2005 advisory opinion in the *Wall Case*, Israel, under the administration of Prime Minister Benjamin Netanyahu, has continued to support the wall/security fence and Israeli settlements on the West Bank. By 2016 the number of Israeli settlers in the West Bank and East Jerusalem had reached an estimated 550,000. See Luke Baker, "Israel's Settlement Drive is Becoming Irreversible, Diplomats Fear," *Reuters*, June 1, 2016, *available at* www.reuters.com. International opposition to Israeli resettlement and the wall/security fence has continued. In December 2016, during the last month of the Obama administration, the United States refused to veto U.N. Security Council Resolution 2234, which reaffirmed that the Israeli settlements in occupied Palestinian territory "constitute[d] a flagrant violation under international law and a major obstacle to the achievement of the two-State solution and a just, lasting and comprehensive peace." U.N. Doc. S/RES/2234, ¶ 1 (2016). See Somini Sengupta & Rick Gladstone, "Rebuffing

Israel, U.S. Allows Censure Over Settlements," *New York Times*, Dec. 23, 2016. Might the Court's decision still affect—for better or worse—prospects for any political solution, by emphasizing what courses of conduct are legal and illegal at international law?

C. THE PROLIFERATION OF INTERNATIONAL COURTS AND TRIBUNALS[1]

One reason why the work of the International Court of Justice has not expanded in recent times is the creation of other international courts with a regional or a specialized jurisdiction. When the Permanent Court of International Justice was established in 1921, there were no other permanent international tribunals, save the Permanent Court of Arbitration, which the PCIJ largely supplanted. The ICJ, too, had a virtually exclusive position as *the* international court until late in the 1950s. Since then, new international courts have been added at an ever-quickening pace. There are now several dozen international courts and tribunals. See the listing of the Project on International Courts and Tribunals at http://www.pict-pcti.org/.

The Variety of International Courts and Tribunals. Several global tribunals consider only specific subject matters, such as international trade (*e.g.*, the World Trade Organization's Dispute Settlement Body) or the law of the sea (the International Tribunal for the Law of the Sea). See Chapter 8. There are also regional courts, such as the European Court of Human Rights and the Inter-American Court of Human Rights. See Chapter 7.

One could differentiate international courts not only by region and subject matter, but also by function. Some help to resolve disputes between parties, while others, instead or in addition, apply international criminal law and impose criminal penalties, or review the consistency of national laws and actions with international law.

International courts and tribunals also reflect significant procedural differences. Some, like the International Court of Justice, permit only states to be parties, while others allow suits to be brought by or against individuals. The busiest international courts and tribunals boast appellate structures or other procedures to handle hundreds or thousands of cases. For example, the

---

[1]   Portions of the first, eighth, and ninth paragraphs of this Part C are adapted from Mark Weston Janis, *International Law* 164–65 (6th ed. 2012).

European Court of Human Rights and the European Court of Justice have two-tier structures to manage their heavy caseloads.

We explore several different international courts and tribunals in this book, including the European Court of Human Rights in Chapters 1 and 7, the European Court of Justice in Chapter 2, the Nuremberg Tribunal and the International Criminal Court in Chapter 7, the International Criminal Tribunal for the former Yugoslavia in Chapters 2 and 6, the Inter-American Commission on Human Rights in Chapter 2, the International Tribunal for the Law of the Sea in Chapter 8, and various arbitral tribunals in this chapter and Chapters 2 and 8.

Who Pays for International Courts? International courts are created by or under the authority of treaties, and treaty parties pay for a court's personnel and operating costs. The International Court of Justice, as an organ of the United Nations, is funded by all U.N. member states out of the general U.N. budget. In 2010, each ICJ judge received a salary of $166,596, with the President earning a supplement of $15,000. By comparison, the 2010 salary of the Chief Justice of the U.S. Supreme Court was $223,500, the salary of each Associate Justice $213,900, and the salary of each of the hundreds of U.S. federal district court judges $174,000, while the salaries of U.S. state court judges ranged between $104,170 and $228,856.

Advantages and Disadvantages of Multiple International Courts and Tribunals. Does the existence of so many international courts and tribunals create too many opportunities for forum shopping? Recall from the discussion following the *Rainbow Warrior* decisions earlier in this chapter just how many different forums were called on to address aspects of that incident. Even when we consider only interstate disputes in international courts and tribunals, multiple forums may be available. For example, during 2001–2008 four different international courts and tribunals—the International Tribunal for the Law of the Sea, an arbitral tribunal constituted under the 1982 Convention on the Law of the Sea, the European Court of Justice, and an arbitral tribunal created pursuant to the 1992 Convention for the Protection of the Marine Environment of the North-East Atlantic—heard aspects of a dispute between Ireland and the United Kingdom concerning possible pollution of the Irish Sea from a British mixed oxide plant. In another 21st-century dispute, Chile challenged European Community practices of harvesting swordfish in the International Tribunal for the Law of the Sea in 2000; the EC responded by bringing a World Trade Organization case against Chile for restricting imports of swordfish. Case Concerning the Conservation and Sustainable Exploitation of Swordfish Stocks in the South-Eastern Pacific Ocean, ITLOS Case No. 7 (2000), *available at* www.itlos.org; Case on Measures Affecting the Transit and Importing of Swordfish (EC v. Chile), WTO Doc. WT/DS193 (suspended Mar. 23, 2001). The swordfish dispute was eventually resolved by negotiation. But suppose negotiations are not successful. What techniques or mechanisms might moderate conflicts between international courts?

One way out of the dilemma is for a regional or specialized dispute settlement forum to develop rules of abstention or deference to another forum. But it is not likely to be easier to resolve conflicts of jurisdiction among international forums than it has been to resolve conflicts of jurisdiction among municipal courts. How to resolve conflicts between the judicial jurisdictions of municipal courts or between national laws has long been a concern in municipal legal systems. Although these conflicts typically arise in cases involving private parties, the underlying question of the international scope of application of national laws may involve sensitive questions of international relations. This area of international law is known as conflict of laws or private international law.

The International Court of Justice and the Proliferation of International Courts. With so many tribunals, is there a risk of divergent interpretations of international law? What role should the International Court of Justice—the principal judicial organ of the United Nations—play in this complex institutional world of multiple courts and tribunals? Faced with the new international courts, some, like former President Guillaume of the ICJ, fear that international law will become fragmented unless the ICJ is recognized as a kind of supreme court for international law. One can envision a range of possibilities that would increase a role for the International Court. Should municipal courts be allowed to refer questions about international law to the ICJ? There is such a mechanism, called a preliminary ruling, in European Union law. See Article 267 of the 2012 Consolidated Versions of the Treaty on European Union and the Treaty on the Functioning of the European Union. Should international courts also be authorized to refer legal questions to the ICJ? Should referrals from the Secretary-General of the United Nations be permitted? Should individuals be allowed to bring cases or questions to the ICJ?

It is doubtful that the world community would agree to a hierarchy granting the ICJ increased authority, much less the role of an international "supreme court." Such changes as allowing individuals access to the International Court seem politically unlikely, and any changes to the ICJ's jurisdiction would require amending the U.N. Charter or the Court's Statute, a difficult process. Establishing the international judicial supremacy of the ICJ would also undermine many of the advantages of the new regional and international courts, such as their more limited state memberships and more expert areas of competence. Some international courts do cite and rely on rulings of other courts, especially those of the ICJ. But it seems inevitable that, despite such judicial cross-fertilization, the new international courts will develop their own areas of the law with a resulting diversity of international legal jurisprudence.

Should the International Court of Justice make changes on its own—changes not involving formal amendments to its jurisdiction—to enhance its influence? For example, when the ICJ is hearing a case, should it become more proactive, reaching out to pronounce on substantive legal issues of great importance? Would becoming more proactive help or hurt the ICJ's influence?

CHAPTER 5

International Law and Municipal Law

In most instances when international legal rules are applied in judicial practice, they are incorporated and applied by municipal courts. In this chapter, we look at the U.S. constitutional rules governing the incorporation of international law into U.S. law. Rules about incorporation are traditionally grouped into those involving treaties (Part A) and those concerning all other forms of international law, a category sometimes called, in countries of the common law, "the law of nations" (Part B).

A. TREATIES AND THE CONSTITUTION

As we noted in our discussion of the 1783 Peace of Paris in Chapter 2, one of the principal reasons why the United States abandoned the Articles of Confederation for the Constitution of 1787 was the failure of the several states to honor their treaty obligations to the United Kingdom. Accordingly, the new Constitution made explicit provision for the national enforcement of treaty obligations, notably including U.S. treaties within the Constitution's Article VI's Supremacy Clause. Our first case below, *Ware v. Hylton* from 1796, saw the Supreme Court enforcing the Supremacy Clause against a recalcitrant Virginia.

WARE V. HYLTON
3 U.S. (3 Dall.) 199 (1796)

The Facts

CHASE, JUSTICE—The Defendants In Error [Hylton and Eppes], on the [7th] day of July, 1774, passed their penal bond to Farrell & Jones [now their administrator, Ware], for the payment of £2,976 11s 6d, of good British money. . . .

On the 20th of October, 1777, the legislature of the commonwealth of Virginia, passed a law to sequester British property. In the 3d section of the law, it was enacted, "that it should be lawful for any citizen of Virginia, owing money to a subject of Great Britain, to pay the same, or any part thereof, from time to time, as he should think fit, into the loan office, taking thereout a certificate for the same, in the name of the creditor, with an endorsement, under the hand of the commissioner of the said office, expressing the name of the payer; and shall deliver such certificate to the governor and the council, whose receipt shall discharge him from so much of the debt. And the governor and the council shall, in like manner, lay before the General Assembly, once in every year, an account of these certificates, specifying the names of the persons by, and for whom they were paid; and shall see to the safe keeping of the same; subject to the future directions of the legislature; provided, that the governor and the council may make such allowance, as they shall think reasonable, out of the interest of the money so paid into the loan office, to the wives and children, residing in the state, of such creditor."

On the 26th of April, 1780, the Defendants in error, paid into the loan office of Virginia, part of their debt, to wit, 3,111 1/9 dollars, equal to £933 14s 0d Virginia currency; and obtained a certificate from the commissioners of the loan office, and a receipt from the governor [Thomas Jefferson] and the council of Virginia, agreeably to the above, in part recited law.

The Defendants in error being sued, on the above bond, in the Circuit Court of Virginia, pleaded the above law, and the payment above stated, in bar of so much of the Plaintiff's debt. The plaintiff, to avoid this bar, replied the fourth article of the Definitive Treaty of Peace, between Great Britain and the United States, of the 3rd September, 1783. . . . The circuit court [ruled for the defendants in error], and the plaintiff brought the present writ of error.

The case is of very great importance, not only from the property that depends on the decision, but because the effect and operation of the treaty are necessarily involved.

The Political Importance of Ware v. Hylton. In Chapter 2 we considered the 1783 Treaty of Paris between Great Britain and the United States. The plaintiff in *Ware* relied on Article IV, which reads: "It is agreed, that creditors on either side shall meet with no lawful impediment to the recovery of the full value, in sterling money, of all *bona fide* debts heretofore contracted." Remember how difficult it would have been for the new republic if the Court had found for Virginia:

[T]he Court had to face the practical situation then existing. . . . The Court knew that the United States must somehow satisfy Great

> Britain on the subject and the very national existence of the United
> States might depend upon it. The realism of this becomes apparent
> when it is recalled that the British had stated that they would not
> evacuate their troops from the western forts until Article 4 [of the
> Peace treaty] was actually being carried out.
>
> Willard Bruce Cowles, *Treaties and Constitutional Law: Property Interferences and Due
> Process of Law* 84 (1941). A judgment unfavorable to the United Kingdom might
> have even led to war. Michael D. Ramsey, "The Power of the States in Foreign
> Affairs: The Original Understanding of Foreign Policy Federalism," 75 *Notre
> Dame Law Review* 341, 422 (1999).

Ware v. Hylton
The Law

It appears to me that the plea, by the Defendant, of the act of Assembly, and
the payment agreeably to its provisions, which is admitted, is a bar to the plaintiff's
action, for so much of his debt as he paid into the loan office; unless the plea is
avoided, or destroyed, by the Plaintiff's replication of the fourth article of the
Definitive Treaty of Peace, between Great Britain and the United States on the
3rd September, 1783.

The question then may be stated thus: Whether the 4th article of the said
treaty nullifies the law of Virginia, passed on the 20th of October, 1777; destroys
the payment made under it; and revives the debt, and gives a right of recovery
thereof, against the original debtor?

It was doubted by one of the counsel for the Defendants in error (Mr. [John]
Marshall) whether Congress had a power to make a treaty, that could operate to
annul a legislative act of any of the states, and to destroy rights acquired by, or
vested in individuals, in virtue of such acts. Another of the Defendant's counsel
(Mr. Campbell) expressly, and with great zeal, denied that Congress possessed
such power.

But a few remarks will be necessary to show the inadmissibility of this
objection to the power of Congress.

1st. The legislatures of all the states, have often exercised the power of taking
the property of its citizens for the use of the public, but they uniformly
compensated the proprietors. The principle to maintain this right is for the public
good, and to that the interest of individuals must yield. The instances are many,
and among them are lands taken for forts, magazines, or arsenals; or for public
roads, or canals; or to erect towns.

2nd. The legislatures of all the states have often exercised the power of divesting rights vested; and even of impairing, and, in some instances, of almost annihilating the obligation of contracts, as by tender laws, which made an offer to pay, and a refusal to receive, paper money, for a specie debt, an extinguishment, to the amount tendered.

3rd. If the Legislature of Virginia could, by a law, annul any former law; I apprehend that the effect would be to destroy all rights acquired under the law so nullified.

4th. If the Legislature of Virginia could not by ordinary acts of legislation, do these things, yet possessing the supreme sovereign power of the state, she certainly could do them, by a treaty of peace; if she had not parted with the power or making such treaty. If Virginia had such power before she delegated it to Congress, it follows, that afterwards, that body possessed it. Whether Virginia parted with the power of making treaties of peace, will be seen by a perusal of the ninth article of the Confederation (ratified by all the states on the 1st of March, 1781), in which it was declared, That "the United States in Congress assembled, shall have the sole and exclusive right and power of determining on peace, or war, except in the two cases mentioned in the 6th article; and of entering into treaties and alliances, with a proviso, when made, respecting commerce." . . .

If doubts could exist before the establishment of the present national government, they must be entirely removed by the 6th article of the Constitution, which provides "That all treaties made, or which shall be made under the authority of the United States, shall be the supreme law of the land; and the Judges in every State shall be bound thereby, anything in the Constitution or laws, of any state to the contrary notwithstanding." There can be no limitation on the power of the people of the United States. By their authority, the state constitutions were made, and by their authority the Constitution of the United States was established: and they had the power to change or abolish the State Constitutions, or to make them yield to the general government, and to treaties made by their authority. A treaty cannot be the Supreme law of the land, that is of all the United States, if any act of a State Legislature can stand in its way. If the Constitution of a State (which is the fundamental law of the State, and paramount to its Legislature) must give way to a treaty, and fall before it; can it be questioned, whether the less power, an act of the State Legislature, must not be prostrate? It is the declared will of the people of the United States that every treaty made, by the authority of the United States, shall be superior to the Constitution and laws of any individual State; and their will alone is to decide. If a law of a State, contrary to a treaty, is not void, but voidable only by a repeal, or nullification by a State Legislature, this certain consequence follows, that the will of a small part of the United States may control or defeat the will of the whole. . . .

On the best investigation I have been able to give the fourth article of the treaty, I cannot conceive, that the wisdom of men could express their meaning in more accurate and intelligible words, or in words more proper and effectual to carry their intention into execution. I am satisfied, that the words, in their natural import, and common use, give a recovery to the British creditor from his original debtor of the debt contracted before the treaty, notwithstanding the payment thereof into the public treasuries, or loan offices, under the authority of any state law; and, therefore, I am of opinion, that the judgment of the circuit court ought to be reversed, and that judgment ought to be given . . . for the Plaintiff in error[.]

John Marshall and Nationalism. Ware v. Hylton was the only case where the future Chief Justice, John Marshall, argued before the Supreme Court. It was ironic that he "had to argue a cause [Virginia's] that ran counter to his deeply felt nationalist sentiments." Marshall's legal strategy allowed "him to fulfill his duty to his client without sacrificing his personal view," *i.e.*, by attempting to avoid the Supremacy Clause and instead striving to reconcile the national 1783 treaty and the Virginia state law. "Editorial Note to Ware, Administrator of Jones, v. Hylton, 1790–1796," in 5 *The Papers of John Marshall* 295, 298–99 (Charles F. Hobson *et al.* eds. 1987). Marshall persuaded the circuit court to take this path but not the Supreme Court. Marshall was, of course, a strong nationalist once on the Court, as we see in *Foster & Elam* below.

The Role of Congress in Executing Treaties. On its face, Article VI's Supremacy Clause addresses issues of American federalism, limiting the powers of the several states, *e.g.*, respecting treaties. But does Article VI also limit the powers of Congress in "executing" treaties? Must Congress always pass implementing legislation for treaties to have authority in domestic law? This was and is the rule in English law. In *Foster v. Neilson* below, Chief Justice John Marshall charted a new course for U.S. constitutional law, with what became the doctrine of "self-executing treaties."

———

Figure 5.A
U.S. Supreme Court Chief Justice John Marshall

JOHN MARSHALL LLD.

Did *Ware* provide a foundation for the self-executing treaty doctrine? Even Professor Yoo, a critic, admitted that *Ware* "stands as the most authoritative declaration of self-executing treaties from the Framing Period." Yoo, however, maintained that *Ware* only rejected the powers of Virginia and other states *vis-à-vis* treaties; it did not concern the role of Congress. John C. Yoo, "Globalism and the Constitution: Treaties, Non-Self-Execution, and the Original Understanding," 99 *Columbia Law Review* 1955, 2079 (1999). Professor Vázquez remarked that Yoo's view—"that treaties can be self-executing [only] if they regulate matters outside Article I['s legislative powers]" is based on "no discernible textual or structured reason" and is unsupported by "subsequent judicial doctrine." Carlos Manuel Vázquez, "Laughing at Treaties," 99 *Columbia Law Review* 2154, 2213–14 (1999). Keep this debate in mind as you read *Foster & Elam* and the other following cases. Is it Yoo or Vázquez who has a better understanding of the importance of *Ware*?

Self-executing Treaties. Perhaps the most important U.S. constitutional law decision concerning the relationship of international law and U.S. municipal law is *Foster & Elam*, where Chief Justice Marshall introduced the concept, though not the exact term, of "self-executing treaties." Besides noting how and why Chief Justice Marshall employed the concept of self-executing treaties, pay particular attention to why the litigants and the U.S. Supreme Court in *Foster & Elam* needed to know whether the treaty provision in question could serve as a rule of decision. This part also considers cases addressing additional complications to treaty reception introduced in the United States by the doctrines of federalism and separation of powers.

FOSTER & ELAM V. NEILSON

27 U.S. (2 Pet.) 253 (1829)

The Facts

MR. CHIEF JUSTICE MARSHALL delivered the opinion of the Court.

This suit was brought by the plaintiffs in error [Foster & Elam], in the court of the United States for the eastern district of Louisiana, to recover a tract of land lying in that district, about 30 miles east of the Mississippi, and in the possession of the defendant [Neilson]. The plaintiffs claimed under a grant for 40,000 arpents of land, made by the Spanish governor, on the 2d of January 1804, to Jayme Joydra, and ratified by the king of Spain on the 29th of May 1804. . . . The defendant excepted to the petition of the plaintiffs, alleging that it does not show a title on which they can recover; that the territory within which the land claimed is situated, had been ceded, before the grant, to France, and by France to the United States; and that the grant is void, being made by persons who had no authority to make it. . . .

The case presents this very intricate, and, at one time, very interesting question: To whom did the country between the Iberville and the Perdido rightfully belong, when the title now asserted by the plaintiffs was acquired? This question has been repeatedly discussed, with great talent and research, by the government of the United States and that of Spain. The United States have perseveringly and earnestly insisted, that by the treaty of St. Ildefonso, made on the 1st of October, in the year 1800, Spain ceded the disputed territory, as part of Louisiana, to France; and that France, by the treaty of Paris, signed on the 30th of April 1803, and ratified on the 21st of October, in the same year, ceded it to the United States. Spain has, with equal perseverance and earnestness, maintained, that her cession to France comprehended that territory only which was, at that time, denominated Louisiana, consisting of the island of New Orleans, and the country she received from France, west of the Mississippi.

[Marshall introduces and discusses the complicated negotiations among France, Spain, Great Britain, and the United States over the territory and then suggests that perhaps the Court need not actually answer the question about ownership.]

The Application of International Law by Municipal Courts. We have moved from the legislative process of international law—how international legal rules are made—to the discipline's judicial and executive process—who applies the rules of international law and how such decisions are made effective. In Chapter 4 we considered international courts and tribunals, and now turn to municipal courts. The great majority of international law cases that are settled by formal judicial process are decided by domestic courts, not by international courts or tribunals. For most lawyers practicing international law, domestic law courts are the usual fora foreseen in negotiations and employed in litigation. Here for reasons of space and audience we look only at the municipal practice of the United States. *American International Law Cases* publishes cases in which U.S. state and federal courts have used international law; there are over 7,500 such cases, just from the years 1990–2013.

The overwhelming majority of U.S. court cases involving international law concern treaties; the most important case is *Foster & Elam v. Neilson.* Not only did the case establish the proposition of the "self-executing" treaty in U.S. law, but it introduced the notion into international law generally, making *Foster & Elam* one of the most significant U.S. contributions to the discipline world-wide.

Figure 5.B
Southeast United States

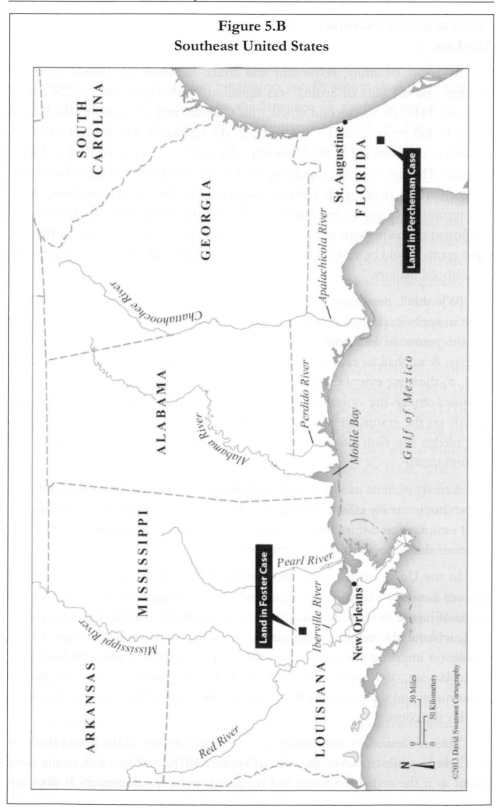

©2013 David Swanson Cartography

Washington. The rule of equality established by it cannot be rendered nugatory in any part of the United States by municipal ordinances or state laws. It stands on the same footing of supremacy as do the provisions of the Constitution and laws of the United States. It operates of itself without the aid of any legislation, state or national; and it will be applied and given authoritative effect by the courts.

The purpose of the ordinance complained of is to regulate, not to prohibit, the business of pawnbroker. But it makes it impossible for aliens to carry on the business. It need not be considered whether the State, if it sees fit, may forbid and destroy the business generally. Such a law would apply equally to aliens and citizens, and no question of conflict with the treaty would arise. The grievance here alleged is that plaintiff in error, in violation of the treaty, is denied equal opportunity. . . .

By definition contained in the ordinance, pawnbrokers are regarded as carrying on a "business." A feature of it is the lending of money upon the pledge or pawn of personal property which, in case of default, may be sold to pay the debt. While the amounts of the loans made in that business are relatively small and the character of property pledged as security is different, the transactions are similar to loans made by banks on collateral security. . . . We have found no state legislation abolishing or forbidding the business. Most, if not all, of the States provide for licensing pawnbrokers and authorize regulation by municipalities. While regulation has been found necessary in the public interest, the business is not on that account to be excluded from the trade and commerce referred to in the treaty. Many worthy occupations and lines of legitimate business are regulated by state and federal laws for the protection of the public against fraudulent and dishonest practices. There is nothing in the character of the business of pawnbroker which requires it to be excluded from the field covered by the above quoted provision, and it must be held that such business is "trade" within the meaning of the treaty. The ordinance violates the treaty. The question in the present case relates solely to Japanese subjects who have been admitted to this country. We do not pass upon the right of admission or the construction of the treaty in this respect, as that question is not before us and would require consideration of other matters with which it is not now necessary to deal. We need not consider other grounds upon which the ordinance is attacked.

Decree reversed.

Treaties and State Law. Asakura is an example of a state law being repudiated by a U.S. treaty rule. The case cited *Foster & Elam* for the proposition that a treaty "operates of itself without the aid of any legislation, state or national; and it will be applied and given authoritative effect by the courts." But did the *Asakura* Court analyze the problem of self-execution? Was it plain that the treaty norm applied in *Asakura* was self-executing by the test set out in *Foster & Elam*? What arguments might be made for and against it being self-executing?

Deteriorating U.S.-Japanese Relations. U.S.-Japanese relations only worsened. In July 1937, Japan invaded China. As one measure of protest, the United States served notice on July 26, 1939, that the U.S.-Japanese Treaty of Commerce and Navigation, at issue in *Asakura*, would be terminated in six months, permitting the United States, *inter alia*, to restrict U.S. exports to and imports from Japan. Herbert Feis, *The Road to Pearl Harbor* 8, 21–23 (1965). On December 7, 1941, the Japanese Navy launched a devastating surprise attack on the U.S. naval base at Pearl Harbor, an act of aggression that united the formerly neutrality-prone U.S. House and Senate with President Roosevelt, and the United States declared war on Japan. Anti-Japanese sentiment remained strong in the United States after the end of the Second World War in 1945, as witnessed by the next case, *Sei Fujii*. The California Supreme Court was no longer bound, of course, by the now-repudiated 1911 commerce and navigation treaty applied by the U.S. Supreme Court in *Asakura*.

SEI FUJII V. CALIFORNIA

38 Cal.2d 718, 242 P.2d 617 (1952)

The Facts

GIBSON, CHIEF JUSTICE.

Plaintiff, an alien Japanese who is ineligible to citizenship under our naturalization laws, appeals from a judgment declaring that certain land purchased by him in 1948 had escheated to the state. There is no treaty between this country and Japan which confers upon plaintiff the right to own land, and the sole question presented on this appeal is the validity of the California alien land law.

The California Alien Land Law. The 1920 California Alien Land Law had originally aimed at preventing the ownership of land by Asian nationals. By 1952, however, it affected principally Japanese aliens, since by then nationals of the Philippines, China, and India could effectively seek U.S. naturalization. See Lawrence E. Davies, "California's Law on Land is Upset," *New York Times*, Apr. 18, 1952, at 7.

Sei Fujii v. California
The Law

It is first contended that the land law has been invalidated and superseded by the provisions of the United Nations Charter pledging the member nations to promote the observance of human rights and fundamental freedoms without distinction as to race. Plaintiff relies on statements in the preamble and in articles 1, 55 and 56 of the Charter.

It is not disputed that the charter is a treaty, and our federal Constitution provides that treaties made under the authority of the United States are part of the supreme law of the land and that the judges in every state are bound thereby. U.S. Const., art. VI. A treaty, however, does not automatically supersede local laws which are inconsistent with it unless the treaty provisions are self-executing. In the words of Chief Justice Marshall: A treaty is "to be regarded in courts of justice as equivalent to an act of the Legislature, whenever it operates of itself, without the aid of any legislative provision. But when the terms of the stipulation import a contract—when either of the parties engages to perform a particular act, the treaty addresses itself to the political, not the judicial department; and the Legislature must execute the contract, before it can become a rule for the court." Foster v. Neilson, 1829, 2 Pet. (U.S.) 253.

In determining whether a treaty is self-executing courts look to the intent of the signatory parties as manifested by the language of the instrument, and, if the instrument is uncertain, recourse may be had to the circumstances surrounding its execution. . . .

In order for a treaty provision to be operative without the aid of implementing legislation and to have the force and effect of a statute, it must appear that the framers of the treaty intended to prescribe a rule that, standing alone, would be enforceable in the courts. . . .

It is clear that the provisions of the preamble and of Article 1 of the charter which are claimed to be in conflict with the alien land law are not self-executing. They state general purposes and objectives of the United Nations Organization and do not purport to impose legal obligations on the individual member nations or to create rights in private persons. It is equally clear that none of the other provisions relied on by plaintiff is self-executing. Article 55 declares that the United Nations "shall promote: . . . universal respect for, and observance of, human rights and fundamental freedoms for all without distinction as to race, sex, language, or religion," and in Article 56, the member nations "pledge themselves to take joint and separate action in cooperation with the Organization for the achievement of the purposes set forth in Article 55." Although the member nations have obligated themselves to cooperate with the international organization in promoting respect for, and observance of, human rights, it is plain that it was contemplated that future legislative action by the several nations would be required to accomplish the declared objectives, and there is nothing to indicate that these provisions were intended to become rules of law for the courts of this country upon the ratification of the charter.

The language used in articles 55 and 56 is not the type customarily employed in treaties which have been held to be self-executing and to create rights and duties in individuals. For example, the treaty involved in Clark v. Allen, 331 U.S. 503, 507–508, relating to the rights of a national of one country to inherit real property located in another country, specifically provided that "such national shall be allowed a term of three years in which to sell the [property] . . . and withdraw the proceeds . . . " free from any discriminatory taxation. In Nielsen v. Johnson, 279 U.S. 47, 50, the provision treated as being self-executing was equally definite. There each of the signatory parties agreed that "no higher or other duties, charges, or taxes of any kind, shall be levied" by one country on removal of property therefrom by citizens of the other country "than are or shall be payable in each state, upon the same, when removed by a citizen or subject of such state respectively." In other instances treaty provisions were enforced without implementing legislation where they prescribed in detail the rules governing rights and obligations of individuals or specifically provided that citizens of one nation shall have the same rights while in the other country as are enjoyed by that country's own citizens. Asakura v. Seattle, 265 U.S. 332, 340[.]

It is significant to note that when the framers of the charter intended to make certain provisions effective without the aid of implementing legislation they employed language which is clear and definite and manifests that intention. For example, Article 104 provides: "The Organization shall enjoy in the territory of each of its Members such legal capacity as may be necessary for the exercise of its functions and the fulfillment of its purposes." Article 105 provides: "1. The Organization shall enjoy in the territory of each of its Members such privileges and immunities as are necessary for the fulfillment of its purposes. 2. Representatives of the Members of the United Nations and officials of the Organization shall similarly enjoy such privileges and immunities as are necessary for the independent exercise of their functions in connection with the Organization." In Curran v. City of New York, 77 N.Y.S.2d 206, 212, these articles were treated as being self-executory.

The provisions in the charter pledging cooperation in promoting observance of fundamental freedoms lack the mandatory quality and definiteness which would indicate an intent to create justiciable rights in private persons immediately upon ratification. Instead, they are framed as a promise of future action by the member nations. Secretary of State Stettinius, Chairman of the United States delegation at the San Francisco Conference where the charter was drafted, stated in his report to President Truman that Article 56 "pledges the various countries to cooperate with the organization by joint and separate action in the achievement of the economic and social objectives of the organization without infringing upon their right to order their national affairs according to their own best ability, in their own way, and in accordance with their own political and economic institutions and processes." . . .

The humane and enlightened objectives of the United Nations Charter are, of course, entitled to respectful consideration by the courts and legislatures of every member nation, since that document expresses the universal desire of thinking men for peace and for equality of rights and opportunities. The charter represents a moral commitment of foremost importance, and we must not permit the spirit of our pledge to be compromised or disparaged in either our domestic or foreign affairs. We are satisfied, however, that the charter provisions relied on by plaintiff were not intended to supersede existing domestic legislation, and we cannot hold that they operate to invalidate the alien land law.

[The court concludes, however, that the California Alien Land Law is invalid, because it violates the 14th Amendment to the U.S. Constitution.]

The Self-executing Treaty Doctrine and the U.N. Charter. Is it clear that the *Sei Fujii* court was correct in holding the U.N. Charter provisions at issue not to be self-executing? The District Court of Appeal of California had found the Charter provisions self-executing. See Sei Fujii v. State, 217 P.2d 481 (Cal. App. 1950), *rehearing denied,* 218 P.2d 595 (Cal. App. 1950). When treaty provisions concerning individual rights conflict with state legislation, does a better case exist for finding the treaty to be self-executing than when a treaty conflicts with congressional action? Quincy Wright noted that Article 56 of the U.N. Charter imposes obligations on the United States as a party, and that Charter provisions do not prevent U.S. courts from interpreting and enforcing its obligations. The critical question then became, in Wright's view, whether Charter obligations were of a character that U.S. courts "can apply." Wright thought that the reference to "separate action in cooperation with the organization" in Article 56 "implies, as a minimum, abstention from separate action, such as enforcement of racially discriminating land laws, which would oppose the purposes of the organization." He considered national courts "more likely to be guided by general principles than are local legislatures" in interpreting and applying human rights treaty obligations, and saw "no fundamental reason why the function of incorporating international law into municipal law should be regarded as a legislative rather than a judicial function." Quincy Wright, "National Courts and Human Rights—The Fujii Case," 45 *American Journal of International Law* 62, 72, 80–81 (1951).

Professor Lockwood surveyed the use of the United Nations Charter in state and federal courts from 1946 to 1955 and found that "the Charter played a significant role in helping American courts find the United States Constitution—to redefine the due process and equal protection clauses of the 14th Amendment and the due process clause of the Fifth Amendment to reflect antiracial discrimination norms central to the Charter." Lockwood examined *Sei Fujii* and the seminal U.S. Supreme Court civil rights cases, in which human rights provisions of the Charter were raised but not addressed by the Court, and concluded that the Charter was "an important influence on the judiciary, *sub silentio*." Bert B. Lockwood, Jr., "The United Nations Charter and United States Civil Rights Litigation: 1946–1955," 69 *Iowa Law Review* 901, 902, 949 (1984).

Applying the Self-executing Treaty Rule. If the 1911 treaty analyzed in *Asakura* had been still in force in 1948, would it have conferred upon Sei Fujii the right to own land? Why was the *Sei Fujii* court more concerned than the *Asakura* court to question whether a treaty rule, in this case the U.N. Charter, was self-executing?

If the U.S. Senate, in the course of giving its advice and consent to a treaty, expresses an opinion as to whether a treaty is self-executing, should a U.S. court defer to that opinion? Should it defer to a Senate declaration that a treaty is not self-executing if the language of the treaty would otherwise suggest that it is? Should the positions of other countries, expressed during the negotiation of a treaty, be taken into account in determining the incorporation of a treaty into U.S. municipal law?

What position should a U.S. court take if the evidence concerning whether a treaty is self-executing is ambiguous? Should a U.S. court presume that a treaty provision is or is not self-executing? Is the court under an obligation to try to give effect to treaty purposes if the language of the treaty can be read both ways? See the judicial debate in *Medellín* below.

> *Treaties and State Law.* A treaty is deemed supreme over state law only when the treaty provision is incorporated in U.S. law either because it is self-executing or because it has been implemented by congressional legislation. In *Missouri v. Holland*, which follows, the Supreme Court did not need to address the self-executing treaty doctrine because Congress had passed a statute implementing the treaty at issue.

MISSOURI V. HOLLAND

252 U.S. 416 (1920)

MR. JUSTICE HOLMES delivered the opinion of the court.

This is a bill in equity brought by the State of Missouri to prevent a game warden of the United States from attempting to enforce the Migratory Bird Treaty Act of July 3, 1918, and the regulations made by the Secretary of Agriculture in pursuance of the same. The ground of the bill is that the statute is an unconstitutional interference with the rights reserved to the States by the Tenth Amendment, and that the acts of the defendant done and threatened under that authority invade the sovereign right of the State and contravene its will manifested in statutes. . . .

On December 8, 1916, a treaty between the United States and Great Britain was proclaimed by the President. It recited that many species of birds in their annual migrations traversed certain parts of the United States and of Canada, that they were of great value as a source of food and in destroying insects injurious to vegetation, but were in danger of extermination through lack of adequate protection. It therefore provided for specified close seasons and protection in other forms, and agreed that the two powers would take or propose to their law-making bodies the necessary measures for carrying the treaty out. The above mentioned Act of July 3, 1918, entitled an act to give effect to the convention, prohibited the killing, capturing or selling any of the migratory birds included in the terms of the treaty except as permitted by regulations compatible with those terms, to be made by the Secretary of Agriculture. Regulations were proclaimed on July 31, and October 25, 1918. It is unnecessary to go into any details, because, as we have said, the question raised is the general one whether the treaty and statute are void as an interference with the rights reserved to the States.

To answer this question it is not enough to refer to the Tenth Amendment, reserving the powers not delegated to the United States, because by Article II, § 2, the power to make treaties is delegated expressly, and by Article VI treaties made under the authority of the United States, along with the Constitution and laws of the United States made in pursuance thereof, are declared the supreme law of the land. If the treaty is valid there can be no dispute about the validity of the statute under Article I, § 8, as a necessary and proper means to execute the powers of the Government. The language of the Constitution as to the supremacy of treaties being general, the question before us is narrowed to an inquiry into the ground upon which the present supposed exception is placed.

It is said that a treaty cannot be valid if it infringes the Constitution, that there are limits, therefore, to the treaty-making power, and that one such limit is that what an act of Congress could not do unaided, in derogation of the powers reserved to the States, a treaty cannot do. An earlier act of Congress [of March 4, 1913] that attempted by itself and not in pursuance of a treaty to regulate the killing of migratory birds within the States had been held bad in the District Court. *United States v. Shauver*, 214 Fed. Rep. 154. *United States v. McCullagh*, 221 Fed. Rep. 288. Those decisions were supported by arguments that migratory birds were owned by the States in their sovereign capacity for the benefit of their people, and that under cases like *Geer v. Connecticut*, 161 U.S. 519, this control was one that Congress had no power to displace. The same argument is supposed to apply now with equal force.

Whether the two cases cited were decided rightly or not they cannot be accepted as a test of the treaty power. Acts of Congress are the supreme law of the land only when made in pursuance of the Constitution, while treaties are declared to be so when made under the authority of the United States. It is open to question whether the authority of the United States means more than the formal acts prescribed to make the convention. We do not mean to imply that there are no qualifications to the treaty-making power; but they must be ascertained in a different way. It is obvious that there may be matters of the sharpest exigency for the national well being that an act of Congress could not deal with but that a treaty followed by such an act could, and it is not lightly to be assumed that, in matters requiring national action, "a power which must belong to and somewhere reside in every civilized government" is not to be found. *Andrews v. Andrews*, 188 U.S. 14. What was said in that case with regard to the powers of the States applies with equal force to the powers of the nation in cases where the States individually are incompetent to act. We are not yet discussing the particular case before us but only are considering the validity of the test proposed. With regard to that we may add that when we are dealing with words that also are a constituent act, like the Constitution of the United States, we must realize that they have called into life a being the development of which could not have been foreseen completely by the most gifted of its begetters. It was enough for them to realize or to hope that they had created an organism; it has taken a century and has cost their successors much sweat and blood to prove that they created a nation. The case before us must be considered in the light of our whole experience and not merely in that of what was said 100 years ago. The treaty in question does not contravene any prohibitory words to be found in the Constitution. The only question is whether it is forbidden by some invisible radiation from the general terms of the Tenth Amendment. We must consider what this country has become in deciding what that Amendment has reserved.

The State as we have intimated founds its claim of exclusive authority upon an assertion of title to migratory birds, an assertion that is embodied in statute. No doubt it is true that as between a State and its inhabitants the State may regulate the killing and sale of such birds, but it does not follow that its authority is exclusive of paramount powers. To put the claim of the State upon title is to lean upon a slender reed. Wild birds are not in the possession of anyone; and possession is the beginning of ownership. The whole foundation of the State's rights is the presence within their jurisdiction of birds that yesterday had not arrived, tomorrow may be in another State and in a week a thousand miles away. If we are to be accurate we cannot put the case of the State upon higher ground than that the treaty deals with creatures that for the moment are within the state borders, that it must be carried out by officers of the United States within the same territory, and that but for the treaty the State would be free to regulate this subject itself.

As most of the laws of the United States are carried out within the States and as many of them deal with matters which in the silence of such laws the State might regulate, such general grounds are not enough to support Missouri's claim. Valid treaties of course "are as binding within the territorial limits of the States as they are elsewhere throughout the dominion of the United States." No doubt the great body of private relations usually fall within the control of the State, but a treaty may override its power. We do not have to invoke the later developments of constitutional law for this proposition; it was recognized as early as *Hopkirk v. Bell*, 3 Cranch, 454, with regard to statutes of limitation, and even earlier, as to confiscation, in *Ware v. Hylton*, 3 Dall. 199. It was assumed by Chief Justice Marshall with regard to the escheat of land to the State in *Chirac v. Chirac*, 2 Wheat. 259, 275. So as to a limited jurisdiction of foreign consuls within a State. *Wildenhus's Case*, 120 U.S. 1. Further illustration seems unnecessary, and it only remains to consider the application of established rules to the present case.

Here a national interest of very nearly the first magnitude is involved. It can be protected only by national action in concert with that of another power. The subject matter is only transitorily within the State and has no permanent habitat therein. But for the treaty and the statute there soon might be no birds for any powers to deal with. We see nothing in the Constitution that compels the Government to sit by while a food supply is cut off and the protectors of our forests and our crops are destroyed. It is not sufficient to rely upon the States. The reliance is vain, and were it otherwise, the question is whether the United States is forbidden to act. We are of opinion that the treaty and statute must be upheld.

Decree affirmed.

Constitution-based Limits to the Treaty-making Power. Justice Holmes wrote that "we do not mean to imply that there are no qualifications to the treaty-making power; but they must be ascertained in a different way." How well did he explicate that way? Is the problem here that Missouri's alleged constitutional prohibition was via "some invisible radiation from the general terms of the Tenth Amendment"? Would a specific constitutional prohibition, *e.g.*, respecting rights to a jury trial in criminal cases, suffice as a qualification on or a limitation to the treaty-making power? In *Reid v. Covert*, which concerned rights to a jury trial under Article III and the Fifth and Sixth Amendments, the Supreme Court held that "no agreement with a foreign nation can confer power on the Congress, or on any other branch of Government, which is free from the restraints of the Constitution." 354 U.S. 1, 16 (1957).

Justice Holmes in *Missouri v. Holland* justified the Supreme Court's decision in part because "a national interest of very nearly the first magnitude is involved." The Treaty was commended in the press as "probably the most important movement for the protection of birds ever instituted in this country or the Dominion." "Safety for the Birds," *New York Times*, Dec. 5, 1916, at 10. Would Missouri's authority to regulate migratory birds have been greater if the national need had been less?

In *Missouri v. Holland*, questions about the scope of the treaty-making power were posed starkly because a federal statute regulating migratory birds, passed before the 1916 treaty was concluded, had been struck down. Did Holmes mean to say that the federal government could achieve ends by way of treaty-making when it cannot do so by simple legislation?

The Historical Context. Note Holmes's language about Americans' cost in "sweat and blood to prove that they created a nation." Holmes had fought in the Civil War as a Union Army officer in the 20th Massachusetts Volunteer Regiment. He was shot twice, at Ball's Bluff in 1861 and at Antietam in 1862.

Both times Holmes was near death. Many of his friends served alongside him and were killed or injured. When his close friend, Henry Abbott, was killed in the 1864 Wilderness Campaign, Holmes wrote, "nearly every Regimental [officer] I know or cared for is dead or wounded." Altogether, about 360,000 died for the Union; about 200,000 more died for the Confederacy. Is it hard to understand why Holmes was committed to the national union of the United States? See Mark W. Janis, "*Missouri v. Holland*: Birds, Wars, and Rights," in *International Law Stories* 207, 216–17 (John E. Noyes, Laura A. Dickinson & Mark W. Janis eds. 2007).

The Politics and Law of Federalism. There have always been political and legal tensions between the several states and the United States. The Civil War was, in large measure, about whether the federal government, increasingly dominated by the North and West, would be permitted to interfere with and perhaps even prohibit the South's "peculiar institution," slavery. The controversy over state or federal regulation of migratory birds detailed in *Missouri v. Holland* took place within the context of this larger issue. Holmes's nationalistic judgment was immediately controversial, and so it has remained. *Missouri v. Holland* was at the center of legal and political debates about whether the federal government and its treaties should limit state laws providing for "separate-but-equal" treatment of minorities and prohibiting inter-racial marriages. Advocating the states-rights point of view, the President of the American Bar Association complained in 1949 that *Missouri v. Holland* promoted what he disparagingly termed "so-called human rights." Frank E. Holman, "International Proposals affecting So-Called Human Rights," 14 *Law and Contemporary Problems* 479 (1949).

Nowadays, the debate over Holmes's judgment in *Missouri v. Holland* focuses on such states-rights issues as women's rights, affirmative action, and the death penalty. See David M. Golove, "Treaty-Making and the Nation: The Historical Foundations of the Nationalist Conception of the Treaty Power," 98 *Michigan Law Review* 1075 (2000); Oona A. Hathaway *et al.*, "The Treaty Power: Its History, Scope, and Limits," 98 *Cornell Law Review* 239 (2013). For the Supreme Court's contrasting views on the power of the states in foreign affairs, compare its judgment in *Missouri v. Holland* with *Medellín* below.

State Law and Foreign Affairs. Federalism limits states in their attempts to legislate respecting foreign affairs. In *Crosby v. National Foreign Trade Council*, 530 U.S. 363 (2000), the U.S. Supreme Court struck down a statute of Massachusetts prohibiting state agencies from purchasing goods or services from companies doing business with Burma. In 2012 the Supreme Court held that an Arizona statute aimed at curbing illegal aliens was preempted by national powers to regulate immigration. Arizona v. United States, 567 U.S. 387 (2012).

Some commentators have argued that it would be appropriate for states to take a larger role in international politics. See Curtis A. Bradley, "The Treaty Power and American Federalism," 97 *Michigan Law Review* 390 (1998). Most, however, have supported the long-standing position that the United States should speak with one voice in foreign affairs. See Martin S. Flaherty, "Are We to be a Nation? Federal Power vs. 'States' Rights' in Foreign Affairs," 70 *University of Colorado Law Review* 1277 (1999).

Treaties and Federal Law. With *Asakura, Sei Fujii,* and *Missouri* we have been looking at the relation between the states and treaties. What is the status of treaties *vis-à-vis* federal law? *Whitney* and *Belmont* below explore this issue.

WHITNEY V. ROBERTSON

124 U.S. 190 (1888)

MR. JUSTICE FIELD delivered the opinion of the court.

The plaintiffs are merchants, doing business in the city of New York, and in August, 1882, they imported a large quantity of "centrifugal and molasses sugars," the produce and manufacture of the island of San Domingo. These goods were similar in kind to sugars produced in the Hawaiian Islands, which are admitted free of duty under the treaty with the king of those islands, and the act of Congress, passed to carry the treaty into effect. They were duly entered at the custom house at the port of New York, the plaintiffs claiming that by the treaty with the Republic of San Domingo the goods should be admitted on the same terms, that is, free of duty, as similar articles, the produce and manufacture of the Hawaiian Islands. The defendant, who was at the time collector of the port, refused to allow this claim, treated the goods as dutiable articles under the acts of Congress, and exacted duties on them to the amount of $21,936. The plaintiffs appealed from the collector's decision to the Secretary of the Treasury, by whom the appeal was denied. They then paid under protest the duties exacted, and brought the present action to recover the amount. . . .

The treaty with the king of the Hawaiian Islands [of January 30, 1875] provides for the importation into the United States, free of duty, of various articles, the produce and manufacture of those islands, in consideration, among other things, of like exemption from duty, on the importation into that country, of sundry specified articles which are the produce and manufacture of the United States. 19 Stat. 625. The language of the first two articles of the treaty, which recite the reciprocal engagements of the two countries, declares that they are made in consideration "of the rights and privileges" and "as an equivalent therefor," which one concedes to the other.

The plaintiffs rely for a like exemption of the sugars imported by them from San Domingo upon the 9th article of the treaty with the Dominican Republic [of February 8, 1867], which is as follows: "No higher or other duty shall be imposed on the importation into the United States of any article the growth, produce, or manufacture of the Dominican Republic, or of her fisheries; and no higher or other duty shall be imposed on the importation into the Dominican Republic of any article the growth, produce, or manufacture of the United States, or their fisheries, than are or shall be payable on the like articles the growth, produce, or manufacture of any other foreign country, or its fisheries." 15 Stat. 473, 478. . . .

But . . . there is [a] complete answer to the pretensions of the plaintiffs. The [1870] Act of Congress under which the duties were collected authorized their exaction. It is of general application, making no exceptions in favor of goods of any country. It was passed after the Treaty with the Dominican Republic; and if there be any conflict between the stipulations of the Treaty and the requirements of the law the latter must control. . . . By the Constitution a treaty is placed on the same footing, and made of like obligation, with an act of legislation. Both are declared by that instrument to be the supreme law of the land, and no superior efficacy is given to either over the other. When the two relate to the same subject, the courts will always endeavor to construe them so as to give effect to both, if that can be done without violating the language of either; but if the two are inconsistent, the one last in date will control the other, provided always the stipulation of the treaty on the subject is self-executing. If the country with which the treaty is made is dissatisfied with the action of the legislative department, it may present its complaint to the executive head of the government, and take such other measures as it may deem essential for the protection of its interests. The courts can afford no redress. Whether the complaining nation has just cause of complaint, or our country was justified in its legislation, are not matters for judicial cognizance.

Judgment affirmed.

The Last-in-time Rule. With *Whitney* we move to the second sort of conflicts between treaties and U.S. domestic law—clashes with national law and institutions. Though the Court in *Whitney* refused to enforce a U.S. treaty promising to provide most-favored-nation treatment to imports from San Domingo (present-day Dominican Republic), it made the general proposition that in case of a conflict between a federal statute and a treaty, "the one last in date will control," a proposition generally favorable to the status of international agreements. Does Article VI(2) of the Constitution, the Supremacy Clause, itself prescribe any rule as to the relationship between federal law and treaties? Is any other solution preferable to the last-in-time rule? How far should the courts go as they "always endeavor to construe" treaties and federal statutes "so as to give effect to both"?

Self-executing Treaties. Would the Supreme Court in *Whitney* have needed to apply the last-in-time rule if the 1867 treaty with the Dominican Republic were not self-executing? Should the 1875 treaty with Hawaii, which entered into effect in 1876, have allowed the plaintiffs to import sugar duty-free, overriding the 1870 statute that the Court used as its rule of decision? Why was the treaty with Hawaii not self-executing? See David Sloss, "Non-Self-Executing Treaties: Exposing a Constitutional Fallacy," 36 *U.C. Davis Law Review* 1, 32–35 (2002).

Dualism, Treaties, and the Role of Courts. Note that the Supreme Court took a dualistic view of the relationship between international law and municipal law: "If the country with which the treaty is made is dissatisfied with the action of the legislative department, it may present its complaint to the executive head of the government, and take such other measures as it may deem essential for the protection of its interests." Dualism remains popular in the United States as a way to protect the U.S. democratic decision-making process, especially the domestic legislative process.

In the United Kingdom, where no treaty is considered self-executing, the courts have taken a comparable stand about the dualistic nature of international law and municipal law. For example, in *The Parlement Belge*, a British court refused to incorporate a treaty provision that gave immunity to a Belgian packet-boat conveying mails because the immunity had not been enacted into statutory form by the British Parliament. Responding to an objection that this broke faith with Belgium, the judge wrote: "I acknowledge the hardship, but the remedy, in my opinion, is not to be found in depriving the British subject without his consent, direct or implied, of his right of action against a wrong-doer, but by the agency of diplomacy, and proper measures of compensation arrangement, between the Governments of Great Britain and Belgium." 4 P.D. 129, 155 (1879). Where, then, in the *Whitney Case* should the government of San Domingo have gone to complain about the actions of the United States?

Many civil law jurisdictions take an opposite tack from the tradition in the United Kingdom and provide that treaties, and indeed international law in general, are supreme over municipal law in municipal courts, even if not incorporated by legislation. See Mark Weston Janis, *International Law* 112–13 (7th ed. 2016).

Does it matter if the "treaty" is, in fact, an international agreement that binds the United States in international law, but has never been submitted to the Senate? *Belmont* below addressed that question.

UNITED STATES V. BELMONT

301 U.S. 324 (1937)

The Facts

MR. JUSTICE SUTHERLAND delivered the opinion of the Court.

This is an action at law brought by petitioner against respondents in a federal district court to recover a sum of money deposited by a Russian corporation (Petrograd Metal Works) with August Belmont, a private banker doing business in New York City under the name of August Belmont & Co. August Belmont died in 1924; and respondents are the duly-appointed executors of his will. A motion to dismiss the complaint for failure to state facts sufficient to constitute a cause of action was sustained by the district court, and its judgment was affirmed by the court below. The facts alleged, so far as necessary to be stated, follow.

The corporation had deposited with Belmont, prior to 1918, the sum of money which petitioner seeks to recover. In 1918, the Soviet Government duly enacted a decree by which it dissolved, terminated and liquidated the corporation (together with others), and nationalized and appropriated all of its property and assets of every kind and wherever situated, including the deposit account with Belmont. As a result, the deposit became the property of the Soviet Government, and so remained until November 16, 1933, at which time the Soviet Government released and assigned to petitioner all amounts due to that government from American nationals, including the deposit account of the corporation with Belmont. Respondents failed and refused to pay the amount upon demand duly made by petitioner.

The assignment was effected by an exchange of diplomatic correspondence between the Soviet Government and the United States. The purpose was to bring about a final settlement of the claims and counterclaims between the Soviet Government and the United States; and it was agreed that the Soviet Government would take no steps to enforce claims against American nationals; but all such claims were released and assigned to the United States, with the understanding that the Soviet Government was to be duly notified of all amounts realized by the

United States from such release and assignment. The assignment and requirement for notice are parts of the larger plan to bring about a settlement of the rival claims of the high contracting parties. The continuing and definite interest of the Soviet Government in the collection of assigned claims is evident; and the case, therefore, presents a question of public concern, the determination of which well might involve the good faith of the United States in the eyes of a foreign government. The court below held that the assignment thus effected embraced the claim here in question; and with that we agree.

That court, however, took the view that the situs of the bank deposit was within the State of New York; that in no sense could it be regarded as an intangible property right within Soviet territory; and that the nationalization decree, if enforced, would put into effect an act of confiscation. And it held that a judgment for the United States could not be had, because, in view of that result, it would be contrary to the controlling public policy of the State of New York. The further contention is made by respondents that the public policy of the United States would likewise be infringed by such a judgment.

The Roosevelt-Litvinov Agreement. Belmont validated the Roosevelt-Litvinov Agreement, a matter of some importance in U.S.-U.S.S.R. relations. At the time of the Supreme Court's decision there were 15 similar lawsuits in the U.S. courts involving more than $8,000,000. The Petrograd Metal Works deposit with August Belmont & Co. was itself only $25,438. "Pact with Soviet on Claims Upheld," *New York Times*, May 4, 1937, at 14. To gain U.S. recognition of the Soviet Union, Maxim Litvinov, the Soviet Foreign Minister, not only assigned assets, like those in this case, to the United States, but pledged that the U.S.S.R. would not propagandize in the United States and that it would give religious freedom to U.S. citizens resident in the Soviet Union. The Soviet Union also gave up its claims against the United States for damage caused by U.S. troops during a 1918 intervention in Siberia. The exchange of letters comprising the Roosevelt-Litvinov Agreement appears at 28 *American Journal of International Law* 1 (Supp. 1934).

United States v. Belmont
The Law

We do not pause to inquire whether in fact there was any policy of the State of New York to be infringed, since we are of opinion that no state policy can prevail against the international compact here involved. . . .

We take judicial notice of the fact that coincident with the assignment set forth in the complaint, the President recognized the Soviet Government, and normal diplomatic relations were established between that government and the Government of the United States, followed by an exchange of ambassadors. The effect of this was to validate, so far as this country is concerned, all acts of the Soviet Government here involved from the commencement of its existence. The recognition, establishment of diplomatic relations, the assignment, and agreements with respect thereto, were all parts of one transaction, resulting in an international compact between the two governments. That the negotiations, acceptance of the assignment and agreements and understandings in respect thereof were within the competence of the President may not be doubted. Governmental power over internal affairs is distributed between the national government and the several states. Governmental power over external affairs is not distributed, but is vested exclusively in the national government. And in respect of what was done here, the Executive had authority to speak as the sole organ of that government. The assignment and the agreements in connection therewith did not, as in the case of treaties, as that term is used in the treaty making clause of the Constitution (Art. II, § 2), require the advice and consent of the Senate.

A treaty signifies "a compact made between two or more independent nations with a view to the public welfare." *Altman & Co. v. United States*, 224 U.S. 583, 600. But an international compact, as this was, is not always a treaty which requires the participation of the Senate. There are many such compacts, of which a protocol, a modus vivendi, a postal convention, and agreements like that now under consideration are illustrations. [A]lthough this might not be a treaty requiring ratification by the Senate, it was a compact negotiated and proclaimed under the authority of the President, and as such was a "treaty" within the meaning of the Circuit Court of Appeals Act, the construction of which might be reviewed upon direct appeal to this court.

Plainly, the external powers of the United States are to be exercised without regard to state laws or policies. The supremacy of a treaty in this respect has been recognized from the beginning. Mr. Madison, in the Virginia Convention, said that if a treaty does not supersede existing state laws, as far as they contravene its operation, the treaty would be ineffective. "To counteract it by the supremacy of the state laws, would bring on the Union the just charge of national perfidy, and involve us in war." 3 Elliot's Debates 515. And see *Ware v. Hylton*, 3 Dall. 199, 236–237. And while this rule in respect of treaties is established by the express language of cl. 2, Art. VI, of the Constitution, the same rule would result in the case of all international compacts and agreements from the very fact that complete power over international affairs is in the national government and is not and cannot be subject to any curtailment of interference on the part of the several states. In respect of all international negotiations and compacts, and in respect of our foreign relations generally, state lines disappear. As to such purposes the State of New York does not exist. Within the field of its powers, whatever the United States rightfully undertakes, it necessarily has warrant to consummate. And when judicial authority is invoked in aid of such consummation, state constitutions, state laws, and state policies are irrelevant to the inquiry and decision. It is inconceivable that any of them can be interposed as an obstacle to the effective operation of a federal constitutional power. Cf. *Missouri v. Holland*, 252 U.S. 416; *Asakura v. Seattle*, 265 U.S. 332, 341.

Executive Agreements and the Constitution. Is it plain that the Constitution meant to give all international agreements supremacy over state laws? Or only those that had been favorably reviewed by the Senate? As a result of cases like *Belmont*, the term "treaty" really has two meanings in the U.S. Constitution. First, there is the "treaty" in Article II(2) that requires the "advice and consent" of the Senate. Second, there is the "treaty" in Article VI(2) that, along with the Constitution and U.S. law, is given supremacy. Should executive agreements benefit from *Foster*'s doctrine of self-execution or *Whitney*'s last-in-time rule? Although scholars have exhaustively explored the original intent of the drafters of the Constitution, it is far from agreed whether it was originally intended that executive agreements have much the same force in domestic law as treaties approved by the Senate.

In practice, executive agreements have proven to be enormously important. Between 1980 and 1992, some 4,510 new executive agreements were made against only 218 treaties that received the advice and consent of the Senate. It is hard to see how the U.S. could honor its international obligations in practice if every international agreement required Senate approval. As Professor Vagts has observed, "[r]unning the likes of 6,500 agreements through the Senate for its advice and consent would be enormously disruptive and would likely prevent the conduct of almost all other business, unless some massive unanimous consent operation could be mounted." Detlev F. Vagts, "International Agreements, the Senate and the Constitution," 36 *Columbia Journal of Transnational Law* 143, 145 (1997).

DAMES & MOORE V. REGAN

453 U.S. 654 (1981)

The Facts

JUSTICE REHNQUIST delivered the opinion of the Court.

The questions presented by this case touch fundamentally upon the manner in which our Republic is to be governed. Throughout the nearly two centuries of our Nation's existence under the Constitution, this subject has generated considerable debate. We have had the benefit of commentators such as John Jay, Alexander Hamilton, and James Madison writing in The Federalist Papers at the Nation's very inception, the benefit of astute foreign observers of our system such as Alexis de Tocqueville and James Bryce writing during the first century of the Nation's existence, and the benefit of many other treatises as well as more than 400 volumes of reports of decisions of this Court. As these writings reveal it is doubtless both futile and perhaps dangerous to find any epigrammatical explanation of how this country has been governed.

. . . We are confined to a resolution of the dispute presented to us. That dispute involves various Executive Orders and regulations by which the President nullified attachments and liens on Iranian assets in the United States, directed that these assets be transferred to Iran, and suspended claims against Iran that may be presented to an International Claims Tribunal. This action was taken in an effort to comply with an Executive Agreement between the United States and Iran. We granted certiorari before judgment in this case, and set an expedited briefing and argument schedule, because lower courts had reached conflicting conclusions on the validity of the President's actions and, as the Solicitor General informed us, unless the Government acted by July 19, 1981, Iran could consider the United States to be in breach of the Executive Agreement.

[T]he decisions of the Court in this area have been rare, episodic, and afford little precedential value for subsequent cases. The tensions present in any exercise of executive power under the tripartite system of Federal Government established by the Constitution have been reflected in opinions by Members of this Court more than once. The Court stated in *United States* v. *Curtiss-Wright Export Corp.*, 299 U.S. 304, 319–320 (1936):

> [W]e are here dealing not alone with an authority vested in the President by an exertion of legislative power, but with such an authority plus the very delicate, plenary and exclusive power of the President as the sole organ of the federal government in the field of international relations— a power which does not require as a basis for its exercise an act of

Congress, but which, of course, like every other governmental power, must be exercised in subordination to the applicable provisions of the Constitution.

And yet 16 years later, Justice Jackson in his concurring opinion in *Youngstown [Sheet & Tube Co. v. Sawyer*, 343 U.S. 579 (1952)], which both parties agree brings together as much combination of analysis and common sense as there is in this area, focused not on the "plenary and exclusive power of the President" but rather responded to a claim of virtually unlimited powers for the Executive by noting:

> The example of such unlimited executive power that must have most impressed the forefathers was the prerogative exercised by George III, and the description of its evils in the Declaration of Independence leads me to doubt that they were creating their new Executive in his image.

As we now turn to the factual and legal issues in this case, we freely confess that we are obviously deciding only one more episode in the never-ending tension between the President exercising the executive authority in a world that presents each day some new challenge with which he must deal and the Constitution under which we all live and which no one disputes embodies some sort of system of checks and balances.

On November 4, 1979, the American Embassy in Tehran was seized and our diplomatic personnel were captured and held hostage. In response to that crisis, President Carter, acting pursuant to the International Emergency Economic Powers Act, 91 Stat. 1626, 50 U.S.C. §§ 1701–1706 (1976 ed., Supp. III) (hereinafter IEEPA), declared a national emergency on November 14, 1979, and blocked the removal or transfer of "all property and interests in property of the Government of Iran, its instrumentalities and controlled entities and the Central Bank of Iran which are or become subject to the jurisdiction of the United States. . . . " Exec. Order No. 12170, 3 CFR 457 (1980). President Carter authorized the Secretary of the Treasury to promulgate regulations carrying out the blocking order. On November 15, 1979, the Treasury Department's Office of Foreign Assets Control issued a regulation providing that "[u]nless licensed or authorized . . . any attachment, judgment, decree, lien, execution, garnishment, or other judicial process is null and void with respect to any property in which on or since [November 14, 1979,] there existed an interest of Iran." 31 CFR § 535.203(e) (1980). The regulations also made clear that any licenses or authorizations granted could be "amended, modified, or revoked at any time." § 535.805.

On November 26, 1979, the President granted a general license authorizing certain judicial proceedings against Iran but which did not allow the "entry of any judgment or of any decree or order of similar or analogous effect. . . . " § 535.504(a). On December 19, 1979, a clarifying regulation was issued stating that "the general authorization for judicial proceedings contained in § 535.504(a) includes pre-judgment attachment." § 535.418.

On December 19, 1979, petitioner Dames & Moore filed suit in the United States District Court for the Central District of California against the Government of Iran, the Atomic Energy Organization of Iran, and a number of Iranian banks. In its complaint, petitioner alleged that its wholly owned subsidiary, Dames & Moore International, S. R. L., was a party to a written contract with the Atomic Energy Organization, and that the subsidiary's entire interest in the contract had been assigned to petitioner. Under the contract, the subsidiary was to conduct site studies for a proposed nuclear power plant in Iran. As provided in the terms of the contract, the Atomic Energy Organization terminated the agreement for its own convenience on June 30, 1979. Petitioner contended, however, that it was owed $3,436,694.30 plus interest for services performed under the contract prior to the date of termination. The District Court issued orders of attachment directed against property of the defendants, and the property of certain Iranian banks was then attached to secure any judgment that might be entered against them.

On January 20, 1981, the Americans held hostage were released by Iran pursuant to an Agreement entered into the day before and embodied in two Declarations of the Democratic and Popular Republic of Algeria. The Agreement stated that "[i]t is the purpose of [the United States and Iran] . . . to terminate all litigation as between the Government of each party and the nationals of the other, and to bring about the settlement and termination of all such claims through binding arbitration." In furtherance of this goal, the Agreement called for the establishment of an Iran-United States Claims Tribunal which would arbitrate any claims not settled within six months. Awards of the Claims Tribunal are to be "final and binding" and "enforceable . . . in the courts of any nation in accordance with its laws." Under the Agreement, the United States is obligated

> to terminate all legal proceedings in United States courts involving
> claims of United States persons and institutions against Iran and its state
> enterprises, to nullify all attachments and judgments obtained therein,
> to prohibit all further litigation based on such claims, and to bring about
> the termination of such claims through binding arbitration.

In addition, the United States must "act to bring about the transfer" by July 19, 1981, of all Iranian assets held in this country by American banks. One billion dollars of these assets will be deposited in a security account in the Bank of England, to the account of the Algerian Central Bank, and used to satisfy awards rendered against Iran by the Claims Tribunal.

On January 19, 1981, President Carter issued a series of Executive Orders implementing the terms of the agreement. These Orders revoked all licenses permitting the exercise of "any right, power, or privilege" with regard to Iranian funds, securities, or deposits; "nullified" all non-Iranian interests in such assets acquired subsequent to the blocking order of November 14, 1979; and required those banks holding Iranian assets to transfer them "to the Federal Reserve Bank of New York, to be held or transferred as directed by the Secretary of the Treasury." Exec. Order No. 12279, 46 Fed. Reg. 7919.

On February 24, 1981, President Reagan issued an Executive Order in which he "ratified" the January 19th Executive Orders. Exec. Order No. 12294, 46 Fed. Reg. 14111. Moreover, he "suspended" all "claims which may be presented to the . . . Tribunal" and provided that such claims "shall have no legal effect in any action now pending in any court of the United States." The suspension of any particular claim terminates if the Claims Tribunal determines that it has no jurisdiction over that claim; claims are discharged for all purposes when the Claims Tribunal either awards some recovery and that amount is paid, or determines that no recovery is due.

Meanwhile, on January 27, 1981, petitioner moved for summary judgment in the District Court against the Government of Iran and the Atomic Energy Organization, but not against the Iranian banks. The District Court granted petitioner's motion and awarded petitioner the amount claimed under the contract plus interest. Thereafter, petitioner attempted to execute the judgment by obtaining writs of garnishment and execution in state court in the State of Washington, and a sheriff's sale of Iranian property in Washington was noticed to satisfy the judgment. However, by order of May 28, 1981, as amended by order of June 8, the District Court stayed execution of its judgment pending appeal by the Government of Iran and the Atomic Energy Organization. The District Court also ordered that all prejudgment attachments obtained against the Iranian defendants be vacated and that further proceedings against the bank defendants be stayed in light of the Executive Orders discussed above.

On April 28, 1981, petitioner filed this action in the District Court for declaratory and injunctive relief against the United States and the Secretary of the Treasury, seeking to prevent enforcement of the Executive Orders and Treasury Department regulations implementing the Agreement with Iran. . . .

The Hostages Crisis. Dames & Moore grew out of the 1979–1981 hostages crisis. We also looked at the U.S.-Iran conflict when we read the *Diplomatic and Consular Staff Case* in Chapter 4. Why did President Carter block all Iranian assets in the United States? Why did he initially permit private suits against Iran like that brought by Dames & Moore? Did the executive branch "use" private litigants to further the goals of American foreign policy? On President Carter's attempt to end the hostages crisis before he left office, see Jimmy Carter, *Keeping Faith: Memoirs of a President* 580–95 (1982). President Carter wrote that the "release of the American hostages had almost become an obsession with me." *Id.* at 594.

Dames & Moore v. Regan
The Law

The parties and the lower courts, confronted with the instant questions, have all agreed that much relevant analysis is contained in *Youngstown Sheet & Tube Co. v. Sawyer*, 343 U.S. 579 (1952). Justice Black's opinion for the Court in that case, involving the validity of President Truman's effort to seize the country's steel mills in the wake of a nationwide strike, recognized that "[t]he President's power, if any, to issue the order must stem either from an act of Congress or from the Constitution itself." Justice Jackson's concurring opinion elaborated in a general way the consequences of different types of interaction between the two democratic branches in assessing Presidential authority to act in any given case. When the President acts pursuant to an express or implied authorization from Congress, he exercises not only his powers but also those delegated by Congress. In such a case the executive action "would be supported by the strongest of presumptions and the widest latitude of judicial interpretation, and the burden of persuasion would rest heavily upon any who might attack it." When the President acts in the absence of congressional authorization he may enter "a zone of twilight in which he and Congress may have concurrent authority, or in which its distribution is uncertain." In such a case the analysis becomes more complicated, and the validity of the President's action, at least so far as separation-of-powers principles are concerned, hinges on a consideration of all the circumstances which might shed light on the views of the Legislative Branch toward such action, including "congressional inertia, indifference or quiescence." Finally, when the President acts in contravention of the will of Congress, "his power is at its lowest ebb," and the Court can sustain his actions "only by disabling the Congress from acting upon the subject." . . .

In nullifying post-November 14, 1979, attachments and directing those persons holding blocked Iranian funds and securities to transfer them to the Federal Reserve Bank of New York for ultimate transfer to Iran, President Carter cited five sources of express or inherent power. The Government, however, has principally relied on § 1702(a)(1) [of the IEEPA], as authorization for these actions.

[Justice Rehnquist concludes that Section 1702(a)(1) of the IEEPA explicitly authorized the President to nullify the attachments and transfer the assets.]

Because the President's action in nullifying the attachments and ordering the transfer of the assets was taken pursuant to specific congressional authorization, it is "supported by the strongest of presumptions and the widest latitude of judicial interpretation, and the burden of persuasion would rest heavily upon any who might attack it." *Youngstown,* 343 U.S., at 637 (Jackson, J., concurring). Under the circumstances of this case, we cannot say that petitioner has sustained that heavy burden. A contrary ruling would mean that the Federal Government as a whole lacked the power exercised by the President, and that we are not prepared to say.

IV

Although we have concluded that the IEEPA constitutes specific congressional authorization to the President to nullify the attachments and order the transfer of Iranian assets, there remains the question of the President's authority to suspend claims pending in American courts. Such claims have, of course, an existence apart from the attachments which accompanied them. In terminating these claims through Executive Order No. 12294, the President purported to act under authority of both the IEEPA and 22 U.S.C. § 1732, the so-called "Hostage Act." 48 Fed. Reg. 14111 (1981).

We conclude that although the IEEPA authorized the nullification of the attachments, it cannot be read to authorize the suspension of the claims. The claims of American citizens against Iran are not in themselves transactions involving Iranian property or efforts to exercise any rights with respect to such property. An *in personam* lawsuit, although it might eventually be reduced to judgment and that judgment might be executed upon, is an effort to establish liability and fix damages and does not focus on any particular property within the jurisdiction. The terms of the IEEPA therefore do not authorize the President to suspend claims in American courts.

[Similarly, the Hostage Act does not authorize the President to suspend the claims.]

Although we have declined to conclude that the IEEPA or the Hostage Act directly authorizes the President's suspension of claims for the reasons noted, we cannot ignore the general tenor of Congress' legislation in this area in trying to determine whether the President is acting alone or at least with the acceptance of Congress. As we have noted, Congress cannot anticipate and legislate with regard to every possible action the President may find it necessary to take or every possible situation in which he might act. . . .

Not infrequently in affairs between nations, outstanding claims by nationals of one country against the government of another country are "sources of friction" between the two sovereigns. *United States v. Pink,* 315 U.S. 203, 225 (1942). To resolve these difficulties, nations have often entered into agreements settling the claims of their respective nationals. As one treatise writer puts it, international agreements settling claims by nationals of one state against the government of another "are established international practice reflecting traditional international theory." L. Henkin, Foreign Affairs and the Constitution 262 (1972). Consistent with that principle, the United States has repeatedly exercised its sovereign authority to settle the claims of its nationals against foreign countries. Though those settlements have sometimes been made by treaty, there has also been a longstanding practice of settling such claims by executive agreement without the advice and consent of the Senate. Under such agreements, the President has agreed to renounce or extinguish claims of United States nationals against foreign governments in return for lump-sum payments or the establishment of arbitration procedures. . . . It is clear that the practice of settling claims continues today. Since 1952, the President has entered into at least 10 binding settlements with foreign nations, including an $80 million settlement with the People's Republic of China.

Crucial to our decision today is the conclusion that Congress has implicitly approved the practice of claim settlement by executive agreement. This is best demonstrated by Congress' enactment of the International Claims Settlement Act of 1949, 22 U.S.C. § 1621 *et seq.* . . . By creating a procedure to implement future settlement agreements, Congress placed its stamp of approval on such agreements. . . .

In addition to congressional acquiescence in the President's power to settle claims, prior cases of this Court have also recognized that the President does have some measure of power to enter into executive agreements without obtaining the advice and consent of the Senate. In *United States v. Pink*, 315 U.S. 203 (1942), for example, the Court upheld the validity of the Litvinov Assignment, which was part of an Executive Agreement whereby the Soviet Union assigned to the United

States amounts owed to it by American nationals so that outstanding claims of other American nationals could be paid. The Court explained that the resolution of such claims was integrally connected with normalizing United States relations with a foreign state:

> Power to remove such obstacles to full recognition as settlement of claims of our nationals . . . certainly is a modest implied power of the President. . . . No such obstacle can be placed in the way of rehabilitation of relations between this country and another nation, unless the historic conception of the powers and responsibilities . . . is to be drastically revised.

Similarly, Judge Learned Hand recognized:

> The constitutional power of the President extends to the settlement of mutual claims between a foreign government and the United States, at least when it is an incident to the recognition of that government; and it would be unreasonable to circumscribe it to such controversies. The continued mutual amity between the nation and other powers again and again depends upon a satisfactory compromise of mutual claims; the necessary power to make such compromises has existed from the earliest times and been exercised by the foreign offices of all civilized nations. [*Ozanic v. United States*, 188 F.2d 228, 231 (2d Cir. 1951).]

In light of all of the foregoing—the inferences to be drawn from the character of the legislation Congress has enacted in the area, such as the IEEPA and the Hostage Act, and from the history of acquiescence in executive claims settlement—we conclude that the President was authorized to suspend pending claims pursuant to Executive Order No. 12294. As Justice Frankfurter pointed out in *Youngstown*, 343 U.S., at 610–611, "a systematic, unbroken, executive practice, long pursued to the knowledge of the Congress and never before questioned . . . may be treated as a gloss on 'Executive Power' vested in the President by § 1 of Art. II." Past practice does not, by itself, create power, but "long-continued practice, known to and acquiesced in by Congress, would raise a presumption that the [action] had been [taken] in pursuance of its consent. . . . " *United States v. Midwest Oil Co.*, 236 U.S. 459, 474 (1915). Such practice is present here and such a presumption is also appropriate. In light of the fact that Congress may be considered to have consented to the President's action in suspending claims, we cannot say that action exceeded the President's powers.

The Youngstown *Test.* The test articulated by Justice Jackson in *Youngstown Sheet & Tube Co. v. Sawyer*, 343 U.S. 579 (1952), was used quite effectively by

Justice Rehnquist in *Dames & Moore*. In *Youngstown*, the test was employed to invalidate President Truman's seizure of steel mills during the Korean War because the presidential act conflicted with congressional intent. However, in *Dames & Moore*, the test was used to validate the acts of Presidents Carter and Reagan to end the Iranian hostage crisis. The presidential acts easier to validate were those nullifying attachments of Iranian property and transferring the assets to the Federal Reserve Bank. Here it seems that the President acted well within the specific authorization of Congress in the International Emergency Economic Powers Act. More difficult for the Court were the presidential acts suspending U.S. litigation in favor of claims arbitration before an international tribunal in The Hague. How persuasive need evidence be that suspension of claims was an ordinary feature of U.S. international practice? The "10 binding settlements with foreign nations" noted by the Court can be distinguished from the suspension of claims in *Dames & Moore*, *e.g.*, because those ten settlements were made pursuant to powers specifically delegated to the President in peace treaties or because they involved lump sum payments to the United States for distribution to claimants. But even if there was sufficient relevant evidence that suspension of claims was customary, how did that custom make the suspension constitutional?

The Constitution and U.S. International Legal Obligations. If the Supreme Court had found that the executive branch could not lawfully terminate the legal suits against Iran in U.S. courts, would this have affected the international legal obligations of the United States? What would have been the practical effect? The possibility that the United States might not be able to honor its international legal commitment to Iran persuaded the Supreme Court to hold a rare special session to decide the case. Linda Greenhouse, "High Court Hears Iran Assets Case," *New York Times*, June 25, 1981, at D3. *Dames & Moore* is a satisfying case for an international lawyer, demonstrating the Supreme Court's commitment to upholding the international legal obligations of the United States. Much more disquieting is the case that follows, *Medellín*, where the Supreme Court seemed all too ready to disregard the nation's international legal responsibilities.

MEDELLÍN V. TEXAS

552 U.S. 491 (2008)

The Facts

ROBERTS, C.J., delivered the opinion of the Court, in which SCALIA, KENNEDY, THOMAS, and ALITO, JJ., joined. STEVENS, J., filed an opinion concurring in the judgment. BREYER, J., filed a dissenting opinion, in which SOUTER and GINSBURG, JJ., joined.

CHIEF JUSTICE ROBERTS delivered the opinion of the Court.

The International Court of Justice (ICJ), located in the Hague, is a tribunal established pursuant to the United Nations Charter to adjudicate disputes between member states. In the *Case Concerning Avena and Other Mexican Nationals (Mex. v. U.S.)*, 2004 I.C.J. 12 (Judgment of Mar. 31) (*Avena*), that tribunal considered a claim brought by Mexico against the United States. The ICJ held that, based on violations of the Vienna Convention, 51 named Mexican nationals were entitled to review and reconsideration of their state-court convictions and sentences in the United States. This was so regardless of any forfeiture of the right to raise Vienna Convention claims because of a failure to comply with generally applicable state rules governing challenges to criminal convictions.

In *Sanchez-Llamas v. Oregon*, 548 U.S. 331 (2006)—issued after *Avena* but involving individuals who were not named in the *Avena* judgment—we held that, contrary to the ICJ's determination, the Vienna Convention did not preclude the application of state default rules. After the *Avena* decision, President George W. Bush determined, through a Memorandum to the Attorney General (Feb. 28, 2005), that the United States would "discharge its international obligations" under *Avena* "by having the State courts give effect to the decision."

Petitioner José Ernesto Medellín, who had been convicted and sentenced in Texas state court for murder, is one of the 51 Mexican nationals named in the *Avena* decision. Relying on the ICJ's decision and the President's Memorandum, Medellín filed an application for a writ of habeas corpus in state court. The Texas Court of Criminal Appeals dismissed Medellín's application as an abuse of the writ under state law, given Medellín's failure to raise his Vienna Convention claim in a timely manner under state law. We granted certiorari to decide two questions. *First*, is the ICJ's judgment in *Avena* directly enforceable as domestic law in a state court in the United States? *Second*, does the President's Memorandum independently require the States to provide review and reconsideration of the claims of the 51 Mexican nationals named in *Avena* without regard to the state procedural default rules? We conclude that neither *Avena* nor the President's Memorandum constitutes directly enforceable federal law that pre-empts state limitations on the filing of successive habeas petitions. We therefore affirm the decision below.

I

A

In 1969, the United States, upon the advice and consent of the Senate, ratified the Vienna Convention on Consular Relations (Vienna Convention or Convention), Apr. 24, 1963, [1970] 21 U.S.T. 77, and the Optional Protocol Concerning the Compulsory Settlement of Disputes to the Vienna Convention (Optional Protocol or Protocol), Apr. 24, 1963, [1970] 21 U.S.T. 325. The preamble to the Convention provides that its purpose is to "contribute to the development of friendly relations among nations." Toward that end, Article 36 of the Convention was drafted to "facilitat[e] the exercise of consular functions." It provides that if a person detained by a foreign country "so requests, the competent authorities of the receiving State shall, without delay, inform the consular post of the sending State" of such detention, and "inform the [detainee] of his righ[t]" to request assistance from the consul of his own state.

The Optional Protocol provides a venue for the resolution of disputes arising out of the interpretation or application of the Vienna Convention. Under the Protocol, such disputes "shall lie within the compulsory jurisdiction of the International Court of Justice" and "may accordingly be brought before the [ICJ] . . . by any party to the dispute being a Party to the present Protocol."

The ICJ is "the principal judicial organ of the United Nations." United Nations Charter, Art. 92, 59 Stat. 1051 (1945). It was established in 1945 pursuant to the United Nations Charter. The ICJ Statute—annexed to the U.N. Charter— provides the organizational framework and governing procedures for cases brought before the ICJ.

Under Article 94(1) of the U.N. Charter, "[e]ach Member of the United Nations undertakes to comply with the decision of the [ICJ] in any case to which it is a party." The ICJ's jurisdiction in any particular case, however, is dependent upon the consent of the parties. See Art. 36, 59 Stat. 1060. The ICJ Statute delineates two ways in which a nation may consent to ICJ jurisdiction: It may consent generally to jurisdiction on any question arising under a treaty or general international law, Art. 36(2), or it may consent specifically to jurisdiction over a particular category of cases or disputes pursuant to a separate treaty. Art. 36(1). . . . By ratifying the Optional Protocol to the Vienna Convention, the United States consented to the specific jurisdiction of the ICJ with respect to claims arising out of the Vienna Convention. On March 7, 2005, subsequent to the ICJ's judgment in *Avena*, the United States gave notice of withdrawal from the

Optional Protocol to the Vienna Convention. Letter from Condoleezza Rice, Secretary of State, to Kofi A. Annan, Secretary-General of the United Nations.

B

Petitioner José Ernesto Medellín, a Mexican national, has lived in the United States since preschool. A member of the "Black and Whites" gang, Medellín was convicted of capital murder and sentenced to death in Texas for the gang rape and brutal murders of two Houston teenagers.

On June 24, 1993, 14-year-old Jennifer Ertman and 16-year-old Elizabeth Pena were walking home when they encountered Medellín and several fellow gang members. Medellín attempted to engage Elizabeth in conversation. When she tried to run, petitioner threw her to the ground. Jennifer was grabbed by other gang members when she, in response to her friend's cries, ran back to help. The gang members raped both girls for over an hour. Then, to prevent their victims from identifying them, Medellín and his fellow gang members murdered the girls and discarded their bodies in a wooded area. Medellín was personally responsible for strangling at least one of the girls with her own shoelace.

Medellín was arrested at approximately 4 a.m. on June 29, 1993. A few hours later, between 5:54 and 7:23 a.m., Medellín was given *Miranda* warnings; he then signed a written waiver and gave a detailed written confession. Local law enforcement officers did not, however, inform Medellín of his Vienna Convention right to notify the Mexican consulate of his detention. Medellín was convicted of capital murder and sentenced to death; his conviction and sentence were affirmed on appeal.

Medellín first raised his Vienna Convention claim in his first application for state postconviction relief. The state trial court held that the claim was procedurally defaulted because Medellín had failed to raise it at trial or on direct review. The trial court also rejected the Vienna Convention claim on the merits, finding that Medellín had "fail[ed] to show that any non-notification of the Mexican authorities impacted on the validity of his conviction or punishment." The Texas Court of Criminal Appeals affirmed.

Medellín then filed a habeas petition in Federal District Court. The District Court denied relief, holding that Medellín's Vienna Convention claim was procedurally defaulted and that Medellín had failed to show prejudice arising from the Vienna Convention violation.

While Medellín's application for a certificate of appealability was pending in the Fifth Circuit, the ICJ issued its decision in *Avena*. The ICJ held that the United States had violated Article 36(1)(b) of the Vienna Convention by failing to inform the 51 named Mexican nationals, including Medellín, of their Vienna Convention rights. In the ICJ's determination, the United States was obligated "to provide, by means of its own choosing, review and reconsideration of the convictions and sentences of the [affected] Mexican nationals." The ICJ indicated that such review was required without regard to state procedural default rules.

[Following additional procedural steps in U.S. courts,] President George W. Bush issued his Memorandum to the United States Attorney General, providing:

> I have determined, pursuant to the authority vested in me as President by the Constitution and the laws of the United States of America, that the United States will discharge its international obligations under the decision of the International Court of Justice in [*Avena*], by having State courts give effect to the decision in accordance with general principles of comity in cases filed by the 51 Mexican nationals addressed in that decision.

Medellín, relying on the President's Memorandum and the ICJ's decision in *Avena*, filed a second application for habeas relief in state court. Because the state-court proceedings might have provided Medellín with the review and reconsideration he requested, and because his claim for federal relief might otherwise have been barred, we dismissed his petition for certiorari as improvidently granted.

The Texas Court of Criminal Appeals subsequently dismissed Medellín's second state habeas application as an abuse of the writ. In the court's view, neither the *Avena* decision nor the President's Memorandum was "binding federal law" that could displace the State's limitations on the filing of successive habeas applications. We again granted certiorari.

The Supreme Court and the Vienna Convention on Consular Relations. The Supreme Court has long been troubled by problems caused by U.S. states failing to comply with the Vienna Convention. In *Breard v. Greene*, a 6–3 majority of the Court refused to stay Virginia's execution of a Paraguayan citizen who had not been informed of his right to contact the Paraguayan consulate. Moreover, a Paraguayan complaint against the United States was pending before the International Court of Justice. The Supreme Court majority held that "[e]ven were Breard's Vienna Convention claim properly raised and proved, it is extremely doubtful that the violation should result in the overturning of a final judgment of conviction without some showing that the violation had an effect on the trial." 523 U.S. 371, 377 (1998). The three dissenting judges were ready to hear the international legal issues raised by the case.

Despite an order of the ICJ to delay, Virginia executed Breard. Virginia's Governor noted both the U.S. Supreme Court opinion and the conflicting advice of President Clinton's Secretary of State and Attorney General (Madeline Albright urged a stay; but Janet Reno argued that Virginia was not bound to listen to the International Court). "Statement by Governor Jim Gilmore concerning the Execution of Angel Breard," Commonwealth of Virginia Office of the Governor Press Release, Apr. 14, 1998. However, "[u]nder the international law of state responsibility, compliance with the internal laws of the Commonwealth of Virginia and of the federal laws of the United States cannot relieve the U.S. from international responsibility for an admitted violation of the Vienna Convention and a potential violation of the UN Charter." Peter H.F. Bekker & Keith Highet, "International Court of Justice Orders United States to Stay Execution of Paraguayan National in Virginia," 3 *ASIL Insights*, Issue 4 (1998). Why would the Supreme Court be more concerned with honoring its international legal obligations to Iran in *Dames & Moore* than with honoring those to Paraguay in *Breard* or to Mexico in *Medellín*?

Medellín v. Texas
The Law

No one disputes that the *Avena* decision—a decision that flows from the treaties through which the United States submitted to ICJ jurisdiction with respect to Vienna Convention disputes—constitutes an *international* law obligation on the part of the United States. But not all international law obligations automatically constitute binding federal law enforceable in United States courts. The question we confront here is whether the *Avena* judgment has automatic *domestic* legal effect such that the judgment of its own force applies in state and federal courts.

This court has long recognized the distinction between treaties that automatically have effect as domestic law, and those that—while they constitute international law commitments—do not by themselves function as binding federal law. The distinction was well explained by Chief Justice Marshall's opinion in *Foster v. Neilson*, 2 Pet. 253, 315 (1829), overruled on other grounds *United States v. Percheman*, 7 Pet. 51 (1833), which held that a treaty is "equivalent to an act of the legislature," and hence self-executing, when it "operates of itself without the aid of any legislative provision." When, in contrast, "[treaty] stipulations are not self-executing they can only be enforced pursuant to legislation to carry them into effect." *Whitney v. Robertson*, 124 U.S. 190, 194 (1888). In sum, while treaties "may comprise international commitments . . . they are not domestic law unless Congress has either enacted implementing statutes or the treaty itself conveys an intention that it be 'self-executing' and is ratified on those terms." *Igartúa-De La Rosa* v. *United States*, 417 F.3d 145, 150 (CA1 2005) (en banc) (Boudin, C.J.).[2] . . .

Medellín and his *amici* nonetheless contend that the Optional Protocol, United Nations Charter, and ICJ Statute supply the "relevant obligation" to give the *Avena* judgment binding effect in the domestic courts of the United States. Because none of these treaty sources creates binding federal law in the absence of implementing legislation, and because it is uncontested that no such legislation exists, we conclude that the *Avena* judgment is not automatically binding domestic law.

A

The interpretation of a treaty, like the interpretation of a statute, begins with its text. Because a treaty ratified by the United States is "an agreement among sovereign powers," we have also considered as "aids to its interpretation" the negotiation and drafting history of the treaty as well as "the postratification understanding" of signatory nations.

As a signatory to the Optional Protocol, the United States agreed to submit disputes arising out of the Vienna Convention to the ICJ. The Protocol provides: "Disputes arising out of the interpretation or application of the [Vienna] Convention shall lie within the compulsory jurisdiction of the International Court of Justice." Of course, submitting to jurisdiction and agreeing to be bound are two different things. A party could, for example, agree to compulsory nonbinding arbitration. Such an agreement would require the party to appear before the arbitral tribunal without obligating the party to treat the tribunal's decision as binding. . . .

The most natural reading of the Optional Protocol is as a bare grant of jurisdiction. . . . The Protocol says nothing about the effect of an ICJ decision and does not itself commit signatories to comply with an ICJ judgment. The Protocol is similarly silent as to any enforcement mechanism.

The obligation on the part of signatory nations to comply with ICJ judgments derives not from the Optional Protocol, but rather from Article 94 of the United Nations Charter—the provision that specifically addresses the effect of ICJ

---

2   The label "self-executing" has on occasion been used to convey different meanings. What we mean by "self-executing" is that the treaty has automatic domestic effect as federal law upon ratification. Conversely, a "non-self-executing" treaty does not by itself give rise to domestically enforceable federal law. Whether such a treaty has domestic effect depends upon implementing legislation passed by Congress.

decisions. Article 94(1) provides that "[e]ach Member of the United Nations *undertakes to comply* with the decision of the [ICJ] in any case to which it is a party." The Executive Branch contends that the phrase "undertakes to comply" is not "an acknowledgment that an ICJ decision will have immediate legal effect in the courts of U.N. members," but rather "a *commitment* on the part of U.N. Members to take *future* action through their political branches to comply with an ICJ decision."

We agree with this construction of Article 94. The Article is not a directive to domestic courts. It does not provide that the United States "shall" or "must" comply with an ICJ decision, nor indicate that the Senate that ratified the U.N. Charter intended to vest ICJ decisions with immediate legal effect in domestic courts. . . .

The remainder of Article 94 confirms that the U.N. Charter does not contemplate the automatic enforceability of ICJ decisions in domestic courts.[6] Article 94(2)—the enforcement provision—provides the sole remedy for noncompliance: referral to the United Nations Security Council by an aggrieved state.

The U.N. Charter's provision of an express diplomatic—that is, nonjudicial—remedy is itself evidence that ICJ judgments were not meant to be enforceable in domestic courts. And even this "quintessentially *international* remed[y]" is not absolute. First, the Security Council must "dee[m] necessary" the issuance of a recommendation or measure to effectuate the judgment. Second, as the President and Senate were undoubtedly aware in subscribing to the U.N. Charter and Optional Protocol, the United States retained the unqualified right to exercise its veto of any Security Council resolution. . . .

If ICJ judgments were instead regarded as automatically enforceable domestic law, they would be immediately and directly binding on state and federal courts pursuant to the Supremacy Clause. Mexico or the ICJ would have no need to proceed to the Security Council to enforce the judgment in this case. Noncompliance with an ICJ judgment through exercise of the Security Council veto—always regarded as an option by the Executive and ratifying Senate during and after consideration of the U.N. Charter, Optional Protocol, and ICJ Statute—would no longer be a viable alternative. There would be nothing to veto. In light

---

6   Article 94(2) provides in full: "If any party to a case fails to perform the obligations incumbent upon it under a judgment rendered by the Court, the other party may have recourse to the Security Council, which may, if it deems necessary, make recommendations or decide upon measures to be taken to give effect to the judgment."

of the U.N. Charter's remedial scheme, there is no reason to believe that the President and Senate signed up for such a result. . . .

In this case, the dissent—for a grab bag of no less than seven reasons—would tell us that this *particular* ICJ judgment is federal law. That is no sort of guidance. Nor is it any answer to say that the federal courts will diligently police international agreements and enforce the decisions of international tribunals only when they *should* be enforced. The point of a non-self-executing treaty is that it "addresses itself to the political, *not* the judicial department; and the legislature must execute the contract before it can become a rule for the Court." The dissent's contrary approach would assign to the courts—not the political branches—the primary role in deciding when and how international agreements will be enforced. To read a treaty so that it sometimes has the effect of domestic law and sometimes does not is tantamount to vesting with the judiciary the power not only to interpret but also to create the law. . . .

D

Our holding does not call into question the ordinary enforcement of foreign judgments or international arbitral agreements. Indeed, we agree with Medellín that, as a general matter, "an agreement to abide by the result" of an international adjudication—or what he really means, an agreement to give the result of such adjudication domestic legal effect—can be a treaty obligation like any other, so long as the agreement is consistent with the Constitution. The point is that the particular treaty obligations on which Medellín relies do not of their own force create domestic law.

III

Medellín next argues that the ICJ's judgment in *Avena* is binding on state courts by virtue of the President's February 28, 2005 Memorandum. The United States contends that while the *Avena* judgment does not of its own force require domestic courts to set aside ordinary rules of procedural default, that judgment became the law of the land with precisely that effect pursuant to the President's Memorandum and his power "to establish binding rules of decision that preempt contrary state law." Accordingly, we must decide whether the President's declaration alters our conclusion that the *Avena* judgment is not a rule of domestic law binding in state and federal courts.

A

The United States maintains that the President's constitutional role "uniquely qualifies" him to resolve the sensitive foreign policy decisions that bear on compliance with an ICJ decision and "to do so expeditiously." We do not question these propositions. In this case, the President seeks to vindicate the United States interests in ensuring the reciprocal observance of the Vienna Convention, protecting relations with foreign governments, and demonstrating commitment to the role of international law. These interests are plainly compelling.

Such considerations, however, do not allow us to set aside first principles. The President's authority to act, as with the exercise of any governmental power, "must stem either from an act of Congress or from the Constitution itself." *Youngstown* [*Sheet & Tube Co. v. Sawyer*, 343 U.S. 579, 585 (1952)]; *Dames & Moore v. Regan*, 453 U.S. 654, 668 (1981).

Justice Jackson's familiar tripartite scheme provides the accepted framework for evaluating executive action in this area. First, "[w]hen the President acts pursuant to an express or implied authorization of Congress, his authority is at its maximum, for it includes all that he possesses in his own right plus all that Congress can delegate." *Youngstown*, 343 U.S., at 635 (Jackson, J., concurring). Second, "[w]hen the President acts in absence of either a congressional grant or denial of authority, he can only rely upon his own independent powers, but there is a zone of twilight in which he and Congress may have concurrent authority, or in which its distribution is uncertain." *Id.* at 637. In this circumstance, Presidential authority can derive support from "congressional inertia, indifference or quiescence." *Ibid.* Finally, "[w]hen the President takes measures incompatible with the expressed or implied will of Congress, his power is at its lowest ebb," and the Court can sustain his actions "only by disabling the Congress from acting upon the subject." *Id.* at 637–638.

B

The United States marshals two principal arguments in favor of the President's authority "to establish binding rules of decision that preempt contrary state law." The Solicitor General first argues that the relevant treaties give the President the authority to implement the *Avena* judgment and that Congress has acquiesced in the exercise of such authority. The United States also relies upon an "independent" international dispute-resolution power wholly apart from the asserted authority based on the pertinent treaties. Medellín adds the additional argument that the President's Memorandum is a valid exercise of his power to take care that the laws be faithfully executed.

1

The United States maintains that the President's Memorandum is authorized by the Optional Protocol and the U.N. Charter. That is, because the relevant treaties "create an obligation to comply with *Avena*," they "*implicitly* give the

President authority to implement that treaty-based obligation." As a result, the President's Memorandum is well grounded in the first category of the *Youngstown* framework.

We disagree. The President now has an array of political and diplomatic means available to enforce international obligations, but unilaterally converting a non-self-executing treaty into a self-executing one is not among them. The responsibility for transforming an international obligation arising from a non-self-executing treaty into domestic law falls to Congress. As this Court has explained, when treaty stipulations are "not self-executing they can only be enforced pursuant to legislation to carry them into effect." *Whitney, supra*, at 194. Moreover, "[u]ntil such act shall be passed, the Court is not at liberty to disregard the existing laws on the subject." *Foster, supra*, at 315.

The requirement that Congress, rather than the President, implement a non-self-executing treaty derives from the text of the Constitution, which divides the treaty-making power between the President and the Senate. The Constitution vests the President with the authority to "make" a treaty. Art. II, § 2. If the Executive determines that a treaty should have domestic effect of its own force, that determination may be implemented "in mak[ing]" the treaty, by ensuring that it contains language plainly providing for domestic enforceability. If the treaty is to be self-executing in this respect, the Senate must consent to the treaty by the requisite two-thirds vote, consistent with all other constitutional restraints. . . .

A non-self-executing treaty, by definition, is one that was ratified with the understanding that it is not to have domestic effect of its own force. That understanding precludes the assertion that Congress has implicitly authorized the President—acting on his own—to achieve precisely the same result. We therefore conclude, given the absence of congressional legislation, that the non-self-executing treaties at issue here did not "express[ly] or implicit[ly]" vest the President with the unilateral authority to make them self-executing. Accordingly, the President's Memorandum does not fall within the first category of the *Youngstown* framework.

[E]ven if we were persuaded that congressional acquiescence could support the President's asserted authority to create domestic law pursuant to a non-self-executing treaty, such acquiescence does not exist here. The United States first locates congressional acquiescence in Congress's failure to act following the President's resolution of prior ICJ controversies. A review of the Executive's actions in those prior cases, however, cannot support the claim that Congress acquiesced in this particular exercise of Presidential authority, for none of them remotely involved transforming an international obligation into domestic law and thereby displacing state law.

The United States also directs us to the President's "related" statutory responsibilities and to his "established role" in litigating foreign policy concerns as support for the President's asserted authority to give the ICJ's decision in *Avena* the force of domestic law. Congress has indeed authorized the President to represent the United States before the United Nations, the ICJ, and the Security Council, but the authority of the President to represent the United States before such bodies speaks to the President's *international* responsibilities, not any unilateral authority to create domestic law. [N]one of the sources of authority identified by the United States supports the President's claim that Congress has acquiesced in his asserted power to establish on his own federal law or to override state law.

None of this is to say, however, that the combination of a non-self-executing treaty and the lack of implementing legislation precludes the President from acting to comply with an international treaty obligation. It is only to say that the Executive cannot unilaterally execute a non-self-executing treaty by giving it domestic effect. That is, the non-self-executing character of a treaty constrains the President's ability to comply with treaty commitments by unilaterally making the treaty binding on domestic courts. The President may comply with the treaty's obligations by some other means, so long as they are consistent with the Constitution. But he may not rely upon a non-self-executing treaty to "establish binding rules of decision that preempt contrary state law."

2

We thus turn to the United States' claim that—independent of the United States' treaty obligations—the Memorandum is a valid exercise of the President's foreign affairs authority to resolve claims disputes with foreign nations. The United States relies on a series of cases in which this Court has upheld the authority of the President to settle foreign claims pursuant to an executive agreement. See [*Am. Ins. Ass'n. v.*] *Garamendi*, 539 U.S. [396, 415 (2003)]; *Dames & Moore*, 453 U.S., at 679–680; *United States v. Pink*, 315 U.S. 203, 229 (1942); *United States v. Belmont*, 301 U.S. 324, 330 (1937). In these cases this Court has explained that, if pervasive enough, a history of congressional acquiescence can be treated as a "gloss on 'Executive Power' vested in the President by § 1 of Art. II." *Dames & Moore, supra,* at 686. . . .

The President's Memorandum is not supported by a "particularly longstanding practice" of congressional acquiescence, but rather is what the

United States itself has described as "unprecedented action." Indeed, the Government has not identified a single instance in which the President has attempted (or Congress has acquiesced in) a Presidential directive issued to state courts, much less one that reaches deep into the heart of the State's police powers and compels state courts to reopen final criminal judgments and set aside neutrally applicable state laws. The Executive's narrow and strictly limited authority to settle international claims disputes pursuant to an executive agreement cannot stretch so far as to support the current Presidential Memorandum.

3

Medellín argues that the President's Memorandum is a valid exercise of his "Take Care" power. The United States, however, does not rely upon the President's responsibility to "take Care that the Laws be faithfully executed." U.S. Const., Art. II, § 3. We think this is a wise concession. This authority allows the President to execute the laws, not make them. For the reasons we have stated, the *Avena* judgment is not domestic law; accordingly, the President cannot rely on his Take Care powers here.

The judgment of the Texas Court of Criminal Appeals is affirmed.

JUSTICE STEVENS, concurring in the judgment.

There is a great deal of wisdom in Justice Breyer's dissent. I agree that the text and history of the Supremacy Clause, as well as this Court's treaty-related cases, do not support a presumption against self-execution. I also endorse the proposition that the Vienna Convention on Consular Relations "is itself self-executing and judicially enforceable." Moreover, I think this case presents a closer question than the Court's opinion allows. In the end, however, I am persuaded that the relevant treaties do not authorize this Court to enforce the judgment of the International Court of Justice (ICJ) in *Case Concerning Avena and Other Mexican Nationals.* . . .

Absent a presumption one way or the other, the best reading of the words "undertakes to comply" is, in my judgment, one that contemplates future action by the political branches.

[T]he costs of refusing to respect the ICJ's judgment are significant. The entire Court and the President agree that breach will jeopardize the United States' "plainly compelling" interests in "ensuring the reciprocal observance of the Vienna Convention, protecting relations with foreign governments, and demonstrating commitment to the role of international law." When the honor of the Nation is balanced against the modest cost of compliance, Texas would do well to recognize that more is at stake than whether judgments of the ICJ, and the principled admonitions of the President of the United States, trump state procedural rules in the absence of implementing legislation.

The Court's judgment, which I join, does not foreclose further appropriate action by the State of Texas.

JUSTICE BREYER, with whom JUSTICE SOUTER and JUSTICE GINSBURG join, dissenting.

The Constitution's Supremacy Clause provides that "all Treaties . . . which shall be made . . . under the Authority of the United States, shall be the supreme Law of the Land; and the Judges in every State shall be bound thereby." Art. VI, cl. 2. The Clause means that the "courts" must regard "a treaty . . . as equivalent to an act of the legislature, whenever it operates of itself without the aid of any legislative provision." *Foster v. Neilson*, 2 Pet. 253, 314 (1829) (majority opinion of Marshall, C.J. . . .

I believe the treaty obligations, and hence the judgment, resting as it does upon the consent of the United States to the ICJ's jurisdiction, bind the courts no less than would "an act of the [federal] legislature." [*Ibid.*]

I.

The critical question here is whether the Supremacy Clause requires Texas to follow, *i.e.*, to enforce, this ICJ judgment. The Court says "no." And it reaches its negative answer by interpreting the labyrinth of treaty provisions as creating a legal obligation that binds the United States internationally, but which, for Supremacy Clause purposes, is not automatically enforceable as domestic law. . . .

In my view, the President has correctly determined that Congress need not enact additional legislation. . . .

A

Supreme Court case law stretching back more than 200 years helps explain what, for present purposes, the Founders meant when they wrote that "all Treaties . . . shall be the supreme Law of the Land." Art. VI, cl. 2. In 1796, for example, the Court decided the case of *Ware v. Hylton*, 3 Dall. 199. A British creditor sought payment of an American's Revolutionary War debt. . . . The Court, with each Justice writing separately, agreed with the British creditor, held the Virginia statute invalid, and found that the American debtor remained liable for the debt.

The key fact relevant here is that Congress had not enacted a specific statute enforcing the treaty provision at issue. Hence the Court had to decide whether the provision was (to put the matter in present terms) "self-executing." Justice Iredell, a member of North Carolina's Ratifying Convention, addressed the matter specifically, setting forth views on which Justice Story later relied to explain the Founders' reasons for drafting the Supremacy Clause. 3 J. Story, Commentaries on the Constitution of the United States 696–697 (1833). . . .

"Under this Constitution," Justice Iredell concluded, "so far as a treaty constitutionally is binding, upon principles of *moral obligation*, it is also by the vigour of its own authority to be executed in fact. It would not otherwise be the *Supreme law* in the new sense provided for." . . .

Some 30 years later, the Court returned to the "self-execution" problem. In *Foster*, 2 Pet. 253, the Court examined a provision in an 1819 treaty with Spain ceding Florida to the United States; the provision said that " 'grants of land made' " by Spain before January 24, 1818, " 'shall be ratified and confirmed' " to the grantee. Chief Justice Marshall, writing for the Court, noted that, as a general matter, one might expect a signatory nation to execute a treaty through a formal exercise of its domestic sovereign authority (*e.g.*, through an act of the legislature). But in the United States "*a different principle*" applies. (emphasis added). The Supremacy Clause means that, here, a treaty is "the law of the land . . . to be regarded in Courts of justice as equivalent to an act of the legislature" and "operates of itself without the aid of any legislative provision" unless it specifically contemplates execution by the legislature and thereby "*addresses itself to the political, not the judicial department*." (emphasis added). The Court decided that the treaty provision in question was *not* self-executing; in its view, the words "shall be ratified" demonstrated that the provision foresaw further legislative action.

The Court, however, changed its mind about the result in *Foster* four years later, after being shown a less legislatively oriented, less tentative, but equally authentic Spanish-language version of the treaty. See *United States v. Percheman*, 7 Pet. 51, 88–89 (1833). And by 1840, instances in which treaty provisions automatically became part of domestic law were common enough for one Justice to write that "it would be a bold proposition" to assert "that an act of Congress must be first passed" in order to give a treaty effect as "a supreme law of the land." *Lessee of Pollard's Heirs v. Kibbe*, 14 Pet. 353, 388 (1840) (Baldwin, J., concurring).

Since *Foster* and *Pollard*, this Court has frequently held or assumed that particular treaty provisions are self-executing, automatically binding the States without more. . . .

All of these cases make clear that self-executing treaty provisions are not uncommon or peculiar creatures of our domestic law; that they cover a wide range of subjects; that the Supremacy Clause itself answers the self-execution question by applying many, but not all, treaty provisions directly to the States; and that the

Clause answers the self-execution question differently than does the law in many other nations. The cases also provide criteria that help determine *which* provisions automatically so apply—a matter to which I now turn.

B

1

The case law provides no simple magic answer to the question whether a particular treaty provision is self-executing. But the case law does make clear that, insofar as today's majority looks for language about "self-execution" in the treaty itself and insofar as it erects "clear statement" presumptions designed to help find an answer, it is misguided. . . .

The many treaty provisions that this Court has found self-executing contain no textual language on the point. Few, if any, of these provisions are clear. Those that displace state law in respect to such quintessential state matters as, say, property, inheritance, or debt repayment, lack the "clea[r] state[ment]" that the Court today apparently requires. This is also true of those cases that deal with state rules roughly comparable to the sort that the majority suggests require special accommodation. These many Supreme Court cases finding treaty provisions to be self-executing cannot be reconciled with the majority's demand for textual clarity. . . .

In a word, for present purposes, the absence or presence of language in a treaty about a provision's self-execution proves nothing at all. At best the Court is hunting the snark. At worst it erects legalistic hurdles that can threaten the application of provisions in many existing commercial and other treaties and make it more difficult to negotiate new ones.

C . . .

I would find the relevant treaty provisions self-executing as applied to the ICJ judgment before us (giving that judgment domestic legal effect) for the following reasons, taken together.

First, the language of the relevant treaties strongly supports direct judicial enforceability, at least of judgments of the kind at issue here. The Optional Protocol bears the title "Compulsory Settlement of Disputes," thereby emphasizing the mandatory and binding nature of the procedures it sets forth. The body of the Protocol says specifically that "any party" that has consented to the ICJ's "compulsory jurisdiction" may bring a "dispute" before the court against any other such party. Art. I. And the Protocol contrasts proceedings of the compulsory kind with an alternative "conciliation procedure," the recommendations of which a party may decide "not" to "accep[t]." Art. III. Thus, the Optional Protocol's basic objective is not just to provide a forum for *settlement* but to provide a forum for *compulsory* settlement.

Moreover, in accepting Article 94(1) of the Charter, "[e]ach Member . . . undertakes to comply with the decision" of the ICJ "in any case to which it is a party." 59 Stat. 1051. And the ICJ Statute (part of the U.N. Charter) makes clear that a decision of the ICJ between parties that have consented to the ICJ's compulsory jurisdiction has "*binding force* . . . between the parties and in respect of that particular case." Art. 59 (emphasis added). Enforcement of a court's judgment that has "binding force" involves quintessential judicial activity.

. . . A leading contemporary dictionary defined ["undertakes"] in terms of "lay[ing] oneself under obligation . . . to perform or to execute." And that definition is just what the equally authoritative Spanish version of the provision (familiar to Mexico) says directly: The words "compromete a cumplir" indicate a present obligation to execute, without any tentativeness of the sort the majority finds in the English word "undertakes." . . .

The upshot is that treaty language says that an ICJ decision is legally binding, but it leaves the implementation of that binding legal obligation to the domestic law of each signatory nation. In this Nation, the Supremacy Clause, as long and consistently interpreted, indicates that ICJ decisions rendered pursuant to provisions for binding adjudication must be domestically legally binding and enforceable in domestic courts *at least sometimes*. And for purposes of this argument, that conclusion is all that I need. The remainder of the discussion will explain why, if ICJ judgments *sometimes* bind domestic courts, then they have that effect here.

Second, the Optional Protocol here applies to a dispute about the meaning of a Vienna Convention provision that is itself self-executing and judicially enforceable. The Convention provision is about an individual's "rights," namely, his right upon being arrested to be informed of his separate right to contact his nation's consul. See Art. 36(1)(b). The provision language is precise. The dispute arises at the intersection of an individual right with ordinary rules of criminal procedure; it consequently concerns the kind of matter with which judges are familiar. The provisions contain judicially enforceable standards. . . .

Third, logic suggests that a treaty provision providing for "final" and "binding" judgments that "settl[e]" treaty-based disputes is self-executing insofar as the judgment in question concerns the meaning of an underlying treaty provision that is itself self-executing. Imagine that two parties to a contract agree to binding arbitration about whether a contract provision's word "grain" includes rye. They would expect that, if the arbitrator decides that the word "grain" does include rye, the arbitrator will then simply read the relevant provision as if it said "grain including rye." They would also expect the arbitrator to issue a binding award that embodies whatever relief would be appropriate under that circumstance. . . .

Fourth, the majority's very different approach has seriously negative practical implications. The United States has entered into at least 70 treaties that contain provisions for ICJ dispute settlement similar to the Protocol before us. Many of these treaties contain provisions similar to those this Court has previously found self-executing—provisions that involve, for example, property rights, contract and commercial rights, trademarks, civil liability for personal injury, rights of foreign diplomats, taxation, domestic-court jurisdiction, and so forth. If the Optional Protocol here, taken together with the U.N. Charter and its annexed ICJ Statute, is insufficient to warrant enforcement of the ICJ judgment before us, it is difficult to see how one could reach a different conclusion in any of these other instances. And the consequence is to undermine longstanding efforts in those treaties to create an effective international system for interpreting and applying many, often commercial, self-executing treaty provisions. I thus doubt that the majority is right when it says, "We do not suggest that treaties can never afford binding domestic effect to international tribunal judgments." In respect to the 70 treaties that currently refer disputes to the ICJ's binding adjudicatory authority, some multilateral, some bilateral, that is just what the majority has done.

Nor can the majority look to congressional legislation for a quick fix. Congress is unlikely to authorize automatic judicial enforceability of *all* ICJ judgments, for that could include some politically sensitive judgments and others better suited for enforcement by other branches: for example, those touching upon military hostilities, naval activity, handling of nuclear material, and so forth. Nor is Congress likely to have the time available, let alone the will, to legislate judgment-by-judgment enforcement of, say, the ICJ's (or other international tribunals') resolution of non-politically-sensitive commercial disputes. And as this Court's prior case law has avoided laying down bright-line rules but instead has adopted a more complex approach, it seems unlikely that Congress will find it easy to develop legislative bright lines that pick out those provisions (addressed to the Judicial Branch) where self-execution seems warranted. But, of course, it is not necessary for Congress to do so—at least not if one believes that this Court's Supremacy Clause cases *already* embody criteria likely to work reasonably well. It is those criteria that I would apply here.

Fifth, other factors, related to the particular judgment here at issue, make that judgment well suited to direct judicial enforcement. The specific issue before the ICJ concerned " 'review and reconsideration' " of the "possible prejudice" caused in each of the 51 affected cases by an arresting State's failure to provide the defendant with rights guaranteed by the Vienna Convention. This review will call for an understanding of how criminal procedure works, including whether, and how, a notification failure may work prejudice. As the ICJ itself recognized, "it is the judicial process that is suited to this task." Courts frequently work with criminal procedure and related prejudice. Legislatures do not. Judicial standards are readily available for working in this technical area. Legislative standards are not readily available. Judges typically determine such matters, deciding, for example, whether further hearings are necessary, after reviewing a record in an individual case. Congress does not normally legislate in respect to individual cases. Indeed, to repeat what I said above, what kind of special legislation does the majority believe Congress ought to consider?

Sixth, to find the United States' treaty obligations self-executing as applied to the ICJ judgment (and consequently to find that judgment enforceable) does not threaten constitutional conflict with other branches; it does not require us to engage in nonjudicial activity; and it does not require us to create a new cause of action. The only question before us concerns the application of the ICJ judgment as binding law applicable to the parties in a particular criminal proceeding that Texas law creates independently of the treaty. [T]he question before us does not involve the creation of a private right of action[.]

Seventh, neither the President nor Congress has expressed concern about direct judicial enforcement of the ICJ decision. To the contrary, the President favors enforcement of this judgment. Thus, insofar as foreign policy impact, the interrelation of treaty provisions, or any other matter within the President's special treaty, military, and foreign affairs responsibilities might prove relevant, such factors *favor*, rather than militate against, enforcement of the judgment before us.

For these seven reasons, I would find that the United States' treaty obligation to comply with the ICJ judgment in *Avena* is enforceable in court in this case without further congressional action beyond Senate ratification of the relevant treaties. The majority reaches a different conclusion because it looks for the wrong thing (explicit textual expression about self-execution) using the wrong standard (clarity) in the wrong place (the treaty language). Hunting for what the text cannot contain, it takes a wrong turn. It threatens to deprive individuals, including businesses, property owners, testamentary beneficiaries, consular officials, and others, of the workable dispute resolution procedures that many treaties, including commercially oriented treaties, provide. In a world where commerce, trade, and travel have become ever more international, that is a step in the wrong direction.

Were the Court for a moment to shift the direction of its legal gaze, looking instead to the Supremacy Clause and to the extensive case law interpreting that Clause as applied to treaties, I believe it would reach a better supported, more felicitous conclusion. That approach, well embedded in Court case law, leads to the conclusion that the ICJ judgment before us is judicially enforceable without further legislative action. . . .

III

Because the majority concludes that the Nation's international legal obligation to enforce the ICJ's decision is not automatically a domestic legal obligation, it must then determine whether the President has the constitutional authority to enforce it. And the majority finds that he does not.

In my view, that second conclusion has broader implications than the majority suggests. The President here seeks to implement treaty provisions in which the United States agrees that the ICJ judgment is binding with respect to the *Avena* parties. Consequently, his actions draw upon his constitutional authority in the area of foreign affairs. In this case, his exercise of that power falls within that middle range of Presidential authority where Congress has neither specifically authorized nor specifically forbidden the Presidential action in question. See *Youngstown Sheet & Tube Co. v. Sawyer*, 343 U.S. 579, 637 (1952) (Jackson, J., concurring). At the same time, if the President were to have the authority he asserts here, it would require setting aside a state procedural law.

It is difficult to believe that in the exercise of his Article II powers pursuant to a ratified treaty, the President can *never* take action that would result in setting aside state law. Suppose that the President believes it necessary that he implement a treaty provision requiring a prisoner exchange involving someone in state custody in order to avoid a proven military threat. Or suppose he believes it necessary to secure a foreign consul's treaty-based rights to move freely or to contact an arrested foreign national. Does the Constitution require the President in each and every such instance to obtain a special statute authorizing his action? On the other hand, the Constitution must impose significant restrictions upon the President's ability, by invoking Article II treaty-implementation authority, to circumvent ordinary legislative processes and to pre empt state law as he does so.

Previously this Court has said little about this question. It has held that the President has a fair amount of authority to make and to implement executive agreements, at least in respect to international claims settlement, and that this authority can require contrary state law to be set aside. See, *e.g.*, [*United States v.*] *Pink*, [315 U.S. 203,] 223, 230–231, 233–234 [(1942)]; *United States v. Belmont*, 301 U.S. 324, 326–327 (1937). It has made clear that principles of foreign sovereign immunity trump state law and that the Executive, operating without explicit legislative authority, can assert those principles in state court. See *Ex parte Peru*, 318 U.S. 578, 588 (1943). It has also made clear that the Executive has inherent power to bring a lawsuit "to carry out treaty obligations." *Sanitary Dist. of Chicago v. United States*, 266 U.S. 405, 425, 426 (1925). But it has reserved judgment as to "the scope of the President's power to preempt state law pursuant to authority delegated by . . . a ratified treaty"—a fact that helps to explain the majority's inability to find support in precedent for its own conclusions. *Barclays Bank PLC v. Franchise Tax Bd. of Cal.*, 512 U.S. 298, 329 (1994).

Given the Court's comparative lack of expertise in foreign affairs; given the importance of the Nation's foreign relations; given the difficulty of finding the proper constitutional balance among state and federal, executive and legislative, powers in such matters; and given the likely future importance of this Court's efforts to do so, I would very much hesitate before concluding that the Constitution implicitly sets forth broad prohibitions (or permissions) in this area.

I would thus be content to leave the matter in the constitutional shade from which it has emerged. Given my view of this case, I need not answer the question. And I shall not try to do so. That silence, however, cannot be taken as agreement with the majority's Part III conclusion.

IV

The majority's two holdings taken together produce practical anomalies. They unnecessarily complicate the President's foreign affairs task insofar as, for example, they increase the likelihood of Security Council *Avena* enforcement proceedings, of worsening relations with our neighbor Mexico, of precipitating actions by other nations putting at risk American citizens who have the misfortune to be arrested while traveling abroad, or of diminishing our Nation's reputation abroad as a result of our failure to follow the "rule of law" principles that we preach. The holdings also encumber Congress with a task (postratification legislation) that, in respect to many decisions of international tribunals, it may not want and which it may find difficult to execute. At the same time, insofar as today's holdings make it more difficult to enforce the judgments of international tribunals, including technical non-politically-controversial judgments, those holdings weaken that rule of law for which our Constitution stands.

These institutional considerations make it difficult to reconcile the majority's holdings with the workable Constitution that the Founders envisaged. They reinforce the importance, in practice and in principle, of asking Chief Justice Marshall's question: Does a treaty provision address the "Judicial" Branch rather than the "Political Branches" of Government. And they show the wisdom of the well-established precedent that indicates that the answer to the question here is "yes."

V

In sum, a strong line of precedent, likely reflecting the views of the Founders, indicates that the treaty provisions before us and the judgment of the International Court of Justice address themselves to the Judicial Branch and consequently are self-executing. In reaching a contrary conclusion, the Court has failed to take proper account of that precedent and, as a result, the Nation may well break its word even though the President seeks to live up to that word and Congress has done nothing to suggest the contrary.

For the reasons set forth, I respectfully dissent.

Deference to International Law and International Tribunals. After choosing to disregard the International Court of Justice proceedings in *Breard*, U.S. courts responded similarly to the International Court proceedings and judgments in *LaGrand* (Germany v. United States), 2001 I.C.J. 466, and *Avena* (Mexico v. United States), 2004 I.C.J. 12. When should a U.S. court give effect to the rulings of an international court or tribunal? Some commentators believe it is a mistake to take U.S. violations of international law too seriously. "All states violate international law some of the time." Ann Bradford & Eric A. Posner, "Universal Exceptionalism in International Law," 52 *Harvard International Law Journal* 3, 53 (2011). Do you agree? What are the bad, as well as the good, outcomes for a state when it fails to comply with international law or the judgments of an international court?

Texas and Medellín. Notwithstanding the Supreme Court's adverse judgment in *Medellín*, the United States still tried to persuade Texas to comply with the ICJ decision. In line with the suggestion in Justice Stevens's concurring opinion, U.S. Secretary of State Rice and U.S. Attorney General Mukasey wrote to Governor Perry of Texas asking "that Texas take the steps necessary to give full effect to the *Avena* decision." However, Texas was adamant in its refusal to comply. The Texas Governor's office maintained that the "world court has no standing in Texas and Texas is not bound by a ruling or edict from a foreign court." *Quoted in* John R. Crook, "Contemporary Practice of the United States

Relating to International Law," 102 *American Journal of International Law* 860, 862 (2008). Texas executed Medellín in early August 2008. James C. McKinley, Jr., "Texas Executes Mexican Despite Objections from Bush and International Court," *New York Times*, Aug. 6, 2008, at A6.

Medellín *and Self-execution.* Does *Medellín* contribute to our understanding about when a treaty provision is self-executing? Chief Justice Roberts conceded that "[n]o one disputes that the *Avena* decision—a decision that flows from the treaties through which the United States submitted to ICJ jurisdiction with respect to Vienna Convention disputes—constitutes an *international* law obligation on the part of the United States," but argued that because the United States could block Security Council enforcement of *Avena*, the U.S. international obligation was not intended to be self-executing and a part of domestic law. Justice Breyer's dissent gave seven reasons why he felt the treaty terms at issue in the case were self-executing: i) mandatory and binding language; ii) relation to a specific individual right; iii) logic; iv) diplomatic imperatives; v) judicial nature of the task; vi) no non-judicial activity required; and vii) no presidential or congressional concern with judicial enforcement of the treaty.

Chief Justice Roberts dismissed Justice Breyer's seven reasons for self-execution as "a grab bag" that give "no sort of guidance." Chief Justice Roberts quoted the 1884 *Head Money Cases*: "a treaty is, of course, 'primarily a contract between nations,'" which "ordinarily 'depends for the enforcement of its provisions on the interest and the honor of the governments which are party to it.'" Does that passage suggest it is rare for U.S. treaties to be self-executing? Note that the *Head Money* Court, immediately following the passage quoted by Roberts, went on to find that "a treaty may also contain provisions which confer certain rights upon the citizens or subjects of one of the nations residing in the territorial limits of the other." 112 U.S. 580, 598–99 (1884). Why did Chief Justice Roberts not analyze the Supremacy Clause and its history? What was his alternative to Justice Breyer's "grab bag"? Do you agree with Professor McGuinness's critique: "Given the Court's mode of determining when a treaty is self-executing, there is no clear guidance for predicting the likely outcomes of future cases"? Margaret E. McGuinness, "International Decision: *Medellín v. Texas*," 102 *American Journal of International Law* 622, 627 (2008). Did Roberts or Breyer better reflect U.S. precedent about the incorporation of treaties in U.S. law?

Medellín *and Presidential Powers.* Chief Justice Roberts did "not question" the proposition "that the President's constitutional role 'uniquely qualifies' him to resolve the sensitive foreign policy decisions that bear on compliance with an ICJ decision and 'to do so expeditiously.' " However, he held that the "responsibility for transforming an international obligation rising from a non-self-executing treaty into domestic law falls to Congress." Does this logic show traditional or proper judicial deference to the determinations of the President in foreign affairs? Did the Supreme Court give less deference in *Medellín* to presidential efforts to carry out an obligation arising under an Article II treaty approved with the advice and consent of the U.S. Senate—the U.N. Charter—than it did in *Dames & Moore* to presidential implementation of an executive agreement? Would Chief Justice Roberts have ordered Texas to comply with a U.S. executive agreement with Mexico, in which the President pledged to carry out the ICJ's *Avena* order?

The Supreme Court and the International Reputation of the United States. Has *Medellín* sullied the reputation of the United States? Is the U.S. Supreme Court an institution that can be trusted to comply with America's international legal obligations? The majority opinion admitted that the United States was legally bound to comply both with the Vienna Convention and with the ICJ judgment in *Avena*, but found that, in the circumstances of this case, a U.S. federal state, Texas, was permitted to reject both international law and a presidential order. The Court's admission of national weakness and disunity might well have dismayed Benjamin Franklin, who once famously said: "We must all hang together, or assuredly we will all hang separately." Benjamin Franklin, "At the Signing of the Declaration of Independence (July 4, 1776)," in *Bartlett's Familiar Quotations* 348 (Emily Morison Beck *et al.* eds., 15th ed. 1980). Compare Chief Justice Roberts's states-rights stance in *Medellín* with Justice Holmes's nationalistic posture in *Missouri v. Holland.* Is *Medellín* simply yet another instance in the centuries-long battle between American nationalists and states-rights advocates?

The emotive force of *Medellín* divided the *Wall Street Journal.* Its news article on the case was generally hostile to the majority opinion. Jess Bravin, "Court Deals Blow to International Treaties," *Wall Street Journal,* Mar. 28, 2008, at A3. Its editorial lauded Chief Justice Roberts: "the *Medellín* majority has delivered a victory for legal modesty and the U.S. Constitution." Editorial, "International Law and Domestic Order," *Wall Street Journal,* Mar. 28, 2008, at A14.

The Supreme Court's recent willingness to disregard the international legal commitments of the United States has, in the view of some, contributed to the Court being taken less seriously abroad. See Adam Liptak, "U.S. Court, a Longtime Beacon, Is Now Guiding Fewer Nations," *New York Times,* Sept. 18,

2008, at A1. As long ago as 1994, Justice Blackmun lamented: "At best, I would say that the present Supreme Court enforced *some* principles of international law and *some* of its obligations *some* of the time." Harry A. Blackmun, "The Supreme Court and the Law of Nations," 104 *Yale Law Journal* 39, 49 (1994) (emphasis in original). Looking at recent cases, how would you now characterize the record of the Court?

B. THE LAW OF NATIONS IN U.S. LAW

Long before 1789, when the English philosopher Jeremy Bentham coined the word *international* to distinguish *internal* from *international* jurisprudence, English law recognized two ancestors of what we now call *international law*: the law of treaties and the law of nations. M.W. Janis, "Jeremy Bentham and the Fashioning of 'International Law,' " 78 *American Journal of International Law* 405 (1984). More than two hundred years after Bentham's linguistic invention, Anglo-American law still solves problems about incorporating rules of international law into municipal law with doctrinal answers set in these two traditional categories. We have already studied the American approach to incorporation of treaties (a path directed by the U.S. Constitution and much at odds with the English approach). Now we ask how the U.S. legal system incorporates the law of nations (a route in this case similar to that of other common law countries). In the United States, the *law of nations* has come to include more or less all of the modern sorts of non-treaty rules we examined in Chapter 2, most notably customary international law, general principles of law, and *jus cogens*. We begin our story in 1784 with the classic pre-Constitutional American case, *Respublica v. De Longchamps*. Pay special attention to how American judges since the 18th century have used precedent and principle to give body to the concept of the *law of nations*.

RESPUBLICA V. DE LONGCHAMPS

Court of Oyer and Terminer at Philadelphia
1 U.S. (1 Dall.) 111 (1784)

CHARLES JULIAN DE LONGCHAMPS, commonly called the *Chevalier de Longchamps*, was indicted, that "he, on the 17th of May 1784, in the dwelling-house of his excellency the French minister plenipotentiary, in the presence of Francis Barbe Marbois, unlawfully and insolently did threaten and menace bodily harm and violence to the person of the said Francis Barbe Marbois, he being consul-general of France to the United States, consul for the state of Pennsylvania, Secretary of the French legation &c. resident in the house aforesaid, and under the protection of the law of nations and this commonwealth." And that "afterwards, to wit on the 19th of May, in the public street, &c., he, said Charles Julian de Longchamps, unlawfully, premeditatedly and violently, in and upon the person of the said Francis Barbe Marbois, under the protection of the laws of the nations, and in the peace of this commonwealth, then and there being, an assault did make, and him, the said Francis Barbe Marbois unlawfully and violently did strike and otherwise, &c., in violation of the laws of nations, against the peace and dignity of the United States and of the commonwealth of Pennsylvania."—To these charges, the defendant pleaded not guilty.

The evidence in support of the first count, was, that on the 17th of May, de Longchamps went to the house of the minister of France, and after some conversation with Monsieur Marbois, was heard to exclaim in a loud and menacing tone, "*Je vous deshonnerera, Policon, Coquin,*" addressing himself to that gentleman. That the noise being heard by the minister, he repaired to the room from which it issued, and that, in his presence, the defendant repeated the insult offered to Monsieur Marbois, in nearly the same terms.

In support of the second count, it appeared, that de Longchamps and Monsieur Marbois, having met in Market street, near the coffee-house, entered into a long conversation, in the course of which, the latter said, that he would complain to the civil authority, and the former replied, "you are a blackguard." The witnesses generally deposed, that de Longchamps struck the cane of Monsieur Marbois, before that gentleman used any violent gestures, or even appeared incensed; but that as soon as the stroke was given, Monsieur Marbois employed his stick with great severity, until the spectators interfered and separated the parties. One of the witnesses, indeed, said, that previously to engaging with their canes, he observed the two gentlemen, at the same instant, lay their hands on each others shoulders, in a manner so gentle, that he, who had heard it was customary among the French to part with mutual salutations, imagined a ceremony of that kind was about to take place, and was surprised to see de Longchamps step back, and strike the cane of Monsieur Marbois.

On the part of the defendant, evidence was produced of his having served with honour in the French armies, and his commission of sub-brigadier in the dragoons of Noailles, was read. It appeared, that the occasion of his calling on Monsieur Marbois, was to obtain authentications of these, and some other papers relative to his family, his rank in France, and his military promotions, in order to refute several publications, which had been made in the newspapers, injurious to his character and pretensions. The refusal of Monsieur Marbois to grant the authentications required, was the ground of de Longchamps' resentment, and the immediate cause of his menaces at the minister's house.

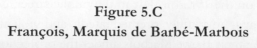

Figure 5.C
François, Marquis de Barbé-Marbois

McKEAN, CHIEF JUSTICE.—This is a case of the first impression in the United States. It must be determined on the principles of the laws of nations, which form a part of the municipal law of Pennsylvania; and, if the offenses charged in the indictment have been committed, there can be no doubt, that those laws have been violated. The words used in the minister's house (which is to be considered as a foreign domicil, where the minister resides in full representation of his sovereign, and where the laws of the state do not extend), may be compared to the same words applied to the Judges in a court of justice, where they sit in representation of the majesty of the people of Pennsylvania. In that case, the offender would be immediately committed to jail, without the preliminary process of an indictment by a grand jury; and, in the case before us, if the offender is convicted, he may certainly be punished by fine and imprisonment.

In actions of slander, words were formerly construed in the mildest sense they would admit; but reason has superceded such forced interpretations, and words are now to be taken according to their ordinary import and meaning. Those expressed by the defendant are evidently of a tendency so opprobrious and violent, that they cannot fail to aggravate the outrage which has been committed.

As to the assault, this is, perhaps, one of that kind, in which the insult is more to be considered, than the actual damage; for, though no great bodily pain is suffered by a blow on the palm of the hand, or the skirt of the coat, yet these are clearly within the legal definition of assault and battery, and among gentlemen, too often, induce duelling, and terminate in murder. As, therefore, anything attached to the person, partakes of its inviolability; de Longchamps' striking Monsieur Marbois' cane, is a sufficient justification of that gentleman's subsequent conduct. . . .

Charles Julian de Longchamps: You have been indicted for unlawfully and violently threatening and menacing bodily harm and violence to the person of the Honorable Francis Barbe de Marbois, secretary to the legation from France, and consul-general of France to the United States of America, in the mansion-house of the minister plenipotentiary of France; and for an assault and battery committed upon the said secretary and consul, in a public street in the City of Philadelphia. To this Indictment you have pleaded, that you were not guilty, and for trial put yourself upon the country; an unbiased jury, upon a fair trial, and clear evidence, have found you guilty.

These offenses having been thus legally ascertained and fixed upon you, his Excellency the President, and the Honorable the Supreme Executive Council, attentive to the honor and interest of this state, were pleased to inform the judges of this court, as they had frequently done before, that the minister of France had earnestly repeated a demand, that you, having appeared in his house in the uniform of a French regiment, and having called yourself an officer in the troops of his Majesty, should be delivered up to him for these outrages, as a Frenchman to be sent to France; and wished us in this stage of your prosecution, to take into mature consideration, and in the most solemn manner to determine:—

1. Whether you could be legally delivered up by council, according to the claim made by the late minister of France?

2. If you could not be thus legally delivered up, whether your offenses in violation of the law of nations, being now ascertained and verified according to the laws of this commonwealth, you ought not to

be imprisoned, until his most Christian Majesty shall declare, that the reparation is satisfactory? . . .

To these questions we have given the following answers in writing:—. . .

1. And as to the first question, we answer, That it is our opinion, that, in this case, Charles Julian de Longchamps cannot be legally delivered up by council, according to the claim made by the minister of France. Though, we think, cases may occur, where council could, *pro bono publico*, and to prevent atrocious offenders evading punishment, deliver them up to the justice of the country to which they belong, or where the offenses were committed.

2. Punishments must be inflicted in the same county where the criminals were tried and convicted, unless the record of the attainder be removed into the supreme court, which may award execution in the county where it sits; they must be such as the laws expressly prescribe; or where no stated or fixed judgment is directed, according to the legal discretion of the court; but judgments must be certain and definite in all respects. Therefore, we conclude, that the defendant cannot be imprisoned, until his most Christian Majesty shall declare that the reparation is satisfactory. . . .

The foregoing answers having been given, it only remains for the court to pronounce sentence upon you. This sentence must be governed by a due consideration of the enormity and dangerous tendency of the offenses you have committed, of the willfulness, deliberation, and malice, wherewith they were done, of the quality and degree of the offended and offender, the provocation given, and all other circumstances which may any way aggravate or extenuate the guilt.

The first crime in the indictment is an infraction of the law of nations. This law, in its full extent, is part of the law of this state, and is to be collected from the practice of different nations, and the authority of writers. The person of a public minister is sacred and inviolable. Whoever offers any violence to him, not only affronts the sovereign he represents, but also hurts the common safety and well-being of nations—he is guilty of a crime against the whole world.

All the reasons, which establish the independency and inviolability of the person of a minister, apply likewise to secure the immunities of his house. It is to be defended from all outrage; it is under a peculiar protection of the laws; to invade its freedom, is a crime against the state and all other nations.

The *comites* of a minister, or those of his train, partake also of his inviolability. The independency of a minister extends to all his household; these are so connected with him, that they enjoy his privileges and follow his fate. The secretary to the embassy has his commission from the sovereign himself; he is the most distinguished character in the suite of a public minister, and is in some instances considered as a kind of public minister himself. Is it not, then, an extraordinary insult, to use threats of bodily harm to his person, in the domicil of the minister plenipotentiary? If this is tolerated, his freedom of conduct is taken away, the business of his sovereign cannot be transacted, and his dignity and grandeur will be tarnished.

You then have been guilty of an atrocious violation of the law of nations; you have grossly insulted gentlemen, the peculiar objects of this law (gentlemen of amiable characters, and highly esteemed by the government of this state), in a most wanton and unprovoked manner: and it is now the interest as well as duty of the government, to animadvert upon your conduct with a becoming severity— such a severity as may tend to reform yourself, to deter others from the commission of the like crime, preserve the honor of the state, and maintain peace with our great and good ally, and the whole world. . . .

Upon the whole THE COURT, after a most attentive consideration of every circumstance in this case, do award, and direct me to pronounce the following sentence:—

That you pay a fine of 100 French crowns to the commonwealth; that you be imprisoned until the 4th day of July 1786, which will make a little more than two years imprisonment in the whole; that you then give good security to keep the peace, and be of good behaviour to all public ministers, secretaries to embassies, and consuls, as well as to all the liege people of Pennsylvania, for the space of seven years, by entering into a recognisance, yourself in a thousand pounds, and two securities in 500 pounds each: that you pay the costs of this prosecution, and remain committed until this sentence be complied with.

The Political Context. Would American sovereignty have been imperiled if the new United States had delivered up De Longchamps to be shipped off to France as was sought by the French Minister? Or if the United States had imprisoned De Longchamps for so long as the French King should dictate? Was it politically useful to rely on the law of nations in refusing the French requests? The Marbois-De Longchamps affair was a cause of concern among leading Americans, including Benjamin Franklin, George Washington, Thomas Jefferson, James Madison, John Adams, James Monroe, John Jay, Benjamin

Harrison, and Charles Pinckney. See William R. Casto, "The Federal Courts' Protective Jurisdiction Over Torts Committed in Violation of the Law of Nations," 18 *Connecticut Law Review* 467, 492 n.143 (1986). A little over a week after De Longchamps assaulted Marbois, Thomas Jefferson wrote to James Madison to complain that Pennsylvania was "so indecisive" in taking steps with respect to the case: "They have not yet declared what they can or will do. . . . The affair is represented to Congress who will have the will but not the power to interpose. It will probably go next to France and bring on serious consequences." Letter of May 25, 1784, *quoted in id.* at 493 n.146. The *De Longchamps Case* provided ammunition for those favoring the creation of a federal judiciary under the U.S. Constitution with jurisdiction to hear cases involving foreign citizens. See Article III(2) of the Constitution.

The Law of Nations in the Common Law. The *De Longchamps Case* preceded the establishment of the federal judiciary. McKean, Chief Justice of Pennsylvania, recited Blackstone's familiar 18th-century formula of the English common law: "the law of nations . . . forms a part of the municipal law." This doctrine about the incorporation of the law of nations into the common law predates the Constitution and the Supremacy Clause of Article VI. What are we to make of the fact that the Supremacy Clause mentions treaties but not the law of nations? Was or is the law of nations the same as customary international law?

Crimes in Violation of the Law of Nations. Was it fair to De Longchamps that he should be subjected to a fine of 100 French crowns and more than two years' imprisonment for an infraction of the law of nations, a law "collected from the practice of different nations, and the authority of writers"? How certain was that law? Should the law have been found in some specific statute of the United States or Pennsylvania? After *United States v. Hudson & Goodwin*, 11 U.S. (7 Cranch) 32 (1812), and *United States v. Coolidge*, 14 U.S. (1 Wheat.) 415 (1816), the doctrine of "common law crimes" lost favor. Defendants today are prosecuted in the United States only for violations of criminal statutes.

An Evolving Doctrine. The very antiquity of the doctrine that the law of nations is part of the common law raises important questions. How has the practice evolved over time? How should a domestic legal system reconcile the traditional doctrine with modern principles of constitutional and statutory law?

In the United States, looking, *inter alia*, at *De Longchamps* and *Smith*, in Chapter 2, the Supreme Court has held that Congress intended the 1789 Alien Tort Statute, refreshed in 1980 by *Filartiga*, one of the cases we read in Chapter 1, to provide another avenue, without further act of Congress, of redress for international law violations committed by individuals. Such wrongs must be at least as definite as the traditional international offences involving ambassadors and piracy. See *Sosa v. Alvarez-Machain* and *Kiobel v. Royal Dutch Petroleum Co.* below. The incorporation doctrine has also evolved in other common law countries. For the United Kingdom, see Philip Sales & Joanne Clement, "International Law in Domestic Courts: The Developing Framework," 124 *Law Quarterly Review* 388, 413–20 (2008).

The Roles of the Law of Nations in U.S. Municipal Law. The relationship between the law of nations and U.S. municipal law was also explored in two cases already considered, *Filartiga v. Pena-Irala* (in Chapter 1) and *The Paquete Habana* (in Chapter 2). In *Filartiga* the court looked to the law of nations because it was construing a U.S. statute that expressly referred to that law.

In *The Paquete Habana*, the Supreme Court derived a common law rule of decision directly from the law of nations, even without a statutory reference. It is *The Paquete Habana* where the famous quote, "International law is part of our law," appears. How should U.S. courts today use the law of nations when no statute expressly requires its application? The doctrine that the law of nations is part of the common law of the United States is discussed in Mark Weston Janis, *International Law* 105–12 (7th ed. 2016).

Yet another function of the law of nations is illustrated by a U.S. Supreme Court decision, *The Charming Betsy*. Here in holding that a vessel was to be treated as belonging to a citizen of Denmark, a neutral country, and hence not subject to forfeit, Chief Justice John Marshall famously ruled: "[A]n act of congress ought never to be construed to violate the law of nations, if any other possible construction remains, and consequently, can never be construed to violate neutral rights, or to affect neutral commerce, further than is warranted by the law of nations as understood in this country." Murray v. Charming Betsy, 6 U.S. (2 Cranch) 64, 118 (1809).

The PLO *Case.* A judgment that may have overly "stretched" the interpretation of a treaty so as to avoid conflict with U.S. domestic law was *United States v. Palestine Liberation Organization*, 695 F.Supp. 1456 (S.D.N.Y. 1988). In that case a U.S. district court judge ruled that the 1987 Anti-Terrorism Act would not be applied to close down the New York office of the Palestine Liberation Organization (PLO) because, as a Permanent Observer to the United Nations, the PLO was protected by the 1947 U.S.-U.N. Headquarters Agreement. Rejecting the U.S. government's argument that the Anti-Terrorism Act trumped the Headquarters Agreement because of the later-in-time rule expressed in *Whitney*, the judge held there was insufficient proof that Congress meant to override the treaty obligations of the United States.

The Reagan administration was split in the aftermath of the *PLO Case*. A high Justice Department official told the *New York Times* that "[t]here is a unanimous belief in this department that the decision should be appealed," but the State Department's Legal Adviser, Abraham Sofaer, countered: "It was a grave mistake for Congress to attempt to close the P.L.O. office. It would violate the United Nations Headquarters Agreement." Clovis Maksoud, the representative of the Arab League in the United States, stated that an appeal "would erode the credibility of the United States in the Middle East." Robert Pear, "U.S. Officials Split Over Whether to Appeal Ruling on P.L.O.," *New York Times*, Aug. 28, 1988, § 1, at 5.

Finally, President Reagan himself resolved the dispute between Justice and State, deciding not to appeal the district court's judgment. On August 29, 1988, the Justice Department issued the following statement: "It is the Administration's normal policy to appeal adverse district court decisions of this kind. But it was decided, in light of foreign policy considerations, including the U.S. role as host to the United Nations organization, not to appeal in this instance." Robert Pear, "U.S. Will Allow P.L.O. to Maintain Its Office at U.N.," *New York Times*, Aug. 30, 1988 at A1. Professor Rosalyn Higgins, later a judge on the International Court of Justice, called the *PLO Case* "a remarkable piece of judicial reasoning, at once admirably purpose-oriented but unpersuasive." Rosalyn Higgins, *Problems and Process: International Law and How We Use It* 215 (1994). Did the *PLO Case* go too far in attempting to reconcile U.S. law and international law?

The Political Question Doctrine. U.S. courts sometimes invoke the "political question doctrine" to abstain from deciding sensitive foreign policy questions. According to Justice Powell, the doctrine involves a three-part inquiry: "(i) Does the issue involve resolution of questions committed by the text of the Constitution to a coordinate branch of Government? (ii) Would resolution of the question demand that a court move beyond areas of judicial expertise? (iii) Do prudential considerations counsel against judicial intervention?" Goldwater v. Carter, 444 U.S. 996, 998 (1979) (Powell, J., concurring). In the *PLO Case* discussed above, the court, although acknowledging that "not all questions touching upon international relations are automatically political questions," nevertheless relied on the political question doctrine to conclude that it would not order the executive branch to arbitrate its dispute concerning the PLO mission. 695 F.Supp. at 1463. The International Court of Justice had ruled, in an advisory opinion, that arbitration of the dispute concerning the PLO mission was required under the U.S.-U.N. Headquarters Agreement. Applicability of the Obligation to Arbitrate Under Section 21 of the United Nations Headquarters Agreement of 26 June 1947, 1988 I.C.J. 12.

SOSA V. ALVAREZ-MACHAIN

542 U.S. 692 (2004)

The Facts

JUSTICE SOUTER delivered the opinion of the Court. . . .

We have considered the underlying facts before, *United States v. Alvarez-Machain*, 504 U.S. 655 (1992). In 1985, an agent of the Drug Enforcement Administration (DEA), Enrique Camarena-Salazar, was captured on assignment in Mexico and taken to a house in Guadalajara, where he was tortured over the course of a 2-day interrogation, then murdered. Based in part on eyewitness testimony, DEA officials in the United States came to believe that respondent Humberto Alvarez-Machain (Alvarez), a Mexican physician, was present at the house and acted to prolong the agent's life in order to extend the interrogation and torture.

In 1990, a federal grand jury indicted Alvarez for the torture and murder of Camarena-Salazar, and the United States District Court for the Central District of California issued a warrant for his arrest. The DEA asked the Mexican Government for help in getting Alvarez into the United States, but when the requests and negotiations proved fruitless, the DEA approved a plan to hire Mexican nationals to seize Alvarez and bring him to the United States for trial. As so planned, a group of Mexicans, including petitioner Jose Francisco Sosa, abducted Alvarez from his house, held him overnight in a motel, and brought him by private plane to El Paso, Texas, where he was arrested by federal officers.

Once in American custody, Alvarez moved to dismiss the indictment on the ground that his seizure was "outrageous governmental conduct," and violated the extradition treaty between the United States and Mexico. The District Court agreed, the Ninth Circuit affirmed, and we reversed, holding the fact of Alvarez's forcible seizure did not affect the jurisdiction of a federal court. The case was tried in 1992, and ended at the close of the Government's case, when the District Court granted Alvarez's motion for a judgment of acquittal.

In 1993, after returning to Mexico, Alvarez began the civil action before us here. He sued Sosa, Mexican citizen and DEA operative Antonio Garate-Bustamante, five unnamed Mexican civilians, the United States, and four DEA agents. So far as it matters here, Alvarez sought damages from the United States under the [Federal Tort Claims Act (FTCA)], alleging false arrest, and from Sosa under the [Alien Tort Statute (ATS)], for a violation of the law of nations. The former statute authorizes suit "for . . . personal injury . . . caused by the negligent or wrongful act or omission of any employee of the Government while acting within the scope of his office or employment." 28 U.S.C. § 1346(b)(1). The latter provides in its entirety that "[t]he district courts shall have original jurisdiction of any civil action by an alien for a tort only, committed in violation of the law of nations or a treaty of the United States." § 1350.

The District Court granted the Government's motion to dismiss the FTCA claim but awarded summary judgment and $25,000 in damages to Alvarez on the ATS claim. A three-judge panel of the Ninth Circuit then affirmed the ATS judgment, but reversed the dismissal of the FTCA claim.

A divided en banc court came to the same conclusion. As for the ATS claim, the court called on its own precedent, "that [the ATS] not only provides federal courts with subject matter jurisdiction, but also creates a cause of action for an alleged violation of the law of nations." The Circuit then relied upon what it called the "clear and universally recognized norm prohibiting arbitrary arrest and detention," to support the conclusion that Alvarez's arrest amounted to a tort in violation of international law. On the FTCA claim, the Ninth Circuit held that, because "the DEA had no authority to effect Alvarez's arrest and detention in Mexico," the United States was liable to him under California law for the tort of false arrest.

We granted certiorari in these companion cases to clarify the scope of both the FTCA and the ATS. We now reverse in each.

The Aftermath of Alvarez-Machain. The opinions in *Sosa* briefly recounted the facts and judgment in *United States v. Alvarez-Machain*, 504 U.S. 655 (1992), where the Supreme Court ruled that a U.S.-government kidnapping in Mexico did not violate the terms of the U.S.-Mexican extradition treaty. What *Sosa* could only hint at was the overwhelming outrage with which *Alvarez-Machain* was greeted. Mexico especially was deeply upset with the decision. Tim Golden, "After Court Ruling, Mexico Tells U.S. Drug Agents to Halt Activity," *New York Times*, June 16, 1992, at 19. Political leaders in the Caribbean, Latin America, Canada, Australia, and Europe also objected. See Jonathan A. Bush, "How Did We Get Here? Foreign Abduction After *Alvarez-Machain*," 45 *Stanford Law Review* 939, 941–42 & nn.11–15 (1993). The Supreme Court's judgment in *Alvarez-Machain* appeared all the more preposterous when the trial judge ultimately acquitted the Mexican doctor on the grounds that the U.S. government's evidence against him "had been based on 'hunches' and the 'wildest speculation' and had failed to support the charges that he had participated in the torture of the drug agent." Seth Mydans, "Judge Clears Mexican in Agent's Killing," *New York Times*, Dec. 15, 1992, at A20. President-elect Bill Clinton condemned *Alvarez-Machain*: "I think that in the absence of some evidence the [Mexican] government was actually taking a dive or trying to thwart us that the principle the Supreme Court articulated was way too broad." *Quoted in* Frank J. Murray, "Clinton Hits Court's Kidnapping Decision," *The Washington Times*, Dec. 16, 1992, at A4. The *Washington Post* opined that "the U.S. government's performance was both embarrassing and badly misguided." "The Collapse of the Alvarez Case," *Washington Post*, Dec. 17, 1992, at A22. As President, Mr. Clinton promised Mexico that the United States government would not conduct any cross-border kidnapping. Steven A. Holmes, "U.S. Gives Mexico Abduction Pledge," *New York Times*, June 22, 1993, at A11.

Alvarez-Machain *and International Law.* Professor Louis Henkin, then President of the American Society of International Law, wrote:

> During its past term, the U.S. Supreme Court had one of its infrequent opportunities to take international law seriously and to assure that the Executive Branch takes international law seriously. The Supreme Court failed. The Attorney General was "gratified."

> [T]he "victory" for the Department of Justice may prove to be pyrrhic. The judicial-executive distortion of standard extradition treaties is remediable, and our treaty partners will no doubt find their remedies. In reaction to general outrage, the United States will—at the least—have to disown that interpretation if it is to maintain its network of extradition treaties, as important to the United States as to any state in the world.

> The larger, longer question is whether the Government of the United States—all branches—is prepared to commit itself to taking international law seriously. . . .

> If the Attorney General continues to refuse to take international law seriously, if the Supreme Court refuses to compel the Department of Justice to take international law seriously, it is up to the President of the United States. . . .

> If the President will not act, it will be up to Congress. The Constitution put international law in the special care of Congress when it gave to that branch the power to define offenses against the Law of Nations.
>
> Louis Henkin, "Will the U.S. Supreme Court Fail International Law?," *Newsletter of the American Society of International Law*, Aug.–Sept. 1992, at 1, 1–2. Should Congress have responded to *Alvarez-Machain* by making it a federal crime for any U.S. official to kidnap any person in violation of international law? Under Article I(8) of the U.S. Constitution, Congress has the power to "define and punish . . . Offences against the Law of Nations."

Sosa v. Alvarez-Machain
The Law

[The Court finds that "the liability asserted here falls within the FTCA exception to waiver of sovereign immunity for claims 'arising in a foreign country,'" and holds that "the exception bars all claims based on any injury suffered in a foreign country, regardless of where the tortious act or omission occurred."]

III

Alvarez has also brought an action under the ATS against petitioner, Sosa, who argues (as does the United States supporting him) that there is no relief under the ATS because the statute does no more than vest federal courts with jurisdiction, neither creating nor authorizing the courts to recognize any particular right of action without further congressional action. Although we agree the statute is in terms only jurisdictional, we think that at the time of enactment the jurisdiction enabled federal courts to hear claims in a very limited category defined by the law of nations and recognized at common law. We do not believe, however, that the limited, implicit sanction to entertain the handful of international law *cum* common law claims understood in 1789 should be taken as authority to recognize the right of action asserted by Alvarez here.

A

Judge Friendly called the ATS a "legal Lohengrin," *IIT v. Vencap, Ltd.*, 519 F.2d 1001, 1015 (C.A.2 1975); "no one seems to know whence it came," and for over 170 years after its enactment it provided jurisdiction in only one case. The first Congress passed it as part of the Judiciary Act of 1789, in providing that the new federal district courts "shall also have cognizance, concurrent with the courts of the several States, or the circuit courts, as the case may be, of all causes where an alien sues for a tort only in violation of the law of nations or a treaty of the United States." Act of Sept. 24, 1789, ch. 20, § 9*(b)*, 1 Stat. 79.

The parties and *amici* here advance radically different historical interpretations of this terse provision. Alvarez says that the ATS was intended not simply as a jurisdictional grant, but as authority for the creation of a new cause of action for torts in violation of international law. We think that reading is implausible. As enacted in 1789, the ATS gave the district courts "cognizance" of certain causes of action, and the term bespoke a grant of jurisdiction, not power to mold substantive law. See *e.g.,* The Federalist No. 81, pp. 447, 451 (J. Cooke ed. 1961) (A. Hamilton) (using "jurisdiction" interchangeably with "cognizance"). The fact that the ATS was placed in § 9 of the Judiciary Act, a statute otherwise exclusively concerned with federal-court jurisdiction, is itself support for its strictly jurisdictional nature. Nor would the distinction between jurisdiction and cause of action have been elided by the drafters of the Act or those who voted on it. As Fisher Ames put it, "there is a substantial difference between the jurisdiction of courts and rules of decision." 1 Annals of Cong. 807 (Gales ed. 1834). It is unsurprising, then, that an authority on the historical origins of the ATS has written that "section 1350 clearly does not create a statutory cause of action," and that the contrary suggestion is "simply frivolous." Casto, The Federal Courts' Protective Jurisdiction Over Torts Committed in Violation of the Law of Nations, 18 Conn. L.Rev. 467, 479, 480 (1986) (hereinafter Casto, Law of Nations); Cf. Dodge, The Constitutionality of the Alien Tort Statute: Some Observations on Text and Context, 42 Va. J. Int'l L. 687, 689 (2002). In sum, we think the statute was intended as jurisdictional in the sense of addressing the power of the courts to entertain cases concerned with a certain subject.

But holding the ATS jurisdictional raises a new question, this one about the interaction between the ATS at the time of its enactment and the ambient law of the era. Sosa would have it that the ATS was stillborn because there could be no claim for relief without a further statute expressly authorizing adoption of causes of action. *Amici* professors of federal jurisdiction and legal history take a different tack, that federal courts could entertain claims once the jurisdictional grant was on the books, because torts in violation of the law of nations would have been recognized within the common law of the time. We think history and practice give the edge to this latter position.

1

"When the *United States* declared their independence, they were bound to receive the law of nations, in its modern state of purity and refinement." *Ware v. Hylton*, 3 Dall. 199, 281 (1796) (Wilson, J.). In the years of the early Republic, this law of nations comprised two principal elements, the first covering the general norms governing the behavior of national states with each other: "*the science which teaches the rights subsisting between nations or states, and the obligations correspondent to those rights,*" E. de Vattel, The Law of Nations, Preliminaries § 3 (J. Chitty et al. transl. and ed. 1883) (hereinafter Vattel), or "that code of public instruction which defines the right and prescribes the duties of nations, in their intercourse with each other," 1 James Kent Commentaries 1. This aspect of the law of nations thus occupied the executive and legislative domains, not the judicial. See 4 W. Blackstone, Commentaries on the Laws of England 68 (1769) (hereinafter Commentaries) ("[O]ffenses against" the law of nations are "principally incident to whole states or nations").

The law of nations included a second, more pedestrian element, however, that did fall within the judicial sphere, as a body of judge-made law regulating the conduct of individuals situated outside domestic boundaries and consequently carrying an international savor. To Blackstone, the law of nations in this sense was implicated "in mercantile questions, such as bills of exchange and the like; in all marine causes, related to freight, average, demurrage, insurances, bottomry . . .; [and] in all disputes relating to prizes, to shipwrecks, to hostages, and ransom bills." *Id.,* at 67. The law merchant emerged from the customary practices of international traders and admiralty required its own transnational regulation. And it was the law of nations in this sense that our precursors spoke about when the Court explained the status of coast fishing vessels in wartime grew from "ancient usage among civilized nations, beginning centuries age, and gradually ripening into a rule of international law . . . " *The Paquete Habana,* 175 U.S. 677, 686 (1900).

There was, finally a sphere in which these rules binding individuals for the benefit of other individuals overlapped with the norms of state relationships. Blackstone referred to it when he mentioned three specific offenses against the law of nations addressed by the criminal law of England: violation of safe conducts, infringements of the rights of ambassadors, and piracy. 4 Commentaries 68. An assault against an ambassador, for example, impinged upon the sovereignty of the foreign nation and if not adequately redressed could rise to an issue of war. See Vattel 463–464. It was this narrow set of violations of the law of nations, admitting of a judicial remedy and at the same time threatening serious consequences in international affairs, that was probably on the minds of the men who drafted the ATS with the reference to tort.

2

Before there was any ATS, a distinctly American preoccupation with these hybrid international norms had taken shape owing to the distribution of political power from independence through the period of confederation. The Continental Congress was hamstrung by its inability to "cause infractions of treaties, or of the law of nations to be punished," J. Madison, Journal of the Constitutional Convention 60 (E. Scott ed. 1893), and in 1781 the Congress implored the States to vindicate rights under the law of nations. In words that echo Blackstone, the congressional resolution called upon state legislatures to "provide expeditious, exemplary, and adequate punishment" for "the violation of safe conducts or passports, . . . of hostility against such as are in amity, . . . with the United States, . . . infractions of the immunities of ambassadors and other public ministers . . . [and] infractions of treaties and conventions to which the United States are a party." 21 Journals of the Continental Congress 1136–1137 (G. Hunt ed. 1912) (hereinafter Journals of the Continental Congress). The resolution recommended that the States "authorise suits . . . for damages by the party injured, and for compensation to the United States for damage sustained by them from an injury done to a foreign power by a citizen." *Id.*, at 1137[.] Apparently only one State acted upon the recommendation, see First Laws of the State of Connecticut 82, 83 (J. Cushing ed. 1982) (1784 compilation; exact date of Act unknown), but Congress had done what it could to signal a commitment to enforce the law of nations.

Appreciation of the Continental Congress's incapacity to deal with this class of cases was intensified by the so-called Marbois incident of May 1784, in which a French adventurer, Longchamps, verbally and physically assaulted the Secretary of the French Legion in Philadelphia. See *Respublica v. De Longchamps*, 1 Dall. 111 (O.T. Phila. 1784).[11] Congress called again for state legislation addressing such matters, and concern over the inadequate vindication of the law of nations persisted through the time of the constitutional convention. During the Convention itself, in fact, a New York City constable produced a reprise of the Marbois affair and Secretary Jay reported to Congress on the Dutch Ambassador's protest, with the explanation that "the federal government does not appear . . . to be vested with any Judicial Powers competent to the Cognizance and Judgment of such Cases." Casto, Law of Nations 494, and n. 152.

---

[11] The French minister plenipotentiary lodged a formal protest with the Continental Congress, 27 Journals of the Continental Congress 478, and threatened to leave Pennsylvania "unless the decision on Longchamps Case should give them full satisfaction." Letter from Samuel Hardy to Gov. Benjamin Harrison of Virginia, June 24, 1784, in 7 Letters of Members of the Continental Congress 558, 559 (E. Burnett ed. 1934). Longchamps was prosecuted for a criminal violation of the law of nations in state court.

The Congress could only pass resolutions, one approving the state-court proceedings, 27 Journals of the Continental Congress 503, another directing the Secretary of Foreign Affairs to apologize and to "explain to Mr. De Marbois the difficulties that may arise . . . from the nature of a federal union," 28 Journals of the Continental Congress 314, and to explain to the representative of Louis XVI that "many allowances are to be made for" the young Nation. *Ibid.*

The Framers responded by vesting the Supreme Court with original jurisdiction over "all Cases affecting Ambassadors, other public ministers and Consuls." U.S. Const., Art. III, § 2, and the First Congress followed through. The Judiciary Act reinforced this Court's original jurisdiction over suits brought by diplomats, created alienage jurisdiction, and, of course, included the ATS.

3

[D]espite considerable scholarly attention, it is fair to say that a consensus understanding of what Congress intended has proven elusive.

Still, the history does tend to support two propositions. First, there is every reason to suppose that the First Congress did not pass the ATS as a jurisdictional convenience to be placed on the shelf for use by a future Congress or state legislature that might, some day, authorize the creation of causes of action or itself decide to make some element of the law of nations actionable for the benefit of foreigners. The anxieties of the preconstitutional period cannot be ignored easily enough to think that the statute was not meant to have a practical effect. Consider that the principal draftsman of the ATS was apparently Oliver Ellsworth,[13] previously a member of the Continental Congress that had passed the 1781 resolution and a member of the Connecticut Legislature that made good on that congressional request. Consider, too, that the First Congress was attentive enough to the law of nations to recognize certain offenses expressly as criminal, including the three mentioned by Blackstone. See An Act for the Punishment of Certain Crimes Against the United States, § 8, 1 Stat. 113–114 (murder or robbery, or other capital crimes, punishable as piracy if committed on the high seas), and § 28, *id.*, at 118 (violation of safe conducts and assaults against ambassadors punished by imprisonment and fines described as "infract[ions of] the law of nations"). It would have been passing strange for Ellsworth and this very Congress to vest federal courts expressly with jurisdiction to entertain civil causes brought by aliens alleging violations of the law of nations, but to no effect whatever until the Congress should take further action. There is too much in the historical record to believe that Congress would have enacted the ATS only to leave it lying fallow indefinitely.

The second inference to be drawn from the history is that Congress intended the ATS to furnish jurisdiction for a relatively modest set of actions alleging violations of the law of nations. Uppermost in the legislative mind appears to have been offenses against ambassadors; violations of safe conduct were probably understood to be actionable, and individual actions arising out of prize captures

---

[13]   The ATS appears in Ellsworth's handwriting in the original version of the bill in the National Archives. Casto, Law of Nations 498, n. 169.

and piracy may well have also been contemplated. But the common law appears to have understood only those three of the hybrid variety as definite or actionable, or at any rate, to have assumed only a very limited set of claims. As Blackstone had put it, "offenses against this law [of nations] are principally incident to whole states or nations," and not individuals seeking relief in court. 4 Commentaries 68.

4

The sparse contemporaneous cases and legal materials referring to the ATS tend to confirm both inferences, that some, but few, torts in violation of the law of nations were understood to be within the common law. . . .

B

Against these indications that the ATS was meant to underwrite litigation of a narrow set of common law actions derived from the law of nations, Sosa raises two main objections. First, he claims that this conclusion makes no sense in view of the Continental Congress's 1781 recommendation to state legislatures to pass laws authorizing such suits. Sosa thinks state legislation would have been "absurd," if common law remedies had been available. Second, Sosa juxtaposes Blackstone's treatise mentioning violations of the law of nations as occasions for criminal remedies, against the statute's innovative reference to "tort," as evidence that there was no familiar set of legal actions for exercise of jurisdiction under the ATS. Neither argument is convincing.

The notion that it would have been absurd for the Continental Congress to recommend that States pass positive law to duplicate remedies already available at common law rests on a misunderstanding of the relationship between common law and positive law in the late 18th century, when positive law was frequently relied upon to reinforce and give standard expression to the "brooding omnipresence" of the common law then thought discoverable by reason. As Blackstone clarified the relation between positive law and the law of nations, "those acts of parliament, which have from time to time been made to enforce this universal law, or to facilitate the execution of [its] decisions, are not to be considered as introductive of any new rule, but merely as declaratory of the old fundamental constitutions of the kingdom; without which it must cease to be a part of the civilized world." 4 Commentaries 67. Indeed, Sosa's argument is undermined by the 1781 resolution on which he principally relies. Notwithstanding the undisputed fact (per Blackstone) that the common law afforded criminal law remedies for violations of the law of nations, the Continental Congress encouraged state legislatures to pass criminal statutes to the same effect, and the first Congress did the same.

Nor are we convinced by Sosa's argument that legislation conferring a right of action is needed because Blackstone treated international law offenses under the rubric of "public wrongs," whereas the ATS uses a word, "tort," that was relatively uncommon in the legal vernacular of the day. It is true that Blackstone did refer to what he deemed the three principal offenses against the law of nations in the course of discussing criminal sanctions, observing that it was in the interest of sovereigns "to animadvert upon them with a becoming severity, that the peace of the world may be maintained," 4 Commentaries 68. But Vattel explicitly linked the criminal sanction for offenses against ambassadors with the requirement that the state, "at the expense of the delinquent, give full satisfaction to the sovereign who has been offended in the person of his minister." Vattel 463–464. . . .

In sum, although the ATS is a jurisdictional statute creating no new causes of action, the reasonable inference from the historical materials is that the statute was intended to have practical effect the moment it became law. The jurisdictional grant is best read as having been enacted on the understanding that the common law would provide a cause of action for the modest number of international law violations with a potential for personal liability at the time.

IV

We think it is correct, then, to assume that the First Congress understood that the district courts would recognize private causes of action for certain torts in violation of the law of nations, though we have found no basis to suspect Congress had any examples in mind beyond those torts corresponding to Blackstone's three primary offenses: violation of safe conducts, infringement of the rights of ambassadors, and piracy. We assume, too, that no development in the two centuries from the enactment of § 1350 to the birth of the modern line of cases beginning with *Filartiga v. Pena-Irala*, 630 F.2d 876 (C.A.2 1980), has categorically precluded federal courts from recognizing a claim under the law of nations as an element of common law; Congress has not in any relevant way amended § 1350 or limited civil common law power by another statute. Still, there are good reasons for a restrained conception of the discretion a federal court should exercise in considering a new cause of action of this kind. Accordingly, we think courts should require any claim based on the present-day law of nations to rest on a norm of international character accepted by the civilized world and defined with a specificity comparable to the features of the 18th century paradigms we have recognized. This requirement is fatal to Alvarez's claim.

A

A series of reasons argue for judicial caution when considering the kinds of individual claims that might implement the jurisdiction conferred by the early statute. First, the prevailing conception of the common law has changed since 1789 in a way that counsels restraint in judicially applying internationally generated norms. When § 1350 was enacted, the accepted conception was of the common law as "a transcendental body of law outside of any particular State but obligatory within it unless and until changed by statute." *Black and White Taxicab & Transfer Co. v. Brown and Yellow Taxicab & Transfer Co.,* 276 U.S. 518, 533 (1928) (Holmes J., dissenting). Now, however, in most cases where a court is asked to state or formulate a common law principle in a new context, there is a general understanding that the law is not so much found or discovered as it is either made or created. Holmes explained famously in 1881 that

> in substance the growth of the law is legislative . . . [because t]he very considerations which judges most rarely mention, and always with an apology, are the secret root from which the law draws all the juices of life. I mean, of course, considerations of what is expedient for the community concerned. [The Common Law 31–32 (Howe ed. 1963).]

One need not accept the Holmesian view as far as its ultimate implications to acknowledge that a judge deciding reliance on an international norm will find a substantial element of discretionary judgment in the decision.

Second, along with, and in part driven by, that conceptual development in understanding common law has come an equally significant rethinking of the role of the federal courts in making it. *Erie R. Co. v. Tompkins,* 304 U.S. 64 (1938), was the watershed in which we denied the existence of any federal "general" common law, *id.,* at 78, which largely withdrew to havens of specialty, some of them defined by express congressional authorization to devise a body of law directly. Elsewhere, this Court has thought it was in order to create federal common law rules in interstitial areas of particular federal interest. [W]e have even assumed competence to make judicial rules of decision of particular importance to foreign relations, such as the act of state doctrine[;] the general practice has been to look for legislative guidance before exercising innovative authority over substantive law. It would be remarkable to take a more aggressive role in exercising a jurisdiction that remained largely in shadow for much of the prior two centuries.

Third, this Court has recently and repeatedly said that a decision to create a private right of action is one better left to legislative judgment in the great majority of cases. . . .

Fourth, the subject of those collateral consequences is itself a reason for a high bar to new private causes of action for violating international law, for the potential implications for the foreign relations of the United States of recognizing such causes should make courts particularly wary of impinging on the discretion of the Legislative and Executive Branches in managing foreign affairs. It is one thing for American courts to enforce constitutional limits on our own State and Federal Governments' power, but quite another to consider suits under rules that would go so far as to claim a limit on the power of foreign governments over their own citizens, and to hold that a foreign government or its agent has transgressed those limits. Yet modern international law is very concerned with just such questions, and apt to stimulate calls for vindicating private interests in § 1350 cases. Since many attempts by federal courts to craft remedies for the violation of new norms of international law would raise risks of adverse foreign policy consequences, they should be undertaken, if at all, with great caution.

The fifth reason is particularly important in light of the first four. We have no congressional mandate to seek out and define new and debatable violations of the law of nations, and modern indications of congressional understanding of the judicial role in the field have not affirmatively encouraged greater judicial creativity. . . .

C

We must still, however, derive a standard or set of standards for assessing the particular claim Alvarez raises, and for this case it suffices to look to the historical antecedents. Whatever the ultimate criteria for accepting a cause of action subject to jurisdiction under § 1350, we are persuaded that federal courts should not recognize private claims under federal common law for violations of any international law norm with less definite content and acceptance among civilized nations than the historical paradigms familiar when § 1350 was enacted. See, *e.g. United States v. Smith*, 5 Wheat. 153, 163–180, n. a. (1820) (illustrating the specificity with which the law of nations defined piracy). This limit upon judicial recognition is generally consistent with the reasoning of many of the courts and judges who faced the issue before it reached this Court. See *Filartiga, supra*, at 890 ("[F]or purposes of civil liability, the torturer has become—like the pirate and slave trader before him—*hostis humani generis*, an enemy of all mankind"); *Tel-Oren* [*v. Libyan Arab Republic*, 726 F.2d 774, 781 (C.A.D.C. 1984)] (Edwards, J., concurring) (suggesting that the "limits of section 1350's reach" be defined by "a handful of heinous actions—each of which violates definable, universal and obligatory norms"); see also *In re Estate of Marcos Human Rights Litigation*, 25 F.3d 1467, 1475 (C.A.9 1994) ("Actionable violations of international law must be of a norm that is specific, universal, and obligatory"). And the determination whether a norm is sufficiently definite to support a cause of action[20] should (and, indeed, inevitably must) involve an element of judgment about the practical consequences of making that cause available to litigants in the federal courts.

Thus, Alvarez's detention claim must be gauged against the current state of international law, looking to those sources we have long, albeit cautiously, recognized.

> [W]here there is no treaty, and no controlling executive or legislative act or judicial decision, resort must be had to the customs and usages of civilized nations; and, as evidence of these, to the works of jurists and commentators, who by years of labor, research and experience, have made themselves peculiarly well acquainted with the subjects of which they treat. Such works are resorted to by judicial tribunals, not for the speculations of their authors concerning what the law ought to be, but for trustworthy evidence of what the law really is. [*The Paquete Habana*, 175 U.S. at 700.]

To begin with, Alvarez cites two well-known international agreements that, despite their moral authority, have little utility under the standard set out in this opinion. He says that his abduction by Sosa was an "arbitrary arrest" within the meaning of the Universal Declaration of Human Rights (Declaration), G.A. Res. 217A (III), U.N. Doc. A/810 (1948). And he traces the rule against arbitrary arrest not only to the Declaration, but also to article nine of the International Covenant on Civil and Political Rights (Covenant), Dec. 19, 1996, 999 U.N.T.S. 171, to which the United States is a party, and to various other conventions to which it is not. But the Declaration does not of its own force impose obligations as a matter of international law. See Humphrey, The UN Charter and the Universal Declaration of Human Rights, in The International Protection of Human Rights 39, 50 (E. Luard ed. 1967) (quoting Eleanor Roosevelt calling the Declaration " 'a statement of principles . . . setting up a common standard of achievement for all peoples and all nations' " and " 'not a treaty or international agreement . . . impos[ing] legal obligations' "). And, although the Covenant does bind the United States as a matter of international law, the United States ratified the Covenant on the express understanding that it was not self-executing and so did not itself create

---

[20] A related consideration is whether international law extends the scope of liability for a violation of a given norm to the perpetrator being sued, if the defendant is a private actor such as a corporation or an individual. Compare *Tel-Oren v. Libyan Arab Republic*, 726 F.2d 774, 791–795 (C.A.D.C.1984) (Edwards, J., concurring) (insufficient consensus in 1984 that torture by private actors violates international law), with *Kadic v. Karadžić*, 70 F.3d 232, 239–241 (C.A.2 1995) (sufficient consensus in 1995 that genocide by private actors violates international law).

obligations enforceable in the federal courts. Accordingly, Alvarez cannot say that the Declaration and Covenant themselves establish the relevant and applicable rule of international law. He instead attempts to show that prohibition of arbitrary arrest has attained the status of binding customary international law. . . .

Alvarez's failure to marshal support for his proposed rule is underscored by the Restatement (Third) of Foreign Relations Law of the United States (1987), which says in its discussion of customary international human rights law that a "state violates international law if, as a matter of state policy, it practices, encourages, or condones . . . prolonged arbitrary detention." *Id.,* § 702. Although the Restatement does not explain its requirements of a "state policy" and of "prolonged" detention, the implication is clear. Any credible invocation of a principle against arbitrary detention that the civilized world accepts as binding customary international law requires a factual basis beyond relatively brief detention in excess of positive authority. Even the Restatement's limits are only the beginning of the enquiry, because although it is easy to say that some policies of prolonged arbitrary detentions are so bad that those who enforce them become enemies of the human race, it may be harder to say which policies cross that line with the certainty afforded by Blackstone's three common law offenses. In any event, the label would never fit the reckless policeman who botches his warrant, even though that same officer might pay damages under municipal law.

Whatever may be said for the broad principle Alvarez advances, in the present, imperfect world, it expresses an aspiration that exceeds any binding customary rule having the specificity we require. Creating a private cause of action to further that aspiration would go beyond any residual common law discretion we think is appropriate to exercise. It is enough to hold that a single illegal detention of less than a day, followed by the transfer of custody to lawful authorities and a prompt arraignment, violates no norm of customary international law so well defined as to support the creation of a federal remedy. . . .

The judgment of the Court of Appeals is

Reversed.

Dr. Alvarez-Machain Revisited. Twelve years after its controversial judgment in *United States v. Alvarez-Machain,* the Supreme Court revisited Dr. Alvarez-Machain. Released and returned to Mexico, Alvarez-Machain sued both the U.S. government and the individuals involved in his kidnapping. As we saw in *Sosa,* the Supreme Court decided in 2004 that Alvarez-Machain could not recover damages, either against the United States under the Federal Tort Claims Act or against the individual kidnappers under the Alien Tort Statute. Though

Alvarez-Machain was again disappointed by the Supreme Court, international law was much better served in the second judgment.

Filartiga v. Pena-Irala *Revisited*. The Court's judgment in *Sosa* was authored by Justice Souter, who conducted a masterful analysis of the Alien Tort Statute, writing an opinion that is careful and sophisticated with respect to international law. Justice Souter reaffirmed much of Judge Kaufman's 1980 opinion in *Filartiga* that ushered in so much human rights litigation in the next three decades. *Sosa* is based on an elegant and nuanced reading of the cases and commentary that have appeared since *Filartiga*. For the purposes of the Alien Tort Statute, it is the judgment's Part III, which dealt with the Alien Tort Statute as it was in 1789, and Part IV, which dealt with a reading of the Alien Tort Statute in today's law, that are most important. Justice Souter's interpretation of the Statute in 1789 represented the unanimous(!) opinion of the Court, while his interpretation of the modern Statute marshaled the support of six of the nine Justices. The judgment preserved the Alien Tort Statute as a living, albeit limited, part of U.S. federal law relating to the law of nations.

"Definite" Violations of the Law of Nations. The *Sosa* Court unanimously agreed that three violations of the law of nations were definite enough in 1789 (and presumably today?) to be prosecuted under the Alien Tort Statute: offenses against ambassadors (the subject matter of *De Longchamps*), violations against safe conducts, and piracy (the subject matter of *Smith* in Chapter 2). Justice Souter (for six members of the Court) also accepted that new violations may become definite enough in modern international law to qualify for Alien Tort Statute protection, but, he said, "we think courts should require any claim based on the present-day law of nations to rest on a norm of international character accepted by the civilized world and defined with a specificity comparable to the features of the 18th-century paradigms we have recognized." Evaluate the Court's rejection of Alvarez-Machain's claim to such a violation. What now is the status of other kinds of violations accepted as definite enough by earlier lower courts, *e.g.*, *Filartiga* in Chapter 1?

Proving the Law of Nations in U.S. Law. *Sosa* is an excellent example of proving the law of nations in the common law, specifically in the federal law of the United States. Locate the different evidences employed to show what a "tort" committed in violation of the "law of nations" meant in 1789 and what it means today. Justice Souter used evidences drawn at least from the following categories: the legislative histories of the Congress before the Constitution, the founding fathers drafting the Constitution, and the First Congress; writers on the law of nations from Blackstone to modern law review articles; judicial decisions from the Supreme Court and other courts; U.S. executive branch and legislative branch practice; and international conventions and declarations. Compare the proof of the law of nations in *Sosa* with some of the other judicial decisions proving international, but non-treaty, rules: *Filartiga*, *Paquete Habana*, *Lotus*, *AM & S*, *Smith*, and *De Longchamps*.

KIOBEL V. ROYAL DUTCH PETROLEUM CO.

133 S.Ct. 1659 (2013)

The Facts

CHIEF JUSTICE ROBERTS delivered the opinion of the Court.

Petitioners, a group of Nigerian nationals residing in the United States, filed suit in federal court against certain Dutch, British, and Nigerian corporations. Petitioners sued under the Alien Tort Statute, 28 U.S.C. § 1350, alleging that the corporations aided and abetted the Nigerian Government in committing violations of the law of nations in Nigeria. The question presented is whether and under what circumstances courts may recognize a cause of action under the Alien Tort Statute, for violations of the law of nations occurring within the territory of a sovereign other than the United States.

I

Petitioners were residents of Ogoniland, an area of 250 square miles located in the Niger delta area of Nigeria and populated by roughly half a million people. When the complaint was filed, respondents Royal Dutch Petroleum Company and Shell Transport and Trading Company, p.l.c., were holding companies incorporated in the Netherlands and England, respectively. Their joint subsidiary, respondent Shell Petroleum Development Company of Nigeria, Ltd. (SPDC), was incorporated in Nigeria, and engaged in oil exploration and production in Ogoniland. According to the complaint, after concerned residents of Ogoniland began protesting the environmental effects of SPDC's practices, respondents enlisted the Nigerian Government to violently suppress the burgeoning demonstrations. Throughout the early 1990's, the complaint alleges, Nigerian military and police forces attacked Ogoni villages, beating, raping, killing, and arresting residents and destroying or looting property. Petitioners further allege that respondents aided and abetted these atrocities by, among other things, providing the Nigerian forces with food, transportation, and compensation, as well as by allowing the Nigerian military to use respondents' property as a staging ground for attacks.

Following the alleged atrocities, petitioners moved to the United States where they have been granted political asylum and now reside as legal residents. They filed suit in the United States District Court for the Southern District of New York, alleging jurisdiction under the Alien Tort Statute and requesting relief under customary international law. . . .

The Second Circuit dismissed the entire complaint, reasoning that the law of nations does not recognize corporate liability. We granted certiorari to consider that question. After oral argument, we directed the parties to file supplemental briefs addressing an additional question: "Whether and under what circumstances the [ATS] allows courts to recognize a cause of action for violations of the law of nations occurring within the territory of a sovereign other than the United States." 132 S.Ct. 1738 (2012). We heard oral argument again and now affirm the judgment below, based on our answer to the second question.

From Filartiga *to* Sosa *to* Kiobel. It has been quite a jurisprudential ride from *Filartiga* in 1980 to *Sosa* in 2004 to *Kiobel* in 2013. What happened? In brief, *Filartiga* inaugurated modern Alien Tort Statute litigation, tens of cases were litigated in the federal district courts, and some reached the federal courts of appeals. Many, though not all, courts followed *Filartiga* and were "friendly" toward international human rights cases brought under the ATS. However, in the 1990s ATS litigation began to change. Suits broadened from those brought against individual foreign aliens to include new claims against large corporations—"Barclay National Bank, Chevron, Del Monte, Ford, IBM, Rio Tinto, Talisman Energy, and Unocal"—and plaintiffs' lawyers were no longer only those working for non-governmental human rights organizations, but also "private, for-profit lawyers working on a contingency fee." Ingrid Woerth, "International Decision: *Kiobel v. Royal Dutch Petroleum Co.*: The Supreme Court and the Alien Tort Statute," 107 *American Journal of International Law* 601, 604 (2013). How might the perception of the public policy value of ATS litigation change with these new defendants and these new plaintiffs' lawyers? Had the ATS envelope been pushed too far? Not remarkably, those defending a corporate point of view applauded *Kiobel*, while human rights advocates deplored the judgment. Mark Walsh, "Global Warning: High Court Limits the Alien Tort Statute, Slowing Suits Against U.S. Companies for Action Overseas," 99 *ABA Journal,* July 2013, at 17, 17–18. See "Agora: Reflections on *Kiobel*," 107 *American Journal of International Law* 829 (2013).

Kiobel v. Royal Dutch Petroleum Co.
The Law

II . . .

The question here is not whether petitioners have stated a proper claim under the ATS, but whether a claim may reach conduct occurring in the territory of a foreign sovereign. Respondents contend that claims under the ATS do not, relying primarily on a canon of statutory interpretation known as the presumption against extraterritorial application. That canon provides that "[w]hen a statute gives no clear indication of an extraterritorial application, it has none," *Morrison v. National Australia Bank Ltd.,* 130 S.Ct. 2869, 2878 (2010), and reflects the "presumption that United States law governs domestically but does not rule the world." *Microsoft Corp. v. AT & T Corp.,* 550 U.S. 437, 454 (2007).

This presumption "serves to protect against unintended clashes between our laws and those of other nations which could result in international discord." *EEOC v. Arabian American Oil Co.,* 499 U.S. 244 (1991) (*Aramco*). As this Court has explained:

> "For us to run interference in . . . a delicate field of international relations there must be present the affirmative intention of the Congress clearly expressed. It alone has the facilities necessary to make fairly such an important policy decision where the possibilities of international discord are so evident and retaliative action so certain." *Benz v. Compania Naviera Hidalgo, S.A.,* 353 U.S. 138 (1957). The presumption against extraterritorial application helps ensure that the Judiciary does not erroneously adopt an interpretation of U.S. law that carries foreign policy consequences not clearly intended by the political branches.

We typically apply the presumption to discern whether an Act of Congress regulating conduct applies abroad. The ATS, on the other hand, is "strictly jurisdictional." *Sosa* [*v. Alvarez-Machain,* 542 U.S. 692, 713 (2004)]. It does not directly regulate conduct or afford relief. It instead allows federal courts to recognize certain causes of action based on sufficiently definite norms of international law. But we think the principles underlying the canon of interpretation similarly constrain courts considering causes of action that may be brought under the ATS. . . .

These concerns are not diminished by the fact that *Sosa* limited federal courts to recognizing causes of action only for alleged violations of international law norms that are " 'specific, universal, and obligatory.' " *Id.,* at 732. As demonstrated by Congress's enactment of the Torture Victim Protection Act of 1991, 106 Stat.

73, identifying such a norm is only the beginning of defining a cause of action. See *id.,* § 3 (providing detailed definitions for extrajudicial killing and torture); *id.,* § 2 (specifying who may be liable, creating a rule of exhaustion, and establishing a statute of limitations). Each of these decisions carries with it significant foreign policy implications.

The principles underlying the presumption against extraterritoriality thus constrain courts exercising their power under the ATS.

III

Petitioners contend that even if the presumption applies, the text, history, and purposes of the ATS rebut it for causes of action brought under that statute. It is true that Congress, even in a jurisdictional provision, can indicate that it intends federal law to apply to conduct occurring abroad. See, *e.g.,* 18 U.S.C. § 1091(e) (providing jurisdiction over the offense of genocide "regardless of where the offense is committed" if the alleged offender is, among other things, "present in the United States"). But to rebut the presumption, the ATS would need to evince a "clear indication of extraterritoriality." *Morrison,* 130 S.Ct., at 2883. It does not.

To begin, nothing in the text of the statute suggests that Congress intended causes of action recognized under it to have extraterritorial reach. The ATS covers actions by aliens for violations of the law of nations, but that does not imply extraterritorial reach—such violations affecting aliens can occur either within or outside the United States. Nor does the fact that the text reaches "*any* civil action" suggest application to torts committed abroad; it is well established that generic terms like "any" or "every" do not rebut the presumption against extraterritoriality.

[N]othing in the text of the ATS evinces the requisite clear indication of extraterritoriality.

Nor does the historical background against which the ATS was enacted overcome the presumption against application to conduct in the territory of another sovereign. We explained in *Sosa* that when Congress passed the ATS, "three principal offenses against the law of nations" had been identified by Blackstone: violation of safe conducts, infringement of the rights of ambassadors, and piracy. 542 U.S., at 723, 724; see 4 W. Blackstone, Commentaries on the Laws of England 68 (1769). The first two offenses have no necessary extraterritorial application. Indeed, Blackstone—in describing them—did so in terms of conduct occurring within the forum nation. See *ibid.* (describing the right of safe conducts for those "who are here"); 1 *id.,* at 251 (1765) (explaining that safe conducts grant a member of one society "a right to intrude into another"); *id.,* at 245–248 (recognizing the king's power to "receiv[e] ambassadors at home" and detailing their rights in the state "wherein they are appointed to reside"); see also E. De Vattel, Law of Nations 465 (J. Chitty et al. transl. and ed. 1883) ("[O]n his entering the country to which he is sent, and making himself known, [the ambassador] is under the protection of the law of nations . . .").

Two notorious episodes involving violations of the law of nations occurred in the United States shortly before passage of the ATS. Each concerned the rights of ambassadors, and each involved conduct within the Union. In 1784, a French adventurer verbally and physically assaulted Francis Barbe Marbois—the Secretary of the French Legion—in Philadelphia. The assault led the French Minister Plenipotentiary to lodge a formal protest with the Continental Congress and threaten to leave the country unless an adequate remedy were provided. *Respublica v. De Longchamps,* 1 Dall. 111 (O.T.Phila.1784). And in 1787, a New York constable entered the Dutch Ambassador's house and arrested one of his domestic servants. See Casto, The Federal Courts' Protective Jurisdiction over Torts Committed in Violation of the Law of Nations, 18 Conn. L.Rev. 467, 494 (1986). At the request of Secretary of Foreign Affairs John Jay, the Mayor of New York City arrested the constable in turn, but cautioned that because " 'neither Congress nor our [State] Legislature have yet passed any act respecting a breach of the privileges of Ambassadors,' " the extent of any available relief would depend on the common law. See Bradley, The Alien Tort Statute and Article III, 42 Va. J. Int'l L. 587, 641–642 (2002) (quoting 3 Dept. of State, The Diplomatic Correspondence of the United States of America 447 (1837)). The two cases in which the ATS was invoked shortly after its passage also concerned conduct within the territory of the United States. See *Bolchos,* 3 F. Cas. 810 (wrongful seizure of slaves from a vessel while in port in the United States); *Moxon,* 17 F. Cas. 942 (wrongful seizure in United States territorial waters).

These prominent contemporary examples—immediately before and after passage of the ATS—provide no support for the proposition that Congress expected causes of action to be brought under the statute for violations of the law of nations occurring abroad.

The third example of a violation of the law of nations familiar to the Congress that enacted the ATS was piracy. Piracy typically occurs on the high seas, beyond the territorial jurisdiction of the United States or any other country. See 4 Blackstone, *supra,* at 72 ("The offence of piracy, by common law, consists of committing those acts of robbery and depredation upon the high seas, which, if committed upon land, would have amounted to felony there"). . . . Petitioners contend that because Congress surely intended the ATS to provide jurisdiction for actions against pirates, it necessarily anticipated the statute would apply to conduct occurring abroad.

Applying U.S. law to pirates, however, does not typically impose the sovereign will of the United States onto conduct occurring within the territorial jurisdiction of another sovereign, and therefore carries less direct foreign policy consequences. Pirates were fair game wherever found, by any nation, because they generally did not operate within any jurisdiction. We do not think that the existence of a cause of action against them is a sufficient basis for concluding that other causes of action under the ATS reach conduct that does occur within the territory of another sovereign; pirates may well be a category unto themselves. See *Morrison,* 130 S.Ct., at 2883 ("[W]hen a statute provides for some extraterritorial application, the presumption against extraterritoriality operates to limit that provision to its terms."). . . .

Finally, there is no indication that the ATS was passed to make the United States a uniquely hospitable forum for the enforcement of international norms. As Justice Story put it, "No nation has ever yet pretended to be the custos morum of the whole world. . . ." *United States v. The La Jeune Eugenie,* 26 F. Cas. 832, 847 (No. 15,551) (C.C.Mass.1822). It is implausible to suppose that the First Congress wanted their fledgling Republic—struggling to receive international recognition—to be the first. Indeed, the parties offer no evidence that any nation, meek or mighty, presumed to do such a thing.

The United States was, however, embarrassed by its potential inability to provide judicial relief to foreign officials injured in the United States. Such offenses against ambassadors violated the law of nations, "and if not adequately redressed could rise to an issue of war." *Sosa,* 542 U.S., at 715; cf. The Federalist No. 80, p. 536 (J. Cooke ed. 1961) (A. Hamilton) ("As the denial or perversion of justice . . . is with reason classed among the just causes of war, it will follow that the federal judiciary ought to have cognizance of all causes in which the citizens of other countries are concerned"). The ATS ensured that the United States could provide a forum for adjudicating such incidents. Nothing about this historical context suggests that Congress also intended federal common law under the ATS to provide a cause of action for conduct occurring in the territory of another sovereign.

Indeed, far from avoiding diplomatic strife, providing such a cause of action could have generated it. Recent experience bears this out. See *Doe v. Exxon Mobil Corp.,* 654 F.3d 11, 77–78 (C.A.D.C. 2011) (Kavanaugh, J., dissenting in part) (listing recent objections to extraterritorial applications of the ATS by Canada,

execution); Lawrence v. Texas, 539 U.S. 558, 573 (2003) (Justice Kennedy, looking to the judgment of the European Court of Human Rights in *Dudgeon v. United Kingdom*, respecting consensual homosexual conduct); and Roper v. Simmons, 543 U.S. 551, 578 (2005) (according to Justice Kennedy, "[t]he opinion of the world community, while not controlling our outcome, does provide respected and significant confirmation for our own conclusions" concerning the unconstitutionality of the juvenile death penalty). In 2010 in *Graham v. Florida*, Justice Kennedy wrote: "There is support for our conclusion" that imposing life without parole sentences on juveniles who did not commit homicide is unconstitutional in "the fact that . . . the United States adheres to a sentencing practice rejected the world over." Although "[t]he judgments of other nations and the international community are not dispositive as to the meaning of the Eighth Amendment," they are also "not irrelevant." 560 U.S. 48, 80 (2010). See "Agora: The United States Constitution and International Law," 98 *American Journal of International Law* 42 (2004).

The use of international law to interpret the U.S. Constitution is long-standing. For example, in the infamous case of *Dred Scott v. Sandford*, 60 U.S. (19 How.) 393 (1857), the Justices of the Supreme Court employed international law extensively as they bitterly divided in a 7–2 judgment holding that African-Americans could never be U.S. citizens and that Congress had not had constitutional power to abolish slavery in the territories in the 1820 Missouri Compromise. "[A]t no time in U.S. history was the gap between our human rights rhetoric and our human rights practice so great." Mark W. Janis, "*Dred Scott* and International Law," 43 *Columbia Journal of Transnational Law* 763, 810 (2005).

CHAPTER 6

International Law and the Use of Force

Rules about the use of force are among the oldest in international law. Classical categories are *jus ad bellum*, *i.e.*, laws about when it is legal to resort to force, and *jus in bello*, *i.e.*, laws concerning the conduct of hostilities. First in Part A we consider *jus ad bellum*, and in Part B *jus in bello*, also known as international humanitarian law and sometimes as the law of war.

A. *JUS AD BELLUM*

Section 1 of this Part A explores traditional limits on resort to force, and Section 2 provides an overview of *jus ad bellum* as embodied in the 1945 U.N. Charter and as conceptualized during the Cold War (1945–1989). The remainder of Part A examines several modern issues related to resort to force in cases of interstate invasions (Section 3), terrorism (Section 4), humanitarian intervention (Section 5), and peacekeeping (Section 6).

1. Traditional Limits on Resort to Force

Just War. For centuries, theologians and jurists have worked to define legal and moral limits on the use of force. St. Augustine, writing in the 5th century, developed a concept of "just war," war pursued to avenge injuries against an enemy who "has neglected either to punish wrongs committed by its own citizens or to restore what has been unjustly taken by it. Further that kind of war is undoubtedly just which God Himself ordains." *Quoted in* Ian Brownlie, *International Law and the Use of Force by States* 5 (1963). The 16th-century Spanish Catholic jurists Vitoria and Suarez, along with the Dutch Protestant theorist Hugo Grotius, who wrote during the Thirty Years War (1618–1648), were among those who refined the just war doctrine, believing there ought to be both humane means and right ends in the prosecution of war.

According to one recent formulation, six principles define a just war:

(1) just cause, including both "humanitarian catastrophes" and "[i]mminent, present and recent acts of aggression (against one's own country or an 'ally')";

(2) last resort, requiring "a series of efforts to avoid war";

(3) proportionality, meaning that "the potential participants to a war should estimate that, if successful, the benefits definitely outweigh the costs of going to war";

(4) likelihood of success, which "advises that a war should not be entered into if there is little or no chance that it will meet with some degree of success";

(5) right intentions, which are usually linked to just cause; a country will have right intentions if it "intends to act in order to correct an injustice, and does not act additionally in ways that lead to its own aggression or to exploitation"; and

(6) legitimate authority, which requires "that only those who are legally designated to make decisions about going to war be permitted to do so."

Nicholas Fotion, *War & Ethics* 19–20 (2007). Not every just war theorist has accepted all of these requirements. Grotius, for example, found "right intentions" too indeterminate to be useful. See Hugo Grotius, *The Law of War and Peace* Book 2, chap. 22, part XVII (Francis W. Kelsey trans. 1985). But the list does reflect typical principles about when it is just to resort to force. The listed principles do not concern the limits on the conduct of hostilities (*i.e., jus in bello*) considered in Part B.

Do national leaders consider just war principles in determining whether to use force? If not, what is their utility? Do they provide a basis for observers to debate and judge the rightness of recourse to force? Are there historical instances of recourse to force that may be generally deemed unjust? Consider these questions as you read about the various examples of recourse to force in this Part A.

War as a Legitimate Exercise of Sovereign Authority. Just war doctrine fell into disfavor in many international legal circles in the 19th and early 20th centuries. International law commentators writing then often regarded war—a formal status that depended on the declaration or intention of one of the parties—as a legitimate exercise of sovereign power. William Hall, for example, claimed that international law has "no alternative but to accept war, independently of the justice of its origin, as a relation which the parties to it may set up, if they choose." W.E. Hall, *A Treatise on International Law* § 16, at 64–65 (4th ed. 1895). Indeed, a traditional way for a state to acquire territory was by conquest followed by occupation and effective control, a method consistent with discretionary unilateral use of force. Nowadays, as we shall see, the legality of recourse to force is suspect, except in cases of self-defense or when authorized by the United Nations Security Council.

International Law Rules Limiting Recourse to Force. Even when war was generally regarded as legal, international law rules limited resort to force. Two types of limits were notable during the 19th and early 20th centuries. First, some treaties constrained states in their resort to force. For example, parties to the 1907 Hague Convention No. II agreed "not to have recourse to armed force for the recovery of contract debts claimed from the Government of one country by the Government of another country as being due to its nationals," although the limitation did not apply if the debtor state refused to submit to arbitration or to comply with a resulting arbitral award. Other agreements limited the size of forces that could be placed along borders. In addition, an extensive body of law concerned the rights of neutrals during wartime.

Second, general international law limited the use of force short of war. An arbitral tribunal in the 1928 *Naulilaa Case*, for example, discussed limits on the use of force in a reprisal. Reprisals—responses that would be illegal but for another state's internationally wrongful act—need not involve fighting; detaining a foreign vessel in port or peacefully blockading foreign vessels could be forms of reprisal. But some reprisals did involve force, as seen in the *Naulilaa Case*. Due to a misunderstanding, a Portuguese garrison killed three Germans on the border between the Portuguese colony of Angola and the German colony of Southwest Africa (present-day Namibia). German forces responded by invading Angola, attacking several Portuguese outposts, and inflicting numerous casualties and significant property damage. The *Naulilaa* tribunal found that Germany's forceful reprisal violated international law. The tribunal held that three conditions were required for a lawful reprisal, none of which had been met: 1) Portugal had not committed "a prior act contrary to the law of nations"; 2) Germany had made no demand for redress, and a "reprisal is only lawful when it has been preceded by an unsatisfied demand," thus showing the "necessity" to resort to force; and 3) Germany's response had been excessive, violating the requirement that there be "proportionality between the reprisal and the offense." Portugal v. Germany, Special Arbitral Tribunal,

[handwritten margin note: Vergeltung - reprisal]

Judgment of 31 July 1928, 2 *Reports of International Arbitral Awards* 1011, 1027–28 (2006) (authors' translation from the French).

Limits on the Use of Force as a Countermeasure or in Self-defense. International lawyers today often use the term "countermeasures" rather than "reprisals." A body of law has developed to gauge the legality of countermeasures, including their proportionality to a prior illegal act. Although the *Naulilaa* tribunal indicated that an armed reprisal might be legal if the conditions noted in the preceding paragraph were met, use of force as a reprisal is legally suspect today. According to the International Court of Justice in its advisory opinion in the *Legality of the Threat or Use of Nuclear Weapons Case*, "armed reprisals in time of peace . . . are considered to be unlawful." 1996 I.C.J. 226, 246. See Derek Bowett, "Reprisals Involving Recourse to Armed Force," 66 *American Journal of International Law* 1 (1972). Provisions of the Charter of the United Nations, which we consider in Section 2 below, help explain this conclusion.

Prior to the U.N. Charter, international legal constraints also applied to recourse to force as a matter of self-preservation or self-defense. 19th-century diplomatic correspondence concerning the *Caroline* dispute concerned such limits.

The Caroline *Incident.* During an 1837 Canadian insurrection against the British government, rebels urged Americans to help their cause. Despite the efforts of U.S. authorities to prevent U.S. citizens from cooperating with the uprising, many from the Buffalo, New York area volunteered. In December 1837 a force of 800–1,000 men, mostly U.S. citizens, took possession of Navy Island, a Canadian island in the Niagara River, which formed the boundary between the United States and Canada. This base was used to fire on Canadian houses and vessels. The *Caroline*, a privately owned American ship, delivered ammunition and supplies from U.S. territory to Navy Island. One night in late December 1837, British forces attacked the *Caroline*, which at the time was docked on the U.S. shore. At least one American was killed. The British lit the ship on fire and then set it adrift; it broke apart.

This incident gave rise to diplomatic exchanges between the U.S. and British governments during the period 1838–1842. U.S. Secretary of State Daniel Webster wrote the April 1841 letter excerpted below to Henry Fox, the British Minister in Washington. Lord Ashburton, sent from Britain to the United States as a special minister to address several outstanding disputes between the two countries, gave the eventual British reply.

THE *CAROLINE* DISPUTE

29 British and Foreign State Papers 1129; 30 British and Foreign State Papers 195

Mr. Webster to Mr. Fox. Washington, April 24, 1841.

[T]he act of destroying the *Caroline* [cannot] be justified by any reasonable application or construction of the right of self-defence under the laws of nations. It is admitted that a just right of self-defence attaches always to nations as well as to individuals, and is equally necessary for the preservation of both. But the extent of this right is a question to be judged of by the circumstances of each particular case, and when its alleged exercise has led to the commission of hostile acts within the territory of a Power at peace, nothing less than a clear and absolute necessity can afford ground of justification.

[I]t will be for Her Majesty's Government . . . to show a necessity of self-defence, instant, overwhelming, leaving no choice of means, and no moment for deliberation. It will be for it to show, also, that the local authorities of Canada, even supposing the necessity of the moment authorized them to enter the territories of The United States at all, did nothing unreasonable or excessive; since the act, justified by the necessity of self-defence, must be limited by that necessity, and kept clearly within it. It must be shown that admonition or remonstrance to the persons on board the Caroline was impracticable, or would have been unavailing; it must be shown that day-light could not be waited for; that there could be no attempt at discrimination between the innocent and the guilty; that it would not have been enough to seize and detain the vessel; but that there was a necessity, present and inevitable, for attacking her in the darkness of the night, while moored to the shore, and while unarmed men were asleep on board, killing some and wounding others, and then drawing her into the current, above the cataract, setting her on fire, and, careless to know whether there might not be in her the innocent with the guilty, or the living with the dead, committing her to a fate which fills the imagination with horror. A necessity for all this, the Government of the United States cannot believe to have existed.

Lord Ashburton to Mr. Webster. Washington, July 28, 1842. . . .

It is so far satisfactory to perceive that we are perfectly agreed as to the general principles of international law applicable to this unfortunate case. Respect for the inviolable character of the territory of independent nations is the most essential foundation of civilization. It is useless to strengthen a principle so generally acknowledged by any appeal to authorities on international law, and you may be assured, Sir, that Her Majesty's Government set the highest possible value on this principle, and are sensible of their duty to support it by their conduct and example for the maintenance of peace and order in the world.

[But] a strong overpowering necessity may arise when this great principle may and must be suspended. It must be so for the shortest possible period during the continuance of an admitted overruling necessity, and strictly confined within the narrowest limits imposed by that necessity. "Self" defence is the first law of our nature, and it must be recognized by every code which professes to regulate the conditions and relations of man. Upon this modification, if I may so call it, of the great general principle, we seem also to be agreed[.]

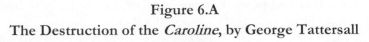

Figure 6.A
The Destruction of the *Caroline*, by George Tattersall

The Outcome of the Caroline *Dispute.* In parts of his July 1842 letter not reproduced above, Lord Ashburton attempted, in good lawyerly fashion, to justify the attack on the *Caroline* within the framework of the rules Webster had set forth. Ashburton also expressed regret for the need to violate U.S. territory, and apologized for not expressing that regret earlier. Webster replied on August 6, 1842. He accepted the apology, noting "with pleasure that your Lordship fully admits those great principles of public law, applicable to cases of this kind, which this government has expressed; and that on your part, as on ours, respect for the inviolable character of the territory of independent states is the most essential foundation of civilization." According to Webster, President Tyler found Ashburton's letter "sufficient to warrant forbearance from any further remonstrance against what took place[.]" *Quoted in* 2 Moore, *Digest of International Law* § 217, at 412–13 (1906).

The Trial of Alexander McLeod. The trial of Alexander McLeod contributed significantly to U.S.-British tensions over the *Caroline* affair. McLeod, a British deputy sheriff, was arrested in New York in 1840 and charged with murder and arson for allegedly participating in the attack on the *Caroline*. His imprisonment and trial in New York state court greatly upset Britain, which regarded the attack on the *Caroline* as a necessary government-authorized act. Secretary of State Webster and other U.S. leaders, including Presidents Harrison and Tyler, agreed with the British that McLeod should not be individually responsible if he was following British orders to attack the *Caroline*. Nevertheless, federal officials were powerless to stop the trial, and conceded that any defenses had to be raised in state court. McLeod was ultimately acquitted when the prosecution could not establish that he had even been present when the *Caroline* was destroyed. McLeod's acquittal helped pave the way for the diplomatic resolution of the *Caroline* dispute. For more background on McLeod's trial and the *Caroline* affair, see John E. Noyes, "*The Caroline*: International Law Limits on Resort to Force," in *International Law Stories* 263 (John E. Noyes, Laura A. Dickinson & Mark W. Janis eds. 2007).

Self-defense and the Caroline *Rule.* When Daniel Webster formulated the *Caroline* rule, he was well aware of a natural law tradition that recognized that states could, in narrow circumstances, use force defensively before they had actually been attacked. See Mark Totten, *First Strike: America, Terrorism, and Moral Tradition* (2010). Some commentators have argued that Webster was articulating a legal test applicable to situations of "self-preservation," *i.e.*, where the continued existence or independence of a country was at stake. But Webster's language and the context of the *Caroline* incident suggest that he was concerned with "self-defense" against attacks that did not necessarily threaten a state's existence. In formulating the *Caroline* rule so restrictively, Webster also emphasized the respect due U.S. neutrality in a conflict between British rebels and the British government.

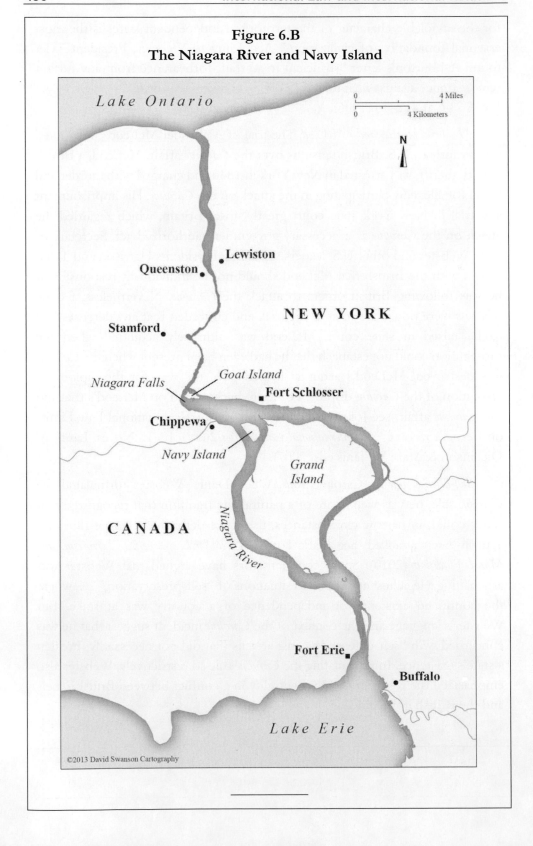

Figure 6.B
The Niagara River and Navy Island

Scholars, political leaders, and a few jurists have continued to invoke the *Caroline* rule in the 20th and 21st centuries, albeit in different political and legal contexts. The Nuremberg Tribunal (see Chapter 7) cited the *Caroline* rule when rejecting German leaders' arguments that it was legitimate to attack Norway in self-defense. International Military Tribunal (Nuremberg), Judgment and Sentences, Oct. 1, 1946, *reprinted in* 41 *American Journal of International Law* 172, 205–07 (1947). Is the *Caroline* rule still legally relevant after adoption of Article 51 of the U.N. Charter, considered below? Which aspects, if any, of the rule are suited to today's world?

2. The United Nations, Self-Defense, and Recourse to Force During the Cold War

States reacted to the excesses of World War I by adopting new legal constraints on the use of force. The 1919 Covenant of the League of Nations provided procedural mechanisms encouraging a cooling-off period before hostilities could commence. Members of the League promised to submit "any dispute likely to lead to a rupture" to arbitration or judicial settlement, or to the League's Council for inquiry. They also agreed "in no case to resort to war until three months after the award by the arbitrators or the judicial decision, or the report by the Council." League of Nations Covenant, arts. 12(1), 15(1). In addition, the 1928 Kellogg-Briand Pact, reproduced in Chapter 2, condemned "recourse to war for the solution of international controversies" and renounced war "as an instrument of national policy." These restraints proved futile in the 1930's and during the Second World War. Following the carnage of World War II, the United Nations Charter in 1945 introduced a general prohibition on the unilateral use of force by states.

The U.N. Charter and Recourse to Force. Articles 2(3) and 33 of the Charter oblige U.N. member states to settle disputes by peaceful means, and Article 2(4) requires members to refrain "from the threat or use of force against the territorial integrity or political independence of any state." The Charter sets out two exceptions to this Article 2(4) proscription: the right of self-defense (Article 51) and collective security measures authorized by the U.N. Security Council (Chapter VII of the U.N. Charter). The U.N. Security Council has more legal authority under Chapter VII to respond to threats to international peace and security, through economic sanctions or forceful measures, than did the Council of the League of Nations under the League Covenant. Review the material about the origins of the United Nations in Chapter 3.

Collective Security. The core of the notion of collective security is that all states should join together to prevent or counteract—forcefully if necessary—one state's use of coercion for its advantage. The U.N. Charter promises an active multilateral form of collective security, but this promise proved more or less a dead letter during the 45 years of the Cold War, 1945–1989. Divided into opposing camps, the West led by the United States and the East led by the Soviet Union, the world's states stymied most collective security efforts attempted during the period. Efforts to promote collective security have taken different turns since 1989, as we will explore in Sections 3–6 of this chapter.

In addition to Cold War divisions, what other factors complicate efforts to build an effective collective security system? Are there some states against which even collective action would be too dangerous or otherwise unavailing? Do collective sanctions harm only the target of sanctions, and might imposing them prove too costly in some situations? Will the international community deem each state that is the victim of aggression equally worth defending?

In theory, three factors determine whether a collective security measure will be successful. First, the members of a collective security arrangement must reach a consensus that a situation threatens international peace and security. Second, they must commit to a response and related contingency plans, and be willing to bear the costs of that response—typically sanctions or the use of force. Third, those members must organize their response, determining what rules and procedures to use in implementing, monitoring, and enforcing it. See Thomas G. Weiss, David P. Forsythe, Roger A. Coate & Kelly-Kate Pease, *The United Nations and Changing World Politics* 27–29 (7th ed. 2014). We consider next the roles that various organs of the United Nations play in promoting international peace, especially through collective security measures.

The U.N. Secretary-General, the Secretariat, and the Promotion of International Peace. Although the U.N. Security Council, in the words of Article 24 of the U.N. Charter, has "primary responsibility for the maintenance of international peace and security"—and we take a closer look at the Council and this responsibility below—other organs also play significant roles in promoting peace. According to Article 99 of the U.N. Charter, the Secretary-General of the United Nations, the Organization's executive leader who supervises the professional staff that comprises the Secretariat, may bring to the Security Council's attention "any matter which in his opinion may threaten the maintenance of international peace and security." The Secretary-General may also take a direct role in efforts to ease tensions and resolve disputes. In Chapter 4.A we saw the Secretary-General's personal involvement in the *Rainbow Warrior* dispute between France and New Zealand. The *Reparation Case* (Chapter 3.B) was decided in the context of U.N. mediation efforts in Israel. The Secretariat is also instrumental in organizing the deployment of peacekeeping forces once they have been authorized. We examine peacekeeping in Section 6 below.

The General Assembly and International Peace and Security. Although the U.N. Charter authorizes the General Assembly to discuss matters related to international peace and security, Article 12 provides that, "[w]hile the Security Council is exercising in respect of any dispute or situation the functions assigned to it in the present Charter, the General Assembly shall not make any recommendation with regard to that dispute or situation," absent a Council request. In the *Wall Case* (Chapter 4.B), the International Court of Justice outlined the relative responsibilities of the General Assembly and the Security Council concerning international peace and security.

One historically important General Assembly recommendation was the Uniting for Peace Resolution (377(A), 1950). The impetus for it was the Communist incursion on the Korean peninsula. The Security Council, with the Soviet Union boycotting its meetings because China's Communist government had not been seated on the Council, condemned the incursion and authorized military action against Communist North Korea. However, when the Soviet Union returned to the Security Council, the Council faced Soviet vetoes and gave no further instructions concerning the Korean military action. The United States then persuaded the General Assembly to authorize steps to unify Korea and hold democratic elections there, and, in order to achieve those ends, to recommend that forces operating "under the auspices of the United Nations" take "[a]ll appropriate steps . . . to ensure conditions of stability throughout Korea." Resolution 376 (1950). This Resolution sidestepped the Security Council. In addition to pushing for Korea-specific General Assembly resolutions, the United States successfully led efforts to adopt the Uniting for Peace Resolution, which provides:

> if the Security Council, because of lack of unanimity of the permanent members, fails to exercise its primary responsibility for the maintenance of international peace and security in any case where there appears to be a threat to the peace, breach of the peace, or act of aggression, the General Assembly shall consider the matter immediately with a view to making appropriate recommendations to Members for collective measures, including in the case of a breach of the peace or act of aggression the use of armed force when necessary, to maintain or restore international peace and security.

The Uniting for Peace Resolution provided the basis for General Assembly approval of peacekeeping initiatives in 1956 (relating to a crisis over the Suez Canal, where British and French opposition blocked Security Council action) and 1960 (in the Congo, where the United States and the Soviet Union supported opposing factions). See Thomas M. Franck, *Nation Against Nation* 38–42 (1985).

The General Assembly today may take certain steps relating to matters of international peace and security without relying on the Uniting for Peace Resolution. As we saw in the *Wall Case*, the Assembly may request an advisory opinion from the ICJ that touches on security matters, even with respect to situations pending before the Security Council. The Assembly also has adopted provisions calling for "voluntary sanctions," and it serves as a forum for debates over matters of peace and security. See Larry D. Johnson, "'Uniting for Peace': Does It Still Serve Any Useful Purpose?," *AJIL Unbound*, July 15, 2014, *available at* https://www.asil.org/blogs/%E2%80%9Cuniting-peace%E2%80%9D-does-it-still-serve-any-useful-purpose. Despite the General Assembly's roles concerning peace and security, however, the Security Council retains key authority. Modern peacekeeping depends on Security Council authorization (see Section 6), and the Council is the organ that can approve legally binding collective security measures under Chapter VII of the U.N. Charter.

The Security Council and International Peace and Security. The Security Council's 15 members (expanded from 11 by a 1965 amendment to the U.N. Charter) include five permanent members (China, France, Russia, the United Kingdom, and the United States), plus 10 states from different regions of the world, elected for two-year terms. A Security Council measure will be adopted if nine states vote in favor of it and no permanent member vetoes it. When the Council considers matters related to international peace and security, it typically turns first to Chapter VI of the Charter, concerning the pacific settlement of disputes, making recommendations to parties concerning dispute resolution. Chapter VI recommendations, however, are approved against the background of Chapter VII, under which the Council may adopt legally binding decisions that impose sanctions or other measures against states threatening international peace and security. The remaining material in this section compares "recommendations" to legally binding Security Council "decisions"; examines provisions of the U.N. Charter related to collective security; introduces the Charter's vision of self-defense; and considers how the Cold War affected views about the legality of recourse to force.

U.N. Recommendations and Decisions. Under Chapter IV of the U.N. Charter, the General Assembly, in adopting resolutions, may make "recommendations." Some of these resolutions may contribute to customary international law (see the *Texaco/Libya Case* in Chapter 2). Security Council resolutions may also contain recommendations, but in addition the Council may make "decisions." This term of art is legally significant, because pursuant to Article 25 of the U.N. Charter, member states "agree to accept and carry out the decisions of the Security Council in accordance with the present Charter." Furthermore, Charter obligations, including this Article 25 obligation, supersede states' other treaty obligations. See Article 103 of the U.N. Charter and the discussion in Chapter 3, Part C. Does the text of Article 25 require automatic deference to every Security Council decision?

Figure 6.C
U.N. Security Council Chamber, U.N. Headquarters, New York City

U.N. Charter Provisions on Recourse to Force. Diplomats and foreign affairs leaders, as well as international lawyers, consult U.N. Charter provisions regulating when it is legal to use force. The core provision is Article 2(4), which sets out the general prohibition on recourse to force. Also reproduced below are portions of Chapter VII, including Article 51, which concerns self-defense, and other provisions related to collective security.

CHARTER OF THE UNITED NATIONS

June 26, 1945, 59 Stat. 1031, T.S. No. 993, 3 Bevans 1153

Article 2 . . .

4.   All Members shall refrain in their international relations from the threat or use of force against the territorial integrity or political independence of any state, or in any manner inconsistent with the Purposes of the United Nations. . . .

7.   Nothing contained in the present Charter shall authorize the United Nations to intervene in matters which are essentially within the domestic jurisdiction of any state or shall require the Members to submit such matters to settlement under the present Charter; but this principle shall not prejudice the application of enforcement measures under Chapter VII.

Chapter VII: Action with Respect to Threats to the Peace,
Breaches of the Peace, and Acts of Aggression

Article 39

The Security Council shall determine the existence of any threat to the peace, breach of the peace, or act of aggression and shall make recommendations, or decide what measures shall be taken in accordance with Articles 41 and 42, to maintain or restore international peace and security.

Article 40

In order to prevent an aggravation of the situation, the Security Council may, before making the recommendations or deciding upon the measures provided for in Article 39, call upon the parties concerned to comply with such provisional measures as it deems necessary or desirable. . . .

Article 41

The Security Council may decide what measures not involving the use of armed force are to be employed to give effect to its decisions, and it may call upon the Members of the United Nations to apply such measures. These may include complete or partial interruption of economic relations and of rail, sea, air, postal, telegraphic, radio, and other means of communication, and the severance of diplomatic relations.

Article 42

Should the Security Council consider that measures provided for in Article 41 would be inadequate or have proved to be inadequate, it may take such action by air, sea, or land forces as may be necessary to maintain or restore international peace and security. Such action may include demonstrations, blockade, and other operations by air, sea, or land forces of Members of the United Nations.

Article 43

1.   All Members of the United Nations, in order to contribute to the maintenance of international peace and security, undertake to make available to the Security Council, on its call and in accordance with a special agreement or agreements, armed forces, assistance, and facilities, including rights of passage, necessary for the purpose of maintaining international peace and security. . . .

Article 45

In order to enable the United Nations to take urgent military measures, Members shall hold immediately available national air-force contingents for combined international enforcement action. The strength and degree of readiness of these contingents and plans for their combined action shall be determined within the limits laid down in the special agreement or agreements referred to in Article 43, by the Security Council with the assistance of [a] Military Staff Committee [as provided in Articles 46 and 47].

Article 48

1.   The action required to carry out the decisions of the Security Council for the maintenance of international peace and security shall be taken by all the Members of the United Nations or by some of them, as the Security Council may determine.

2.   Such decisions shall be carried out by the Members of the United Nations directly and through their action in the appropriate international agencies of which they are members.

Article 49

The Members of the United Nations shall join in affording mutual assistance in carrying out the measures decided upon by the Security Council. . . .

Article 51

Nothing in the present Charter shall impair the inherent right of individual or collective self-defense if an armed attack occurs against a Member of the United Nations until the Security Council has taken the measures necessary to maintain international peace and security. Measures taken by Members in the exercise of this right of self-defense shall be immediately reported to the Security Council and shall not in any way affect the authority and responsibility of the Security Council under the present Charter to take at any time such action as it deems necessary in order to maintain or restore international peace and security.

Article 2(4). The carefully negotiated language of Article 2(4) appears in what is now a nearly universally accepted treaty, the U.N. Charter. Article 2(4) is invoked not only as treaty law but also as customary international law and, often, as *jus cogens.* Compare Article 2(4) and the U.N. Charter to the text and status of 1928 Kellogg-Briand Pact in Chapter 2.

Can you spot any ambiguities in the text of Article 2(4)? The following excerpts explore some of the questions about its meaning. What is the efficacy of Article 2(4)? It has not stopped all wars and armed conflicts! Is it only aspirational? We revisit this question at the end of this section.

Self-defense. The text of Article 51 of the U.N. Charter may at first reading seem straightforward, but it has given rise to numerous questions. For example, what prerequisites attach to collective self-defense? What is the "inherent right" of self-defense that Article 51 preserves? Natural law and customary law concepts of necessity and proportionality inform the meaning of that right, but its exact contours are debatable.

In addition to limits embodied in the inherent right of self-defense, what other constraints are suggested by the text of Article 51? There is no indication that self-defense encompasses uses of force designed to punish an enemy, as a measure of revenge. The text of Article 51 also apparently limits self-defense by including the phrase "if an armed attack occurs." But what constitutes an "armed attack"? Those who accord Article 51 a narrow scope stress that the state exercising self-defense must have been the victim of a significant attack; that the armed attack is underway or, if it has already occurred, that there is clear evidence additional attacks are planned; and that the defender's target is responsible for the armed attack. Is self-defense only permissible if an armed attack has actually been launched? What if an attack appears to be imminent? Is self-defense only available in response to attacks by states? We consider these questions when we explore terrorism in Section 4.

Article 51, located in the Charter's Chapter VII on collective security, refers to Security Council measures. Is the use of force in self-defense therefore ancillary to the collective security system of the United Nations? See Section 3.

Collective Security and Constitutional Change. Article 24 of the U.N. Charter provides that the Security Council has "primary responsibility for the maintenance of international peace and security." If the Council's suggestions, made pursuant to Chapter VI of the Charter entitled "Pacific Settlement of Disputes," fail to resolve a dispute, the Council may turn to Chapter VII. If it "determine[s] the existence of any threat to the peace, breach of the peace, or act of aggression" (Article 39), the Council may—even absent an armed attack by the offending state—impose economic sanctions or take other measures. Security Council "decisions" concerning such sanctions or measures are, as we have noted, not mere recommendations. They are legally binding on states, pursuant to Article 25 of the U.N. Charter.

However, the Chapter VII system of collective security has not functioned as originally envisioned. For example, the Security Council, should it authorize the use of force, may not directly call on military units provided by states pursuant to Article 43 of the U.N. Charter, because states have never entered into any Article 43 special agreements. And the innovation of U.N. peacekeeping, discussed in Section 6 below, is nowhere mentioned in the Charter. We explore the issue of "constitutional change" in the United Nations throughout this chapter. Constitutional law is always a complex subject. It becomes even more so in an international context with so many states and legal cultures involved.

The Cold War and Challenges to the Charter Vision of Collective Security. Cold War politics challenged the original vision of the U.N. Charter concerning the maintenance of international peace and security. That original vision was based on the premise that the world's major powers would agree on sanctions, and ultimately approve the use of force, to counter threats to the peace and breaches of the peace. However, the Security Council's permanent members— China, France, the Soviet Union, the United Kingdom, and the United States— were often divided, and the veto blocked many possible Council measures. How did this development affect the scope of permissible uses of force in self-defense, or otherwise affect the law governing recourse to force? Consider this question as you read the following essays. The authors, Professors Louis Henkin and Michael Reisman, took different views of Article 2(4) and the legality of unilateral use of force in light of the inability of the Security Council to respond effectively to threats to peace and acts of aggression.

LOUIS HENKIN, USE OF FORCE:
LAW AND U.S. POLICY

Right v. Might: International Law and the Use of Force 37 (1989)

. . . The Charter remains the authoritative statement of the law on the use of force. It is the principal norm of international law of this century.

The crucial norm is set forth in article 2(4). . . .

The Charter reflected universal agreement that the status quo prevailing at the end of World War II was not to be changed by force. Even justified grievances and a sincere concern for "national security" or other "vital interests" would not warrant any nation's initiating war. Peace was the paramount value. The Charter and the organization were dedicated to realizing other values as well—self-determination, respect for human rights, economic and social development, justice, and a just international order. But those purposes could not justify the use of force between states to achieve them; they would have to be pursued by other means. Peace was more important than progress and more important than justice. The purposes of the United Nations could not in fact be achieved by war. War inflicted the greatest injustice, the most serious violations of human rights, and the most violence to self-determination and to economic and social development. War was inherently unjust. In the future, the only "just war" would be war against an aggressor—in self-defense by the victim, in collective defense of the victim by others, or by all. Nations would be assured independence, the undisturbed enjoyment of autonomy within their territory, and their right to be let alone. Change—other than internal change through internal forces—would have to be achieved peacefully by international agreement. Henceforth there would be order so that international society could concentrate on meeting better the needs of justice and human welfare.

EFFORTS TO RECONSTRUE THE CHARTER

During the early postwar years there was general agreement as to what the prescriptions of article 2(4) meant. Clearly, the article outlaws war and other acts of armed aggression by one state against another; it also forbids lesser forms of intervention by force by one state in the territory of another. Apart from collective action under the auspices of the United Nations to enforce the peace, the only lawful use of force by a state is that contemplated under the limited exception in article 51 permitting the use of force in self-defense against an armed attack. In time, the language of article 2(4) proved to be not without ambiguities and not invulnerable to claims that intervention by force is permitted for certain "benign" purposes.

One initial ambiguity appears on the face of article 2(4). Does the prohibition of the use of force against "the territorial integrity" of another state forbid only a use of force designed to deprive that state of territory, or does it also prohibit force that violates the territorial borders of that state, however temporarily and for whatever purpose? Does the prohibition of the use of force against "the political independence" of another state outlaw only a use of force that aims to end that state's political independence by annexing it or rendering it a puppet, or does it also prohibit force designed to coerce that state to follow a particular policy or take a particular decisions? In what other circumstances would a use or threat of force be "inconsistent with the purposes of the United Nations"? Another debate concerned whether economic pressure—an oil embargo, a boycott, or other sanctions—designed to derogate from a state's territorial integrity or political independence is a "use of force" prohibited by article 2(4).

An effective United Nations system, or a court with comprehensive jurisdiction and recognized authority, might have answered these and other questions by developing the law of the Charter through construction and case-by-case application. In the absence of such authoritative interpretation, the meaning of the Charter has been shaped by the actions and reactions of states and by the opinions of publicists and scholars. Scholars have debated the ambiguities of the Charter that I have cited and other questions of interpretation; a government occasionally has sought to shape the law to justify an action it has taken. But governments generally have insisted on the interpretations most restrictive of the use of force: the Charter outlaws war for any reason; it prohibits the use of armed force by one state on the territory of another or against the forces, vessels, or other public property of another state located anywhere, for any purpose, in any circumstances. Virtually every use of force in the years since the Charter was signed has been clearly condemned by virtually all states. Virtually every putative justification of a use of force has been rejected. Over the years since the Charter's adoption, even states that have perpetrated acts of force, when seeking to justify their acts, have not commonly urged a relaxed interpretation of the prohibition. Rather, they have asserted facts and circumstances that might have rendered their actions not unlawful. For example, in 1950, North Korea claimed that the South Korean army had initiated hostilities, permitting North Korea to act in self-defense; in Czechoslovakia in 1948 and 1968, and in Hungary in 1956, the USSR claimed that its troops had been invited by the legitimate authorities to help preserve order.

Indeed, the community of states has acted formally to tighten the Charter's restrictions. The Declaration on Principles of International Law concerning

Friendly Relations and Cooperation among States in Accordance with the Charter of the United Nations, adopted by consensus in the General Assembly in 1970, and the Definition of Aggression, adopted by consensus in 1974, have restated and expanded the law of the Charter as prohibiting armed intervention and aggression, broadly conceived. The resolution defining aggression made it clear that prohibited forms of aggression include not only invasion, but also attack or military occupation, however temporary; sending armed bands or mercenaries that carry out grave acts of armed force; bombarding a state's territory; blocking its ports; and attacking the forces of another state (wherever they are).

SUGGESTED EXCEPTIONS TO THE PROHIBITIONS OF ARTICLE 2(4)

In time, however, some states claimed exceptions to the absolute prohibitions of article 2(4), as permitting intervention by force for certain "benign" purposes (in addition to the self-defense exception under article 51). None of the "benign exceptions" has been formally accepted; only one has brought wide acquiescence.

Humanitarian intervention. On several occasions states have claimed the right to use force in "humanitarian intervention." The paradigmatic case was the action of Israel in 1976 to extricate hostages held on a hijacked plane at Entebbe (Uganda). The United States claimed its unsuccessful attempt in 1980 to liberate the diplomatic hostages held in Teheran also came within the exception. States have been reluctant to adopt this exception to article 2(4) formally, but the legal community has widely accepted that the Charter does not prohibit humanitarian intervention by use of force strictly limited to what is necessary to save lives.

The exception, I believe, is not restricted to actions by a state on behalf of its own nationals. But it is a right to liberate hostages if the territorial state cannot or will not do so. It has not been accepted, however, that a state has a right to intervene by force to topple a government or occupy its territory even if that were necessary to terminate atrocities or to liberate detainees. Entebbe was acceptable, but the occupation of Cambodia by Vietnam was not. The U.S. invasion and occupation of Grenada, even if in fact designed to protect the lives of U.S. nationals, also was widely challenged.

Intervention to support self-determination. The suggestion that a state may intervene by force to help a people achieve "self-determination" in some circumstances has received some support.

Self-determination is a powerful political dogma that has been accepted as a principle of international law. It is incorporated in widely accepted treaties, including both the International Covenant on Civil and Political Rights and the

International Covenant on Economic, Social and Cultural Rights. The concept of self-determination cries for definition, . . . but all agree that it includes at least the right of peoples in Asia and Africa to be free from colonial domination, Western style.

Neither article 2(4) of the Charter nor any other provision of international law forbids authentic revolution and wars of independence. Indeed, there is a strong case that it is now unlawful for a state to maintain an unwilling people in colonial status, and such unlawfulness is compounded if a colony is maintained by force. A very different question, however, is whether an external power is permitted to intervene by force to help expel the colonial power or hasten its departure.

On various theories, many states have supported the right to intervene by force to help an entity achieve independence from colonial rule. The United States has firmly rejected any such right. In addressing India's invasion and occupation of Goa (Portuguese India) in 1961, Ambassador Adlai Stevenson said:

> What is at stake today is not colonialism; it is a bold violation of one of the most basic principles in the United Nations Charter. . . . But if our Charter means anything, it means that states are obligated to renounce the use of force, are obligated to seek a solution of their differences by peaceful means.

India used force to end Portuguese control in Goa and claimed the territory for itself; later, other states asserted a general right to intervene by force to help a people achieve independence. In a famous statement, attributed to Leonid Brezhnev, defending the Soviet invasion of Czechoslovakia in 1968, the USSR decried those who "regard the notion of sovereignty as prohibiting support for the struggle of progressive forces." He added: "Genuine revolutionaries, being internationalists, cannot but support progressive forces in their just struggle for national and social liberation."

The world rejected Brezhnev's invasion of Czechoslovakia; even the Third World was not persuaded by the "national liberation" justification. General Assembly resolutions, however, have confirmed the right of colonial peoples to achieve independence by force if necessary and included ambiguous declarations that suggested a right of other states to intervene to help them.

With colonialism no longer an important concern, the pressure for a "self-determination exception" to the law of the Charter has subsided, and the potential significance of such an exception, if recognized, is sharply reduced.

Intervention for socialism: The Brezhnev Doctrine. The Brezhnev regime also asserted generally the right of any socialist state to intervene in another when socialism there is threatened. It said:

> Just as, in Lenin's words, a man living in a society cannot be free from the society, a particular socialist state, staying in a system of other states composing the socialist community, cannot be free from the common interests of that community.
>
> The sovereignty of each socialist country cannot be opposed to the interests of the world of socialism, of the world revolutionary movement. . . .
>
> Discharging their internationalist duty toward the fraternal peoples of Czechoslovakia and defending their own socialist gains, the U.S.S.R. and other socialist states had to act decisively and they did act against the antisocialist forces in Czechoslovakia.

The Brezhnev Doctrine has been generally condemned. The USSR itself appears to have disavowed it in the Helsinki accords.

Intervention for democracy. Self-determination as a justification for the use of force to end colonialism has lost its raison d'être, but some have invoked a people's right to "internal self-determination" to support the use of force by one state to preserve or impose democracy in another. One suggestion, for example, is that article 2(4) permits the use of force to "enhance opportunities of ongoing self-determination . . . to increase the probability of the free choice of peoples about their government and political structure." Some see this view as the foundation of the so-called Reagan Doctrine, construed as including a claim of the right to intervene by force in another state to preserve or impose democracy.

The claim has received no support by any other government. Like the use of force to impose or maintain socialism or any other ideology, the use of force for democracy clearly would be contrary to the language of article 2(4), to the intent of its framers, and to the construction long given to that article by the United States.

At bottom, all suggestions for exceptions to article 2(4) imply that, contrary to the assumptions of the Charter's framers, there are universally recognized values higher than peace and the autonomy of states. In general, the claims of peace and state autonomy have prevailed.

Self-defense under the Charter . . .

The original intent of article 51 seems clear: despite the prohibition on the unilateral use of force in article 2(4), a victim of an armed attack may use force to defend itself, and others may join to use force in collective self-defense of the victim, pending action by the Security Council. No one has doubted that the right of individual or collective self-defense against armed attack continues to apply if the Security Council does not act, or if—as later proved to be the case—the Security Council becomes generally incapable of acting. It has also been accepted that the right of self-defense, individual or collective, is subject to limitations of "necessity" and "proportionality," but that self-defense includes a right both to repel the armed attack and to take the war to the aggressor state in order effectively to terminate the attack and prevent a recurrence. It is generally accepted, too, that states are permitted to organize themselves in advance in bona fide collective self-defense arrangements (such as the North Atlantic Treaty Organization) for possible response if one of the members should become the victim of an armed attack.

The right of self-defense is available "if an armed attack occurs." In the wake of Suez-Sinai (1956), however, some publicists began to argue that the "inherent right of self-defense" recognized by article 51 is the traditional right of self-defense, predating the Charter, which was not limited to defense against "armed attack." They argued that the right of self-defense "if an armed attack occurs" does not mean "only if an armed attack occurs." The only limitation on self-defense, they said, was that implied in the famous *Caroline* dictum: that the right of self-defense was available only when "the necessity of that self-defense is instant, overwhelming, and leaving no choice of means, and no moment for deliberation."

This more permissive interpretation of article 51 found favor with some commentators, but little with governments. The United States rejected it when its allies in effect invoked it at Suez (1956). During the Cuban missile crisis (1962), the United States, though eager to justify its blockade of Cuba, pointedly refrained from adopting the "loose" construction of article 51 and did not claim as justification a right to act in "inherent self-defense." To this day, the United States has not claimed a right to act in self-defense where no armed attack has occurred. In 1985, however, the United States interpreted the concept of armed attack to include certain terrorist activities. Declaring the Libyan government responsible for terrorist acts in Europe, including the bombing of a Berlin nightclub frequented by U.S. servicemen in which one was killed and many wounded, the United States launched a bomb attack on targets in Libyan territory. President

Reagan described the attack as "fully consistent with Article 51 of the UN Charter," presumably because, in the American view, the terrorist act was an "armed attack" justifying the bombing as a use of force in self-defense.

. . . Publicists have debated whether, under article 51, a state may use force in . . . "anticipatory" self-defense, particularly in the context of nuclear strategy. Some have suggested that if a state has strong reasons to believe it is about to be the target of a nuclear strike, the "armed attack has occurred" and the victim need not wait but may "respond" in "anticipatory self-defense." Fortunately, that issue has remained academic. [T]he attack on Libya . . . was not designed to "beat Libya to the punch," but, President Reagan said, it "will not only diminish Colonel Quadhafi's capacity to export terror, it will provide him with incentives and reasons to alter his criminal behavior."

The bombing of Libya by the United States was widely condemned and the claimed justification widely rejected.

Intervention and Counterintervention

Before the UN Charter, the law seemed to be that a state may provide military assistance to the government of another state, even to help it suppress rebellion, but a state could not assist rebels against the incumbent government of another state. If rebellion succeeded sufficiently to achieve the status of "belligerent" and constitute a civil war, the law probably forbade assistance to either side. That law, confirmed by special Non-Intervention Agreements in the 1930s, was battered during the Spanish Civil War as states intervened on both sides. The United States, however, honored the principle of nonintervention, helping neither side.

The United Nations Charter did not expressly address intervention in civil wars. Nothing in article 2(4) forbids sending military assistance to an incumbent government, but the use of force in support of rebels against an incumbent government would be a use of force against the territorial integrity of the state and, presumably, against its political independence. Under the Charter, a state probably may not send troops into the territory of another state to support either side in a civil war, since that too would violate the latter's territorial integrity and compromise its political independence. Assistance not involving the use of force, however—for example, providing advice, selling arms, or giving financial assistance to one (or both) sides in a civil war—seems not to be covered by article 2(4), but may violate norms against nonintervention that predate the Charter and have been strongly restated in numerous General Assembly resolutions.

W. MICHAEL REISMAN, CRITERIA FOR THE LAWFUL USE OF FORCE IN INTERNATIONAL LAW

10 *Yale Journal of International Law* 279 (1985)

Law includes a system of authorized coercion in which force is used to maintain and enhance public order objectives and in which unauthorized coercions are prohibited. . . . Law acknowledges the utility and the inescapability of the use of coercion in social processes, but seeks to organize, monopolize, and economize it.

The international legal system diverges from these general legal features only in terms of degree of organization and centralization of the use of coercion. In national systems, coercion is organized, relatively centralized, and, for the most part, monopolized by the apparatus of the state. In the international system, it is not. Individual actors historically have reserved the right to use force unilaterally to protect and vindicate legal entitlements.

Political and jurisprudential principles such as these must be kept in mind in an examination and rational interpretation of Article 2(4) of the United Nations Charter. Its sweeping prohibition of the threat or use of force in international politics was not an autonomous ethical affirmation of nonviolence[.] Article 2(4) was embedded in and made initially plausible by a complex security scheme, established and spelled out in the United Nations Charter. If the scheme had operated, it would have obviated the need for the unilateral use of force. States with a grievance could have repaired to the Security Council, which could then apply the appropriate quantum and form of authoritative coercion and thereby vindicate collectively the rights it found had been violated. Under these circumstances, the need for and justification of a unilateral resort to force ceased. Even then, . . . the Charter acknowledged the inherent limits of its structures in the prevailing international politics by reserving to states the right of self-defense.

But the security system of the United Nations was premised on a consensus between the permanent members of the Security Council. Lamentably, that consensus dissolved early in the history of the organization. Thereafter, for almost all cases but those in which there was a short-term interest in collaboration, the Security Council could not operate as originally planned. Part of the systemic justification for the theory of Article 2(4) disappeared. At the same time, the Soviet Union announced, in effect, that it did not accept Article 2(4): "Wars of national liberation," an open-textured conception essentially meaning wars the Soviets supported, were not, in the Soviet conception, violations of Article 2(4). . . .

The international political system has largely accommodated itself to the indispensability of coercion in a legal system, on the one hand, and the deterioration of the Charter system, on the other, by developing a nuanced code for appraising the lawfulness of individual unilateral uses of force. The net result is not the value sterility of nineteenth century international legal conceptions of coercion, but neither is it Article 2(4). Some sense of the complexity of the code can be gained by examining, in a single time period, 1979, forceful unilateral interventions without the prior authorization of the United Nations.

In 1979, forces of Tanzania invaded Uganda, expelled the government of Idi Amin, and ultimately restored the government of Milton Obote. In the same year, French forces, in a quick and bloodless coup, expelled the government of Jean-Bedel Bokassa from the Central African Republic and installed a different president. In the same year, forces of the government of Vietnam entered Cambodia and sought to unseat the Pol Pot government and to replace it with a Vietnamese-backed government led by Heng Samrin. And in the same year, Soviet forces entered Afghanistan to support a government which, it seemed, would not have survived had it not been for the timely intervention and continued presence and operation of a foreign military force. . . .

Although efforts were made to arouse the United Nations to criticize the first two of these interventions, the organization resisted. But the organization condemned the latter two. Since all of these interventions, like all unilateral actions, were motivated in key part by the self-interest of the actors concerned, we must assume that there were some additional ingredients that rendered some of them internationally acceptable. I submit that it is in the identification of those factors that one can begin to describe the contemporary international law on the use of force.

The deterioration of the Charter security regime has stimulated a partial revival of a type of unilateral *jus ad bellum*. But in sharp contrast to the nineteenth century conception, which was value-neutral and ultimately power-based, the contemporary doctrine relates only to the vindication of rights which the international community recognizes but has, in general or in a particular case, demonstrated an inability to secure or guarantee. Hence, appraisals of state resort to coercion can no longer simply condemn them by invoking Article 2(4), but must test permissibility or lawfulness by reference to a number of factors, including the objective and the contingency for which coercion is being applied.

Nine basic categories appear to have emerged in which one finds varying support for unilateral uses of force. They are self-defense, which has been construed quite broadly; self-determination and decolonization; humanitarian intervention by the military instrument to replace an elite in another state; uses of the military instrument within spheres of influence and critical defense zones; treaty-sanctioned interventions within the territory of another state; use of the military instrument for the gathering of evidence in international proceedings; use of the military instrument to enforce international judgments; and counter-measures such as reprisals and retorsions. The categories themselves, however, are not determinative. . . .

In the determination of any action, a key and constant factor—less a criterion of lawfulness and more a sine qua non of survival—is the need for the maintenance of minimum order in a precarious international system. Will a particular use of force, whatever its justification otherwise, enhance or undermine world order?

When this requirement is met, attention may be directed to the fundamental principle of political legitimacy in contemporary international politics. It is, as anyone familiar with the UN Charter and with such key constitutive decisions as *Namibia* and *Western Sahara* knows, the enhancement of the ongoing right of peoples to determine their own political destinies. That obvious point bears renewed emphasis, for it is, in my view, the main purpose of contemporary international law: Article 2(4) is the means. The basic policy of contemporary international law has been to maintain the political independence of territorial communities so that they can continue to be able to express their ongoing desire for political organization in a form appropriate to them. Article 2(4), like so much in the Charter and in contemporary international politics, supports and must be interpreted in terms of this key postulate. Each application of Article 2(4) must enhance opportunities for ongoing self-determination. Though all interventions are lamentable, the fact is that some may serve, in terms of aggregate consequences, to increase the probability of the free choice of peoples about their government and political structure. Others have the manifest objective and consequence of doing exactly the opposite.

There is, thus, neither need nor justification for treating in a mechanically equal fashion, Tanzania's intervention in Uganda to overthrow the Amin despotism, on the one hand, and Soviet intervention in Hungary or Czechoslovakia to overthrow popular governments and to impose an undesired regime on a coerced population, on the other. Nor should the different appraisal of these cases by the international legal system occasion any surprise.

[N]orms are instruments devised by human beings to precipitate desired social consequences. One should not seek a point-for-point conformity to a rule without constant regard for the policy or principle that animated its prescription, with appropriate regard for the factual constellation in the minds of the drafters. . . . The expression of Article 2(4), in the form of a rule, is premised, I submit, on a political context and a technological environment which has been changing inexorably since the end of the nineteenth century. The rule assumes that the only threat to or usurpation of the right of political independence of a people within a particular territorial community is from external and overt invasion. It makes a historicist assumption as well: internal changes are deemed to be personnel changes in the composition of an elite which do not bring about basic changes in systems of public order within the country or in its external political alignments; governments come and go but the life of the people continues in its traditional fashion. Most important, it does not presuppose division, maintained by a precarious nuclear equipoise, between two contending public order systems, either of which might find itself substantially disadvantaged and pressed to intense coercion by the defection of a particular community from its own critical defense zone.

The rule-formulation of Article 2(4) is oblivious to these factors. . . .

The net effect of a mechanical interpretation of Article 2(4) may be to superimpose on an unwilling polity an elite, an ideology, and an external alignment alien to its wishes. This may entail far-reaching social and economic changes and grave deprivations of human rights for substantial numbers and strata of the population.

Contrasting Views of Article 2(4) and Permissible Uses of Force. Contrast the views of Professors Henkin and Reisman, both writing near the end of the Cold War, concerning the international law governing the use of force. What for each is the role of Article 2(4)? What are permissible exceptions to 2(4)? What instances of the use of force would both regard as illegal? How does each explain the many examples of the use of force involving territorial incursions since World War II?

For Professor Henkin, the prohibition against unilateral state use of force is a fundamental norm necessary in a dangerous, nuclearized world. Promoting peace and security is the paramount goal, best furthered by upholding the territorial integrity of states. Implicitly, Henkin suggested that the major purpose of the U.N. Charter is to preserve the integrity of states and, consequently, to maintain peace and stability through the state system; human rights, self-determination, and other Charter goals are best pursued in a stable, peaceful world. He argued that even without an effectively functioning Security Council, the prohibition on the use of force should remain a strong rule—clear, comprehensive, and resistant to self-serving interpretations such as the Brezhnev and Reagan doctrines. Henkin denied that decisions to comply with a rule against unilateral use of force rest on reciprocity. The fact that the Soviet Union may have failed to comply with the rule did not permit the United States to abandon it.

For Henkin, the situations in which the use of force might be allowed are few and narrowly construed: self-defense (including collective self-defense); Chapter VII enforcement actions authorized by the U.N. Security Council; and one state inviting another to use force in its territory, *e.g.*, to combat an insurrection. Henkin narrowly construed the self-defense exception, insisting, for instance, that an armed attack is a necessary prerequisite for self-defense. Henkin noted and discounted various suggested exceptions to Article 2(4). His view that permissible exceptions to 2(4) are limited also links the preservation of peace to the preservation of existing governments and states. For example, Henkin wrote, "Nothing in article 2(4) forbids sending military assistance to an incumbent government, but the use of force in support of rebels against an incumbent government would be a use of force against the territorial integrity of the state and, presumably, against its political independence."

Professor Reisman's views differed on three fundamental levels. First, Reisman was uncomfortable with a black letter rule limiting the use of force. Although he rejected the 19th-century "value sterility" that accepted uses of force, Reisman found in the latter 20th century a "nuanced code for appraising the lawfulness of individual unilateral uses of force." Second, Reisman accepted the central importance of values other than a prohibition on the unilateral use force—notably "the enhancement of the ongoing right of peoples to determine their own political destinies." Third, he criticized the "historicist assumptions" lying behind a strict reading of Article 2(4), which he thought depended on the idea that the United Nations could work as originally envisioned in Chapter VII of the U.N. Charter. Is Reisman's view so highly contextual that it permits too much manipulation? Does he compromise too much the principle restricting unilateral uses of force?

The Relevance of International Law on Recourse to Force. When is international law relating to the use of force taken into account? Certainly the legality of recourse to force is debated in the U.N. General Assembly and Security Council. Debates over the use of force are often carried out in other political fora as well, with states in armed conflicts often making opposing assertions about the legality of each other's recourse to force. In highly political contexts, how is the law on the use of force relevant? Are the legal rules too indeterminate to matter? Do they sometimes provide at least a framework for debate and perhaps a structure for the formulation of policy positions? States using force tend to argue that their use of force is legal. These states either rely on self-defense or cite a particular "exception" to Article 2(4)'s prohibition. States also use legal arguments to condemn uses of force by other states, and historical judgments may rely on legal constructs.

Do legal rules limiting recourse to force matter less to powerful countries than to weaker ones? In the United States, as in many other countries, government lawyers advise political leaders about international law. What is the efficacy of legal advice concerning recourse to force in the United States? Several former U.S. State Department Legal Advisers have shared their views on that question. Abraham D. Sofaer, Legal Adviser from 1985–1990 during the administrations of Ronald Reagan and George H.W. Bush, recalled occasions—"once at the very highest level imaginable"—when he advised against the use of force and his advice was taken. Conrad Harper, Legal Adviser from 1993–1996 during the Clinton administration, recounted his discussions about a proposed use of force with the General Counsel of the Central Intelligence Agency and lawyers from the Departments of Justice and Defense. Although these government lawyers found it difficult to "go back to our principals and say that the proposed action 'probably wasn't a good idea,' " they became persuaded that the action would have been illegal. "And having been persuaded, we all went back to our principals and convinced them—and the action was never taken." Michael J. Matheson, Legal Adviser during part of the George H.W. Bush administration, found it unrealistic "to think Presidents are often going to refrain from the use of force on what they consider to be essential security grounds because of the views of the Legal Adviser." However, according to Matheson, Legal Advisers can accomplish "important things . . . with respect to the use of force. One is to see to it that the modalities used are as consistent with international law as possible. For example, the actions we took in Nicaragua, which were gratuitously in violation of international law need not necessarily have been so." In addition, "when the decision is made to use force, it's important what argument is made to justify that decision." Some justifications "will open up entirely new open-ended doctrines," while other justifications "are more consistent with past practices; the Legal Adviser can have a considerable amount of influence on what arguments are made, which in turn greatly influences what precedential effect that use of force might have." *Quoted in* Michael P. Scharf & Paul R. Williams, *Shaping Foreign Policy in Times of*

Crisis: The Role of International Law and the State Department Legal Adviser 164–65 (2010).

How else might international law relating to the use of force be relevant? States sometimes have refused to recognize a government that has come into existence because of an illegal use of force. See the *Goldberg Case* in Chapter 3. The international law on the use of force has also influenced such varied matters as the law of treaties, the content of treaties, rules of engagement written by states for their armed forces, and the content of municipal laws and constitutions. See Ian Brownlie, "The United Nations Charter and the Use of Force, 1945–1985," in *The Current Legal Regulation of the Use of Force* 491 (A. Cassese ed. 1986). Furthermore, as we shall see in Section 3, a state's illegal use of force may trigger a response of the U.N. Security Council toward that state.

Judicial Interpretations. The International Court of Justice and arbitral tribunals have occasionally addressed the legality of uses of force and self-defense. See Case Concerning Military and Paramilitary Activities In and Against Nicaragua (Nicaragua v. United States), 1986 I.C.J. 14; Legality of the Threat or Use of Nuclear Weapons, Advisory Opinion, 1996 I.C.J. 226; Oil Platforms (Iran v. United States), 2003 I.C.J. 161; the 2004 *Wall Case* (see Chapter 4); Armed Activities on the Territory of the Congo (Congo v. Uganda), 2005 I.C.J. 168.; *Jus ad Bellum* (Ethiopia v. Eritrea), Ethiopia's Claims 1–8, Partial Award (Eritrea-Ethiopia Claims Commission, 2005), 45 *International Legal Materials* 430 (2006); Delimitation of Maritime Boundary (Guyana v. Suriname) ¶¶ 78–81, 140–44, 165 (Law of the Sea Convention Annex VII Arbitral Tribunal, 2007), *available at* www.pca-cpa.org. What are the advantages and disadvantages of the International Court or international arbitral tribunals hearing and deciding cases involving the use of force and intervention? Compare the ICJ decisions in Chapter 4, as well as the Permanent Court of Arbitration's *Dogger Bank Case* in the same chapter.

3. Interstate Invasions

When the Berlin Wall fell in 1989, the bell tolled on the Cold War. East Germany, along with Poland, Czechoslovakia, Hungary, Romania, and Bulgaria left the Soviet bloc. The Soviet Union itself began to disintegrate. More than a dozen republics within the Soviet Union—Estonia, Latvia, Lithuania, the Ukraine, Armenia, and Kazakhstan among them—declared their independence. Communist Yugoslavia, too, dissolved into new sovereign states. These developments loosened the logjam in the U.N. Security Council, which was now freer to act and perhaps to deliver on its original promise in 1945 to provide for collective security. The "new" Security Council's first major test was not long in coming.

Iraq's 1990 Invasion of Kuwait and the Security Council's Responses. On August 2, 1990, over 100,000 Iraqi troops attacked neighboring Kuwait. The greatly outnumbered Kuwaiti forces were routed, and the Emir of Kuwait fled the country. The invasion followed the collapse of talks in which Iraq had asserted financial and territorial claims. On the same day as the invasion, the U.N. Security Council passed Resolution 660 by a vote of 14–0, with Yemen abstaining, to condemn the invasion and to demand immediate and unconditional withdrawal of all Iraqi forces. In Resolution 661, adopted on August 6, 1990 by a vote of 13–0 (Cuba and Yemen abstaining), the Council "decide[d] that all States shall" prevent Iraqi imports and impose other economic sanctions on Iraq. Three days later the Council voted unanimously to declare Iraq's asserted annexation of Kuwait null and void. S.C. Res. 662 (1990).

Council Resolution 678, excerpted below, was adopted in November 1990 following a massive buildup of U.S. and other military forces in Saudi Arabia and the region. Beginning on January 16, 1991, when Iraq refused to comply with a U.S. deadline for withdrawing from Kuwait, the air strikes and ground assault of "Operation Desert Storm" began. These led, by the end of February, to the restoration of Kuwaiti sovereignty within the territory of Kuwait.

SECURITY COUNCIL RESOLUTION 678

Nov. 28, 1990, 29 *International Legal Materials* 1565 (1990)

The Security Council,

Recalling, and reaffirming its resolutions 660 (1990) of 2 August 1990, 661 (1990) of 6 August 1990, 662 (1990) of 9 August 1990, 664 (1990) of 18 August 1990, 665 (1990) of 25 August 1990, 666 (1990) of 13 September 1990, 667 (1990) of 16 September 1990, 669 (1990) of 24 September 1990, 670 (1990) of 25 September 1990, 674 (1990) of 29 October 1990 and 677 (1990) of 28 November 1990,

Noting that, despite all efforts by the United Nations, Iraq refuses to comply with its obligation to implement resolution 660 (1990) and the above mentioned subsequent relevant resolutions, in flagrant contempt of the Security Council,

Mindful of its duties and responsibilities under the Charter of the United Nations for the maintenance and preservation of international peace and security,

Determined to secure full compliance with its decisions,

Acting under Chapter VII of the Charter,

1.   *Demands* that Iraq comply fully with resolution 660 (1990) and all subsequent relevant resolutions, and decides, while maintaining all its decisions, to allow Iraq one final opportunity, as a pause of goodwill, to do so;

2.   *Authorizes* Member States co-operating with the government of Kuwait, unless Iraq on or before 15 January 1991 fully implements, as set forth in paragraph 1 above, the foregoing resolutions, to use all necessary means to uphold and implement resolution 660 (1990) and all subsequent relevant resolutions and to restore international peace and security in the area;

3.   *Requests* all States to provide appropriate support for the actions undertaken in pursuance of paragraph 2 above;

4.   *Requests* the States concerned to keep the Security Council regularly informed on the progress of actions undertaken pursuant to paragraphs 2 and 3 above;

5.   *Decides* to remain seized of the matter.

Figure 6.D
U.S. Air Force Fighters over Kuwaiti Oil Fires Set by Retreating Iraqi Forces, Operation Desert Storm, 1991

> *Debating the Legal Basis for the Use of Force Against Iraq.* States understood Resolution 678's phrase "all necessary means" to refer to the use of force. Was Operation Desert Storm an exercise of collective self-defense, or was it instead a proper exercise of Council authority under Chapter VII of the U.N. Charter? The authors of the two following excerpts debated that question.

THOMAS M. FRANCK & FAIZA PATEL, UN POLICE ACTION IN LIEU OF WAR: "THE OLD ORDER CHANGETH"

85 *American Journal of International Law* 63 (1991)

The new alternative to traditional wars of self-defense is collective police actions by the members of the international community. Exceptionally, these could be implemented by regional organizations. Usually, they would take the form of global action. Either way, the police action must be authorized specifically by the Security Council under Article 53 (for regional action) or Article 42 (for global action).

If states use armed force under the self-defense rubric of Article 51, their individual activities are subsumed by, or incorporated into, the global police response once it is activated. That is, the old way is licensed only until the new way begins to work: "until," in the words of Article 51, "the Security Council has taken the necessary measures to maintain international peace and security."

. . . A new-style, UN-authorized police action functioning alongside a traditional sovereign exercise of war powers is conceptually and operationally untenable, the more so when states seeking the freedom to act unilaterally have forces committed alongside others in a Security Council police action. As a textual matter, it is obvious on its face that the Charter, in creating the new police power, intended to establish an exclusive alternative to the old war system. The old system was retained only as a fallback, available when the new system could not be made to work; not, as some U.S. hawks argue, as an equal alternative, to be chosen at the sole discretion of the members. . . .

The delegates to the San Francisco Conference recognized that the enforcement provisions of chapter VII of the Charter provided "the teeth of the United Nations." The committee considering its military enforcement measures adopted Article 42 unanimously. In so doing, delegates intended to give the Security Council "the power, when diplomatic, economic, or other measures are considered by the Council to be inadequate, to undertake such aerial, naval, or other operations as may be necessary to maintain or restore international peace and security." This article was thought to remedy the principal defect of the League Covenant and the committee's rapporteur observed that "this unanimous vote . . . renders sacred the obligation of all states to participate in the operations." Thus, "[m]ilitary assistance, in case of aggression, ceases to be a *recommendation* made to member states; it becomes for us an *obligation* which none can shirk."

This record is entirely inconsistent with the notion that, once the Security Council has taken measures, individual members are supposed to remain free to design their own military responses.

. . . Just as Congress nowadays does not grant letters of marque and reprisal (Constitution, Article I, section 8(11)) or establish post roads (Article I, section 8(7)), so the Security Council has not made use of Article 43 of the Charter, which authorizes it to negotiate agreements with consenting member states that, preemptively, would have placed designated national military contingents at the Council's disposal. That no such agreements were made, owing to the Cold War, does not signify a lapse in the Organization's general police power, set out in Article 42, any more than the abstinence by Congress in matters of post roads signifies a lapse in its power to legislate on other matters pertaining to the Postal Service. Rather, the practice of the Security Council has evolved other means for taking coercive measures, including the use of police forces raised ad hoc in response to a specific threat to the peace. Both the Korean and the Kuwaiti situations are examples. What emerges from the institutional history of the years of stasis is not evidence that the Council's policing functions have fallen into desuetude but, on the contrary, that the central idea of a globally sanctioned police action was never abandoned; that the failure to implement Article 43 merely led to organic growth and the alternative creation of police action through invocation of Article 42, which does not require special agreements.

This is as one would expect. The UN Charter is not merely a treaty, but also the constitutive instrument of a living global organization. Its organs were designed both to implement important tasks and to interpret their own authority. Such organic growth is desirable and inevitable.

EUGENE V. ROSTOW, UNTIL WHAT? ENFORCEMENT ACTION OR COLLECTIVE SELF-DEFENSE?

85 *American Journal of International Law* 506 (1991)

Should the Persian Gulf war of 1990–1991 be characterized as an "international enforcement action" of the United Nations Security Council or as a campaign of collective self-defense approved, encouraged, and blessed by the Security Council?

This is not simply a nice and rather metaphysical legal issue, but an extremely practical one. The question it presents is whether the control and direction of hostilities in the gulf, their termination, and the substance of the settlement they produce were handled by the Council as the Korean War was handled, that is, as a campaign of collective self-defense, or as the United Nations' first "international enforcement action." . . .

On paper, the powers of the UN Security Council go beyond those possessed by the League of Nations. The Council can call on the members to apply measures not involving the use of armed force in order to deal with situations of aggression, and, if such measures are deemed inadequate, it "may take such action by air, sea, or land forces as may be necessary to maintain or restore international peace and security." Provision was made for the formation of a standing United Nations force, and of a Military Staff Committee to advise and assist the Security Council on these and cognate questions. The Military Staff Committee exists in a state of suspended animation at the present time, although it may be revived. Military actions to restore peace taken under Article 42 and 43 of the Charter are called "international enforcement actions."

Finally, after the Charter outlined the peacekeeping procedures of the Security Council under chapter VII in Articles 39–50, it provided in Article 51 that "[n]othing in the present Charter shall impair the inherent right of individual or collective self-defense if an armed attack occurs . . . until the Security Council has taken measures necessary to maintain international peace and security." In the narrowest sense, the present controversy is about the meaning of the word "until" in Article 51.

The coercive powers conferred on the Security Council have not yet become a working part of the process for managing the state system. The fate of these coercive powers thus far reflects the nature of the United Nations as a hybrid political entity superimposed on the system of sovereign states: not a superpower or a world government, but an instrumentality for achieving cooperation among the nations in the interest of peace; an instrumentality, a catalyst, to which certain powers have been tentatively delegated by those nations. Diplomacy and conciliation are the normal methods of the Security Council. . . .

While some eminent authorities consider the Korean War to have been a Security Council "enforcement action," they press the term too hard. In the Korean episode, the Security Council was able to function for two months because the Soviet Union was boycotting the Organization at the time. Even under those circumstances, however, the Council did not use the language of "decision" which would have activated Article 25. The Council's resolutions simply recommended that the members refrain from helping North Korea and urged them to "furnish such assistance to the Republic of Korea as may be necessary to repel the armed attack and to restore international peace and security in the area." For all their symbolic panoply of the United Nations flag and other emblems, the forces which finally prevailed in Korea were national forces carrying out a mission of collective self-defense under American direction, not a Security Council enforcement action.

In Rhodesia, the Security Council made a number of legally binding "decisions" favoring economic sanctions but rejected proposals to employ armed forces under its own control, and the affair was finally settled not by economic sanctions but by military force.

In the Persian Gulf crisis, Security Council Resolution 678 "[a]uthorizes Member States co-operating with the Government of Kuwait . . . to use all necessary means to uphold [the earlier resolutions] and to restore international peace and security in the area." Except for the word "authorizes," the resolution is clearly one designed to encourage and support a campaign of collective self-defense, and therefore not a Security Council enforcement action. Instead of attempting to direct such an operation itself, the Council "requests the States concerned" to keep it regularly informed about their progress. The Security Council held no meetings on the gulf crisis between November 29, 1990, when Resolution 678 was adopted, and February 14, 1991, when it met in secret session to discuss the political aspects of the end of the war. And the initial cease-fire in the gulf war was achieved as a practical matter not by an agreed Security Council resolution but by President Bush's ultimatum of February 28, 1991. . . .

During the period of active hostilities, neither the Secretary-General nor any other part of the United Nations Secretariat attempted to exercise control over military operations, although a committee of the Council actively supervised the program of economic sanctions.

Thus, the practice followed in implementing Resolution 678 and in terminating hostilities has been that of an allied military campaign in defense of Kuwait directed by officers of the United States and the associated nations. Does the word "authorized" in Resolution 678 mean that the member states which cooperated with Kuwait in driving Iraq out of that country could not have done so without the Council's "authority"? As Professor Glennon points out, Resolution 678 is in fact permissive, like Resolution 83 of June 27, 1950, adopted by the Security Council during the Korean War. It imposes no legally binding obligation under Article 25 of the Charter. In Glennon's words, it "merely exhorts, authorizes or recommends," leaving to the member states the decision whether to cooperate in the effort of the allied coalition to liberate Kuwait. The word "authorizes" in Resolution 678 should not therefore be considered to transform a military campaign of self-defense into an enforcement action.

Thus far, the nominal authority of the Security Council to engage in military "enforcement actions" has not been tested. This is not a state of affairs to be deplored. Political relations among the members of the Council—permanent and temporary alike—are not sufficiently stable to make so radical a step politically feasible or desirable. Although the diplomacy of the gulf crisis in 1990 and 1991 has shown some movement in a promising direction, it remains to be seen whether these hints of progress are followed by more substantial changes.

Collective Self-defense or Chapter VII Enforcement? Rostow believed that the use of force against Iraq was an exercise of collective self-defense in accordance with Article 51 of the U.N. Charter. Rostow took the position that Security Council authorization added nothing of legal value to actions Kuwait and its allies could have taken under the theory of collective self-defense. In his view, no Security Council "blessing" in advance was necessary. Note that Security Council Resolution 678 neither set time limits on the use of force nor required an accounting to the Security Council. These features may suggest that states wanted to be free to take whatever action they—rather than the U.N. organization—thought best against Iraq (so long as their action was acceptable as collective self-defense). States guard their prerogatives to use force, as indicated also by their unwillingness, as discussed in Section 2, to conclude Article 43 special agreements for military forces the Security Council could call on by itself.

Did Security Council Resolution 678 instead authorize a type of Chapter VII enforcement action, as Franck and Patel suggested? In their view, changes in the conception of the U.N. Charter allow us to regard Resolution 678 and the use of force against Iraq as U.N. actions. In effect, the Charter permits the Security Council to delegate to states the authority to respond to crises, sometimes by resorting to force. Resolution 678 was only one of a series of Security Council resolutions and decisions affecting Iraq; viewed in context, 678 was a proper exercise of the Council's general Article 42 authority to "take such action . . . as may be necessary to maintain or restore international peace and security." After Iraq had occupied Kuwait, the United States and other states did not use force until they had sought and obtained Security Council authorization. In this view, the Council exercises essential roles under Chapter VII of the U.N. Charter: determining that a threat to the peace or a breach of the peace has occurred, imposing sanctions, and authorizing states to use force as a matter of collective security.

If the use of force against Iraq in 1991 was an exercise of collective self-defense, why did the United States and other members of the Security Council find it necessary to approve Resolution 678? Why might the choice of one or the other justification make a difference?

The Relationship Between Self-defense and the Security Council. According to Article 51 of the U.N. Charter, the right of self-defense is preserved "until the Security Council has taken measures necessary to maintain international peace and security." When is the right of states to use force in self-defense suspended? When the Security Council passes any resolutions under Chapter VII? When the Security Council decides U.N. member states must impose comprehensive sanctions against a state that has used force? Security Council Resolution 661 explicitly affirmed "the inherent right of individual or collective self-defense, in response to the armed attack by Iraq against Kuwait, in accordance with Article 51 of the Charter." But what if references to Article 51 were absent in a comprehensive sanctions resolution? At some point—*e.g.*, at least when the Security Council explicitly rules that "self defense" steps must cease—arguments that force is authorized in self-defense will be legally suspect. The line between when the Security Council has taken the requisite "measures necessary" and when it has not is blurred. States, rather than any authoritative third party, are likely to decide for themselves where the line is drawn.

Post-Desert Storm Security Council Resolutions. After Iraq was driven out of Kuwait, the Security Council approved several resolutions containing bold provisions. For example, states normally settle boundary disputes by agreement or by authorizing a tribunal to decide them, but in Resolutions 687 (1991) and 833 (1993) the Security Council itself imposed a settlement for an Iraq-Kuwait boundary dispute.

Parts of Resolution 687 affected matters normally left to municipal legal systems. In paragraph 29, the Security Council effectively required all states to apply a *force majeure* defense to Iraqi claims made when otherwise valid transactions were not carried out because of the Security Council's economic sanctions against Iraq. Paragraph 29 was, in short, a type of "legislation" directed at the practices of municipal courts.

Some paragraphs of Resolution 687 related to humanitarian measures, as did Resolution 688 (1991), which condemned Iraq's repression of Kurds in northern Iraq and sought to promote humanitarian relief measures in Iraq.

Other provisions of Resolution 687 concerned Iraqi armaments. The Security Council decided Iraq would accept destruction or removal of certain weapons, submit to on-site inspections of its weapons systems, and take other steps related to its military capabilities. The Council called on the Secretary-General and the International Atomic Energy Agency to carry out measures concerning Iraqi weapons, nuclear material, and nuclear facilities.

Paragraph 19 of Resolution 687 also contemplated a Compensation Commission to assess Iraq's liability for damages due to the invasion of Kuwait. This Commission—formally created as a subsidiary organ of the Security Council by Resolution 692 (1991)—operated as a fact-finding and quasi-adjudicatory body. The Commission completed its work in 2005, having resolved over 2.6 million claims and having awarded approximately $52.4 billion to successful claimants; by 2014 the Commission had disbursed all but $4.63 billion of these awards from a fund created by taking five percent of Iraq's sales of its oil exports. See U.N. Office of Internal Oversight Services, "Internal Audit Division Report 2015/016: Audit of the United Nations Claims Commission Claims Payments" (2015), *available at* https://oios.un.org/.

Was Resolution 687 an appropriate exercise of the Security Council's authority? Did the Council provide "institutionalized countermeasures" as a means of responding to Iraq's illegal actions and thus enforcing international law? Was the Compensation Commission's primary goal instead to provide justice to victims of Iraq's aggression? See Vera Gowlland-Debbas, "Security Council Enforcement Action and Issues of State Responsibility," 43 *International and Comparative Law Quarterly* 55 (1994); David D. Caron & Brian Morris, "The UN Compensation Commission: Practical Justice, not Retribution," 13 *European Journal of International Law* 183 (2002).

We excerpt here a few of Security Council Resolution 687's provisions that became particularly important in arguments about the legal basis for a second invasion of Iraq in 2003. That invasion toppled the Iraqi government led by Saddam Hussein.

SECURITY COUNCIL RESOLUTION 687

Apr. 3, 1991, 30 *International Legal Materials* 846 (1991)

The Security Council, . . .

Conscious of the need to take the following measures acting under Chapter VII of the Charter,

1. *Affirms* [13 previous Security Council resolutions], except as expressly changed below to achieve the goals of this resolution, including a formal cease-fire; . . .

6. *Notes* that as soon as the Secretary-General notifies the Security Council of the completion of the deployment of the United Nations observer unit, the conditions will be established for the Member States cooperating with Kuwait in accordance with resolution 678 (1990) to bring their military presence in Iraq to an end consistent with resolution 686 (1991); . . .

22. *Decides* that upon the approval by the Security Council of the [claims compensation] programme called for in paragraph 19 above and upon Council agreement that Iraq has completed all actions contemplated in paragraphs 8, 9, 10, 11, 12 and 13 above [concerning Iraqi weapons and on-site inspections], the prohibitions against the import of commodities and products originating in Iraq and the prohibitions against financial transactions related thereto contained in resolution 661 (1990) shall have no further force or effect; . . .

24. *Decides* that, in accordance with resolution 661 (1990) and subsequent related resolutions and until a further decision is taken by the Security Council, all States shall continue to prevent the sale or supply, or the promotion or facilitation of such sale or supply, to Iraq by their nationals, or from their territories or using their flag vessels or aircraft, of [military equipment, arms, and related technology and support services;]

33. *Declares* that, upon official notification by Iraq to the Secretary-General and to the Security Council of its acceptance of the provisions above, a formal cease-fire is effective between Iraq and Kuwait and the Member States cooperating with Kuwait in accordance with resolution 678 (1990);

34. *Decides* to remain seized of the matter and to take such further steps as may be required for the implementation of the present resolution and to secure peace and security in the area.

Iraqi Sanctions. The U.N. Security Council maintained numerous sanctions against Iraq after Desert Storm, with exceptions for certain foodstuffs and other materials required for essential civilian needs. The sanctions were not completely successful. For example, some countries resumed civilian air travel to Iraq, avoiding the Security Council's economic sanctions. Smugglers also evaded sanctions, even supplying Iraq with conventional weapons and, on occasion, material that might be useful for chemical or biological weapons production. See John F. Murphy, *The Evolving Dimensions of International Law* 126–32 (2010); Barbara Crossette, "French Flight Tests Ban Against Iraq," *New*

York Times, Sept. 23, 2000, at A7. A U.N. program authorizing Iraq to sell oil to raise funds to purchase humanitarian goods was beset by fraud. See Independent Inquiry Committee into the United Nations Oil-for-Food Programme, *Manipulation of the Oil-for-Food Programme by the Iraqi Regime* (2005). For an overview of the efficacy of U.N. sanctions against Iraq during the 1990s, see David Cartright & George A. Lopez, *The Sanctions Decade: Assessing UN Strategies in the 1990s*, at 37–61 (2000). For discussion of Iraq's responses to sanctions, including to the inspections provided for in Security Council Resolution 1441 (2002) discussed below, see Kevin Woods, James Lacey & Williamson Murray, "Saddam's Delusions: The View from the Inside," 85 *Foreign Affairs*, May–June 2006, at 2.

The Efficacy of Security Council Decisions. What steps can the Security Council take to help assure that its legally binding decisions, such as those imposing sanctions on aggressor states, will be effective? Why are Security Council sanctions given even partial effect? It is hard to deny that the Council achieves some concrete results. Consider, for example, the Council's creation of the Iraq Compensation Commission, noted above, which awarded over 50 billion dollars to successful claimants, or the establishment of the International Criminal Tribunal for the former Yugoslavia in The Hague (see the *Furundžija Case* in Chapter 2 and the *Tadić Case* in Part B of this chapter).

Terminating Security Council Decisions. Paragraph 24 of Resolution 687 provided that some Security Council sanctions imposed against Iraq were to continue in effect "until a further decision is taken by the Security Council." Since any of the Council's permanent members could veto a proposal to lift sanctions, should the Council specify that any sanctions it imposes expire if they are not renewed by some date certain? Or require that an initial sanctions resolution include a modified voting procedure to determine when the sanctions can be lifted? See David D. Caron, "The Legitimacy of the Collective Authority of the Security Council," 87 *American Journal of International Law* 552, 577–88 (1993).

Security Council Resolution 1441. The Security Council adopted Resolution 1441 in November 2002 amidst concerns that Iraq might be developing weapons of mass destruction. Here are some key provisions of Resolution 1441:

SECURITY COUNCIL RESOLUTION 1441

Nov. 8, 2002, 42 *International Legal Materials* 250 (2003)

The U.N. Security Council, *acting under* Chapter VII of the U.N. Charter:

1. *Decides* that Iraq has been and remains in material breach of its obligations under relevant resolutions, including resolution 687 (1991), in particular through Iraq's failure to cooperate with United Nations inspectors and the IAEA [International Atomic Energy Commission], and to complete the actions required under paragraphs 8 to 13 of resolution 687 (1991);

2. *Decides*, while acknowledging paragraph 1 above, to afford Iraq, by this resolution, a final opportunity to comply with its disarmament obligations under relevant resolutions of the Council; and accordingly decides to set up an enhanced inspection regime with the aim of bringing to full and verified completion the disarmament process established by resolution 687 (1991) and subsequent resolutions of the Council; . . .

4. *Decides* that false statements or omissions in the declarations submitted by Iraq pursuant to this resolution and failure by Iraq at any time to comply with, and cooperate fully in the implementation of, this resolution shall constitute a further material breach of Iraq's obligations and will be reported to the Council for assessment in accordance with paragraphs 11 and 12 below; . . .

11. *Directs* the Executive Chairman of UNMOVIC [the United Nations Monitoring, Verification and Inspection Commission] and the Director-General of the IAEA to report immediately to the Council any interference by Iraq with inspection activities, as well as any failure by Iraq to comply with its disarmament obligations, including its obligations regarding inspections under this resolution;

12. *Decides* to convene immediately upon receipt of a report in accordance with paragraphs 4 or 11 above, in order to consider the situation and the need for full compliance with all of the relevant Council resolutions in order to secure international peace and security[.]

Invading Iraq Again. "Enhanced inspections" had not found any proscribed Iraqi weapons by early 2003. (Indeed, the U.S. Central Intelligence Agency later concluded, following a thorough search for weapons of mass destruction in Iraq, that Iraq had "essentially destroyed" all of its chemical and biological weapons and its nuclear weapons program by the end of 1991 and had destroyed its last biological weapons plant in 1996. See *Comprehensive Report of the Special Advisor to the DCI [Director of Central Intelligence] on Iraq's WMD* (2004), *available at* https://www.cia.gov/library/reports/general-reports-1/iraq_wmd_

2004.) Nevertheless, U.S. and British forces, along with forces from a few other states, invaded Iraq on March 20, 2003, ousting the Iraqi leader, Saddam Hussein. As you read the following materials, ask whether this second invasion of Iraq was either legally or politically justified.

The British Iraq Inquiry. The British government established the Iraq Inquiry in June 2009 to review the United Kingdom's decision to join the United States in invading Iraq in 2003. The Inquiry interviewed numerous officials, reviewed over 150,000 government documents, and studied information in the public domain. According to the Inquiry's chair, Sir John Chilcot, the 12-volume *Report of the Iraq Inquiry* (known as the *Chilcot Report*), issued in July 2016, was intended "to establish, as accurately as possible, what happened and to identify the lessons that can be learned." The *Report* "concluded that the UK chose to join the invasion of Iraq before the peaceful options for disarmament had been exhausted. Military action at that time was not a last resort." Furthermore, the process for deciding "that there was a legal basis for UK military action" was "far from satisfactory." Statement by Sir John Chilcot: 6 July 2016, at 1, 4, *available at* http://www.iraqinquiry.org.uk/media/247010/2016-09-06-sir-john-chilcots-public-statement.pdf.

The Inquiry took no position on whether this invasion of Iraq was legal. It did, however, pay significant attention to how British Attorney General Goldsmith's advice concerning the legality of invading Iraq changed over time, and how that advice was communicated within the British government.

Legal Justifications for the 2003 Invasion of Iraq. In a detailed March 7, 2003 memo, Attorney General Goldsmith set out for Prime Minister Tony Blair "three possible bases for the use of force." The first two bases—the use of force in self-defense and "to avert overwhelming humanitarian catastrophe" ("emerging as a further, and exceptional, basis for the use of force")—did not apply. Humanitarian intervention remained a "controversial" justification for recourse to force, and Goldsmith saw "no reason" to believe "it would be an appropriate basis for action in present circumstances." Attorney General Peter Goldsmith to Prime Minister Tony Blair, Mar. 7, 2003, ¶¶ 2–4, *available at* http://news.bbc.co.uk/2/shared/bsp/hi/pdfs/28_04_05_attorney_general.pdf. Self-defense, as traditionally conceived under the U.N. Charter regime, seemed at least equally implausible as a justification. Review the legality of the invasion of Iraq on the grounds of self-defense and humanitarian intervention under the approach outlined by Professor Henkin in Section 2.

However, the U.N. Security Council, acting under Chapter VII of the U.N. Charter, also could legally authorize the use of force. Goldsmith evaluated possible interpretations of Security Council Resolution 1441. The central question was whether Resolution 1441 "revived" the authority to use force set out in Resolution 678, reproduced above. Goldsmith also stressed the importance of proportionality: even if the Security Council had authorized the use of force, the force used must be proportional to the Council's objective of "securing compliance with Iraq's disarmament obligations. [R]egime change cannot be the objective of military action." *Id.* ¶ 32.

The following excerpt from the *Chilcot Report* summarizes findings concerning Attorney General Goldsmith's legal advice.

THE CHILCOT REPORT

5 The Report of the Iraq Inquiry, Section 5 (July 2016), *available at* http://www.iraqinquiry.org.uk/media/246506/the-report-of-the-iraq-inquiry_section-50.pdf

On 9 December [2002], formal "instructions" to provide advice were sent to Lord Goldsmith. They were sent by the [Foreign and Commonwealth Office (FCO)] on behalf of the FCO and the [Ministry of Defence] as well as [the Prime Minister's Office, No. 10 Downing Street (No. 10)]. . . .

Lord Goldsmith provided draft advice to [British Prime Minister Tony] Blair on 14 January 2003. [This draft advice provided "that a further decision by the Security Council would be required to revive the authorisation to use force contained in resolution 678 (1990)."] As instructed he did not, at that time, provide a copy of his advice to [Secretary of State for Foreign and Commonwealth Affairs Jack] Straw or to [Secretary of State for Defence Geoffrey] Hoon. . . .

Lord Goldsmith discussed the negotiating history of resolution 1441 with Mr Straw, [with U.K. Permanent Representative to the United Nations] Sir Jeremy Greenstock, with White House officials and the State Department's Legal Advisers. They argued that resolution 1441 could be interpreted as not requiring a second resolution. The US Government's position was that it would not have agreed to resolution 1441 had its terms required one.

When Lord Goldsmith met No. 10 officials on 27 February, he told them that he had reached the view that a "reasonable case" could be made that resolution 1441 was capable of reviving the authorisation to use force in resolution 678 (1990) without a further resolution, if there were strong factual grounds for concluding that Iraq had failed to take the final opportunity offered by resolution 1441.

rules relating to the material breach of a treaty equally apply to the material breach of a Security Council resolution." It is up to "the Security Council to decide upon the measures to be taken, and who should take them, in the event that a state breaches a Security Council resolution."

5)   Security Council practice subsequent to Resolution 687 also did not support a "revival" theory. Resolution 1441's threat was "fully consistent with a concomitant intention to obtain further Security Council authorization at a future date, once the Security Council determines that the final opportunity" for Iraq's compliance "has passed." States both "favoring and disfavoring an authorization to use force in Resolution 1441 sought to include language expressly reflecting their positions; neither side succeeded and in this sense the resolution was left intentionally ambiguous." In such a situation, "the default rule—no use of force—remained intact." In sum, "contemporary legal restraints on the unilateral use of force do not dissipate whenever the Security Council fails to reach consensus."

Are Professor Murphy's arguments persuasive? Do technical arguments construing Resolution 1441 and other Security Council resolutions lessen or enhance the significance of international law in debates about the 2003 invasion of Iraq?

Evaluating the U.N. Collective Security System. According to Professor Michael Glennon, such developments as NATO's bombing of Kosovo in 1999 and U.S. attitudes toward the 2003 invasion of Iraq demonstrate that "the Charter provisions governing use of force are simply no longer regarded as binding international law. [T]he Charter has, tragically, gone the way of the 1928 Kellogg-Briand pact which purported to outlaw war." Michael J. Glennon, "How War Left the Law Behind," *New York Times*, Nov. 21, 2002, at A33. Do you agree? Consider several possible counterarguments. Is it a sufficient response to point out that the U.N. Security Council was never intended to restrain the actions of the major powers, but that it has always been available to counter threats to the peace by lesser powers? Or, does the U.N. system of collective security present such a compelling normative vision that occasional (or even frequent) violations of its requirements leave the edifice in place? Did this U.N. system in fact affect U.S. decisions concerning the 2003 invasion of Iraq, because it compelled the United States to articulate a legal justification for the invasion, and because several major allies refused to support the invasion? Is the U.N. collective security system ineffective when many international actors appear to believe that Security Council approval confers legitimacy on uses of force not undertaken in self-defense? Is skepticism about the continued legal significance of the U.N. collective security system a product of a particular strand of U.S. views about law and international relations—a position that does not resonate in other parts of the world? See the essays by Edward C. Luck, Anne-Marie Slaughter, and Ian Hurd in "Stayin' Alive: The Rumors of the UN's Death Have Been Exaggerated," *Foreign Affairs*, July–Aug. 2003, at 201; John E. Noyes, "American Hegemony, U.S. Political Leaders, and General International Law," 19 *Connecticut Journal of International Law* 293, 304–08 (2004); Richard H. Pildes, "Conflicts Between American and European Views of Law: The Dark Side of Legalism," 44 *Virginia Journal of International Law* 145 (2003).

4. Terrorism

The United States and other countries have responded forcefully to terrorist attacks, often asserting self-defense in justification. Should the challenges posed by terrorist attacks give rise to new legal paradigms governing recourse to force? Does Article 51 of the U.N. Charter need to be refashioned in light of terrorist attacks? What are appropriate limits on states' counter-terrorism activities? The U.N. Security Council has also made "legislative" decisions to respond to instances of terrorism. Are there limits on such decisions? We explore these questions in this section. Terrorism also poses challenges for the *jus in bello*, as discussed in Part B of this chapter.

9/11. The terrorist attacks of September 11, 2001 on U.S. soil prompted quick and forceful responses. The United States emphasized that it was exercising its right of individual and collective self-defense. The United States submitted the following letter to the United Nations, pursuant to the requirement in Article 51 of the U.N. Charter that "[m]easures taken by Members in the exercise of this right of self-defence shall be immediately reported to the Security Council."

LETTER FROM THE PERMANENT REPRESENTATIVE OF THE UNITED STATES OF AMERICA TO THE UNITED NATIONS ADDRESSED TO THE PRESIDENT OF THE SECURITY COUNCIL

Oct. 7, 2001, *available at* avalon.law.yale.edu/sept11/un_006.asp

In accordance with Article 51 of the Charter of the United Nations, I wish, on behalf of my Government, to report that the United States of America, together with other States, has initiated actions in the exercise of its inherent right of individual and collective self-defence following the armed attacks that were carried out against the United States on 11 September 2001.

On 11 September 2001, the United States was the victim of massive and brutal attacks in the states of New York, Pennsylvania and Virginia. These attacks were specifically designed to maximize the loss of life; they resulted in the death of more than 5,000 persons, including nationals of 81 countries, as well as the destruction of four civilian aircraft, the World Trade Center towers and a section of the Pentagon. Since 11 September, my Government has obtained clear and compelling information that the Al-Qaeda organization, which is supported by the Taliban regime in Afghanistan, had a central role in the attacks. . . .

The attacks on 11 September 2001 and the ongoing threat to the United States and its nationals posed by the Al-Qaeda organization have been made possible by the decision of the Taliban regime to allow the parts of Afghanistan that it controls to be used by this organization as a base of operation. Despite every effort by the United States and the international community, the Taliban regime has refused to change its policy. From the territory of Afghanistan, the Al-Qaeda organization continues to train and support agents of terror who attack innocent people throughout the world and target United States nationals and interests in the United States and abroad.

In response to these attacks, and in accordance with the inherent right of individual and collective self-defence, United States armed forces have initiated actions designed to prevent and deter further attacks on the United States. These actions include measures against Al-Qaeda terrorist training camps and military installations of the Taliban regime in Afghanistan. In carrying out these actions, the United States is committed to minimizing civilian casualties and damage to civilian property. In addition, the United States will continue its humanitarian efforts to alleviate the suffering of the people of Afghanistan. We are providing them with food, medicine and supplies.

John D. Negroponte

Armed Attacks. After 9/11 the United States relied on the doctrine of self-defense to justify the massive military aerial and land Operation Enduring Freedom against the Taliban and Al Qaeda in Afghanistan. Article 51 of the U.N. Charter recognizes the use of force in self-defense "if an armed attack occurs." What constitutes an "armed attack"? The International Court of Justice considered this question in the 1986 *Nicaragua Case*, where it ruled that

> the U.S. use of force against Nicaragua was not justified as an exercise of collective self-defense.

CASE CONCERNING MILITARY AND PARAMILITARY ACTIVITIES IN AND AGAINST NICARAGUA

Nicaragua v. United States, 1986 I.C.J. 14, 103–04

[An armed attack] includ[es] not merely action by regular armed forces across an international border, but also "the sending by or on behalf of a State of armed bands, groups, irregulars or mercenaries, which carry out acts of armed force against another State of such gravity as to amount to" (*inter alia*) an actual armed attack conducted by regular forces, "or its substantial involvement therein." [T]he prohibition of armed attacks may apply to the sending by a State of armed bands to the territory of another State, if such an operation, because of its scale and effects, would have been classified as an armed attack rather than as a mere frontier incident had it been carried out by regular armed forces. But the Court does not believe that the concept of "armed attack" includes not only acts by armed bands where such acts occur on a significant scale but also assistance to rebels in the form of the provision of weapons or logistical or other support.

> *A High Threshold for "Armed Attacks."* Why was the International Court concerned to set a high threshold of gravity for an armed attack that could justify the use of force in self-defense? A low threshold would make "defensive" uses of force legal in more circumstances. Did the Court set too high a bar? Suppose, instead of one or a few significant attacks, terrorists are responsible for only small incidents. Some commentators have argued that small incidents, if in a series, may be aggregated to satisfy the threshold requirement of gravity to constitute an "armed attack," thus justifying the use of force in self-defense. See Christopher Greenwood, "International Law and the United States' Air Operation Against Libya," 89 *West Virginia Law Review* 933, 954–56 (1987).
>
> *Who May Commit an Armed Attack?* Another question, in addition to the scale of operations required to constitute an armed attack, is whether only states may commit armed attacks. When Article 51 of the U.N. Charter was drafted, some proposals referred to self-defense in response to "an attack *by any State* against a member state"; as finally adopted, however, Article 51 only refers to responses to armed attacks, without specifying the source of attacks. The negotiating history of Article 51 is, however, "at best ambiguous" concerning whether the armed attacks that could give rise to defensive uses of force may

come from a non-state actor. See Kimberley N. Trapp, "Can Non-state Actors Mount an Armed Attack?," in *The Oxford Handbook of the Use of Force in International Law* 679, 685 (Marc Weller ed. 2015).

Attribution and State Responsibility for Armed Attacks by Non-state Actors. The ICJ's characterization of "armed attack," set out in the *Nicaragua Case* excerpt above, referred to attacks by "groups" or "irregulars," but the Court also contemplated such groups being sent "by or on behalf of a State." What connection between a state and a non-state actor must exist for an attack by a non-state actor to be attributed to the state? This question of "attribution" is often raised under the rubric of state responsibility in international law. The International Court discussed attribution in the *Diplomatic and Consular Immunity Case* in Chapter 5, and we examine state responsibility further in Chapter 7.

The Effective Control Test. In the *Nicaragua Case* the ICJ ruled that the United States was not responsible for violations of international humanitarian law allegedly committed by rebel *contras* in Nicaragua. According to the Court, "[f]or this conduct to give rise to legal responsibility of the United States, it would in principle have to be proved that that State had effective control of the military or paramilitary operations in the course of which the alleged violations were committed." 1986 I.C.J. at 65. In justifying its response to the 9/11 attacks, did the United States argue that the Taliban, which governed Afghanistan, "effectively controlled" Al-Qaeda's operations? Opinions have differed on whether links between the Taliban and Al Qaeda were sufficiently close that Al Qaeda's attacks could be legally attributable to the Taliban. Compare Kimberley N. Trapp, *State Responsibility for International Terrorism* 53–54 (2011) (questioning whether armed attacks carried out by Al Qaeda were attributable to the Taliban), with Mary Ellen O'Connell, "Lawful Self-Defense to Terrorism," 63 *University of Pittsburgh Law Review* 889, 901–02 (2002) (Taliban responsible).

Is the *Nicaragua* effective control test too restrictive, given the nature of the terrorist threat? Professor Sean Murphy saw deleterious consequences from continued reliance on the ICJ's *Nicaragua* approach:

> (1) a state may provide weapons, logistical support, and safe haven to a terrorist group; (2) that group may then inflict violence of any level of gravity on another state, even with weapons of mass destruction; (3) the second state has no right to respond in self-defense against the first state because the first state's provision of such assistance is not an "armed attack" within the meaning of Article 51; and (4) the second state has no right to respond in self-defense against the terrorist group because its conduct cannot be imputed to the first

state, absent a showing that the first state "sent" the terrorist group on its mission.

Sean D. Murphy, "Self-Defense and the Israeli Wall Advisory Opinion: An *Ipse Dixit* from the Court?," 99 *American Journal of International Law* 62, 66 (2005). The hidden nature of terrorist communications and the organizational structure of terrorist units also may make it difficult or impossible to prove that a terrorist group has acted under the specific control of a state.

Why should there be resistance to loosening the effective control test? Consider the pros and cons of using an alternative test of attribution set out by the International Criminal Tribunal for the former Yugoslavia in *Prosecutor v. Tadić*: "The control required by international law may be deemed to exist when a State . . . *has a role in organising, coordinating or planning the military actions* of the military group, in addition to financing, training and equipping or providing operational support to that group." 38 *International Legal Materials* 1518, 1545 (1999) (emphasis in original).

Self-defense Against Terrorist Armed Attacks Not Attributable to a State. Must a terrorist armed attack be attributable to a state in order for a victim state legally to use force in self-defense in the territory of the state from which the attack originated? Why require attribution at all? Suppose a government tolerates a terrorist group based in its territory, but does not help finance the group or help plan its actions, much less effectively control its operations. Should that government at least be subject to a duty to cooperate in suppressing the terrorist group? Should a victim state be allowed to use force in self-defense in the territory of the state that tolerates the presence of the terrorist group? What if a state is willing, but simply unable, to control terrorist activities in its territory? If the defensive use of force against terrorist groups abroad is deemed legal in such situations, how can the territorial integrity of states, a value emphasized in Article 2(4) of the U.N. Charter, be protected? Recall the fact situation and legal test used in the *Caroline* dispute (Section 1). For an intriguing account of the continuing importance of guerilla warfare, see Max Boot, "The Evolution of Irregular War: Insurgents and Guerillas from Akkadia to Afghanistan," 92 *Foreign Affairs*, Mar./Apr. 2013, at 100.

Defining Terrorism. According to the 2002 U.S. National Security Strategy, excerpted below, terrorism is "premeditated, politically motivated violence perpetrated against innocents." Is this definition satisfactory?

Agreement on an international law definition of terrorism has proven elusive. The 2004 report of the U.N. Secretary-General's High-level Panel on

Threats, Challenges and Change highlighted features of terrorism that may help future efforts to arrive at a generally applicable definition. The Panel regarded terrorism as

> any action, in addition to actions already specified by the existing conventions on aspects of terrorism, the Geneva Conventions and Security Council resolution 1566 (2004), that is intended to cause death or serious bodily harm to civilians or non-combatants, when the purpose of such an act, by its nature or context, is to intimidate a population or to compel a government or an international organization to do or to abstain from doing any act.

A More Secure World: Our Shared Responsibility ¶ 164(d), U.N. Doc. A/59/565 (2004). Resolution 1566 provided in part

> that criminal acts, including against civilians, committed with the intent to cause death or serious bodily injury, or taking of hostages, with the purpose to provoke a state of terror in the general public or in a group of persons or particular persons, intimidate a population or compel a government or an international organization to do or to abstain from doing any act, which constitute offences within the scope of and as defined in the international conventions and protocols relating to terrorism, are under no circumstances justifiable by considerations of a political, philosophical, ideological, racial, ethnic, religious or other similar nature.

In 2011, the Special Tribunal for Lebanon, a hybrid international court established by the Security Council in 2007 (see Chapter 7), though acknowledging that "many scholars and other legal experts" believe "that no widely accepted definition of terrorism has evolved in the world society," nevertheless unanimously concluded:

> [A] number of treaties, UN resolutions, and the legislative and judicial practice of States evince the formation of a general *opinio juris* in the international community, accompanied by a practice consistent with such *opinio,* to the effect that a customary rule of international law regarding the international crime of terrorism, at least *in time of peace,* has indeed emerged. This customary rule requires the following three key elements: (i) the perpetration of a criminal act (such as murder, kidnapping, hostage-taking, arson, and so on), or threatening such an act; (ii) the intent to spread fear among the population (which would generally entail the creation of public danger) or directly or

indirectly coerce a national or international authority to take some action, or to refrain from taking it; (iii) when the act involves a transnational element.

Ayyash *et al.*, Interlocutory Decision on the Applicable Law: Terrorism, Conspiracy, Homicide, Perpetration, Cumulative Charging, Case No. STL–11–01/I, ¶ 85 (Feb. 16, 2011).

How successful have been these attempts to define terrorism at international law? Why has it been so difficult to agree on a definition of terrorism? Is it important to arrive at an international law definition?

The U.S. National Security Strategy. The U.S. executive periodically prepares a National Security Strategy to communicate—to Congress, foreign governments, and domestic constituencies—the administration's views of major U.S. national security concerns and how it intends to deal with them. The document also promotes internal consensus within the executive branch on foreign policy, and is implemented by more detailed plans, such as the National Military Strategy. Note the assertion, in the 2002 National Security Strategy, that preemptive use of force is a permissible self-defense action against terrorists.

THE 2002 NATIONAL SECURITY STRATEGY OF THE UNITED STATES OF AMERICA

Sept. 17, 2002, *available at* http://georgewbush-whitehouse.archives.gov/nsc/nss/2002

The United States of America is fighting a war against terrorists of global reach. The enemy is not a single political regime or person or religion or ideology. The enemy is terrorism—premeditated, politically motivated violence perpetrated against innocents. . . .

Our priority will be first to disrupt and destroy terrorist organizations of global reach and attack their leadership; command, control, and communications; material support; and finances. This will have a disabling effect upon the terrorists' ability to plan and operate.

. . . We will disrupt and destroy terrorist organizations by:

—direct and continuous action using all the elements of national and international power[;]

—defending the United States, the American people, and our interests at home and abroad by identifying and destroying the threat before it reaches our borders. While the United States will constantly strive to enlist the support of the international community, we will not hesitate to act alone, if necessary, to exercise our right of self defense by acting preemptively against such terrorists, to prevent them from doing harm against our people and our country; and

—denying further sponsorship, support, and sanctuary to terrorists by convincing or compelling states to accept their sovereign responsibilities.

We will also wage a war of ideas to win the battle against international terrorism. This includes:

—using the full influence of the United States, and working closely with allies and friends, to make clear that all acts of terrorism are illegitimate so that terrorism will be viewed in the same light as slavery, piracy, or genocide: behavior that no respectable government can condone or support and all must oppose[.]

In the Cold War, especially following the Cuban missile crisis, we faced a generally status quo, risk-averse adversary. Deterrence was an effective defense. But deterrence based only upon the threat of retaliation is less likely to work against leaders of rogue states more willing to take risks, gambling with the lives of their people, and the wealth of their nations. . . .

—Traditional concepts of deterrence will not work against a terrorist enemy whose avowed tactics are wanton destruction and the targeting of innocents; whose so-called soldiers seek martyrdom in death and whose most potent protection is statelessness. The overlap between states that sponsor terror and those that pursue [weapons of mass destruction] compels us to action.

For centuries, international law recognized that nations need not suffer an attack before they can lawfully take action to defend themselves against forces that present an imminent danger of attack. Legal scholars and international jurists often conditioned the legitimacy of preemption on the existence of an imminent threat—most often a visible mobilization of armies, navies, and air forces preparing to attack.

We must adapt the concept of imminent threat to the capabilities and objectives of today's adversaries. Rogue states and terrorists do not seek to attack us using conventional means. They know such attacks would fail. Instead, they rely on acts of terror and, potentially, the use of weapons of mass destruction—weapons that can be easily concealed, delivered covertly, and used without warning. . . .

The United States has long maintained the option of preemptive actions to counter a sufficient threat to our national security. The greater the threat, the greater is the risk of inaction—and the more compelling the case for taking anticipatory action to defend ourselves, even if uncertainty remains as to the time and place of the enemy's attack. To forestall or prevent such hostile acts by our adversaries, the United States will, if necessary, act preemptively.

> *Debating the Preemptive Use of Force.* What are the arguments against "preemptive" use of force, as articulated in the 2002 U.S. National Security Strategy? Does preemptive force conform to international law concerning self-defense? Does the legality of preemptive force depend on the viability of the U.N. collective security system? Consider the view of the 2004 U.N. High-level Panel on Threats, Challenges and Change:

A MORE SECURE WORLD

Report of the High-level Panel on Threats, Challenges and Change, U.N. Doc. A/59/565 (2004)

The language of [Article 51] is restrictive: "Nothing in the present Charter shall impair the inherent right of individual or collective self-defense if an armed attack occurs against a member of the United Nations, until the Security Council has taken measures to maintain international peace and security." However, a threatened State, according to long established international law, can take military action as long as the threatened attack is *imminent*, no other means would deflect it and the action is proportionate. The problem arises where the threat in question is not imminent but still claimed to be real: for example the acquisition, with allegedly hostile intent, of nuclear weapons-making capability.

Can a State, without going to the Security Council, claim in these circumstances the right to act, in anticipatory self-defence, not just pre-emptively (against an imminent or proximate threat) but preventively (against a non-imminent or non-proximate one)? Those who say "yes" argue that the potential harm from some threats (e.g., terrorists armed with a nuclear weapon) is so great that one simply cannot risk waiting until they become imminent, and that less harm may be done (e.g., avoiding a nuclear exchange or radioactive fallout from a reactor destruction) by acting earlier.

The short answer is that if there are good arguments for preventive military action, with good evidence to support them, they should be put to the Security Council, which can authorize such action if it chooses to. If it does not so choose, there will be, by definition, time to pursue other strategies, including persuasion, negotiation, deterrence and containment—and to visit again the military option.

For those impatient with such a response, the answer must be that, in a world full of perceived potential threats, the risk to the global order and the norm of non-intervention on which it continues to be based is simply too great for the legality of unilateral preventive action, as distinct from collectively endorsed action, to be accepted. Allowing one to so act is to allow all.

We do not favour the rewriting or reinterpretation of Article 51.

Reinterpreting Self-defense. The "Bush doctrine" of preemptive self-defense, asserted in the 2002 U.S. National Security Strategy (a doctrine the U.N. *More Secure World* report refers to as preventive self-defense), raises a host of questions for international law and international relations. Does the Bush doctrine represent a claim that customary international law governing the use of force in self-defense be changed? See Chapter 2. Should at least the literal "if an armed attack occurs" limit of Article 51 of the U.N. Charter be abandoned? Should an "imminent attack" requirement, which was included in the *Caroline* formulation (Section 1) and which, as suggested in *A More Secure World*, has been accepted by many modern international lawyers, suffice to trigger the use of force in self-defense? Should the criterion of "imminence" itself be reinterpreted, in light of the expected gravity of a terrorist attack, the capabilities of modern attackers, and the likelihood that attacks may come without warning? May all states engage in preemptive/preventive self-defense? Could Russia, for example, have invoked such a "right" to launch attacks anywhere in the world against those supporting rebels in Chechnya? Chechnya is a Russian province in the oil-rich North Caucasus, where in recent decades insurgents have sought independence.

Would the United States have been better advised not to have articulated a new policy of preemptive/preventive self-defense but to have reaffirmed U.N. Charter-based rules governing the use of force in self-defense? See Jane G. Dalton, "The United States National Security Strategy: Yesterday, Today, and Tomorrow," 52 *Naval Law Review* 60 (2005). Could the United States have justified its defensive uses of force against terrorists under existing, standard legal limits? What did the United States hope to gain by articulating its new policy?

The Obama Administration's National Security Strategy. President Obama's first National Security Strategy, issued in 2010, did not explicitly refer to "preemptive actions." It provided, "The United States must reserve the right to act unilaterally if necessary to defend our nation and our interests, yet we will also seek to adhere to standards that govern the use of force. Doing so strengthens those who act in line with international standards, while isolating and weakening those who do not." *National Security Strategy* 22 (2010), *available at* http://nssarchive.us/. According to a later (2015) National Security Strategy, the United States "will continue to embrace the post-World War II legal architecture—from the U.N. Charter to the multilateral treaties that govern the conduct of war, respect for human rights, nonproliferation, and many other topics of global concern—as essential to the ordering of a just and peaceful world." *National Security Strategy* 23 (2015), *available at* http://nssarchive.us/.

Targeted Killings. Are "secret [U.S.] military missions against suspected Al Qaeda targets in as many as twenty countries," including attacks by unmanned remotely-operated drone aircraft, legally justified under "an expansive interpretation of the right of self-defense"? John R. Crook, "Contemporary Practice of the United States Relating to International Law," 103 *American Journal of International Law* 132, 161 (2009). Is there any other possible legal justification? The United States has conducted drone attacks against individual Al Qaeda and ISIL (Islamic State of Iraq and the Levant) targets, using missiles capable of inflicting significant damage, in Libya, Pakistan, Somalia, Syria, and Yemen. Those countries have not launched armed attacks against the United States. Should the use of new technologies conform to traditional legal constraints? If a drone attack were a legal exercise of self-defense, would that excuse violations of international humanitarian law (Part B) or human rights law (Chapter 7) caused by the attack? Even if targeted killings are legal, is it wise to engage in them? See *Report of the Special Rapporteur on Extrajudicial, Summary or Arbitrary Executions, Philip Alston: Study on Targeted Killings*, U.N. Doc. A/HRC/14/24/Add.6 (2010); Thomas Michael McDonnell, "Sow What You Reap: Using Predator and Reaper Drones to Carry Out Assassinations of Suspected Islamic Terrorists," 44 *George Washington International Law Journal* 243 (2012); Mary Ellen O'Connell, "Game of Drones," 109 *American Journal of International Law* 889 (2015).

Evaluating Legal Limits on the Use of Force. Are the legal rules relating to use of force in self-defense either inappropriate or unacceptably vague? How might they be changed or clarified? For one restatement of the law of self-defense in light of modern threats, based on a survey of British international law academics, practitioners, and international relations scholars, see "The Chatham House Principles of International Law on the Use of Force in Self-Defence," 55 *International and Comparative Law Quarterly* 963 (2006). Should the law governing self-defense be abandoned? Should the world return to a (modified?) just war doctrine (see Section 1) to assess the permissibility of recourse to force?

Alternatives to Using Force to Counter Terrorism. What measures, other than using force in self-defense or when invited by a state harboring terrorists, may a state victimized by terrorist attacks legally take against a terrorist organization? Such actions as municipal criminal prosecutions and cooperative interstate agreements to suppress terrorism and gather evidence would be permissible. States may also take proportional countermeasures such as imposing economic sanctions. Professor Mary Ellen O'Connell, in assessing permissible countermeasures, has noted limited support for the view that "a state may be able to send agents to apprehend terrorists from another state that refuses to extradite or try them. A police action or incursion is short of armed force and is arguably proportional to the wrong of harboring terrorists." Mary Ellen O'Connell, "Lawful Self-Defense to Terrorism," 63 *University of Pittsburgh Law Review* 889, 907 (2002).

The U.N. Security Council's Responses to Terrorism. The U.N. Security Council also responded to 9/11. On September 28, 2001, acting under Chapter VII of the Charter, the Council adopted the U.S.-proposed Resolution 1373, which set out a variety of measures "that all States shall" take, and which established a monitoring Counter-Terrorism Committee. Resolution 1373 was remarkable because it did not focus on sanctions against one state, such as the Iraqi resolutions considered in Section 3, but instead ordered all countries to comply with certain requirements. Recall from Section 2 that the Council, pursuant to Articles 25 and 48(1) of the U.N. Charter, may adopt legally binding decisions; those decisions may apply to all states.

Resolution 1373 notably contained provisions, designed to block financing for terrorists, that were based on the 1999 International Convention for the Suppression of the Financing of Terrorism. When the Security Council acted, Paul Szasz noted, "only four states had ratified the Convention (Botswana, Sri Lanka, the United Kingdom, and Uzbekistan) and forty-six others had signed it[.] By making only a few substantive provisions of the 1999 Convention obligatory," the Council avoided "imposing on states various other substantive requirements of that treaty, in particular" its detailed provisions relating "to the prosecution or extradition of offenders." According to Szasz, the Council in principle could, however, have imposed such provisions, "either by making participation in the Convention obligatory rather than optional, or by providing that all the provisions of the Convention . . . are binding on all states." Paul C. Szasz, "The Security Council Starts Legislating," 96 *American Journal of*

International Law 901, 903 (2002). Should we regard the U.N. Security Council as an international legislature?

Each of the U.N.'s then 191 member states submitted the initial reports called for in Security Council Resolution 1373—an astounding record of compliance. What challenges arise in attempting to achieve continuing compliance with the requirements of this Resolution? See Eric Rosand, "Security Council Resolution 1373, the Counter-Terrorism Committee, and the Fight Against Terrorism," 97 *American Journal of International Law* 333 (2003). If there is compliance failure, is the failure that of the United Nations, or of various states?

A Security Council sanctions regime, established in 1999 by Security Council Resolution 1267 to respond to the Taliban in Afghanistan, was also expanded to encompass Al Qaeda and its leader, Osama bin Laden. Under this regime, a "1267 Committee," composed of representatives from states on the Security Council, lists individuals and entities believed to support terrorism. U.N. member states are required to implement specified sanctions against those on the list, such as freezing their assets and imposing travel bans. For more on U.N. counterterrorism efforts and the work of the 1267 Committee, see John F. Murphy, *The Evolving Dimensions of International Law* 216–26 (2010).

European Rights, U.N. Sanctions, and the Intersection of International Legal Systems. Should those on the U.N. 1267 Committee's sanctions list have some sort of due process protection? In the 2008 European Court of Justice *Kadi Case*, Yassin Abdullah Kadi and the Al Barakaat International Foundation disputed their listing under a European Community (EC) regulation that implemented the 1267 Committee's measures. Kadi and Al Barakaat claimed violations of fundamental individual rights under EC law, including the right to property, the right to be heard by a court, and the right of effective judicial review. The *Kadi* court noted that, as of early 2007, the 1267 Committee's procedures were "still in essence diplomatic and intergovernmental." Counsel could not represent listees before the Committee. The Committee also need not "communicate to the applicant the reasons and evidence justifying his appearance in the summary list," grant "him access, even restricted, to that information," or provide reasons when rejecting a delisting request. Kadi & Al Barakaat International Foundation v. Council of the European Union & European Commission, 2008 E.C.R. I–06351 (European Court of Justice, Grand Chamber, 2008), 47 *International Legal Materials* 927, 961 (2008).

Despite these concerns, should the European Court of Justice have deferred to the targeted sanctions of the 1267 Committee, because all states are required to comply with Security Council decisions? See the discussion of U.N. Charter Articles 25 and 103 in Section 2. Did the ECJ's decision undermine respect for the U.N. Charter? According to the *Kadi* court, the ECJ's own governing treaty provided "no immunity" for the contested European regulation on the grounds that it implemented Security Council resolutions. The court did not conclude that the Council's actions were illegal because somehow inconsistent with the U.N. Charter or *jus cogens* standards. The court instead found a violation of appellants' fundamental rights under EC law. *Kadi* is an example of dualism, a concept used in the *Medellín Case* in Chapter 5. See Gráinne de Búrca, "The European Court of Justice and the International Legal Order After *Kadi*," 51 *Harvard Journal of International Law* 1 (2010). The U.N. Security Council, for its part, has modified the 1267 Committee's procedures to provide some protections for individuals.

U.N. Constraints on the Security Council. Is there a risk the Security Council may become too active as a legislative body? What constrains the Security Council's ability to act as a legislature? Some limits relate to power politics. For example, a proposed Security Council action must please the existing permanent members, or else it will suffer a veto. Also, any proposal must gain the approval of nine of the fifteen members of the Council (the so-called "sixth veto"). Do required processes or deliberations constrain Council actions? The U.N. Charter requires certain findings; in order to act under Chapter VII, the Security Council must find a "threat to the peace, breach of the peace, or act of aggression." Perhaps more significant are informal limits on the Council's authority, derived from a desire to insure that Council decisions are effective.

International Judicial Constraints on the Security Council. What other international judicial institutions might review Security Council decisions? Does the International Court of Justice have the authority to judicially review the "legality" of Security Council decisions, *i.e.*, their compliance with U.N. Charter standards or *jus cogens* norms? Despite hints in a few ICJ opinions that the International Court might engage in some judicial review, no such system formally exists that is similar to the judicial review of the constitutionality of legislation found in the U.S. and some other municipal legal systems. The ICJ may be concerned that (a) such review would give judges too much power; (b) the *jus cogens* or U.N. Charter norms that would be used to evaluate Security Council measures are indeterminate; (c) the difficulty of establishing jurisdiction in the ICJ would make judicial review too haphazard to be of utility; (d) the Charter and its *travaux* do not provide for judicial review; (e) Article 59 of the ICJ's Statute formally limits the precedential effect of ICJ decisions in contentious cases; (f) the Security Council might not heed ICJ criticisms of Council actions. If there were to be ICJ review of Security Council decisions, it need not take the form of judicial nullification. Any judicial oversight would not likely lead the Court flatly to declare Security Council actions illegal. Rather, the Court, emphasizing its role as a coordinate organ of the United Nations charged with interpreting international law, might itself suggest the legal limits of application of a Council decision. See Bernd Martenczuk, "The Security Council, the International Court and Judicial Review: What Lessons from Lockerbie?," 10 *European Journal of International Law* 517 (1999); Stefan Talmon, "The Security Council as World Legislature," 99 *American Journal of International Law* 175 (2005).

5. Humanitarian Intervention

Is it permissible under international law to use force to promote humanitarian causes? May states engage in humanitarian intervention unilaterally, or only collectively through the collective security system of the United Nations? This section introduces some of the key legal questions about humanitarian intervention, focusing on developments in Libya and Syria following the so-called "Arab Spring" of 2010.

The Legality of Humanitarian Intervention. From at least the 16th century and into the 21st century, some scholars have argued that states may unilaterally intervene abroad to protect indigenous populations or foreign citizens subjected to gross abuses. See Stephen C. Neff, *Justice Among Nations* 124–25, 178, 296–97 (2014). Since the U.N. Charter was adopted, unilateral humanitarian intervention has been debated as a possible "exception" to Article 2(4)'s prohibition on the use of force. Some contemporary theorists have denied the legality of unilateral humanitarian intervention. Recall Professor Henkin's views in Section 2 above. Others have treated humanitarian intervention "not as a new legal right . . . but as a mitigating circumstance that does not create law and which is recognized as purely circumstantial and discretionary relief, rather like the early uses of equity." Thomas M. Franck, *Recourse to Force* 190 (2002). Yet others have been willing to recognize the legality of unilateral uses of force in aid of human rights. Recall Professor Reisman's views (Section 2) and British Attorney General Goldsmith's claim that humanitarian intervention, though "controversial," was an "emerging" and "exceptional" doctrine (Section 3). See also Dino Kritsiotis, "Reappraising Policy Objections to Humanitarian Intervention," 19 *Michigan Journal of International Law* 1005 (1998); Sir Nigel Rodley, " 'Humanitarian Intervention,' " in *The Oxford Handbook of the Use of Force in International Law* 775 (Marc Weller ed. 2015).

Recent atrocities in Rwanda, the former Yugoslavia, Libya, and Syria have kept the debate over humanitarian intervention alive. If unilateral humanitarian intervention is sometimes legal, in what circumstances is that the case? For example, how extensive must human rights violations be to justify humanitarian intervention? Should a state be precluded from intervening if it has other significant interests of its own that would be furthered by entering the fray? Does humanitarian intervention gain legitimacy when undertaken by a group of states rather than by a single state? Is it more legitimate if those states are democratic? Should the force used for humanitarian ends be proportional to the suffering being endured? Must humanitarian intervention have a reasonable chance of ameliorating the situation? Some have argued that the 1999 Kosovo bombing campaign, a response to Serbian human rights abuses there, worsened the condition of ethnic Albanians in Kosovo. Michael Mandelbaum, "A Perfect Failure: NATO's War Against Yugoslavia," 78 *Foreign Affairs*, Sept.-Oct. 1999, at 2.

The Security Council and the Responsibility to Protect. Does the U.N. Security Council alone have the authority to approve the use of force to avert a humanitarian disaster? Does it have the responsibility to do so? According to the U.N. Secretary-General's 2004 High-level Panel on Threats, Challenges and Change, humanitarian disasters in Somalia, Bosnia and Herzegovina, Rwanda, Kosovo, and Darfur, Sudan, led to "a growing acceptance that while sovereign Governments have the primary responsibility to protect their own citizens from such catastrophes, when they are unable or unwilling to do so that responsibility should be taken up by the wider international community." Responses could vary from prevention to responding to violence to rebuilding devastated societies. The High-level Panel endorsed "the emerging norm that there is a collective international responsibility to protect, exercisable by the Security Council authorizing military intervention as a last resort, in the event of genocide and other large-scale killing, ethnic cleansing or serious violations of international humanitarian law which sovereign Governments have proved powerless or unwilling to prevent." *A More Secure World: Our Shared Responsibility*, U.N. Doc. A/59/565 (2004). Both the U.N. General Assembly and Security Council have affirmed "R2P." G.A. Res. 60/1, ¶¶ 138–39 (2005) (adopting the 2005 World Summit Outcome); S.C. Res. 1674, ¶ 4 (2006). Does R2P articulate a legal duty to act? What aspects of R2P are controversial? What could be done to help assure that this responsibility is carried out effectively? See *Implementing the Responsibility to Protect: Report of the Secretary-General*, U.N. Doc. A/63/677 (2009).

   The Use of Force in Libya. Was the intervention by the United States and its allies in Libya in 2011 an example of R2P? When President Obama justified his decision to attack he stressed that Libyan President Muammar Qaddafi's troops were poised to slaughter thousands of innocent civilians. Harold Hongju Koh, the Legal Adviser to the U.S. Department of State, argued that "United States military actions rest on ample legal authority." He cited to Chapter VII of the U.N. Charter—specifically to Articles 39, 41, and 42—and noted that Security Council Resolution 1973 authorized states to take "all necessary measures" to enforce a no-fly zone over Libya, to protect Libyan civilians, and to carry out inspections for an arms embargo. Koh also submitted that U.S. policy was "aimed at preventing an imminent humanitarian catastrophe." Harold Hongju Koh, "Statement Regarding Use of Force in Libya," American Society of International Law Annual Meeting, Washington, DC, Mar. 26, 2011, *available at* http://www.state.gov. Punished by the air strikes of the United States, the United Kingdom, and France, the Qaddafi government in Libya fell, and Qaddafi himself was killed by opposing Libyan forces.

   Whether the Libyan intervention is an example of a new principle of collective humanitarian intervention is questionable. Noting that the Security Council had authorized forceful measures equivalent to R2P as early as 1992 in Somalia and 1993 in Srbenicia, Simon Chesterman argued that "by the time RtoP was endorsed by the World Summit in 2005, its normative content had been emasculated to the point where it essentially provided that the Security Council could authorize, on a case-by-case basis, things that it had been authorizing for more than a decade." Simon Chesterman, "'Leading From Behind': The Responsibility to Protect, The Obama Doctrine, and Humanitarian Intervention After Libya," 25 *Ethics & International Affairs* 279, 280 (2011). In Chesterman's view, the story of the Libyan intervention added little to the right to intervene. Rather, that story was all about the political will and military ability of states to intervene.

   Was the Libyan intervention as much about regime change as it was about humanitarianism? If so, who should decide whether humanitarian abuses justify and trigger outside intervention? As Chesterman pointed out, Qaddafi may have been particularly vulnerable to outside intervention, first because he was so forthright about an "impending massacre," and second because he had lost support not only in the West but among African and Arab states and was thus politically isolated. See *id.* at 282.

The Libyan intervention was costly for the United States—more than $1 billion. Moreover, there was heated opposition to President Obama's use of force without Congressional approval. Following Qaddafi's downfall, Libya also has seen an outflow of refugees to Europe, economic turmoil, continuing strife among warring factions, and an environment in which Islamic militants operate. See Suliman Ali Zway & Carlotta Gall, "Libyan Factions Reject Unity Government Plans," *New York Times*, Oct. 21, 2015, at A10.

BARACK OBAMA, STATEMENT ON SYRIA

The White House, Office of the Press Secretary, Aug. 31, 2013, *available at* https://obamawhitehouse.archives.gov/

THE PRESIDENT: Good afternoon, everybody. Ten days ago, the world watched in horror as men, women and children were massacred in Syria in the worst chemicals attack of the 21st century. Yesterday the United States presented a powerful case that the Syrian government was responsible for this attack on its own people.

Our intelligence shows the Assad regime and its forces preparing to use chemical weapons, launching rockets in the highly populated suburbs of Damascus, and acknowledging that a chemical attack took place. And all of this corroborates what the world can plainly see—hospitals overflowing with victims, terrible images of the dead. All told well over 1,000 people were murdered. Several hundred of them were children—young girls and boys gassed to death by their own government.

This attack is an assault on human dignity[;] it also presents a serious danger to our national security. It risks making a mockery of the global prohibition on the use of chemical weapons. It endangers our friends and our partners along Syria's borders, including Israel, Jordan. Turkey, Lebanon and Iraq. It could lead to escalating use of chemical weapons, or their proliferation to terrorist groups who would do our people harm.

In a world with many dangers, this menace must be confronted.

Now after careful deliberation, I have decided that the United States should take military action against Syrian regime targets. This would not be an open-ended intervention. We would not put boots on the ground. Instead, our action would be designed to be limited in duration and scope. But I am confident we can hold the Assad regime accountable for their use of chemical weapons, deter this kind of behavior, and degrade their capacity to carry it out.

Our military has positioned assets in the region. The Chairman of the Joint Chiefs has informed me that we are prepared to strike whenever we choose. Moreover, the Chairman has indicated to me that our capacity to execute this mission is not time-sensitive: it will be effective tomorrow, or next week, or one month from now. And I'm prepared to give that order.

But having made my decision as Commander-in-Chief based on what I am convinced is our national security interests. I'm also mindful that I'm the President of the world's oldest constitutional democracy. I've long believed that our power is rooted not just in our military might but in our example as a government of the people, by the people, and for the people. And that's why I've made a second decision: I will seek authorization for the use of force from the American people's representatives in Congress. . . .

I'm confident in the case our government has made without waiting for U.N. inspectors. I'm comfortable going forward without the approval of a United Nations Security Council that, so far, has been completely paralyzed and unwilling to hold Assad accountable. As a consequence, many people have advised against taking this decision to Congress, and undoubtedly, they were impacted by what we saw happen in the United Kingdom this week when the Parliament of our closest ally failed to pass a resolution with a similar goal, even as the Prime Minister supported taking action.

Yet, while I believe I have the authority to carry out this military action without specific congressional authorization. I know that the country will be stronger if we take this course, and our actions will be even more effective. . . .

A country faces few decisions as grave as using military force, even when that force is limited. I respect the views of those who call for caution, particularly as our country emerges from a time of war that I was elected in part to end. But if we really do want to turn away from taking appropriate action in the face of such an unspeakable outrage, then we must acknowledge the costs of doing nothing.

Here's my question for every member of Congress and every member of the global community: What message will we send if a dictator can gas hundreds of children to death in plain sight and pay no price? What's the purpose of the international system that we've built if a prohibition on the use of chemical weapons that has been agreed to by the governments of 98 percent of the world's people and approved overwhelmingly by the Congress of the United States is not enforced?

Make no mistake—this has implications beyond chemical warfare. If we won't enforce accountability in the face of this heinous act, what does it say about our resolve to stand up to others who flout fundamental international rules? To governments who would choose to build nuclear arms? To terrorist[s] who would spread biological weapons? To armies who carry out genocide?

We cannot raise our children in a world where we will not follow through on the things we say, the accords we sign, the values that define us.

[T]he American people have the good sense to know we cannot resolve the underlying conflict in Syria with our military. In that part of the world, there are ancient sectarian differences, and the hopes of the Arab Spring have unleashed forces of change that are going to take many years to resolve. And that's why we're not contemplating putting our troops in the middle of someone else's war.

Instead, we'll continue to support the Syrian people through our pressure on the Assad regime, our commitment to the opposition, our care for the displaced, and our pursuit of a political resolution that achieves a government that respects the dignity of its people.

But we are the United States of America, and we cannot and must not turn a blind eye to what happened in Damascus. Out of the ashes of world war, we built an international order and enforced the rules that gave it meaning And we did so because we believe that the rights of individuals to live in peace and dignity depend on the responsibilities of nations. We aren't perfect, but this nation more than any other has been willing to meet those responsibilities. . . .

Ultimately, this is not about who occupies this office at any given time, it's about who we are as a country. I believe that the people's representatives must be invested in what America does abroad, and now is the time to show the world that America keeps our commitments. We do what we say. And we lead with the belief that right makes might—not the other way around. We all know there are no easy options. But I wasn't elected to avoid hard decisions. And neither were the members of the House and the Senate. I've told you what I believe, that our security and our values demand that we cannot turn away from the massacre of countless civilians with chemical weapons. And our democracy is stronger when the President and the people's representatives stand together.

I'm ready to act in the face of this outrage. Today I'm asking Congress to send a message to the world that we are ready to move forward together as one nation.

The Use of Force in Syria. As this book goes to press, the conflict in Syria is in its sixth year. At least 250,000 people have been killed, millions have fled Syria as refugees, and millions more are internally displaced. The situation in Syria is politically complicated: scores of rebel groups, including Al Qaeda and

ISIL (the Islamic State of Iraq and the Levant), oppose the Syrian government, while other states and private donors support various actors.

Although President Obama backtracked on his August 2013 pledge to take military action against Syrian regime targets when U.S. Congressional support seemed doubtful, a year later the United States began conducting air strikes against ISIL in Syria. Might various legal arguments support recourse to force in Syria? See "Statement by the President on Airstrikes in Syria," Sept. 23, 2014, *available at* http://www.obamawhitehouse.archives.gov. Is the bombing of ISIL targets in Syria legally justified as an exercise of individual or collective self-defense? See "Letter dated 23 September 2014 from the Permanent Representative of the United States of America to the United Nations addressed to the Secretary-General," U.N. Doc. S/2014/695. Recall the discussion of self-defense in response to terrorist acts in Section 3.

May a country legally use military force to help a government being attacked by rebels, when that government requests assistance? In September 2015, Russia provided arms and a strike force to the Syrian government, and Russian jets began bombing rebel forces. Although Russia may well have had a variety of motivations for entering the fray—including deflecting adverse attention from its invasion of the Ukraine, creating some diplomatic leverage with the West, and responding to threats that ISIL poses to Russia—its efforts bolstered President Assad's regime in Syria. See "Syria, Russia and the West: A Game-changer in Latakia?," *The Economist*, Sept. 26, 2015, at 45.

Our focus in this section has been on the use of force for humanitarian purposes, rather than on self-defense or the use of outside force to bolster a government against rebels. What facts might justify humanitarian intervention? The Syrian government attacked pro-democracy protesters in 2011, used chemical weapons as recounted in President Obama's August 2013 "Statement on Syria," and more recently bombed a hospital, killing 55 people. See "Syria's War: Spiralling Out of Control," *The Economist*, May 7, 2016, at 42. Considering especially Syria's use of chemical weapons, would it have been either wise or legal for the United States or the United Kingdom to use force in Syria in 2013, even if not authorized by the Security Council? Some commentators felt that U.S.-U.K. intervention would be unwise but lawful. See Joshua Rozenberg, "Syria Intervention: It may not be Wise, but Using Force may be Lawful," *The Guardian* (London), Aug. 28, 2013. Others felt that such action might not be lawful, but it would be wise. Professor Hurd argued, "[t]here are moral reasons for disregarding the law." Ian Hurd, "Bomb Syria, Even if It is Illegal," *New York Times*, Aug. 28, 2013, at A23. Do you agree that morality should sometimes trump international law when making national policy decisions? If so, who should judge the morality of such acts? Was President Obama right or wrong to apparently give up on his moral argument of humanitarian intervention? These questions echo controversies about unilateral humanitarian intervention—noted at the start of this section—that international lawyers and government officials have faced for many years.

U.N. Responses in Syria. The United Nations has struggled to respond to the tragedy in Syria. U.N. Secretary-General Ban Ki-Moon lamented that the stalemate over Syria in the Security Council had harmed not only the Syrian people but also the reputation of the United Nations: "We cannot look the other way while the increasing sectarian violence spirals out of control, the humanitarian emergency escalates and the crisis spills over borders." *Quoted in* Michele Nichols, "U.N. Chief Says Security Council Paralysis Harming Syrian People," Reuters, Sept. 5, 2012, *available at* http://www.reuters.com. In lieu of authorizing the use of force in Syria, the Council has promoted a temporary cessation of hostilities and has sought to facilitate political negotiations and the delivery of humanitarian assistance. See S.C. Res. 2268 (2016). The efficacy of R2P is called into question if the Security Council is hamstrung by virtue of vetoes by its permanent members.

Syria, Chemical Weapons, and Arms Control Regimes. The Syrian government's use of chemical weapons did prompt some international law measures. Two weeks after President Obama's "Statement on Syria," Russia and the United States concluded an agreement—the September 14, 2013 Framework for Elimination of Syrian Chemical Weapons—that called for procedures to destroy those weapons. On September 27, 2013 the U.N. Security Council decided it would "impose measures under Chapter VII" of the U.N. Charter should Syria use chemical weapons or transfer them without authorization. S.C. Res. 2118, ¶ 21 (2013). See John R. Crook, "Contemporary Practice of the United States Relating to International Law," 107 *American Journal of International Law* 899, 900–07 (2013). In addition, Syria—one of the few countries in the world that had not accepted the 1992 Chemical Weapons Convention, which prohibits the development, production, stockpiling, and use of such weapons, and which authorizes inspections—ratified that Convention in September 2013. The Organization for the Prohibition of Chemical Weapons (OPCW) oversees inspections under the Convention, which is one of dozens of treaties regulating arms control and disarmament. In October 2014, the OPCW, which was awarded the 2013 Nobel Peace Prize "for its extensive efforts to eliminate chemical weapons," "The Nobel Peace Prize 2013," http://www.nobelprize.

org/nobel_prizes/peace/laureates/2013/, announced "that almost all of Syria's declared chemical agents and precursor chemicals had been" removed from Syria and "safely and irreversibly destroyed." Paul F. Walker, "Syrian Chemical Weapons Destruction: Taking Stock and Looking Ahead," Dec. 4, 2014, http://www.armscontrol.org. For background on the OPCW, see http://www.opcw.org, and for a general introduction to arms control and disarmament, see Mark Weston Janis, *International Law* 186-94 (7th ed. 2016). However, observers have documented some toxic chemical and chemical weapons attacks in Syria in 2015, 2016, and 2017. See "Timeline of Syrian Chemical Weapons Activity, 2012–2017," https://www.armscontrol.org/factsheets/Timeline-of-Syrian-Chemical-Weapons-Activity.

Figure 6.E

Headquarters of the Organization for the Prohibition of Chemical Weapons, The Hague

Regional Organizations and the Use of Force. That regional organizations may have a role in promoting international peace and security is explicitly recognized in Chapter VIII of the U.N. Charter. But the authority of Chapter VIII regional organizations to use force formally depends on Security Council authorization per Article 53 of the Charter. Does the world need to rely more on regional organizations to respond to humanitarian crises or to help maintain international security? Regional organizations have taken on some roles in peacekeeping operations, a topic to which we now turn.

6. Peacekeeping

U.N. peacekeeping evolved as a mechanism to further the U.N.'s mandate to promote peace and security. Although U.N. peacekeepers generally may use force only defensively, the U.N. Security Council in 2013 authorized them to use force offensively to counter summary executions, sexual violence, and the recruitment of children by armed groups in the Democratic Republic of the Congo. After introducing traditional peacekeeping and how peacekeeping forces are authorized, we turn to recent challenges and possible improvements for the institution of peacekeeping.

Traditional Peacekeeping. Between 1948 and 1978, the United Nations authorized 13 peacekeeping operations, which, since there was and is no standing U.N. army, utilized forces contributed by U.N. member states. Early peacekeeping operations followed a traditional pattern: peacekeepers were stationed along a cease-fire line, interposed between belligerents, or assigned to observe boundaries; they could use force only to defend themselves or to remain in positions taken in accordance with U.N. authorization; they operated under U.N. command; and they included no representatives from any of the permanent members of the Security Council. Such peacekeeping operations were established only with the consent of the states in which they were to be deployed. See Eric Suy, "Peace-Keeping Operations," in *A Handbook on International Organizations* 539 (René-Jean Dupuy ed., 2d ed. 1998).

Consent counters any formal legal objection that peacekeeping forces constitute impermissible outside intervention in the affairs of the states involved. As a practical matter, peacekeeping forces are not likely to be able to function effectively absent the consent of all combatants. However, a state, in giving its consent to the presence of U.N. peacekeepers, may not be speaking for all combatants, if rebels or military units of other states are active where peacekeepers are deployed.

The Legal Authority for Peacekeeping. What is the legal justification for peacekeeping? It is not mentioned in the U.N. Charter. According to a former U.N. Under-Secretary-General for Political Affairs, peacekeeping "was discovered, like penicillin," while the U.N. was "looking for something else, during an investigation of the guerrilla fighting in northern Greece in 1947." Brian Urquhart, "The United Nations, Collective Security, and International Peacekeeping," in *Negotiating World Order: The Artisanship and Architecture of Global Diplomacy* 59, 62 (Alan K. Henrikson ed. 1986). Some have found sufficient U.N. Charter authority for peacekeeping operations in Chapter VII's Article 40, under which the Security Council may call on states to comply with provisional measures; others analogize peacekeeping to "peacemaking" and rely on provisions in Chapter VI, concerning the pacific settlement of disputes. Former U.N. Secretary-General Dag Hammerskjöld said that, in truth, peacekeeping derived from a Chapter "six-and-a-half" of the Charter, since it bridged Chapter VII, dealing with enforcement measures, and Chapter VI. See John F. Murphy, "Force and Arms," in 1 *United Nations Legal Order* 247, 292–96 (Oscar Schachter & Christopher C. Joyner eds. 1995).

The General Assembly, the Security Council, and Peacekeeping. Who is entitled to authorize peacekeeping operations? In the 1950 Uniting for Peace Resolution, noted in Section 2, the General Assembly asserted its authority to help maintain international peace and security if the Security Council failed "to discharge its responsibilities," and in 1956 the Assembly authorized a peacekeeping force (the United Nations Emergency Force (UNEF)) to patrol an armistice line in the wake of a conflict between Israel and Egypt. Some states challenged the legality of UNEF and another peacekeeping operation and refused to pay their share of expenditures authorized by the General Assembly for the operations. In response, the General Assembly requested an advisory opinion from the International Court of Justice, which in the 1962 *Certain Expenses Case* found that "the operations were undertaken to fulfil a prime purpose of the United Nations, that is, to promote and to maintain a peaceful settlement of the situation," and that associated expenses were legally incurred. The ICJ distinguished "Chapter VII enforcement actions," which the Security Council alone could take, from other "measures" relating to international peace and security, such as the authorization of peacekeeping operations, which were not within the exclusive purview of the Council. But the Court, echoing Article 12 of the U.N. Charter, also ruled that "the Assembly should not recommend measures while the Security Council is dealing with the same matter unless the Council requests it to do so." Certain Expenses of the United Nations (Article 17, Paragraph 2 of the Charter), Advisory Opinion, 1962 I.C.J. 151, 163, 170–71.

For many decades the Security Council has asserted control over peacekeeping operations. Indeed, when authorizing modern "peacemaking" or "peacebuilding" initiatives in volatile post-conflict situations—considered below—the Security Council has invoked Chapter VII of the U.N. Charter, thus blurring the traditional distinction between peacekeeping and Chapter VII enforcement actions. For more discussion of the authority of the General Assembly and the Security Council with respect to matters of peace and security, see the *Wall Case* in Chapter 4.

Modern Peacekeeping. In recent decades states have called on the U.N. Security Council to send peacekeepers to undertake a variety of complex tasks. The Council has approved many operations, particularly since the end of the Cold War in 1989; 16 peacekeeping operations were in the field in 2015. A 2015 report to the United Nations by the Independent Panel on Peace Operations, excerpted below, examined challenges facing complex peacekeeping operations.

REPORT OF THE HIGH-LEVEL INDEPENDENT PANEL ON PEACE OPERATIONS ON UNITING OUR STRENGTHS FOR PEACE

U.N. Doc. A/70/95–S/2015/446 (2015)

In 1948, the first peacekeeping mission and the first high-profile mediator were deployed as innovative efforts by a young United Nations as provisional solutions for particular problems. Nearly 70 years later, United Nations peace operations, including peacekeeping and special political missions as well as good offices and mediation initiatives, are now central to the Organization's peace and security efforts. Member States have turned increasingly to those tools to address evolving threats to international peace and security. . . .

The United Nations is today the largest provider of international peace operations, with more than 128,000 civilian and uniformed personnel serving in 39 missions across four continents, and United Nations envoys working assiduously to prevent or resolve armed conflicts. . . .

However, many of those operations and their personnel face significant challenges. They are deployed in complex conflict settings, often in insecure environments. All too often they do not have the capabilities required to implement their mandates and, in some cases, they operate in the absence of an underpinning peace process. In such conditions, peace operations struggle to achieve their objectives. . . .

Despite the overall spread of peace over the past quarter century, there has been a reversal of the positive recent trends in the past three years, and conflicts have been on the rise again. Most worryingly, the number of civil wars has increased in the last few years and attacks perpetrated by Governments and armed groups against civilians have risen for the first time in a decade. That increase is compounded by the rise in violent extremism, which can be conducive to terrorism. A historic high of more than 50 million uprooted people today suffer the fate of internal displacement or refuge abroad, resulting in a significant burden for host countries and severely stretching the capacity of humanitarian agencies to respond.

In addition to indiscriminate killing, appalling abuses are perpetrated against civilians in the midst of today's armed conflicts. Sexual violence remains a pervasive tactic of modern war. Women and girls are subject to mass abduction, as well as forced conversion, marriage and sexual slavery. Men and boys are more often forcibly recruited to fight or face extrajudicial execution. . . .

Many of today's armed conflicts are more intractable and less conducive to political resolution. Many of them result from entrenched long-term conflict punctuated by episodic relapse into large-scale violence. . . .

Complex linkages at the local, national, regional and global levels shape conflicts and demand a more nuanced approach to their resolution. Transnational illicit networks trafficking in drugs, weapons, people and money have embedded themselves in many conflicts, feeding on them, and fuelling them with funds and weapons. They now span continents, and prey upon less resilient conflict-affected and post-conflict States, where they become entrenched through corruption, rent-seeking and predation. . . .

A growing number of violent extremist and terrorist groups represent a particularly malignant threat to international peace and security. Their use of shocking violence, exploitation of distorted but powerful religious symbolism and absolutism presents a grave challenge to peace. In some cases their maximalist objectives directly threaten the very existence of nation States. The militant groups harness localized grievances to radical transnational agendas, and use today's global connectedness to move information, money, fighters and weapons across States and into and between conflict areas.

At the same time, many conflicts are caused by bad governance, where the State is captured by elites who monopolize its levers for power and enrichment and use the security apparatus to contain social and political challenges to their rule. When peaceful protests and efforts at conflict prevention fail to bring about compromise, violence often ensues and, in its path, the reopening of historic wounds, the hardening of religious or ethnic competitive identities, regional entanglements and, at times, the accentuation of international rivalries. . . .

Looking to the future, the rise of civil society and the growing voice of the people are creating strong momentum for the spread of democracy and human rights across the globe. The growth of the world economy has supported unprecedented levels of wealth and lifted millions out of poverty. In addition, the spread of technology, especially social media networks, is bringing citizens of the world closer together and awakening them to the indivisible nature of human freedoms, strengthening their resolve to address global challenges together.

At the same time, many of today's dynamics with the potential for conflict will likely intensify. . . . In many countries, the struggle for political inclusion and respect for human rights is challenging the status quo. . . . Economic inequality has widened both within and across States and is creating the potential for political frictions. More broadly, a rapidly growing population is creating ever-higher demands on food, energy and water, which calls for new solutions for the management and distribution of those scarce resources. Changing climatic conditions and the overuse of land and waterways will further exacerbate tensions and expand the number of potential hot spots.

. . . United Nations peace operations can and do make important and at times decisive contributions to conflict prevention and resolution, but they cannot and should not be asked to respond to all threats. . . .

Increased reliance on United Nations peace operations has led to an all-time high level of deployment. The United Nations has 16 peacekeeping operations in the field. The numbers of military and police have more than tripled since the year 2000 from 34,000 to 106,000, and civilian staff in peacekeeping operations now number more than 19,000. The United Nations also provides logistical support to more than 20,000 African Union personnel. Contemporary missions last on average three times longer than their predecessors, reflecting challenging operating environments and slow progress in the political processes they are supposed to support. Smaller civilian political missions have grown in number, size and responsibilities, with 23 political missions now in place with more than 3,000 personnel[.]

United Nations peace operations have proven to be effective and cost-efficient tools when accompanied by a political commitment to peace. In the past decade, the United Nations has supported relatively successful peace processes and political transitions, including in Nepal, Sierra Leone and Timor-Leste. United Nations peace operations in Côte d'Ivoire, Guinea-Bissau, Haiti and Liberia have accompanied those countries during turbulent but overall successful transitions. . . .

The record of some other missions, however, has been less positive. Missions have ended when Government consent for their presence was withdrawn or because the patience of the Security Council wore thin. In some cases, departed missions have later been forced to return in the face of renewed conflict. An older generation of small ceasefire-monitoring missions has endured for decades with no exit in sight. Lack of any serious progress in resolving the decades-old political situations underpinning them raises the question of whether they should be ended.

Today, many contemporary United Nations missions are struggling in more complex political contexts and difficult operating environments. A decade ago, many peace operations were deployed following the end of hostilities and the signing of a comprehensive peace agreement. Today, a growing number of missions operate in remote and austere environments where no political agreement exists, or where efforts to establish or re-establish one have faltered. They face ongoing hostilities and parties who are unwilling to negotiate or otherwise undermine the presence of a mission by condoning or inflicting restrictions on its ability to operate. . . . Logistical supply lines in vast, landlocked and often insecure operating environments are often stretched thin and left vulnerable to disruption.

Several missions fall into those scenarios. For example, the United Nations mission deployed in Mali is struggling to maintain an effective presence in the conflict zone, and its peacekeepers are facing persistent deadly attacks from extremist groups. In the Democratic Republic of the Congo, the mission has, for 16 years, been buffeted between regional- and community-level conflicts, and has recently been given a mandate to conduct offensive operations. In Darfur, the hybrid African Union-United Nations mission is a mere shadow of its original purpose, restricted to delivering on the narrow objectives of monitoring conflict, patrolling camps and stimulating local efforts to build dialogue. In South Sudan, an ambitious agenda to support the newly independent country collapsed in an outbreak of civil war, and the mission has been largely forced into a reactive posture protecting civilians, including tens of thousands of people sheltering within United Nations compounds. In each of those cases, the United Nations

The Panel is convinced of the importance of the core principles of peacekeeping to guide successful United Nations peacekeeping operations in observing ceasefires and implementing peace agreements. At the same time, the Panel stresses its concern that the principles of peacekeeping should never be used as an excuse for failure to protect civilians or defend the mission proactively. Moreover, two decades of peacekeeping experience in more volatile settings calls for a flexible and progressive interpretation of those principles.

As the [2000] Brahimi Report [of the Panel on U.N. Peace Operations] stated, "impartiality" is not the same as neutrality or equal treatment of all parties in all cases for all time, when in some cases local parties consist not of moral equals but of obvious aggressors and victims. Impartiality must mean adherence to the principles of the Charter and to the objectives of a mission mandate that is rooted in Charter principles. . . . Missions should protect civilians irrespective of the origin of the threat. They should promote respect by all actors for the human rights of the local population and the combatants regardless of affiliation. . . .

"Consent of the main parties" had a clear meaning when peacekeepers were deployed in the context of a ceasefire or peace agreement in an inter-State conflict or between clear parties in a civil war. In conflict management settings today, where fighting continues and is not confined to two parties, there may be practical obstacles to obtaining consent beyond that of the Government. Clearly the consent of the Government is fundamental for the deployment of a mission, and that should be reinforced. Obtaining and maintaining the consent of the other parties remains an important objective of any mission and should be pursued to the extent possible. . . .

"Self-defence" is a well-recognized concept and is thoroughly defined in United Nations rules of engagement. However, the concept of "defence of the mandate" requires clarity as to which tasks within the mandate may require the use of force. . . .

The United Nations is the sum of what its Member States place at its disposal. The Panel's consultations revealed a strong interest in strengthening United Nations capabilities for peace operations for the future. That interest must now translate into commitment. In the spirit of Article 43 of the Charter, in which Member States are called upon to make arrangements to make available armed forces, assistance and facilities to the Security Council to maintain international peace and security, it is time for Member States to support new arrangements for mobilizing the requisite capabilities and strengthening systems to deliver on the mandates of peace operations in more austere and insecure environments. . . .

Slow deployment is one of the greatest impediments to more effective peace operations. When a mission trickles into a highly demanding environment, it is dangerously exposed on the ground and initial high expectations turn to disappointment, frustration and anger.

The Security Council has no standing army to call upon. Reliance on ad hoc solutions for rapidly deploying new missions and for crisis response has limited the timeliness and effectiveness of international response. However, repeated calls for a global on-call standby capacity have foundered time and again on concerns about predictability, availability and cost.

Truly rapid and effective deployment capacities will always come at a cost, but a more reliable system for responding quickly to save lives and arrest emerging conflicts can potentially avoid a larger, more costly response later. [T]he Secretariat and Member States should agree on a suite of tools on which the Security Council can draw to respond to crises, including both United Nations and non-United Nations capabilities. This should include at least four modalities: (a) a small United Nations rapid reinforcement/deployment capability; (b) arrangements for the transfer of personnel and assets in a crisis; (c) a rapidly deployable integrated United Nations headquarters; and (d) national and regional standby arrangements. . . .

With 106,000 uniformed personnel from 121 contributing countries deployed in the field, training should be a major priority for United Nations peace operations, yet training is significantly underresourced. The United Nations should serve as a central point in coordinating a stronger global training partnership. . . .

The drafters of the Charter were prescient when they included the role of regional arrangements in Chapter VIII. Regional entities have emerged progressively as important and significant actors with considerable influence over conflict dynamics and regional politics. Although United Nations peace operations have long collaborated with regional entities, the United Nations should now strengthen such partnerships[.]

[T]he United Nations should move ahead with regional partners where there is interest and capacity to forge a strong partnership, as is the case with the African Union today. The centrality of Africa for United Nations peace operations is evident: 62.5 per cent of United Nations peace operations and 87 per cent of all uniformed United Nations peacekeepers are in Africa, and more than 80 per cent of the annual peacekeeping budget is spent on missions in Africa. Over the past decade, the African Union and its regional economic communities and regional mechanisms have worked towards a coherent continental peace and security architecture, including in building the African Standby Force and the African Capacity for Immediate Response to Crises for the future.

Recent experience . . . shows that troops from regional and neighbouring countries are essential as first responders and often bring political commitment, understanding of the context and a direct link to regional political influence and leverage. Yet, as many in the region itself have cautioned, there are also potential political risks to regional engagement in managing conflict situations where national interests of neighbouring countries may not be compatible with the intended direction of peace efforts.

Modern Peacekeeping's Successes and Failures. Despite the difficulties recounted by the Independent Panel, some post-conflict operations have achieved at least some success. For example, in the early 1990s the U.N. Transitional Authority in Cambodia (UNTAC), along with the U.N. High Commissioner for Refugees, coordinated the repatriation of more than 360,000 refugees living in camps in Thailand. UNTAC also was charged with controlling the civil administration of Cambodia's government (in particular in the areas of defense, public security, finance, information, and foreign affairs), developing a civilian police force, and organizing and monitoring free elections. With respect to military issues, UNTAC's mandate included the demobilization and disarming of the armed forces of the various Cambodian factions. During its 18 months of operation, UNTAC employed about 22,000 international personnel and cost about $1.7 billion. The verdict on UNTAC is mixed. It successfully organized an election in 1993, for example, but was less successful in its disarmament efforts. One observer characterized UNTAC's achievements as "little short of miraculous" given the political climate in Cambodia. Trevor Findlay, *Cambodia: The Legacy and Lessons of UNTAC* 161 (1995). For other assessments of UNTAC's successes and failures, see Michael W. Doyle, *UN Peacekeeping in Cambodia: UNTAC's Civil Mandate* (1995), and Steven R. Ratner, *The New UN Peacekeeping* 135–206 (1995).

Improving Peacekeeping. What would improve peacekeeping operations directed at interstate conflicts, terrorism, and humanitarian crises? Are failures due to insufficient consensus on the need for such operations, insufficient commitment to them, or insufficient organization? Is it important to maintain what the Independent Panel on Peace Operations termed "the three core principles of peacekeeping, *i.e.,* consent of the parties, impartiality and the non-use of" offensive force? Does responsibility for peacekeeping failures lie with the United Nations Security Council? With the permanent members of the

Council, for not vetoing overly ambitious operations? With the U.N. General Assembly, which establishes peacekeeping budgets? With the states voting on those budgets? With U.N. commanders of peacekeeping forces? With troop-contributing states? With other states? Consider the comments of former U.N. Secretary-General Dag Hammerskjöld:

> [W]e often hear it said that the United Nations has succeeded here, or has failed there. What do we mean? Do we refer to the purposes of the Charter? They are expressions of universally shared ideals, which cannot fail us, though we, alas, often fail them. Or do we think of the institutions of the United Nations? They are our tools. We fashioned them. We use them. It is our responsibility to remedy any flaws there may be in them. It is our responsibility to correct any failures in our use of them.

"Address at New York University Hall of Fame Ceremony on the Unveiling of the Bust and Tablet for Woodrow Wilson, May 20, 1956," *available at* http://www.un.org/depts/dhl/dag/docs/nyuwoodrow.pdf.

The Independent Panel recommended a host of specific improvements, set out in the full Report. Some relate to peacekeeping, and some relate to a broad array of other peace operations, including mediation carried out by the U.N. Secretary-General and Secretariat—see the *Reparation Case* in Chapter 3 and the *Rainbow Warrior Case* in Chapter 4—and efforts of other U.N. envoys. Various entities, including the independent Global Policy Forum, the United Nations Peacebuilding Commission, and other U.N. bodies have also proposed reforms. See http://www.un.org/en/peacekeeping/operations/peacekeeping.shtml and the websites of the United Nations Peacebuilding Commission, http://www.un.org/en/peacebuilding/, and the Global Policy Forum, http://globalpolicy.org/security-council/peacekeeping.html.

Rapid Response Forces. One possible reform, highlighted in the Independent Panel's Report, is that states should, "in the spirit of" Article 43 of the U.N. Charter, negotiate arrangements to make armed forces immediately available to the Organization. We looked at Article 43 in Section 2. Would Article 43-type agreements be a good idea? Another possibility is for the Security Council to establish a globally recruited volunteer force, using its authority under Article 29 of the U.N. Charter to "establish such subsidiary organs as it deems necessary for the performance of its functions." See Thomas Franck, "The United Nations as Guarantor of International Peace and Security: Past, Present and Future," in *The United Nations at Age Fifty: A Legal Perspective* 25, 33–35 (Christian Tomuschat ed. 1995).

Regional Organizations and Peacekeeping. The Independent Panel also recognized the importance of partnerships with regional organizations in conducting peacekeeping operations. Should coordination with the U.N. Security Council be required? Chapter VIII of the U.N. Charter addresses regional arrangements. According to Article 52(1), "Nothing in the present Charter precludes the existence of regional arrangements or agencies for dealing with such matters relating to the maintenance of international peace and security as are appropriate for regional action provided that such arrangements or agencies and their activities are consistent with" U.N. purposes and principles. Article 53(1) provides that "[t]he Security Council shall, where appropriate, utilize such regional arrangements or agencies for enforcement action under its authority. But no enforcement action shall be taken under regional arrangements or by regional agencies without the authorization of the Security Council." There are also regional self-defense organizations, such as the North Atlantic Treaty Organization.

Responsibility for U.N. Peacekeeper Abuses. As noted in the Report of the Independent Panel, some peacekeepers themselves have committed abuses. What should be done to prevent and to remedy such abuses? The Independent Panel, referring to immunities generally accorded the United Nations and its agents, asserted that "[i]mmunity was never intended and does not apply to provide immunity from prosecution to United Nations personnel alleged to have committed sexual exploitation and abuse; the immunity privileges are functional, that is, related to the exercise of his or her professional duty as a United Nations employee." The Panel called on "Member States, in particular troop-contributing countries that have exclusive criminal jurisdiction over the members of their contingents" to "immediately and vigorously investigate and prosecute all credible allegations of misconduct and crime, especially sexual violence involving rape and minors." Report of the High-level Independent Panel on Peace Operations on Uniting Our Strengths for Peace, U.N. Doc. A/70/95–S/2015/446, ¶¶ 284–85 (2015). See also Ryan McCarrel, "The United Nations and Sexual Abuse," *Foreign Affairs*, Snapshot, Feb. 14, 2016, *available at* https://www.foreignaffairs.com.

Even if individual peacekeepers may, at least in theory, face national legal sanctions for committing abuses, should the United Nations itself be responsible if a U.N. commander oversees troops that commit abuses, or if a peacekeeping force fails to provide a feasible safe haven for persecuted civilians? More generally, should the United Nations be legally responsible for some or all of its representatives' acts under either national or international law? There is much debate over the scope of the immunities recognized in Articles 104 and 105 of the U.N. Charter and the 1946 Convention on the Privileges and Immunities of the United Nations. The issue has gained the attention, *inter alia*, of the International Law Commission. See Chapter 3.C and the Draft Articles on the Responsibility of International Organizations, in *Report of the International Law Commission on its Sixty-third Session*, U.N. GAOR, 66th Sess., Supp. No. 10, U.N. Doc. A/66/10, at 52 (2011).

The particular issue of the responsibility of peacekeepers or U.N. commanders for rapes and other atrocities may raise questions of international humanitarian law, if the peacekeeping operations occur during armed conflicts. See Daphne Shraga, "UN Peacekeeping Operations: Applicability of International Humanitarian Law and Responsibility for Operations-Related Damage," 94 *American Journal of International Law* 406 (2000). We turn next to international humanitarian law, or *jus in bello*.

B. *JUS IN BELLO*

As we explained in Part A, *jus ad bellum* concerns the legality of recourse to force. By contrast, *jus in bello* also known as international humanitarian law or the law of armed conflict—regulates how states and their armed forces ought to treat combatants, civilians, and prisoners once armed conflicts are underway. Today, widely accepted treaties specify protections for civilians during hostilities and proscribe conduct that would cause combatants and prisoners unnecessary suffering.

Treaties and the Jus in Bello. Treaties have supplemented customary law concerning *jus in bello*. Conventions emerged from the Hague Peace Conferences of 1899 and 1907, as well as from 1864, 1906, 1929, and 1949 codification efforts in Geneva, Switzerland. "Hague law" is generally associated with the methods of conducting hostilities and permissible types of armaments, while 1949 "Geneva law" focuses on protecting victims of armed conflict. The four Geneva Conventions of 1949, responses to the atrocities of World War II, detail protections due (1) the wounded and sick in armed forces in the field; (2) wounded, sick, and shipwrecked members of the armed forces at sea; (3) prisoners of war; and (4) civilians in times of war or armed conflict. Two 1977 Protocols to these 1949 Conventions, applicable respectively to "international armed conflicts" and "armed conflicts not of an international character," update international humanitarian law. The statutes of international criminal tribunals—for example, the International Criminal Tribunal for the former Yugoslavia, the International Criminal Tribunal for Rwanda, and the International Criminal Court (see Chapter 7)—help specify the content of this body of law.

International Humanitarian Law as Lex Specialis. International humanitarian law, or the law of armed conflict, has traditionally been regarded as *lex specialis*, displacing rules of general international law during wartime. International lawyers have long believed that the legality of acts should be judged by different rules in times of war than in times of peace. Hugo Grotius published his famous *De Jure Belli ac Pacis (On the Law of War and Peace)* in 1625, and for scholars thereafter the law of war and the law of peace have been fundamental organizing constructs. Today international lawyers typically refer to the "law of armed conflict" instead of the "law of war," reflecting the fact that modern "wars" typically lack a requisite formal declaration.

Comparing Human Rights Law and International Humanitarian Law. Conduct that would be an impermissible infringement of human rights law during peacetime may be legal during an armed conflict. *Jus in bello* allows killing, not only of combatants, but of civilians when such "collateral damage" falls within legal parameters. *Jus in bello* also allows some individuals to be detained without a judicial conviction, and authorizes military authorities to limit free expression and assembly. Although international humanitarian law has moved in the direction of increasing protections for individuals, human rights law remains in large measure a distinct field. It applies among unequal parties, limiting what governments may do to citizens outside the realm of armed conflicts, while international humanitarian law applies to formally equal contestants. See Geoffrey S. Corn, "Mixing Apples and Hand Grenades: The Logical Limit of Applying Human Rights Norms to Armed Conflict," 1 *Journal of International Humanitarian Legal Studies* 52 (2010); Theodor Meron, "The Humanization of Humanitarian Law," 94 *American Journal of International Law* 239, 248 (2000).

Comparing Jus ad Bellum *and* Jus in Bello. Under *jus ad bellum*, one side in a conflict may be acting illegally by using force. Any such illegality does not, however, justify violations of *jus in bello* by a victim state. That is, international humanitarian law applies neutrally; both an aggressor state and a victim state are legally bound by its requirements. This separation of *jus ad bellum* and *jus in bello* means that applying rules of international humanitarian law does not depend on resolving the often difficult question of whether a war is just or legal. Combatants on any side of an armed conflict may be guilty of war crimes.

Basic Principles of International Humanitarian Law. In a 1996 advisory opinion, the International Court of Justice identified two "cardinal principles" of international humanitarian law:

> The first is aimed at the protection of the civilian population and civilian objects and establishes the distinction between combatants and non-combatants; States must never make civilians the object of attack and must consequently never use weapons that are incapable of distinguishing between civilian and military targets. According to the second principle, it is prohibited to cause unnecessary suffering to combatants: it is accordingly prohibited to use weapons causing them such harm or uselessly aggravating their suffering. In application of that second principle, States do not have unlimited freedom of choice of means in the weapons they use.

Legality of the Threat or Use of Nuclear Weapons, 1996 I.C.J. 226, 257.

What are the implications of the principle never to "make civilians the object of attack"? This principle prohibits targeting civilians, but killing civilians has never been completely forbidden under international humanitarian law if, for example, they are near a military target. The Council of the International Institute of Humanitarian Law, a non-governmental organization based in Italy, has suggested some corollaries of the cardinal principle that outlaws the targeting of civilians, including "the prohibition of attacks on dwellings and other installations which are used only by the civilian population" and "the prohibition to attack, destroy, remove or render useless objects indispensable to the survival of the civilian population." Declaration on the Rules of International Humanitarian Law Governing the Conduct of Hostilities in Non-International Armed Conflicts, *International Review of the Red Cross*, Sept.–Oct. 1990, at 404, 406.

Another basic, conceptual feature of international humanitarian law concerns its nonreciprocal character. All four 1949 Geneva Conventions contain the same Article 1, which many authorities regard as reflecting customary international law, and which provides that "the High Contracting Parties undertake to respect and ensure respect for the present Convention in all circumstances." According to Judge Meron, this "all circumstances" language "epitomiz[es] the rejection of reciprocity and insistence on the automatic application of the Conventions." Theodor Meron, "The Humanization of Humanitarian Law," 94 *American Journal of International Law* 239, 248 (2000). The 1952 *Commentary* of the International Committee of the Red Cross (ICRC) to the First Geneva Convention stressed that "[a] State does not proclaim the principle of the protection due to wounded and sick combatants in the hope of saving a certain number of its own nationals. It does so out of respect for the human person as such." *Available at* www.icrc.org.

Who may challenge violations of the Geneva Conventions? The ICRC's 2016 *Commentary* to the Geneva Conventions asserted that "[t]he interests protected by the Conventions are of such fundamental importance to the human person that every High Contracting Party has a legal interest in their observance, wherever a conflict may take place and whoever its victims may be." ¶ 119, *available at* www.icrc.org. Judge Meron, while acknowledging disputes over "the exact scope of third-party rights under common Article 1," found that it "can already be seen as the humanitarian law analogue to the human rights *erga omnes* principle." Meron, *supra*, at 249. For discussion of obligations *erga omnes*, see Chapter 2, Part E.

The Efficacy of International Humanitarian Law. It is easy to become cynical about the efficacy of international humanitarian law in light of continuing, visible atrocities during armed conflicts. Improving compliance, in the words of Judge Meron, is not a job to be "left to the law alone": "In the long run, humanitarian norms must become a part of public consciousness everywhere. Education, training, persuasion, and emphasis on values . . . such as ethics, honor, mercy, and shame, must be vigorously pursued." Theodor Meron, "The Humanization of Humanitarian Law," 94 *American Journal of International Law* 239, 278 (2000). Still, violations of international humanitarian law are occasionally brought before national or international courts and tribunals. What other legal mechanisms could promote the efficacy of international humanitarian law? What are the roles of the International Committee of the Red Cross, discussed in Chapter 3, Part C? What are the possibilities for humanitarian interventions by states, or for decisions by the U.N. Security Council seeking to avert humanitarian disasters during armed conflicts—issues addressed in Part A of this chapter? Consider, as you read the next excerpt, what roles military lawyers play in promoting compliance with the *jus in bello*.

MIKE NEWTON, THE MILITARY LAWYER: NUISANCE OR NECESSITY?

Human Dignity Protection in Armed Conflict: Strengthening Measures for the Respect and Implementation of International Humanitarian Law and Other Rules Protecting Human Dignity in Armed Conflict 107 (International Institute of Humanitarian Law, Guido Ravasi & Gian Luca Beruto eds. 2006)

LAWYERS AS A MILITARY NECESSITY

[C]ommanders have relied on sound legal advice precisely *because* of their need to accomplish the mission rather than as an unfortunate impediment. Military lawyers and good commanders develop a very special relationship of trust precisely because the lawyer provides necessary technical advice that the commander relies upon in solving some of the most complex problems posed by the military mission itself.

For example, even during [the U.S. Civil War], the tactical uncertainty faced by Union forces in waging a campaign against the rebel forces thrust lawyers into the spotlight. The first comprehensive effort to describe the law of war in a written code . . . began as a request from the General-in-Chief of the Union Armies, based on his confusion over the distinction between lawful and unlawful combatants. . . . On August 6, 1862, General [Henry] Halleck wrote to Dr. Francis Lieber, a highly regarded law professor at the then Columbia College in New York, to request his assistance in defining guerrilla warfare. This request, which can justly be described as the catalyst that precipitated more than one hundred years of legal effort resulting in the modern web of international agreements regulating the conduct of hostilities, read as follows:

> My Dear Doctor: Having heard that you have given much attention to the usages and customs of war as practiced in the present age, and especially to the matter of guerrilla war, I hope you may find it convenient to give to the public your views on that subject. The rebel authorities claim the right to send men, in the garb of peaceful citizens, to waylay and attack our troops, to burn bridges and houses and to destroy property and persons within our lines. They demand that such persons be treated as ordinary belligerents, and that when captured they have extended to them the same rights as other prisoners of war; they also threaten that if such persons be punished as marauders and spies they will retaliate by executing our prisoners of war in their possession. I particularly request your views on these questions.

Based on the stimulus of Confederate conduct, the Union Army issued a disciplinary code governing the conduct of hostilities (known worldwide as the

Lieber Code) as "General Orders 100: Instructions for the Government of the Armies of the United States in the Field" in April 1863. This was the first comprehensive military code of discipline that sought to define the precise parameters of permissible conduct during conflict. The principle endures in the law today that persons who do not enjoy lawful combatant status are not entitled to the benefits of legal protections derived from the laws of war (including prisoner of war status) and are subject to punishment for their warlike acts. The law of war is therefore integral to the very notion of military professionalism because it defines the class of persons against whom professional military forces can lawfully apply violence based on principles of military necessity and reciprocity. . . .

Though the detailed prescriptions of the law of armed conflict evolved in response to the demands of military pragmatism and the impetus of changing technology, lawyers were also a necessary ingredient in developing the norms that have come to define the very essence of professionalism. Commanders must balance the need to accomplish the mission against an internalized awareness of the larger legal and ethical context for their actions. As a consequence, military professionals developed legal codes in order to increase military efficiency by defining appropriate bounds that served to facilitate the accomplishment of the mission. . . . Any unit that is ripped apart by allegations of illegality and indiscipline cannot be combat effective simply because its members are focused on the details of sworn statements, self preservation, and self interest rather than the overall accomplishment of operational goals.

[T]he modern law of armed conflict . . . serves as the firebreak between being a hero in the service of your nation and a criminal who brings disgrace to your nation, dishonor to the unit, and disruption to the military mission.

In the wake of the Lieber Code, other states issued similar manuals: Prussia, 1870; The Netherlands, 1871; France, 1877; Russia, 1877 and 1904; Serbia, 1878; Argentina, 1881; Great Britain, 1883 and 1904; and Spain, 1893. Over time, military codes and the more thorough military manuals that followed served to communicate the "gravity and importance" of behavioral norms to commanders and soldiers. Legal norms continue to form the rallying point of moral and professional clarity that guides soldiers in the midst of incredibly nuanced missions, no matter how tired they are, or how much adrenaline is flowing in the impetus of the moment. . . .

THE LAW OF LAWYERS

As the law became more complex, and its implementation on the battlefield more problematic, it is unsurprising and perhaps inevitable that the role for lawyers became embedded in the law itself. . . .

For [states party to Geneva Protocol I], Article 82 imposes an affirmative obligation to provide legal advisors to military forces.

. . . The unstated but necessary corollary to [Article 82] is that the Parties to the Protocol have an obligation to ensure that the selected legal advisors "get the appropriate training." In addition, the creation of an office or section exclusively devoted to international law applicable in armed conflict is an "apparently essential prerequisite for the implementation of Article 82."

. . . Article 83 included [training and dissemination] provisions focused on closing the gap between the textual provisions of law and their realization in practice:

> 1.   The High Contracting Parties undertake, in time of peace as in time of armed conflict, to disseminate the Conventions and this Protocol as widely as possible in their respective countries and, in particular, to include the study thereof in their programmes of military instruction and to encourage the study thereof by the civilian population, so that those instruments may become known to the armed forces and to the civilian population.
>
> 2.   Any military or civilian authorities who, in time of armed conflict, assume responsibilities in respect of the application of the Conventions and this Protocol shall be fully acquainted with the text thereof.

Taken together, these provisions are intended to effect a comprehensive mechanism for training military professionals in the obligations inherent in the law of armed conflict as well as a systematic and authoritative implementation of those principles.

BACK TO THE FUTURE:
THE CONTINUED NECESSITY FOR MILITARY LAWYERS

The Lawyer as Trainer—Recent events in Iraq serve as a stark reminder that the efforts of commanders and lawyers to achieve a well-trained and disciplined force can never be taken for granted. Unfortunately, this is not a new lesson. Lieutenant General William R. Peers reported that one of the contributing factors to the crimes committed at My Lai was that "[n]either units nor individual members of Task Force Barker and the 11th Brigade received the proper training in the Law of War (Hague and Geneva conventions), the safeguarding of noncombatants, or the Rules of Engagement." . . .

In practice, the lawyer must have a hand in the drafting, training, dissemination, inspection, and enforcement of the Rules of Engagement and command policies that provide the linkage from the classroom to the field. This, in turn, requires that lawyers work closely with commanders and staffs to ensure proper targeting[.] The Rules of Engagement must be disseminated to every corner of the command; equally important, the lawyer must be constantly on the move to reinforce the legal component of the Rules of Engagement, answer questions, and help fill the gaps in soldiers' minds regarding the interface of law and tactics.

Some soldiers from the Vietnam era reported that a lackadaisical approach to legal training caused them to take the otherwise sound command guidance they received on pocket cards and put the cards into their pockets unread and hence ignored. The United States Army continues to develop and disseminate such cards, as do many of our allies. The card is not an end in itself, but serves as the commander's tool to help instill compliance with legal norms, which is in turn reinforced by the active role of military lawyers.

In contrast to simply preparing a card for distribution to soldiers, lawyers with the Third Infantry Division during Operation Iraqi Freedom developed a matrix that was disseminated and used at command levels down to the smallest tactical force. The matrix (see Figure [6.F] below) gave commanders and soldiers a quick and ready reference with which to consider and implement the obligations of international humanitarian law. Anecdotal evidence shows that the Third Infantry Division filled out these cards and kept records of their efforts to comply with the law as long as it was physically possible given the demands of the battle.

The Lawyer as Negotiator—Military lawyers must continue to play a central role in the negotiation of new legal norms. The Official [International Committee of the Red Cross] Commentary on Protocol I notes with some understatement, "a good military legal advisor should have some knowledge of military problems." In a similar vein, the law cannot be allowed to drift into an atrophied state in which its objectives are seen as romanticized and unattainable in the operational context. If Humanitarian Law becomes separated from the everyday experience and practice of professional military forces around the world, it is in danger of being relegated to the remote pursuit of ethereal goals. As the Third Infantry Division matrix illustrates so well, the law takes form and shape in the practice of soldiers and the thinking of commanders on the ground rather than in the textbooks and scholarly opinions.

. . . Failure to keep the legal norms anchored in the real world of practice would create a great risk of superimposing the humanitarian goals of the law as the dominant and perhaps only legitimate objective in times of conflict. This trend could result in principles and documents that would become increasingly divorced from military practice and therefore increasingly irrelevant to the actual conduct of operations. . . .

The Lawyer as Enforcer—The importance of enforcing the substantive body of norms through criminal investigations and prosecutions when appropriate cannot be overstated. As early as 1842, Secretary of State Daniel Webster articulated the idea that a nation's sovereignty also entails "the strict and faithful observance of all those principles, laws, and usages which have obtained currency among civilized states, and which have for their object the mitigation of the miseries of war." Military lawyers are at the forefront of such efforts precisely because they are in the best position to evaluate the culpability of commanders in light of the "reasonable commander" standard that is built into the law of armed conflict. Moreover, the same experts who advise commanders on the proper implementation of the law should find a great deal of professional satisfaction in helping to ensure that the law retains its influence and credibility. Their expertise forms the basis of effective prosecutions that are legally sound, but fair and credible from the perspective of soldiers in the field.

The events at Abu Ghraib have served to remind military professionals of the visceral linkage between their actions and the achievement of the mission. Abu Ghraib represents a sharp departure from American ideals precisely because some soldiers forgot about their overarching mission to defend justice and human dignity. At the same time, it is worth recalling that the crimes were made public because one young soldier, Specialist Joseph Darby, alerted appropriate authorities when he became aware of the activities inside Abu Ghraib.

The investigation and administration of appropriate discipline against culpable individuals serves an important deterrent purpose in the legal regime by helping to strengthen the resolve of the next Joseph Darby who may be forced to choose between loyalty to his comrade-in-arms and the principles of law and professionalism.

Figure 6.F

Matrix for U.S. Third Infantry Division, Operation Iraqi Freedom

Commanders are responsible for assessing proportionality before authorizing indirect fire into a populated area or protected place (NFA/RFA). Refer to ROE; seek legal advice; copy SJA, G5 and FSE.

POPULATED AREA TARGETING RECORD
(Military Necessity – Collateral Damage – Proportionality Assessment)

I. MILITARY NECESSITY – What are we shooting at and why?

1. DTG of mission: _____
2. Location – Grid Coordinates: _____
3. Enemy Target (WMD, CHEM, SCUD, ARTY, ARMOR, C2, LOG)
     a. Type and Unit: _____
     b. Importance to Mission: _____
4. Target Intel:
     a. How Observed: UAV, FIST, SOF, other: _____
     b. Unobserved: Q36, Q37, ELINT, other: _____
     c. Last Known DTG of Observation or Detection: _____
5. Other Concerns as applicable:
     a. US Casualties: Number: _____ Location: _____
     b. Receiving Enemy Fire: Unit: _____ Location: _____

II. COLLATERAL DAMAGE – Who or what is there now?

6. City: _____ Original Population: _____
7. Estimated Population Now in Target Area (if known): _____
8. Cultural, Economic, or Other Significance and Effects:
_____

III. MUNITIONS SELECTION – Mitigate civilian casualties and civilian property destruction

9. Available Delivery Systems Within Range:
     155, MLRS, ATACMS, AH64, CAS, other:_____
10. Munitions: DPICM, Precision-Guided Munitions (PGM),
     other:_____

IV. COMMANDER'S AUTHORIZATION TO FIRE – Proportionality analysis

11. Legal Advisor's Rank and Name: _____
12. Civil Affairs/G5 Advisor: _____
13. Is the anticipated loss of life and damage to civilian property acceptable in relation to the military advantage expected to be gained? _____ Yes/No _____
14. Commander or Representative's Rank, Name, and Position:
_____
15. Optional Comments: _____
16. DTG of Decision: _____

[M]any of the prosecutions of those who strayed so far from accepted professional norms in Iraq are based on the principle of dereliction of duty. Reflecting a concept of military law recognized around the world, Article 92 of the Uniform Code of Military Justice makes it a crime to fail to perform a known duty, either willfully or through neglect. The necessary base of knowledge that supports subsequent enforcement efforts was built by the military lawyers who taught the units, rehearsed them, and integrated legal considerations into the operational flow.

The Lawyer as Reporter—Lawyers who advise commanders on the proper application of Humanitarian Law have a vested interest in helping to ensure that those norms are respected and implemented in the future. In order to achieve that fundamental objective, legal advisors must be engaged at all levels to bring the light of truth and proper legal analysis to allegations of war crimes. . . .

Lawyers must be proactive in responding to allegations that humanitarian norms have been violated by collecting the relevant facts and eyewitness accounts, and analyzing them in light of their particular expertise in the law. . . .

For example, no responsible commander intentionally targets civilian populations, and the law on this matter is clear and fundamental. In the era of mass communications, the media often creates a perception that the normative content of the law is meaningless by conveying an automatic presumption that any instance of collateral damage is based on illegal conduct by military commanders. This perception is, of course, completely without foundation in Humanitarian Law. [N]othing would erode compliance with Humanitarian Law faster than . . . distorted allegations that permissible conduct in fact represents willful defiance of international norms.

. . . If the exposure of illegal acts on the part of the adversary helps sway social and political opinion away from supporting lawless thugs, they may in turn recognize that their unlawful actions are a barrier to achieving their ends.

The Goals of International Humanitarian Law. The law of war undeniably serves humanitarian goals. Professor Newton stressed that a well-developed *jus in bello* also promotes battlefield discipline and efficiency, and that it can connect to traditional notions of military honor. Military officers are particularly attuned to the dangers of moral corrosion troops experience when the laws of war are not reinforced and obeyed. See Geoffrey Corn, "The Corrosive Risks of Lawless Leadership," Nov. 30, 2016, http://opiniojuris.org/2016/11/30/the-corrosive-risks-of-lawless-leadership/.

Figure 6.G
Francis Lieber, Author of the Lieber Code

Individual Responsibility for Violations of the Jus in Bello. Professor Newton's discussion of the military lawyer's role as "enforcer" points to how individuals—both soldiers and their commanders—may violate the law of armed conflict. Individual responsibility may attach to prohibited acts directed at combatants on the battlefield, prisoners of war, and civilians outside of combat.

What sorts of excuses might individuals, having committed an act violating international humanitarian law, appropriately invoke? If, for example, a commanding officer were to order a soldier to violate the law of war, could a soldier who complied with that order be held accountable? According to the Nuremberg judgment (see Chapter 7), "[t]hat a soldier was ordered to kill or torture in violation of the international law of war has never been recognized as a defense to such acts of brutality, though . . . the order may be urged in mitigation of the punishment." The same standard is incorporated in the Statutes of the International Criminal Tribunal for the former Yugoslavia (ICTY), the International Criminal Tribunal for Rwanda (ICTR), and the International Criminal Court (ICC).

The Nuremberg judgment and decisions of the ICTY and the ICTR provide numerous examples of commanding military officers themselves being tried and convicted for violating the law of war. According to Article 6(3) of the Statute of the ICTR, the fact that a subordinate committed a proscribed act may not relieve his commanding officer from criminal responsibility. If the officer "knew or had reason to know that the subordinate was about to commit" such an act, or if the subordinate committed the act and the officer had failed to take "necessary and reasonable" preventive measures, the officer may be responsible. Should civilian leaders also be liable for violations of international humanitarian law? Under what circumstances? See *Prosecutor v. Musema*, No. 96–13–1 (ICTR, 2000), *available at* http://www.unictr.unmict.org/en/cases.

Process. Although international courts occasionally try individuals for violations of the law of war when municipal procedures are unavailable, international humanitarian law is most often implemented at the national level. Rules of international humanitarian law may be incorporated into municipal law. In the United States, these rules are set out in U.S. military manuals, *e.g.*, *The Law of Land Warfare* (FM 27–10, 1976) and *Human Intelligence Collector Operations* (FM 2–22.3 (FM 34–52), 2006). Soldiers and commanders may be prosecuted for proscribed conduct under the Uniform Code of Military Justice, codified as a U.S. statute. 10 U.S.C. §§ 801 *et seq.* As Professor Newton noted, soldiers may be found liable for "dereliction of duty" under their own state's military disciplinary procedures if they have violated military orders that incorporate rules of international humanitarian law. Is not some such incorporation mechanism necessary if this body of law is ever to be truly effective?

Of course, as suggested by Professor Newton's references to the My Lai incident in Vietnam and to the abuses at Abu Ghraib in Iraq, not all violations have been deterred. See Michal R. Belknap, *The Vietnam War on Trial: The My Lai Massacre and Court-Martial of Lieutenant Calley* (2002); Seymour M. Hersch,

Chain of Command: The Road from 9/11 to Abu Ghraib (2004). What additional measures at the national level might encourage greater compliance? See Laura A. Dickinson, "Military Lawyers on the Battlefield: An Empirical Account of International Law Compliance," 104 *American Journal of International Law* 1 (2010).

Characterization Issues. Applying the *jus in bello* requires classifying types of conflicts and groups of people. According to Professor Newton, the law of war "defines the class of persons against whom professional military forces can lawfully apply violence." It is essential, for example, to know who is a civilian and who is a combatant. Professor Dinstein has concluded that "the hallmark of civilians is that they are neither members of the armed forces nor do they actively participate in hostilities." Yoram Dinstein, *The Conduct of Hostilities under the Law of International Armed Conflict* 113 (2004).

In what types of conflicts do international humanitarian law protections apply? According to the 1977 Protocols to the 1949 Geneva Conventions and current conceptions of customary international law, international humanitarian law only relates to "armed conflicts," and it is thus important to determine what constitutes an armed conflict. Since legal obligations may vary depending on whether an armed conflict is "international" or "not of an international character," it is also important to consider that distinction. In the *Tadić Case* from the International Criminal Tribunal for the former Yugoslavia, excerpted below, the judges discussed the doctrine of "armed conflict," so central to the operation of international humanitarian law.

The Tadić Case *and the International Criminal Tribunal for the former Yugoslavia.* The U.N. Security Council established the ICTY in Security Council Resolution 827 (1993). The Tribunal's Statute confers jurisdiction to prosecute individuals for certain international law offenses alleged to have been committed in the territory of the former Yugoslavia since January 1, 1991. Article 2 of the Statute provides that the Tribunal has "the power to prosecute persons committing or ordering to be committed grave breaches of the Geneva Conventions of 12 August 1949." Article 3 provides for "the power to prosecute persons violating the laws or customs of war," and Article 5 "the power to prosecute persons responsible for" specified crimes against humanity "when committed in armed conflict, whether international or internal in character." Dusko Tadić challenged the Tribunal's jurisdiction in part on the grounds that the offenses listed in Articles 2, 3, and 5 could only be committed during an armed conflict; he argued that no such conflict was ongoing in the region of Prijedor, where he was alleged to have violated the ICTY Statute. For more discussion of international criminal tribunals, see Chapter 7.

PROSECUTOR V. TADIĆ

Decision on the Defence Motion for Interlocutory Appeal on Jurisdiction, Case No. IT–94–1 (Appeals Chamber, International Criminal Tribunal for the former Yugoslavia, 1995), 35 *International Legal Materials* 32 (1996)

Armed Conflicts

Appellant now asserts the new position that there did not exist a legally cognizable armed conflict—either internal or international—at the time and place that the alleged offences were committed. . . .

International humanitarian law governs the conduct of both internal and international armed conflicts. Appellant correctly points out that for there to be a violation of this body of law, there must be an armed conflict. The definition of "armed conflict" varies depending on whether the hostilities are international or internal but, contrary to Appellant's contention, the temporal and geographical scope of both internal and international armed conflicts extends beyond the exact time and place of hostilities. With respect to the temporal frame of reference of international armed conflicts, each of the four Geneva Conventions contains language intimating that their application may extend beyond the cessation of fighting. For example, both Conventions I and III apply until protected persons who have fallen into the power of the enemy have been released and repatriated.

Although the Geneva Conventions are silent as to the geographical scope of international "armed conflicts," . . . at least some of the provisions of the Conventions apply to the entire territory of the Parties to the conflict, not just to the vicinity of actual hostilities. . . . With respect to prisoners of war, the Convention applies to combatants in the power of the enemy; it makes no difference whether they are kept in the vicinity of hostilities. In the same vein, Geneva Convention IV protects civilians anywhere in the territory of the Parties. [T]he very nature of the Conventions—particularly Conventions III and IV— dictates their application throughout the territories of the parties to the conflict; any other construction would substantially defeat their purpose.

The geographical and temporal frame of reference for internal armed conflicts is similarly broad. This conception is reflected in the fact that beneficiaries of common Article 3 of the Geneva Conventions are those taking no active part (or no longer taking active part) in the hostilities. This indicates that the rules contained in Article 3 also apply outside the narrow geographical context of the actual theatre of combat operations. [The Tribunal discusses other examples involving detainee protections, which continue even after the end of hostilities.]

On the basis of the foregoing, we find that an armed conflict exists whenever there is a resort to armed force between States or protracted armed violence between governmental authorities and organized armed groups or between such groups within a State. International humanitarian law applies from the initiation of such armed conflicts and extends beyond the cessation of hostilities until a general conclusion of peace is reached; or, in the case of internal conflicts, a peaceful settlement is achieved. Until that moment, international humanitarian law continues to apply in the whole territory of the warring States or, in the case of internal conflicts, the whole territory under the control of a party, whether or not actual combat takes place there.

Applying the foregoing concept of armed conflicts to this case, we hold that the alleged crimes were committed in the context of an armed conflict. Fighting among the various entities within the former Yugoslavia began in 1991, continued through the summer of 1992 when the alleged crimes are said to have been committed, and persists to this day. . . . These hostilities exceed the intensity requirements applicable to both international and internal armed conflicts.

Armed Conflicts. Deciding whether an armed conflict exists is critical in determining whether international humanitarian law applies. The status of armed conflict may also be important, *e.g.*, with respect to rights of asylum, the law of neutrality, the activities of U.N. peacekeepers, and the interpretation of arms control treaties. What features characterize armed conflicts? According to Article 1(2) of the 1977 Protocol II to the Geneva Conventions, "situations of internal disturbances and tensions, such as riots [and] isolated and sporadic acts of violence" are not covered. How about "sporadic" international violence? Did France's sinking of the *Rainbow Warrior* in a New Zealand harbor (Chapter 4) constitute an armed conflict? Is an international border incident, such as occurred in the *Naulilaa Case* discussed in Part A, Section 1 above, an armed conflict? What about the "Cod Wars" between the United Kingdom and Iceland, considered in the *Fisheries Jurisdiction Case* in Chapter 8? Such isolated and relatively minor incidents probably would not amount to "armed conflicts." Are criteria of intensity and duration equally significant in determining the existence of an armed conflict? According to the International Tribunal for the former Yugoslavia in *Prosecutor v. Haradinaj*, "[t]he criterion of protracted armed violence" refers "more to the intensity of the armed violence than to its duration." Judgment, Case No. IT–04–84–T, ¶ 49 (Trial Chamber I, 2008). What factors should be used to judge intensity?

In *Haradinaj* the ICTY recognized that "an armed conflict can exist only between parties that are sufficiently organized to confront each other with military means." *Id.* ¶ 60. When is a group sufficiently well organized to engage in armed conflict? See International Law Association Committee on Use of Force, "Final Report on the Meaning of Armed Conflict in International Law," in International Law Association, *Report of the Seventy-Fourth Conference (The Hague)* 676 (2010); "How is the Term 'Armed Conflict' Defined in International Humanitarian Law?," International Committee of the Red Cross Opinion Paper, Mar. 2008, *available at* http://www.icrc.org.

In international humanitarian law, it may be important to know whether an armed conflict is "international" or "not of an international character," *i.e.*, "internal." The *Tadić* Tribunal continued by examining the distinction between the two categories of armed conflicts. Why do the rules applicable to each category differ? Is it always easy to distinguish the two categories?

Prosecutor v. Tadić
International Versus Internal Armed Conflicts

There has been protracted, large-scale violence between the armed forces of different States and between governmental forces and organized insurgent groups. [W]e conclude that the conflicts in the former Yugoslavia have both internal and international aspects[.]

Whenever armed violence erupted in the international community, in traditional international law the legal response was based on a stark dichotomy: belligerency or insurgency. The former category applied to armed conflicts between sovereign States (unless there was recognition of belligerency in a civil war), while the latter applied to armed violence breaking out in the territory of a sovereign State. Correspondingly, international law treated the two classes of conflict in a markedly different way: interstate wars were regulated by a whole body of international legal rules, governing both the conduct of hostilities and the protection of persons not participating (or no longer participating) in armed violence (civilians, the wounded, the sick, shipwrecked, prisoners of war). By contrast, there were very few international rules governing civil commotion, for States preferred to regard internal strife as rebellion, mutiny and treason coming within the purview of national criminal law and, by the same token, to exclude any possible intrusion by other States into their own domestic jurisdiction. This dichotomy was clearly sovereignty-oriented and reflected the traditional configuration of the international community, based on the coexistence of sovereign States more inclined to look after their own interests than community concerns or humanitarian demands.

Since the 1930s, however, the aforementioned distinction has gradually become more and more blurred, and international legal rules have increasingly emerged or have been agreed upon to regulate internal armed conflict. There exist various reasons for this development. First, civil wars have become more frequent, not only because technological progress has made it easier for groups of individuals to have access to weaponry but also on account of increasing tension, whether ideological, inter-ethnic or economic; as a consequence the international community can no longer turn a blind eye to the legal regime of such wars. Secondly, internal armed conflicts have become more and more cruel and protracted, involving the whole population of the State where they occur: the all-out resort to armed violence has taken on such a magnitude that the difference with international wars has increasingly dwindled (suffice to think of the Spanish civil war, in 1936–39, of the civil war in the Congo, in 1960–1968, the Biafran conflict in Nigeria, 1967–70, the civil strife in Nicaragua, in 1981–1990, or El Salvador, 1980–1993). Thirdly, the large-scale nature of civil strife, coupled with the increasing interdependence of States in the world community, has made it more and more difficult for third States to remain aloof: the economic, political and ideological interests of third States have brought about direct or indirect involvement of third States in this category of conflict, thereby requiring that international law take greater account of their legal regime in order to prevent, as much as possible, adverse spill-over effects. Fourthly, the impetuous development and propagation in the international community of human rights doctrines, particularly after the adoption of the Universal Declaration of Human Rights in 1948, has brought about significant changes in international law, notably in the approach to problems besetting the world community. A State-sovereignty-oriented approach has been gradually supplanted by a human-being-oriented approach. . . . It follows that in the area of armed conflict the distinction between interstate wars and civil wars is losing its value as far as human beings are concerned. Why protect civilians from belligerent violence, or ban rape, torture or the wanton destruction of hospitals, churches, museums or private property, as well as proscribe weapons causing unnecessary suffering when two sovereign States are engaged in war, and yet refrain from enacting the same bans or providing the same protection when armed violence has erupted "only" within the territory of a sovereign State? If international law, while of course duly safeguarding the legitimate interests of States, must gradually turn to the protection of human beings, it is only natural that the aforementioned dichotomy should gradually lose its weight.

[T]he violations at issue here . . . entail individual criminal responsibility, regardless of whether they are committed in internal or international armed conflicts. Principles and rules of humanitarian law reflect "elementary considerations of humanity" widely recognized as the mandatory minimum for conduct in armed conflicts of any kind. No one can doubt the gravity of the acts at issue, nor the interest of the international community in their prohibition.

International Versus Internal Armed Conflicts. The distinction between international and internal armed conflicts remains significant. As a matter of treaty law, for example, Protocol I to the Geneva Conventions (accepted by 174 parties, not including the United States, as of May 2017) applies to international armed conflicts, while Protocol II (168 parties, not including the United States) applies only to armed conflicts "not of an international character," *e.g.,* civil wars. With respect to customary international law, the Tribunal in the 1995 *Tadić Case* found that "(i) only a number of rules and principles governing international armed conflicts have gradually been extended to apply to internal conflicts; and (ii) this extension has not taken place in the form of a full and mechanical transplant of those rules to internal conflicts." 35 *International Legal Materials* at 69. See also International Committee of the Red Cross, 1–2 *Customary International Humanitarian Law* (Jean-Marie Henckaerts & Louise Doswald-Beck eds. 2005), and the exchange between U.S. government lawyers and the ICRC at 46 *International Legal Materials* 514, 959 (2007). Broadening the category of international armed conflicts and correspondingly narrowing the category of conflicts "not of an international character" would increase the circumstances in which the most extensive *jus in bello* protections apply.

What distinguishes an international conflict from an internal one? Is it too simplistic to say that all international armed conflicts are fought between states? The International Criminal Court in the *Lubanga Case* (Chapter 7) ruled that an internal armed conflict could become international not only when another state directly intervened, but when "some of the participants in the internal armed conflict act on behalf of that other State (indirect intervention)." Case No. ICC–01/04 01/06, Decision on the Confirmation of Charges ¶ 209 (ICTY, 2007). How are we to determine when participants in an armed conflict "act on behalf of" another state? See *id.* ¶ 201 the discussion of attribution in Part A, Section 4 above.

Armed Conflict and Terrorists. Is the struggle against global terrorism an armed conflict? To answer yes, the fight must be with a "sufficiently organized" entity, as noted above. This formula suggests there could be no armed conflict with an individual terrorist. If a fight against a terrorist group is an armed conflict, is it an international armed conflict, an armed conflict "not of an international character," or an armed conflict of some different sort? International humanitarian law provides rights for those engaged in international armed conflicts and non-international armed conflicts (traditionally civil wars), but what rights must be accorded suspected terrorists under international law? The following case excerpt and discussion explore some of these questions.

The Hamdan Case. In its 2006 decision in *Hamdan v. Rumsfeld*, the U.S. Supreme Court ruled on whether the Geneva Conventions applied to the conflict with Al Qaeda. The case involved a *habeas corpus* petition by Salim Ahmed Hamdan, a Yemeni national who was seized in Afghanistan after the September 11, 2001 terrorist attacks and held in custody at the U.S. prison in Guantánamo Bay, Cuba. He was to be tried for conspiracy by a U.S. military commission convened by the President. The alleged conspiracy involved Hamdan's transporting weapons and working as a bodyguard and personal driver for the Al Qaeda leader Osama bin Laden.

The *Hamdan* Court found that the 1949 Geneva Conventions are, "as the Government does not dispute, part of the law of war. And compliance with the law of war is the condition upon which the authority set forth in Article 21 [of the U.S. Uniform Code of Military Justice (UCMJ)], authorizing a presidential order to establish a military commission] is granted." The Supreme Court ultimately ruled for Hamdan, concluding "that the military commission convened to try Hamdan lacks power to proceed because its structure and procedures"—*e.g.*, the authority to exclude the defendant and his counsel from the trial, and to allow use of hearsay evidence and evidence obtained through coercion—"violate both the UCMJ and the Geneva Conventions." 548 U.S. 557, 567, 628 (2006). In the course of discussing the protections provided by the Geneva Conventions, the Supreme Court considered the nature of the armed conflict with Al Qaeda.

Figure 6.H
Map of U.S. Naval Base, Guantánamo Bay, Cuba

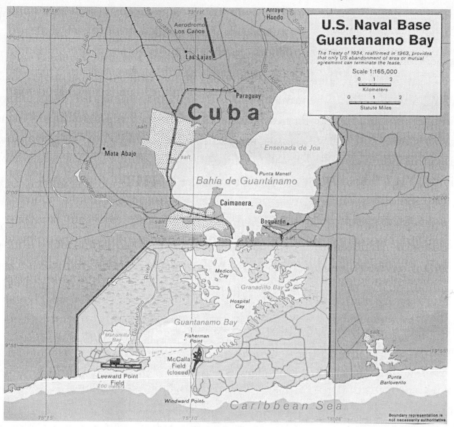

Figure 6.I
Entrance to Detention Camp 1, Guantánamo Bay's Delta Camp

HAMDAN V. RUMSFELD

548 U.S. 557 (2006)

The conflict with al Qaeda is not, according to the Government, a conflict to which the full protections afforded detainees under the 1949 Geneva Conventions apply because Article 2 of those Conventions (which appears in all four Conventions) renders the full protections applicable only to "all cases of declared war or of any other armed conflict which may arise between two or more of the High Contracting Parties." Since Hamdan was captured and detained incident to the conflict with al Qaeda and not the conflict with the Taliban [*i.e.,* the government of Afghanistan], and since al Qaeda, unlike Afghanistan, is not a "High Contracting Party" . . . the protections of those Conventions are not, it is argued, applicable to Hamdan.

We need not decide the merits of this argument because there is at least one provision of the Geneva Conventions that applies here even if the relevant conflict is not one between signatories. Article 3, often referred to as Common Article 3 because, like Article 2, it appears in all four Geneva Conventions, provides that in a "conflict not of an international character occurring in the territory of one of the High Contracting Parties, each Party to the conflict shall be bound to apply, as a minimum," certain provisions protecting "[p]ersons taking no active part in the hostilities, including members of armed forces who have laid down their arms and those placed *hors de combat* by . . . detention." One such provision prohibits "the passing of sentences and the carrying out of executions without previous judgment pronounced by a regularly constituted court affording all the judicial guarantees which are recognized as indispensable by civilized peoples."

The Court of Appeals thought, and the Government asserts, that Common Article 3 does not apply to Hamdan because the conflict with al Qaeda, being " 'international in scope,' " does not qualify as a " 'conflict not of an international character.' " That reasoning is erroneous. The term "conflict not of an international character" is used here in contradistinction to a conflict between nations. . . . Common Article 3 . . . affords some minimal protection, falling short of full protection under the Conventions, to individuals associated with neither a signatory nor even a nonsignatory "Power" who are involved in a conflict "in the territory of" a signatory. The latter kind of conflict is distinguishable from the conflict described in Common Article 2 chiefly because it does not involve a clash between nations (whether signatories or not). In context, then, the phrase "not of an international character" bears its literal meaning. See, *e.g.,* J. Bentham, Introduction to the Principles of Morals and Legislation 6, 296 (J. Burns & H.

Hart eds. 1970) (using the term "international law" as a "new though not inexpressive appellation" meaning "betwixt nation and nation"; defining "international" to include "mutual transactions between sovereigns as such").

Although the official commentaries accompanying Common Article 3 indicate that an important purpose of the provision was to furnish minimal protection to rebels involved in one kind of "conflict not of an international character," *i.e.*, a civil war, the commentaries also make clear "that the scope of application of the Article must be as wide as possible." . . .

Common Article 3, then, is applicable here and, as indicated above, requires that Hamdan be tried by a "regularly constituted court affording all the judicial guarantees which are recognized as indispensable by civilized peoples." . . . At a minimum, a military commission "can be 'regularly constituted' by the standards of our military justice system only if some practical need explains deviations from court-martial practice." [N]o such need has been demonstrated here. . . .

Common Article 3 obviously tolerates a great degree of flexibility in trying individuals captured during armed conflict; its requirements are general ones, crafted to accommodate a wide variety of legal systems. But *requirements* they are nonetheless. The commission that the President has convened to try Hamdan does not meet those requirements.

Common Article 3. If the *Hamdan* Court had accepted the government's argument that the "war" with Al Qaeda was neither an "international armed conflict" (because not between states) nor a "non-international armed conflict" (because not a civil war), would there have been a gap in the law? The U.S. Supreme Court avoided that outcome by finding that Common Article 3 had a broad scope of application. Was the Court's rationale convincing? Common Article 3 by its terms applies to "the case of armed conflict not of an international character occurring in the territory of one of the High Contracting Parties," and delegates negotiating the article focused on insurgents resisting the established government inside one state. Terrorist activities are neither always localized in one territory nor always targeted at one government. Did the Court grapple sufficiently with the possibility that the "global war on terror" might be a new sort of armed conflict— international in scope, though not between nation states? If existing international humanitarian law did not apply in this global war, would other international law apply? If international human rights law (see Chapter 7) applied, it might provide terrorists with more protections than international humanitarian law. See John B. Bellinger III & Vijay M. Padmanabahn,

"Detention Operations in Contemporary Conflicts: Four Challenges for the Geneva Conventions and Other Existing Law," 105 *American Journal of International Law* 201 (2011); Geoffrey S. Corn, "Hamdan, Lebanon, and the Regulation of Hostilities: The Need to Recognize a Hybrid Category of Armed Conflict," 40 *Vanderbilt Journal of Transnational Law* 295 (2007).

Types of Combatants. International humanitarian law accords different protections to different categories of individuals, distinguishing combatants from civilians. During international armed conflicts, lawful combatants may be targeted based on their status; they may not be prosecuted for acts of war during military operations (except for violations of international humanitarian law such as war crimes); and, when captured, they enjoy prisoner of war status, a status discussed in the next paragraph. Many would also distinguish "lawful" from "unlawful" combatants. "[T]he term unlawful combatant describes all persons taking a direct part in hostilities without being entitled to do so." Knut Dörmann, "Combatants, Unlawful," in 2 *Max Planck Encyclopedia of Public International Law* 360, ¶ 4 (Rüdiger Wolfrum ed. 2012). What criteria determine whether a civilian is "taking a direct part in hostilities"? Was Hamdan—allegedly Osama bin Laden's bodyguard and personal driver—an unlawful combatant? Do combatants include financiers, recruiters, trainers, those collecting intelligence, or those selling goods or providing services to Al Qaeda? See "Forum: The ICRC Interpretive Guidance on the Notion of Direct Participation in Hostilities Under International Humanitarian Law," 42 *New York University Journal of International Law and Politics* 637 (2010); Faiza Patel, "Who Can Be Detained in the 'War on Terror'? The Emerging Answer," 13 *ASIL Insights*, Issue 18 (2009).

Prisoners of War. A lawful combatant is entitled to prisoner of war (POW) status when captured, and hence to the full protections of the (Third) 1949 Geneva Convention Relative to the Treatment of Prisoners of War. These protections include the right not to be interrogated without consent, and the associated rights not to be subjected to torture or coercion to secure information, or to be subjected to "any unpleasant or disadvantageous treatment of any kind" for failure to answer questions. Art. 17. The view that lawful combatants have committed no legal wrong merely by fighting in an armed conflict suggests their detention is not penal. As the U.S. Supreme Court stated in 2004 in *Hamdi v. Rumsfeld*, citing Article 118 of the Third Geneva Convention, "[t]he purpose of detention is to prevent captured individuals from returning to the field of battle and taking up arms once again. [Under] the law of war . . . detention may last no longer than active hostilities."

542 U.S. 507, 518 (2004). When POWs are alleged to have committed an offense, they generally have the right to be tried for the offence "only by a military court" offering "essential guarantees of independence and impartiality." Third Geneva Convention, art. 84.

Who Is Entitled to POW Status? Not all combatants are entitled to POW status. Article 4(A)(1) of the Third Geneva Convention provides that POWs include "[m]embers of the armed forces of a Party to [an international armed] conflict as well as members of militias or volunteer corps forming part of such armed forces," once they "have fallen into the power of the enemy." Members of militia "belonging to" a party to an international armed conflict may also qualify for POW status under Article 4(A)(2) if they meet additional criteria: openly carrying arms; wearing a uniform or a distinctive sign; being under the command of a leader responsible for his subordinates; and conducting "operations in accordance with the laws and customs of war."

President George W. Bush unilaterally determined that none of the Guantánamo detainees seized after the 9/11 terrorist attacks—including individuals fighting for the Taliban, the then-government of Afghanistan— was entitled to POW status. Was that determination consistent with the Third Geneva Convention? Article 5 of the Convention provides in part that if there is "any doubt" about "whether persons, having committed a belligerent act and having fallen into the hands of the enemy, belong to" a category of prisoner of war listed in Article 4, "such persons shall enjoy the protection of the present Convention until such time as their status has been determined by a competent tribunal." According to one commentator, "the most difficult element to defend of the decisions made by President Bush . . . with respect to the status of prisoners taken in Afghanistan is the blanket nature of the decision to deny POW status to the Taliban prisoners." George H. Aldrich, "The Taliban, Al Qaeda, and the Determination of Illegal Combatants," 96 *American Journal of International Law* 891, 897 (2002). Should some entity also have determined whether any of those seized in Afghanistan after 9/11 were civilians who had committed no belligerent act at all?

The Treatment of Detainees in the "War on Terror." Assuming a suspected Al Qaeda or ISIL (Islamic State of Iraq and the Levant) terrorist is captured and detained, what legal standards should apply to his treatment? Should he be treated in accordance with domestic criminal procedures? Do the risks to the prosecution of revealing sources, the difficulties of proving a case against a suspected terrorist who may have resided abroad, and the dangers of releasing suspected terrorists from prison suggest that a due process, criminal justice model cannot work? Is a "prisoner of war model" preferable? According to Professor Franck, the Geneva Conventions reflect several premises:

> first, that humane treatment of prisoners of war will encourage other combatants to surrender peaceably. Second, it is assumed that, when one party to a conflict treats its prisoners humanely, the other will reciprocate. Third, it is probably an unspoken conjecture that ordinary prisoners of war do not have much information that is likely, whether revealed or unrevealed, to have a great impact on the outcome of the conflict. Simply stating these underlying assumptions of the law of war is to suggest that they are not so evidently applicable to an international terrorist conspiracy like Al Qaeda.

Thomas M. Franck, "Criminals, Combatants, or What? An Examination of the Role of Law in Responding to the Threat of Terror," 98 *American Journal of International Law* 686, 687 (2004). If Al Qaeda or ISIL members are neither treated as criminals in a domestic legal system, nor given full protections as POWs, what international legal standards apply to them?

Before the *Hamdan* decision, some officials in the George W. Bush administration, including Justice Department attorneys, argued that "enemy combatants"—a term neither defined in the Geneva Conventions nor commonly used in international humanitarian law—were not entitled to the protection of Common Article 3 of the Geneva Conventions. This Article *inter alia* provides for sentencing by a regularly constituted court as elaborated in the *Hamdan Case*, and proscribes both "cruel treatment and torture" and "humiliating and degrading treatment" of those within its scope. In February 2002, President George W. Bush determined that enemy combatants should be granted some protections, but only "[a]s a matter of policy": the U.S. military "shall continue to treat detainees humanely and, to the extent appropriate and consistent with military necessity, in a manner consistent with the principles of" the Third Geneva Convention of 1949. *Reprinted in The Torture Papers: The Road to Abu Ghraib* 134, 135 (Karen J. Greenberg & Joshua L. Dratel eds. 2005). The references to "policy" and "military necessity" suggest that this determination did not regard application of the Third Geneva Convention to all detainees as legally mandated. After the *Hamdan* decision, the U.S. Department of Defense affirmed that all armed service members "shall observe the requirements of the law of war, and shall apply, without regard to a detainee's legal status, at a minimum the standards articulated in Common Article 3." Directive 2310.01E, "The Department of Defense

Detainee Program," ¶ 4.2 (2006), *quoted in* Gary D. Solis, *The Law of Armed Conflict* 166–67 (2010).

Other U.S. practices have been controversial as well. Was it legal to engage in "extraordinary renditions," *i.e.*, sending detainees to countries where they might well be tortured? See Leila Nadya Sadat, "Ghost Prisoners and Black Sites: Extraordinary Rendition under International Law," 37 *Case Western Reserve Journal of International Law* 309 (2006). May the United States escape its legal responsibilities by delegating military functions to private contractors who engage in abuses? See Laura A. Dickinson, *Outsourcing War and Peace: Preserving Public Values in a World of Privatized Foreign Affairs* (2011).

Government Attorneys. Was it ethical for U.S. Justice Department lawyers to prepare memoranda supporting President Bush's decision to deny POW status to all Guantánamo detainees, a decision discussed above? In addition, some government attorneys broadly construed presidential authority and narrowly interpreted prohibitions on torture and inhumane interrogation techniques, prohibitions mandated for example in the 1984 Convention Against Torture and Other Cruel, Inhuman or Degrading Treatment or Punishment. Justice Department memoranda allegedly contributed to abuses of U.S. detainees in Guantánamo and Iraq. See Laura A. Dickinson, "Abu Ghraib: The Battle Over Institutional Culture and Respect for International Law within the U.S. Military," in *International Law Stories* 405 (John E. Noyes, Laura A. Dickinson & Mark W. Janis eds. 2007).

The Justice Department memoranda did not go unchallenged. Other U.S. government lawyers found them "legally and morally unsupportable, likely to endanger our own military personnel, and damaging to our country's reputation and national interest." Richard B. Bilder & Detlev F. Vagts, "Speaking Law to Power: Lawyers and Torture," 98 *American Journal of International Law* 689, 690 (2004). In 2004, the U.S. Department of Justice withdrew one notorious memorandum that had narrowly interpreted the definition of torture. U.S. Department of Justice, Office of Legal Counsel, Memorandum for James B. Comey, Deputy Attorney General, from Acting Assistant Attorney General Daniel Levin, Dec. 30, 2004, *available at* https://www.aclu.org/files/torturefoia/released/082409/olcremand/2004olc96.pdf.

Were the Justice Department attorneys insufficiently familiar with historical links between international law and U.S. foreign policy? Should the President instead have relied on advice from State Department and military lawyers, who more routinely face issues of international law? John Bellinger, the State Department Legal Adviser during President Bush's second term

(2005–2009), argued "that the United States should have provided all detainees in the conflict with Al Qaeda and the Taliban the protections of common Article 3 . . . from the outset of the conflict." John B. Bellinger III & Vijay M. Padmanabahn, "Detention Operations in Contemporary Conflicts: Four Challenges for the Geneva Conventions and Other Existing Law," 105 *American Journal of International Law* 201, 207 (2011). Consider also the views of William H. Taft IV, who served as Legal Adviser to the U.S. Department of State from 2001 to 2005:

WILLIAM H. TAFT IV, A VIEW FROM THE TOP: AMERICAN PERSPECTIVES ON INTERNATIONAL LAW AFTER THE COLD WAR

31 *Yale Journal of International Law* 503, 509–10 (2006)

[B]oth the civilian and military leadership of the Department of Defense proposed to follow the U.S. practice in Vietnam of treating all detainees in accordance with the [Geneva] Conventions, regardless of whether they were entitled to such treatment or not. It was the lawyers from the Department of Justice who pressed for a determination that the Conventions and other standards of international law and practice did not govern the conflict. Bearing an abstract hostility to international law, developed in the sheltered environment of academic journals, and equally unfamiliar and unconcerned with our broader policy interests in promoting respect for the rule of law among states as well as within them, these lawyers proposed to create a regime in which detainees were deprived of all legal rights and the conditions of their treatment were a matter of unreviewable executive discretion. Why lawyers, of all people, should want to establish the point that such a lawless regime could legally exist, even as a theoretical matter, much less recommend that one actually be created, is, I confess, beyond me, and in itself is a sad commentary on the extent to which sophistry has penetrated what used to be widely regarded as an honorable and learned profession.

[I]t was a mistake to disconnect as large an organization as the U.S. Army from a system of rules under which it had been operating for many years, tell it that there are no legal requirements for its future conduct, and give it no more guidance than to act humanely. Even when rules for how to treat detainees are well settled and troops are trained and disciplined to comply with them, the tension and the high passion involved in combat can easily result in abuses. When the rules are changing and their legal authority is in doubt, such abuses are virtually inevitable.

[During the Bush] Administration's consideration of how to treat detainees in the conflict with al Qaeda . . . lawyers effectively turned what should have been, as it was in Vietnam, a question of how we wanted to treat the detainees into a debate about what our minimal obligations were under the law. The nation's foreign policy on which our liberty and prosperity depend . . . became simply the occasion for lawyers with but slight experience in and no responsibility for these matters to obtain official endorsement of an exotic legal proposition. Even if the proposition had been correct, which the Supreme Court determined it was not, this abstract exercise would have been a mistake. Of course, it's important to know what the law is, but it's even more important to know what it is in your interest to do. When you know that, it is time to ask the lawyers whether it is lawful, and if it is, you go ahead with it. This is the way foreign and national security policy have generally been made and carried out in the past, and international law has developed consistent with state practice determined by policymaking officials.

Enforcing International Humanitarian Law. Detainees in the "war on terror" have challenged their detention and treatment in U.S. and foreign courts. What forum can best help ensure respect for international humanitarian law? How efficacious are national courts? Review the material in Chapter 5 and consider what obstacles there may be to U.S. judicial enforcement of this body of international law. Are the Geneva Conventions self-executing? Did the *Hamdan* Court find Common Article 3 of the Geneva Conventions self-executing?

Are international courts, such as the International Tribunal for the former Yugoslavia, which decided *Tadić*, better able to promote compliance with the law of war? Should the military be left to enforce this law? Reconsider the essay by Professor Newton above. What might the International Committee of the Red Cross, discussed in Chapter 3, contribute? How else may compliance with international humanitarian law be promoted?

Jus Cogens. The proscription against official torture has often been cited as an example of a *jus cogens* norm. See *Filartiga* in Chapter 1. Why is it important to determine whether an alleged act of torture also constitutes a violation of international humanitarian law? First, some international lawyers may regard the concept of *jus cogens*, discussed in Chapter 2, as problematic, and may be more comfortable looking to treaties that embody international humanitarian law and human rights law. Second, the public is more aware of the Geneva Conventions than of *jus cogens*; public concern with a governmental policy that allows torture may be heightened if such conduct is seen as contravening the venerable Geneva Conventions. *Jus cogens* today is often associated with fundamental human rights.

Human Rights

The legal status of individuals has long been controversial in international law. In the narrow positivist doctrine of the 19th and early 20th centuries individuals were treated as mere objects of international law, but by the mid-20th century they became proper subjects (Part A). One of the most exciting developments in the later 20th and early 21st centuries has been the emergence of international human rights law (Part B). Two important modern aspects of the role of individuals in international law are European Human Rights Law (Part C) and the International Criminal Court (Part D).

A. INDIVIDUALS AS OBJECTS AND SUBJECTS OF INTERNATIONAL LAW

→ old status

In the traditional positivistic international law of the 19th and early 20th centuries, individuals were viewed as "objects" of international law. Although individuals were not deemed to be "subjects" of international law (and so had neither international legal rights nor duties), they could be objects of the law in state versus state litigation. So grew up doctrines of state protection of individuals and state responsibility for injuries done to individuals. However, those traditional doctrines have at least two significant limitations. First, as we see in *Nottebohm* below, individuals could only be protected by their national states, and national links may be elusive. Second, and more important, the objective view leaves individuals open to abuse by their own states, since it is impractical to conceive of a state protecting its own nationals in international proceedings against itself.

THE NOTTEBOHM CASE

Liechtenstein v. Guatemala, 1955 I.C.J. 4

The Facts

[Nottebohm, born German, obtained Liechtenstein citizenship in 1939, but nonetheless was treated as a German enemy alien during the Second World War.

561

As a consequence, Guatemala deported Nottebohm to the United States where he was interned; his Guatemalan properties were expropriated. Liechtenstein sued Guatemala on Nottebohm's behalf in the International Court of Justice, arguing that Nottebohm was a citizen of neutral Liechstenstein, not of belligerent Germany. Guatemala objected that Liechtenstein could not legitimately protect Nottebohm before the Court.]

Nottebohm was born at Hamburg on September 16th, 1881. He was German by birth, and still possessed German nationality when, in October 1939, he applied for naturalization in Liechtenstein.

In 1905 he went to Guatemala. He took up residence there and made that country the headquarters of his business activities, which increased and prospered; these activities developed in the field of commerce, banking and plantations. Having been an employee in the firm of Nottebohm Hermanos, which had been founded by his brothers Juan and Arturo, he became their partner in 1912 and later, in 1937, he was made head of the firm. After 1905 he sometimes went to Germany on business and to other countries for holidays. He continued to have business connections in Germany. He paid a few visits to a brother who had lived in Liechtenstein since 1931. Some of his other brothers, relatives and friends were in Germany, others in Guatemala. He himself continued to have his fixed abode in Guatemala until 1943, that is to say, until the occurrence of the events which constitute the basis of the present dispute.

In 1939, after having provided for the safeguarding of his interests in Guatemala by a power of attorney given to the firm of Nottebohm Hermanos on March 22nd, he left that country . . . at approximately the end of March or the beginning of April, when he seems to have gone to Hamburg, and later to have paid a few brief visits to Vaduz where he was at the beginning of October 1939. It was then, on October 9th, a little more than a month after the opening of the second World War marked by Germany's attack on Poland, that his attorney, Dr. Marxer, submitted an application for naturalization on behalf of Nottebohm. . . .

On October 9th, 1939, Nottebohm, "resident in Guatemala since 1905 (at present residing as a visitor with his brother, Hermann Nottebohm, in Vaduz)," applied for admission as a national of Liechtenstein and, at the same time, for the previous conferment of citizenship in the Commune of Mauren. He sought dispensation from the condition of three years' residence as prescribed by law, without indicating the special circumstances warranting such waiver. He submitted a statement of the *Crédit Suisse* in Zurich concerning his assets, and undertook to pay 25,000 Swiss francs to the Commune of Mauren, 12,500 Swiss francs to the State, to which was to be added the payment of dues in connection with the proceedings. He further stated that he had made "arrangements with the Revenue Authorities of the Government of Liechtenstein for the conclusion of a formal agreement to the effect that he will pay an annual tax of naturalization amounting to Swiss francs 1,000 of which Swiss francs 600 are payable to the Commune of Mauren and Swiss francs 400 are payable to the Principality of Liechtenstein, subject to the proviso that the payments of these taxes will be set off against ordinary taxes which will fall due if the applicant takes up residence in one of the Communes of the Principality." He further undertook to deposit as security a sum of 30,000 Swiss francs. He also gave certain general information as to his financial position and indicated that he would never become a burden to the Commune whose citizenship he was seeking.

Lastly, he requested "that naturalization proceedings be initiated and concluded before the Government of the Principality and before the Commune of Mauren without delay, that the application be then placed before the Diet with a favourable recommendation and, finally, that it be submitted with all necessary expedition to His Highness the Reigning Prince."

On the original typewritten application which has been produced in a photostatic copy, it can be seen that the name of the Commune of Mauren and the amounts to be paid were added by hand, a fact which gave rise to some argument on the part of Counsel for the Parties. There is also a reference to the "*Vorausverständnis*" of the Reigning Prince obtained on October 13th, 1939, which Liechtenstein interprets as showing the decision to grant naturalization, which interpretation has, however, been questioned. Finally, there is annexed to the application an otherwise blank sheet bearing the signature of the Reigning Prince, "Franz Josef," but without any date or other explanation.

A document dated October 15th, 1939, certifies that on that date the Commune of Mauren conferred the privilege of its citizenship upon Mr. Nottebohm and requested the Government to transmit it to the Diet for approval. A certificate of October 17th, 1939, evidences the payment of the taxes required to be paid by Mr. Nottebohm. On October 20th, 1939, Mr. Nottebohm took the oath of allegiance and a final arrangement concerning liability to taxation was concluded on October 23rd.

This was the procedure followed in the case of the naturalization of Nottebohm.

A certificate of nationality has also been produced, signed on behalf of the Government of the Principality and dated October 20th, 1939, to the effect that

Nottebohm was naturalized by Supreme Resolution of the Reigning Prince dated October 13th, 1939.

Having obtained a Liechtenstein passport, Nottebohm had it visa-ed by the Consul General of Guatemala in Zurich on December 1st, 1939, and returned to Guatemala at the beginning of 1940, where he resumed his former business activities and in particular the management of the firm of Nottebohm Hermanos.

Relying on the nationality thus conferred on Nottebohm, Liechtenstein considers itself entitled to seize the Court of its claim on his behalf, and its Final Conclusions contain two submissions in this connection. Liechtenstein requests the Court to find and declare, first, "that the naturalization of Mr. Frederic Nottebohm in Liechtenstein on October 13th, 1939, was not contrary to international law," and secondly, "that Liechtenstein's claim on behalf of Mr. Nottebohm as a national of Liechtenstein is admissible before the Court."

The Final Conclusions of Guatemala, on the other hand, request the Court "to declare that the claim of the Principality of Liechtenstein is inadmissible," and set forth a number of grounds relating to the nationality of Liechtenstein granted to Nottebohm by naturalization.

Thus, the real issue before the Court is the admissibility of the claim of Liechtenstein in respect of Nottebohm.

Nottebohm. Friedrich Nottebohm, born in Hamburg in 1881, moved to Guatemala in 1905. There he worked with his brothers, Arturo and Juan, in a family company engaged in commerce, banking, and growing coffee. It became "one of the oldest, wealthiest, and most influential families in Guatemala and Central America." Cindy C. Buys, "Nottebohm's Nightmare: Have We Exorcised the Ghosts of WWII Detention Programs or Do They Still Haunt Guantanamo?," 11 *Chicago-Kent Journal of International & Comparative Law* 1, 4 (2011). For more on confiscation of German assets in Latin America during World War II, see J. Fred Rippy, "German Investments in Guatemala," 20 *Journal of Business of the University of Chicago* 212 (1947).

The Nottebohm Case
The Law

In order to decide upon the admissibility of the Application, the Court must ascertain whether the nationality conferred on Nottebohm by Liechtenstein by means of a naturalization which took place in the circumstances which have been described, can be validly invoked as against Guatemala, whether it bestows upon Liechtenstein a sufficient title to the exercise of protection in respect of

Nottebohm as against Guatemala and therefore entitles it to seize the Court of a claim relating to him. . . .

Since no proof has been adduced that Guatemala has recognized the title to the exercise of protection relied upon by Liechtenstein as being derived from the naturalization which it granted to Nottebohm, the Court must consider whether such an act of granting nationality by Liechtenstein directly entails an obligation on the part of Guatemala to recognize its effect, namely, Liechtenstein's right to exercise its protection. In other words, it must be determined whether that unilateral act by Liechtenstein is one which can be relied upon against Guatemala in regard to the exercise of protection. The Court will deal with this question without considering that of the validity of Nottebohm's naturalization according to the law of Liechtenstein.

It is for Liechtenstein, as it is for every sovereign State, to settle by its own legislation the rules relating to the acquisition of its nationality, and to confer that nationality by naturalization granted by its own organs in accordance with that legislation. It is not necessary to determine whether international law imposes any limitations on its freedom of decision in this domain. Furthermore, nationality has its most immediate, its most far-reaching and, for most people, its only effects within the legal system of the State conferring it. Nationality serves above all to determine that the person upon whom it is conferred enjoys the rights and is bound by the obligations which the law of the State in question grants to or imposes on its nationals. This is implied in the wider concept that nationality is within the domestic jurisdiction of the State.

But the issue which the Court must decide is not one which pertains to the legal system of Liechtenstein. It does not depend on the law or on the decision of Liechtenstein whether that State is entitled to exercise its protection, in the case under consideration. To exercise protection, to apply to the Court, is to place oneself on the plane of international law. It is international law which determines whether a State is entitled to exercise protection and to seize the Court.

The naturalization of Nottebohm was an act performed by Liechtenstein in the exercise of its domestic jurisdiction. The question to be decided is whether that act has the international effect here under consideration. . . .

In the present case it is necessary to determine whether the naturalization conferred on Nottebohm can be successfully invoked against Guatemala, whether, as has already been stated, it can be relied upon as against that State, so that Liechtenstein is thereby entitled to exercise its protection in favour of Nottebohm against Guatemala. . . .

International arbitrators have decided . . . numerous cases of dual nationality, where the question arose with regard to the exercise of protection. They have given their preference to the real and effective nationality, that which accorded with the facts, that based on stronger factual ties between the person concerned and one of the States whose nationality is involved. Different factors are taken into consideration, and their importance will vary from one case to the next: the habitual residence of the individual concerned is an important factor, but there are other factors such as the centre of his interests, his family ties, his participation in public life, attachment shown by him for a given country and inculcated in his children, etc.

Similarly, the courts of third States, when they have before them an individual whom two other States hold to be their national, seek to resolve the conflict by having recourse to international criteria and their prevailing tendency is to prefer the real and effective nationality. . . .

The character thus recognized on the international level as pertaining to nationality is in no way inconsistent with the fact that international law leaves it to each State to lay down the rules governing the grant of its own nationality. The reason for this is that the diversity of demographic conditions has thus far made it impossible for any general agreement to be reached on the rules relating to nationality, although the latter by its very nature affects international relations. It has been considered that the best way of making such rules accord with the varying demographic conditions in different countries is to leave the fixing of such rules to the competence of each State. On the other hand, a State cannot claim that the rules it has thus laid down are entitled to recognition by another State unless it has acted in conformity with this general aim of making the legal bond of nationality accord with the individual's genuine connection with the State which assumes the defence of its citizens by means of protection as against other States. . . .

According to the practice of States, to arbitral and judicial decisions and to the opinions of writers, nationality is a legal bond having as its basis a social fact of attachment, a genuine connection of existence, interests and sentiments, together with the existence of reciprocal rights and duties. It may be said to constitute the juridical expression of the fact that the individual upon whom it is conferred, either directly by the law or as the result of an act of the authorities, is in fact more closely connected with the population of the State conferring nationality than with that of any other State. Conferred by a State, it only entitles that State to exercise protection vis-à-vis another State, if it constitutes a translation into juridical terms of the individual's connection with the State which has made him its national.

Diplomatic protection and protection by means of international judicial proceedings constitute measures for the defence of the rights of the State. As the Permanent Court of International Justice has said and has repeated, "by taking up the case of one of its subjects and by resorting to diplomatic action or international judicial proceedings on his behalf, a State is in reality asserting its own rights—its right to ensure, in the person of its subjects, respect for the rules of international law."

Since this is the character which nationality must present when it is invoked to furnish the State which has granted it with a title to the exercise of protection and to the institution of international judicial proceedings, the Court must ascertain whether the nationality granted to Nottebohm by means of naturalization is of this character or, in other words, whether the factual connection between Nottebohm and Liechtenstein in the period preceding, contemporaneous with and following his naturalization appears to be sufficiently close, so preponderant in relation to any connection which may have existed between him and any other State, that it is possible to regard the nationality conferred upon him as real and effective, as the exact juridical expression of a social fact of a connection which existed previously or came into existence thereafter.

Naturalization is not a matter to be taken lightly. To seek and to obtain it is not something that happens frequently in the life of a human being. It involves his breaking a bond of allegiance and his establishment of a new bond of allegiance. It may have far-reaching consequences and involve profound changes in the destiny of the individual who obtains it. It concerns him personally, and to consider it only from the point of view of its repercussions with regard to his property would be to misunderstand its profound significance. In order to appraise its international effect, it is impossible to disregard the circumstances in which it was conferred, the serious character which attaches to it, the real and effective, and not merely the verbal preference of the individual seeking it for the country which grants it to him.

At the time of his naturalization does Nottebohm appear to have been more closely attached by his tradition, his establishment, his interests, his activities, his family ties, his intentions for the near future to Liechtenstein than to any other State? . . .

The essential facts are as follows:

At the date when he applied for naturalization Nottebohm had been a German national from the time of his birth. He had always retained his connections with members of his family who had remained in Germany and he had always had business connections with that country. His country had been at war for more than a month, and there is nothing to indicate that the application for naturalization then made by Nottebohm was motivated by any desire to dissociate himself from the Government of his country.

He had been settled in Guatemala for 34 years. He had carried on his activities there. It was the main seat of his interests. He returned there shortly after his naturalization, and it remained the centre of his interests and of his business activities. He stayed there until his removal as a result of war measures in 1943. He subsequently attempted to return there, and he now complains of Guatemala's refusal to admit him. There, too, were several members of his family who sought to safeguard his interests.

In contrast, his actual connections with Liechtenstein were extremely tenuous. No settled abode, no prolonged residence in that country at the time of his application for naturalization: the application indicates that he was paying a visit there and confirms the transient character of this visit by its request that the naturalization proceedings should be initiated and concluded without delay. No intention of settling there was shown at that time or realized in the ensuing weeks, months or years—on the contrary, he returned to Guatemala very shortly after his naturalization and showed every intention of remaining there. If Nottebohm went to Liechtenstein in 1946, this was because of the refusal of Guatemala to admit him. No indication is given of the grounds warranting the waiver of the condition of residence, required by the 1934 Nationality Law, which waiver was implicitly granted to him. There is no allegation of any economic interests or of any activities exercised or to be exercised in Liechtenstein, and no manifestation of any intention whatsoever to transfer all or some of his interests and his business activities to Liechtenstein. It is unnecessary in this connection to attribute much importance to the promise to pay the taxes levied at the time of his naturalization. The only links to be discovered between the Principality and Nottebohm are the short sojourns already referred to and the presence in Vaduz of one of his brothers: but his brother's presence is referred to in his application for naturalization only as a reference to his good conduct. Furthermore, other members of his family have asserted Nottebohm's desire to spend his old age in Guatemala.

These facts clearly establish, on the one hand, the absence of any bond of attachment between Nottebohm and Liechtenstein and, on the other hand, the existence of a long-standing and close connection between him and Guatemala, a link which his naturalization in no way weakened. That naturalization was not based on any real prior connection with Liechtenstein, nor did it in any way alter the manner of life of the person upon whom it was conferred in exceptional circumstances of speed and accommodation. In both respects, it was lacking in the genuineness requisite to an act of such importance, if it is to be entitled to be respected by a State in the position of Guatemala. It was granted without regard to the concept of nationality adopted in international relations.

Naturalization was asked for not so much for the purpose of obtaining a legal recognition of Nottebohm's membership in fact in the population of Liechtenstein, as it was to enable him to substitute for his status as a national of a belligerent State that of a national of a neutral State, with the sole aim of thus coming within the protection of Liechtenstein but not of becoming wedded to its traditions, its interests, its way of life or of assuming the obligations—other than fiscal obligations—and exercising the rights pertaining to the status thus acquired.

Guatemala is under no obligation to recognize a nationality granted in such circumstances. Liechtenstein consequently is not entitled to extend its protection to Nottebohm vis-à-vis Guatemala and its claim must, for this reason, be held to be inadmissible. . . .

For these reasons,

THE COURT,

by eleven votes to three,

Holds that the claim submitted by the Government of the Principality of Liechtenstein is inadmissible.

State Responsibility and State Protection. Guatemala's alleged violation of international law in *Nottebohm* involved a duty often characterized as state responsibility. State responsibility is a complex and multifaceted legal concept, deserving of its own substantive note below. A counterpart of state responsibility is state protection, a doctrine permitting but not obliging a state to protect its nationals. State protection of individuals in international proceedings is especially common in investment disputes. Despite the negative outcome for Nottebohm himself, there are in practice a great many examples of successful state protection of individuals not only in the International Court, but in *ad hoc* commissions and tribunals. See Timothy G. Nelson, "Passport, S'il

Vous Plaît?: Investment Treaty Protection and the Individual Investor's Citizenship," 32 *Suffolk Transnational Law Review* 451 (2009).

Given that Liechtenstein in the *Nottebohm Case* was under no legal obligation to protect Nottebohm, why did Liechtenstein go to the trouble and expense of suing Guatemala in the International Court? Was it because of the government's concern for Nottebohm? Because of the threat to Liechtenstein's reputation as a safe haven? If Liechtenstein had refused to pursue Nottebohm's claim, how else could Nottebohm have sought redress? What were his chances for real success in Guatemala's courts? Liechtenstein's courts? Diplomatic negotiations? International arbitration?

Opposability. The ICJ was careful to rule that Nottebohm's Liechtenstein nationality was not "opposable" to Guatemala, and that Liechtenstein could not "extend its protection to Nottebohm vis-à-vis Guatemala." Did this leave open the possibility that Liechtenstein might have effectively taken up Nottebohm's claims against other states?

Reparations. When one state successfully claims that another state is responsible for injuring the claimant state's national, does the notion that the claimant state is "in reality asserting its own right" extend to issues of reparation? For example, if Liechtenstein had been successful in obtaining compensation from Guatemala for injuries done to Nottebohm, should Liechtenstein have had to turn the proceeds it obtained over to Nottebohm?

In 2012, the ICJ ruled in favor of claims made by the Republic of Guinea on behalf of its national, Ahmadon Sadio Diallo, against the Democratic Republic of the Congo (the DRC). 2012 I.C.J. 324. This was the ICJ's first judgment awarding damages in a human rights case. The Court had previously found that Diallo had been illegally arrested by the DRC and that the DRC had wrongfully seized Diallo's property. Although Guinea sought reparations of more than $11.5 million, the ICJ ordered the DRC to pay only a total of $95,000 for both non-material and material injury. Mads Adenas, "International Decision: *Ahmadon v. Democratic Republic of Congo*," 107 *American Journal of International Law* 178 (2013). Is this a landmark ruling? Or does the small award show a continued reluctance of the ICJ to act meaningfully to protect human rights?

Stateless Persons. Do stateless people have rights? How can stateless individuals pursue claims against states for violating their rights? In 1958 in *Trop v. Dulles* the U.S. Supreme Court found that depriving a military deserter of his

U.S. citizenship was a violation of the Eighth Amendment's protection against cruel and unusual punishment:

> There may be involved no physical mistreatment, no primitive torture. There is instead the total destruction of the individual's status in organized society. It is a form of punishment more primitive than torture, for it destroys for the individual the political existence that was centuries in the development. The punishment strips the citizen of his status in the national and international political community. His very existence is at the sufferance of the country in which he happens to find himself. . . . In short, the expatriate has lost the right to have rights.
>
> This punishment . . . subjects the individual to a fate of ever-increasing fear and distress. He knows not what discriminations may be established against him, what proscriptions may be directed against him, and when and for what cause his existence in his native land may be terminated. He may be subject to banishment, a fate universally decried by civilized people. He is stateless, a condition deplored in the international community of democracies. . . .
>
> The civilized nations of the world are in virtual unanimity that statelessness is not to be imposed as punishment for crime.

356 U.S. 86, 101–02 (1956).

In 1948, the U.N. General Assembly resolved in Article 15 of the Universal Declaration of Human Rights that "[e]veryone has the right to a nationality" and that "[n]o one shall be arbitrarily deprived of his nationality nor denied the right to change his nationality."

Multiple Nationality. Is there an exclusive relationship between an individual and a state, or may an individual be eligible to be a dual national? Or a national of many states? Sometimes, the answer to both questions is "yes." See Linda Bosniak, "Multiple Nationality and the Postnational Transformation of Citizenship," 42 *Virginia Journal of International Law* 979 (2002). Professor Sloane has concluded "it is past time to liberate international law . . . from the fiction of the genuine link as a generic, broadly applicable norm regulating the ascription of nationality." Instead, "the form that the international legal regulation of nationality takes today should be responsive to its diverse contemporary functions." Robert D. Sloane, "Breaking the Genuine Link: The Contemporary International Legal Regulation of Nationality," 50 *Harvard International Law Journal* 1, 60 (2009). Is this more relativistic approach a sensible guideline? How would it, for example, be applied in the *Nottebohm Case* itself? Would it lead to more equitable, but less predictable, results?

Exhaustion of Local Remedies. In espousal cases like *Nottebohm*, or in cases brought directly by corporations or individuals to an international court (such as the *McCann Case* in Chapter 1), international law may require an individual to exhaust domestic remedies before an international panel takes up a case. The doctrine of exhaustion of local remedies raises difficult issues: Is exhaustion required in an espousal case if the applicant country is seeking to recover for "its own" injuries, sufficiently distinct from its espousal claims? At what point in the domestic legal process are remedies to be deemed exhausted? When will pursuing local remedies be considered futile, so that no domestic proceedings are necessary? When are an individual's domestic claims sufficiently "like" the international court claim, such that local remedies must be pursued before the international court is allowed to proceed with the merits? If an international claim is based on a treaty violation, and the respondent country does not allow treaty claims to be brought directly in its courts—recall the self-executing treaty doctrine in U.S. law in Chapter 5—is exhaustion required? Why is exhaustion of local remedies generally required in international law?

NOTE: STATE RESPONSIBILITY

There is no easy definition of "state responsibility" in international law— the term is used to describe several related concepts—but it might help to begin with a little history. Professor Brownlie identified seven "strands" to the doctrine, marking a rough chronology: (1) the emergence of the law of nations in the 16th century necessitated, albeit obscurely, a consideration of "the issue of liability"; (2) the close connection between natural law and the law of nations in the 17th and 18th centuries meant that the law of nations turned to "concepts of responsibility for injuries inflicted"; (3) Roman law and national law in the 16th and 17th centuries were concerned with issues of "fault"; (4) just war, a medieval concept, was important to Vittoria in the 16th century, Grotius in the 17th century, and Vattel in the 18th century, all of whom viewed war as a legal procedure to redress "injuries sustained or complained of"; (5) hence followed the doctrine that a denial of justice enabled "the issue of letters of reprisal by princes in cases where their subjects had failed to obtain redress for legal wrongs in the domestic forum of principality"; (6) after the Jay Treaty arbitrations, the United States engaged in 17 more commissions and courts of international arbitration between 1794 and 1871, "which gave rise to an articulate and reasonably sophisticated law of international claims"; and (7) led by the United States, there was increasing reference "to legal bases of claim[s] in [19th-century] diplomatic correspondence." Ian Brownlie, *State Responsibility (Part I)*, at 2–6 (1983).

Much of the modern international law of state responsibility developed from state practice and tribunal decisions relating to states taking up the claims of their citizens for harm done to those citizens by another state; the *Nottebohm Case* is an example. In the 1924 *Mavrommatis Palestine Concessions Case* the Greek government sued the United Kingdom for denial of contractual rights of a Greek national to operate public works in Jerusalem and Jaffa in the British mandate of Palestine. Answering the British objection that Mavrommatis was merely a private person, the Permanent Court of International Justice held:

> [I]t is true that the dispute was at first between a private person and a State—i.e. between M. Mavrommatis and Great Britain. Subsequently the Greek Government took up the case. The dispute then entered upon a new phase; it entered into the domain of international law, and became a dispute between two States.

1924 P.C.I.J., Ser. A, No. 2, at 12.

In the latter part of the 20th century, new procedural mechanisms developed allowing individuals to pursue claims at international law in international tribunals against states directly on their own behalf. We have already seen several examples, *e.g., McCann* in Chapter 1, and the *Texaco/Libya Arbitration* and the *Domingues Case* in Chapter 2. We explore more examples later in this chapter.

Issues of state responsibility may also concern general questions of the liability of states, arising in contexts other than injuries to aliens. States may be responsible for violating the territorial integrity of other states, as in the *Rainbow Warrior Case* in Chapter 4, or for unlawfully using force against another state (Chapter 6). States may be responsible for harming the environment, breaching their treaty obligations, or violating the rights of their own citizens, *e.g.,* when states breach certain *erga omnes* obligations (Chapter 2) or when they violate international conventions, *e.g.,* the European Human Rights Convention considered in Part C.

Since 1949, the International Law Commission (ILC), a U.N. body of experts of various nationalities that works on the codification and progressive development of international law, has extensively studied basic principles of the law of state responsibility. The task has been politically sensitive. Philip Allott, a notable critic of the ILC's effort, maintained there was a clash between Western international lawyers who viewed the ILC's work as "codifying the obligations of states in the treatment of aliens" and Third World international lawyers who saw it as "a matter of confirming the diplomatic protection of aliens within limits that respected the sovereignty of all states." Philip Allott, "State Responsibility and the Unmasking of International Law," 29 *Harvard International Law Journal* 1, 10 (1988). A political impasse was broken in 1963 when Roberto Ago, a newly selected Rapporteur for the project, decided not to focus on "primary" rules concerning, *e.g.*, protections for aliens. Ago decided instead to set out broad, generally worded principles of responsibility. This decision calmed some opposition, and the ILC project continued, culminating in the adoption in 2001 of its Draft Articles on the Responsibility of States for Internationally Wrongful Acts.

The ILC's General Commentary sets out the Commission's basic approach, which is to treat matters of state responsibility at a high level of generality:

> These articles seek to formulate, by way of codification and progressive development, the basic rules of international law concerning the responsibility of States for their internationally wrongful acts. The emphasis is on the secondary rules of State responsibility: that is to say, the general conditions under international law for the State to be considered responsible for wrongful actions or omissions, and the legal consequences which flow therefrom. The articles do not attempt to define the content of international obligations, the breach of which gives rise to responsibility. This is the function of the primary rules, whose codification would involve restating most of substantive customary and conventional international law.

"Report of the International Law Commission on the Work of its Fifty-third Session," U.N. Doc. A/56/10 (2001), in 2 *Yearbook of the International Law Commission*, U.N. Doc. A/CN.4/SER.A/2001/Add.1 (Part 2), at 20, 31 (U.N. Sales No. O4.V.17 Pt 2, 2008).

However, it may well be that the ILC has only added to the confusion surrounding the doctrine of state responsibility. Philip Allott commented: "There is reason to believe that the Commission's long and laborious work on state responsibility is doing serious long-term damage to international law and international society." For Allott, even trying to define state responsibility has become a "dangerous fiction," both because it assigns legal responsibility to "legal persons known as states" rather than to "human beings" who should be morally responsible and because the ILC's concept of state responsibility leaves too much room for unnecessary argument about "every conceivable case of potential responsibility." Allott, *supra*, at 10, 14-15.

The ILC's 2001 Draft Articles address several general topics. Among them are "invocation of the responsibility of a state," relating in part to the issue of standing that arose in *Nottebohm*, "countermeasures," a principle we met in Chapter 6, and distress and other "circumstances precluding wrongfulness," seen in *Rainbow Warrior* in Chapter 4.

We close this Note on State Responsibility by highlighting a few other traditional issues of state responsibility: attribution, due diligence, and reparation. Attribution raises the question, for whose acts is a state responsible? The case law illustrates the considerable reach of the state responsibility doctrine. The United Kingdom was held responsible in the *Union Bridge Co. Case* (1924), 6 *Reports of International Arbitral Awards* 138 (2006), for the acts of a low-level railway official in South Africa who wrongly interfered with property belonging to a U.S. citizen in 1900 when the United States was a neutral during the Anglo-Boer War. The ILC, after surveying state practice, judicial decisions, and the writings of publicists, concluded that a state may be held responsible for the acts of all of its organs—executive, legislative, and judicial. "Report of the International Law Commission on the Work of Its Fifty-third Session," *supra*, at 26 (Article 4), 40–42. Some cases pose difficult questions about whether the actions of individuals or groups may be attributed to a state. In *Yeager v. Iran*, 17 *Iran-U.S. Claims Tribunal Reports* 92 (1987), Iran was held responsible for the actions of Revolutionary Guards when they harassed U.S. citizens out of their employment in the country. See also the *Diplomatic and Consular Staff Case* in Chapter 4.

Tribunals sometimes have relied on notions of due diligence to find states responsible for failing to prevent individuals from harming foreign nationals, or for failing to apprehend or punish the perpetrators. For example, in *Janes (U.S.A.) v. United Mexican States* (1925), 4 *Reports of International Arbitral Awards* 82 (2006), an international claims commission found Mexico responsible for the failure of Mexican authorities to exercise due diligence in their efforts to apprehend a mine company employee who in 1918 shot and killed Byron Janes, a U.S. citizen who was a superintendent of mines.

Within the law of state responsibility, every breach of a state's legal obligations gives rise to a duty to make full reparation. Reparation may take the form, alternatively or in combination, of restitution, compensation, or satisfaction. As we saw in the *Rainbow Warrior Case* in Chapter 4, satisfaction may include, for example, apology or a declaration that a responsible state engaged in wrongdoing.

MARK W. JANIS, INDIVIDUALS AS SUBJECTS OF INTERNATIONAL LAW

17 *Cornell International Law Journal* 61 (1984)

Legal positivism has long provided the usual theory for comprehending international law. The typical positivist definition of international law is grounded on a subject-based differentiation between international and municipal rules. Positivism views international law as a set of rules with states as its subjects. Municipal law is thought of as pertaining to individuals who are subjects of a single state. . . .

Before positivism, there was no theoretical insistence that the rules of the law of nations applied only to states. William Blackstone reflected the sentiment of the middle eighteenth century. For Blackstone, individuals and states were both proper subjects of the law of nations. He drew no dividing line between what later came to be called public and private international law. Blackstone distinguished his law of nations from other sorts of law not on the basis of its subjects but because of its sources. He saw the rules of the law of nations as universal, emanating either from natural justice or from the practice of many states. Municipal legal rules, however, emanated from a single state.

In 1789, Jeremy Bentham created the term "international law" in his *Introduction to the Principles of Morals and Legislation*. Bentham defined the new concept as the law which relates to "the mutual transactions between sovereigns as such." He thought that "as to any transactions which may take place between individuals who are subjects of different states, these are regulated by the internal laws, and decided upon by the internal tribunals" of individual sovereign states. Categorizing laws on the basis of "the persons whose conduct is the object of the law," Bentham concluded that international law had only states as its subjects. While categorizing rules on the basis of the subjects to be governed is logical enough, it plainly was wrong for Bentham to assume that international law so defined was equivalent to the traditional law of nations. There were significant differences between the two.

Two early nineteenth-century positivists promoted the notion that the individual was not a proper subject of international law. Joseph Story, complaining that no treatises existed on the subject, crafted "private" international law to parallel Bentham's "public" international law. Public international law went to international matters affecting states, while private international law concerned international matters between individuals. John Austin argued that because public international law claimed to regulate matters between sovereign states which as sovereigns could not be regulated by any outside authority, international law was just a form of "positive morality" and not really law at all.

Legal positivism had taken the eighteenth-century law of nations, a law common to individuals and states, and transformed it into public and private international law. The former was deemed to apply to states, the latter to individuals. Positivists scorned both sides of the discipline. Public international law was "international" but not really "law." Private international law was "law" but not really "international." Even so insightful a modern positivist as H.L.A. Hart assumed that the essence of international law was that it addressed states. Although Hart saw persuasive similarities between international and municipal law, he accepted uncritically Bentham's subject-based approach to the field.

The positivist definition of international law has had an enormous impact on modern perceptions concerning the individual and international law. With few exceptions, the theory rejects the notion that individuals are proper subjects of public international law. Originally, the subject-based approach was merely Bentham's attempt to provide a rational way of explaining that law may have different subjects: individuals and states. While law can be categorized on the basis of its subjects, in practice the law of nations and international law have concerned more than the legal rights of states. . . .

A prominent example of the failure of positivism to describe adequately the reality of the individual as a subject of international law comes from the time of Bentham himself. In *Respublica v. De Longchamps*, an American municipal court indicted the defendant for assaulting the Consul General of France to the new United States. It was held that the case "must be determined on the principles of the laws of nations." There was, following Blackstone, no doubt that an individual could be guilty of an infraction of the law of nations. De Longchamps, for his violation of the law of nations, was ordered to pay a fine of one hundred French crowns to the Commonwealth of Pennsylvania and to be imprisoned for "a little more" than two years.

Even during the high tide of positivism, the United States Supreme Court had no difficulty seeing individuals as subjects of international law. In *The Paquete Habana*, the United States Navy had seized two Cuban fishing smacks in the opening days of the Spanish-American War. A lower federal court condemned the boats as prizes of war. The masters for themselves, their crews, and their owners, argued before the Supreme Court that peaceful fishing craft were exempt from seizure under the rules of international law. In perhaps the most famous statement ever made about international law by a United States court, the Supreme Court held that "[i]nternational law is part of our law, and must be ascertained and administered by the courts of justice of appropriate jurisdiction, as often as questions of right depending upon it are duly presented for their determination." The Court held that:

> By an ancient usage among civilized nations, beginning centuries ago, and gradually ripening into a rule of international law, coast fishing vessels, pursuing their vocation of catching and bringing in fresh fish, have been recognized as exempt, with their cargoes and crews, from capture as prize of war.

Individuals had a right to rely on this rule as against the United States. The Court ordered the government to pay over the proceeds of the sale of the vessels and their cargoes to the individual claimants.

However inadequately subject-based theory accounted for individual rights and obligations in international law in the eighteenth and nineteenth centuries, positivism has done an even poorer job in explaining the practices of the twentieth century. The trials of Nazi war criminals after the Second World War highlighted the limitations of positivism. Faced with the excesses of a seemingly "civilized" state, those formulating and applying international law discarded any pretense that international rules applied only to state behavior.

The Charter of the International Military Tribunal at Nuremberg explicitly made individuals subject to international rules relating to crimes against peace, war crimes, and crimes against humanity. At Nuremberg and in other war trials, thousands of individuals were tried and convicted; hundreds were executed. Nuremberg re-established plainly and forcefully that the rules of international law should and do apply to individuals. The Nuremberg Tribunal held that "[c]rimes against international law are committed by men, not by abstract entities, and only by punishing individuals who commit such crimes can the provisions of international law be enforced." . . .

All of these examples—*De Longchamps*, *Paquete Habana*, the Nuremberg trials, the European and American human rights systems, the European [Union], and *Filartiga*—demonstrate that a large and important part of international law practice establishes individual rights and obligations and provides international and municipal procedures for enforcing these rights and obligations. The reality of practice contradicts the positivist insistence that international law applies only to relations among states. Insofar as the purpose of theory is to describe reality, the positivist, subject-based theory is inadequate.

Furthermore, restricting international law to states fails a second test by which positivism may be measured—its prescriptive worth. Surely, it is counter to the proper values of international law to prescribe that individuals may not be the subjects of international law. It was, at the time of the Nuremberg trials, politically and morally unacceptable to say that individuals within the German State between 1933 and 1945 were subjects only of German law to whom international rights and obligations could not pertain. In light of the atrocities of Nazi Germany, it would have been reprehensible to leave victims without legal rights and perpetrators without legal obligations. The lesson of Nuremberg is that there are individual international rights and obligations that transcend state boundaries.

Similar considerations pertain to international communities such as the Council of Europe and the European [Union]. These groups have recognized the need to extend certain basic human and economic rights and obligations directly to individuals even though these rights and obligations emanate not from municipal law but from international law. Given the difficulty of addressing some issues, such as human rights and economic development, through municipal legal systems alone, such an extension of international law rules to individuals makes sense. It is impressive that, with the European Human Rights system and the legal system of the [European Union], the Europeans have begun to open international legal processes to individuals.

It is wrong, both in terms of describing reality and in terms of preferential expression, for the theory of international law to hold that individuals are outside the ambit of international law rules. Individuals are and should be within this realm. The positivist notion that individuals are not fit subjects for international law springs not from a description of reality, but from a jurisprudential philosophy most concerned with a subject-based categorization of types of law. In so categorizing international law, the positivist theorists simply discarded the more inclusive notions of the law of nations. Whatever the impact of positivist theory, it never absolutely represented the practice of any time. Today, reality and preference have so revealed the weakness and obsolescence of subject-based theory that the sooner we rid ourselves of it the better. . . .

If we reject the positivist's subject-based definition of international law, then what should be our new concept of the nature of international law? What are the objections to reverting to Blackstone's understanding that the discipline should be characterized by its reliance on universal and multinational sources?

One might say that, so characterized, international law is not properly "international," but this is a rather superficial problem. Bentham supposed international law to be the equivalent of the law of nations, but it was not. So, the fault, if any, in matching the term and the content of international law must rest with its creator. We could easily use the old term, law of nations, and eliminate the linguistic quibble. But the term "international law" is too much in use to abandon it now. I suggest that we continue using the word international but understand "nation" to mean not only the national state but also the individuals who are the nationals of state. This meaning is both true to the word "nation" and finally makes sense of Bentham's equivalence between the law of nations and international law.

> *Individuals, International Law, and U.S. Law.* U.S. law has been relatively favorable over time in recognizing and prescribing the international rights and duties of individuals—*e.g.*, *De Longchamps*, *Smith*, *Paquete Habana*, *Asakura*, *Filartiga*, and *Sosa*, excerpted in Chapters 2 and 4. Why did U.S. law more or less resist the restrictive notions of 19th- and early 20th-century legal positivism? Was it because U.S. lawyers and judges were common lawyers, moving along in the conservative stream of case law and judicial precedent, while their European counterparts were civil lawyers, more likely to be affected by the changing currents of legal philosophy and academic doctrine? Whatever the cause, the readiness of the classical 18th-century law of nations to acknowledge individuals as subjects of its law was better preserved in U.S. law than in civil law, which had to rediscover individual rights and duties in modern international law. Note how important U.S. precedent on this matter was in the Nuremberg judgment below.
>
> *Individual Rights and State Sovereignty.* Are individual rights at international law a challenge to the sovereignty of states? We saw in the Treaty of Westphalia, discussed in Chapters 2 and 3, that one of the cornerstones of the Westphalian system of international relations is the principle that sovereign states should be free of outside interference in regulating their own citizens in their own territories, albeit subject to some international legal limits respecting religious minorities. Individual rights at international law, of course, permeate state sovereignty, permitting outsiders to evaluate how well a state does protecting the rights of individuals, citizens as well as aliens, in its own territory. The challenge is particularly acute with respect to international human rights law, the topic to which we now turn.

B. INTERNATIONAL HUMAN RIGHTS LAW

The concept that individuals can be subjects, as well as objects, of international law logically divides into individual *rights* at international law and individual *duties*. The next two parts primarily explore individual human rights: Part B looks at international human rights law in general, and Part C addresses the particularly successful European regional international human rights legal system. Part D then turns to individual duties with an introduction to international criminal law. Note how much progress has been made over the last seven decades in establishing individuals as true subjects of international law.

Part B's Section 1 is a short introduction to the antecedents of international human rights law in municipal (domestic) human rights law. Section 2 examines the Nuremberg trial, which helped inaugurate modern international human rights law in the 1940's. Section 3 discusses the evolution of international human rights law, using a sample case, *Damian Thomas*, before the U.N. Human Rights Committee to show some of the strengths and weaknesses of general international human rights law under the auspices of the United Nations.

1. Human Rights and Municipal Law

The principle that law should protect the rights of individuals against the abuses of governments can at least be dated back to John Locke's *Two Treatises of Government*, published in 1690. Locke believed that human rights, not governments, came first in the natural order of things. Locke's prose celebrated the rights to life, liberty, and property of the English under the limited government won by the Glorious Revolution of 1688. The particular advantages of England's unwritten constitution in the 18th century, especially the separation and balance of powers among the executive, legislative, and judicial branches of government, were elaborated and popularized by the French political philosopher Montesquieu in the *Spirit of the Laws* in 1748. In 1762, the revolutionary potential of human rights—"Man is born free; and everywhere he is in chains"—was proclaimed by Jean Jacques Rousseau. Democratic revolutions soon followed in America and throughout Europe.

> *The American Declaration of Independence.* On July 4, 1776, the American Declaration of Independence issued from Philadelphia. The intellectual influences of Locke, Montesquieu, and Rousseau on Thomas Jefferson's document were plain to see. In a ringing affirmation of human rights and the duty of governments to protect them, the delegates of the 13 United States of America proclaimed:
>
> > We hold these truths to be self-evident, that all men are created equal, that they are endowed by their Creator with certain unalienable Rights, that among these are Life, Liberty and the pursuit of Happiness. That to secure these rights, Governments are instituted among Men, deriving their just powers from the consent of the

governed. That whenever any Form of Government becomes destructive of these ends, it is the Right of the People to alter or to abolish it, and to institute new Government, laying its foundation on such principles and organizing its powers in such form, as to them shall seem most likely to effect their Safety and Happiness.

Bills of Rights. The last decades of the 18th century were a good time for political affirmations of human rights. As the constitutions of the newly independent American states were drafted in 1776, bills of rights enumerating specific rights were directly incorporated therein, even, as for Virginia, making up its first part. The fashion of bills of rights spread to Europe. Jefferson wrote James Madison from Paris on January 12, 1789: "Everybody here is trying their hands at forming declarations of rights." Thomas Jefferson, Letter of Jan. 12, 1789, 14 *The Papers of Thomas Jefferson* 436, 437 (Julian P. Boyd ed. 1958). Jefferson continued to play his part, reading and critiquing Lafayette's draft of what on August 27, 1789, a few weeks after the fall of the Bastille, would become the National Assembly's Declaration of the Rights of Man and Citizen. Thomas Jefferson, Letter of June 3, 1789, to Rabaut de St. Etienne, 15 *id.* at 166. The French Declaration's indebtedness to Rousseau's philosophy and Philadelphia's practice was widely acknowledged.

On September 25, 1789, less than a month after the promulgation of the French Declaration, the first Congress of the new Federal Government of the United States of America proposed the first ten amendments to the United States Constitution. These amendments came into force following the tenth state ratification (Virginia's) on December 15, 1791, and are known as the Bill of Rights.

Many of the rights enunciated in the French Declaration and the U.S. Bill of Rights are similar. For example, Article 11 of the French Declaration reads: "Free communication of ideas and opinions is one of the most precious of the rights of man. Consequently, every citizen may speak, write, and print freely subject to responsibility for the abuse of such liberty in the cases determined by law"; while Article 1 of the U.S. Bill of Rights provides: "Congress shall make no law . . . abridging the freedom of speech, or of the press[.]"

The Legacy of Municipal Declarations and Bills of Rights. Close in kinship, the American Declaration of Independence, the French Declaration of the Rights of Man and Citizen, and the U.S. Bill of Rights make up the 18th-century documentary foundation on which two centuries of legal protection of human rights in municipal law have been built. Constitutional guarantees of human rights are now widespread. In many countries, such as the United Kingdom, the principal responsibility for protecting human rights has ordinarily been vested in a democratically elected legislature. In others, such as the United States, that role has been assumed by the courts.

2. The Nuremberg Judgment

The idea that human rights could be protected by international, as well as municipal, law developed slowly. Throughout the 19th and early 20th centuries, the prevalent conception of state sovereignty proved a stumbling block to efforts to impose international legal obligations on states to protect individuals. Instead, the doctrine of state responsibility examined above in *Nottebohm* provided partial protection, but only so long as the claim of a foreign national injured by a state was effectively espoused at the international level by that individual's national state. However, neither the doctrine of state sovereignty nor its counterpart, the doctrine of state protection, could shield individuals from abuses committed by their own governments. In practice, this fault excluded international review of most instances of governmental violations of human rights.

The turning point for this traditional approach in international law came in the 1940s in the midst of the extreme human rights abuses in war-torn Europe. In the Moscow Declaration of German Atrocities of October 30, 1943, the United States, the United Kingdom, France, and the Soviet Union declared that individual Germans would be held responsible for their violations of international law. U.N. Doc. A/CN.4/5, at 87–88 (1949). In the August 8, 1945, Charter of the International Military Tribunal, the same four Allies established the Nuremberg Tribunal.

THE NUREMBERG JUDGMENT

The United States of America, the French Republic, the United Kingdom of Great Britain and Northern Ireland, and the Union of Soviet Socialist Republics v. Hermann Wilhelm Goering, Rudolf Hess, Joachim von Ribbentrop [and 24 Other Named Defendants], 6 F.R.D. 69 (1946)

On the 8th August 1945, the Government of the United Kingdom of Great Britain and Northern Ireland, the Government of the United States of America, the Provisional Government of the French Republic, and the Government of the Union of Soviet Socialist Republics entered into an agreement establishing this Tribunal for the trial of War Criminals whose offences have no particular geographical location. In accordance with Article 5, the following Governments of the United Nations have expressed their adherence to the Agreement:

Greece, Denmark, Yugoslavia, the Netherlands,

Czechoslovakia, Poland, Belgium, Ethiopia, Australia,

Honduras, Norway, Panama, Luxemburg, Haiti, New Zealand,

India, Venezuela, Uruguay, and Paraguay.

By the Charter annexed to the Agreement, the constitution, jurisdiction and functions of the Tribunal were defined.

The Tribunal was invested with power to try and punish persons who had committed crimes against peace, war crimes and crimes against humanity as defined in the Charter.

The Charter also provided that at the trial of any individual member of any group or organization the Tribunal may declare (in connection with any act of which the individual may be convicted) that the group or organization of which the individual was a member was a criminal organization.

In Berlin, on the 18th October 1945, in accordance with Article 14 of the Charter, an indictment was lodged against the defendants[,] who had been designated by the Committee of the Chief Prosecutors of the signatory Powers as major war criminals. . . .

This indictment charges the defendants with crimes against peace by the planning, preparation, initiation and waging of wars of aggression, which were also wars in violation of international treaties, agreements and assurances; with war crimes; and with crimes against humanity. The defendants are also charged with participating in the formulation or execution of a common plan or conspiracy to commit all these crimes. The Tribunal was further asked by the Prosecution to declare all the named groups or organizations to be criminal within the meaning of the Charter. . . .

In accordance with Articles 16 and 23 of the Charter, Counsel were either chosen by the defendants in custody themselves, or at their request were appointed by the Tribunal. In his absence the Tribunal appointed Counsel for the defendant Bormann, and also assigned Counsel to represent the named groups or organizations.

The trial which was conducted in four languages—English, Russian, French and German—began on the 20th November 1945, and pleas of "Not Guilty" were made by all the defendants except Bormann.

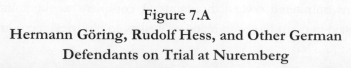

Figure 7.A
Hermann Göring, Rudolf Hess, and Other German
Defendants on Trial at Nuremberg

The hearing of evidence and the speeches of Counsel concluded on 31st August 1946.

403 open sessions of the Tribunal have been held. 33 witnesses gave evidence orally for the Prosecution against the individual defendants, and 61 witnesses, in addition to 19 of the defendants, gave evidence for the Defense.

A further 143 witnesses gave evidence for the Defense by means of written answers to interrogatories.

The Tribunal appointed Commissioners to hear evidence relating to the organizations, and 101 witnesses were heard for the Defense before the Commissioners, and 1,809 affidavits from other witnesses were submitted. Six reports were also submitted, summarizing the contents of a great number of further affidavits.

38,000 affidavits signed by 155,000 people were submitted on behalf of the Political Leaders, 136,213 on behalf of the SS, 10,000 on behalf of the SA, 7,000 on behalf of the SD, 3,000 on behalf of the General Staff and OKW, and 2,000 on behalf of the Gestapo.

The Tribunal itself heard 22 witnesses for the organizations. The documents tendered in evidence for the prosecution of the individual defendants and the organizations numbered several thousands. A complete stenographic record of everything said in court has been made, as well as an electrical recording of all the proceedings. . . .

Much of the evidence presented to the Tribunal on behalf of the Prosecution was documentary evidence, captured by the Allied armies in German army headquarters, Government buildings, and elsewhere. Some of the documents were found in salt mines, buried in the ground, hidden behind false walls and in other places thought to be secure from discovery. The case, therefore against the defendants rests in a large measure on documents of their own making, the authenticity of which has not been challenged except in one or two cases.

THE CHARTER PROVISIONS

The individual defendants are indicted under Article 6 of the Charter, which is as follows:

> Article 6. The Tribunal established by the Agreement referred to in Article 1 hereof for the trial and punishment of the major war criminals of the European Axis countries shall have the power to try and punish persons who, acting in the interests of the European Axis countries, whether as individuals or as members of organizations, committed any of the following crimes.
>
> The following acts, or any of them, are crimes coming within the jurisdiction of the Tribunal for which there shall be individual responsibility:
>
> (a)   Crimes Against Peace: namely planning, preparation, initiation or waging a war of aggression, or a war in violation of international treaties, agreements or assurances, or participation in a common plan or conspiracy for the accomplishment of any of the foregoing;
>
> (b)   War Crimes: namely, violations of the laws or customs of war. Such violations shall include, but not be limited to, murder, ill-treatment or deportation to slave labor or for any other purpose of civilian population of or in occupied territory, murder or ill-treatment of prisoners of war or persons on the seas, killing of hostages, plunder of public or private property, wanton destruction of cities, towns or villages, or devastation not justified by military necessity;
>
> (c)   Crimes Against Humanity: namely, murder, extermination, enslavement, deportation, and other inhumane acts committed against any civilian population, before or during the war, or persecutions on

political, racial or religious grounds in execution of or in connection with any crime within the jurisdiction of the Tribunal, whether or not in violation of the domestic law of the country where perpetrated.

Leaders, organizers, instigators and accomplices participating in the formulation or execution of a common plan or conspiracy to commit any of the foregoing crimes are responsible for all acts performed by any persons in execution of such plan. . . .

THE LAW OF THE CHARTER

The jurisdiction of the Tribunal is defined in the Agreement and Charter, and the crimes coming within the jurisdiction of the Tribunal, for which there shall be individual responsibility, are set out in Article 6. The law of the Charter is decisive, and binding upon the Tribunal.

The making of the Charter was the exercise of the sovereign legislative power by the countries to which the German Reich unconditionally surrendered; and the undoubted right of these countries to legislate for the occupied territories has been recognized by the civilized world. The Charter is not an arbitrary exercise of power on the part of the victorious nations, but in the view of the Tribunal, as will be shown, it is the expression of international law existing at the time of its creation; and to that extent is itself a contribution to international law.

The Signatory Powers created this Tribunal, defined the law it was to administer, and made regulations for the proper conduct of the Trial. In doing so, they have done together what any one of them might have done singly; for it is not to be doubted that any nation has the right thus to set up special courts to administer law. With regard to the constitution of the court, all that the defendants are entitled to ask is to receive a fair trial on the facts and the law.

The Charter makes the planning or waging of a war of aggression or a war in violation of international treaties a crime; and it is therefore not strictly necessary to consider whether and to what extent aggressive war was a crime before the execution of the London Agreement. But in view of the great importance of the questions of law involved, the Tribunal has heard full argument from the Prosecution and the Defense, and will express its view on the matter.

It was urged on behalf of the defendants that a fundamental principle of all law—international and domestic—is that there can be no punishment of crime without a pre-existing law. *Nullum crimen sine lege, nulla poena sine lege*. It was submitted that *ex post facto* punishment is abhorrent to the law of all civilized nations, that no sovereign power had made aggressive war a crime at the time the alleged criminal acts were committed, that no statute had defined aggressive war, that no penalty had been fixed for its commission, and no court had been created to try and punish offenders.

In the first place, it is to be observed that the maxim *nullum crimen sine lege* is not a limitation of sovereignty, but is in general a principle of justice. To assert that it is unjust to punish those who in defiance of treaties and assurances have attacked neighboring states without warning is obviously untrue, for in such circumstances the attacker must know that he is doing wrong, and so far from it being unjust to punish him, it would be unjust if his wrong were allowed to go unpunished. Occupying the positions they did in the government of Germany, the defendants, or at least some of them must have known of the treaties signed by Germany, outlawing recourse to war for the settlement of international disputes; they must have known that they were acting in defiance of all international law when in complete deliberation they carried out their designs of invasion and aggression. On this view of the case alone, it would appear that the maxim has no application to the present facts.

This view is strongly reinforced by a consideration of the state of international law in 1939, so far as aggressive war is concerned. The General Treaty for the Renunciation of War of August 27th 1928, more generally known as the Pact of Paris or the Kellogg-Briand Pact, was binding on sixty-three nations, including Germany, Italy and Japan at the outbreak of war in 1939. In the preamble, the signatories declared that they were:—

> Deeply sensible of their solemn duty to promote the welfare of mankind; persuaded that the time has come when a frank renunciation of war as an instrument of national policy should be made to the end that the peaceful and friendly relations now existing between their peoples should be perpetuated . . . all changes in their relations with one another should be sought only be pacific means . . . thus uniting civilised nations of the world in a common renunciation of war as an instrument of their national policy . . .

The first two articles are as follows:

> Article I: the High Contracting Parties solemnly declare in the names of their respective peoples that they condemn recourse to war for the solution of international controversies and renounce it as an instrument of national policy in their relations to one another.

> Article II: The High Contracting Parties agree that the settlement or solution of all disputes or conflicts of whatever nature or of whatever

origin they may be, which may arrive among them, shall never be sought except by pacific means.

The question is, what was the legal effect of this pact? The nations who signed the pact or adhered to it unconditionally condemned recourse to war for the future as an instrument of policy, and expressly renounced it. After the signing of the pact, any nation resorting to war as an instrument of national policy breaks the pact. In the opinion of the Tribunal, the solemn renunciation of war as an instrument of national policy necessarily involves the proposition that such a war is illegal in international law and that those who plan and wage such a war, with its inevitable and terrible consequences, are committing a crime in so doing. War for the solution of international controversies undertaken as an instrument of national policy certainly includes a war of aggression, and such a war is therefore outlawed by the pact. As Mr. Henry L. Stimson, then Secretary of State of the United States, said in 1932:

> War between nations was renounced by the signatories of the Kellogg-Briand Treaty. This means that it has become throughout practically the entire world . . . an illegal thing. Hereafter, when nations engage in armed conflict, either one or both of them must be termed violators of this general treaty law. . . . We denounce them as law breakers.

But it is argued that the pact does not expressly enact that such wars are crimes, or set up courts to try those who make such wars. To that extent the same is true with regard to the laws of war contained in the Hague Convention. The Hague Convention of 1907 prohibited resort to certain methods of waging war. These included the inhumane treatment of prisoners, the employment of poisoned weapons, the improper use of flags of truce, and similar matters. Many of these prohibitions had been enforced long before the date of the Convention; but since 1907 they have certainly been crimes, punishable as offences against the laws of war; yet the Hague Convention nowhere designates such practices as criminal, nor is any sentence prescribed, nor any mention made of a court to try and punish offenders. For many years past, however, military tribunals have tried and punished individuals guilty of violating the rules of land warfare laid down by this Convention. In the opinion of the Tribunal, those who wage aggressive war are doing that which is equally illegal, and of much greater moment than a breach of one of the rules of the Hague Convention. In interpreting the words of the Pact, it must be remembered that international law is not the product of an international legislature, and that such international agreements as the Pact of Paris have to deal with general principles of law, and not with administrative matters of procedure. The law of war is to be found not only in treaties, but in the customs and practices of states which gradually obtained universal recognition and from the general principles of justice applied by jurists and practised by military courts. This law is not static, but by continual adaptation follows the needs of a changing world. Indeed, in many cases treaties do no more than express and define for more accurate reference the principles of law already existing. . . .

It was submitted that international law is concerned with the actions of sovereign states, and provides no punishment for individuals; and further, that where the act in question is an act of state, those who carry it out are not personally responsible, but are protected by the doctrine of the sovereignty of the State. In the opinion of the Tribunal, both these submissions must be rejected. That international law imposes duties and liabilities upon individuals as well as upon states has long been recognized. In the recent case of Ex parte Quirin (1942, 317 U.S. 1), before the Supreme Court of the United States, persons were charged during the war with landing in the United States for purposes of spying and sabotage. The late Chief Justice Stone, speaking for the Court, said:

> From the very beginning of its history this Court has applied the law of war as including that part of the law of nations which prescribes for the conduct of war, the status, rights and duties of enemy nations as well as enemy individuals.

He went on to give a list of cases tried by the Courts, where individual offenders were charged with offences against the laws of nations, and particularly the laws of war. Many other authorities could be cited, but enough has been said to show that individuals can be punished for violations of international law. Crimes against international law are committed by men, not by abstract entities, and only by punishing individuals who commit such crimes can the provisions of international law be enforced.

The provisions of Article 228 of the Treaty of Versailles . . . illustrate and enforce this view of individual responsibility.

The principle of international law, which under certain circumstances, protects the representatives of a state, cannot be applied to acts which are condemned as criminal by international law. The authors of these acts cannot shelter themselves behind their official position in order to be freed from punishment in appropriate proceedings. Article 7 of the Charter expressly declares:

The official position of defendants, whether as heads of state, or responsible officials in government departments, shall not be considered as freeing them from responsibility, or mitigating punishment.

On the other hand the very essence of the Charter is that individuals have international duties which transcend the national obligations of obedience imposed by the individual state. He who violates the laws of war cannot obtain immunity while acting in pursuance of the authority of the state if the state in authorizing action moves outside its competence under International Law.

It was also submitted on behalf of most of these defendants that in doing what they did they were acting under the orders of Hitler, and therefore cannot be held responsible for the acts committed by them in carrying out these orders. The Charter specifically provides in Article 3:

The fact that the defendant acted pursuant to orders of his Government or of a superior shall not free him from responsibility, but may be considered in mitigation of punishment.

The provisions of this article are in conformity with the law of all nations. That a soldier was ordered to kill or torture in violation of the international law of war has never been recognized as a defense to such acts of brutality, though, as the Charter here provides, the order may be urged in mitigation of the punishment. The true test, which is found in varying degrees in the criminal law of most nations, is not the existence of the order, but whether moral choice was in fact possible.

The Nuremberg Judgment. The 1946 judgment of the Nuremberg Tribunal confirmed the classical norm that individuals, as well as states, were proper subjects of international law. The Nuremberg judgment has come to stand not only for the moral and political imperative that individuals be made legally responsible for violations of international law but also for the proposition that individual human rights ought to be protected at the level of international law. In the words of Professor Henry King, one of the prosecuting attorneys at Nuremberg: "Nuremberg was designed to change the anarchic context in which the nations and peoples of the world related to one another." Henry T. King, "The Meaning of Nuremberg," 30 *Case Western Journal of International Law* 143, 143–44 (1998). As the judgment emphasized, punishment of individuals for war crimes by military tribunals was long-standing.

Though some, like George Kennan, lamented the effect of Nuremberg on the United States' post-war relations with Germany, see George F. Kennan, *Memoirs 1925–1950*, at 175 (1967), nowadays most applaud the Tribunal's work.

The very term "Nuremberg" has become a shorthand for both modern international criminal law and international human rights law. Professor Sadat described what she called the "Nuremberg principles," which laid the foundation for modern international human rights law: "They eschew collective responsibility in favor of individual criminal responsibility; provide that no human being (even a head of state or other responsible government official) is above the law with respect to the most serious crimes of concern to humanity as a whole: war crimes, crimes against humanity, and the crime of aggressive war; and that reliance upon internal law is no defense to a crime for which an individual may have responsibility under international law." Leila Nadya Sadat, "Shattering the Nuremberg Consensus: U.S. Rendition Policy and International Criminal Law," *Yale Journal of International Affairs,* Winter 2008, at 65, 66–67. For additional background on the creation of the Nuremberg Tribunal, the trials, and their lasting significance, see Theodor Meron & Jean Galbraith, "Nuremberg and Its Legacy," in *International Law Stories* 13 (John E. Noyes, Laura A. Dickinson & Mark W. Janis eds. 2007).

Human Rights and the U.N. Charter. In the Preamble of the 1945 Charter of the United Nations, the People of the United Nations reaffirm their "faith in fundamental human rights." Charter Article 55 calls on the Organization to promote "universal respect for, and observance of, human rights and fundamental freedoms for all without distinction as to race, sex, language, or religion." We saw that these norms were held not self-executing in U.S. law by the California Supreme Court in *Sei Fujii* in Chapter 5.

Human Rights After Nuremberg. The emergence of international human rights law in the mid-20th century has been described as the most "radical development in the whole history of international law" since it so speedily reestablished individuals as well as states as subjects of international law. John P. Humphrey, "The Revolution in the International Law of Human Rights," 4 *Human Rights* 205, 208 (1975). Is it any surprise that the experience of Nazi-occupied Europe destroyed the moral foundations of the positivist theory that international law and legal process should not be available to individuals?

However rapid the emergence of the rules of international human rights law, the development of effective international human rights legal process has been much more gradual. Need there necessarily be a greater political consensus to create effective legal machinery than to promulgate rules of substantive law? In cases where there is no formal international legal process, *i.e.,* no court or executive to enforce international human rights law, how is international human rights law to be made efficacious? What is the influence of public pronouncements by governments or private groups critical of a state's human rights practices? How can such pronouncements be made more forceful, *e.g.*, by economic or political sanctions? As we see below, some progress has been made in creating enforcement mechanisms at the level of the United Nations. More progress, however, is to be seen in regional human rights systems, especially in Europe, explored in Part C.

3.   Human Rights and the United Nations

The transformation of the substantive norms of human rights law from national to international law was made complete in 1948 in the Universal Declaration of Human Rights, where the U.N. General Assembly followed in the footsteps of Jefferson and the drafters of the French Declaration of the Rights of Man and Citizen and the U.S. Bill of Rights. The Universal Declaration is generally said to enumerate human rights norms at the level of international law. Among the sources of international law surveyed in Chapter 2, which would most strongly support the assertion that the various articles in the Universal Declaration constitute international legal norms? Is the fact that the norms are embodied in a General Assembly resolution that was adopted unanimously (the vote was 48 states in favor, none against, and 8 abstaining) itself sufficient? Does every article of the Universal Declaration have an equal claim to be an international legal norm?

The system of human rights law at the United Nations has evolved from a preoccupation with the development of norms to an emphasis on procedures for implementing those norms, an evolution traced in the first excerpt in this section. Following this excerpt is an opinion in the *Damian Thomas Case* brought to one of the forums available at the United Nations for pursuing complaints of human rights abuses, along with discussion of the efficacy of the U.N. human rights system.

THOMAS BUERGENTHAL, THE NORMATIVE AND INSTITUTIONAL EVOLUTION OF INTERNATIONAL HUMAN RIGHTS

19 *Human Rights Quarterly* 703 (1997)

II.   STAGE ONE: THE NORMATIVE FOUNDATION

The first stage in this process begins with the entry into force of the UN Charter and continues at least through the adoption in 1966 of the International Covenants on Human Rights. By this time, the Universal Declaration of Human Rights had been adopted by the United Nations, as had the Genocide Convention and the Convention on the Elimination of All Forms of Racial Discrimination, to mention only the principal human rights instruments. During this same period, the European Convention on Human Rights entered into force; the Organization of American States proclaimed the American Declaration on the Rights and Duties of Man; and UNESCO and the ILO, respectively, promulgated the Convention against Discrimination in Education and the Convention Concerning Discrimination in Respect of Employment and Occupation.

This period, in short, witnessed the normative consolidation of international human rights law. It is true, of course, that this process continues to this day. It is equally true, however, that in these first 20 years following the establishment of the UN the process had become irreversible. . . .

III. STAGE TWO: INSTITUTION BUILDING . . .

The period here under consideration also saw the emergence and consolidation of universal and regional treaty-based institutions for the protection of human rights. In the mid to late 1970s the UN Human Rights Committee and the Committee on the Elimination of Racial Discrimination (CERD) came into being with the entry into force of the International Covenant on Civil and Political Rights and the International Convention on the Elimination of All Forms of Racial Discrimination. The entry into force in 1978 of the American Convention on Human Rights brought with it the establishment of the Inter-American Commission and Court of Human Rights. Although the European Convention of Human Rights came into effect as early as 1953, it was not until the late 1960s and early 1970s that the institutions it created, particularly the Court, began to play an important role in the implementation of the Convention. In 1978, moreover, UNESCO adopted a special mechanism for dealing with human rights violations falling within its sphere of competence. ILO institutions for dealing with human rights issues predate those referred to above, whereas those established under the African Charter on Human and Peoples' Rights did not come into being until after the entry into force of that instrument in 1986. . . .

IV. STAGE THREE: IMPLEMENTATION IN
THE POST COLD WAR ERA

The institutions referred to in the preceding section did not come fully into their own until the mid to late 1980s when they could begin to focus on adopting effective measures to ensure state compliance with their international obligations. This process continues to this day. It is one thing to establish institutions on the international plane to promote and protect human rights, it is quite another to give them the authority and tools they need to achieve their objective. States are more likely to agree to the creation of human rights institutions than to cooperate with these institutions when they or their allies are charged with human rights violations. It must be recognized, however, that the political factors which contributed in large measure to the creation of human rights institutions in the first place—the ideas that inspired the international human rights movement and captured the imagination of mankind—make it increasingly more difficult for states not to comply with their human rights obligations.

During the period here under consideration, the world underwent dramatic changes to which the human rights revolution contributed significantly and from which the revolution also benefitted significantly. The end of the Cold War freed many nations in Europe from Communist rule, permitting them to embark on a process of democratic transformation. What is more, it liberated international efforts to promote human rights from the debilitating ideological conflicts and political sloganeering of the past. These developments have enabled the UN to focus increasingly on obstacles to the implementation of human rights. . . .

In some regions of the world considerable progress has nevertheless been made in the implementation of human rights. During the period here under consideration the human rights system established under the European Convention of Human Rights gained institutional maturity. In fact, by the time the Soviet Union collapsed, the European Court of Human Rights had for all practical purposes become the constitutional court of Western Europe. The recent accession to the European Convention of the former Eastern and Central European allies of the Soviet Union as well as some of the new Soviet Republics has the potential of transforming the Court into the constitutional court of all Europe. This process may take longer, however, than one might assume at first glance because the newer members face many serious political, economic and social problems that few, if any, of the Western European members confronted when they first joined the Convention system.

The inter-American human rights system, which came into being later than its European counterpart, was unable for many years to play a major role in improving the human rights situation in the Americas. For decades the region was in the grips of oppressive regimes that engaged in massive violations of human rights behind a veil of impunity sustained at the height of the Cold War by superpower protection. With the onset of the process of transition to democracy in that region, which began in the mid-1980s, the inter-American human rights system could finally focus on implementation. The judgments of the Inter-American Court of Human Rights in the late 1980s, exposing the heinous practice of disappearances for all the world to see, opened the way for the Court and the

Inter-American Commission on Human Rights to play a much more active role in protecting human rights in the Americas. Unlike Western Europe, however, the Americas is a region still very much in the process of development, with serious social and economic problems, poverty, and corruption. Moreover, there are some countries where the military, while ostensibly no longer in power, remains a real force to be reckoned with. Transition to democracy has a long way to go in the region, despite the impressive progress made in the past few years. It is clear, though, that those who believed in the 1960s and 1970s that oppressive military regimes were the only obstacle to the effective protection of human rights and genuine democracy in the region proved to be only partially right. By the same token, it is probably true that the process of democratization is now irreversible. Moreover, while the human rights problems of the region cannot be solved by merely substituting a freely elected government for a military regime, the inter-American human rights system has in recent years been able to point to some real successes.

The same cannot be said as yet of the African human rights system. It still faces many of the problems that afflicted the inter-American system two decades ago as far as repressive regimes are concerned and even greater economic, social, and political obstacles. The poverty, corruption, underdevelopment, disease, tribal conflicts, and many other scourges that affect African society today make the task of the African Commission on Human and Peoples' Rights extremely difficult. The liberation of South Africa from apartheid—in itself probably the greatest victory to date of the human rights revolution—and that country's emergence as the foremost democratic nation on the African continent, as well as some promising trends towards democracy in the region, cannot in the long run do anything but strengthen the role of the African Commission.

The African Commission, the human rights organs of the inter-American system, and the treaty bodies established within the UN framework all suffer from a very serious lack of financial resources. This fact has very harmful consequences for their ability to discharge their responsibilities. The real tragedy here is that at precisely the moment in history when conditions are, on the whole, more favorable than ever before for the implementation of human rights on the global and regional levels, the institutions assigned the task of promoting and supervising this process are for financial reasons not able to do so satisfactorily. Here it should be said that while resources are scarce everywhere, the real reasons for at least some budget-cutting activities affecting human rights bodies have more to do with a desire of certain governments to limit the power of these institutions than with genuine budgetary concerns. Given the contemporary human rights revolution, it is politically easier today to cut the budget of a human rights body by pointing to a lack of funds than by suggesting that its activities are not important.

> *Human Rights Norms, Institutions, and Implementation.* Professor Buergenthal, who served from 2000 to 2010 as the U.S. judge on the International Court of Justice, divided the history of international human rights law into three eras: norm-building between 1945 and 1966, institution-building between 1966 and 1989, and implementation-building since 1989. Of course, not all international human rights systems have developed at the same pace. On the one hand, the most effective system of all—European human rights law—explored in Part C below, effectively implemented the European Human Rights Convention beginning in the 1970s. On the other hand, most U.N.-based human rights systems—the Human Rights Committee, which considered the *Damian Thomas Case* below, being just one example—seem still to fall well short of effective implementation.

DAMIAN THOMAS V. JAMAICA

U.N. Human Rights Committee Communication No. 800/1998,
U.N. Doc. CCPR/65/D/800/1998

The Facts

The Human Rights Committee, established under article 28 of the International Covenant on Civil and Political Rights, [m]eeting on 8 April 1999 [a]dopts the following:

Views under article 5, paragraph 4, of the Optional Protocol

The author of the communication is Damian Thomas, a Jamaican minor (16 years old at the time of submission of the communication), currently at St. Catherine's District Prison, Jamaica. The author was born on 21 November 1980. . . . He is not represented by counsel.

The author was arrested on 9 May 1995 and convicted on 3 May 1996. On 5 May 1996 he was placed in the General Penitentiary, Kingston.

By a further submission the author informed the Committee that he was 15 years old when he was arrested. He was brought before the Gun Court for two murders, where only one of those allegations was sent to trial. He was tried before the Home Circuit Court, convicted and sentenced to be detained during her Majesty's pleasure. . . .

While at the General Penitentiary, the author wrote to the Commissioner for Prisons requesting that he be removed from the adult prison. It appears that someone within the prison system, one Mr. Dawkins, informed him that he was to be moved to a juvenile institution. However, when the author was moved it was to St. Catherine District Prison, once again among adults. The author claims that he is being held in a prison with adult inmates in violation of the Covenant.

By submission dated 23 March 1998, the State party contends that the circumstances under which the author is being held are not clear. It requests that the author provide information on the offence for which he was convicted, as well as any other relevant information, e.g. how old was he at the time of his sentence and whether the judicial authorities were made aware of his age. . . .

The author in a letter dated 11 May 1998, informed the Committee that he was tried at the Gun Court for two murders, that he lost his appeal, being sentenced to detention during her Majesty's pleasure. He informs the Committee that he was born on 21 November 1980, and was only 15 at the time of his arrest.

He further submits that since he has been in detention both at the General Penitentiary and at St. Catherine District Prison he has been systematically beaten by warders. He refers to several incidents; one on 8 November 1996, where he was kicked by several warders; Mr. Norris, Mr. Dwight and Sergeant Brown. On 20 March 1997 a warder called Mr. Waugh boxed him round the ears and threatened him. On 16 December 1997 he was thumped on the back and beaten by a Mr. Campbell and a corporal Ferguson while taking him to the overseer's office. They told the overseer that they were taking him to the hospital allegedly because he had lice. He was never taken to the hospital but rather he was beaten and kicked about by the warders and a warder called Mr. Mcdermatt cut off his Rastafarian hair. On 20 July 1997, he was beaten by several warders including a Mr. Gardener allegedly because the author was from the same area where the warder's aunt had been killed.

These new allegations were transmitted to the State party with a request that any comments be submitted to the Committee before 30 January 1999, since the case would be put before the Committee at its 65th session. To date, 25 March 1999, no response has been received from the State party.

Accounting for the Weakness of the U.N. Human Rights System. Professor Mutua has criticized "official international human rights bodies such as the Human Rights Committee [as] basically weak and ineffectual." The causes are many, including poor funding, "organizational and bureaucratic constraints," and a choice of "the UN institutional culture which emphasizes compromise, consensus and diplomacy" rather than a disinterested "application of norm to fact." Makau wa Mutua, "Looking Past the Human Rights Committee: An

Argument for De-Marginalizing Enforcement," 4 *Buffalo Human Rights Law Review* 211, 223 (1998). Might some of weakness of the system be due to state parties, which establish and fund the system, and which often have treaty reporting obligations? As of April 2012, half of the reports that the 167 parties to the International Covenant on Civil and Political Rights (ICCPR) owed to the ICCPR's Human Rights Committee were overdue, and some states had never submitted a report. Navanethem Pillay, *Strengthening the United Nations Human Rights Treaty Body System: A Report by the United Nations High Commissioner for Human Rights* 22–23 (2012), *available at* http://www2.ohchr.org/english/ bodies/HRTD/docs/HCReportTBStrengthening.pdf. In *Damian Thomas*, what can the Human Rights Committee really do?

The Damian Thomas Case
The Law

With regard to the author's alleged ill-treatment at the General Penitentiary and St. Catherine District Prison, the Committee notes that the author has made precise allegations that he was brutalized by several wardens on 8 November 1996; 20 March 1997; 16 December 1997 and 20 July 1997. The Committee also notes that the author has complained to the prison authorities. His claims have not been refuted by the State party, which has promised to investigate these, but has failed to forward to the Committee its findings, eleven months after promising to do so, in spite of a reminder sent on 30 October 1998. The Committee recalls that a State party is under the obligation to investigate seriously allegations of violations of the Covenant made under the Optional Protocol. However, in the present case the Committee notes that these allegations were transmitted to the State party after Jamaica's denunciation of the Optional Protocol came into force on 23 January 1998. Consequently, the Committee considers that these claims are inadmissible under article 1 of the Optional Protocol.

With respect to the remaining allegations the Committee observes that the State party has not raised objections to the admissibility of the communication. It further observes that, given the name, date of birth, date of arrest and of conviction and the location in 1998 in St. Catherine's District Prison, all in relation to the author, the State party should have no difficulty in identifying the details relevant to this matter. Accordingly the Committee decides that the remaining allegations are admissible and proceeds, without further delay, to an examination of the substance of the author's claims, in the light of all the information made available to it by the parties. . . .

With respect to the non segregation of the author from adult prisoners both at the General Penitentiary and at St. Catherine's District Prison, the Committee once again regrets the State party's lack of cooperation in this matter. The Committee considers that it is incumbent upon the State party where a complaint such as this is submitted to it in respect of a serving prisoner, to verify whether that prisoner is, or has at any relevant stage, been a minor. The Committee notes from the information before it and not refuted by the State party, that the author was born in November 1980, making him seventeen years old when his communication was submitted to the Committee and 15, when he was sentenced. The Committee considers that the State party has failed to discharge its obligations under the Covenant in respect of Damian Thomas, in so far as he has been kept among adult prisoners when still a minor, and consequently, finds that there has been a violation of article 10, paragraphs 2 and 3.

The Committee further observes that the facts as described in the present case, also constitute a violation of article 24 of the Covenant, since the State party has failed to provide to Damian Thomas such measures of protection as are required by his status as a minor.

The Human Rights Committee, acting under article 5, paragraph 4, of the Optional Protocol to the International Covenant on Civil and Political Rights, is of the view that the facts before it disclose a violation of articles 10, paragraphs 2 and 3, and 24 of the Covenant.

In accordance with article 2, paragraph 3(a), of the Covenant, the State party is under an obligation to provide Mr. Thomas with an effective remedy, entailing his placement in a juvenile institution, separated from adult prisoners if Jamaican legislation authorises it, and including compensation for his non segregation from adult prisoners while a minor. The State party is under an obligation to ensure that similar violations do not occur in the future.

On becoming a State party to the Optional Protocol, Jamaica recognized the competence of the Committee to determine whether there has been a violation of the Covenant or not. This case was submitted for consideration before Jamaica's denunciation of the Optional Protocol became effective on 23 January 1998; in accordance with article 12(2) of the Optional Protocol it is subject to the continued application of the Optional Protocol. Pursuant to article 2 of the Covenant, the State party has undertaken to ensure to all individuals within its territory or subject to its jurisdiction the rights recognized in the Covenant and to provide an effective and enforceable remedy in case a violation has been established. The Committee wishes to receive from the State party, within 90 days, information about the measures taken to give effect to the Committee's views.

Shaming. Unlike some of the regional human rights systems, most U.N.-based bodies lack any enforcement power; their decisions are not legally binding. The U.N. Human Rights Committee can only hope to "shame" a government with bad publicity. See Markus Schmidt, "Treaty-Based Human Rights Complaints Procedures in the UN—Remedy or Mirage for Victims of Human Rights Violations?," 1998 *Human Rights*, No. 2, at 13, 15–16. "Shaming" can, of course, still sometimes be an important goal in human rights litigation, as we saw in *Filartiga* in Chapter 1. When might a government be more or less susceptible to pressure from an adverse opinion of an international body such as the U.N. Human Rights Committee?

Withdrawal from the Right of Individual Petition. What has Jamaica lost by repudiating the right of individual petition to the U.N. Human Rights Committee? Will criticism, such as that below from Natalia Schiffrin, Senior Legal Officer at the International Centre for the Legal Protection of Human Rights (Interights), a non-governmental organization based in London, have an international economic or political impact? Might it encourage domestic dissatisfaction with government policies?

Although Jamaica remains a party to the ICCPR, "and to that end the rights enshrined in it are still guaranteed to its people," the country's decision to withdraw from the right of individual petition was "a sad day for human rights." Schiffren lamented that "[t]he system is only as strong as its members. Its effectiveness will be significantly reduced if countries pull out whenever they perceive the Committee as posing an obstacle to domestic practice." Natalia Schiffrin, "Jamaica Withdraws the Right of Individual Petition Under the International Covenant on Civil and Political Rights," 92 *American Journal of International Law* 563, 568 (1998). What might the U.N. Committee do differently?

U.N. Human Rights Bodies. The ICCPR's Human Rights Committee is not the only U.N. human rights body to be criticized for its lack of efficacy. A 53-member U.N. Commission on Human Rights, established in 1946 to hear and respond to human rights complaints, had been roundly condemned, and in 2006 the U.N. General Assembly replaced it with a new 47-member Human Rights Council. Although immediately acknowledged to be imperfect, the new Human Rights Council, with its system of "Universal Periodic Review" of every country's human rights practices, was hoped to be "transparent, fair and impartial." Scott R. Lyons, "The New United Nations Human Rights Council," 10 *ASIL Insights,* Issue 7 (2006). However, within a year the Council was criticized for "again fail[ing] to address many egregious human-rights abuses around the world," even declining to condemn Sudan for its conduct in Darfur.

"Human Rights: Bad Counsel: The UN Adrift on Human Rights," *The Economist*, Apr. 7, 2007, at 58. The Council on Foreign Relations reported in 2009 that "bloc voting, loose membership standards, and bias against Israel are keeping the two-year-old council from living up to expectations as a responsible watchdog over global human rights norms." Sixty years after adoption of the Universal Declaration of Human Rights, "many see the new rights council as a stain on the UN's reputation." Lauren Vriens, "Troubles Plague UN Human Rights Council," Council on Foreign Relations, *Backgrounder*, May 13, 2009, at 1. In 2010 seven of the 14 countries elected to the Human Rights Council— Libya, Angola, Malaysia, Thailand, Uganda, Mauritania, and Qatar—were criticized by human rights organizations for poor human rights records. All 14 ran unopposed. Does the fault really rest with the United Nations? Can a more or less universal institution be expected to surmount the ideological and cultural divides among states with at all as much success as regional institutions such as the Council of Europe and the European Court of Human Rights explored below?

A Confusion of Norms and Institutions. Is it fair to say that the United Nations has too often substituted words and bureaucracies for action on human rights? There are "literally several hundred" U.N. human rights treaties and, besides the U.N. Human Rights Committee, tens of U.N. institutions charged with monitoring human rights. See Gudmundur Alfredsson, "The United Nations and Human Rights," 25 *International Journal of Legal Information* 17 (1997). What can be done to improve the effectiveness of U.N. human rights efforts? For discussion of an intergovernmental process conducted during 2012–2014 that proposed changes to the system, see Christian Broeker, "The Reform of the United Nations' Human Rights Treaty Bodies," 18 *ASIL Insights*, Issue 16 (2014); Navanethem Pillay, *Strengthening the United Nations Human Rights Treaty Body System: A Report by the United Nations High Commissioner for Human Rights* (2012), *available at* http://www2.ohchr.org/english/bodies/HRTD/docs/ HCReportTBStrengthening.pdf.

The Efficacy of International Human Rights Treaties. Critics from different ideological perspectives now wonder whether international human rights treaties necessarily encourage better governmental behavior. Professor Hathaway has documented how frequently governments that have ratified such treaties still flout their obligations. Oona Hathaway, "Do Human Rights Treaties Make a Difference?," 111 *Yale Law Journal* 1935 (2002). However, Professor Hathaway has been challenged by Professors Goodman and Jinks, who dismiss the value of her statistical modeling. They concluded that "the best assumption remains the conventional one: human rights treaties advance the cause they seek to promote, not the other way around." Ryan Goodman & Derek Jinks, "Measuring the Effects of Human Rights Treaties," 14 *European Journal of International Law* 171, 183 (2003).

Regional Protection of International Human Rights. Besides the universal international human rights law of the United Nations and the protection of human rights in domestic legal systems, there are, as Professor Buergenthal noted, several regional international human rights stories to be told. For example, the African Charter on Human and Peoples' Rights and an African Commission on Human and Peoples' Rights date from 1981. In 2006, a new 11-judge African Court on Human and Peoples' Rights based in Arusha, Tanzania, was sworn in. Scott Lyons, "The African Court on Human and Peoples' Rights," 10 *ASIL Insights*, Issue 24 (2006). However, Professor Heyns has concluded that the "African regional human rights system is faced with almost insurmountable challenges: massive violations on a continent of immense diversity, where a tradition of domestic compliance with human rights norms is still to be established." Christof Heyns, "The African Regional Human Rights System: The African Charter," 108 *Penn State Law Review* 679, 701 (2004).

There is somewhat more regional success in the Americas where there are two overlapping regional international human rights systems, one based on the Charter of the Organization of American States, the other created by the American Convention on Human Rights. However, the workload and efficacy of the Inter-American Court of Human Rights, which sits in Costa Rica, by no means rival that of the European Court of Human Rights, which we examine below. Some scholars have doubted that the Inter-American system actually does much to improve the protection of human rights in the Americas. James L. Cavallaro & Stephanie Erin Brewer, "Reevaluating Regional Human Rights Litigation in the Twenty-First Century: The Case of the Inter-American Court," 102 *American Journal of International Law* 768 (2008). Another wondered why domestic courts are so reluctant to respect the judgments of the Inter-American Court. Alexandra Huneeus, "Courts Resisting Courts: Lessons from the Inter-American Court's Struggle to Enforce Human Rights," 44 *Cornell International Law Journal* 493 (2011).

Why do states choose to participate in international organizations protecting human rights? How far are governments willing to bend state sovereignty to permit international supervision of domestic human rights practices? A comprehensive review of many academic studies concluded that state participation is motivated by diverse reasons, sometimes to further deep commitment to human rights, but othertimes to "lock in" domestic reforms, or to "reduce pressure for real change." In most cases the explanation comes from very differing domestic political processes. Emilie M. Hafner-Burton, "International Regimes for Human Rights," 15 *Annual Review of Political Science* 265, 271 (2012).

The United States and Human Rights Law. Sadly, the United States has never itself joined the Inter-American Court of Human Rights. An American Bar Association group, the World Justice Project, concluded in 2009 that though "the courts and other legal institutions in the U.S. generally meet a high standard in most of 15 key measures of adherence to the rule of law," the United States "lags behind its peer nations in its adherence to international rule of law principles." James Podgers, "Survey Says—Study Measures Adherence to Rule of Law by U.S. and Other Nations," 96 *ABA Journal,* Jan. 2010, at 61. American ambivalence toward international law is long-standing, see Mark Weston Janis, *America and the Law of Nations 1776–1939* (2010), but some problems are of recent origin. Writing in 2005, Professor Ignatieff lamented that "[t]o date, the Bush Administration has paid no political price [in domestic politics] for its flouting of the Geneva Convention and other treaties." Michael Ignatieff, "America the Mercurial," *Legal Affairs*, Mar./Apr. 2005, at 68.

We have already seen, in Chapter 5, some of the ways in which U.S. courts do and do not apply international human rights law—*Filartiga, Asakura, Sei Fujii, Medellín, Sosa*, and *Kiobel*. Judge Fletcher of the U.S. Ninth Circuit Court of Appeals, after reviewing the judicial record on implementation of international human rights norms, concluded that the U.S. Supreme Court "has left us with more questions than answers. [T]hose questions can be fully and properly answered only by adapting our jurisprudence to the modern world, just as those who came before us adapted their jurisprudence to what was, for them, their modern world." William A. Fletcher, "International Human Rights in American Courts," 93 *Virginia Law Review* 653, 672–73 (2007).

Why is it that democratic, as well as totalitarian, governments sometimes skirt international human rights law? How much depends on the regard in which international human rights law is held domestically, *e.g.*, by the general public, the political leaders, the lawyers and judges?

C. EUROPEAN HUMAN RIGHTS LAW

The proceedings at Nuremberg had special meaning for those who had witnessed the awful abuses of human rights in Nazi-occupied Europe. For the

Europeans pressing for political union, human rights became an important priority. The European Convention for the Protection of Human Rights and Fundamental Freedoms was signed on November 4, 1950, and came into force on September 3, 1953. Merely as a European bill of rights, the Convention provided little exceptional on the international scene. The heart of the Convention rested in what were, until 1998, two optional clauses, the crucial aspects of the system's enforcement machinery: Article 25 (now mandatory Article 34) gave individuals as well as states the right to petition the European human rights system, and Article 46 (now mandatory Article 32) gave the European Court of Human Rights jurisdiction to hear and try cases already reported on by a Commission to which petitions were submitted.

Historically, the Europeans were familiar with bills of rights, but they were unfamiliar with judicial enforcement of those rights. Domestically, they trusted the legislative and executive branches of government rather than the judiciary to protect fundamental freedoms. Only over time have they been willing to empower international institutions to safeguard the Convention's rights.

Nowadays, the European Court of Human Rights in Strasbourg, France, is the most successful of all the international human rights courts or commissions. Its jurisdiction extends to 47 states, about one-quarter of all the world's nations: Albania, Andorra, Armenia, Austria, Azerbaijan, Belgium, Bosnia and Herzegovina, Bulgaria, Croatia, Cyprus, the Czech Republic, Denmark, Estonia, Finland, France, Georgia, Germany, Greece, Hungary, Iceland, Ireland, Italy, Latvia, Liechtenstein, Lithuania, Luxembourg, Malta, Moldova, Monaco, Montenegro, Netherlands, Norway, Poland, Portugal, Romania, Russia, San Marino, Serbia, Slovakia, Slovenia, Spain, Sweden, Switzerland, The former Yugoslav Republic of Macedonia, Turkey, Ukraine, and the United Kingdom.

The Seven Decades of the European Convention of Human Rights. Looking at the history of the system, it can be said that each of the seven decades of the European Convention on Human Rights has told its own distinctive tale. The 1950s spoke of institutional development but had little actual case law about which to boast. The Convention was signed in 1950 and, ratified by eight states, came into force in 1953. In 1955 the Commission was granted the right to hear individual petitions against consenting states. The Court was constituted in 1958. Only on June 2, 1956, was an application declared admissible by the Commission (by Greece against the United Kingdom respecting Cyprus). Altogether only five applications (two government, three individual) were deemed admissible in the 1950s. No case was heard by the Court.

The 1960s saw both modest triumph and disquieting disobedience. There were some 54 applications admitted by the Commission (five government and 49 individual), and the Court rendered its first ten decisions in seven cases. However, in 1969, following adverse reports by the Commission, Greece withdrew from the Council of Europe and denounced the European Convention on Human Rights. This reduced the total membership in the system from 16 to 15 at the end of the decade. The number of states accepting the right of individual petition had grown to 11. The same number (though not always the same states) accepted the jurisdiction of the Court.

The 1970s showed a solid maturation of the system. Greece rejoined the Convention in 1974. By the end of the decade some 20 countries belonged, 14 accepting individual petition and 17 consenting to the jurisdiction of the Court. One hundred sixty-eight applications (five government, 163 individual) were deemed admissible by the Commission. Twenty-four cases were decided by the Court.

The 1980s witnessed an explosion of activity under the Convention. As of December 31, 1989, 22 states were parties to the Convention. All had accepted the right of individual petition and the jurisdiction of the Court. The Commission deemed 455 applications admissible, and the Court decided 169 cases.

The 1990s evidenced the continuing growth of the system. As of the end of the decade, 41 countries had ratified the European Human Rights Convention and thus accepted the Convention's now-mandatory right of individual petition and jurisdiction of the Court. New member states included many nations from the former Communist bloc: Albania, Bulgaria, Croatia, the Czech Republic, Estonia, Georgia, Hungary, Latvia, Lithuania, Moldova, Poland, Romania, Russia, Slovakia, Slovenia, The former Yugoslav Republic of Macedonia, and Ukraine. In the first eight years of the decade (1990–1997), the Commission admitted 3,491 applications. Between 1990 and 1999, the Court delivered 995 judgments, more in those ten years than in the previous four decades. On November 1, 1998, the Convention was significantly amended by Protocol No. 11, which not only transformed the two critical optional clauses into mandatory provisions, but merged the part-time European Commission and Court of Human Rights into a single full-time European Court of Human Rights.

In the first decade of the 21st century, the European Court of Human Rights became a real work horse. Six more countries—Armenia, Azerbaijan, Bosnia and Herzegovina, Monaco, Montenegro, and Serbia—joined the system, and by 2005 the Strasbourg judges were charged to review the practice of some 47 member states of the European Convention on Human Rights and Fundamental Freedoms. In the ten years 2000–2009, the Strasbourg Court received more than 330,000 applications, roughly 33,000 each year. During this decade, the Court rendered more than 11,000 judgments, an average of more than one thousand judgments every year. The Strasbourg Court delivered more judgments in that one decade than it had rendered in 50 previous years.

Since 2009, the European human rights system has considered mechanisms to help it cope with its burgeoning caseload and to solidify its "constitutional" role with respect to human rights. 2010's Protocol No. 15 tightens the time frame for applications, facilitates the hearing of cases by a chamber of the Court, and articulates limits on the discretion of states when they carry out their obligation to implement the Convention at the national level. Protocol No. 16, adopted in 2013, creates an option for the highest court of a member state to seek an advisory opinion from the European Court of Human Rights. The Court's caseload remains significant, with the Court delivering 1,926 judgments in 2016. However, the number of applications disposed of administratively has increased, and applications pending before a judicial formation decreased from 151,600 in 2011 to 79,750 in 2016. European Court of Human Rights, *Analysis of Statistics 2016*, at 6–7 (2017), *available at* http://echr.coe.int/Documents/Stats_analysis_2016_ENG.pdf.

The Optional Clauses. The story of the success of the European human rights law system is the story of what were the two optional clauses. In 1950, it may have seemed that opponents had "gutted" the Convention by making the right of individual petition and the jurisdiction of the Court optional, but, over time, states "opted into" both procedures. What strategies did the Commission and the Court use to induce states to accept the optional clauses and to maintain their acceptances? Did the example of some European governments accepting the optional clauses make it difficult for other European governments to opt out? Were European governments influenced by human rights abuses in other parts of the world, and did they seek to underline their own commitments to human rights? See Mark W. Janis, Richard S. Kay & Anthony W. Bradley, *European Human Rights Law* 12–23, 103–16 (3d ed. 2008).

The Efficacy of the European Court of Human Rights. Our three cases from the European Court of Human Rights—*McCann* in Chapter 1, and *Sunday Times* and *Soering* below—were all successful challenges to the British government. Did they bolster or weaken the status of the Court?

THE SUNDAY TIMES CASE

Sunday Times v. United Kingdom, European Court of Human Rights,
Judgment of 26 April 1979, Series A, Vol. 30, Application No. 6538/74 (1979) © Council of
Europe/European Court of Human Rights—Conseil de l'Europe/Cour européenne des droits de l'homme

The Facts

Between 1958 and 1961 Distillers Company (Biochemicals) Limited ("Distillers") manufactured and marketed under license in the United Kingdom drugs containing an ingredient initially developed in the Federal Republic of Germany and known as thalidomide. The drugs were prescribed as sedatives for, in particular, expectant mothers. In 1961 a number of women who had taken the drugs during pregnancy gave birth to children suffering from severe deformities; in the course of time there were some 250 such births in all. Distillers withdrew all drugs containing thalidomide from the British market in November of the same year.

[B]y 1971, three hundred and eighty-nine claims in all were pending against Distillers. Apart from a statement of claim in one case and a defence delivered in 1969, no further steps were taken in those actions where writs had been issued. Distillers had announced in February 1968 that they would provide a substantial sum for the benefit of the remaining three hundred and eighty-nine claimants and both sides were anxious to arrive at a settlement out of court. The case in fact raised legal issues of considerable difficulty under English law. Had any of the actions come on for trial, they would have been heard by a professional judge sitting without a jury.

In 1971 negotiations began on a proposal by Distillers to establish a charitable trust fund for all the deformed children other than those covered by the 1968 settlement. The proposal was made subject to the condition that all parents accepted but five refused, one, at least, because payments out of the fund would have been based on need. An application, on behalf of the parents who would have accepted, to replace those five by the Official Solicitor as next friend was refused by the Court of Appeal in April 1972. During subsequent negotiations, the original condition was replaced by a requirement that "a substantial majority" of the parents consented. By September 1972 a settlement involving the setting-up of a £3,250,000 trust fund had been worked out and was expected to be submitted in October to the court for approval.

Reports concerning the deformed children had appeared regularly in *The Sunday Times* since 1967 and in 1968 it had ventured some criticism of the settlement concluded in that year. There had also been comment on the children's circumstances in other newspapers and on television. In particular, in December

1971, the *Daily Mail* published an article which prompted complaints from parents that it might jeopardize the settlement negotiations in hand; the *Daily Mail* was "warned off" by the Attorney-General in a formal letter threatening sanctions under the law of contempt of court but contempt proceedings were not actually instituted. On 24 September 1972, *The Sunday Times* carried an article entitled "Our Thalidomide Children: A Cause for National Shame": this examined the settlement proposals then under consideration, describing them as "grotesquely out of proportion to the injuries suffered," criticized various aspects of English law on the recovery and assessment of damages in personal injury cases, complained of the delay that had elapsed since the births and appealed to Distillers to make a more generous offer. The article contained the following passage:

> . . . the thalidomide children shame Distillers . . . there are times when to insist on the letter of the law is as exposed to criticism as infringement of another's legal rights. The figure in the proposed settlement is to be £3.25 million, spread over 10 years. This does not shine as a beacon against pre-tax profits last year of £64.8 million and company assets worth £421 million. Without in any way surrendering on negligence, Distillers could and should think again.

A footnote in the article announced that "in a future article *The Sunday Times* [would] trace how the tragedy occurred." On 17 November 1972, the Divisional Court of the Queen's Bench Division granted the Attorney-General's application for an injunction restraining publication of this future article on the ground that it would constitute contempt of court[.]

The unpublished article which was the subject of the injunction opened with a suggestion that the manner of marketing thalidomide in Britain left a lot to be desired. It stated that Distillers:

—relied heavily on the German tests and had not completed full trials of its own *before* marketing the drug;

—failed to uncover in its research into medical and scientific literature the fact that a drug related to thalidomide could cause monster births;

—before marketing the drug did no animal tests to determine the drug's effect on the foetus;

—accelerated the marketing of the drug for commercial reasons. Were not deflected by a warning from one of its own staff that thalidomide was far more dangerous than had been supposed;

—were not deflected by the discovery that thalidomide could damage the nervous system, in itself a hint that it might damage the foetus;

—continued to advertise the drug as safe for pregnant women up to a month from when it was withdrawn.

The body of the article described how, after their apparently disappointing initial ventures into pharmaceutics, Distillers learned in 1956 that the German firm of *Chemie Gruenenthal* had developed a sedative considered harmless and unique— thalidomide. The very large market existing at the time for sedatives was becoming overcrowded and Distillers thought it necessary to act quickly. Their decision to market the drug was taken before they had seen technical information, other than the transcript of a German symposium, and before carrying out independent tests. Indeed, they seemed to believe that thalidomide would not need elaborate tests. Distillers put in hand a search of scientific literature but failed to discover the results of research in 1950 by a Dr. Thiersch showing that a chemical related to thalidomide could cause monster births; opinions differed as to whether his work should have been found.

Sales of thalidomide began in Germany in October 1957 and Distillers were committed under their licensing agreement to commence marketing in April 1958. They put the programme for the drug's launch in hand even though clinical trials were behind. Results of the first British trials were published in January 1958: it had been found that thalidomide suppressed the work of the thyroid gland and that its method of action was unknown; the researcher warned that more tests were needed. Distillers did not rely on this advice, basing their decision on "flimsy" evidence, namely other trials in the United Kingdom and assurances concerning the results of research in Germany. The warning about anti-thyroid effects was particularly relevant since it was known that drugs affecting the thyroid could affect unborn children; it was reasonable to argue that Distillers should have delayed launching the drug pending further tests.

On 14 April 1958, continued the article, thalidomide went on sale in Britain, advertised as "completely safe." At the end of 1959, Distillers' pharmacologist discovered that thalidomide in liquid form was highly poisonous and that an overdose might be lethal, but his report was never published and the liquid product went on sale in July 1961. In December 1960, it was reported that patients who had taken thalidomide in the tablet form in which it had firstly been on sale showed symptoms of peripheral neuritis; this news had the result of holding up an application to market thalidomide in the United States of America where it was, in fact, never sold. Further cases of peripheral neuritis were reported in 1961 but Distillers' advertising continued to stress the drug's safety.

Early in 1961 children were born in the United Kingdom with deformities, but there was at the time nothing to connect them with thalidomide. However, between May and October, a doctor in Australia discovered that the common factor in a number of monster births was that the mothers had taken thalidomide during pregnancy. This was reported to *Chemie Gruenenthal* on 24 November who withdrew the drug two days later following newspaper disclosures. Distillers ended the public sale of thalidomide immediately afterwards. Tests on animals, published in April 1962, confirmed that thalidomide caused deformities, but sales to hospitals were not ended until December 1962.

The draft article concluded as follows:

> So the burden of making certain that thalidomide was safe fell squarely on [Distillers]. How did the company measure up to this heavy responsibility? It can be argued that:
>
> 1.   [Distillers] should have found all the scientific literature about drugs related to thalidomide. It did not.
>
> 2.   It should have read Thiersch's work on the effects on the nervous system of drugs related to thalidomide, have suspected the possible action on unborn babies and therefore have done tests on animals for teratogenic effect. It did not.
>
> 3.   It should have done further tests when it discovered that the drug had anti-thyroid activity and unsuspected toxicity. It did not.
>
> 4.   It should have had proof before advertising the drug as safe for pregnant women that this was in fact so. It did not.
>
> For [Distillers] it could be argued that it sincerely believed that thalidomide was free from any toxicity at the time it was first put on the market in Britain; that peripheral neuritis did not emerge as a side effect until the drug had been on sale in Britain for two years; that testing for teratogenic effects was not general in 1958; that if tests had been done on the usual laboratory animals nothing would have shown because it is only in the New Zealand white rabbit that thalidomide produces the same effects as in human beings; and, finally, that in the one clinical report of thalidomide being given to pregnant women no serious results followed (because thalidomide is dangerous only during the first 12 weeks of pregnancy). . . .
>
> There appears to be no neat set of answers[.]

Distillers made a formal complaint to the Attorney-General that the *Sunday Times* article of 24 September 1972 constituted contempt of court in view of the litigation still outstanding and, on 27 September, the Solicitor-General, in the absence of the Attorney-General, wrote to the editor of *The Sunday Times* to ask him for his observations. The editor, in his reply, justified that article and also submitted the draft of the proposed future article for which he claimed complete factual accuracy. . . . On 11 October, the Attorney-General's Office informed *The Sunday Times* that, following representations by Distillers, the Attorney-General had decided to apply to the High Court in order to obtain a judicial decision on the legality of the publication of the proposed article. On the following day, he issued a writ against Times Newspapers Ltd. in which he claimed an injunction "to restrain the defendants . . . by themselves, their servants or agents or otherwise, from publishing or causing or authorizing to be published or printed an article in draft dealing, *inter alia*, with the development, distribution and use of the drug thalidomide, a copy of which article had been supplied to the Attorney-General by the defendants."

The Attorney-General's application was heard by three judges of the Queen's Bench Division from 7 to 9 November 1972; on 17 November the court granted the injunction.

In its judgment the court remarked:

> the article does not purport to express any views as to the legal responsibility of Distillers . . . but . . . is in many respects critical of Distillers and charges them with neglect in regard to their own failure to test the product, or their failure to react sufficiently sharply to warning signs obtained from the tests by others. No one reading the article could . . . fail to gain the impression that the case against Distillers on the footing of negligence was a substantial one.

The editor of the *Sunday Times* had indicated that any libel proceedings following publication would be defended by a plea that the contents of the article were true and the court approached the article on the footing that it was factually accurate.

The reasoning in the court's judgment may be summarised as follows. The objection to unilateral comment, prior to conclusion of the court hearing, was that it might prevent the due and impartial administration of justice by affecting and prejudicing the mind of the tribunal itself, by affecting witnesses who were to be called or by prejudicing the free choice and conduct of a party to the litigation. It was the third form of prejudice that was relevant to the present case. . . .

An appeal by Times Newspapers Ltd. against the Divisional Court's decision was heard by the Court of Appeal from 30 January to 2 February 1973. The court had before it an affidavit by the editor of the Sunday Times setting out developments in the intervening period both in the case itself and in public discussion thereof. With the leave of the court, counsel for Distillers made submissions on the contents of the proposed article, pointing to errors he said it contained. On 16 February, the Court of Appeal discharged the injunction. . . .

Lord Denning said that the proposed article:

> . . . contains a detailed analysis of the evidence against Distillers. It marshals forcibly the arguments for saying that Distillers did not measure up to their responsibility. Though, to be fair, it does summarise the arguments which could be made for Distillers. . . .

"Trial by newspaper," continued Lord Denning, must not be allowed. However, the public interest in a matter of national concern had to be balanced against the interest of the parties in a fair trial or settlement; in the present case the public interest in discussion outweighed the potential prejudice to a party. The law did not prevent comment when litigation was dormant and not being actively pursued. . . .

Following the Court of Appeal's decision, the *Sunday Times* refrained from publishing the proposed article so as to enable the Attorney-General to appeal. [L]eave to appeal . . . was granted by the House of Lords on 1 March 1973. The hearing before the House of Lords was held in May 1973. On 18 July 1973, the House gave judgment unanimously allowing the appeal and subsequently directed the Divisional Court to grant an injunction. . . .

Lord Reid said that the House must try to remove the uncertainty which was the main objection to the present law. The law of contempt had to be founded entirely on public policy; it was not there to protect the rights of parties to a litigation but to prevent interference with the administration of justice and should be limited to what was reasonably necessary for the purpose. Freedom of speech should not be limited more than was necessary but it could not be allowed where there would be real prejudice to the administration of justice. . . .

The Court of Appeal had wrongly described the actions as "dormant" since settlement negotiations were in hand and improper pressure on a litigant to settle could constitute contempt. As for the Court of Appeal's balancing of competing interests, Lord Reid said:

> . . . contempt of court has nothing to do with the private interests of litigants. I have already indicated the way in which I think that a balance

must be struck between the public interest in freedom of speech and the public interest in protecting the administration of justice from interference. I do not see why there should be any difference in principle between a case which is thought to have news value and one which is not. Protection of the administration of justice is equally important whether or not the case involves important general issues.

Lord Reid concluded that publication of the article should be postponed for the time being in the light of the circumstances then prevailing; however, if things dragged on indefinitely, there would have to be a reassessment of the public interest in a unique situation.

[A summary of the concurring opinion of Lord Morris of Booth-y-Gest in the English House of Lords is omitted.]

Lord Diplock said that contempt of court was punishable because it undermined the confidence of the parties and of the public in the due administration of justice. The due administration of justice required that all citizens should have unhindered access to the courts; that they should be able to rely on an unbiased decision based only on facts proved in accordance with the rules of evidence; that, once a case was submitted to a court, they should be able to rely upon there being no usurpation by any other person, for example in the form of "trial by newspaper," of the function of the court. Conduct calculated to prejudice any of these requirements or to undermine public confidence that they would be observed was contempt of court.

[Summaries of the concurring opinions of Lord Simon of Glaisdale and Lord Cross of Chelsea in the English House of Lords are omitted.]

On 25 July 1973, the House of Lords ordered that the cause be remitted to the Divisional Court with a direction to grant the following injunction:

> That ... Times Newspapers Ltd., by themselves, their servants, agents or otherwise, be restrained from publishing, or causing or authorising or procuring to be published or printed, any article or matter which prejudges the issues of negligence, breach of contract or breach of duty, or deals with the evidence relating to any of the said issues arising in any actions pending or imminent against Distillers ... in respect of the development, distribution or use of the drug "thalidomide." ...

On 23 June 1976, the Divisional Court heard an application by the Attorney-General for the discharge of the injunction. It was said on behalf of the Attorney-General that the need for the injunction no longer arose: most of the claims against Distillers had been settled and there were only four extant actions which could by then have been brought before the courts if they had been pursued diligently. As there was a conflicting public interest in the *Sunday Times* being allowed to publish "at the earliest possible date," the Attorney-General submitted the matter to the court as one where the public interest no longer required the restraint. The court, considering that the possibility of pressure on Distillers had completely evaporated, granted the application.

[A discussion of the Phillimore Report on the Law of Contempt, issued in December 1974, is omitted.]

In their application, lodged with the Commission on 19 January 1974, the applicants claimed that the injunction, issued by the High Court and upheld by the House of Lords, to restrain them from publishing an article in the *Sunday Times* dealing with thalidomide children and the settlement of their compensation claims in the United Kingdom constituted a breach of Article 10 of the Convention. They further alleged that the principles upon which the decision of the House of Lords was founded amounted to a violation of Article 10 and asked the Commission to direct or, alternatively, to request the Government to introduce legislation overruling the decision of the House of Lords and bringing the law of contempt of court into line with the Convention.

Balancing the Issues. In *Sunday Times*, there was no doubt that the balancing of the legal issues—weighing the public's right to know and the *Sunday Times*'s right to freedom of expression against Distillers' right to a trial by the courts, not by the media, and the interest of the English government in the integrity of the judicial process—was a very close one. Eight English judges (three at the trial level and five in the House of Lords), five European Human Rights commissioners, and nine European Human Rights judges felt that the scales tilted toward granting an injunction against the *Sunday Times*. Three English judges (in the Court of Appeal), eight European Human Rights commissioners, and eleven European Human Rights judges felt that the balance went for permitting the *Sunday Times* to publish the thalidomide article. Of 44 judges and commissioners who considered the case, half went one way and half the other. Reasonable men and women could and did differ. What is the difference between the standards applied in English law and those in European human rights law?

The Sunday Times Case
The Law

In its report of 18 May 1977, the Commission . . . expressed the opinion:

—by eight votes to five, that the restriction imposed on the applicant's right to freedom of expression was in breach of Article 10 of the Convention[.]

The applicants claim to be the victims of a violation of Article 10 of the Convention which provides:

1.   Everyone has the right to freedom of expression. This right shall include freedom to hold opinions and to receive and impart information and ideas without interference by public authority and regardless of frontiers. This Article shall not prevent States from requiring the licensing of broadcasting, television or cinema enterprises.

2.   The exercise of these freedoms, since it carries with it duties and responsibilities, may be subject to such formalities, conditions, restrictions or penalties as are prescribed by law and are necessary in a democratic society, in the interests of national security, territorial integrity or public safety, for the prevention of disorder or crime, for the protection of health or morals, for the protection of the reputation or rights of others, for preventing the disclosure of information received in confidence, or for maintaining the authority and impartiality of the judiciary. . . .

It is clear that there was an "interference by public authority" in the exercise of the applicants' freedom of expression which is guaranteed by paragraph 1 of Article 10. Such an interference entails a "violation" of Article 10 if it does not fall within one of the exceptions provided for in paragraph 2. The Court, therefore, has to examine in turn whether the interference in the present case was "prescribed by law," whether it had an aim or aims that is or are legitimate under Article 10 § 2 and whether it was "necessary in a democratic society" for the aforesaid aim or aims.

[The European Court holds that there had been an "interference with the applicants' freedom of expression," that it was "prescribed by law," and that "the interference with the applicants' freedom of expression had an aim that is legitimate under Article 10 § 2." The crucial part of the case then follows: "Was the interference 'necessary in a democratic society' for maintaining the authority of the judiciary?"]

[F]reedom of expression constitutes one of the essential foundations of a democratic society; subject to paragraph 2 of Article 10, it is applicable not only to information or ideas that are favourably received or regarded as inoffensive or as a matter of indifference, but also to those that offend, shock or disturb the State or any sector of the population.

These principles are of particular importance as far as the press is concerned. They are equally applicable to the field of the administration of justice, which serves the interests of the community at large and requires the co-operation of an enlightened public. There is general recognition of the fact that the courts cannot operate in a vacuum. Whilst they are the forum for the settlement of disputes, this does not mean that there can be no prior discussion of disputes elsewhere, be it in specialized journals, in the general press or amongst the public at large. Furthermore, whilst the mass media must not overstep the bounds imposed in the interests of the proper administration of justice, it is incumbent on them to impart information and ideas concerning matters that come before the courts just as in other areas of public interest. Not only do the media have the task of imparting such information and ideas: the public also has a right to receive them.

To assess whether the interference complained of was based on "sufficient" reasons which rendered it "necessary in a democratic society," account must thus be taken of any public interest aspect of the case. The Court observes in this connection that, following a balancing of the conflicting interests involved, an absolute rule was formulated by certain of the Law Lords to the effect that it was not permissible to prejudge issues in pending cases: it was considered that the law would be too uncertain if the balance were to be struck anew in each case. Whilst emphasising that it is not its function to pronounce itself on an interpretation of English law adopted in the House of Lords, the Court points out that it has to take a different approach. The Court is faced not with a choice between two conflicting principles but with a principle of freedom of expression that is subject to a number of exceptions which must be narrowly interpreted. In the second place, the Court's supervision under Article 10 covers not only the basic legislation but also the decision applying it. It is not sufficient that the interference involved belongs to that class of the exceptions listed in Article 10 § 2 which has been invoked; neither is it sufficient that the interference was imposed because its subject-matter fell within a particular category or was caught by a legal rule formulated in general or absolute terms: the Court has to be satisfied that the interference was necessary having regard to the facts and circumstances prevailing in the specific case before it.

The thalidomide disaster was a matter of undisputed public concern. It posed the question whether the powerful company which had marketed the drug bore legal or moral responsibility towards hundreds of individuals experiencing an appalling personal tragedy or whether the victims could demand or hope for indemnification only from the community as a whole; fundamental issues concerning protection against and compensation for injuries resulting from scientific developments were raised and many facets of the existing law on these subjects were called in question.

As the Court has already observed, Article 10 guarantees not only the freedom of the press to inform the public but also the right of the public to be properly informed[.]

In the present case, the families of numerous victims of the tragedy, who were unaware of the legal difficulties involved, had a vital interest in knowing all the underlying facts and the various possible solutions. They could be deprived of this information, which was crucially important for them, only if it appeared absolutely certain that its diffusion would have presented a threat to the "authority of the judiciary."

Being called upon to weigh the interests involved and assess their respective force, the Court makes the following observations:

In September 1972, the case had, in the words of the applicants, been in a "legal cocoon" for several years and it was, at the very least, far from certain that the parents' actions would have come on for trial. There had also been no public enquiry[.]

The Government and the minority of the Commission point out that there was no prohibition on discussion of the "wider issues," such as the principles of the English law of negligence, and indeed it is true that there had been extensive discussion in various circles especially after, but also before, the Divisional Court's initial decision[.] However, the Court considers it rather artificial to attempt to divide the "wider issues" and the negligence issue. The question of where responsibility for a tragedy of this kind actually lies is also a matter of public interest.

It is true that, if the *Sunday Times* article had appeared at the intended time, Distillers might have felt obliged to develop in public, and in advance of any trial, their arguments on the facts of the case[;] however, those facts did not cease to be a matter of public interest merely because they formed the background to pending litigation. By bringing to light certain facts, the article might have served as a brake on speculative and unenlightened discussion.

Having regard to all the circumstances of the case . . . the Court concludes that the interference complained of did not correspond to a social need sufficiently pressing to outweigh the public interest in freedom of expression within the meaning of the Convention. The Court therefore finds the reasons for the restraint imposed on the applicants not to be sufficient under Article 10 § 2. That restraint proves not to be proportionate to the legitimate aim pursued; it was not necessary in a democratic society for maintaining the authority of the judiciary.

There has accordingly been a violation of Article 10. . . .

FOR THESE REASONS, THE COURT

holds by eleven votes to nine that there has been a breach of Article 10 of the Convention[.]

The Boldness of the Court. A distinguished British international lawyer, F.A. Mann, felt that the European Court of Human Rights went too far:

However uncertain its definition and scope may be in some respects, contempt of court is undoubtedly one of the great contributions the common law has made to the civilized behaviour of a large part of the world beyond the continent of Europe where the institution is unknown. . . . Yet it is that very branch of the law which the European Court of Human Rights has seriously undermined by, in effect, overturning the unanimous decision of the House of Lords in the *Sunday Times* case—a unique event in the history of English law. In fact it is probably no exaggeration to say that the gravest blow to the fabric of English law has been dealt by the majority of eleven judges coming from Cyprus, Denmark, Eire, France, Germany, Greece, Italy, Portugal, Spain, Sweden and Turkey, who, over the dissent of nine judges from Austria, Belgium, Holland, Iceland, Luxembourg, Malta, Norway, Switzerland and the United Kingdom, decided in favor of the *Sunday Times*. . . .

The reader will have to make up his or her own mind . . . whether the Strasbourg Court arrogated to itself powers of factual appreciation which it cannot possibly exercise convincingly . . . and ask whether according to the standards and traditions of English law and English public life it is the decision of the House of Lords or that of the European Court of Human Rights which more correctly assesses the "social need" and "the legitimate aim" of a civilised society ... and whether the level of judicial reasoning is higher in London or Strasbourg.

F.A. Mann, "Contempt of Court in the House of Lords and the European Court of Human Rights," 95 *Law Quarterly Review* 348, 348–49, 352 (1979).

One can understand Mann's discomfort with the "overturning" of the House of Lords by the Strasbourg Court, but did *Sunday Times* really raise the question of which court's "judicial reasoning" was "higher"? As another observer remarked about another judgment against the United Kingdom, the *Golder Case*: "Membership of a European institution, and submission to the jurisdiction of its organs, means the acceptance of a European way of thinking. The European Commission and Court of Human Rights are likely to construe texts in the 'continental,' not the common law, manner." William Dale, "Human Rights in the United Kingdom—International Standards," 25 *International and Comparative Law Quarterly* 292, 302 (1976).

Continued Acceptance of the Optional Clauses. The United Kingdom was at the time not obliged to accept forever "a European way of thinking." However, states continued to accept both Article 25 and Article 46. At the time of the *Sunday Times Case* 14 of the 21 Council of Europe states had already accepted Article 25 individual petition, and 16 had consented to Article 46 jurisdiction of the Court. Not only did the United Kingdom continue to renew its pledges to both Article 25 and Article 46, but so did the other then-consenting states. Now, the once optional clauses are mandatory. Far from discouraging governments, the *Sunday Times* judgment and cases like it did not slow the accession of states to the legal machinery of European human rights law. Still, a "European way of thinking" is often unpopular. Witness the June 2016 British referendum that favored "Brexit," the severing of ties with the European Union. Will a British rupture with the Strasbourg Court follow?

The Efficacy of European Human Rights Law. How far can the Court go without upsetting the apple cart of state consent? Writing just after the *Sunday Times Case*, Ralph Beddard remarked on the caution exercised by the system's institutions up to that time:

> It is, and always has been, obvious that winning the confidence of the parties and the public was a first step in any attempt to establish judicial determination of the protection of human rights. The last 27 years have not been free of difficulties, however, and the confidence of the parties was won, particularly in the early days, by very careful treading on the part of the Commission. There are cases which, if

presented to the Commission today, would probably make greater progress than they did at the time of application. However, a Commission leaning heavily in favor of governments would have lost the confidence of the public.

Ralph Beddard, *Human Rights and Europe* 4 (2d ed. 1980).

Such caution paid off. In 1980, Sir Humphrey Waldock, then President of the International Court of Justice but previously President of both the European Commission and the European Court of Human Rights, could conclude that "the system set up by the European Convention on Human Rights is, in general, effective is not, I believe, today open to serious question." Humphrey Waldock, "The Effectiveness of the System Set Up by the European Convention on Human Rights," 1 *Human Rights Law Journal* 1 (1980).

How easy is it to judge the "efficacy" of law? Does it matter whether one is testing (1) the efficacy of a particular legal decision, (2) the efficacy of legal rules in practice, or (3) the efficacy of the legal system in the society in general? Most studies evaluating the "efficacy" of European human rights law focus on the efficacy of the judgments of the European Court of Human Rights, but avoid broader efficacy questions. See Mark W. Janis, "The Efficacy of Strasbourg Law," 15 *Connecticut Journal of International Law* 39 (2000).

Remedies at Strasbourg. Sometimes, as in *Sunday Times*, the Court's declaration of a violation of the European Human Rights Convention is the only remedy provided by the Court. Other times, as in the *McCann Case* in Chapter 1, the Court awards damages. However, these damages are ordinarily small or nominal, most typically an award of some of the costs of litigating the case. Recently, the Court has begun experimenting, occasionally ordering the restitution of property or paying applicants its fair market value. See Mark W. Janis, Richard S. Kay & Anthony W. Bradley, *European Human Rights Law* 89–103 (3d ed. 2008). If the Strasbourg Court becomes bolder in awarding damages or in ordering restitution, will this boldness help or hurt the system's efficacy? Will it demonstrate that Strasbourg has clout, or will it induce states to disregard costly judgments?

The Victim of Its Own Success? Is the European Court of Human Rights now a victim of its own success? We noted at the outset of this part how Strasbourg's case load has grown from a handful of rendered judgments in each of its first decades to more than a thousand judgments a year in the last several years. Even so, the European Court of Human Rights is falling behind. In 2009, for example, the Strasbourg Court received about 57,000 applications but was able to deliver "only" about 1,600 judgments. What has accounted for the explosion in applications? Is it due more to "deepening," *i.e.*, that lawyers are more acquainted with the Strasbourg system and, hence, are more likely to apply for review of domestic governmental action, or to "widening," *i.e.*, that the number of member states has grown to more than twice the total less than 30 years ago?

What can be done to handle the onslaught of new applications? Some have suggested that the Court be given new powers "to decline to examine in detail applications that raise no substantial issue under the Convention." Jean-Paul Costa, "The European Court of Human Rights and Its Recent Case Law," 38 *Texas International Law Journal* 455, 467 (2003). The Court may now render a "pilot" judgment instead of issuing a great many similar decisions against a repetitively transgressing state. Whatever the solution to the problem of too much work, Strasbourg's difficulty with its success would be a happy prospect to face for most other international legal tribunals.

THE SOERING CASE

Soering v. United Kingdom, European Court of Human Rights,
Judgment of 7 July 1989, Series A, Vol. 161, Application No. 14038/88 (1989) © Council of
Europe/European Court of Human Rights—Conseil de l'Europe/Cour européenne des droits de l'homme

The Facts

I.   *Particular circumstances of the case*

The applicant, Mr. Jens Soering, was born on 1 August 1966 and is a German national. He is currently detained in prison in England pending extradition to the United States of America to face charges of murder in the Commonwealth of Virginia.

The homicides in question were committed in Bedford County, Virginia, in March 1985. The victims, William Reginald Haysom (aged 72) and Nancy Astor Haysom (aged 53), were the parents of the applicant's girlfriend, Elizabeth Haysom, who is a Canadian national. Death in each case was the result of multiple and massive stab and slash wounds to the neck, throat and body. At the time the applicant and Elizabeth Haysom, aged 18 and 20 respectively, were students at the University of Virginia. They disappeared together from Virginia in October 1985, but were arrested in England in April 1986 in connection with cheque fraud.

The applicant was interviewed in England between 5 and 8 June 1986 by a police investigator from the Sheriff's Department of Bedford County. In a sworn affidavit dated 24 July 1986 the investigator recorded the applicant as having admitted to killings in his presence and in that of two United Kingdom police officers. The applicant had stated that he was in love with Miss Haysom but that her parents were opposed to the relationship. He and Miss Haysom had therefore planned to kill them. They rented a car in Charlottesville and traveled to Washington where they set up an alibi. The applicant then went to the parents' house, discussed the relationship with them and, when they told him they would do anything to prevent it, a row developed during which he killed them with a knife.

On 13 June 1986 a grand jury of the Circuit Court of Bedford County indicted him on charges of murdering the Haysom parents. The charges alleged capital murder of both of them and the separate non-capital murders of each.

On 11 August 1986 the Government of the United States of America requested the applicant's and Miss Haysom's extradition under the terms of the Extradition Treaty of 1972 between the United States and the United Kingdom. On 12 September a Magistrate at Bow Street Magistrates' Court was required by the Secretary of State for Home Affairs to issue a warrant for the applicant's arrest under the provisions of section 8 of the Extradition Act 1870[.] The applicant was subsequently arrested on 30 December at HM Prison Chelmsford after serving a prison sentence for cheque fraud.

On 29 October 1986 the British Embassy in Washington addressed a request to the United States' authorities in the following terms:

> Because the death penalty has been abolished in Great Britain, the Embassy has been instructed to seek an assurance, in accordance with the terms of . . . the Extradition Treaty, that, in the event of Mr. Soering being surrendered and being convicted of the crimes for which he has been indicted . . . , the death penalty, if imposed, will not be carried out.

> Should it not be possible on constitutional grounds for the United States Government to give such an assurance, the United Kingdom authorities ask that the United States Government undertake to recommend to the appropriate authorities that the death penalty should not be imposed or, if imposed, should not be executed.

On 30 December 1986 the applicant was interviewed in prison by a German prosecutor (*Staatsanwalt*) from Bonn. In a sworn witness statement the prosecutor recorded the applicant as having said, *inter alia*, that "he had never had the intention of killing Mr. and Mrs. Haysom and . . . he could only remember having inflicted wounds at the neck on Mr. and Mrs. Haysom which must have had something to do with their dying later;" and that in the immediately preceding days "there had been no talk whatsoever [between him and Elizabeth Haysom] about killing Elizabeth's parents. . . ."

On 11 February 1987 the local court in Bonn issued a warrant for the applicant's arrest in respect of the alleged murders. On 11 March the Government of the Federal Republic of Germany requested his extradition to the Federal Republic under the Extradition Treaty of 1872 between the Federal Republic and the United Kingdom[.]

In a letter dated 20 April 1987 to the Director of the Office of International Affairs, Criminal Division, United States Department of Justice, the Attorney for Bedford County, Virginia (Mr. James W. Updike, Jr.) stated that, on the assumption that the applicant could not be tried in Germany on the basis of admissions alone, there was no means of compelling witnesses from the United States to appear in a criminal court in Germany. On 23 April the United States, by diplomatic note, requested the applicant's extradition to the United States in preference to the Federal Republic of Germany.

On 8 May 1987 Elizabeth Haysom was surrendered for extradition to the United States. After pleading guilty on 22 August as an accessory to the murder of her parents, she was sentenced on 6 October to 90 years' imprisonment (45 years on each count of murder).

On 20 May 1987 the Government of the United Kingdom informed the Federal Republic of Germany that the United States had earlier "submitted a request, supported by *prima facie* evidence, for the extradition of Mr. Soering." The United Kingdom Government notified the Federal Republic that they had "concluded that, having regard to all the circumstances of the case, the court should continue to consider in the normal way the United States' request." They further indicated that they had sought an assurance from the United States' authorities on the question of the death penalty and that "in the event that the court commits Mr. Soering, his surrender to the United States' authorities would be subject to the receipt of satisfactory assurances on this matter."

On 1 June 1987 Mr. Updike swore an affidavit in his capacity as Attorney for Bedford County, in which he certified as follows:

> I hereby certify that should Jens Soering be convicted of the offence of capital murder as charged in Bedford County, Virginia . . . a representation will be made in the name of the United Kingdom to the judge at the time of sentencing that it is the wish of the United Kingdom that the death penalty should not be imposed or carried out.

This assurance was transmitted to the United Kingdom Government under cover of a diplomatic note on 8 June. It was repeated in the same terms in a further affidavit from Mr. Updike sworn on 16 February 1988 and forwarded to the United Kingdom by diplomatic note on 17 May 1988. In the same note the Federal Government of the United States undertook to ensure that the commitment of the appropriate authorities of the Commonwealth of Virginia to make representations on behalf of the United Kingdom would be honored.

During the course of the present proceedings the Virginia authorities have informed the United Kingdom Government that Mr. Updike was not planning to provide any further assurances and intended to seek the death penalty in Mr. Soering's case because the evidence, in his determination, supported such action.

On 16 June 1987 at the Bow Street Magistrates' Court committal proceedings took place before the Chief Stipendiary Magistrate.

The Government of the United States adduced evidence that on the night of 30 March 1985 the applicant killed William and Nancy Haysom at their home in Bedford County, Virginia. In particular, evidence was given of the applicant's own admissions as recorded in the affidavit of the Bedford County police investigator.

On behalf of the applicant psychiatric evidence was adduced from a consultant forensic psychiatrist (report dated 15 December 1986 by Dr. Henrietta Bullard) that he was immature and inexperienced and had lost his personal identity in a symbiotic relationship with his girlfriend—a powerful, persuasive and disturbed young woman. . . .

On 29 June 1987 Mr. Soering applied to the Divisional Court for a writ of habeas corpus in respect of his committal and for leave to apply for judicial review. On 11 December both applications were refused by the Divisional Court (Lord Justice Lloyd and Mr. Justice Macpherson).

In support of his application for leave to apply for judicial review, Mr. Soering had submitted that the assurance received from the United States' authorities was so worthless that no reasonable Secretary of State could regard it as satisfactory under Article IV of the Extradition Treaty between the United Kingdom and the United States[.] In his judgment Lord Justice Lloyd agreed that "the assurance leaves something to be desired":

> Article IV of the Treaty contemplates an assurance that the death penalty will not be carried out. That must presumably mean an assurance by or on behalf of the Executive Branch of Government, which in this case would be the Governor of the Commonwealth of Virginia. The certificate sworn by Mr. Updike, far from being an assurance on behalf

of the Executive, is nothing more than an undertaking to make representations on behalf of the United Kingdom to the judge. I cannot believe that this is what was intended when the Treaty was signed. But I can understand that there may well be difficulties in obtaining more by way of assurance in view of the federal nature of the United States Constitution.

Leave to apply for judicial review was refused because the claim was premature. Lord Justice Lloyd stated:

> The Secretary of State has not yet decided whether to accept the assurance as satisfactory and has certainly not yet decided whether or not to issue a warrant for Soering's surrender. Other factors may well intervene between now and then. This court will never allow itself to be put in the position of reviewing an administrative decision before the decision has been made.

As a supplementary reason, he added:

> Secondly, even if a decision to regard the assurance as satisfactory had already been made by the Secretary of State, then on the evidence currently before us I am far from being persuaded that such a decision would have been irrational. [It was explained that "[t]he test in an extradition case would be that no reasonable Secretary of State could have made an order for return in the circumstances."]

On 30 June 1988 the House of Lords rejected the applicant's petition for leave to appeal against the decision of the Divisional Court.

On 14 July 1988 the applicant petitioned the Secretary of State, requesting him to exercise his discretion not to make an order for the applicant's surrender under section 11 of the Extradition Act 1870[.]

This request was rejected, and on 3 August 1988 the Secretary of State signed a warrant ordering the applicant's surrender to the United States' authorities. However, the applicant has not been transferred to the United States by virtue of the interim measures indicated in the present proceedings firstly by the European Commission and then by the European Court[.]

[The European Court of Human Rights reviews the laws relating to murder in England and Virginia and then turns to the prison conditions in Virginia facing Soering.]

There are currently 40 people under sentence of death in Virginia. The majority are detained in Mecklenburg Correctional Center, which is a modern maximum security institution with a total capacity of 335 inmates. . . .

The size of a death row inmate's cell is 3m by 2.2m. Prisoners have an opportunity for approximately 7 1/2 hours' recreation per week in summer and approximately 6 hours' per week, weather permitting, in winter. The death row area has two recreation yards, both of which are equipped with basketball courts and one of which is equipped with weights and weight benches. Inmates are also permitted to leave their cells on other occasions, such as to receive visits, to visit the law library or to attend the prison infirmary. In addition, death row inmates are given one hour out-of-cell time in the morning in a common area. Each death row inmate is eligible for work assignments, such as cleaning duties. When prisoners move around the prison they are handcuffed with special shackles around the waist.

When not in their cells, death row inmates are housed in a common area called "the pod." The guards are not within this area and remain in a box outside. In the event of disturbance or inter-inmate assault, the guards are not allowed to intervene until instructed to do so by the ranking officer present.

The applicant adduced much evidence of extreme stress, psychological deterioration and risk of homosexual abuse and physical attack undergone by prisoners on death row, including Mecklenburg Correctional Center. This evidence was strongly contested by the United Kingdom Government on the basis of affidavits sworn by administrators from the Virginia Department of Corrections. . . .

A death row prisoner is moved to the death house 15 days before he is due to be executed. The death house is next to the death chamber where the electric chair is situated. Whilst a prisoner is in the death house he is watched 24 hours a day. He is isolated and has no light in his cell. The lights outside are permanently lit. A prisoner who utilizes the appeals process can be placed in the death house several times.

The United Kingdom's Predicament. When Virginia had refused to try Soering for a charge where the death penalty could not be imposed, the United Kingdom was caught between a rock and a hard place in international law. If by the terms of the U.K.-U.S. extradition treaty the U.K. government thought it ought to extradite Soering, but by the terms of the European Convention for the Protection of Human Rights and Fundamental Freedoms the United Kingdom was obligated to follow a contrary judgment of the European Court of Human Rights, what should the United Kingdom do? Should the U.K. government follow the extradition treaty because it is the international agreement later in time? Or should the U.K. government follow the European Human Rights Convention because the Convention concerns more fundamental rights? Is the answer linked to notions about *jus cogens*? See Chapter 2 and look back to *Filartiga* in Chapter 1. As it turned out, Virginia let the United Kingdom off the hook. There is more about international conflict of laws and the specific conflict in *Soering* in David Seymour & Jennifer Tooze, "The *Soering* Case: The Long Reach of the European Convention on Human Rights," in *International Law Stories* 115 (John E. Noyes, Laura A. Dickinson & Mark W. Janis eds. 2007).

The Soering Case
The Law

I.   *Alleged Breach of Article 3*

The applicant alleged that the decision by the Secretary of State for the Home Department to surrender him to the authorities of the United States of America would, if implemented, give rise to a breach by the United Kingdom of Article 3 of the Convention, which provides:

> No one shall be subjected to torture or to inhuman or degrading treatment or punishment.

A.   *Applicability of Article 3 in cases of extradition*

The alleged breach derives from the applicant's exposure to the so-called "death row phenomenon." This phenomenon may be described as consisting in a combination of circumstances to which the applicant would be exposed if, after having been extradited to Virginia to face a capital murder charge, he was sentenced to death.

In its report the Commission reaffirmed "its case-law that a person's deportation or extradition may give rise to an issue under Article 3 of the Convention where there are serious reasons to believe that the individual will be subjected, in the receiving State, to treatment contrary to that Article."

The Government of the Federal Republic of Germany supported the approach of the Commission, pointing to a similar approach in the case-law of the German courts.

The applicant likewise submitted that Article 3 not only prohibits the Contracting States from causing inhuman or degrading treatment or punishment to occur within their jurisdiction but also embodies an associated obligation not to put a person in a position where he will or may suffer such treatment or punishment at the hands of other States. For the applicant, at least as far as Article 3 is concerned, an individual may not be surrendered out of the protective zone of the Convention without the certainty that the safeguards which he would enjoy are as effective as the Convention standard.

The United Kingdom Government, on the other hand, contended that Article 3 should not be interpreted so as to impose responsibility on a Contracting State for acts which occur outside its jurisdiction. In particular, in their submission, extradition does not involve the responsibility of the extraditing State for inhuman or degrading treatment or punishment which the extradited person may suffer outside the State's jurisdiction. To begin with, they maintained, it would be straining the language of Article 3 intolerably to hold that by surrendering a fugitive criminal the extraditing State has "subjected" him to any treatment or punishment that he will receive following conviction and sentence in the receiving State. Further arguments advanced against the approach of the Commission were that it interferes with international treaty rights; it leads to a conflict with the norms of international judicial process, in that it in effect involves adjudication on the internal affairs of foreign States not Parties to the Convention or to the proceedings before the Convention institutions; it entails grave difficulties of evaluation and proof in requiring the examination of alien systems of law and of conditions in foreign States; the practice of national courts and the international community cannot reasonably be invoked to support it; it causes a serious risk of harm in the Contracting State which is obliged to harbour the protected person, and leaves criminals untried, at large and unpunished.

In the alternative, the United Kingdom Government submitted that the application of Article 3 in extradition cases should be limited to those occasions in which the treatment or punishment abroad is certain, imminent and serious. In their view, the fact that by definition the matters complained of are only anticipated, together with the common and legitimate interest of all States in bringing fugitive criminals to justice, requires a very high degree of risk, proved beyond reasonable doubt, that ill-treatment will actually occur.

The Court will approach the matter on the basis of the following considerations.

As results from Article 5 § 1(f), which permits "the lawful . . . detention of a person against whom action is being taken with a view to . . . extradition," no right not to be extradited is as such protected by the Convention. Nevertheless, in so far as a measure of extradition has consequences adversely affecting the enjoyment of a Convention right, it may, assuming that the consequences are not too remote, attract the obligations of a Contracting State under the relevant Convention guarantee. What is at issue in the present case is whether Article 3 can be applicable when the adverse consequences of extradition are, or may be, suffered outside the jurisdiction of the extraditing State as a result of treatment or punishment administered in the receiving State.

Article 1 of the Convention, which provides that "the High Contracting Parties shall secure to everyone within their jurisdiction the rights and freedoms defined in Section I," sets a limit, notably territorial, on the reach of the Convention. In particular, the engagement undertaken by a Contracting State is confined to "securing" ("*reconnaître*" in the French text) the listed rights and freedoms to persons within its own "jurisdiction." Further, the Convention does not govern the actions of States not Parties to it, nor does it purport to be a means of requiring the Contracting States to impose Convention standards on other States. Article 1 cannot be read as justifying a general principle to the effect that, notwithstanding its extradition obligations, a Contracting State may not surrender an individual unless satisfied that the conditions awaiting him in the country of destination are in full accord with each of the safeguards of the Convention. Indeed, as the United Kingdom Government stressed, the beneficial purpose of extradition in preventing fugitive offenders from evading justice cannot be ignored in determining the scope of application of the Convention and of Article 3 in particular.

In the instant case it is common ground that the United Kingdom has no power over the practices and arrangements of the Virginia authorities which are the subject of the applicant's complaints. It is also true that in other international instruments cited by the United Kingdom Government—for example the 1951 United Nations Convention relating to the Status of Refugees (Article 33), the 1957 European Convention on Extradition (Article 11) and the 1984 United Nations Convention against Torture and Other Cruel, Inhuman and Degrading Treatment or Punishment (Article 3)—the problems of removing a person to another jurisdiction where unwanted consequences may follow are addressed expressly and specifically.

These considerations cannot, however, absolve the Contracting Parties from responsibility under Article 3 for all and any foreseeable consequences of extradition suffered outside their jurisdiction.

In interpreting the Convention regard must be had to its special character as a treaty for the collective enforcement of human rights and fundamental freedoms. Thus, the object and purpose of the Convention as an instrument for the protection of individual human beings require that its provisions be interpreted and applied so as to make its safeguards practical and effective. In addition, any interpretation of the rights and freedoms guaranteed has to be consistent with "the general spirit of the Convention, an instrument designed to maintain and promote the ideals and values of a democratic society."

Article 3 makes no provision for exceptions and no derogation from it is permissible under Article 15 in time of war or other national emergency. This absolute prohibition of torture and of inhuman or degrading treatment or punishment under the terms of the Convention shows that Article 3 enshrines one of the fundamental values of the democratic societies making up the Council of Europe. It is also to be found in similar terms in other international instruments such as the 1966 International Covenant on Civil and Political Rights and the 1969 American Convention on Human Rights and is generally recognised as an internationally accepted standard.

The question remains whether the extradition of a fugitive to another State where he would be subjected or be likely to be subjected to torture or to inhuman or degrading treatment or punishment would itself engage the responsibility of a Contracting State under Article 3. That the abhorrence of torture has such implications is recognised in Article 3 of the United Nations Convention Against Torture and Other Cruel, Inhuman or Degrading Treatment or Punishment, which provides that "no State Party shall . . . extradite a person where there are substantial grounds for believing that he would be in danger of being subjected to torture." The fact that a specialised treaty should spell out in detail a specific obligation attaching to the prohibition of torture does not mean that an essentially similar obligation is not already inherent in the general terms of Article 3 of the European Convention. It would hardly be compatible with the underlying values of the Convention, that "common heritage of political traditions, ideals, freedom and the rule of law" to which the Preamble refers, were a Contracting State knowingly to surrender a fugitive to another State where there were substantial grounds for believing that he would be in danger of being subjected to torture, however heinous the crime allegedly committed. Extradition in such circumstances, while not explicitly referred to in the brief and general wording of Article 3, would plainly be contrary to the spirit and intendment of the Article, and in the Court's view this inherent obligation not to extradite also extends to cases in which the fugitive would be faced in the receiving State by a real risk of exposure to inhuman or degrading treatment or punishment proscribed by that Article.

What amounts to "inhuman or degrading treatment or punishment" depends on all the circumstances of the case. Furthermore, inherent in the whole of the

Convention is a search for a fair balance between the demands of the general interest of the community and the requirements of the protection of the individual's fundamental rights. As movement about the world becomes easier and crime takes on a larger international dimension, it is increasingly in the interest of all nations that suspected offenders who flee abroad should be brought to justice. Conversely, the establishment of safe havens for fugitives would not only result in danger for the State obliged to harbour the protected person but also tend to undermine the foundations of extradition. These considerations must also be included among the factors to be taken into account in the interpretation and application of the notions of inhuman and degrading treatment or punishment in extradition cases.

It is not normally for the Convention institutions to pronounce on the existence or otherwise of potential violations of the Convention. However, where an applicant claims that a decision to extradite him would, if implemented, be contrary to Article 3 by reason of its foreseeable consequences in the requesting country, a departure from this principle is necessary, in view of the serious and irreparable nature of the alleged suffering risked, in order to ensure the effectiveness of the safeguard provided by that Article.

In sum, the decision by a Contracting State to extradite a fugitive may give rise to an issue under Article 3, and hence engage the responsibility of that State under the Convention, where substantial grounds have been shown for believing that the person concerned, if extradited, faces a real risk of being subjected to torture or to inhuman or degrading treatment or punishment in the requesting country. The establishment of such responsibility inevitably involves an assessment of conditions in the requesting country against the standards of Article 3 of the Convention. Nonetheless, there is no question of adjudicating on or establishing the responsibility of the receiving country, whether under general international law, under the Convention or otherwise. In so far as any liability under the Convention is or may be incurred, it is liability incurred by the extraditing Contracting State by reason of its having taken action which has as a direct consequence the exposure of an individual to proscribed ill-treatment.

B.   *Application of Article 3 in the particular circumstances of the present case*

[The Court first determines that it was not unlikely that Soering would be charged with and convicted of a crime that would expose him to the "death row phenomenon."]

*2.   Whether in the circumstances the risk of exposure to the "death row phenomenon"
would make extradition a breach of Article 3*

(a)   General considerations

As is established in the Court's case-law, ill-treatment, including punishment,
must attain a minimum level of severity if it is to fall within the scope of Article
3. The assessment of this minimum is, in the nature of things, relative; it depends
on all the circumstances of the case, such as the nature and context of the
treatment or punishment, the manner and method of its execution, its duration,
its physical or mental effects and, in some instances, the sex, age and state of
health of the victim.

Treatment has been held by the Court to be both "inhuman" because it was
premeditated, was applied for hours at a stretch and "caused, if not actual bodily
injury, at least intense physical and mental suffering," and also, "degrading"
because it was "such as to arouse in [its] victims feelings of fear, anguish and
inferiority capable of humiliating and debasing them and possibly breaking their
physical or moral resistance." In order for a punishment or treatment associated
with it to be "inhuman" or "degrading," the suffering or humiliation involved
must in any event go beyond that inevitable element of suffering or humiliation
connected with a given form of legitimate punishment. In this connection,
account is to be taken not only of the physical pain experienced but also, where
there is a considerable delay before execution of the punishment, of the sentenced
person's mental anguish of anticipating the violence he is to have inflicted on him.

Capital punishment is permitted under certain conditions by Article 2 § 1 of
the Convention, which reads:

> Everyone's right to life shall be protected by law. No one shall be
> deprived of his life intentionally save in the execution of a sentence of a
> court following his conviction of a crime for which this penalty is
> provided by law.

In view of this wording, the applicant did not suggest that the death penalty
per se violated Article 3. He, like the two Government Parties, agreed with the
Commission that the extradition of a person to a country where he risks the death
penalty does not in itself raise an issue under either Article 2 or Article 3. On the
other hand, Amnesty International in their written comments . . . argued that the
evolving standards in Western Europe regarding the existence and use of the
death penalty required that the death penalty should now be considered as an
inhuman and degrading punishment within the meaning of Article 3.

Certainly, "the Convention is a living instrument which ... must be interpreted in the light of present-day conditions"; and, in assessing whether a given treatment or punishment is to be regarded as inhuman or degrading for the purposes of Article 3, "the Court cannot but be influenced by the developments and commonly accepted standards in the penal policy of the member States of the Council of Europe in this field." *De facto* the death penalty no longer exists in time of peace in the Contracting States to the Convention. In the few Contracting States which retain the death penalty in law for some peacetime offences, death sentences, if ever imposed, are nowadays not carried out. This "virtual consensus in Western European legal systems that the death penalty is, under current circumstances, no longer consistent with regional standards of justice," to use the words of Amnesty International, is reflected in Protocol No. 6 to the Convention, which provides for the abolition of the death penalty in time of peace. Protocol No. 6 was opened for signature in April 1983, which in the practice of the Council of Europe indicates the absence of objection on the part of any of the Member States of the Organization; it came into force in March 1985 and to date has been ratified by thirteen Contracting States to the Convention, not however including the United Kingdom.

Whether these marked changes have the effect of bringing the death penalty *per se* within the prohibition of ill-treatment under Article 3 must be determined on the principles governing the interpretation of the Convention.

The Convention is to be read as a whole and Article 3 should therefore be construed in harmony with the provisions of Article 2. On this basis Article 3 evidently cannot have been intended by the drafters of the Convention to include a general prohibition of the death penalty since that would nullify the clear wording of Article 2 § 1.

Subsequent practice in national penal policy, in the form of a generalized abolition of capital punishment, could be taken as establishing the agreement of the Contracting States to abrogate the exception provided for under Article 2 § 1 and hence to remove a textual limit on the scope for evolutive interpretation of Article 3. However, Protocol No. 6, as a subsequent written agreement, shows that the intention of the Contracting Parties as recently as 1983 was to adopt the normal method of amendment of the text in order to introduce a new obligation to abolish capital punishment in time of peace and, what is more, to do so by an optional instrument allowing each State to choose the moment when to undertake such an engagement. In these conditions, notwithstanding the special character of the Convention, Article 3 cannot be interpreted as generally prohibiting the death penalty.

That does not mean however that circumstances relating to a death sentence can never give rise to an issue under Article 3. The manner in which it is imposed or executed, the personal circumstances of the condemned person and a disproportionality to the gravity of the crime committed, as well as the conditions of detention awaiting execution, are examples of factors capable of bringing the treatment or punishment received by the condemned person within the proscription under Article 3. Present-day attitudes in the Contracting States to capital punishment are relevant for the assessment whether the acceptable threshold of suffering or degradation has been exceeded.

(b) The particular circumstances

The applicant submitted that the circumstances to which he would be exposed as a consequence of the implementation of the Secretary of State's decision to return him to the United States, namely the "death row phenomenon," cumulatively constitute such serious treatment that his extradition would be contrary to Article 3. He cited in particular the delays in the appeal and review procedures following a death sentence, during which time he would be subject to increasing tension and psychological trauma; the fact, so he said, that the judge or jury in determining sentence is not obliged to take into account the defendant's age and mental state at the time of the offence; the extreme conditions of his future detention on "death row" in Mecklenburg Correctional Center, where he expects to be the victim of violence and sexual abuse because of his age, color and nationality; and the constant spectre of the execution itself, including the ritual of execution. He also relied on the possibility of extradition or deportation, which he would not oppose, to the Federal Republic of Germany as accentuating the disproportionality of the Secretary of State's decision.

The Government of the Federal Republic of Germany took the view that, taking all the circumstances together, the treatment awaiting the applicant in Virginia would go so far beyond treatment inevitably connected with the imposition and execution of a death penalty as to be "inhuman" within the meaning of Article 3.

On the other hand, the conclusion expressed by the Commission was that the degree of severity contemplated by Article 3 would not be attained.

The United Kingdom Government shared this opinion. In particular, they disputed many of the applicant's factual allegations as to the conditions on death row in Mecklenburg and his expected fate there.

i.   Length of detention prior to execution

The period that a condemned prisoner can expect to spend on death row in Virginia before being executed is on average six to eight years[.] This length of time awaiting death is, as the Commission and the United Kingdom Government noted, in a sense largely of the prisoner's own making in that he takes advantage of all avenues of appeal which are offered to him by Virginia law. The automatic appeal to the Supreme Court of Virginia normally takes no more than six months[.] The remaining time is accounted for by collateral attacks mounted by the prisoner himself in habeas corpus proceedings before both the State and Federal courts and in applications to the Supreme Court of the United States for certiorari review, the prisoner at each stage being able to seek a stay of execution[.] The remedies available under Virginia law serve the purpose of ensuring that the ultimate sanction of death is not unlawfully or arbitrarily imposed.

Nevertheless, just as some lapse of time between sentence and execution is inevitable if appeal safeguards are to be provided to the condemned person, so it is equally part of human nature that the person will cling to life by exploiting those safeguards to the full. However well-intentioned and even potentially beneficial is the provision of the complex of post-sentence procedures in Virginia, the consequence is that the condemned prisoner has to endure for many years the conditions on death row and the anguish and mounting tension of living in the ever-present shadow of death.

ii.   Conditions on death row

As to conditions in Mecklenburg Correctional Center, where the applicant could expect to be held if sentenced to death, the Court bases itself on the facts which were uncontested by the United Kingdom Government, without finding it necessary to determine the reliability of the additional evidence adduced by the applicant, notably as to the risk of homosexual abuse and physical attack undergone by prisoners on death row.

The stringency of the custodial regime in Mecklenburg, as well as the services (medical, legal and social) and the controls (legislative, judicial and administrative) provided for inmates, are described in some detail above. In this connection, the United Kingdom Government drew attention to the necessary requirement of extra security for the safe custody of prisoners condemned to death for murder. Whilst it might thus well be justifiable in principle, the severity of a special regime such as that operated on death row in Mecklenburg is compounded by the fact of inmates being subject to it for a protracted period lasting on average six to eight years.

iii. *The applicant's age and mental state*

At the time of the killings, the applicant was only 18 years old and there is some psychiatric evidence, which was not contested as such, that he "was suffering from [such] an abnormality of mind . . . as substantially impaired his mental responsibility for his acts."

Unlike Article 2 of the Convention, Article 6 of the 1966 International Covenant on Civil and Political Rights and Article 4 of the 1969 American Convention on Human Rights expressly prohibit the death penalty from being imposed on persons aged less than 18 at the time of commission of the offence. Whether or not such a prohibition be inherent in the brief and general language of Article 2 of the European Convention, its explicit enunciation in other, later international instruments, the former of which has been ratified by a large number of States Parties to the European Convention, at the very least indicates that as a general principle the youth of the person concerned is a circumstance which is liable, with others, to put in question the compatibility with Article 3 of measures connected with a death sentence.

It is in line with the Court's case-law to treat disturbed mental health as having the same effect for the application of Article 3.

Virginia law, as the United Kingdom Government and the Commission emphasised, certainly does not ignore these two factors. Under the Virginia Code account has to be taken of mental disturbance in a defendant, either as an absolute bar to conviction if it is judged to be sufficient to amount to insanity or, like age, as a fact in mitigation at the sentencing stage[.] Additionally, indigent capital murder defendants are entitled to the appointment of a qualified mental health expert to assist in the preparation of their submissions at the separate sentencing proceedings[.] These provisions in the Virginia Code undoubtedly serve, as the American courts have stated, to prevent the arbitrary or capricious imposition of the death penalty and narrowly to channel the sentencer's discretion[.] They do not however remove the relevance of age and mental condition in relation to the acceptability, under Article 3, of the "death row phenomenon" for a given individual once condemned to death.

Although it is not for this Court to prejudge issues of criminal responsibility and appropriate sentence, the applicant's youth at the time of the offence and his then mental state, on the psychiatric evidence as it stands, are therefore to be taken into consideration as contributory factors tending, in his case, to bring the treatment on death row within the terms of Article 3.

iv.   Possibility of extradition to the Federal Republic of Germany

For the United Kingdom Government and the majority of the Commission, the possibility of extraditing or deporting the applicant to face trial in the Federal Republic of Germany, where the death penalty has been abolished under the Constitution[,] is not material for the present purposes. Any other approach, the United Kingdom Government submitted, would lead to a "dual standard" affording the protection of the Convention to extraditable persons fortunate enough to have such an alternative destination available but refusing it to others not so fortunate.

This argument is not without weight. Furthermore, the Court cannot overlook either the horrible nature of the murders with which Mr. Soering is charged or the legitimate and beneficial role of extradition arrangements in combating crime. The purpose for which his removal to the United States was sought, in accordance with the Extradition Treaty between the United Kingdom and the United States, is undoubtedly a legitimate one. However, sending Mr. Soering to be tried in his own country would remove the danger of a fugitive criminal going unpunished as well as the risk of intense and protracted suffering on death row. It is therefore a circumstance of relevance for the overall assessment under Article 3 in that it goes to the search for the requisite fair balance of interests and to the proportionality of the contested extradition decision in the particular case.

(c)   Conclusion

For any prisoner condemned to death, some element of delay between imposition and execution of the sentence and the experience of severe stress in conditions necessary for strict incarceration are inevitable. The democratic character of the Virginia legal system in general and the positive features of Virginia trial, sentencing and appeal procedures in particular are beyond doubt. The Court agrees with the Commission that the machinery of justice to which the applicant would be subject in the United States is in itself neither arbitrary nor unreasonable, but, rather, respects the rule of law and affords not inconsiderable procedural safeguards to the defendant in a capital trial. Facilities are available on death row for the assistance of inmates, notably through provision of psychological and psychiatric services[.]

However, in the Court's view, having regard to the very long period of time spent on death row in such extreme conditions, with the ever present and mounting anguish of awaiting execution of the death penalty, and to the personal circumstances of the applicant, especially his age and mental state at the time of the offence, the applicant's extradition to the United States would expose him to a real risk of treatment going beyond the threshold set by Article 3. A further consideration of relevance is that in the particular instance the legitimate purpose of extradition could be achieved by another means which would not involve suffering of such exceptional intensity or duration.

Accordingly, the Secretary of State's decision to extradite the applicant to the United States would, if implemented, give rise to a breach of Article 3.

This finding in no way puts in question the good faith of the United Kingdom Government, who have from the outset of the present proceedings demonstrated their desire to abide by their Convention obligations, firstly by staying the applicant's surrender to the United States authorities in accord with the interim measures indicated by the Convention institutions and secondly by themselves referring the case to the Court for a judicial ruling[.]

For These Reasons, the Court Unanimously

1.   *Holds* that, in the event of the Secretary of State's decision to extradite the applicant to the United States of America being implemented, there would be a violation of Article 3[.]

Soering's Fate. Soon after the judgment of the Court, the United States represented to the United Kingdom that Soering would not be tried for a crime for which the death penalty could be imposed. Soering was then extradited to the United States, tried in Virginia, and found guilty on two counts of first-degree murder; it was recommended by the jury that he serve two life terms. Richard Lillich & Hurst Hannum, *International Human Rights* 768 (3d ed. 1995). Might the Court have differed from the Commission because it thought that Virginia would be willing to reduce the charge only if the United Kingdom were ordered not to extradite Soering?

Jens Soering tells his own version of the murders, his conviction, and his life in prison at http://www.jenssoering.com. Soering's conviction is still headline news. See Laura Vozzella, "In 1985, a Gruesome Double Murder Shocked Virginia. Was the Wrong Man Convicted?," *Washington Post Magazine*, Mar. 9, 2017.

The Extraterritorial Effect of the Soering *Judgment.* Is it fair to impose the human rights obligations of the European Convention on a non-party such as the United States? According to one extradition expert, the *Soering* decision "is having an impact on U.S. domestic criminal procedure at a very basic level"; officials of U.S. states seeking to extradite from Europe a fugitive accused of murder must essentially "prove to the Departments of State and Justice that the document [seeking extradition] is signed by the state official who has authority to bind the state to the commitment not to pursue or impose the death penalty." Christopher L. Blakesley, "The *Pinochet Extradition Case* and Beyond: Human Rights Clauses Compared to Traditional Derivative Protections Such as Double Criminality," 1999–2000 *Proceedings of the American Branch of the International Law Association* 370, 402. Why should U.S. death row conditions be a fit topic for consideration by the Strasbourg Court? Compare *Soering*'s extraterritorial reach to the extraterritorial implications of *Filartiga* in Chapter 1 where conduct in Paraguay was adjudicated in the United States. The U.S. Supreme Court also considered the extraterritorial application of human rights law in the Alien Tort Statute cases in Chapter 5.

D. INTERNATIONAL CRIMINAL LAW

Besides rights individuals also have duties at international law. Indeed, as we have seen, the modern transformation of the role of individuals in international law began after World War II with the Nuremberg criminal trials of individual defendants. After Nuremberg, it was the hope of many to establish a permanent international criminal tribunal. It took a long time, though, for the International Criminal Court (ICC) to emerge. Only in 1998 did states draft the Rome Statute, which, coming into force in 2002, finally established the ICC. The readings below introduce the negotiations leading to the Rome Statute and one of the first decisions of the ICC, the *Lubanga Case*. We then review developments at the ICC and at some of the other new international criminal tribunals.

LEILA NADYA SADAT & S. RICHARD CARDEN, THE NEW INTERNATIONAL CRIMINAL COURT: AN UNEASY REVOLUTION

88 *Georgetown Law Journal* 381 (2000)

I.   PROLOGUE: THE LAST INTERNATIONAL INSTITUTION OF THE TWENTIETH CENTURY

From June 15 through July 17, 1998, representatives of 160 countries, closely watched by 250 non-governmental organizations (NGOs), met in Rome to negotiate a Treaty that would establish a permanent international criminal court. The Conference was held in the United Nations Food and Agricultural Organization building ("la FAO" in Italian), a large, rather plebeian structure from the Mussolini period, with a splendid view of *Il Palatino* from the top floor terrace. The weather was hot, the mood alternated between exhilaration and anxiety, the work was hard. Issues that had been debated for more than two years during the Preparatory Committee meetings leading up to the Rome Conference (PrepComI) remained on the table unresolved. The starting point of the negotiations was a complex consolidated text containing 116 articles, including some 1300 phrases in brackets. It was extremely difficult to read, let alone understand. As is by now well known, after five weeks of grueling negotiations, the Diplomatic Conference adopted a Statute for the Court in an emotional vote of 120 to 7, with 21 countries abstaining. The United States, whose delegation was instrumental in the development of the Statute throughout the PrepComI meetings and the Rome Conference, was one of the seven countries voting against the Treaty.

The adoption of the International Criminal Court (ICC) Statute is the result of more than seventy-five years of hard work and false starts. As the Preamble to the Treaty notes, the purpose of the Court is to end impunity for the perpetrators of "atrocities that deeply shock the conscience of humanity." And the Twentieth Century witnessed atrocities on a truly unprecedented scale. The estimate of 170 million dead in 250 conflicts that have occurred since World War II is a grim testament to the failure of the international community to create a viable mechanism to prevent aggression and enforce international humanitarian law.

It was thus appropriate and somehow fortuitous that the Diplomatic Conference was held in Rome. Once the center of an empire that stretched, during the Hadrianic period, across an area the size of the Continental United States and Alaska, Rome is a city rich in historic and cultural treasures. It has also been repeatedly devastated by war. And what delegate, gazing out over *Il Palatino* and the ruins of the Forum, or seeing *Castel Sant'Angelo*, where Pope Clement was besieged for months while soldiers looted the city and tormented and killed its inhabitants, could not feel the weight of history upon him or her, or understand the historic purpose for which all were gathered? Indeed, what better place in which to argue, on behalf of humanity, that the excesses of war should be restrained by the Rule of Law?

The International Criminal Court is the last great international institution of the Twentieth Century. It is no exaggeration to suggest that its creation has the potential to reshape our thinking about international law. For if many aspects of the Rome Treaty demonstrate the tenacity of traditional Westphalian notions of State sovereignty, there are nonetheless elements of supranationalism and efficacy (in spite of the complementarity principle [under which states may try individuals for crimes within the ICC's jurisdiction, in place of the ICC]) in the Statute that could prove extremely powerful. Not only does the Statute place State and non-State actors side-by-side in the international arena, but the Court will put real people in real jails. Indeed, the establishment of the Court raises hopes that the lines between international law on the one hand, and world order, on the other, are blurring and that the normative structure being created by international law might influence or even restrain the Hobbesian order established by the politics of States.

Given the unsuccessful history of previous efforts to establish an international criminal court, and the tepid support of many of the major powers during the Preparatory Committee meetings leading up to the Diplomatic Conference, the adoption of the Statute by the Diplomatic Conference comes as a surprise. It can be credited, at least in part, to the enormous lobbying and informational efforts of NGO's, which conducted a tireless campaign in support of the Court and came together as new evidence of global civil society. Another important factor was the emergence of a so-called "like-minded" group of States, which, although individually holding quite divergent views on many issues, were united in their view that the Court's ultimate establishment was a priority. Moreover, strong support from European countries and other traditional U.S. allies rallied the West behind the Court even without U.S. participation. . . .

But classic ideas about sovereignty die hard, and if the road to Rome was long and difficult, the journey to the seat of the Court at the Hague may be even more arduous. First, sixty States must ratify the Treaty before the Court can come into existence. In addition, before the Court can exercise its functions, the Preparatory Commission, established by the Diplomatic Conference at Rome, must prepare draft texts of Rules of Procedure and Evidence, Elements of Crimes, a relationship agreement between the Court and the United Nations, basic principles of the headquarters agreement, financial regulations and rules, an agreement on the privileges and immunities of the Court, a budget for the first financial year, and the rules of procedure for the Assembly of States Parties. Much of this work will be the subject of Preparatory Commission meetings held over the next two years.

Developments at the International Criminal Court. The Rome Statute came into force in July 2002. Judges, 18 in all, were elected to serve on the International Criminal Court (ICC) in March 2003. As of May 2017, there were 124 states parties to the Rome Statute. According to the President of the ICC, over its first two and a half years, the ICC built "the Court's physical structure" and established "the Court's judicial structure," *e.g.,* "the adoption by the judges of the Regulations of the Court." Philippe Kirsch, "Building an Effective & Efficient Court," *ICC Newsletter #3*, Feb. 2005, at 1. The pace gradually picked up. By 2015, the ICC Office of the Prosecutor was seized of 21 cases and eight situations, all in Africa. There were also preliminary examinations of situations in Afghanistan, Colombia, Georgia, Guinea, Honduras, Iraq, Nigeria, and Ukraine. The ICC Secretary-General in 2013 hinted at some practical challenges when he stressed it was "particularly crucial that States provide timely and full cooperation to the Court in accordance with their legal obligations, and that appropriate action be taken in cases of non-cooperation." *Report of the International Criminal Court for 2012–13*, U.N. Doc. A/68/314, at 2, 21 (2013). In 2015 the Court submitted that it "faced a heavy workload," expecting "that 2016 will be a very busy year for the Court, with the unprecedented number of four trials taking place simultaneously. Those trials alone cover alleged crimes involving more than 10,000 victims, reflecting the fact that the scope of cases at the Court is typically far broader than that of trials in national jurisdictions." *Report of the International Criminal Court on its activities in 2014/15*, U.N. Doc. A/70/350, at 2 (2015).

U.S. Hostility Toward the International Criminal Court. The United States, with its many international military engagements exposing overseas U.S. personnel to possible prosecution, has been especially doubtful about turning over prosecutorial and adjudicatory powers to the ICC. Although President Clinton did finally authorize the signing of the Rome Statute, he did so only on December 31, 2000, the last day that the treaty was open to signature and very near the end of his term in office. And rather than submit the treaty to the Senate for its advice and consent to ratification, President Clinton emphasized what he saw as the treaty's "significant flaws." Sean D. Murphy, "Contemporary Practice of the United States Relating to International Law," 95 *American Journal of International Law* 387, 399 (2001). Even less friendly to the ICC, President Bush's administration notified the United Nations on May 6, 2002, "that the United States does not intend to become a party to the [Rome] treaty [and that accordingly] the United States has no legal obligations arising from its signature on December 31, 2001." Sean D. Murphy, "Contemporary Practice of the United States Relating to International Law," 96 *American Journal of International Law* 706, 724 (2002). The United States did not join the ICC during the eight years of the Obama administration.

What motivates U.S. hostility to the ICC? Central to U.S. opposition is the U.S. "policy of ensuring that no U.S. national will ever be tried before the International Criminal Court." John F. Murphy, "Gulliver No Longer Quivers: U.S. Views on and the Future of the International Criminal Court," 44 *The International Lawyer* 1123, 1128 (2010). Besides this, there have been doubts expressed about the constitutionality of U.S. adherence to the Rome Statute.

For a comprehensive review, see David Scheffer & Ashley Cox, "The Constitutionality of the Rome Statute of the International Criminal Court," 98 *Journal of Criminal Law & Criminology* 983 (2008).

Important, too, is the preference the United States has for *ad hoc* rather than permanent international criminal tribunals. The *ad hoc* tribunals established at The Hague for the former Yugoslavia in 1993 and at Arusha for Rwanda in 1994 were created by the U.N. Security Council and thus much more sure to be controlled by the Council's permanent members—the United States, China, France, Russia, and the United Kingdom—than is an independent permanent international criminal court. See William A. Schabas, "United States Hostility to the International Criminal Court: It's All About the Security Council," 15 *European Journal of International Law* 701 (2004). Adding to U.S. anxieties, ICC Chief Prosecutor Luis Moreno Campo warned that international corporate officers could face charges at The Hague if they facilitate government or insurgent conduct that violates international human rights law. James Podgers, "Corporations in Line of Fire: International Prosecutor Says Corporate Officials Could Face War Crimes Charges," 90 *ABA Journal,* Jan. 2004, at 13. Even given these drawbacks, Professor Sievert has argued that the United States ought to modify its opposition to the ICC: "it is far better that the U.S. controls the process in the future and use it to its advantage than stand alone as its own rogue state against ninety-nine civilized nations." Ron Sievert, "A New Perspective on the International Criminal Court: Why the Right Should Embrace the ICC and How America Can Use It," 63 *University of Pittsburgh Law Review* 77, 129 (2006).

Has the United States tempered its opposition to the International Criminal Court? In 2005, the George W. Bush administration did not oppose a U.N. Security Council resolution referring the situation in Darfur, in the Sudan, to the ICC Prosecutor. In 2011, the United States under the Obama administration joined a unanimous Security Council vote referring the situation in Libya after February 15, 2011 to the Prosecutor. See U.N. Doc. S/RES/1595 (2005); U.N. Doc. S/RES/1970 (2011). Is a critical issue for the United States the extent of discretion of the ICC Office of the Prosecutor to investigate situations and pursue cases without Security Council authorization? If a Security Council resolution were the only route to ICC jurisdiction, any permanent member of the Council, including the United States, could block ICC investigations or cases.

The Jurisdiction of the ICC. Referral from the Security Council acting under Chapter VII of the U.N. Charter is not the only basis for the Court's exercise of jurisdiction. State parties may refer cases to the ICC, and the Prosecutor may also investigate proceedings *proprio motu*, if authorized by the Pre-Trial Chamber. See Rome Statute, arts. 13–15. As of February 2017, four countries— Uganda, the Democratic Republic of the Congo, the Central African Republic, and Mali—had referred situations in their territories to the ICC Prosecutor for investigation. The Prosecutor has also been authorized to conduct *proprio motu* investigations in Kenya, the Ivory Coast, and Georgia. The Court may exercise jurisdiction only with respect to war crimes, crimes against humanity, and the crime of aggression, and then "only with respect to crimes committed after the entry into force of" the Rome Statute. *Id.* art. 10.

The Utility of International Criminal Courts. There seem to be four kinds of goals advanced for the creation of international criminal courts: (1) justice and punishment, (2) deterrence, (3) record-keeping, and (4) the progressive development of international law. So far, practice shows that achievement of the first two goals—justice/punishment and deterrence—has been spotty at best. However, the utility of international criminal tribunals has been surer for the other two aims—record-keeping and the progressive development of international law. See Mark W. Janis, "The Utility of International Criminal Courts," 12 *Connecticut Journal of International Law* 161 (1997). When reading the *Lubanga Case* below, ask which of these four goals may or may not be advanced by the ICC proceeding and judgment.

SITUATION IN THE DEMOCRATIC REPUBLIC OF THE CONGO IN THE CASE OF THE PROSECUTOR V. THOMAS LUBANGA DYILO (2007)

Decision on the Confirmation of Charges, International Criminal Court
Pre-trial Chamber I, ICC–01/04–01/06, Jan. 29, 2007

The District of Ituri before 1 July 2002

Ituri is a district in the Orientale Province of the Democratic Republic of the Congo (the DRC). It is bordered by Uganda to the east and Sudan to the north. Its population is between 3.5 and 5.5 million people, of whom only about 100,000 live in Bunia, the district capital. Ituri's population consists of some 20 different ethnic groups, the largest being the Hemas, the Alurs, the Biras, the Lendus and their southern sub-group, the Ngitis.

Ituri is rich in natural resources, such as gold, oil, timber, coltan and diamonds. For example, the Mongwalu mine, which is located about forty-five kilometres north-west of Bunia, is the most important gold mine in the DRC and one of the most important in Central Africa.

The majority of the population of Ituri makes its living from agriculture, and the rest from trade, animal husbandry and fishing. Agriculture is the principal economic activity of the Lendus, while the Hemas are more active in livestock farming.

In the summer of 1999, tensions developed as a result of disputes over the allocation of land in Ituri and the appropriation of natural resources. During the second half of 2002, there was renewed violence in various parts of the district.

Thomas Lubanga Dyilo

Thomas Lubanga Dyilo was born in 1960 in Jiba (Djugu territory of Ituri, Orientale Province, DRC), and belongs to the Hema ethnic group. He studied at the University of Kisangani, where he obtained a degree in psychology. From 1986 to 1997, he allegedly headed an organisation called "Votura." From 1990 to 1994, he was also allegedly assistant at the CEPROMAD University. Throughout that period, he also engaged in other income-generating activities, ranging from farming to gold trading.

On the evidence presented for the purpose of the confirmation hearing, it would appear that Thomas Lubanga Dyilo entered politics between late 1999 and early 2000. Soon thereafter, he was elected to the Ituri District Assembly.

On 15 September 2000, the statutes of the *Union des Patriotes Congolais* (UPC) were signed by Thomas Lubanga Dyilo, as the first signatory, and several other persons who subsequently held leadership positions within the party and its armed military wing, the *Forces Patriotiques pour la Liberation du Congo* (FPLC). In August 2002, the UPC took control of Bunia.

In early September 2002, the UPC was renamed *Union des Patriotes Congolais/Reconciliation et Paix* (UPC/RP) and Thomas Lubanga Dyilo appointed its President. A few days later, in Bunia, Thomas Lubanga Dyilo signed the decree appointing the members of the first UPC/RP executive for the Ituri District. At the same time, a second decree officially established the FPLC. Immediately after the establishment of the FPLC, Thomas Lubanga Dyilo became its Commander-in-Chief.

Prosecution allegations against Thomas Lubanga Dyilo

In the "Document Containing the Charges, Article 61(3)(a)," filed on 28 August 2006, the Prosecution charges Thomas Lubanga Dyilo under articles 8(2)(e)(vii) and 25(3)(a) of the [ICC] Statute with the war crimes of conscripting and enlisting children under the age of fifteen years into an armed group (in this case, the FPLC, military wing of the UPC since September 2002) and using them to participate actively in hostilities. The Prosecution submits that "the crimes occurred in the context of an armed conflict not of an international character."

The Prosecution asserts that even prior to the founding of the FPLC, the UPC actively recruited children under the age of fifteen years in significant numbers and subjected them to military training in its military training camp in Sota, amongst other places.

The Prosecution further submits that, after its founding and until the end of 2003, the FPLC continued to systematically enlist and conscript children under the age of fifteen years in large numbers in order to provide them with military training, and use them subsequently to participate actively in hostilities, including as bodyguards for senior FPLC military commanders. The FPLC military training camps included camps in Centrale, Mandro, Rwampara, Irumu and Bule.

The Prosecution submits that Thomas Lubanga Dyilo is criminally responsible for the crimes listed in the Document Containing the Charges as a co-perpetrator, jointly with other FPLC officers and UPC members and supporters.

[T]he Chamber has concluded that . . . there was sufficient evidence to establish substantial grounds to believe that from early September 2002 to the end of 2003:

i. the FPLC repeatedly admitted into its ranks young recruits, including children under the age of fifteen years, who wished to voluntarily join the FPLC;

ii. the FPLC repeatedly forcibly recruited into its ranks young recruits, including children under the age of fifteen years;

iii. the FPLC encouraged the practice whereby each Hema family was to contribute to the war effort, in particular, by supplying young recruits, including children under the age of fifteen years;

iv. the FPLC sent its young recruits, including children under the age of fifteen years, to the FPLC military training camps in Centrale, Rwampara, Mandro, Irumu, Bule, Bogoro, and Sota;

v. the aim of the military training was to prepare the young FPLC recruits, including those under the age of fifteen years, to participate actively in military operations; the training lasted up to two months, and included physical exercises like learning to salute, march, run, take up positions and use firearms;

vi. the young FPLC recruits, including those under the age of fifteen years, were subject to strict military discipline and the instructors sought to boost their morale by making them sing aggressive military songs;

vii.   the most senior FPLC commanders—Thomas Lubanga Dyilo, Floribert Kisembo and Bosco Ntaganda—regularly visited FPLC military training camps where young recruits, including those under the age of fifteen years, were being trained;

viii. upon completion of their military training, Floribert Kisembo and Bosco Ntaganda and other senior commanders (such as Tchalingonza) provided the young recruits, including those under the age of fifteen years, with a military uniform and a personal weapon (usually a firearm), and soon thereafter ordered them into combat on the front line in military operations conducted in Libi and Mbau in October 2002, in Largu in early 2003, in Lipri and Bogoro in February and March 2003, in Bunia in May 2003 and in Djugu and Mongwalu in June 2003;

ix.   it was common practice among the most senior FPLC commanders (i.e. Thomas Lubanga Dyilo, Floribert Kisembo and Bosco Ntaganda) and other senior commanders (such as Tchalingonza) to use young recruits, including those under the age of fifteen years, as bodyguards to protect military objectives, such as their physical safety (including during military operations) and FPLC military quarters.

[T]he Chamber finds that there is sufficient evidence to establish substantial grounds to believe that from early September 2002 to 13 August 2003, Thomas Lubanga Dyilo incurred criminal responsibility as a co-perpetrator within the meaning of article 25(3)(a) of the Statute[.]

Lubanga: *The Belated First Judgment.* The *Lubanga* judgment was long-anticipated. By 2008, a newspaper columnist lamented: "as it celebrates its 10th anniversary, the ICC is facing its own indictment. Its critics charge that its work is often counter-productive, politicised and plain incompetent." Among the criticisms: that the ICC had not completed a prosecution, that its defendants were all African, and that its work complicated peace efforts. Gideon Rachman, "When Peace and Justice Collide," *Financial Times*, July 7, 2008. The slow progress of the *Lubanga Case* illustrates some of the ICC's problems. In 2003, the ICC's Chief Prosecutor underlined that the Ituri situation in the Democratic Republic of the Congo ought to be "the most urgent situation to be followed" by the ICC. Lubanga, who had been arrested by the Congolese government in

2005, was transferred to The Hague in 2006. In 2007, as we see, a pre-trial chamber decided there was sufficient evidence for the Prosecutor to proceed. In 2009, the trial finally began. In July 2010, however, the trial chamber stayed the proceedings, ruling that "because of the Prosecutor's clearly evinced intention not to implement the Chamber's orders[,] the fair trial of the accused is no longer possible." Decision of July 8, 2010, ¶ 31. The trial chamber's order to release Lubanga was reversed on appeal, and the trial recommenced in December 2010—only to be interrupted again to hear (and ultimately reject) a defense motion to dismiss the case on the grounds that the Office of the Prosecutor had allegedly bribed and coached witnesses. The trial chamber eventually rendered its judgment in 2012.

SITUATION IN THE DEMOCRATIC REPUBLIC OF THE CONGO IN THE CASE OF THE PROSECUTOR V. THOMAS LUBANGA DYILO (2012)

International Criminal Court
Trial Chamber 1, ICC–01/04–01/06, Mar. 14, 2012

The Chamber concludes beyond reasonable doubt that the accused, by virtue of his position as President and Commander-in-Chief from September 2002 onwards, was able to shape the policies of the UPC/FPLC and to direct the activities of his alleged co-perpetrators. The established reporting structures; the lines of communication within the UPC/FPLC; and the meetings and close contact between the accused and at least some of the alleged co-perpetrators, support the conclusion that he was kept fully informed throughout the relevant period and he issued instructions relating to the implementation of the common plan. Thomas Lubanga personally assisted in the military affairs of the UPC/FPLC in a variety of ways. He was involved in planning military operations and he exercised a key role in providing logistical support, by ensuring weapons, ammunition, food, uniforms and military rations and other supplies were available for the troops. . . .

Viewed in its entirety, the evidence demonstrates that the accused and his alleged co-perpetrators, including particularly Floribert Kisembo, Chief Kahwa and Bosco Ntaganda, worked together and each of them made an essential contribution to the common plan that resulted in the enlistment, conscription and use of children under the age of 15 to participate actively in hostilities.

In light of the evidence above, the Chamber is persuaded beyond reasonable doubt that the accused made an essential contribution to the common plan for the purposes of Article 25(3)(a). . . .

The accused and his co-perpetrators agreed to, and participated in a common plan to build an army for the purpose of establishing and maintaining political and military control over Ituri. This resulted, in the ordinary course of events, in the conscription and enlistment of boys and girls under the age of 15, and their use to participate actively in hostilities. . . .

The accused and at least some of his co-perpetrators were involved in the takeover of Bunia in August 2002. Thomas Lubanga, as the highest authority within the UPC, appointed Chief Kahwa, Floribert Kisembo and Bosco Ntaganda to senior positions within the UPC/FPLC. The evidence has established that during this period, the leaders of the UPC/FPLC, including Chief Kahwa, and Bosco Ntaganda, and Hema elders such as Eloy Mafuta, were active in mobilization and recruitment campaigns aimed at persuading Hema families to send their children to join the UPC/FPLC. Those children recruited before the formal creation of the FPLC were incorporated into that group, and a number of training camps were added to the original facility at Mandro. The Chamber has concluded that between 1 September 2002 and 13 August 2003, a significant number of high-ranking members of the UPC/FPLC and other personnel conducted a large-scale recruitment exercise directed at young people, including children under the age of 15, whether voluntarily or by coercion.

The Chamber is satisfied beyond reasonable doubt that as a result of the implementation of the common plan to build an army for the purpose of establishing and maintaining political and military control over Ituri, boys and girls under the age of 15 were conscripted and enlisted into the UPC/FPLC between 1 September 2002 and 13 August 2003. Similarly, the Chamber is satisfied beyond reasonable doubt that the UPC/FPLC used children under the age of 15 to participate actively in hostilities, including during battles. They were also used, during the relevant period, as soldiers and as bodyguards for the senior officials, including the accused.

Thomas Lubanga was the President of the UPC/FPLC, and the evidence demonstrates that he was simultaneously the Commander-in-Chief of the army and its political leader. He exercised an overall coordinating role over the activities of the UPC/FPLC. He was informed, on a substantive and continuous basis, of the operations of the FPLC. He was involved in planning military operations, and he played a critical role in providing logistical support, including as regards weapons, ammunition, food, uniforms, military rations and other general supplies for the FPLC troops. He was closely involved in making decisions on recruitment policy and he actively supported recruitment initiatives, for instance by giving speeches to the local population and the recruits. In his speech at the Rwampara camp, he encouraged children, including those under the age of 15 years, to join the army and to provide security for the populace once deployed in the field following their military training. Furthermore, he personally used children below the age of 15 amongst his bodyguards and he regularly saw guards of other UPC/FPLC members of staff who were below the age of 15. The Chamber has concluded that these contributions by Thomas Lubanga, taken together, were essential to a common plan that resulted in the conscription and enlistment of girls and boys below the age of 15 in to the UPC/FPLC and their use to actively participate in hostilities.

The Chamber is satisfied beyond reasonable doubt, as set out above, that Thomas Lubanga acted with the intent and knowledge necessary to establish the charges (the mental element required by Article 30). He was aware of the factual circumstances that established the existence of the armed conflict. Furthermore, he was aware of the nexus between those circumstances and his own conduct, which resulted in the enlistment, conscription and use of children below the age of 15 to participate actively in hostilities.

For the foregoing reasons and on the basis of the evidence submitted and discussed before the Chamber at trial, and the entire proceedings, pursuant to Article 74(2) of the Statute, the Chamber finds Mr. Thomas Lubanga Dyilo:

> GUILTY of the crimes of conscripting and enlisting children under the age of fifteen years into the FPLC and using them to participate actively in hostilities within the meaning of Articles 8(2)(e)(vii) and 25(3)(a) of the Statute from early September 2002 to 13 August 2003.

The Lubanga *Judgment.* When the ICC finally did deliver its first judgment in 2012, it was not generally praised. There were three ICC decisions altogether, numbering hundreds of pages: the verdict convicting Lubanga, a ruling on his sentence, and an outline on awarding reparations to victims. "[P]rovoking concern was the fact that it took the ICC six years to render a trial verdict in a case involving a single defendant accused only of the war crime of child soldiering." Moreover, despite its length, "the decision did not meet the bar . . . of 'a fully reliable record' established 'so that future generations can remember and be made fully cognizant of what happened.'" Diane Marie Amann, "International Decision: *Prosecutor v. Lubanga,*" 106 *American Journal of International Law* 809, 815, 817 (2012). Nevertheless, one observer commended the ICC for "shedding light on the conscription, enlistment, and use of child soldiers." Triestino Mariniello, *"Prosecutor v. Thomas Lubanga Dyilo*: The First Judgment of the International Criminal Court's Trial Chamber," 1 *International*

Human Rights Law Review 137, 138 (2012). But even this triumph was warped: "[T]he [ICC] was not satisfied that even a single one of the witnesses whom the prosecution called purporting to be victims had, in fact, been child soldiers. In other words, not a single one of Lubanga's victims ever got a chance to tell his or her story to the Court and have it count." Caroline Buisman, "Delegating Investigations: Lessons to be Learned from the Lubanga Judgment," 11 *Northwestern Journal of International Human Rights* 30, 82 (2013).

The saga has continued. Lubanga's guilty verdict and 14-year sentence were affirmed on appeal in December 2014, and a year later Lubanga began serving his sentence at a prison facility in the Democratic Republic of the Congo. As of May 2017, hearings and a decision on a plan for reparations to victims were pending. Why has the ICC been so slow, and so relatively unsuccessful?

The Fate of the International Criminal Court. What will be the fate of the ICC? The ICC has been criticized for focusing exclucively on prosecutions against Africans. Several African countries have threatened to leave the Court. David Kaye, "Who's Afraid of the International Criminal Court?," 90 *Foreign Affairs*, May/June 2011, at 1, 2. Finally, in January 2016, the ICC opened an investigation outside Africa. International Criminal Court, "ICC Pre-Trial Chamber I Authorizes the Prosecutor to Open an Investigation into the Situation in Georgia" (Press Release 27 January 2016), www.icc-cpi.int. Will broadening the ICC's geographical ambit help or hurt its reputation?

Ad Hoc *International Criminal Tribunals.* Although a permanent international criminal court is an innovation, *ad hoc* international criminal courts set up for a specific region or problem are longstanding. Besides the Nuremberg trials explored above, there have been *ad hoc* international criminal tribunals in Tokyo for the trial of Japanese World War II war criminals, in The Hague (beginning in 1993) for crimes in the former Yugoslavia, and in Arusha (beginning in 1994) for crimes in Rwanda. There are significant differences among the four *ad hoc* tribunals. Among other things, the Nuremberg and Tokyo trials, following the Allied defeat of Germany and Japan, proceeded immediately against the principal leaders of those governments; the Hague and Arusha trials, with no conquests in hand, had to begin with proceedings against figures of lesser consequence. Louis B. Sohn, "From Nazi Germany and Japan to Yugoslavia and Rwanda: Similarities and Differences," 12 *Connecticut Journal of International Law* 209 (1997).

Much criticism has been launched at the Arusha proceedings of the International Criminal Tribunal for Rwanda (ICTR). See Paul J. Magnarella,

Justice in Africa: Rwanda's Genocide, Its Courts, and the UN Criminal Tribunal (2000). In four short months in 1994, Hutus in Rwanda killed almost three quarters of the country's Tutsi minority population. Tutsi exiles in Uganda then invaded Rwanda, overthrew the Hutu regime, and, in turn, committed mass killings. Leslie Haskell & Lars Waldorf, "The Impunity Gap of the International Criminal Tribunal for Rwanda: Causes and Consequences," 34 *Hastings International and Comparative Law Review* 49, 49–50 (2011). As of 2009, all the ICTR prosecutions—90 in all—were of individuals from the overthrown Hutu regime. As one commentator has remarked, "the tribunal's failure to prosecute the [present Tutsi government] would inevitably lead to the objective conclusion that the ICTR was a form of victor's justice." Thierry Cruvellier, *Court of Remorse: Inside the International Criminal Tribunal for Rwanda* 164 (2010). May the ICTR nevertheless usefully contribute to prosecutions, in municipal courts in Rwanda and elsewhere, of those accused of genocide? See Leila Sadat, "Transjudicial Dialogue and the Rwandan Genocide: Aspects of Antagonism and Complementarity," 22 *Leiden Journal of International Law* 543 (2009).

More progress has been made at the International Criminal Tribunal for the former Yugoslavia (ICTY). The ICTY reached out to try some, though not all, of the principal suspected actors, including former Yugoslav President Slobodan Milošević. Milošević's trial was criticized for taking so long—he died in March 2006, when his trial had been underway for more than four years—and for its high costs and procedural confusions. See "Former Yugoslavia: Justice on Trial," *The Economist*, Feb. 28, 2004, at 47. The ICTY was also criticized for being unwilling to rein in "truculent defendants." See Marlise Simons, "As a Defendant Bullies and Boasts, Questions Arise on a Court's Limits," *New York Times*, Apr. 17, 2012, at A3. One commentator concluded: The ICTY "weaves a sad end to the story of a court that was founded by little hope, encouraged some, then jettisoned it all." Eric Gordy, "What Happened to the Hague Tribunal?," *International Herald Tribune*, June 3, 2013, at 6. Nonetheless, the ICTY proceedings constitute the most significant example of an international criminal court's prosecutions since Nuremberg. ICTY case law is voluminous. See the collections of cases, largely ICTY, compiled in *Annotated Leading Cases of International Criminal Tribunals*, vols. 1–50 (André Klip *et al.* eds. 1999–2017).

What political factors contribute to the ability of an international criminal court to work successfully? Will such a court be successful only if it is established and run by occupying powers after a war? Did the states that emerged after the breakup of Yugoslavia cooperate with the ICTY because of the prospect of membership in the European Union? To what extent does the "success" of an international criminal court depend on the court itself?

International Criminal Law in National Courts and Tribunals. National courts, special and ordinary, are also used to prosecute international crimes. We have seen several examples of prosecutions and tort claims in U.S. courts: *Filartiga* in Chapter 1, *Smith* in Chapter 2, and *De Longchamps, Sosa,* and *Kiobel* in Chapter 5. Other countries have been active as well, notably Belgium. See Marlise Simons, "Human Rights Cases Begin to Flood Into Belgian Courts," *New York Times International,* Dec. 27, 2001, at A8. In Spain, a prominent investigating judge, Baltasar Garzón, indicted, among others, the 9/11 terrorist, Osama bin Laden, and Chile's dictator, Augusto Pinochet. However, Garzón himself was indicted in a Spanish court when he opened an investigation into the disappearance of tens of thousands of people during the Spanish Civil War and General Franco's dictatorship. Spanish authorities complained that Garzón's investigation would violate an amnesty granted after Franco's death in 1975 that sought to promote national reconciliation. Graham Keeley, "Judge Baltasar Garzón in the Dock Over Inquiry Into Franco-Era Killings," *The Times (London),* Sept. 10, 2009, *available at* http://www.thetimes.co.uk.

Apparently bolder, a trial court in Guatemala convicted the former dictator of the country for crimes against humanity and genocide for massacres of Ixil villagers in the early 1980s. Elisabeth Malkin, "Former Leader of Guatemala is Guilty of Genocide Against Mayan Group," *New York Times,* May 11, 2013, at A6. However, Guatemala's Constitutional Court vacated the judgment and ordered a retrial, which has been suspended. "Genocide Trial for Guatemala Ex-Dictator Rios Montt Suspended," Reuters, Jan. 11, 2016, http://www.reuters.com/articles/us-guatemala-trial-idUSKCN0UP21F20160111.
Another national approach to reconciliation is the South African process of "transitional justice," involving "truth commissions" that assess allegations of mass violations of human rights by former officials of an ousted government. Truth commissions have also been employed in Latin America and elsewhere. See Ruti G. Teitel, *Transitional Justice* (2000). National prosecutions of international crimes are sometimes ordered and supervised by regional human rights courts such as the European and Inter-American courts of human rights. See Alexandra Huneeus, "International Law by Other Means: The Quasi-Criminal Jurisdiction of Human Rights Courts," 107 *American Journal of International Law* 1 (2013).

Hybrid Courts. An approach used in Bosnia-Herzegovina, East Timor, and Kosovo, "hybrid courts," mixes national and foreign judges on hybrid national/international criminal tribunals. See Laura A. Dickinson, "The Promise of Hybrid Courts," 97 *American Journal of International Law* 295 (2003). The first hybrid court, the Special Court for Sierra Leone, was established in 2002 and transitioned to a residual mechanism in 2013. Although this court was criticized for its slow and expensive pace, it prosecuted and convicted a number of military leaders for crimes against humanity, war crimes, and violations of international humanitarian law. And significantly, in 2012, the Special Court for Sierra Leone found Charles Taylor, the former President of Liberia, guilty of aiding and abetting war crimes and crimes against humanity. Taylor was the first African president to be prosecuted by an international court. The British Foreign Secretary, William Hague, termed the Taylor conviction a "landmark verdict." *Quoted in* Owen Bowcott & Monica Mark, "Charles Taylor Found Guilty of Abetting Sierra Leone War Crimes," *The Guardian*, Apr. 26, 2012. Another hybrid tribunal, the Special Tribunal for Lebanon, addresses certain Lebanese crimes, including terrorism, rather than international law crimes. See Olivia Swaak-Goldman, "Introductory Note to Security Council Resolution 1757 Establishing the Special Tribunal for Lebanon," 46 *International Legal Materials* 989 (2007). Yet another national/international hybrid court, the Extraordinary Chambers in the Courts of Cambodia, was established in 2005 to try former leaders of the Khmer Rouge, accused of killing an estimated 1.7 million Cambodians between 1975 and 1979. For its, at best, mixed record, see Abby Seif, "Seeking Justice in the Killing Fields," 99 *ABA Journal*, Mar. 2013, at 50.

A Toothless Tiger? Forecasting dire consequences in anticipation of the Supreme Court's opinion in *Kiobel* (see Chapter 5), Second Circuit Judge Pierre Leval lamented, "over 65 years after Nuremberg, although the world remains awash in these atrocities, the prohibitions of international law are largely toothless." Pierre N. Leval, "The Long Arm of International Law: Giving Victims of Abuse Their Day in Court," 92 *Foreign Affairs*, Mar./Apr. 2013, at 16. After your study of the various courts and processes devoted to international human rights and criminal law, do you agree? For an excellent review of the work of the ad hoc criminal tribunals and the ICC, see Leila Nadya Sadat, "Crimes Against Humanity in the Modern Era," 107 *American Journal of International Law* 334 (2013).

CHAPTER 8

The Law of the Sea

Much of the oceans—the high seas—has long been regarded as common space, subject to no state's sovereignty. For many years, international law recognized coastal state rights only in internal waters, such as ports, and in a narrow band of oceans near the coast known as the territorial sea. In the mid-20th century, however, what had been a relatively stable customary legal system for the oceans began to disintegrate. Some states asserted jurisdiction over broad coastal zones, seeking to take advantage of advances in technology that allowed mining and drilling for oil and gas on the continental shelf. The ability of foreign trawlers and factory ships to capture and process huge quantities of fish near the shores of coastal states also contributed to proclamations of wide coastal zones. Such coastal state assertions disquieted maritime powers, which feared infringements on traditional navigational freedoms.

The law of the sea has evolved from a set of general rules based on natural law and customary international law into often complex treaty-based regimes involving international organizations and international tribunals. The modern law of the sea was molded by the Third United Nations Conference on the Law of the Sea (UNCLOS III), which officially convened in 1973, following six years of studies and preparatory work by U.N. bodies. After numerous formal negotiating sessions and inter-sessional meetings, the Conference generated the 1982 Convention on the Law of the Sea. The Convention codified many principles previously accepted in customary and treaty law. It also introduced or affirmed new concepts, concerning the exclusive economic zone, fishing rights, the continental shelf, marine scientific research, pollution, transit passage through straits, the breadth of the territorial sea, and rights of landlocked states. Controversial provisions about mining the seabed beyond national jurisdiction delayed the entry into force of the Convention until November 1994, but as of May 2017 there were 168 parties, including most developed states though not the United States. Hundreds of other treaties also shape the modern law of the sea.

In thinking about law of the sea issues, a helpful starting point is to ask where in the oceans an event occurred or a dispute arose. Some controversies occur between ships of different countries on the high seas, a region under no state's sovereignty. We look at the traditional topics of the high seas in Part A and vessels in Part B. There are also a variety of coastal zones. A coastal state's authority depends on the zone in which an incident or activity occurs; the nature of that incident or activity; and the nationality, type, and conduct of any vessels involved. Part C explores assertions of coastal state jurisdiction over parts of the commons and over resources on the continental shelf, in the exclusive economic zone, and in fisheries zones. Part D addresses the territorial sea and straits. Part E turns to a part of the oceans beyond the limits of national jurisdiction—the deep seabed—and in particular to the regime governing deep seabed mining.

It can be misleading to think about the law of the sea in terms of a single legal regime. Law of the sea issues are too diverse. It probably is more helpful to recognize that different regimes govern, for example, marine pollution, warships, and deep seabed mining. In each, the forums available to resolve legal problems and the relative importance of municipal and international law may vary.

A. THE HIGH SEAS

The high seas have traditionally been regarded as international common space, open to all vessels and subject to the sovereignty of no state. The excerpts in this part are separated by three and a half centuries. Hugo Grotius's 1633 treatise was influential in shaping conceptions of the legal status of the high seas. Articles from the 1982 Law of the Sea Convention provide a modern vantage point from which to assess some of the changes in the law governing the high seas.

Hugo Grotius. Grotius (1583–1645), the author of our first reading, was a prodigy. He knew Latin and Greek by age 8, entered university at age 11, edited an encyclopedia at 15, was a lawyer pleading cases in the highest court of the Netherlands at 16, and became Attorney General of the Netherlands by the time he was 24. Grotius gained fame not only as a lawyer but as a diplomat and a political and legal theorist. He is one of the most important figures in the history of international law; we have noted his contributions to modern conceptions of international law in Chapters 2 and 3. Grotius's most famous work, *De Jure Belli ac Pacis* (*On the Law of War and Peace*), was published in 1625.

Grotius and High Seas Freedoms. Grotius's *De Mare Liberum* (*The Freedom of the Seas*), excerpted below, was originally a chapter of *De Jure Praede* (*Commentary on the Law of Prize and Booty*), a work written in 1604–1605. Grotius wrote *De Jure Praede* to support Dutch access to the East Indian trade and to dispute Spanish and Portuguese claims over the high seas. *De Mare Liberum* was separately published in 1609, probably in anticipation of a proclamation by King James I of England that prohibited foreigners from fishing in "British seas" unless they obtained a British license. The translation below is of a 1633 Latin version of the work. Grotius supported his view of the legal regime of the high seas by drawing on natural law reasoning. Recall the discussion of natural law, one of the traditional sources of international law, in Chapter 2.

HUGO GROTIUS, THE FREEDOM OF THE SEAS (1633)

Ralph van Deman Magoffin trans. & James Brown Scott ed. 1916

The delusion is as old as it is detestable with which many men, especially those who by their wealth and power exercise the greatest influence, . . . try to persuade themselves, that justice and injustice are distinguishable the one from the other not by their own nature, but in some fashion merely by the opinion and custom of mankind. . . .

But . . . there have stood forth in every age independent and wise and devout men able to root out this false doctrine from the minds of the simple, and to convict its advocates of shamelessness. . . .

My intention is to demonstrate briefly and clearly that the Dutch—that is to say, the subjects of the United Netherlands—have the right to sail to the East Indies, as they are now doing, and to engage in trade with the people there. I shall base my argument on the following most specific and unimpeachable axiom of the Law of Nations, called a primary rule or first principle, the spirit of which is self-evident and immutable, to wit; Every nation is free to travel to every other nation, and to trade with it.

God Himself says this speaking through the voice of nature; and inasmuch as it is not His will to have Nature supply every place with all the necessaries of life, He ordains that some nations excel in one art and others in another. Why is this His will, except it be that He wished human friendships to be engendered by mutual needs and resources, lest individuals deeming themselves entirely sufficient unto themselves should for that very reason be rendered unsociable? . . . Those therefore who deny this law, destroy this most praiseworthy bond of human fellowship, remove the opportunities for doing mutual service, in a word do violence to Nature herself. For do[es] not the ocean, navigable in every direction with which God has encompassed all the earth, and the regular and the occasional winds which blow now from one quarter and now from another, offer sufficient proof that Nature has given to all peoples a right of access to all other peoples?

[L]et us consider whether [Portugal has] been able to obtain exclusive jurisdiction over the sea and its navigation or over trade. Let us first consider the case of the sea.

Now, in the legal phraseology of the Law of Nations, the sea is called indifferently the property of no one (*res nullius*), or a common possession (*res communis*), or public property (*res publica*). It will be most convenient to explain the signification of these terms if we follow the practice of all the poets since Hesiod, of the philosophers and jurists of the past, and distinguish certain epochs, the divisions of which are marked off perhaps not so much by intervals of time as by obvious logic and essential character. And we ought not to be criticized if in our explanation of a law deriving from nature, we use the authority and definition of those whose natural judgment admittedly is held in the highest esteem.

[C]ommon possession relates to use, as is seen from a quotation from Seneca:

> Every path was free, All things were used in common.

According to his reasoning there was a kind of sovereignty, but it was universal and unlimited. For God had not given all things to this individual or to that, but to the entire human race, and thus a number of persons, as it were *en masse*, were not debarred from being substantially sovereigns or owners of the same thing, which is quite contradictory to our modern meaning of sovereignty. For it now implies particular or private ownership, a thing which no one then had.

[T]he transition to the present distinction of ownerships did not come violently, but gradually, nature herself pointing out the way. For since there are some things, the use of which consists in their being used up, either because having become part of the very substance of the user they can never be used again, or because by use they become less fit for future use, it has become apparent, especially in dealing with the first category, such things as food and drink for example, that a certain kind of ownership is inseparable from use. For "own" implies that a thing belongs to some one person, in such a way that it cannot belong to any other person. By the process of reasoning this was next extended to things of the second category, such as clothes and movables and some living things. . . .

This occupation or possession, however, in the case of things which resist seizure, like wild animals for example, must be uninterrupted or perpetually maintained, but in the case of other things it is sufficient if after physical possession is once taken the intention to possess is maintained. Possession of movables implies seizure, and possession of immovables either the erection of buildings or some determination of boundaries, such as fencing in. . . .

Two conclusions may be drawn from what has thus far been said. The first is, that which cannot be occupied, or which never has been occupied, cannot be the property of any one, because all property has arisen from occupation. The second is, that all that which has been so constituted by nature that although serving some one person it still suffices for the common use of all other persons, is today and ought in perpetuity to remain in the same condition as when it was first created by nature. . . .

The air . . . is not susceptible of occupation; and . . . its common use is destined for all men. For the same reasons the sea is common to all, because it is so limitless that it cannot become a possession of any one, and because it is adapted for the use of all, whether we consider it from the point of view of navigation or of fisheries. . . .

These things therefore are what the Romans call "common" to all men by natural law, or as we have said, "public" according to the law of nations; and indeed they call their use sometimes common, sometimes public. Nevertheless, although those things are with reason said to be *res nullius*, so far as private ownership is concerned, still they differ very much from those things which, though also *res nullius*, have not been marked out for common use, such for example as wild animals, fish, and birds. For if any one seizes those things and assumes possession of them, they can become objects of private ownership, but the things in the former category by the consensus of opinion of all mankind are forever exempt from such private ownership on account of their susceptibility to universal use; and as they belong to all they cannot be taken away from all by any one person any more than what is mine can be taken away from me by you. . . .

The nature of the sea . . . differs from that of the shore, because the sea, except for a very restricted space, can neither easily be built upon, nor inclosed; if the contrary were true yet this could hardly happen without hindrance to the general use. Nevertheless, if any small portion of the sea can be thus occupied, the occupation is recognized. . . .

Now Celsus holds that piles driven into the sea belong to the man who drove them. But such an act is not permissible if the use of the sea be thereby impaired. . . . Labeo . . . holds that in case any . . . construction should be made in the sea, the following injunction is to be enforced: "Nothing may be built in the sea whereby the harbor, the roadstead, or the channel be rendered less safe for navigation."

Now the same principle which applies to navigation applies also to fishing, namely, that it remains free and open to all. Nevertheless there shall be no prejudice if any one shall by fencing off with stakes an inlet of the sea make a fish pond for himself, and so establish a private preserve.

. . . But outside of an inlet this will not hold, for then the common use of the sea might be hindered.

. . . The Portuguese claim as their own the whole expanse of the sea which separates two parts of the world so far distant the one from the other, that in all the preceding centuries neither one has so much as heard of the other. Indeed, if we take into account the share of the Spaniards, whose claim is the same as that of the Portuguese, only a little less than the whole ocean is found to be subject to two nations, while all the rest of the peoples in the world are restricted to the narrow bounds of the northern seas. . . . If in a thing so vast as the sea a man were to reserve to himself from general use nothing more than mere sovereignty, still he would be considered a seeker after unreasonable power. If a man were to enjoin other people from fishing, he would not escape the reproach of monstrous greed. But the man who even prevents navigation, a thing which means no loss to himself, what are we to say of him?

. . . For it is most outrageous for you to appropriate a thing, which both by ordinance of nature and by common consent is as much mine as yours, so exclusively that you will not grant me a right of use in it which leaves it no less yours than it was before. . . .

The last defense of injustice is usually a claim or plea based on prescription or on custom. To this defense therefore the Portuguese have resorted. But the best established reasoning of the law precludes them from enjoying the protection of either plea.

[I]t is impossible to acquire by usucaption or prescription things which cannot become property, that is, which are not susceptible of possession or of quasi-possession, and which cannot be alienated. All of which is true of the sea and its use.

[S]ince the law of nature arises out of Divine Providence, it is immutable; but a part of this natural law is the primary or primitive law of nations, differing from the secondary or positive law of nations, which is mutable. For if there are customs incompatible with the primary law of nations, then, according to the judgment of Vasquez, they are not customs belonging to men, but to wild beasts, customs which are corruptions and abuses, not laws and usages. Therefore those customs cannot become prescriptions by mere lapse of time, cannot be justified by the passage of any law, cannot be established by the consent, the protection, or the practice even of many nations. . . .

The conclusion of the whole matter therefore is that the Portuguese are in possession of no right whereby they may interdict to any nation whatsoever the navigation of the Ocean to the East Indies.

Reasons Supporting Freedom of the Seas. Grotius's view of the high seas, grounded in natural law, was defined fundamentally by the notion of "freedom of the seas": all were to have access to the oceans for various uses; no state could subject the oceans or their resources to its exclusive sovereignty. What did Grotius discern in natural law to support his position that the oceans were *res communis?* He relied on several principles: it was unfair to exclude others from using the oceans' "inexhaustible" resources; the oceans could not be bounded and were an indivisible whole; the oceans could not be occupied or possessed, and things that could not be occupied or seized could not become the property of anyone; and free navigation and commerce were to be preserved, because God "wished human fellowships to be engendered by mutual needs and resources." Which, if any, of these reasons still resonate today?

John Selden and Closed Seas. Grotius's views did not go unchallenged. The best-known response was that of the Englishman John Selden, who published *Mare Clausum* in 1635. Selden argued that the seas could be appropriated, and that various uses of the oceans could diminish the owner's rights. Selden's work supported such British practices as requiring foreigners to obtain fishing licenses, demanding that foreign ships strike their flags in salute to British ships in "British seas," stopping hostilities by foreign ships in those seas, and imposing certain tolls on the passage of foreign vessels.

British Sea Power and High Seas Freedoms. Grotius's notion of the high seas as not subject to exclusive sovereignty came to be generally accepted:

> During the 19th century, British sea power, then supreme, helped consolidate an international maritime regime based on the freedoms of the high seas, freedoms to travel and to fish without coastal state regulation outside a 3-mile territorial sea. This was a customary legal regime, not written in any convention or treaty. It was, however, remarkably effective, respected by most states in times of peace from the end of the Napoleonic Wars in 1815 to the end of World War II in 1945. As a result, for over a century, navies and other users of the oceans could sail freely on seas covering some 70 percent of the earth's surface. Only within a narrow band of 3 miles, the territorial

sea, did coastal states put some legal limits on the mobility of naval forces.

Mark W. Janis, *Sea Power and the Law of the Sea* xiii–xiv (1976).

The High Seas in the Modern Law of the Sea. The 1982 Convention on the Law of the Sea includes a standard modern formulation of international law governing the high seas. What modifications of the Grotian conception of *mare liberum* do Articles 86–90 of the 1982 Convention reflect?

UNITED NATIONS CONVENTION ON THE LAW OF THE SEA, ARTICLES 86–90, 301

Dec. 10, 1982, Senate Treaty Doc. No. 103–39 (1994), 1833 U.N.T.S. 3

Part VII: High Seas

Article 86: Application of the provisions of this Part

The provisions of this Part apply to all parts of the sea that are not included in the exclusive economic zone, in the territorial sea or in the internal waters of a State, or in the archipelagic waters of an archipelagic State. This article does not entail any abridgement of the freedoms enjoyed by all States in the exclusive economic zone in accordance with article 58.

Article 87: Freedom of the high seas

1. The high seas are open to all States, whether coastal or land-locked. Freedom of the high seas is exercised under the conditions laid down by this Convention and by other rules of international law. It comprises, *inter alia,* both for coastal and land-locked States:

(a) freedom of navigation;

(b) freedom of overflight;

(c) freedom to lay submarine cables and pipelines, subject to Part VI;

(d) freedom to construct artificial islands and other installations permitted under international law, subject to Part VI;

(e) freedom of fishing, subject to the conditions laid down in section 2;

(f) freedom of scientific research, subject to Parts VI and XIII.

2. These freedoms shall be exercised by all States with due regard for the interests of other States in their exercise of the freedom of the high seas, and also

with due regard for the rights under this Convention with respect to activities in the Area.

Article 88: Reservation of the high seas for peaceful purposes

The high seas shall be reserved for peaceful purposes.

Article 89: Invalidity of claims of sovereignty over the high seas

No State may validly purport to subject any part of the high seas to its sovereignty.

Article 90: Right of navigation

Every State, whether coastal or land-locked, has the right to sail ships flying its flag on the high seas.

Part XVI: General Provisions . . .

Article 301: Peaceful uses of the seas

In exercising their rights and performing their duties under this Convention, States Parties shall refrain from any threat or use of force against the territorial integrity or political independence of any State, or in any other manner inconsistent with the principles of international law embodied in the Charter of the United Nations.

High Seas Freedoms Today. Article 2 of the 1958 Geneva Convention on the High Seas explicitly designates navigation, fishing, overflight, and the laying of submarine cables and pipelines as high seas freedoms. These are repeated in Article 87 of the 1982 Convention on the Law of the Sea, which adds the freedom of scientific research and the freedom to build artificial islands and other installations permitted under international law to the list of high seas freedoms. Article 87 qualifies the exercise of high seas freedoms in ways that Grotius did not.

States have, from time to time, employed the high seas for military purposes. Could a state declare a military test site in the oceans? Place weapons or military detection devices on the seabed, invoking the freedom of the high seas? What do you make of Articles 88 and 301 of the 1982 Convention? The Convention's negotiating history suggests that these provisions were not intended to restrict the use of force more stringently than allowed under the U.N. Charter. For discussion of international law limits on recourse to force, see Chapter 6, Part A.

The Law of the Sea Convention nowhere defines the high seas. Article 86 provides that the high seas provisions of the 1982 Convention apply outside various coastal zones, but, significantly, does not say that they do not apply in those coastal zones. Some articles in the high seas part of the Convention, such as those relating to the nationality of vessels and the rights and responsibilities of flag states, are relevant in zones of coastal state control. As we will see in Part C of this chapter, some high seas freedoms also apply in a coastal zone known as the exclusive economic zone.

Controlling Activities on the High Seas. If the high seas are generally open to ships for a variety of purposes, who is responsible for maintaining order there? What if a vessel is in an unsafe operating condition, threatening other vessels or the environment? Or if a ship engages in such egregious practices as slave trading, piracy, or the dumping of dangerous chemicals? Some answers are provided in the next part.

B. VESSELS

Jurisdiction and control over the actions of and activities on board vessels on the high seas have traditionally been left to the ship's "flag state," the state of the vessel's nationality. The first excerpt in this part, taken from a 1905 arbitral decision, explores the concept of vessel nationality. Both that decision and the other readings in this part—a British government report about oil spills from ships, a modern U.S. piracy case, and a decision by the International Tribunal for the Law of the Sea—involve complications that arise in trying to balance high seas freedoms with the need to control vessels.

The Muscat Dhows *Arbitration.* In 1904 Great Britain and France agreed to arbitrate a dispute that arose after Muscat (referred to nowadays as Oman) quarantined five Muscat subjects for medical reasons. The five men escaped, and the British, acting at the request of the Sultan of Muscat, recaptured them. These Muscat subjects held French papers that, according to France, gave France the right to exercise jurisdiction over them; France demanded their release. In negotiations with France, Britain agreed to advise the Sultan that he should release the men if France agreed to arbitrate several matters, including the rights of ships flying the French flag (considered in the excerpt below). The case was set against the broader background of efforts to suppress the slave trade and competing French and British assertions of authority in the Persian Gulf.

The *Muscat Dhows Case* was heard in the Permanent Court of Arbitration, discussed in Chapter 4. Muscat was not a party to the arbitration. The Sultan was reportedly dissuaded from sending a Muscat representative to The Hague because of the cost involved, and he asked Britain to act on Muscat's behalf. France, however, was not willing to arbitrate with Muscat if the British acted as Muscat's agent. Because of this French objection, Muscat was not named as a party in the case.

The Nationality of Ships. During the *Muscat Dhows* arbitral proceedings, Great Britain argued that "Frenchifying" the dhows infringed the independence of the Sultan of Muscat, because dhows owned by Muscat nationals were "thereby withdrawn from their natural jurisdiction" and could not be searched by Muscat warships. *The Times* (London), July 25, 1905, at 5. The arbitral tribunal, however, affirmed the general rule that a state may authorize any vessel to fly its flag, the flag being a symbol of its nationality. States normally register ships to establish their nationality and issue documents that those ships can use to prove their nationality. Nationality is often clear, but it took France and Britain over three years after the decision in the *Muscat Dhows Case* to agree on which particular French protégés and dhows were "grandfathered" under the French flag.

CASE OF THE MUSCAT DHOWS

France-Great Britain, 1905, in *The Hague Arbitration Cases* 64 (George G. Wilson ed. 1915)
and available at http://www.pcacases.com/web/view/93

Whereas generally speaking it belongs to every Sovereign to decide to whom he will accord the right to fly his flag and to prescribe the rules governing such grants, and whereas therefore the granting of the French flag to subjects of His Highness the Sultan of Muscat in itself constitutes no attack on the independence of the Sultan,

Whereas nevertheless a Sovereign may be limited by treaties in the exercise of this right, and . . . whereas therefore the question arises, under what conditions Powers which have acceded to the General Act of the Brussels Conference of July 2, 1890 relative to the African Slave Trade, especially to article 32 of this Act, are entitled to authorize native vessels to fly their flags,

Whereas by article 32 of this Act the faculty of the Signatory Powers to grant their flag to native vessels has been limited for the purpose of suppressing slave trading and in the general interests of humanity, irrespective of whether the applicant for the flag may belong to a state signatory of this Act or not, and whereas at any rate France is in relation to Great Britain bound to grant her flag only under the conditions prescribed by this Act,

Whereas in order to attain the above mentioned purpose, the Signatory Powers of the Brussels Act have agreed in its article 32 that the authority to fly the flag of one of the Signatory Powers shall in future only be granted to such native vessels, which shall satisfy all the three following conditions:

> 1.   Their fitters-out or owners must be either subjects of or persons protected by [protégés of] the Power whose flag they claim to fly,

> 2.   They must furnish proof that they possess real estate situated in the district of the authority to whom their application is addressed, or supply a solvent security as a guarantee for any fines to which they may eventually become liable,

> 3.   Such fitters-out or owners, as well as the captain of the vessel, must furnish proof that they enjoy a good reputation, and especially that they have never been condemned for acts of slave trade, . . .

Whereas the aim of the said article 32 is to admit to navigation in the seas infested by slave trade only those native vessels which are under the strictest surveillance of the Signatory Powers, a condition which can only be secured if the owners, fitters-out and crews of such vessels are exclusively subjected to the sovereignty and jurisdiction of the State, under whose flag they are sailing,

[The tribunal examines the meaning of the term "protégé," which is not defined in the 1890 General Act.]

Whereas the fact of having granted before the ratification of the Brussels Act on January 2, 1892 authorizations to fly the French flag to native vessels not satisfying the conditions prescribed by article 32 of this Act was not in contradiction with any international obligation of France,

FOR THESE REASONS, [the tribunal] decides and pronounces as follows:

> 1.   *before the 2nd of January 1892 France was entitled to authorize vessels belonging to subjects of His Highness the Sultan of Muscat to fly the French flag, only bound by her own legislation and administrative rules;*

> 2.   *owners of dhows, who before 1892 have been authorized by France to fly the French flag, retain this authorization as long as France renews it to the grantee;*

> 3.   *after January 2, 1892 France was not entitled to authorize vessels belonging to subjects of His Highness the Sultan of Muscat to fly the French flag, except on condition that their owners or fitters-out had established or should establish that they had been considered and treated by France as her "protégés" before the year 1863*[.]

> *The Importance of Vessel Nationality.* Why is it important for ships to have nationality? On the high seas, a ship is generally immune from the exercise of

jurisdiction except by the authorities of the ship's flag state. In theory, this system ensures that only the flag state is responsible for a vessel's safety and other administrative and social matters. If more than one state were entitled to exercise responsibility for a vessel, there could be significant interference with navigational and other freedoms.

These considerations help explain the disadvantages associated with unregistered, "stateless" vessels. In *United States v. Marino-Garcia* a U.S. court discussed stateless vessels:

> Vessels without nationality are international pariahs. They have no internationally recognized right to navigate freely on the high seas. Moreover, flagless vessels are frequently not subject to the laws of a flag-state. As such they represent "floating sanctuaries from authority" and constitute a potential threat to the order and stability of navigation on the high seas.
>
> The absence of any right to navigate freely on the high seas coupled with the potential threat to order on international waterways has led various courts to conclude that international law places no restrictions upon a nation's right to subject stateless vessels to its jurisdiction.

679 F.2d 1373, 1382 (11th Cir. 1982). Even if there are no restrictions on who may exercise jurisdiction over a stateless vessel, does that mean that those on board a stateless vessel have no protections under international law? See the material on human rights in Chapter 7.

Open Registry. A system of flag state control poses particular difficulties if a flag state cannot or will not control its ships. The *Muscat Dhows* tribunal, in a portion of the opinion not excerpted above, expressed concern that "slavetraders may easily abuse the French flag, for the purpose of escaping from search." Modern challenges relate to unsafe labor conditions and structural defects associated with vessels registered in "open registry" (also known as "flag of convenience") states. A 1970 British committee headed by Lord Rochdale identified six features common to open registry:

> (i)   The country of registry allows ownership and/or control of its merchant vessels by non-citizens;
>
> (ii) Access to the registry is easy. A ship may usually be registered at a consul's office abroad. Equally important, transfer from the registry at the owner's option is not restricted;

(iii) Taxes on the income from the ships are not levied locally or are low. A registry fee and an annual fee, based on tonnage, are normally the only charges made. A guarantee or acceptable understanding regarding future freedom from taxation may also be given;

(iv) The country of registry is a small power with no national requirement under any foreseeable circumstances for all the shipping registered, but receipts from very small charges on a large tonnage may produce a substantial effect on its national income and balance of payments;

(v) Manning of ships by non-nationals is freely permitted; and

(vi) The country of registry has neither the power nor the administrative machinery effectively to impose any government or international regulations; nor has the country the wish or the power to control the companies themselves.

Committee of Inquiry into Shipping, *Report* 51, Cmnd. 4337 (1970).

The risks of harm from open registry vessels may compound. For example, not long before the Liberian-flag *Braer* ran aground off the Shetlands and spilled huge quantities of crude oil—one of the events that led to Lord Donaldson's *Safer Ships, Cleaner Seas* Report excerpted below—the ship's largely Filipino crew had complained to the International Transport Workers' Federation that the ship was not only aging but was undermanned. Jason Benetto, "The Shetland Oil Disaster: Cut-price Recipe for Catastrophe," *Independent on Sunday*, Jan. 10, 1993, at 22. Although flag-of-convenience vessels are not responsible for all vessel safety and pollution problems—the *Exxon Valdez*, which spilled oil off Alaska in 1989, was registered in the United States—the safety record of many such vessels has been questionable. Massive spills from two Liberian-flagged vessels, the *Torrey Canyon* in the North Sea in 1967 and the *Amoco Cadiz* off the Brittany coast in 1978, alerted the public to modern marine pollution dangers, prompting the adoption of some international safety and pollution prevention measures. Other damaging spills off the coasts of France and Spain from the Maltese-flagged *Erika* in 1999 and the Bahamian-flagged *Prestige* in 2001 raised anew questions about how to respond to the practice of open registry.

Figure 8.A
The *Amoco Cadiz* Oil Spill Off the Coast of Brittany, 1978

As of 2016, over 70 per cent of the world fleet flew the flag of countries different from the nationalities of the ships' owners, and over 76 per cent was registered in developing states. Panama, Liberia, and the Marshall Islands have the largest registries, comprising 41 per cent of the world's tonnage. The Bahamas, Cyprus, and Malta also register many vessels. See U.N. Conference on Trade and Development, *Review of Maritime Transport 2016*, at 44–45, UNCTAD/RMT/2016 (U.N. Sales No. E.16.II.D.7, 2016).

SAFER SHIPS, CLEANER SEAS

Report of Lord Donaldson's Inquiry Into the Prevention of Pollution From Merchant Shipping, Cm. 2560 (1994)

On 5 January 1993 one of the Shetland Islanders' worst nightmares became a reality. The [Liberian-registered] MV *BRAER* went onto the rocks at Garths Ness. She was fully laden with 84,700 tonnes of Norwegian Gullfaks crude oil and some 1,600 tonnes of heavy fuel oil bunkers. The weather was atrocious—storm force winds and mountainous seas. There were all the makings of a major economic and ecological disaster for the local community.

In the event the consequences were serious but miraculously less catastrophic than might have been expected. . . .

It must not be forgotten that on 3 December 1992, only a month before the *BRAER* was wrecked off Shetland, the tanker *AEGEAN SEA* was wrecked off La Coruña in northern Spain. . . .

In an ideal world Flag States, whose flags are worn by the world's shipping, would lay down, and enforce upon their own shipowners, standards of design, maintenance and operation which would ensure a very high standard of safety at sea. Coastal States, along whose coasts shipping passes, and Port States, at whose ports or anchorages shipping calls, would have no cause to concern themselves with the maintenance of such standards.

The present system of Flag State Control falls well short of this ideal. At any one time the fleet of any Flag State will be scattered throughout the world. No Flag State has the resources to police its fleet on a continuous and all-embracing basis. The most that it can do is to insist upon periodic surveys and to undertake *ad hoc* inspection if it learns that a ship has suffered a casualty or, for some other reason such as a Port State Control inspection, it suspects that its ship no longer complies with internationally agreed standards. Good shipowners will maintain the seaworthiness of their ships regardless of whether a Flag State periodical survey is imminent. Regrettably, bad shipowners regard the imminence of such a survey as the only reason for spending money on maintenance or repairs and then only if satisfied that the survey will be thorough.

In this situation, even if Flag States were to comply to the full with their responsibilities, Coastal and Port States would have a part to play. They would, in their own interests, be concerned to detect the few unseaworthy ships which had escaped the Flag State net. Their role would be to supplement and support Flag State Control, but not to substitute for it.

Regrettably it is beyond argument that not all Flag States live up to their responsibilities. Figures for deficiencies and detections revealed by Port State Control inspections show that, for example, of 61 Indian registered ships inspected over one in four were so seriously deficient that they had to be detained in port. Over 85 per cent of the inspections of Indian registered ships uncovered deficiencies. India, although a striking example, is by no means alone and a number of other Flag States also have a poor record.

[The United Kingdom's percentage of the world's shipping has declined significantly. The U.K. now depends heavily on foreign-flag vessels to move its goods.]

A State which confers its nationality upon a ship, and thus authorizes it to fly its flag, has an unfettered right to subject that ship to its laws. This enables it to impose and maintain standards of design, construction, equipment, maintenance and operation. Whilst there is no upper limit to these standards, there are lower limits. These stem from the various international Conventions to which Flag States are parties, such as the SOLAS, MARPOL 73/78 and Load Line Conventions, under which Flag States are required to establish that ships flying their flags comply with the provisions of those Conventions and to issue the necessary certificates of compliance. . . .

Economic and competitive considerations effectively prevent Flag States from imposing standards which are higher than those internationally agreed and any improvement in standards is thus only achievable by international agreement. The machinery for such agreement is provided by the International Maritime Organization (IMO). . . .

It is for Flag States individually to decide how to give effect to their international obligations. In some cases the international Conventions specify precise requirements. SOLAS, for example, requires minimum pressures at fire hydrants and MARPOL includes precise formulae for the calculation of positions of ballast tanks. But in other cases, the Conventions merely specify that equipment must be "approved" by the Flag State or be "to the satisfaction of the Flag State." Sometimes such lack of precision is necessary for technical reasons or to allow for innovation. Regrettably in others it is merely designed to conceal differences of view between the members of IMO. . . .

When the international Conventions were originally drafted, most of the world's merchant fleet was owned by, and flew the flags of, the world's major maritime and trading powers. These States had already established survey and inspection of their ships as a matter of public policy aimed at protecting the safety of crews and passengers. While the setting of such standards was not immune from commercial pressures from shipowning interests, their enforcement was not subject to such pressures. This was presumably in reflection of the fact that in the UK, for example, there had been a long history of regulation through the Board of Trade and the fact that most UK trade was carried in UK ships which were subject to the same standards and accordingly competed fairly with one another. States had little or no direct financial interest in shipping and could apply and enforce standards in the interests of public policy without feeling any pressure to maintain or enhance their merchant fleets.

All that has changed. Today few States regard it as consistent with their national status and dignity to be without a register of national shipping of as large a size as possible. Some also regard such a register as a useful source of income. In seeking to achieve this aim, some see no need to limit eligibility to ships whose owners or operators have any connection with the State. They maintain what are called "open" registers. A few such States are landlocked and have no connection with the sea. Rather more include ships which are never likely to call at a national port. Perhaps in recognition of this fact one of the largest and, it has to be said, one of the most efficient, Liberia, maintains its register and discharges its responsibilities from an office in the USA. Relatively few Liberian ships ever call at Monrovia, their usual port of registry. Another example is Vanuatu, which has few foreign exports and whose register is run from the USA and London.

All this might be unobjectionable if, despite the very considerable difficulties in enforcing standards on ships (and shipowners) which have no real connection with the State whose flag the ships fly, agreed international standards were universally enforced. However they are not. The vice of "open" registers is twofold. First, in practice they lead to varying standards of safety. This is easily demonstrated by [statistics on] the incidence of total losses by flag. Second, the existence of "open" registers and the consequent ease with which ships can be transferred to a different register and flag has led to some shipowners shopping around for the registers which have the lowest standards of enforcement and which, in consequence, involve them in the least expense. This is positively encouraged by some of the Flag States concerned which have even been known to advertise competitive "prices" for their survey and certification work.

Limiting Flag State Grants of Nationality? Would it be appropriate for international law to limit state grants of nationality to vessels, in order to help cure some of the problems seen in the *Muscat Dhows Case* and Lord Donaldson's Report? In *Muscat Dhows*, should France have had an unqualified right to determine the conditions under which a ship was entitled to fly the French flag? Would conditions such as those set forth in Article 32 of the General Act of the Brussels Conference of 1890 make sense today? Should there be restrictions on the authority of modern open registry states to register vessels? States have not accepted significant limitations on their right to grant nationality to vessels.

Genuine Link. One limited response to open registry is the requirement, set forth in Article 91 of the Law of the Sea Convention, that "[t]here must exist a genuine link between" a flag state and a vessel registered in that state. However, this requirement is highly indeterminate. Some authorities consider that this requirement could be met by some minimal connection between the flag state and the vessel's crew, officers, or owner. Other authorities deem the "genuine link" requirement simply an aspect of the general obligation of every flag state—set out in Article 94 of the Law of the Sea Convention—to "effectively exercise its jurisdiction and control in administrative, technical and social matters over ships flying its flag." The International Tribunal for the Law of the Sea has adopted the latter view. M/V "Virginia G" Case (Panama/Guinea-Bissau), ITLOS Case No. 19 (2014), ¶¶ 112–13, *available at* www.itlos.org. On "genuine link," see *Nottebohm* in Chapter 7.

Flag State Obligations Set by Multiple Treaties. Besides the 1982 Law of the Sea Convention, numerous other treaties set rules governing ships and shipboard activities. Many contain specific substantive standards. Lord Donaldson's Report mentioned a few examples.

In taking measures related to pollution and safety, the training of officers and crew members, labor conditions, and jurisdiction over activities on board its ships, a flag state must, per Article 94(5) of the Law of the Sea Convention, "conform to generally accepted international regulations, procedures and practices." Such regulations may be embodied in the growing number of international conventions adopted primarily under the auspices of the International Maritime Organization (IMO). The reference to "generally accepted" standards suggests that a State Party to the Convention may be legally obligated to apply detailed standards developed by the IMO even if that state is not a party to the specific treaty that sets the standards. What determines whether a regulation has been "generally accepted"? Although the answer to that question is debated, the "generally accepted" concept may not be identical to the concept of customary international law because even a persistently objecting state may be bound to comply a "generally accepted" standard. See *Paquete Habana* and the other cases about custom in Chapter 2.

Ensuring Effective Flag State Jurisdiction and Control. Is it appropriate to continue to place significant reliance on the obligation of each flag state to exercise administrative and supervisory responsibilities with respect to ships flying its flag? Would a system of inspections and approvals of ship safety by an international regulatory body be preferable to national supervision of merchant vessels—a task often delegated to private organizations? How else could international law and process respond to the challenges of ineffective flag state control?

Coastal State Control of Foreign Flag Vessels. A coastal state may exercise authority over foreign flag merchant vessels while they are in the territorial sea, absent agreement to the contrary. The territorial sea is a zone of coastal state sovereignty that today may extend up to 12 nautical miles—one nautical mile equals 1.15078 miles—from a state's coastal baselines. (In this chapter "miles" refers to nautical miles.) We further examine coastal state jurisdiction in the territorial sea, as well as the right of foreign flag vessels to "innocent passage" through the territorial sea, in Part D of this chapter. As we see in Part C, a coastal state may also exercise limited authority over foreign flag vessels in broader coastal zones.

Port State Control of Foreign Flag Vessels. As noted in Lord Donaldson's Report, port states may exercise some control over substandard ships by detaining them until essential repairs are made. Should the standards used to detain ships in port be subject to uniform international law? Regional port state memoranda of understanding (MOUs)—such as the Paris MOU, https://www.parismou.org—help regulate port state inspections and detentions of vessels, as well as communications among states about substandard ships.

Exceptions to Flag State Jurisdiction on the High Seas. Many treaties, particularly bilateral ones, authorize countries to exercise some degree of jurisdiction over foreign flag vessels on the high seas with respect, for example, to immigration, drug trafficking, or terrorist-related activities. Article 110 of the 1982 Law of the Sea Convention also provides for a limited right to board and inspect documents where "there is reasonable ground for suspecting" that a ship flying a foreign flag is engaged in the slave trade or unauthorized broadcasting, is stateless, or in reality has the same nationality as a boarding warship. For discussion of flag state jurisdiction and these exceptions, see Louis B. Sohn, Kristen Gustafson Juras, John E. Noyes & Erik Franckx, *Law of the Sea in a Nutshell* 70–96 (2d ed. 2010). Should the list in Article 110 be expanded to grant more authority than document inspection, or to encompass additional topics, such as drug trafficking or transporting weapons of mass destruction? Why was additional authority not approved when the Law of the Sea Convention was negotiated?

One traditional exception to flag state jurisdiction on the high seas, recognized in Article 110 of the Law of the Sea Convention and in customary international law, involves piracy. The 2012 opinion of a U.S. federal court in *United States v. Dire*, excerpted below, explores the circumstances and concept of modern piracy.

UNITED STATES V. DIRE

680 F.3d 446 (4th Cir. 2012), *cert. denied*, 568 U.S. 1145 (2013)

The Facts

Opinion by JUDGE KING:

In the early morning hours of April 1, 2010, on the high seas between Somalia and the Seychelles (in the Indian Ocean off the east coast of Africa), the defendants . . . imprudently launched an attack on the USS Nicholas, having confused that mighty Navy frigate for a vulnerable merchant ship. The defendants, all Somalis, were swiftly apprehended and then transported to the Eastern District of Virginia, where they were convicted of the crime of piracy, as proscribed by 18 U.S.C. § 1651, plus myriad other criminal offenses. In this appeal, the defendants challenge their convictions and life plus-eighty-year sentences on several grounds, including that their fleeting and fruitless strike on the Nicholas did not, as a matter of law, amount to a § 1651 piracy offense. As explained below, we reject their contentions and affirm.

According to the trial evidence, the USS Nicholas was on a counter-piracy mission in the Indian Ocean when, lit to disguise itself as a merchant vessel, it encountered the defendants shortly after midnight on April 1, 2010. The Nicholas was approached by an attack skiff operated by defendant Hasan and also carrying defendants Dire and Ali, while defendants Umar and Gurewardher remained with a larger mother-ship some distance away. From their posts on the Nicholas, crew members could see by way of night-vision devices that Hasan was armed with a loaded rocket-propelled grenade launcher (commonly referred to as an "RPG"), and that Dire and Ali carried AK-47 assault rifles.

. . . When the defendants' attack skiff was within sixty feet of the Nicholas's fantail (its lowest and thus most accessible point), Dire and Ali discharged the first shots—bursts of rapid, automatic fire from their AK-47s aimed at the Nicholas and meant to attain its surrender. The Nicholas's crew responded in kind, resulting in an exchange of fire that lasted less than thirty seconds. Bullets from Dire and Ali's AK-47s struck the Nicholas near two of its crew members, but the defendants' brief attack was (thankfully) casualty-free. Dire, Ali, and Hasan then turned their skiff and fled, with the Nicholas in pursuit.

. . . Dire, Ali, and Hasan threw various items from the skiff overboard into the Indian Ocean, discarding the RPG, the AK-47s, and a ladder that would have enabled them to board the Nicholas. About thirty minutes into the pursuit, the Nicholas captured the three defendants in the skiff. Thereafter, the Nicholas chased and captured the two defendants in the mothership. . . .

The defendants' strike on the USS Nicholas was consistent with an accustomed pattern of Somali pirate attacks, designed to seize a merchant ship and then return with the vessel and its crew to Somalia, where a ransom would be negotiated and secured. Indeed, on April 4, 2010, during questioning aboard the Nicholas, the defendants separately confessed to participating willingly in a scheme to hijack a merchant vessel, and they provided details about their operation.

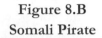

Figure 8.B
Somali Pirate

Municipal Courts and International Law. The *Dire Case* is but one of many examples of municipal courts deciding issues related to the international law of the sea. Another piracy case is *United States v. Smith* in Chapter 2. Municipal courts traditionally have been a force in developing and articulating a uniform maritime law, applicable to a wide range of issues. We see another example later in this chapter, in *Regina v. Keyn*.

Cases arising in municipal courts may involve maritime treaties or municipal statutes embodying such treaties. The *Dire Case* reminds us that these courts may also apply the law of nations. For other examples of U.S. courts interpreting the law of nations or customary international law, see *Filartiga*, which we studied in Chapter 1, *Paquete Habana* and *United States v. Smith* in Chapter 2, and *De Longchamps* and *Sosa v. Alvarez-Machain* in Chapter 5. As you read the next excerpt, consider whether you agree with the *Dire* district court and court of appeals that the meaning of "piracy in violation of the law of nations" as proscribed in 18 U.S.C. § 1651 may change over time. Or, as another federal district court had ruled, should the meaning of piracy be fixed as of 1819, when the U.S. anti-piracy statute was enacted? Recall that in *Sosa*, the U.S. Supreme Court concluded that the meaning of the law of nations, incorporated by reference in the Alien Tort Statute, was not entirely static.

United States v. Dire
The Law

In these consolidated appeals, the defendants first contend that their ill-fated attack on the USS Nicholas did not constitute piracy under 18 U.S.C. § 1651, which provides in full:

> Whoever, on the high seas, commits the crime of piracy as defined by the law of nations, and is afterwards brought into or found in the United States, shall be imprisoned for life.

According to the defendants, the crime of piracy has been narrowly defined for purposes of § 1651 as robbery at sea, i.e., seizing or otherwise robbing a vessel. Because they boarded the Nicholas only as captives and indisputably took no property, the defendants contest their convictions on Count One [piracy], as well as the affixed life sentences.

[The district court, in United States v. Hasan, 747 F. Supp. 2d 599, 602 (E.D. Va. 2010), referred to here as *Hasan I*, denied the defendants' motion to dismiss the piracy count, concluding that "piracy under the law of nations" encompassed acts of violence committed on the high seas for private ends.]

The *Hasan I* opinion was issued on the heels of the August 17, 2010 published opinion in *United States v. Said*, 757 F. Supp. 2d 554 (E.D. Va. 2010), wherein a different judge of the Eastern District of Virginia essentially took these defendants' view of the piracy offense by recognizing a robbery element. Like these defendants, the *Said* defendants have been charged with piracy under 18 U.S.C. § 1651 for attacking—but not seizing or otherwise robbing—a United States Navy ship. The *Said* court . . . dismiss[ed] the piracy count from the indictment because no taking of property was alleged.

As the *Said* court recognized, article I of the Constitution accords Congress the power "[t]o define and punish Piracies and Felonies committed on the high Seas, and Offences against the Law of Nations." . . . Examining the Act of 1819 [the predecessor of 18 U.S.C. § 1651] in its *United States v. Smith* decision of 1820, the Supreme Court [had] "no hesitation in declaring, that piracy, by the law of nations, is robbery upon the sea."

Invoking the principle that a court "must interpret a statute by its ordinary meaning at the time of its enactment," the *Said* court deemed *Smith* to be the definitive authority on the meaning of piracy under 18 U.S.C. § 1651. . . .

The *Said* court . . . noted, "the only substantive change to § 1651 since its enactment has been the removal of the death penalty for the offense as opposed to the current penalty of life imprisonment."

[T]he *Said* court [deemed] contemporary international law sources defining piracy to encompass the *Said* defendants' violent conduct . . . to be too "unsettled" to be authoritative. The court further determined that relying on those international law sources would violate due process, explaining that, if "the definition of piracy [were adopted] from [the] debatable international sources whose promulgations evolve over time, defendants in United States courts would be required to constantly guess whether their conduct is proscribed by § 1651[,] render[ing] the statute unconstitutionally vague." Thereby undeterred from employing the "clear and authoritative" definition in *Smith* "of piracy as sea robbery," the court dismissed the piracy count from the *Said* indictment.

[In *Hasan I*] the district court took a different tack[.] [That] court focused on piracy's unusual status as a crime defined by the law of nations and subject to universal jurisdiction.

The district court began by recognizing that, "[f]or centuries, pirates have been universally condemned as *hostis humani generis*—enemies of all mankind— because they attack vessels on the high seas, and thus outside of any nation's territorial jurisdiction, . . . with devastating effect to global commerce and navigation."

[According to the district court in *Hasan I*,] "general piracy can be prosecuted by any nation, irrespective of the presence of a jurisdictional nexus." (citing *Sosa v. Alvarez-Machain*, 542 U.S. 692, 762 (2004) (Breyer, J., concurring in part and concurring in the judgment) ("[I]n the 18th century, nations reached consensus not only on the substantive principle that acts of piracy were universally wrong but also on the jurisdictional principle that any nation that found a pirate could prosecute him.")). Importantly, though, "because it is created by international consensus, general piracy is restricted in substance to those offenses that the international community agrees constitute piracy."

[A]s the district court recounted, "Congress passed the Act of 1819 to make clear that it wished to proscribe not only piratical acts that had a nexus to the United States, but also piracy as an international offense subject to universal jurisdiction." . . .

Having noted that "[n]o other Supreme Court decision since *Smith* has directly addressed the definition of general piracy," and recognizing the necessity of looking to foreign sources to determine the law of nations, the district court then focused on case law from other countries. The court deemed the Privy Council of England's 1934 decision in *In re Piracy Jure Gentium*, [1934] A.C. 586 (P.C.), to be "[t]he most significant foreign case dealing with the question of how piracy is defined under international law."

[T]he Privy Council [ruled]: "Actual robbery is not an essential element in the crime of piracy jure gentium. A frustrated attempt to commit a piratical robbery is equally piracy jure gentium."

[T]he district court in *Hasan I* [also] examined Kenya's 2006 *Republic v. Ahmed* prosecution of "ten Somali suspects captured by the United States Navy on the high seas"—"[t]he most recent case on [general piracy] outside the United States of which [the district court was] aware." The High Court of Kenya affirmed the *Ahmed* defendants' convictions for piracy *jure gentium*, culling from international treaties a modern definition of piracy that encompasses acts of violence and detention.

As detailed in *Hasan I*, "there are two prominent international agreements that have directly addressed, and defined, the crime of general piracy." The first of those treaties is the Geneva Convention on the High Seas (the "High Seas Convention"), which was adopted in 1958 and ratified by the United States in 1961, rendering the United States one of today's sixty-three parties to that agreement. . . .

The second pertinent treaty is the United Nations Convention on the Law of the Sea (the "UNCLOS"), which has amassed 162 parties since 1982—albeit not the United States, which has not ratified the UNCLOS "but has recognized that its baseline provisions reflect customary international law." [Article 101 of] the UNCLOS provides that

[p]iracy consists of any of the following acts:

(a)   any illegal acts of violence or detention, or any act of depredation, committed for private ends by the crew or the passengers of a private ship or a private aircraft, and directed:

(i)   on the high seas, against another ship or aircraft, or against persons or property on board such ship or aircraft;

(ii)   against a ship, aircraft, persons or property in a place outside the jurisdiction of any State;

(b)   any act of voluntary participation in the operation of a ship or of an aircraft with knowledge of facts making it a pirate-ship or aircraft;

(c)   any act of inciting or of intentionally facilitating an act described in subparagraph (a) or (b).

[T]he UNCLOS . . . "defines piracy in exactly the same terms as the [High Seas Convention], with only negligible stylistic changes." The court also observed that the UNCLOS "represents the most recent international statement regarding the definition . . . of piracy."

"Having concluded that Congress's proscription of 'piracy as defined by the law of nations' in 18 U.S.C. § 1651 necessarily incorporates modern developments in international law," the district court next endeavored to "discern the definition of piracy under the law of nations at the time of the alleged offense in April 2010." In so doing, the court observed that the law of nations is ascertained today via the same path followed in 1820 by the Supreme Court in *Smith*: consultation of " 'the works of jurists, writing professedly on public law[s]' "; consideration of " 'the general usage and practice of nations' "; and contemplation of " 'judicial decisions recognising and enforcing that law.' " (quoting *Smith*, 18 U.S. (5 Wheat.) at 160–61). Engaging in that analysis, the court concluded:

As of April 1, 2010, the law of nations, also known as customary international law, defined piracy to *include* acts of violence committed on the high seas for private ends without an actual taking. More specifically, . . . the definition of general piracy under modern customary international law is, at the very least, reflected in Article 15 of the 1958 High Seas Convention and Article 101 of the 1982 UNCLOS.

[The *Hasan* I] court recognized: "UNCLOS's definition of general piracy has a norm-creating character and reflects an existing norm of customary international law that is binding on even those nations that are not a party to the Convention, including the United States."

[E]ven accepting that "actual robbery on the high seas" was once an essential element of general piracy, "the view that general piracy does not require an actual robbery on the sea has certainly gained traction since the Nineteenth Century, as evidenced by [intervening case law], the Harvard Draft Convention on Piracy, the High Seas Convention, and UNCLOS." Additionally, the court recognized that "[c]ontemporary scholarly sources . . . appear to agree that the definition of piracy in UNCLOS represents customary international law." "While writers on the issue do present disagreements regarding the definition of general piracy," the court acknowledged, "such disagreements do not implicate the core definition provided in UNCLOS" (explaining that "writers [instead] disagree about the outer boundaries of the definition of general piracy, such as whether UNCLOS's requirement of 'private ends' prohibits its application to terrorist activities, or whether piracy can arise in situations involving just one ship rather than two"). . . .

The *Hasan I* opinion further rejected the *Said*-approved theory "that applying the contemporary customary international law definition of general piracy violates fundamental due process protections." According to *Hasan I,* "§ 1651's express incorporation of the definition of piracy provided by 'the law of nations,' which is today synonymous with customary international law, provides fair warning of what conduct is proscribed by the statute." In support of that conclusion, the district court in *Hasan I* recapped the Supreme Court's 1820 holding in *Smith* "that, by incorporating the definition of piracy under the law of nations, Congress had proscribed general piracy as clearly as if it had enumerated the elements of the offense in the legislation itself."

[The district court in *Hasan I* concluded that the facts supported an allegation of piracy against the defendants. At trial, all defendants were convicted of piracy, and they appealed their convictions.]

We . . . agree with the district court that the definition of piracy under the law of nations, at the time of the defendants' attack on the USS Nicholas and continuing today, had for decades encompassed their violent conduct. That definition, spelled out in the UNCLOS, as well as the High Seas Convention before it, has only been reaffirmed in recent years as nations around the world have banded together to combat the escalating scourge of piracy. For example, in November 2011, the United Nations Security Council adopted Resolution 2020, recalling a series of prior resolutions approved between 2008 and 2011 "concerning the situation in Somalia"; expressing "grave[ ] concern[ ] [about] the ongoing threat that piracy and armed robbery at sea against vessels pose"; and emphasizing "the need for a comprehensive response by the international community to repress piracy and armed robbery at sea and tackle its underlying causes." Of the utmost significance, Resolution 2020 reaffirmed "that international law, as reflected in the [UNCLOS], sets out the legal framework applicable to combating piracy and armed robbery at sea." Because the district court correctly applied the UNCLOS definition of piracy as customary international law, we reject the defendants' challenge to their Count One piracy convictions, as well as their mandatory life sentences.

Piracy and Universal Jurisdiction. As the *Dire* court indicated, when a vessel is suspected of piracy, a warship may do more than merely board and inspect documents. According to Article 105 of the Law of the Sea Convention, on the high seas, "every State may seize a pirate ship[,] arrest the persons and seize the property on board[, and] decide upon the penalties to be imposed[.]" States may, in short, exercise universal jurisdiction over pirates. We met the concept of universal jurisdiction when we studied *Filartiga* (Chapter 1), *Smith, Furundžija,* and *jus cogens* (Chapter 2), and *Sosa* and *Kiobel* (Chapter 4). Should piracy be subject to more severe enforcement measures than other egregious conduct at sea? Why was piracy historically singled out for special treatment? Perhaps it was in part because pirates were often cruel, committing despicable acts against those they encountered. But piracy also threatened core values associated with the traditional concepts of the law of the sea. Pirates in control of a vessel would hardly subject themselves to the "flag state control" that was supposed to help assure order on the high seas! And pirates interfered with others' freedom of navigation and with the free flow of commerce.

The Scope of Modern Piracy. Although the *Dire* court affirmed that modern piracy is not limited to "robbery at sea," the scope of piracy is nonetheless restricted. What are the characteristics of modern piracy? Read carefully Article 101 of the Law of the Sea Convention, quoted in *Dire.* Why is the definition of piracy so narrow? The narrow definition may in part reflect the desire to create only a limited exception from traditional principles of flag state control and high seas freedoms.

Other Measures to Control Violence at Sea. When in 1985 terrorists boarded the passenger ship *Achille Lauro* in port, took control of the vessel on the high seas, and threw a passenger overboard, many observers concluded no act of piracy had been committed. In response, the International Maritime Organization prepared the 1988 Convention for the Suppression of Unlawful Acts (SUA) against the Safety of Maritime Navigation, which does apply to such conduct. The SUA Convention has been widely accepted; as of May 2017, there were 166 contracting parties representing 95.16 per cent of the world's shipping tonnage.

Piracy and Armed Conflict. When pirates are seized, then tried and convicted in municipal courts, they are treated as criminals. Why should international law not regard pirate attacks—which justify responses by military forces—as armed attacks and invoke the law of war? If there were a "war on piracy," would pirates be entitled to prisoner of war status or other rights under international humanitarian law? Compare the treatment of terrorists under international humanitarian law, considered in Chapter 6. Do organized terrorists pose more of an existential threat to states than do pirates, thus somehow justifying use of a different international legal paradigm?

Piracy and Privateering. Historically, the United States and other countries commissioned private ships as privateers, issuing letters of marque and reprisal that authorized them to attack and capture enemy vessels as well as pirates. See Article I, Section 8 of the U.S. Constitution. A privateer acting within the scope of its commission could itself avoid charges of piracy, certainly in the courts of its commissioning country. The 1856 Paris Declaration Respecting Maritime Law proclaimed that "[p]rivateering is, and remains abolished," 1 *American Journal of International Law Supplement* 89 (1907), and governments have abandoned its use. Why is privateering no longer tolerated? Why are only government warships authorized to seize pirate or enemy vessels?

Contemporary Piracy. Recent decades have seen an upsurge in piracy, along with what is known as "armed robbery against ships," a phrase referring to piratical acts committed in internal waters or the territorial sea. Hundreds of pirate attacks have occurred off the coast of Somalia, off West Africa, and in the waters of southeast Asia. Efforts to respond to piracy involve complex legal and foreign policy issues related to arms trafficking, networks used to finance pirates, human rights, international development aid, insurance law, criminal law, and the use of military forces, as well as law of the sea issues. International organizations have been involved in anti-piracy efforts. For example, the United Nations Security Council has adopted resolutions authorizing foreign warships to enter the territorial waters of Somalia to repress pirates; the International Maritime Organization has developed anti-piracy guidelines for flag states and shippers; and various U.N. agencies have provided assistance to African countries to train prosecutors and build prisons for pirates. Several treaties and declarations set out cooperative measures to deter or punish acts of piracy. For background, see the websites of the International Maritime Organization, which regularly prepares piracy reports (http://www.imo.org),

Piracy Studies, which provides academic research and commentary (http://piracy-studies.org), and the International Maritime Bureau Piracy Reporting Centre of the International Chamber of Commerce (https://www. icc-ccs.org/piracy-reporting-centre).

Nationality of Claims. What should happen if a non-flag state illegally interferes with a flag state's vessel, *i.e.*, in situations not involving piracy or some other legal basis for interference? If a vessel's crew members, owners, and cargo interests suffer injury through actions of a non-flag state, may the vessel's flag state pursue a claim on behalf of those various entities if they are not of the same nationality as the flag state? The issue arose in the 1999 *Saiga Case*, excerpted below. Although the *Saiga* was flying the flag of Saint Vincent and the Grenadines, a corporation from Cyprus owned the vessel, a Scottish corporation managed it, a Swiss corporation chartered it, its master and crew were Ukrainians, and some Senegalese nationals were employed on board. Guinea argued that Saint Vincent and the Grenadines was not entitled to represent the interests of the *Saiga*'s employees, crew, or cargo owners. As seen in the excerpt below, the International Tribunal for the Law of the Sea (ITLOS) disagreed.

The Saiga Case. The *Saiga*, a tanker flying the flag of Saint Vincent and the Grenadines, was engaged in supplying fuel oil to fishing boats inside Guinea's 200-mile exclusive economic zone but outside the 24-mile limit of the contiguous zone, a zone in which international law recognizes the customs authority of coastal states. We discuss the EEZ and the contiguous zone in Part C. On October 28, 1997, a Guinean patrol craft attacked the *Saiga*, arrested it, and brought the vessel and its crew to port in Conakry, Guinea, where the master was detained and the cargo of fuel oil was discharged. Guinea claimed that supplying fuel to fishing vessels violated Guinean customs laws. Criminal charges were brought in Guinea against the *Saiga*'s master, who received a suspended sentence of six months imprisonment and a fine. The dispute was brought to the ITLOS, where Saint Vincent and the Grenadines claimed, *inter alia*, that Guinea interfered with the navigation rights of a Vincentian vessel and used excessive force in stopping and arresting the vessel. The ITLOS, in its 1999 judgment, ruled in favor of Saint Vincent and the Grenadines on several issues, awarding that state $2,123,357 as compensation. The excerpt below concerns the right of the flag state to seek relief for injuries affecting a range of affected parties.

THE M/V "SAIGA" (NO. 2)

International Tribunal for the Law of the Sea, *M/V "SAIGA" (No. 2) (Saint Vincent and the Grenadines* v. *Guinea), Judgment, ITLOS Reports 1999,* Kluwer Law International, p. 10, at p. 48, paras. 106-107, *available at* http://www.itlos.org

[T]he [1982 Law of the Sea] Convention considers a ship as a unit, as regards the obligations of the flag State with respect to the ship and the right of a flag State to seek reparation for loss or damage. . . . Thus the ship, every thing on it, and every person involved or interested in its operations are treated as an entity linked to the flag State. The nationalities of these persons are not relevant.

[There are] two basic characteristics of modern maritime transport: the transient and multinational composition of ships' crews and the multiplicity of interests that may be involved in the cargo on board a single ship. A container vessel carries a large number of containers, and the persons with interests in them may be of many different nationalities. This may also be true in relation to cargo on board a break-bulk carrier. Any of these ships could have a crew comprising persons of several nationalities. If each person sustaining damage were obliged to look for protection from the State of which such person is a national, undue hardship would ensue.

> *Third-party Settlement of Law of the Sea Disputes and the International Tribunal for the Law of the Sea.* The ITLOS, which decided the *Saiga Case*, is one of several new international courts that have been created in recent decades. See Chapter 5, Part C on the proliferation of international courts and tribunals. The 1982 Convention on the Law of the Sea provides for obligatory reference of certain disputes to third-party tribunals, by unilateral action filed by just one state, if negotiated settlements fail. If states parties to a dispute do not agree on the same forum, the case will usually go to binding arbitration. In the merits stage of the *Saiga Case*, however, the ITLOS obtained jurisdiction because of an agreement between the parties. The ITLOS, a court created by the Law of the Sea Convention, is located in Hamburg, Germany. Open to all countries (and in a few situations to individuals), the subject matters that the ITLOS may hear are limited to ocean law issues. Compare the ITLOS to the International Court of Justice (Chapter 5), the European Court of Human Rights (Chapters 1 and 7), and the International Tribunal for the former Yugoslavia (Chapters 2 and 6).

———————

Figure 8.C
International Tribunal for the Law of the Sea, Hamburg, Germany

Limits of the Vessel-as-Unit Concept. Should the *Saiga Case*'s vessel-as-unit doctrine apply when some of the crew members on a foreign flag vessel are nationals of the coastal state that has detained the vessel? The ITLOS thought so in the *Arctic Sunrise Case* decided late in 2013, involving Russia's seizure of a Greenpeace vessel. Arctic Sunrise Case (Netherlands v. Russia), ITLOS Case No. 22, Prompt Release, *available at* http://www.itlos.org. Suppose that a company with a nationality different from that of the flag state owns cargo on a vessel of the flag state, and that the cargo has been damaged by another state's illegal act. Should the company, or the state of the company's nationality, be precluded from pursuing a claim for that damage? Is only the flag state entitled to pursue the claim? What if the flag state is unwilling to do so? The International Law Commission in its 2006 Draft Articles on Diplomatic Protection concluded that

> [t]he right of the State of nationality of the members of the crew of a
> ship to exercise diplomatic protection is not affected by the right of
> the State of nationality of a ship to seek redress on behalf of such
> crew members, irrespective of their nationality, when they have been

injured in connection with an injury to the vessel resulting from an internationally wrongful act.

Report of the International Law Commission on the Work of its Fifty-eighth Session, art. 18, U.N. Doc. A/61/10 (2006), 2 *Yearbook of the International Law Commission*, U.N. Doc. A/CN.4/SER.A.2006/Add.1 (Part 2), at 25 (2013) (U.N. Sales No. 12.V.13 (Part 2)). Should affected crew members or cargo interests have to rely on a state to pursue claims on their behalf in an international forum, as they did in the *Saiga Case*? Compare *Nottebohm* in Chapter 7.

C. THE CONTINENTAL SHELF, FISHERIES ZONES, AND THE EXCLUSIVE ECONOMIC ZONE

In the mid-20th century, coastal states began to make claims with respect to zones of the oceans beyond the narrow territorial sea over which states traditionally had asserted sovereignty. See Figure 8.D. In this part, we first examine the regime of the continental shelf, initiated through unilateral proclamation but now developed as treaty law. We then look at coastal state claims to fisheries zones. These claims contributed to acceptance of coastal state rights over fisheries in the exclusive economic zone (EEZ). The seaward extension of national jurisdiction has affected both access to and management of ocean resources.

The Truman Proclamation on the Continental Shelf. The Truman Proclamation on the continental shelf was a significant event in the 20th-century movement toward extended coastal state jurisdiction. In June 1943, U.S. Secretary of the Interior Harold Ickes wrote to President Franklin Roosevelt:

> The war has impressed us with the necessity for an augmented supply of natural resources. In this connection I draw your attention to the importance of the Continental Shelf not only to the defense of our country, but more particularly as a storehouse of natural resources. The extent of these resources can only be guessed at and needs careful investigating.

Figure 8.D
Coastal Zones Under the 1982 Convention on the Law of the Sea

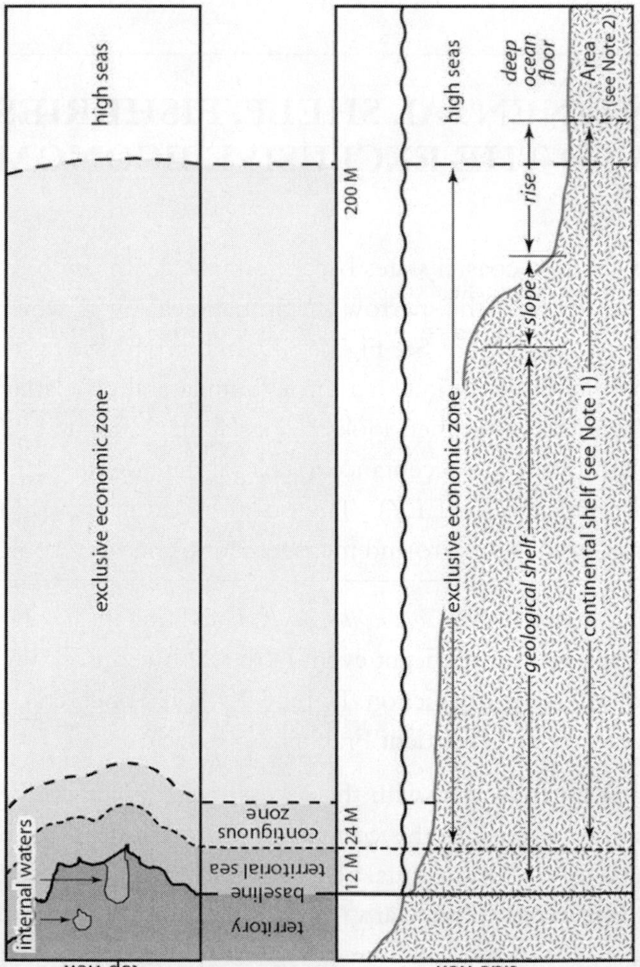

Note 1: The legal continental shelf comprises the seabed and subsoil extending beyond a coastal state's territorial sea to at least 200 miles from that state's baseline; in some areas the legal continental shelf may extend beyond this 200-mile limit. See Article 76, Law of the Sea Convention.

Note 2: The Area is defined as "the seabed and ocean floor and subsoil thereof, beyond the limits of national jurisdiction." Article 1(1), Law of the Sea Convention.

Note 3: "M" refers to nautical miles. One nautical mile equals 6076.115 feet (1852 meters).

The Continental Shelf extending some 100 or 150 miles from our shores forms a fine breeding place for fish of all kinds; it is an excellent hiding place for submarines; and since it is a continuation of our continent, it probably contains oil and other resources similar to those found in our States.

I suggest the advisability of laying the ground work now for availing ourselves fully of the riches in this submerged land and in the waters over them. The legal and policy problems involved, both international and domestic, are many and complex. In the international field, it may be necessary to evolve new concepts of maritime territorial limits beyond three miles, and of rights to occupy and exploit the surface and the subsoil of the open sea.

[1945] 2 *Foreign Relations of the United States* 1481. Ickes referred to "maritime territorial limits beyond three miles" because the United States, like many other states, claimed sovereignty over a three-mile territorial sea. In 1988 the United States extended its territorial sea to 12 miles, a step consistent with Article 3 of the 1982 Convention on the Law of the Sea. See John E. Noyes, "United States of America Presidential Proclamation No. 5298: A 12-Mile U.S. Territorial Sea," 4 *International Journal of Estuarine and Coastal Law* 142 (1989).

President Roosevelt reacted favorably to Ickes's suggestion regarding the continental shelf in a memorandum to Secretary of State Cordell Hull:

I think Harold Ickes has the right slant on this. For many years I have felt that the old three-mile limit . . . should be superseded by a rule of common sense. For instance, the Gulf of Mexico is bounded on the south by Mexico and on the north by the United States. In parts of the Gulf, shallow water extends very many miles offshore. It seems to me that the Mexican Government should be entitled to drill for oil in the southern half of the Gulf and we in the northern half of the Gulf. That would be far more sensible than allowing some European nation, for example, to come in there and drill.

[1945] 2 *Foreign Relations of the United States* 1482.

Treaties or Unilateral Action? The State Department's Office of Economic Affairs, reviewing Ickes's proposal and another proposal to establish U.S. fisheries conservation zones, argued that the proposals constituted "so significant a departure from past practices under the law of nations" that they "could, if proper precautions were not taken, lead to misunderstanding, suspicion, and opposition on the part of many other countries." The Office argued for international consultation with, and the "concurrence" of, various states. One or both of the U.S. proposals were informally communicated to Canada, Cuba, Denmark, France, Iceland, Mexico, the Netherlands, Norway, Portugal, the Soviet Union, and the United Kingdom. *Id.* at 1485–86, 1510. Some states suggested negotiating international agreements concerning resources outside the territorial sea, but the United States proceeded unilaterally. Was this appropriate?

THE TRUMAN PROCLAMATION

Proclamation 2667, Policy of the United States With Respect to the Natural
Resources of the Subsoil and Sea Bed of the Continental Shelf,
Sept. 28, 1945, 3 C.F.R. 67 (1943–1948 Compilation)

WHEREAS the Government of the United States of America, aware of the long range world-wide need for new sources of petroleum and other minerals, holds the view that efforts to discover and make available new supplies of these sources should be encouraged; and

WHEREAS its competent experts are of the opinion that such resources underlie many parts of the continental shelf off the coasts of the United States of America, and that with modern technological progress their utilization is already practicable or will become so at an early date; and

WHEREAS recognized jurisdiction over these resources is required in the interest of their conservation and prudent utilization when and as development is undertaken; and

WHEREAS it is the view of the Government of the United States that the exercise of jurisdiction over the natural resources of the subsoil and sea bed of the continental shelf by the contiguous nation is reasonable and just, since the effectiveness of measures to utilize or conserve those resources would be contingent upon cooperation and protection from the shore, since the continental shelf may be regarded as an extension of the land-mass of the coastal nation and thus naturally appurtenant to it, since these resources frequently form a seaward extension of a pool or deposit lying within the territory, and since self-protection compels the coastal nation to keep close watch over activities off its shores which are of the nature necessary for utilization of these resources;

NOW, THEREFORE, I, HARRY S. TRUMAN, President of the United States of America, do hereby proclaim the following policy of the United States of America with respect to the natural resources of the subsoil and sea bed of the continental shelf.

Having concern for the urgency of conserving and prudently utilizing its natural resources, the Government of the United States regards the natural resources of the subsoil and sea bed of the continental shelf beneath the high seas but contiguous to the coasts of the United States as appertaining to the United States, subject to its jurisdiction and control. In cases where the continental shelf extends to the shores of another State, or is shared with an adjacent State, the boundary shall be determined by the United States and the State concerned in accordance with equitable principles. The character as high seas of the waters above the continental shelf and the right to their free and unimpeded navigation are in no way thus affected.

Latin American Coastal Zones. Following the Truman Proclamation, Mexico issued a proclamation claiming sovereign rights over its adjacent continental shelf and the superjacent resources. Several other Latin American countries, including Argentina, Chile, Costa Rica, El Salvador, and Peru, soon claimed rights up to 200 miles from their coasts. Although those states cited U.S. action as precedent for their assertions of authority over broad coastal zones, each responded to its own set of national goals. Chile, for example, was concerned to protect its new offshore whaling industry when it issued its proclamation, and Peru sought to reserve rich offshore fisheries for its own citizens. The states making these claims typically disavowed any intention of interfering with freedom of navigation. After the Truman Proclamation, could the United States persuasively object to assertions by other coastal states of extensive authority over coastal zones?

Evolution of the Legal Concept of the Continental Shelf. These unilateral proclamations contributed to a process by which the regime of the continental shelf gained recognition in international law. In 1951 the International Law Commission adopted draft articles on the continental shelf, and the ILC's work contributed significantly to the 1958 Geneva Convention on the Continental Shelf. The International Court of Justice addressed the contribution of the 1958 Convention to the crystallization of customary international law in the 1969 *North Sea Continental Shelf Cases*, which appear at the end of Chapter 2. The ICJ emphasized that the continental shelf was to be considered the "natural prolongation" of the land territory of a state.

The Limits of the Continental Shelf. The continental shelf was one of many issues addressed during the Third United Nations Conference on the Law of the Sea (UNCLOS III), where the 1982 Convention on the Law of the Sea was negotiated. One matter in controversy was the definition of the continental shelf. Article 1 of the 1958 Convention on the Continental Shelf defined the continental shelf as the seabed and subsoil "adjacent to the coast" but beyond the territorial sea, extending "to a depth of 200 metres or, beyond that limit, to where the depth of the superjacent waters admits of the exploitation of the natural resources" of the seabed or subsoil. This definition was controversial, in part because of its ambiguities. Could a spot hundreds of miles offshore be "adjacent to the coast"? The phrase "admits of the exploitation of the natural resources" could encompass scooping up a basket of gravel, as well as drilling for oil, which could be more difficult in deeper water. Furthermore, under this definition, the limits of the continental shelf could change as technology changed, perhaps extending even thousands of miles beyond the physical continental shelf.

Article 76 of the 1982 Law of the Sea Convention provides a more certain definition than does Article 1 of the 1958 Convention. According to Article 76, each coastal state is entitled to a continental shelf, beyond its territorial sea, of at least 200 miles from its baselines (discussed below)—a political concession to states with geologically short shelves. A state with a geologically broader shelf must, in setting the legal limits of the shelf beyond 200 miles, apply detailed scientific criteria set out in Article 76. Article 76(8) requires a state seeking to establish an outer limit beyond 200 miles to submit supporting data to the Commission on the Limits of the Continental Shelf (CLCS), a technical body created by the 1982 Convention. If the coastal state sets the outer limit of its continental shelf "on the basis of" recommendations of the CLCS, the resulting outer limit is "final and binding." In no case may the outer limit of the continental shelf extend beyond the further seaward of (a) 350 miles from the baseline, or (b) 100 miles beyond the point at which the ocean depth reaches 2,500 meters.

Rights and Duties on the Continental Shelf. In addition to debating the outer limit of the continental shelf, the delegates to UNCLOS III also addressed the legal status of the shelf. According to Articles 77 and 78 of the 1982 Law of the Sea Convention, set out below, what is the balance struck between coastal state rights and the rights of other states with regard to the continental shelf and activities on and above it?

UNITED NATIONS CONVENTION ON THE
LAW OF THE SEA, ARTICLES 77–78

Dec. 10, 1982, Senate Treaty Doc. No. 103–39 (1994), 1833 U.N.T.S. 3

Article 77: Rights of the coastal State over the continental shelf

1.   The coastal State exercises over the continental shelf sovereign rights for the purpose of exploring it and exploiting its natural resources.

2.   The rights referred to in paragraph 1 are exclusive in the sense that if the coastal State does not explore the continental shelf or exploit its natural resources, no one may undertake these activities without the express consent of the coastal State.

3.   The rights of the coastal State over the continental shelf do not depend on occupation, effective or notional, or on any express proclamation.

4.   The natural resources referred to in this Part consist of the mineral and other non-living resources of the sea-bed and subsoil together with living organisms belonging to sedentary species, that is to say, organisms which, at the harvestable stage, either are immobile on or under the sea-bed or are unable to move except in constant physical contact with the sea-bed or the subsoil.

*Article 78: Legal status of the superjacent waters and airspace
and the rights and freedoms of other States*

1.   The rights of the coastal State over the continental shelf do not affect the legal status of the superjacent waters or of the air space above those waters.

2.   The exercise of the rights of the coastal State over the continental shelf must not infringe or result in any unjustifiable interference with navigation and other rights and freedoms of other States as provided for in this Convention.

Baselines. The lines from which the breadths of a state's coastal zones are measured are known as "baselines." In general, the baseline follows the low-water line along the coast. See Convention on the Law of the Sea, art. 5.

Some states have proclaimed lengthy straight baselines rather than baselines that closely follow the low-water marks of the coastline. In 1951 the International Court of Justice approved Norway's decision to draw a straight baseline along a fringe of islands and rocks, known as a skjærgaard. "Where a coast is deeply indented and cut into, as is that of Eastern Finnmark," the Court stated, "or where it is bordered by an archipelago such as in the 'skjærgaard'[,] the base-line becomes independent of the low-water mark, and can only be determined by means of a geometric construction." The Court also suggested that the coastal state's important economic interests, "clearly evidenced by a long usage," were a relevant consideration supporting straight baselines, in addition to the geographical criteria. In addition, "the drawing of base-lines must not depart to any appreciable extent from the general direction of the coast." Anglo-Norwegian Fisheries Case, 1951 I.C.J. 116, 128–29, 133.

Article 7 of the 1982 Convention on the Law of the Sea, reflecting factors articulated in the *Anglo-Norwegian Fisheries Case*, describes conditions under which a state may draw straight baselines. In a subsequent case, the ICJ observed "that the method of straight baselines, which is an exception to the normal rules for the determination of baselines, may only be applied if a number of conditions are met. This method must be applied restrictively." Case Concerning Maritime Delimitation and Territorial Questions (Qatar v. Bahrain), 2001 I.C.J. 40, ¶ 212.

More than 75 states have drawn straight baselines along all or part of their coasts since 1951. Some of these baselines are many miles distant from the coast. See J. Ashley Roach & Robert W. Smith, *Excessive Maritime Claims* § 4.6 (3d ed. 2012). What are the implications of drawing straight baselines? What mechanisms are available to challenge assertions of straight baselines?

Maritime Boundary Delimitations. Since many law of the sea issues turn on the allocation of rights and responsibilities in coastal zones, it is important to determine the maritime boundaries between adjacent and opposite states. The expansion of coastal zones has precipitated many new maritime boundary delimitation disputes. These are often settled by negotiation, conciliation, or adjudication. Recall the *North Sea Continental Shelf Cases* in Chapter 2. Territorial sovereignty disputes may complicate the determination of maritime boundaries. Recall the *Minquiers and Echrehos Case* in Chapter 4.

U.S. Fisheries Zones. A companion to President Truman's continental shelf proclamation was a 1945 proclamation on coastal fisheries. Proclamation No. 2,668, Policy of the United States with Respect to Coastal Fisheries in Certain Areas of the High Seas, Sept. 28, 1945, 3 C.F.R. 68 (1943–1948 Compilation). The fisheries proclamation asserted sole U.S. authority to conserve and manage fisheries in areas contiguous to U.S. coasts where U.S. nationals historically had fished exclusively, and called for joint regulatory agreements in areas where both U.S. and foreign nationals fished. The United States, however, never established conservation zones under this proclamation, and foreign states were not eager to enter agreements that would limit their fishing practices. The Exclusive Fisheries Zone Act of 1966 established a 12-mile exclusive U.S. fisheries zone. A decade later the 1976 Fishery Conservation and Management

Act established a 200-mile fisheries conservation zone. The American Fisheries Promotion Act of 1980 phased out foreign fishing in this 200-mile zone.

The Fisheries Jurisdiction Case. In the 1974 *Fisheries Jurisdiction Case* between the United Kingdom and Iceland, excerpted below, the International Court of Justice examined problems arising from the expansion of coastal fishing zones in international law. In 1948, Iceland's Parliament passed a law authorizing the Ministry of Fisheries to set "conservation zones within the limits of the continental shelf of Iceland; wherein all fisheries shall be subject to Icelandic rules and control." In 1952, Iceland established a fisheries zone extending four miles from straight baselines and prohibited foreign fishing within the zone. Six years later Iceland proclaimed a 12-mile fisheries zone, again prohibiting foreign fishing within the new limit. British efforts to continue fishing in the 12-mile zone led to "incidents on the fishing grounds." In a 1961 exchange of notes, the United Kingdom acknowledged Iceland's dependence on coastal fisheries for its livelihood and economic development and agreed not to object to the 12-mile zone. Iceland, for its part, promised to give the United Kingdom six months' notice of any further extension of Icelandic fisheries jurisdiction and agreed to refer any dispute over such an extension to the International Court of Justice. When Iceland extended its fisheries jurisdiction to 50 miles in 1972, the United Kingdom brought a claim to the Court. Iceland refused to appear in the case.

The Cod Wars. The *Fisheries Jurisdiction Case* was decided against the background of the "Cod Wars," during which Iceland boarded British vessels, arrested British fishermen, and cut the nets of British trawlers. In response, the United Kingdom deployed naval frigates to escort and protect British trawlers off Iceland. There were shooting and ramming incidents. Tensions were particularly high during 1958–1961, after Iceland extended its fisheries zone from four to 12 miles, and in 1972–1973, after Iceland declared a 50-mile fisheries zone. Iceland's 1972 decisions to extend its fisheries zone and to denounce its 1961 agreement with Great Britain followed the 1971 Icelandic election; the Agrarian Progressive Party, which had made fisheries jurisdiction a major campaign issue, emerged as the head of a new coalition government.

———

Figure 8.E
Clash Between the Icelandic Coast Guard Vessel *Odinn* and the British Warship *Scylla* in the North Atlantic, Early 1970s

THE FISHERIES JURISDICTION CASE

United Kingdom v. Iceland, 1974 I.C.J. 3 (Merits)

The United Kingdom asks the Court to adjudge and declare:

(*a*)   That there is no foundation in international law for the claim by Iceland to be entitled to extend its fisheries jurisdiction by establishing a zone of exclusive fisheries jurisdiction extending to 50 nautical miles from the baselines[;] and that its claim is therefore invalid; and

(*b*)   that questions concerning the conservation of fish stocks in the waters around Iceland are not susceptible in international law to regulation by the unilateral extension by Iceland of its exclusive fisheries jurisdiction to 50 nautical miles from the aforesaid baselines but are matters that may be regulated, as between Iceland and the United Kingdom, by arrangements agreed between those two countries[.]

The Geneva Convention on the High Seas of 1958, which was adopted "as generally declaratory of established principles of international law," defines in Article 1 the term "high seas" as "all parts of the sea that are not included in the territorial sea or in the internal waters of a State." Article 2 then declares that "The high seas being open to all nations, no State may validly purport to subject any part of them to its sovereignty" and goes on to provide that the freedom of the high seas comprises, *inter alia*, both for coastal and non-coastal States, freedom of navigation and freedom of fishing. The freedoms of the high seas are however made subject to the consideration that they "shall be exercised by all States with reasonable regard to the interests of other States in their exercise of the freedom of the high seas."

. . . The question of the breadth of the territorial sea and that of the extent of the coastal State's fishery jurisdiction were left unsettled at the 1958 conference. These questions were referred to the Second Conference on the Law of the Sea, held in 1960. Furthermore, the question of the extent of the fisheries jurisdiction of the coastal State, which had constituted a serious obstacle to the reaching of an agreement at the 1958 Conference, became gradually separated from the notion of the territorial sea. This was a development which reflected the increasing importance of fishery resources for all States.

The 1960 Conference failed by one vote to adopt a text governing the two questions of the breadth of the territorial sea and the extent of fishery rights. However, after that Conference the law evolved through the practice of States on the basis of the debates and near-agreements at the Conference. Two concepts have crystallized as customary law in recent years arising out of the general consensus revealed at that Conference. The first is the concept of the fishery zone, the area in which a State may claim exclusive fishery jurisdiction independently of its territorial sea; the extension of that fishery zone up to a 12-mile limit from the baselines appears now to be generally accepted. The second is the concept of preferential rights of fishing in adjacent waters in favour of the coastal State in a situation of special dependence on its coastal fisheries, this preference operating in regard to other States concerned in the exploitation of the same fisheries[.]

In recent years the question of extending the coastal State's fisheries jurisdiction has come increasingly to the forefront. The Court is aware that a number of States has asserted an extension of fishery limits. The Court is also aware of present endeavours, pursued under the auspices of the United Nations, to achieve in a third Conference on the Law of the Sea the further codification and progressive development of this branch of the law, as it is of various proposals and preparatory documents produced in this framework, which must be regarded as manifestations of the views and opinions of individual States and as vehicles of their aspirations, rather than as expressing principles of existing law. The very fact of convening the third Conference on the Law of the Sea evidences a manifest desire on the part of all States to proceed to the codification of that law on a universal basis, including the question of fisheries and conservation of the living resources of the sea. . . . In the circumstances, the Court, as a court of law, cannot render judgment *sub specie legis ferendae*, or anticipate the law before the legislator has laid it down.

The concept of a 12-mile fishery zone . . . has been accepted with regard to Iceland in the substantive provisions of the 1961 Exchange of Notes, and the United Kingdom has also applied the same fishery limit to its own coastal waters since 1964; therefore this matter is no longer in dispute between the Parties. At the same time, . . . the Applicant has expressly recognized Iceland's preferential rights in the disputed waters and . . . has invoked its own historic fishing rights in these same waters, on the ground that reasonable regard must be had to such traditional rights by the coastal State, in accordance with the generally recognized principles embodied in Article 2 of the High Seas Convention.

. . . The contemporary practice of States leads to the conclusion that the preferential rights of the coastal State in a special situation are to be implemented by agreement between the States concerned, either bilateral or multilateral, and, in case of disagreement, through the means for the peaceful settlement of disputes provided for in Article 33 of the Charter of the United Nations. . . .

State practice on the subject of fisheries reveals an increasing and widespread acceptance of the concept of preferential rights for coastal States, particularly in favour of countries or territories in a situation of special dependence on coastal fisheries. Both [a resolution at the 1958 conference] and [a] 1960 joint amendment concerning preferential rights were approved by a large majority of the Conferences, thus showing overwhelming support for the idea that in certain special situations it was fair to recognize that the coastal State had preferential fishing rights. After these Conferences, the preferential rights of the coastal State were recognized in various bilateral and multilateral international agreements. . . .

There can be no doubt of the exceptional dependence of Iceland on its fisheries. That exceptional dependence was explicitly recognized by the Applicant in the Exchange of Notes of 11 March 1961, and the Court has also taken judicial notice of such recognition[.]

The preferential rights of the coastal State come into play only at the moment when an intensification in the exploitation of fishery resources makes it imperative to introduce some system of catch-limitation and sharing of those resources, to preserve the fish stocks in the interests of their rational and economic exploitation. This situation appears to have been reached in the present case. . . .

The Icelandic regulations challenged before the Court have been issued and applied by the Icelandic authorities as a claim to exclusive rights thus going beyond the concept of preferential rights. Article 2 of the Icelandic Regulations of 14 July 1972 states:

> Within the fishery limits all fishing activities by foreign vessels shall be prohibited in accordance with the provisions of Law No. 33 of 19 June 1922, concerning Fishing inside the Fishery Limits.

Article 1 of the 1922 Law provides: "Only Icelandic citizens may engage in fishing in the territorial waters of Iceland, and only Icelandic boats or ships may be used for such fishing." . . .

The concept of preferential rights is not compatible with the exclusion of all fishing activities of other States. A coastal State entitled to preferential rights is not free, unilaterally and according to its own uncontrolled discretion, to determine the extent of those rights. The characterization of the coastal State's rights as preferential implies a certain priority, but cannot imply the extinction of the concurrent rights of other States, and particularly of a State which, like the Applicant, has for many years been engaged in fishing in the waters in question, such fishing activity being important to the economy of the country concerned. . . .

In this case, the Applicant has pointed out that its vessels have been fishing in Icelandic waters for centuries and that they have done so in a manner comparable with their present activities for upwards of 50 years. Published statistics indicate that from 1920 onwards, fishing of demersal species by United Kingdom vessels in the disputed area has taken place on a continuous basis from year to year, and that, except for the period of the Second World War, the total catch of those vessels has been remarkably steady. Similar statistics indicate that the waters in question constitute the most important of the Applicant's distant-water fishing grounds for demersal species.

The Applicant further states that in view of the present situation of fisheries in the North Atlantic, which has demanded the establishment of agreed catch-limitations of cod and haddock in various areas, it would not be possible for the fishing effort of United Kingdom vessels displaced from the Icelandic area to be diverted at economic levels to other fishing grounds in the North Atlantic. Given the lack of alternative fishing opportunity, it is further contended, the exclusion of British fishing vessels from the Icelandic area would have very serious adverse consequences, with immediate results for the affected vessels and with damage extending over a wide range of supporting and related industries. It is pointed out in particular that wide-spread unemployment would be caused among all sections of the British fishing industry and in ancillary industries and that certain ports—

Hull, Grimsby and Fleetwood—specially reliant on fishing in the Icelandic area, would be seriously affected. . . .

The provisions of the Icelandic Regulations of 14 July 1972 and the manner of their implementation disregard the fishing rights of the Applicant. Iceland's unilateral action thus constitutes an infringement of the principle enshrined in Article 2 of the 1958 Geneva Convention on the High Seas which requires that all States, including coastal States, in exercising their freedom of fishing, pay reasonable regard to the interests of other States. It also disregards the rights of the Applicant as they result from the Exchange of Notes of 1961. The Applicant is therefore justified in asking the Court to give all necessary protection to its own rights, while at the same time agreeing to recognize Iceland's preferential position. Accordingly, the Court is bound to conclude that the Icelandic Regulations of 14 July 1972 establishing a zone of exclusive fisheries jurisdiction extending to 50 nautical miles from baselines around the coast of Iceland, are not opposable to the United Kingdom, and the latter is under no obligation to accept the unilateral termination by Iceland of United Kingdom fishery rights in the area.

. . . Due recognition must be given to the rights of both Parties, namely the rights of the United Kingdom to fish in the waters in dispute, and the preferential rights of Iceland. Neither right is an absolute one: the preferential rights of a coastal State are limited according to the extent of its special dependence on the fisheries and by its obligation to take account of the rights of other States and the needs of conservation; the established rights of other fishing States are in turn limited by reason of the coastal State's special dependence on the fisheries and its own obligation to take account of the rights of other States, including the coastal State, and of the needs of conservation.

[B]oth States have an obligation to take full account of each other's rights and of any fishery conservation measures the necessity of which is shown to exist in those waters. It is one of the advances in maritime international law, resulting from the intensification of fishing, that the former *laissez-faire* treatment of the living resources of the sea in the high seas has been replaced by a recognition of a duty to have due regard to the rights of other States and the needs of conservation for the benefit of all. Consequently, both Parties have the obligation to keep under review the fishery resources in the disputed waters and to examine together, in the light of scientific and other available information, the measures required for the conservation and development, and equitable exploitation, of those resources[.]

The most appropriate method for the solution of the dispute is clearly that of negotiation. Its objectives should be the delimitation of the rights and interests of the Parties, the preferential rights of the coastal State on the one hand and the rights of the Applicant on the other, to balance and regulate equitably questions such as those of catch-limitation, share allocations and "related restrictions concerning areas closed to fishing, number and type of vessels allowed and forms of control of the agreed provisions" (*Fisheries Jurisdiction (United Kingdom v. Iceland), Interim Measures, Order of 12 July 1973, I.C.J. Reports 1973*, p. 303, para. 7). This necessitates detailed scientific knowledge of the fishing grounds. It is obvious that the relevant information and expertise would be mainly in the possession of the Parties. The Court would, for this reason, meet with difficulties if it were itself to attempt to lay down a precise scheme for an equitable adjustment of the rights involved. . . .

For these reasons,

THE COURT,

by ten votes to four,

(1) finds that the Regulations concerning the Fishery Limits off Iceland . . . promulgated by the Government of Iceland on 14 July 1972 and constituting a unilateral extension of the exclusive fishing rights of Iceland to 50 nautical miles from the baselines specified therein are not opposable to the Government of the United Kingdom;

(2) finds that, in consequence, the Government of Iceland is not entitled unilaterally to exclude United Kingdom fishing vessels from areas between the fishery limits agreed to in the Exchange of Notes of 11 March 1961 and the limits specified in the Icelandic Regulations of 14 July 1972, or unilaterally to impose restrictions on the activities of those vessels in such areas;

by ten votes to four,

(3) holds that the Government of Iceland and the Government of the United Kingdom are under mutual obligations to undertake negotiations in good faith for the equitable solution of their differences concerning their respective fishery rights in the areas specified in subparagraph 2;

(4) holds that in these negotiations the Parties are to take into account, *inter alia*:

(*a*) that in the distribution of the fishing resources in the areas specified in subparagraph 2 Iceland is entitled to a preferential share to the extent of the special dependence of its people upon the fisheries in the seas around its coasts for their livelihood and economic development;

(*b*)   that by reason of its fishing activities in the areas specified in subparagraph 2, the United Kingdom also has established rights in the fishery resources of the said areas on which elements of its people depend for their livelihood and economic well-being;

(*c*)   the obligation to pay due regard to the interests of other States in the conservation and equitable exploitation of these resources;

(*d*)   that the above-mentioned rights of Iceland and of the United Kingdom should each be given effect to the extent compatible with the conservation and development of the fishery resources in the areas specified in subparagraph 2 and with the interests of other States in their conservation and equitable exploitation;

(*e*)   their obligation to keep under review those resources and to examine together, in the light of scientific and other available information, such measures as may be required for the conservation and development, and equitable exploitation, of those resources, making use of the machinery established by the North-East Atlantic Fisheries Convention or such other means as may be agreed upon as a result of international negotiations.

The Aftermath of the Fisheries Jurisdiction Case. Rejecting the decision in the *Fisheries Jurisdiction Case*, Iceland extended its fishing limits from 50 to 200 miles in 1975. How does this action by Iceland compare to the reception accorded the ICJ decisions we studied in Chapter 4? This extension of Icelandic fishing limits resulted in further clashes involving British and Icelandic naval units. Other states became concerned that the controversy might lead Iceland to withdraw from the North Atlantic Treaty Organization and to shut down a NATO military base in the country that was used to monitor the Soviet Navy. In June 1976, Iceland and the United Kingdom finally reached an agreement allowing limited British fishing within the 200-mile zone. Iceland also concluded bilateral fishing agreements with Belgium, the Federal Republic of Germany, and Norway.

The ICJ's View of Rights to Fisheries. In the *Fisheries Jurisdiction Case*, the ICJ concluded that Iceland had no unilateral right to extend its fisheries zone to 50 miles. Why did the ICJ not simply rule that British vessels had the freedom to fish outside Iceland's 12-mile fisheries zone? Is the Court's reasoning persuasive? The Court concluded that Iceland and the United Kingdom should negotiate "for the equitable solution of their differences" over rights to fisheries. How does the Court's invocation of equity compare with its use of equity in the *North Sea Continental Shelf Cases* at the end of Chapter 2? The ICJ's recourse to procedure may have reflected the unsettled nature of international law on this issue. The Court did not elaborate a general rule of law while states were in the midst of negotiating the contours of coastal state zones at the then-ongoing Third United Nations Conference on the Law of the Sea (UNCLOS III).

Coastal State Fisheries Jurisdiction and Customary International Law. Judges Forster, Bengzon, Jimenez de Arechaga, Nagendra Singh, and Ruda concurred separately in the *Fisheries Jurisdiction Case*. Although the judges agreed with the result in the majority opinion and found that a 12-mile fisheries zone was generally accepted in international law, they felt that no general rule of customary international law established 12 miles as the maximum limit. The judges argued that 30 to 35 coastal states had extended their fisheries jurisdiction beyond 12 miles, and noted the general lack of protests to such extensions and the existence of public pronouncements inconsistent with making any protest. The concurring judges also cited declarations and proposals made at UNCLOS III. They questioned whether, on "a subject where practice was contradictory and lacks precision," it was "reasonable to discard entirely as irrelevant the evidence of what States are prepared to claim and to acquiesce in, as gathered from the positions taken by them in view of or in preparation for a conference for the codification and progressive development of the law on the subject." 1974 I.C.J. at 48. Finally, the judges lamented the legal uncertainty at the time regarding the maximum limit of coastal state fisheries jurisdiction, and expressed the hope that the matter would be clarified at UNCLOS III. What should a court do if it can establish neither a posited rule of customary international law nor rejection of the rule? Compare the discussion of the *Lotus Case* in Chapter 2.

Multilateral Efforts to Codify the Law of the Sea. The *Fisheries Jurisdiction* decision noted multilateral efforts prior to UNCLOS III to codify the international law of the sea. The excerpt above refers to one of the five 1958 treaties concluded at the First United Nations Conference on the Law of the Sea: the Convention on the High Seas. The other four are the Convention on the Territorial Sea and the Contiguous Zone, the Convention on the Continental Shelf, the Convention on Fishing and Conservation of the Living Resources of the High Seas, and the Optional Protocol of Signature concerning the Compulsory Settlement of Disputes. The United Kingdom, but not Iceland, was party to those five treaties.

UNCLOS III Negotiations Concerning the Exclusive Economic Zone. At the 1974 Caracas session of UNCLOS III, delegates from over 100 states favored a 200-mile coastal state exclusive economic zone (EEZ). Not all issues relating to the EEZ were resolved early in the Conference. Negotiating many of these issues—the legal status of the EEZ, the applicability of the EEZ to archipelagic states and small islands, the relationship between the EEZ and the continental shelf, boundary delimitation, dispute settlement, and coastal state responsibilities concerning fish in their EEZs—took years. Compare the complex negotiations of the 1982 Convention on the Law of the Sea to the relatively simpler bilateral treaty negotiations we examined in Chapter 2.

The Variety of Views about the EEZ. The 1974 UNCLOS III debates revealed considerable variety in the positions of states. Here are just a few examples, drawn from records of meetings between July 31, 1974 and August 6, 1974 in 2 UNCLOS III Official Records 171, 179, 192, 201, 210, 217 (U.N. Sales No. E.75.V.4, 1975). Honduras's delegate claimed "inherent rights" over resources in its adjacent zones, and argued that foreign states had no competence there absent agreement with the coastal state. Kenya and Ecuador, along with many developing countries, favored complete coastal state sovereignty in the EEZ; their delegates advocated 200-mile territorial seas. Somalia's delegate thought that the traditional law of the sea favored the major maritime powers, and that developing coastal states should not "sign away their territorial sovereignty in exchange for lesser rights."

Island states and archipelagic states had particular interests in fisheries. New Zealand's delegate criticized a suggestion that the economic zone of islands should be restricted. Archipelagic states also strongly supported the concept of an EEZ, but did not necessarily favor complete coastal state "sovereignty" over the EEZ.

For other countries, the EEZ concept represented a significant concession. Mr. Ogiso, Japan's delegate, argued that "[f]reedom of access to fishery resources, if it was retained only beyond 200 miles, would become practically meaningless." He urged respect for traditional distant water fishing states whose economies depended on fishing.

Maritime powers, including states in the Soviet bloc, also stressed the importance of coastal states not exercising rights in their EEZs that would interfere with navigational freedoms. The concern was that extensive coastal state EEZ rights or 200-mile territorial seas might well allow coastal states to disrupt navigation by exercising control over pollution, scientific research, customs, fiscal, immigration, or health matters. The delegate of the Ukrainian

Soviet Socialist Republic worried that "[u]nder the pretext of exercising such controls, a coastal State might at any time detain a foreign vessel and reduce to nothing the freedom of navigation in the zone."

Land-locked and geographically disadvantaged states also voiced concerns. Upper Volta (now Burkina Faso) argued for assured access to the sea by land-locked countries and for their right to participate in the exploitation of EEZ resources. Mr. Ballah, the delegate from the Caribbean nation of Trinidad and Tobago, said his country "conditioned its acceptance of the concept of the 200-mile exclusive economic zone on recognition by the Conference of preferential or equal rights for every State within a region or subregion to the living resources of the economic zones of the other States of the region." Turkey noted that, although it was surrounded on three sides by seas, those seas were semi-enclosed and not well stocked with fish. The delegate of the Federal Republic of Germany stressed dual needs—the effective conservation of fisheries and the equitable allocation of those resources—and found "no justification for the reallocation of available resources for the benefit of a limited number of geographically advantaged States." Germany was one of several countries stressing the importance of an obligatory dispute settlement mechanism to review the actions of coastal states.

Resolving Conflicting Interests in the EEZ. How does the 1982 Law of the Sea Convention resolve the Grotius/Selden *mare liberum/mare clausum* debate with regard to the EEZ? Is the EEZ still a part of the high seas? Consider these questions as you read the following articles from the Law of the Sea Convention.

UNITED NATIONS CONVENTION ON THE LAW OF THE SEA, ARTICLES 55–59

Dec. 10, 1982, Senate Treaty Doc. No. 103–39 (1994), 1833 U.N.T.S. 3

Article 55: Specific legal regime of the exclusive economic zone

The exclusive economic zone is an area beyond and adjacent to the territorial sea, subject to the specific legal regime established in this Part [V, concerning the EEZ], under which the rights and jurisdiction of the coastal State and the rights and freedoms of other States are governed by the relevant provisions of this Convention.

Article 56: Rights, jurisdiction and duties of the coastal State
in the exclusive economic zone

1.   In the exclusive economic zone, the coastal State has:

(a)   sovereign rights for the purpose of exploring and exploiting, conserving and managing the natural resources, whether living or non-living, of the waters superjacent to the seabed and of the seabed and its subsoil, and with regard to other activities for the economic exploitation and exploration of the zone, such as the production of energy from the water, currents and winds;

(b)   jurisdiction as provided for in the relevant provisions of this Convention with regard to:

(i)   the establishment and use of artificial islands, installations and structures;

(ii)   marine scientific research;

(iii)   the protection and preservation of the marine environment;

(c)   other rights and duties provided for in this Convention.

2.   In exercising its rights and performing its duties under this Convention in the exclusive economic zone, the coastal State shall have due regard to the rights and duties of other States and shall act in a manner compatible with the provisions of this Convention.

3.   The rights set out in this article with respect to the seabed and subsoil shall be exercised in accordance with Part VI [concerning the continental shelf].

Article 57: Breadth of the exclusive economic zone

The exclusive economic zone shall not extend beyond 200 nautical miles from the baselines from which the breadth of the territorial sea is measured.

Article 58: Rights and duties of other States in the exclusive economic zone

1.   In the exclusive economic zone, all States, whether coastal or land-locked, enjoy, subject to the relevant provisions of this Convention, the freedoms referred to in article 87 of navigation and overflight and of the laying of submarine cables and pipelines, and other internationally lawful uses of the sea related to these freedoms, such as those associated with the operation of ships, aircraft and submarine cables and pipelines, and compatible with the other provisions of this Convention.

2.   Articles 88 to 115 and other pertinent rules of international law apply to the exclusive economic zone in so far as they are not incompatible with this Part.

3.   In exercising their rights and performing their duties under this Convention in the exclusive economic zone, States shall have due regard to the rights and duties of the coastal State and shall comply with the laws and regulations adopted by the coastal State in accordance with the provisions of this Convention and other rules of international law in so far as they are not incompatible with this Part.

Article 59: Basis for the resolution of conflicts regarding the attribution
of rights and jurisdiction in the exclusive economic zone

In cases where this Convention does not attribute rights or jurisdiction to the coastal State or to other States within the exclusive economic zone, and a conflict arises between the interests of the coastal State and any other State or States, the conflict should be resolved on the basis of equity and in the light of all the relevant circumstances, taking into account the respective importance of the interests involved to the parties as well as to the international community as a whole.

Acceptance of the EEZ as Customary International Law. In March 1983 President Reagan proclaimed a 200-mile exclusive economic zone for the United States, asserting that "international law recognizes that . . . a coastal State may assert certain sovereign rights over natural resources and related jurisdiction" in such a zone. Presidential Proclamation No. 5,030, Mar. 10, 1983, 22 *International Legal Materials* 465 (1983). In 1985 the International Court of Justice found it "incontestable that . . . the institution of the exclusive economic zone . . . is shown by the practice of states to have become part of customary law." Continental Shelf (Libya v. Malta) Case, 1985 I.C.J. 13, 33. As of October 1993, according to the U.N. Secretary-General's 1993 annual *Report* on the law of the sea, 91 states had claimed a 200-mile EEZ (or one up to a median line with opposite states), and an additional 15 states had claimed a 200-mile fisheries zone; 11 states claimed a 200-mile territorial sea. Had the 1982 Convention's EEZ regime gained general acceptance as customary international law even before the Convention entered into force in November 1994? What additional information, if any, might be needed to answer the question?

Beneficiaries of the EEZ. Which states benefit most from the concept of the EEZ? Some states that have long coastlines, are located far from other states, or possess distant territories or dependencies may claim huge exclusive economic zones. The United States has the largest area, approximately

3,000,000 square miles. France's EEZ is next with approximately 2,000,000 square miles. Several relatively small states, including Japan, Kiribati, New Zealand, and Papua New Guinea, have extensive EEZs. Indonesia, with its many islands, has an EEZ measuring approximately 1,500,000 square miles.

It is not merely the size of an EEZ that is important. According to Article 56(a), reproduced above, coastal states have sovereign rights over the living resources of the EEZ, but EEZs differ significantly in terms of the amount of fish they support. Among the states noted in the preceding paragraph, the United States and Indonesia topped the list in 2007, with, respectively, an estimated 4,800,000 and 4,900,000 metric tons of fish caught in their EEZs. France's EEZ catch lagged far behind at 500,000 metric tons. See Louis B. Sohn, Kristen Juras, John E. Noyes & Erik Franckx, *Law of the Sea in a Nutshell* 248 (2d ed. 2010).

Control Over EEZ Fisheries. Access to and control over coastal fisheries was an issue of tremendous importance in the debate over the EEZ. Does the 1982 Law of the Sea Convention adhere to the same conception of rights concerning fisheries that the ICJ articulated in the *Fisheries Jurisdiction Case*? Coastal state rights over EEZ fisheries under the 1982 Convention are more extensive than the "preferential rights" the ICJ invoked in *Fisheries Jurisdiction*. Article 56 of the Convention provides generally that the coastal state has "sovereign rights" over EEZ natural resources. The detailed Articles 61 and 62 effectively preserve coastal state control over EEZ fisheries. A coastal state may qualify its conservation obligations in light of economic and social factors, may preclude altogether foreign fishing in the 200-mile EEZ, and, where such fishing is allowed, may license and regulate it.

Promoting the Conservation and Management of Fish Stocks. Do the interests and values associated with EEZ fisheries solely concern coastal states and distant water fishing states? Has giving coastal states "sovereign rights" with respect to EEZ fisheries effectively promoted conservation and management of the 90 percent of fish stocks found in EEZs? According to Professor Christie, "[s]cientific information and management methodologies continue to be inadequate; entry into domestic fisheries has largely not been controlled; enforcement and reporting remain questionable; and the EEZ as a management area has not been an adequate zone for ecosystem management[.] Simply changing jurisdictional zones did not substantially benefit the resources." Donna R. Christie, "It Don't Come EEZ: The Failure and Future of Coastal State Fisheries Management," 14 *Journal of Transnational Law and Policy*

1, 34 (2004). How might international law more effectively promote EEZ fisheries conservation and management?

Other challenges attend the management of fish that swim between the EEZs of different states or between the EEZ of one state and the high seas beyond, and of fish that live only outside EEZs. International actors have tackled these challenges, with mixed success at best, primarily through multilateral treaties, *e.g.*, the 1995 Implementation Agreement relating to the Conservation and Management of Straddling Fish Stocks and Highly Migratory Fish Stocks (accepted by the United States and 85 other parties as of May 2017), soft law instruments, *e.g.*, the 1995 Code of Conduct for Responsible Fisheries adopted by the Food and Agriculture Organization, and regulations of regional fisheries organizations.

Obligatory Third-party Dispute Resolution. Many categories of disputes are subject to the Law of the Sea Convention's provisions for obligatory third-party arbitration or adjudication. See the *Saiga Case* in Part B above. Excluded from such provisions, however, are disputes relating to a coastal state's "sovereign rights with respect to the living resources in the exclusive economic zone or their exercise, including its discretionary powers for determining allowable catch, its harvesting capacity, the allocation of surpluses to other States and the terms and conditions established in its conservation and management laws and regulations." Convention on the Law of the Sea, art. 297(3). What are the implications of this exclusion for the balance of rights and obligations set out in the Convention's EEZ provisions?

Linkages Among Convention Provisions. Look back at the views of states concerning EEZ matters during the UNCLOS III negotiations. If a state was not satisfied with the Convention's EEZ provisions, why might it still accept the Convention? Different parts of the Convention concern protection of the marine environment, marine scientific research, and a wide range of other oceans topics. U.S. complaints about the Convention focused on its deep seabed mining provisions, explored in Part E of this chapter.

The Regime of Islands. At UNCLOS III, states debated which offshore features constituted islands and which coastal zones islands should have. States with many islands were eager to maximize surrounding coastal zones, especially in order to control fisheries. States with navies and distant-water fishing fleets sought to limit expansive zones around islands. The resulting compromise was Article 121 of the Law of the Sea Convention.

UNITED NATIONS CONVENTION ON THE
LAW OF THE SEA, ARTICLE 121

Dec. 10, 1982, Senate Treaty Doc. No. 103–39 (1994), 1833 U.N.T.S. 3

Article 121: Regime of islands

1.   An island is a naturally formed area of land, surrounded by water, which is above water at high tide.

2.   Except as provided for in paragraph 3, the territorial sea, the contiguous zone, the exclusive economic zone and the continental shelf of an island are determined in accordance with the provisions of this Convention applicable to other land territory.

3.   Rocks which cannot sustain human habitation or economic life of their own shall have no exclusive economic zone or continental shelf.

Islands, Rocks, Low-tide Elevations, and Artificial Islands. Why is it significant, under Article 121, whether an island is a "rock" that "cannot sustain human habitation or economic life of [its] own"? What ambiguities accompany the legal definitions of an island and an Article 121(3) rock? May states act unilaterally to upgrade the status of Article 121(3) rocks? May they legally turn submerged features into islands? Convention Article 60(8) provides: "Artificial islands, installations and structures do not possess the status of islands. They have no territorial sea of their own, and their presence does not affect the delimitation of the territorial sea, the exclusive economic zone or the continental shelf." See also Article 13 on low-tide elevations, which are above water only at high tide. Questions about the legal entitlements of islands, rocks, low-tide elevations, and artificial structures have arisen recently amidst political tensions in the South China Sea. See *In re* South China Sea Arbitration (Philippines v. China), Award (Annex VII United Nations Convention on the Law of the Sea Arbitral Tribunal, 2016), *available at* http://www.pcacases.com/pcadocs/PH-CN%20-%2020160712%20-%20Award.pdf.

Comparing the EEZ and the Continental Shelf. Article 56 of the 1982 Convention, which is contained in its Part V on the EEZ, refers to sovereign rights of coastal states to explore, exploit, conserve, and manage non-living, as well as living, natural resources. Why, then, does the Convention include a separate Part VI on the continental shelf? The explanation lies not only in the different historical origins of the two zones, but in their location. The continental shelf sometimes may extend beyond 200 miles from the baseline, which is the maximum permissible breadth of the EEZ. In addition, although a continental shelf is deemed to exist even absent a coastal state proclamation, an EEZ must be proclaimed.

Comparing the EEZ and the Contiguous Zone. The 1958 Convention on the Territorial Sea and the Contiguous Zone provides that states may assert a zone contiguous to the territorial sea. This contiguous zone may extend 12 miles from the baseline; Article 33 of the 1982 Convention increases the limit to 24 miles. Within this zone, according to Article 33, a coastal state "may exercise the control necessary to (a) prevent infringement of its customs, fiscal, immigration or sanitary laws and regulations within its territory or territorial sea; (b) punish infringement of the above laws and regulations committed within its territory or territorial sea." Does the EEZ render the concept of the contiguous zone superfluous?

In the *Saiga Case* excerpted in Part B above, Guinea attempted to justify its arrest of a foreign-flag vessel outside a 24-mile zone. Guinea argued that the vessel's actions in Guinea's EEZ—supplying fuel oil to fishing vessels ("bunkering")—circumvented Guinean customs laws, and that arrest of the vessel was consistent with Article 58(3) of the Law of the Sea Convention. The International Tribunal for the Law of the Sea rejected Guinea's assertion:

> The main public interest which Guinea claims to be protecting by applying its customs laws to the exclusive economic zone is said to be the "considerable fiscal losses a developing country like Guinea is suffering from illegal off-shore bunkering in its exclusive economic zone." . . . In effect, Guinea's contention is that the customary international law principle of "public interest" gives it the power to impede "economic activities that are undertaken [in its EEZ] under the guise of navigation but are different from communication."
>
> According to article 58, paragraph 3, of the Convention, the "other rules of international law" which a coastal State is entitled to apply in the exclusive economic zone are those which are not incompatible with Part V of the Convention. In the view of the Tribunal, recourse to the principle of "public interest," as invoked by Guinea, would entitle a coastal State to prohibit any activities in the exclusive economic zone which it decides to characterize as activities which affect its economic "public interest" or entail "fiscal losses" for it. This would curtail the rights of other States in the exclusive economic zone. The Tribunal is satisfied that this would be incompatible with the provisions of articles 56 and 58 of the

> Convention regarding the rights of the coastal State in the exclusive economic zone.
>
> *M/V "SAIGA" (No. 2) (Saint Vincent and the Grenadines v. Guinea), Judgment, ITLOS Reports 1999,* Kluwer Law International, p. 10, at p. 55, paras. 130–131, *available at* http://www.itlos.org. An arrest of a foreign flag vessel in the EEZ for customs violations may, however, be valid under international law if the arrest follows "hot pursuit" from the territorial sea or the contiguous zone. See Law of the Sea Convention, art. 111.

D. THE TERRITORIAL SEA AND STRAITS

International law today provides that a coastal state has sovereignty over a narrow band of waters adjacent to its coastline, known as the territorial sea. As you read this part, ask what are the relative rights and responsibilities of coastal states and flag states in the territorial sea. We start with a case and a treaty excerpt relating to the exercise of criminal jurisdiction by a coastal state over a person on board a foreign flag vessel in the territorial sea. Later text concerns the rights of vessels to innocent passage through the territorial sea and to transit passage through straits, issues that have been particularly sensitive with respect to warships.

> *Coastal State Authority in the Territorial Sea.* An 1876 British case, *Regina v. Keyn,* highlighted controversies over the concept of the territorial sea and the extent of coastal state control there. The *Franconia,* a German merchant ship, accidentally struck and sunk the *Strathclyde,* a British vessel, less than three miles from the British coast, resulting in the drowning of a woman aboard the *Strathclyde.* Ferdinand Keyn, the German captain of the *Franconia,* was tried for manslaughter in a British criminal court and convicted. On appeal, the British court addressed the issue of the jurisdiction of British courts over acts by foreign nationals aboard foreign vessels in British coastal waters. The court's 13 judges voted, 7 to 6, that British courts had no jurisdiction and that the guilty verdict thus could not stand. The majority held that Parliament could grant the courts jurisdiction over acts committed in a marginal belt of the oceans, but concluded that Parliament had not yet done so. The following excerpt contains brief excerpts from two of the lengthy opinions in this case.

REGINA V. KEYN

Great Britain, Court for Crown Cases Reserved, 2 Law Reports (Exchequer Division) 63 (1876)

SIR R. PHILLIMORE:

[W]ithin [the] term "territory" are certainly comprised the ports and harbours, and the space between the flux and reflux of tide, or the land up to the furthest point at which the tide recedes. But it is at this point that the difficulty presented by the case before us begins, and here the following questions present themselves for solution:

1.   Is a state entitled to any extension of dominion beyond low-water mark?

2.   If so, how far does this territory, or do these territorial waters, as they are usually called, extend?

3.   Has a state the same dominion over these territorial waters as over the territory of her soil and in her ports, or is it of a more limited character and confined to certain purposes?

With respect to the first of these questions the answer may be given without doubt or hesitation, namely, that a state is entitled to a certain extension of territory, in a certain sense of that word, beyond low-water mark.

With respect to the second question, the distance to which the territorial waters extend, it appears on an examination of the authorities that the distance has varied (setting aside even more extravagant claims) from 100 to 3 miles, the present limit. . . .

The third question . . . remains to be substantively considered; it is one of much importance, viz., whether, admitting that the state has a dominion over three miles of adjacent water, it is the same dominion which the possessor has over her land and her ports, or is it of a more limited character—limited to the purpose of protecting the adjacent shore, for which it was granted, and not extending to a general sovereignty over all passing vessels[.]

The consensus of civilised independent states has recognised a maritime extension of frontier to the distance of three miles from low-water mark, because such a frontier or belt of water is necessary for the defence and security of the adjacent state.

It is for the attainment of these particular objects that a dominium has been granted over this portion of the high seas.

This proposition is materially different from the proposition contended for, namely, that it is competent to a state to exercise within these waters the same rights of jurisdiction and property which appertain to it in respect to its lands and its ports. There is one obvious test by which the two sovereignties may be distinguished.

According to modern international law, it is certainly a right incident to each state to refuse a passage to foreigners over its territory by land, whether in time of peace or war. But it does not appear to have the same right with respect to preventing the passage of foreign ships over this portion of the high seas. . . .

The reason of the thing, that is, the defence and security of the state, does not require or warrant the exclusion of peaceable foreign vessels from passing over these waters; and the custom and usage of nations has not sanctioned it.

Consequences fraught with mischief and injustice might flow from the opposite doctrine, which would render applicable to a foreign vessel while in itinere from one foreign port to another, passing over these waters, all the criminal law of the adjacent territory. No single instance has been brought to our notice of the practical exercise by any nation of this jurisdiction. . . .

A foreign merchant vessel going into the port of a foreign state subjects herself to the ordinary law of the place during the period of her commorancy [*i.e.,* stopping] there; she is as much a subditus temporaneus as the individual who visits the interior of the country for the purposes of pleasure or business. . . .

If . . . there be no difference between the jurisdiction by the adjacent state over vessels in ports and over passing and commorant vessels, then the whole criminal law of England was applicable to the crew and those on board the German vessel, so long as she was within a marine league of the English shore.

The consequences of such a position of law appear to me, especially in the absence of any precedent, sufficient to render it untenable.

There is yet another argument, already partially adverted to, which appears to me entitled to great weight in an English court of justice.

Upon the subject of the three-miles belt of territorial water, Parliament has frequently legislated. It might perhaps be not impertinently asked, why, if these waters are territorial in the same sense as the land, and those who traverse them are already subject to the law. But, passing by this observation, it will be found on examination of the statutes that the provisions in them are either framed exclusively for British subjects and ships, or that they relate to the protection and peace of the state. . . .

Upon the whole, I am of opinion that the Court had no jurisdiction over this foreigner for an offence committed on board a foreign ship on the high seas, though within three miles of the coast; that he is governed by the law of the state to which his flag belongs; and that the conviction cannot be sustained. . . .

Cockburn, C.J.

. . . There can be no doubt that the suggestion of Bynkershoek, that the sea surrounding the coast to the extent of cannon-range should be treated as belonging to the state owning the coast, has, with but very few exceptions, been accepted and adopted by the publicists who have followed him during the last two centuries. But it is equally clear that, in the practical application of the rule, in respect of the particular of distance, as also in the still more essential particular of the character and degree of sovereignty and dominion to be exercised, great difference of opinion and uncertainty have prevailed, and still continue to exist. . . .

One set of writers . . . ascribe to the state territorial property and sovereignty over the three miles of sea, to the extent of the right of excluding the ships of all other nations, even for the purpose of passage—a doctrine flowing immediately from the principle of territorial property, but which is too monstrous to be admitted. Another set concede territorial property and sovereignty, but make it subject to the right of other nations to use these waters for the purpose of navigation. Others . . . deny any right of territorial property, but concede "jurisdiction"; by which I understand them to mean the power of applying the law, applicable to persons on the land, to all who are within the territorial water, and the power of legislating in respect of it, so as to bind every one who comes within the jurisdiction, whether subjects or foreigners. Some . . . would confine this jurisdiction to purposes of "safety and police"—by which I should be disposed to understand measures for the protection of the territory, and for the regulation of the navigation, and the use of harbours and roadsteads, and the maintenance of order among the shipping therein, rather than the general application of the criminal law.

Other authors . . . would restrict the jurisdiction to certain specified purposes in which the local state has an immediate interest, namely, the protection of its revenue and fisheries, the exacting of harbour and light dues, and the protection of its coasts in time of war.

Some of these authors . . . make a most important distinction between a commorant and a passing ship. According to [one] author, while the commorant ship is subject to the general law of the local state, the passing ship is liable to the local jurisdiction only in matters of "military and police regulations, made for the safety of the territory and population of the coast." None of these writers, it should be noted, discuss the question, or go the length of asserting that a foreigner in a foreign ship, using the waters in question for the purpose of navigation solely, on its way to another country, is liable to the criminal law of the adjoining country for an offence committed on board.

Now, when it is remembered that it is mainly on the statements and authority of these writers, and to opinions founded upon them, that we are called upon to hold that foreigners on the so-called territorial sea are subject to the general law of this country, the discrepancy of opinion which I have been pointing out becomes very material.

. . . This unanimity of opinion that the littoral sea is, at all events for some purposes, subject to the dominion of the local state, may go far to shew that, by the concurrence of other nations, such a state may deal with these waters as subject to its legislation. But it wholly fails to show that, in the absence of such legislation, the ordinary law of the local state will extend over the waters in question—which is the point which we have to determine.

The Breadth of the Territorial Sea. As the opinions in *Regina v. Keyn* indicate, the breadth of the territorial sea has historically been the subject of disagreement. In the mid-20th century, some Latin American states unilaterally asserted 200-mile territorial seas, and the delegates to the 1958 U.N. Conference on the Law of the Sea could reach no agreement on the maximum permissible breadth of the territorial sea. In 1960, the Second U.N. Conference on the Law of the Sea failed by one vote to adopt a proposal for a six-mile territorial sea and an additional six-mile fisheries zone. Today, as recognized in Article 3 of the 1982 Law of the Sea Convention and (in the view of the International Court of Justice and scholars) customary international law, the territorial sea extends up to 12 miles from a state's baselines. States favoring very broad territorial seas in order to protect their access to living resources were largely satisfied by the provisions for an EEZ in the 1982 Convention.

Coastal State Sovereignty in the Territorial Sea. International law now provides that the coastal state has "sovereignty" over its territorial sea, the airspace above it, and its bed and subsoil. Law of the Sea Convention, art. 2. Are there justifications for sovereign coastal state authority valid today that were not present or not recognized in 1876? Sovereignty in this context reflects an amalgam of coastal state jurisdictional concerns with fisheries, customs, security, health, immigration, and other matters. The coastal state's control over its territorial sea is, however, not absolute, qualified most notably by the right of innocent passage discussed below. Indeed, state sovereignty may be regarded as a relative concept, conditioned by applicable rules of international law and the need for coexistence in a multi-polar world. We introduced sovereignty with the Peace of Westphalia in Chapter 2, Part A, and explored it in Chapter 3, Part A.

Coastal State Exercise of Criminal Jurisdiction on Board Foreign Ships in the Territorial Sea. What state(s) may exercise criminal jurisdiction over those on board foreign vessels in the territorial sea? Even when a coastal state is entitled to exercise jurisdiction with respect to criminal activities on board a foreign flag vessel, it may defer to the flag state's exercise of jurisdiction. When would such deference be appropriate?

The narrow reason precluding the British courts from prosecuting Captain Keyn was cured within two years, when Parliament enacted a law authorizing, *inter alia*, British criminal jurisdiction over acts in a marginal sea. Would Britain's exercise of criminal jurisdiction over Keyn have been both legal and appropriate under Article 27 of the 1982 Law of the Sea Convention, below? In what circumstances is it illegal for a coastal state to exercise jurisdiction over criminals in the territorial sea? See Article 27(5). Is it sensible today, for purposes of the exercise of a coastal state's criminal jurisdiction, to distinguish among vessels passing through the territorial sea on their way to or from one of the coastal state's ports, vessels simply passing by the coastal state's shores, and vessels stopping in the territorial sea?

UNITED NATIONS CONVENTION ON THE LAW OF THE SEA, ARTICLE 27

Dec. 10, 1982, Senate Treaty Doc. No. 103–39 (1994), 1833 U.N.T.S. 3

Criminal jurisdiction on board a foreign ship

1.   The criminal jurisdiction of the coastal State should not be exercised on board a foreign ship passing through the territorial sea to arrest any person or to conduct any investigation in connection with any crime committed on board the ship during its passage, save only in the following cases:

(a)   if the consequences of the crime extend to the coastal State;

(b)   if the crime is of a kind to disturb the peace of the country or the good order of the territorial sea;

(c)   if the assistance of the local authorities has been requested by the master of the ship or by a diplomatic agent or consular officer of the flag State; or

(d)   if such measures are necessary for the suppression of illicit traffic in narcotic drugs or psychotropic substances.

2.   The above provisions do not affect the right of the coastal State to take any steps authorized by its laws for the purpose of an arrest or investigation on board a foreign ship passing through the territorial sea after leaving internal waters.

3.   In the cases provided for in paragraphs 1 and 2, the coastal State shall, if the master so requests, notify a diplomatic agent or consular officer of the flag State before taking any steps, and shall facilitate contact between such agent or officer and the ship's crew. In cases of emergency this notification may be communicated while the measures are being taken.

4.   In considering whether or in what manner an arrest should be made, the local authorities shall have due regard to the interests of navigation.

5.   Except as provided in Part XII [concerning protection of the marine environment] or with respect to violations of laws and regulations adopted in accordance with Part V [concerning the exclusive economic zone], the coastal State may not take any steps on board a foreign ship passing through the territorial sea to arrest any person or to conduct any investigation in connection with any crime committed before the ship entered the territorial sea, if the ship, proceeding from a foreign port, is only passing through the territorial sea without entering internal waters.

Internal Waters. Waters landward of a state's baselines (noted in Part C above) are deemed internal waters, unambiguously within a state's sovereignty. A foreign merchant vessel in internal waters, in Phillimore's words in *Regina v. Keyn,* "subjects herself to the ordinary law of the place during the period of her commorancy there."

However, international law still applies in internal waters. Articles 218 and 219 of the 1982 Law of the Sea Convention specify the enforcement measures port states may take with respect to pollution violations by foreign flag vessels voluntarily in port. International law may limit or specify port state rights with respect to other issues as well. For example, port states often refrain from exercising their jurisdiction with regard to shipboard matters that do not "disturb the public tranquility," leaving such matters to flag state authorities. Wildenhus's Case, 120 U.S. 1, 17 (1887). Bilateral treaties regulate the contours of this "peace of the port" doctrine.

Conflicts of Jurisdiction. The peace of the port doctrine is but one of many examples of the role international law may play in resolving conflicts of jurisdiction between a flag state and a coastal or port state. Conflicts of jurisdiction are not restricted to the maritime realm. International businesses, for example, must determine how to comply with different, and sometimes directly conflicting, national laws. How such conflicts are resolved occupies the attention of international lawyers representing individuals and businesses. At times, such conflicts of jurisdiction also give rise to diplomatic disputes between countries. We saw one example in the *Lotus Case* in Chapter 2, where we introduced the concept of jurisdiction in international law.

Coastal State Jurisdiction over Foreign Vessels in the Territorial Sea. As we have seen, a coastal state may apply its laws to individuals in the territorial sea, and arrest them there for criminal violations. The coastal state may also seek to apply certain national laws to foreign flag vessels in the territorial sea, and to arrest those vessels for pollution, fishing, or other violations. However, foreign vessels have a right of innocent passage in the territorial sea; the contours of that right limit a coastal state's discretion in its own territorial sea.

Innocent Passage. In 1758 Vattel set out the concept of the right of innocent passage through the territorial sea, and this concept was legally established in customary international law by the mid-19th century. See Yoshifumi Tanaka, "Navigational Rights and Freedoms," in *The Oxford Handbook of the Law of the Sea* 536, 539-40 (Donald R. Rothwell, Alex G. Oude Elferink, Karen N. Scott & Tim Stephens eds. 2015). A right of innocent passage for foreign merchant vessels, allowing them to pass continuously and expeditiously through the territorial sea or to and from ports, furthers the goals of free navigation and commerce. This right demonstrates that a coastal state does not exercise absolute control over its territorial sea at international law. The coastal state may not exclude foreign vessels engaged in innocent passage, although where essential to its security, the coastal state may "temporarily" suspend such passage. The coastal state may enact laws related to innocent passage in respect of a range of matters, including, for example, "the safety of navigation and the regulation of maritime traffic." There are limits: coastal state requirements may not "have the practical effect of denying or impairing the right of innocent passage" and may not "discriminate in form or in fact against the ships of any State or against ships carrying cargoes to, from or on behalf of any State." In addition, coastal state laws "shall not apply to the design, construction, manning or equipment of foreign ships unless they are giving effect to generally accepted international rules or standards." Why not? Law of the Sea Convention, arts. 21, 24–25.

Article 19 of the 1982 Law of the Sea Convention reflects an effort to make the concept of innocent passage more objective than it was in the 1958 Convention on the Territorial Sea and Contiguous Zone. The 1958 Convention, in Article 14(4), simply deems passage as innocent "so long as it is not prejudicial to the peace, good order or security of the coastal State"—a phrase repeated in Article 19(1) of the 1982 Convention. But Article 19(2) then provides that "[p]assage of a foreign ship shall be considered to be prejudicial to the peace, good order or security of the coastal State if in the territorial sea it engages in any of" a list of 12 activities, including fishing, research, interference with cables, "wilful and serious" pollution, and a catch-all item: "any other activity not having a direct bearing on passage." See John E. Noyes, "The Territorial Sea and Contiguous Zone," in *The Oxford Handbook of the Law of the Sea* 91 (Donald R. Rothwell, Alex G. Oude Elferink, Karen N. Scott & Tim Stephens eds. 2015).

Innocent Passage of Warships and Cold War Politics. Although innocent passage of merchant vessels is relatively uncontroversial, the question whether warships are entitled to a right of innocent passage has been highly contentious. May foreign warships pass through a territorial sea without at least notifying the coastal state, or without that state giving prior authorization for such passage? Does a right of innocent passage for warships pose unacceptable security risks for coastal states? At the 1930 Hague Codification Conference, the United States was among those denying that such a right existed. By World War II, however, the United States had emerged as a major maritime power, favoring expansive navigation rights for warships as well as for merchant vessels. The United States and NATO member states believed that limitations on warships' navigational rights favored the Soviet Union, which had the largest submarine fleet, able to pass submerged and undetected in territorial waters. Yet when the 1982 Law of the Sea Convention was being negotiated during the 1970s, the Soviet Union and its allies had also come to favor innocent passage of warships through the territorial sea. The United States and the Soviet Union, although opponents during the then-ongoing Cold War, found that their legal interests coincided at UNCLOS III. China and many newly independent and developing states, however, thought notification or authorization essential before a foreign warship could pass through the territorial sea. More broadly, those states believed that the traditional doctrine of "freedom of the seas" disadvantaged them and favored maritime and colonial powers.

Innocent Passage of Warships and the 1982 Convention on the Law of the Sea. Does the 1982 Convention accord foreign warships a right of innocent passage through the territorial sea? Maritime powers stress that some of the activities listed in Article 19(2) that could render passage non-innocent, such as "any exercise or practice with weapons of any kind," "the launching, landing or taking on board of any aircraft," and "the launching, landing or taking on board of any military device," are activities specifically associated with warships. In addition, Article 19 appears in a subsection about innocent passage entitled "rules applicable to all ships"—not just merchant vessels—and Article 20 specifies that "[i]n the territorial sea, submarines," which are typically naval vessels, "are required to navigate on the surface and to show their flag."

In light of these provisions, is a coastal state legally entitled to subject the passage of a foreign warship through the territorial sea to prior notice or authorization? In 1989 the United States and the former Soviet Union concluded a bilateral agreement (the Uniform Interpretation of Norms of International Law Governing Innocent Passage), providing that "neither prior notification nor authorization" is a precondition to warships enjoying the right of innocent passage. A U.N. report notes that such preconditions are "generally considered" incompatible with the Law of the Sea Convention. *Oceans and the Law of the Sea: Report of the Secretary-General*, U.N. Doc. A/59/62, ¶ 12 (2004). However, some 40 parties to the Law of the Sea Convention maintain that passage of foreign warships through the territorial sea requires prior notification to or authorization by the coastal state. Is this position plausible? Does the 1982 Convention reflect an "agreement to disagree" about the innocent passage of warships, or do states that insist on prior notice or authorization simply flout international law? How, in practice, might the conflicting views of coastal states and maritime powers be accommodated with respect to the passage of warships?

Warship Immunity. What may a coastal state do if a foreign warship leaves designated sea lanes or otherwise violates the right of innocent passage? Coastal state enforcement authority is more limited with respect to warships than with respect to merchant vessels. Warships are immune from boarding, arrest, detention, or the institution of legal proceedings. Law of the Sea Convention, art. 32. According to Article 23 of the 1958 Territorial Sea Convention, a provision echoed in Article 30 of the 1982 Law of the Sea Convention, the coastal state may "require" the offending foreign warship "to leave the

through straits, how does the Convention strike a balance between coastal states' claims of sovereignty and maritime powers' claims to high seas freedoms? There are significant differences between the rules governing innocent passage and the rules governing transit passage through straits. For example, transit passage assures that warships may pass in "normal mode," which for surface ships extends to launching and recovering aircraft and deploying radar and sonar devices, and which for submarines includes submerged passage; innocent passage does not allow such "normal mode" activities. Transit passage through straits is not suspendable, while innocent passage may be. Transit passage includes the right of overflight, while innocent passage does not. Sea lanes used for transit passage must be approved by the International Maritime Organization, while the coastal state has more discretion to establish sea lanes for innocent passage.

Strait states remain concerned about potential security threats posed by foreign ships transiting straits. Strait states may still, of course, exercise their right to self-defense (see Chapter 6), and they may take certain enforcement actions against a vessel that does not follow Convention rules governing transit passage. Environmental risks, such as spills from oil tankers or from vessels carrying radioactive material, also concern strait states. According to Article 233 of the 1982 Convention, a strait state may take "appropriate enforcement measures" with respect to vessels that have violated certain environmental laws, "causing or threatening major damage to the marine environment of the straits."

The Regime of Warships. Permitting warships to navigate or conduct exercises in zones of the oceans other than the territorial sea and straits is also, of course, of concern to maritime powers. Professor Oxman found "nothing surprisingly new in the regime of warships under the 1982 Convention":

> The demilitarization pressures were deflected by liberal use of "peaceful purposes" clauses and cross-references to the prohibitions on the threat or use of force in the U.N. Charter that have little, if any, effect on the legal regime. With respect to all the new regimes or geographical expansions of existing regimes, effects on activities of warships are expressly eliminated or mitigated in each case:
>
> —there is a liberal right of archipelagic sea lanes passage in broad sealanes traversing the newly recognized archipelagic waters;

—the regime of innocent passage in the expanded territorial sea is made more objective and is replaced by a more liberal regime of transit passage in straits;

—high seas freedoms of navigation, overflight and the laying of submarine cables and pipelines, and other internationally lawful uses of the sea related to those freedoms, are expressly preserved in the economic zone;

—high seas freedoms are given more explicit protection from infringement by the coastal State in its exercise of continental shelf rights;

—warships are excluded from all environmental provisions;

—regulation of the deep seabeds depends on a definition of the term "activities in the Area" that does not cover military activities or marine scientific research.

Bernard H. Oxman, "The Regime of Warships Under the United Nations Convention on the Law of the Sea," 24 *Virginia Journal of International Law* 809, 861–62 (1984).

A Package Deal? International lawyers debate whether various new provisions in the 1982 Convention amount to customary international law, or whether they are binding only as treaty law. Some argue that acceptance of provisions at UNCLOS III, coupled with state practice, provide the necessary consensus for the bulk of the Convention to be considered customary international law. Others maintain that the Convention is a "package deal," the product of numerous compromises and trade-offs, and that a state cannot claim particular rights concerning the oceans while rejecting certain obligations. Note that the Convention, in Article 309, generally prohibits reservations and exceptions to its provisions.

UNCLOS III negotiations concerning innocent passage and transit passage through straits were not carried out in isolation from negotiations on other issues. Some maritime powers, whose interests, according to many observers, were well-served by the outcome of the negotiations on transit passage through straits, were less pleased by other negotiated compromises. In particular, some developed states criticized the deep seabed mining regime that evolved at UNCLOS III. That regime, which now incorporates significant 1994 changes favored by developed states, is explored in Part E.

The United States and the Law of the Sea Convention. As of May 2017, the United States was not one of the 168 parties to the Law of the Sea Convention. What then are the legal rights of the United States with respect to innocent passage and transit passage through straits? Is the United States, a party to the 1958 Convention on the Territorial Sea, bound by that Convention's navigation provisions in its relations with other 1958 Convention parties, such as Spain? In light of the "package deal" arguments just noted, do the provisions of the 1982 Law of the Sea Convention on innocent passage and transit passage through straits constitute customary international law? Might the customary international law of the sea differ from the provisions of the Law of the Sea Convention?

To promote U.S. navigational freedoms, should the United States negotiate bilateral agreements, rely on assertions of customary international law, or assert U.S. military might? What difference would it make if the United States were to accept the Law of the Sea Convention? Note that the U.S. Department of Defense and both Democratic and Republican administrations from 1994—when the Convention's deep seabed mining regime was changed (see Part E)—into 2017 have advocated U.S. accession. In 2012, John Bellinger, Legal Adviser to the State Department during the second term of President George W. Bush, testified that the Bush administration in February 2002 saw an "urgent need for Senate approval" of the Law of the Sea Convention:

> The Bush Administration decided to support the Law of the Sea Convention [because we] concluded that, on balance, the treaty was clearly in the U.S. national security, economic, and environmental interests.
>
> First and foremost, the Bush Administration concluded that the Convention was beneficial to the United States military, especially during a time of armed conflict, because it provided clear treaty-based navigational rights for our Navy, Coast Guard, and aircraft. This was especially important for the Bush Administration as we asked our military to take on numerous new missions after the 9-11 attacks during the Global War on Terrorism; several countries had challenged U.S. military activities in their territorial waters, and the Administration concluded that it was vital to have a treaty-based legal right to support our freedom of movement and activities.

The Law of the Sea Convention (Treaty Doc. 103–39): Hearing Before the Senate Committee on Foreign Relations, 112th Cong. 181, 184–85 (2013). See also John E.

Noyes, "The Law of the Sea Convention and the United States of America," 47 *Revue belge de droit international* 15 (2014).

E. THE DEEP SEABED

The contours of a legal regime for the seabed beyond the limits of national jurisdiction have taken shape only in the past half century. In 1967, Arvid Pardo, Malta's Ambassador to the United Nations, spoke to the General Assembly on the uses and resources of the seabed, discussing underseas archaeological treasures, offshore natural gas and petroleum, ocean floor sediments, marine scientific research, missile systems and other fixed military installations, and pollution. He stirred the most interest, however, when he turned to the exploitation of the "incredibly vast" mineral resources on and beneath the ocean floor beyond the boundaries of national jurisdiction. Although Pardo underestimated the extent of national jurisdiction over the continental shelf that came to be accepted, many at UNCLOS III shared his vision of great deep seabed wealth. Much attention focused on nodules rich in manganese, nickel, copper, and cobalt that are scattered over about 15 per cent of the seabed at depths of 3,000 to 6,000 meters. Modern technology allows recovery of these nodules, for which companies are actively exploring. In this section we trace the evolution of the complex international legal regime that presently governs deep seabed mining.

The Common Heritage of Mankind. Ambassador Pardo referred to the seabed beyond the limits of national jurisdiction as the "common heritage of mankind," which "should be used and exploited for peaceful purposes and for the exclusive benefit of mankind as a whole." He argued that developing states, "representing that part of mankind which is most in need of assistance, should receive preferential consideration" in the distribution of revenues derived from the exploitation of the seabed, an argument reflected in the U.N. General Assembly's 1970 Declaration of Principles. That resolution, excerpted below, also proclaimed the deep seabed and its resources to be the "common heritage of mankind." For discussion of the common heritage concept, see John E. Noyes, "The Common Heritage of Mankind: Past, Present, and Future," 40 *Denver Journal of International Law and Policy* 447 (2012).

Differing Legal Conceptions of the Deep Seabed. The common heritage notion was not the only theory postulated for deep seabed mining before UNCLOS III. Some argued that the seabed beyond the limits of national jurisdiction was *res nullius,* a conception that would allow unilateral claims of title or sovereignty. Others termed the deep seabed *res communis* and thus not subject to expropriation. Note that Grotius had already distinguished these concepts in the 1633 excerpt in Part A above. In responding to a 1974 claim by Deepsea Ventures, Inc. seeking U.S. recognition of "exclusive rights to develop, evaluate and mine" a claim in the deep seabed, the U.S. State Department, while noting that it did not grant or recognize exclusive mining rights in the deep seabed, declared that "the mining of the seabed beyond the limits of national jurisdiction may proceed as a freedom of the high seas under existing international law." *Digest of U.S. Practice in International Law* § 5, at 342–43 (1974). Would a high seas freedoms regime for seabed minerals be similar to a common heritage regime as outlined in the Principles Resolution? Or would they differ? If so, how?

THE DECLARATION OF PRINCIPLES GOVERNING THE SEA-BED AND THE OCEAN FLOOR, AND THE SUBSOIL THEREOF, BEYOND THE LIMITS OF NATIONAL JURISDICTION

G.A. Res. 2749 (XXV), 25 U.N. GAOR Supp. (No. 28), at 24, U.N. Doc. A/8028 (1970)

The General Assembly, . . .

Affirming that there is an area of the sea-bed and the ocean floor, and the subsoil thereof, beyond the limits of national jurisdiction, the precise limits of which are yet to be determined,

Recognizing that the existing legal régime of the high seas does not provide substantive rules for regulating the exploration of the aforesaid area and the exploitation of its resources,

Convinced that the area shall be reserved exclusively for peaceful purposes and that the exploration of the area and the exploitation of its resources shall be carried out for the benefit of mankind as a whole,

Believing it essential that an international régime applying to the area and its resources and including appropriate international machinery should be established as soon as possible,

Bearing in mind that the development and use of the area and its resources shall be undertaken in such a manner as to foster the healthy development of the world economy and balanced growth of international trade, and to minimize any adverse economic effects caused by fluctuation of prices of raw materials resulting from such activities,

Solemnly declares that:

The sea-bed and ocean floor, and the subsoil thereof, beyond the limits of national jurisdiction (hereinafter referred to as the area), as well as the resources of the area, are the common heritage of mankind.

The area shall not be subject to appropriation by any means by States or persons, natural or juridical, and no State shall claim or exercise sovereignty or sovereign rights over any part thereof.

No State or person, natural or juridical, shall claim, exercise or acquire rights with respect to the area or its resources incompatible with the international régime to be established and the principles of this Declaration.

All activities regarding the exploration and exploitation of the resources of the area and other related activities shall be governed by the international régime to be established.

The area shall be open to use exclusively for peaceful purposes by all States, whether coastal or land-locked, without discrimination, in accordance with the international régime to be established.

States shall act in the area in accordance with the applicable principles and rules of international law[.]

The exploration of the area and the exploitation of its resources shall be carried out for the benefit of mankind as a whole, irrespective of the geographical location of States, whether land-locked or coastal, and taking into particular consideration the interests and needs of the developing countries.

The area shall be reserved exclusively for peaceful purposes, without prejudice to any measures which have been or may be agreed upon in the context of international negotiations undertaken in the field of disarmament and which may be applicable to a broader area. . . .

On the basis of the principles of this Declaration, an international régime applying to the area and its resources and including appropriate international machinery to give effect to its provisions shall be established by an international treaty of a universal character, generally agreed upon. The régime shall, inter alia, provide for the orderly and safe development and rational management of the area and its resources and for expanding opportunities in the use thereof, and ensure the equitable sharing by States in the benefits derived therefrom, taking into particular consideration the interests and needs of the developing countries, whether land-locked or coastal.

New Uses of the Deep Seabed. Much attention recently has focused on living resources discovered at deep-sea hydrothermal vents. The sale of marine biotechnology-related products generates over $100 billion in revenues each year, and several such products use genetic materials from living organisms found at deep-sea hydrothermal vents. This attention has contributed to initiatives for the conservation and sustainable use of marine biodiversity in areas beyond national jurisdiction. Could the ISA regulate the harvesting of living resources at hydrothermal vents in order to protect the fragile environment near polymetallic sulfides? Even if the Authority may not regulate living resources at deep-seabed vents, does the general principle, set out in Article 136 of the Convention, that the Area is the "common heritage of mankind" provide direction with respect to how these living resources are to be treated? Or should the harvesting of such living resources be regarded as a high seas freedom? What rules of international law now apply to this issue? Is a new international regime needed for living resources at hydrothermal vents? How should it be developed? In 2017 a U.N. preparatory committee finalized its recommendations for a new implementing agreement, linked to the 1982 Law of the Sea Convention, to govern marine biological diversity in areas beyond national jurisdiction. See Salvatore Arico & Charlotte Slapin, *UNU-IAS Report: Bioprospecting the Genetic Resources in the Deep Seabed* (2005); Joanna Mossup, "Marine Bioprospecting," in *The Oxford Handbook of the Law of the Sea* 825 (Donald R. Rothwell, Alex G. Oude Elferink, Karen N. Scott & Tim Stephens eds. 2015); Cymie Payne, "Biodiversity in High Seas Areas: An Integrated Legal Approach," 21 *ASIL Insights*, Issue 9 (2017).

Recapping Concepts. How have international law and international legal process affected international relations concerning the oceans, and international relations generally? The law of the sea, a well-developed area of international law, illustrates several concepts introduced in this book. These include the role of unilateral action in spurring developments in international law; the relevance of natural law, customary international law, and treaties, including detailed multilateral lawmaking conventions, in developing rules; roles for soft law; assertions of *erga omnes* obligations; differing treatment of developing and developed states; the use of municipal tribunals to help implement international law; the growth of international institutions and formal third-party international dispute settlement mechanisms; and techniques to promote the efficacy of international law.

Index